DYNAMICS OF
INTERNATIONAL RELATIONS

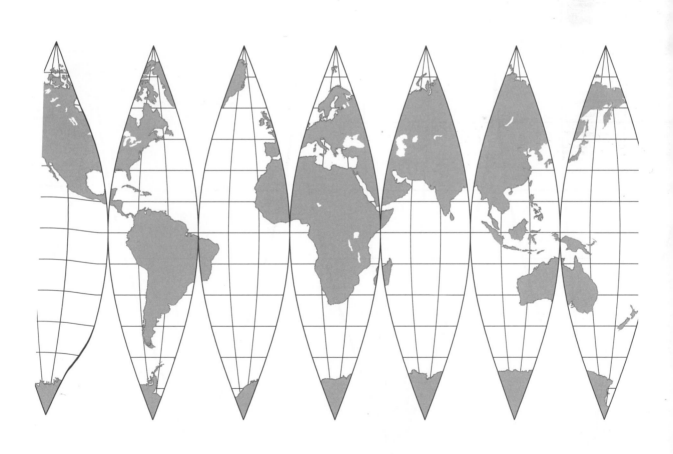

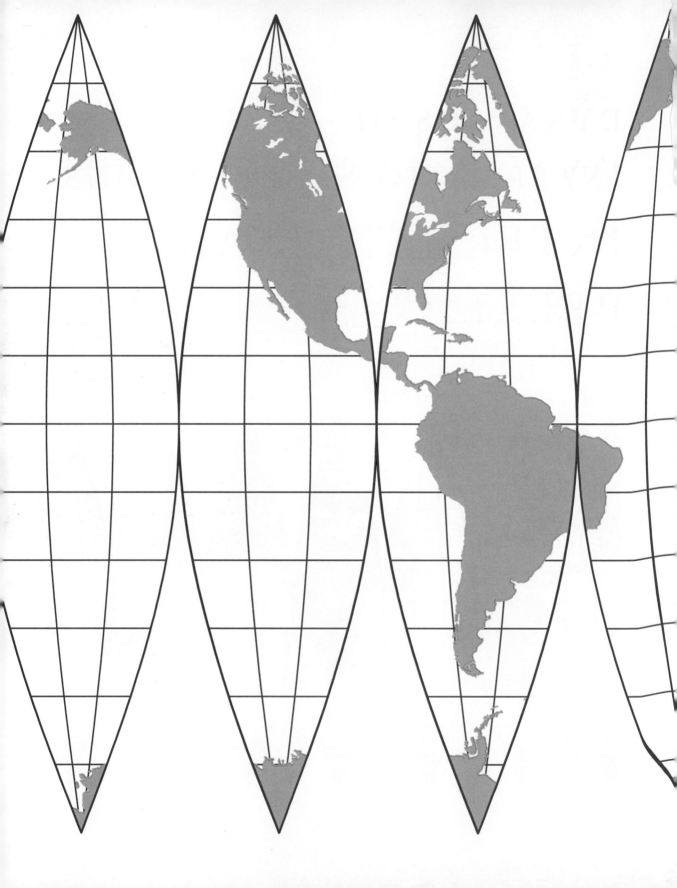

SECOND EDITION

DYNAMICS OF INTERNATIONAL RELATIONS

CONFLICT AND MUTUAL GAIN IN AN ERA
OF GLOBAL INTERDEPENDENCE

Walter C. Clemens, Jr.

ROWMAN & LITTLEFIELD PUBLISHERS, INC.
Lanham • Boulder • New York • Toronto • Oxford

ROWMAN & LITTLEFIELD PUBLISHERS, INC.

Published in the United States of America
by Rowman & Littlefield Publishers, Inc.
A wholly owned subsidiary of The Rowman & Littlefield Publishing Group, Inc.
4501 Forbes Boulevard, Suite 200, Lanham, MD 20706
www.rowmanlittlefield.com

P.O. Box 317, Oxford OX2 9RU, UK

British Library Cataloguing-in-Publication Information Available

Library of Congress Cataloging-in-Publication Data

Clemens, Walter C.
    Dynamics of international relations : conflict and mutual gain in an era
of global interdependence / Walter C. Clemens, Jr.—2nd ed.
        p.   cm.
    Includes bibliographical references and index.
    ISBN 0-7425-2821-9 (paper : alk. paper)
    1. International relations.   I. Title.
JZ1242.C57   2004
327.1′01—dc21
                                    2003006012
Printed in the United States of America

♾™ The paper used in this publication meets the minimum requirements of American
National Standard for Information Sciences—Permanence of Paper for Printed Library
Materials, ANSI/NISO Z39.48-1992.

for
Iolani Lenore Clemens
"Heavenly Bird"

Alle Menschen werden Brüder
Wo dein sanfter Flügel weilt

If I am not for myself, who will be for me? Yet if I am for myself only, what am I?
—Hillel

Let us get out of our grooves and study the rest of the globe.
—Voltaire, "On Toleration"

More and more, the interdependence and complexity of international and political and economic relations render it incumbent on all civilized and orderly powers to insist upon the proper policing of the world.
—Theodore Roosevelt

That people inevitably think in terms of their self-interest is something very little can be done about. But is it not equally tenable that a great deal can be done about influencing people to think and act in terms of their true self-interest? In this dangerous international age, notions of exalted and exaggerated nationalism, national egocentrism and isolationism, of chauvinism, of group superiority and master race, of group exclusiveness, of national self-righteousness, of special privilege, are in the interest of neither the world nor of any particular group in it. They are false views of self-interest and carry us all toward the disaster of war.
—Ralph Bunche, "The International Significance of Human Relations," Lincoln's Day Address, Springfield, Illinois, February 12, 1951

The building of peace is like the building of a beautiful cathedral. It is a work that may not be done in my lifetime nor shall it be done in yours. But you ought to add a stone to it. There ought to be at least one spiral that is yours or one edifice that belongs to you. You ought to be able to point to it and say that I helped place that building block in the cathedral of peace.
—Vice President Hubert H. Humphrey on International Cooperation Year, Washington, D.C., June 2, 1965

At the dawn of the twenty-first century, we face a strange paradox: the more we know about the issues, and about each other, the more we act as if we were strangers.

We all live on the same planet, buffeted by the same winds, influenced by the same currents of change. But instead of acting on what unites us—seizing common opportunities and defending against shared threats—we allow a chasm to persist between us: between rich and poor, free and fettered, privileged and humiliated; between those who benefit from globalization, and those who are marginalized.

This gulf is an affront to human dignity. It leaves all our societies vulnerable, and each of us insecure. We need to mend this great divide with a new fabric of solidarity.
—Secretary-General Kofi Annan, BBC World Service lecture, delivered in New York on December 10, 2002

BRIEF CONTENTS

DETAILED CONTENTS

LIST OF TABLES, FIGURES, AND MAPS

FIGURES

LIST OF SIDEBARS AND TIME LINES

Why study international relations (IR)? Because, like a mountain, it is there—challenging, interesting to explore, sometimes beautiful, potentially useful (with rich ore), and often dangerous. Why attempt the climb? To understand where humanity has come from and where it can go. To survive. To make the world a better place. Also, to get ahead—to find a job. To live and prosper in a world where, as naturalist John Muir noted: "When you touch anything, you find it is hitched to everything else in the universe."

The dynamics of IR—the driving forces behind conflict and cooperation across borders—are important not only to diplomats, soldiers, and peacekeepers. These forces—tangible and intangible—shape the safety and prosperity of everyone. They awaken the imagination of every alert human being, every seeker for patterns in the great chain of being. They are a "must know" for the banker, the commodity trader, the public health worker, the ecologist, and for those working in many other professions. A better understanding of IR can enhance rather than destroy life. We owe it to ourselves and to future generations to seek knowledge that could alter our dance of the dinosaurs—the shortsighted routines that invite extinction.

This book introduces the reader to IR as a fact of life and as a field of study. Both the practice and the study of IR are problem-oriented, focused on issues of survival, development, justice, and the environment. These issues challenge both our minds and our character, pressing us to fuse knowledge from many fields to grasp complex realities and suggest constructive policies.

WHO GETS WHAT, HOW, AND WHY?

The basic IR question is how to enhance the interests of one's own group—whether it be a tribe, nation, party, state, business corporation, social movement, or church—in a global setting where each group's interests may conflict as well as harmonize with others'. Whether we see our group in narrow terms (for example, Bosnian Serbs), broad terms (our community of believers) or in universal terms (all humanity), we still must deal with others whose objectives may parallel but also differ from ours.

Our world is one of escalating interdependencies. How should we cope with our shared vulnerabilities? Governments and other IR actors may seek one-sided or joint gains. They may claim values (wealth, power, influence) for themselves or create and share such goods with others. Which road should IR actors take?

This book suggests that IR actors are more likely to achieve their own objectives in the long run if they cooperate for mutual gain than if they exploit others for one-sided gain. It warns, however, that cooperation among competitors depends upon reciprocation and may require safeguards to promote compliance. In contrast to mutual gain policies, efforts to exploit others may yield short-run benefits but tend, over time, to boomerang against the exploiter. A related finding is that, the more all parties communicate, the more likely they are to find solutions useful to all sides. Secret talks are sometimes useful, but open diplomacy usually trumps closed-door diplomacy.

HOW THIS BOOK IS ORGANIZED FOR BREADTH AND DEPTH

This book tries to provide a "state of the art" picture of what we know about IR *plus* the essential tools for learning more. For breadth, the book's four major parts cover the central issues of IR—from security and political economy to environmental protection and human rights. Depth comes from each chapter's case studies, structured to compare recurring problems. Thus, the chapter "Why Wage War?" examines several comparable wars (among them, Korea, 1950–1953; and the Persian Gulf, 1990–1991). Placing these pairs in a wider context, the chapter also reports on the severity and frequency of all major wars since the late 18th century.

History is our trove and main database, but it is not a perfect laboratory. The global scene refuses to hold still for repeated experiments.[1] The chapter "How to Win at Peace" shows how different were the challenges facing those who sought to rebuild Germany and Japan after 1945, Russia after 1991, and Afghanistan and Iraq after 2002–2003. What worked in past cases may fail in a different time and place.

Theory and experience should nurture each other. Knowledge begins with a quest to answer some basic problem. Scientists start with hunches about what causes what. These hunches become tentative explanations (hypotheses) which can be tested and evaluated.

Adapting this approach, each chapter in this book begins with a tough question: "How can foes become partners?" "What is the role of women in development?" Some chapters ask the reader to don an official hat and look at IR from the standpoint of the UN Secretary-General, the Brazilian foreign minister, or the president of India. Having posed a serious question, each chapter then reviews contending concepts and explanations about the problem. Next, it places theory against reality in several cases. It evaluates what propositions seem to hold and what questions remain. Finally, it applies these insights to the policy problems with which the chapter began.

The universe is large. So how were the cases selected? There were three considerations. First, each exemplifies an important IR problem iterated in various settings; for example, how to defuse explosive confrontations such as the 1962 Cuban missile crisis. What lessons, if any, does Cuba (1962) present for decision makers concerned with North Korea or Iran early in the 21st century?

Second, the cases help us assess competing IR theories and policy guidelines in a variety of contexts—from arms control to environmental protection. A sampling of case studies cannot fully test a hypothesis or theory. But if a theory fails in important cases, we must doubt its validity. If it seems to explain some key cases, we must study it further.

Third, the cases help identify which kinds of policies failed and which met their objectives—an important exercise for the scholar and politician alike. We find that the reconstruction of Europe and Japan after World War II ranks at the top of U.S. successes abroad. On the other hand, both Washington and Moscow failed ignominiously when they tried to keep clients in power in Vietnam and Afghanistan.[2]

All these cases are more interesting because previously top secret documents are becoming available that shed light on what decision makers knew and felt at the time. As still more facts emerge, of course, interpretations of recent history undergo continuous revision.

---

[1] To supplement history, we can mimic the "real world." Each chapter of this book begins and ends with a role-play intended to whet the reader's appetite for the facts and her/his appreciation of how difficult it can be to make wise decisions. Not only students but also generals and corporate executives simulate the real world with human actors, computers, or both. But while simulations can provide insights, they omit important variables, beginning with the moods and physical traits of actual decision makers. Simulated reality is not the same as reality.

[2] The cases used in this book emerged from three surveys of scholars and diplomats, one-third of them non-U.S., conducted by the author at the Woodrow Wilson International Center for Scholars in Washington, the Harvard University Center for Science and International Affairs, and Boston University in 1976–1977, 1987, and 1999. The early results were published in several op–ed and journal articles. A century of U.S. policy was analyzed in Clemens, *America and the World, 1898–2025: Achievements, Failures, Alternative Futures* (New York: Palgrave, 2000); the Soviet experience, in Clemens, *Can Russia Change? The USSR Confronts Global Interdependence* (New York: Routledge, 1990).

TO SOLVE PROBLEMS, DO WE NEED THEORY?

Fed up with study, Goethe's Dr. Faust warns a student that "all theory is gray," while "the tree of life is green." But theory and life—our case studies—can make each other "green." Each informs the other. Scientists in all fields need strong theories to spur and organize their quests. A good IR theory would make sense of the scrambled signals we take in daily from a world pulsing with both conflict and harmony, the brutish and the beautiful. A good theory would lay out principles, rules, and assumptions by which we analyze IR problems and accumulate knowledge. An insightful theory is necessary for wise policy.

How is theory relevant to practice? Every diplomat and politician consults some kind of theory, if only the maxims learned at a parent's knee.[3] Many of the intellectuals shaping policy in the George W. Bush administration claim to be "Straussians"—followers of Leo Strauss, a professor of classic political theory at the University of Chicago.[4] As we shall see in Chapter 1, Strauss provided a set of ideals to guide U.S. policy, while his colleague, Hans J. Morgenthau, taught a generation of foreign policy intellectuals about the realities of power in IR. Their theories were not ivory tower, or "gray." Each man was a German Jew who escaped Hitler's Holocaust.

Every field of knowledge has a dominant image, or paradigm, guiding its explorations. If the image is wrong (the sun circles the earth), we misinterpret what we see. If correct (the earth circles the sun), the phenomena we perceive can fall into their proper places. Many thousands of years passed before humans dropped their image of the earth as the center of the universe. Scholars and statesmen may also hold onto false or misleading images for long periods.

Long before Morgenthau and Strauss, varieties of "realism" and "idealism" dominated the study and practice of IR. Each theory starts from a simplistic, often misleading paradigm. This book proposes a paradigm shift. It contends that global interdependence provides a better lens for analyzing IR than realism/neorealism or idealism and its many "neo" offshoots. The book also suggests how IR can borrow from the "meta" theory of complexity to view IR in the broader framework of evolution and other nonlinear systems. The "fitness" of any organism, including IR actors and the entire IR system, may be seen as the ability to cope with complex challenges. This ability, in turn, depends not just on material assets but also on intangibles. In short, culture matters. Of course, no theory offers the final word—not even in the physical sciences. At a minimum, theories must be continually refined. Sometimes the underlying paradigm is replaced, giving rise to a new process of search and discovery.

Grand, comprehensive theories of IR view the world as through a telescope. There are also partial and medium-range theories that peer at details as through a microscope. A comprehensive theory can give birth to a partial theory. For example, realism implies that wars are inevitable and should be treated as just another tool in the quest for power. Partial theories also help build grand theories. Interdependence draws upon medium-range theories of collective action and negotiation.

The study of IR is in flux. After much searching, our questions will probably outnumber our answers. We must build on and improve one another's findings, making knowledge cumulative. With better data and more insightful models, perhaps we can improve IR theory and in so doing possibly raise the quality of life worldwide.

---

[3] The longest-serving Soviet foreign minister often recalled how his father and a friend traced U.S. wealth to "cunning and wise" presidents such as Theodore Roosevelt. Did the Soviet diplomat see the U.S. presidents he met—from Franklin Roosevelt to George Bush (the elder)—through his father's lens? See Andrei Gromyko, *Memoirs* (New York: Doubleday, 1989), 4.

[4] James Atlas, "A Classicist's Legacy: New Empire Builders," *The New York Times*, May 4, 2003, E1, E4.

Ideas jump political as well as scientific borders resulting in major consequences. The streams and rivers of international studies flow into an ever-expanding effort to comprehend life—its chaos, its complexity, its order. Analysis of IR gains from, and contributes to, many branches of knowledge. We adapt insights and tools from all of the social sciences as well as from statistics, law, and philosophy. To understand the diverse civilizations on the world stage, we also need to study sacred texts such as the *Quran*, epic tales such as *Ramayana*, and novels such as *Bridge on the Drina*, by Ivo Andrić, and *Guerrillas*, by V. S. Naipaul. We must consult other disciplines that bear on IR—from biology (symbiosis) to physics (missiles) to plant genetics (hybrid wheat). Complexity theory, mentioned earlier, spans many disciplines but seeks to build on and modify Darwin's view of evolution.

Recommended books, journals, and Web sites are listed at the end of each chapter. Additional sources and suggestions on how to conduct research may be found on the Student Web site. Besides words and numbers we must also know shapes and sizes—such as those in the *World Bank Atlas* and the many maps presented in this book. The photos, paintings, and cartoons that illustrate this text offer still other ways of learning about IR. But do not be like the student in Goethe's *Faust* who wants to learn but is overwhelmed by the task, which makes his head spin: "How hard it is to array all the study tools in order to get to the bottom of things!" Faust replies with a question: "Do you think that mere paper is the fountain that will quench thirst for all time? If your refreshment does not come from within your own self, you will never gain it."

Consider Voltaire's advice: "Let us get out of our grooves and study the rest of the globe." Do not sit forever before books and computer screens. True, you can communicate far and wide using the Internet, but there is more to life than words. Direct experience is also a valuable teacher.[5] Try to visit distant places and learn how others see and feel about the world—preferably in their own language. Do not be like members of the U.S. House of Representatives in the early 21st century—most of whom had no passport.

Having read much and experienced the world, we may still lack answers to important questions. The human psyche and other factors shaping IR are even more complicated than the "quarks" and "jaguars" studied by other disciplines. Even if we have a good understanding of IR, our policy recommendations will be subjective: Where we stand depends heavily on where we sit. Indeed, we form part of what we are trying to comprehend.

Our efforts to understand IR may resemble the waxed wings of Icarus, bound to melt as he rose toward the sun. But we hope rather that they will rise more like the first flight of the Wright Brothers—primitive, yet aloft and open to improvement.

NEW TO THE SECOND EDITION

The entire text has been updated throughout, with an emphasis on what has changed (and what remains the same) since 9/11. Here are some highlights:

• The second edition of *Dynamics of International Relations* is now packaged—free of charge—with the authoritative *World Bank Atlas*. The Atlas has been a primary resource for scholars and students of international relations for thirty-five years and it serves as a primary source of information for the new edition of this text.

• International relations in an era of global terrorism forms a theme for the new edition.

• Coverage of new and ongoing conflicts in Kosovo, Chechnya, Afghanistan, North Korea, and Iraq is

---

[5] A single Jewish woman in New York learned a great deal from corresponding by e-mail with a gay Iraqi man as Baghdad was bombed in 2003. See Daniel Zalewski, "A Baghdad Blogger," *The New Yorker*, March 31, 2003, pp. 33–34. But another American learned even more as he lived through the bombing and talked to Iraqis under siege. See Jon Lee Anderson, "Letter From Iraq," ibid., pp. 80–85.

included. The 2003 war in Iraq is featured in maps, tables, and text.

• New data are included on war, weapons of mass destruction, defense budgets, peace initiatives, trade flows, human development indices, and environmental degradation.

• New color maps of the world and major world regions are available in the text and to the professor for downloading into classroom presentations.

• New photos, cartoons, figures, tables, sidebars, timelines, and case studies are incorporated throughout.

• New Student Study Guide includes "Learning About International Relations" as well as *The Rowman & Littlefield Guide to Writing with Sources* (ISBN 0-7425-2998-3).

• New student Web site includes chapter-by-chapter links and resources from the text plus activities based on the *World Bank Atlas*.
www.rowmanlittlefield.com/rl/books/ClemensSG

• New password-protected instructor's Web site includes well-reviewed Instructor's Manual by B. Welling Hall, downloadable test questions, and downloadable full color maps from the text.
www.rowmanlittlefield.com/rl/books/ClemensIM

ACKNOWLEDGMENTS

Many individuals and institutions helped stimulate, support, and improve this book—more than can be named here. Thanks to them all, beginning with those noted in the first edition. Two faithful friends have been this book's companions for many years— retired ambassador Hermann Fr. Eilts, founding director of the Boston University Center for International Relations, and J. David Singer, founder of the Correlates of War Project at the University of Michigan. Their encouragement and advice—from the realms of praxis and theory—have been crucial to this second edition. Stuart Kauffman shaped my understanding of complexity theory; Joseph S. Nye, power and interdependence; Stanley Hoffmann, historical sociology; Howard Raiffa, creating and claiming values in bargaining; Lawrence S. Finkelstein, the United Nations. Other colleagues from Boston University, MIT, and Harvard University will see their imprints on the pages that follow. Professors Courtney B. Smith of Seton Hall University and B. Welling Hall of Earlham College reviewed the manuscript for this second edition and made many useful suggestions. Professor Hall has also revised her highly praised instructor's manual, now available on the Professor's Web site. Many students at Boston University and elsewhere have also contributed to the book—among them: Courtney Stockland, Joshua Dubois, and Dino Laverghetta, who prepared tables, Web listings, and bibliographic references. Ali Ho Clemens again helped with graphics and unraveled problems in the human–machine interface. Jeff Danziger's cartoons again supplied abundant tinder. Once again, Jennifer Knerr at Rowman & Littlefield, joined by Renée Legatt and Jehanne Schweitzer, gave this project unstinting support. Christopher Thornton, Terry Lane, and Nikki Phipps reviewed the manuscript and Joanne Bowser oversaw production at TechBooks. Indexing was done by Christopher Thornton.

The book is dedicated to my daughter, Iolani Lenore Clemens. Iolani is Hawaiian for "heavenly bird"—the name given by Queen Emma in 1870 to a school in Honolulu where Sun Yat-sen, father of modern China, began to learn about the West in 1879–1882 and where, some eighty years later, I first taught languages and learned about the East.

Where the gentle wing of Iolani Lenore hovers, all may feel as brothers and sisters—as in Friedrich von Schiller's "Ode to Joy," the text for Beethoven's Ninth Symphony.

PART 1

Hard Realities, High Ideals, and Global Interdependence

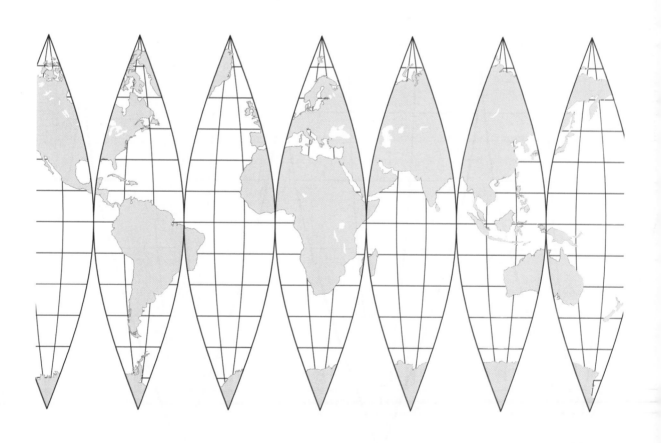

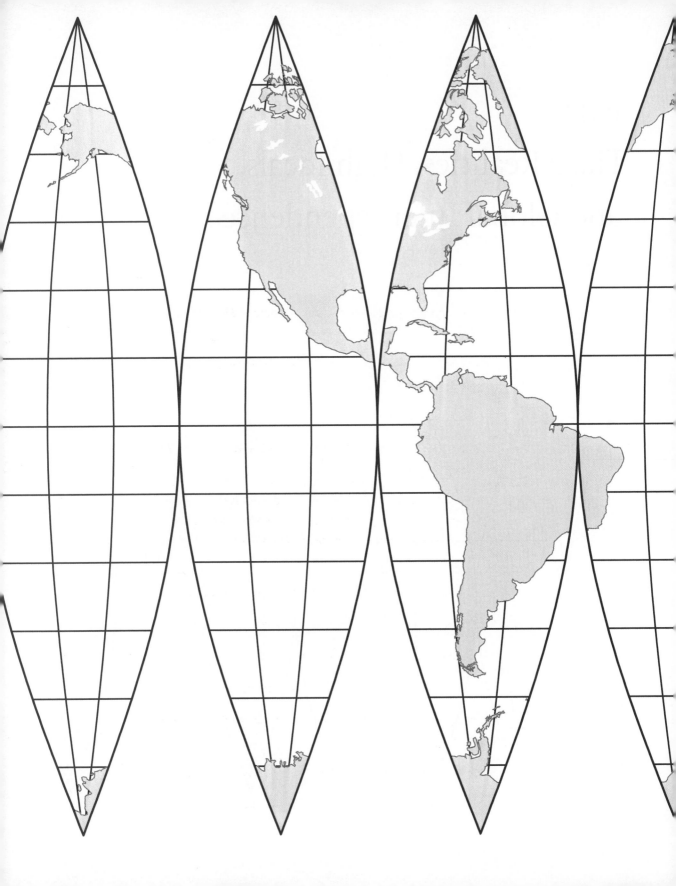

C H A P T E R   O N E

IS IR "WINNER-TAKE-ALL"? CAN IT BE MUTUAL GAIN?

THE BIG QUESTIONS IN CHAPTER 1

- What is international relations (IR)? How does IR differ from foreign policy?

- Who or what are the key players in IR? What and where are the main playing fields?

- What is globalization? Is it good or bad?

- What is interdependence? Is it good or bad? How does it relate to globalization?

- Through what lens should you view IR—the realist focus on the struggle for power, the idealist vision of a world order based on law and morality, or the interdependence image of danger shared with opportunity?

- What is negotiation? What are the main types of negotiators?

- Is it smarter to go it alone or to cooperate with other IR players?

- What happens when players seek a free ride?

- Games that IR actors play: defection or coordination?

- Can agreements serve the interests of both sides if they have divergent interests?

- Is it wiser to do your business behind closed doors or in the open?

- Are there any principles that guide foreign policy?

When You Become National Security Adviser...

Imagine that, not too far into the 21st century, the newly elected president asks you to be her special assistant for national security. She wants you to take the post once held by Henry Kissinger, Zbigniew Brzezinski, Colin Powell, Anthony Lake, and Condoleezza Rice. You direct the National Security Council—the president's own think tank. You help the president make sense of the often conflicting recommendations by the many government agencies concerned with national security—from Commerce and Defense to State and the Treasury Department, as well as the Central Intelligence Agency (CIA) and other intelligence agencies—and chart a course.

Three weeks before her inauguration, the president asks you to outline a strategy for building a world in which U.S. interests can flourish. The president would prefer a world in which cooperation prevailed over conflict, but she sees a reality filled with danger as well as opportunity.

What can we learn from the past, the president asks, when the rules and playing field are in flux? When skyjacked airliners crashed into the World Trade Center, the Pentagon, and a Pennsylvania field on September 11, 2001, did that mean we entered a new stage in human history? Or was this another case where, as French diplomats say, "plus ça change, plus c'est la même chose"—the more things change, the more they stay the same?

The events of "9/11" jolted not just Americans but many people around the globe. Some danced with joy that the vaunted hyperpower had been wounded, but many commiserated. A French newspaper headline read: "We are all Americans." Candlelight condolence processions took place in Iran.

What can—what should—Americans and other people do about these events? The president notes that many voices in the Islamic world as well as China and Singapore boldly assert that Western values are not their values. Why do so many people hate us? Can we mitigate these feelings or should we ignore them? Should we strive to address underlying conditions or get tough and tighten security—or both?

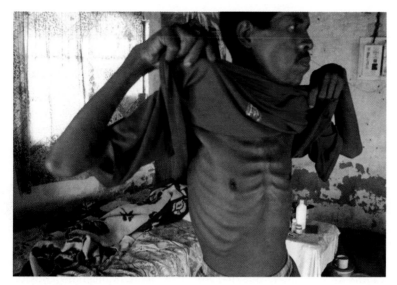

Globalization can add to human misery as well as to greater well-being. The image here reminds us that, by the early 21st century, HIV had become a global pandemic. Just as HIV destroyed the body's immune system, the spread of HIV and AIDS was disabling the body politic. The worst-hit African countries began to suffer a social breakdown. Their capacity to resist famine eroded as hunger and disease reinforced each other.

regarded as matters of "domestic jurisdiction" in which outsiders should not meddle. Corporations dare not ignore global problems such as climate change and HIV.

After 9/11, the dividing line between foreign and domestic policy became further blurred. In the United States, "national security" began to merge with "homeland security."

LEVELS OF ACTION AND ANALYSIS

To analyze any event on the world stage, we must know the cast. Who are the **actors**? They are a multitude—distinct but interacting. In the 20th century, IR focused on three levels: the individual, the state and society, and the state system. In the 21st century, we must include two others—transnational forces and the eco- or biosphere. How they fit together is suggested in Figure 1.1.

Level 1: Individuals and Human Nature

At center stage are individuals—the designers, implementers, beneficiaries, and often the victims of world politics. In this sense, IR remained unchanged by 9/11. It was individuals—not "Islam" or some other abstraction—who financed, organized, and carried out the skyjackings. It was individuals who died; coped with the mayhem; tried to punish those responsible; and labored to thwart, create, or profit from more 9/11s.

Fig. 1.1 Five Levels of IR Action and Analysis

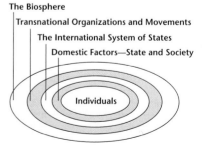

The Biosphere
Transnational Organizations and Movements
The International System of States
Domestic Factors—State and Society
Individuals

So we must learn about key individuals—from Osama bin Laden to George W. Bush—what made or makes them tick. But we must also know about our shared "human nature"—our "wiring" shaped by thousands or millions of years of evolution. Here, 9/11 immediately presents a puzzle. We know that humans are programmed to survive. Why then did the 9/11 skyjackers—educated, healthy, materially comfortable—seek their own destruction? Why did they freely choose self-destruction—banned by some readings of the *Quran*?

The skyjackers registered a huge impact on IR. Though they had little or no backing from any established government, they inflicted great damage on a "superpower" at the price of their nineteen lives and less than a million dollars.

Was this a new development—that individuals not associated with any government could play such decisive roles in world affairs? No—*plus ça change*. Zoroaster, Buddha, Abraham, Jesus, Mohammed, Joseph Smith, and Mary Baker Eddy changed the world. Pope Urban II mobilized the crusades. Gandhi undermined the British Empire.

Assassins have often shifted the path of history. Assassins killed three great liberators—Abraham Lincoln, Tsar Alexander II, and Gandhi. In 1914, a young Serb killed Austria's archduke and catalyzed World War I. Several would-be assassins tried to kill Hitler but failed.

The Nobel Peace Prize has been awarded not only to UN officials such as Ralph Bunche and government ministers such as Henry Kissinger, but also to private individuals such as Jane Addams, Martin Luther King, Jr., Mother Teresa, Elie Wiesel, and Shirin Ebadi. Presidents Theodore Roosevelt and Woodrow Wilson received the prize while still in office, but Jimmy Carter won it in 2002—testimony to his contributions both while U.S. president and later as a private citizen. The man who funded the prizes did a great deal for both war and peace: Alfred Nobel invented dynamite and commercialized the exploitation of Black Sea oil.

Individuals remain the basic actors in IR. Abstractions do not plan and act—not "Islam" or "the West," not the "United States" or "New York," not "terrorism" or "repression."

Level 2: Domestic Factors—State, Society, Culture

States—often called nation-states—became the dominant actors on the world stage in the 17th century when they supplanted tribes, empires, city-states, and princedoms. The 1648 **Treaty of Westphalia** established the state as the basic unit of the international—more precisely, the interstate—system.[2] A state must have four features: a

2. The Treaty of Westphalia affirmed the independence of the United Dutch Provinces and the Swiss cantons from Spanish Hapsburg rule. The treaty ended the Thirty Years War of religion and upheld the principle, "Whoever rules, his religion will prevail."

A new phase in IR became manifest as the second millennium began—a struggle to the death between radical Islamists and the West. Al-Qaeda skyjackers struck major symbols of U.S. power and the American way of life on 9/11/01. When the twin towers of New York's World Trade Center collapsed, a gaping hole was left not just in lower Manhattan but also in America's image. Never in modern warfare had so few, using such limited resources, done so much damage to a major power and—as the repercussions swelled—to the world. Had Goliath been felled? Could it recover? A basic and recurring issue for this book is how 9/11 changed IR and what, despite everything, remained much as before.

defined territory, a permanent population, a stable government, and independence—that is, the sovereign right to deal with other states. This view of the state developed as Protestant princes in northern Europe established their independence from the Catholic Church and as French, Swedish, and other kings asserted their **sovereignty** (supreme power) over feudal lords.

The United States acted promptly after 9/11 to remove the Taliban regime in Afghanistan, which had provided a base to Osama bin Laden and his al-Qaeda network. When the Taliban refused to surrender bin Laden, U.S. forces, joined by anti-Taliban Afghans, drove the Taliban from Afghan cities. A new phase in U.S. policy began after 9/11 in which U.S. forces would not just bomb suspected terrorist targets from afar, as the Clinton administration had done in the 1990s, but would invade, occupy, and reorganize entire countries accused of supporting anti-U.S. terrorists. The United States could be seen as both "liberator" and as "invader" or "occupier." Like some god, it destroyed to create.

But Washington devoted far more resources to destroying the Taliban than to helping Afghans rebuild. The photo shows war-ravaged Kandahar in December 2001. With the Taliban routed, people dared to play music again and many women dropped their veils. By 2003, New Yorkers were planning new buildings, but much of Afghanistan—including Kandahar—still lay in ruins.

Nearly 200 states made up the United Nations as the 21st century began—up from 51 when the UN was formed in 1945. Saudi Arabia and Egypt—birthplaces of the skyjackers—were UN founding members in 1945. Afghanistan, home to bin Laden before 9/11, joined the UN in 1946, but was represented there in 2001 by a government in exile, not by the Taliban theocrats who ruled most of the country and sheltered bin Laden. Palestinians—for whom the skyjackers expressed deep concern—had no state and only "permanent observer" status at the UN.

We often speak of the state as a unified actor, as in "France opposed Germany." But this use is very misleading, for no country is monolithic. The term *nation-state* also leads to muddled thinking, for it implies that every state is homogeneous, with one society and one culture. Most states, however, contain more than one nation. In Canada, for example, many French speakers and Native Americans see themselves as members of distinct nations. Even a relatively homogeneous society such as Japan contains regional, social, and economic groups with special interests in IR. Japanese farmers, for example, resisted free trade that would threaten their subsidized monopolies.

Societies come in many sizes—from families to professions to a possible *Société des Nations*, as the French called the League of Nations in 1919. Many societies contain more than one culture. In Saudi Arabia, modern ways and oil wealth overlap with the much older ways and values of desert nomads. Cultures can unify societies but can also divide them.

Level 3: The System of States and International Organization

World affairs are heavily shaped by the state system—the structure of power among states and the ways they behave, the rules they observe, the patterns of conflict and cooperation that divide and unite them. There are regional subsystems within the larger international system, each with its own pecking order.

Among states there is anarchy—absence of government—except for the rules and customs they accept. But states have created international organizations and laws to regulate trade, limit war, and facilitate cross-border relations. When we speak of international organizations, we usually refer to an **intergovernmental organization (IGO)**, created and funded by states. The United Nations is a multipurpose IGO—meant to promote a variety of political, economic, and social goals. Other IGOs strive to promote narrower, "functional" tasks—from delivering mail across borders (Universal Postal Union) to fostering peaceful uses of atomic energy (International Atomic Energy Agency). Thus, most IGOs belong to the state system and yet can be seen as "nonstate actors" because they are not states.

A supranational organization, if one existed, would stand above and govern states—perhaps on the U.S. or Canadian "federal" models. One of the earliest IGOs with supranational authority was the European Coal and Steel Authority, founded by six states in 1951 to regulate their production and pricing of coal and steel. The United Nations is very far from being a supranational world government. It depends mainly on the voluntary cooperation of its members, though the UN Security Council can make decisions regarding peace and security that, in theory, bind all UN members. In the early 21st century, the **European Union (EU)** was a hybrid—part IGO, part supranational—but it was beginning to behave more like a state, as we shall see in Chapter 15. Other regional organizations, such as those in Africa and the Americas, were much less developed than the EU.

Level 4: Transnational Relations

Most of what we usually call IR takes place between states. Levels 2 and 3 are **state-centric**—focused on actions within or between states. But this way of thinking nearly misses the forest for the trees. How so? The state-centric view neglects Level 4. Transnational actors pass over, ignore, go around, flout, or attack states and their borders. In short, **transnational** relations transcend states and their borders, in contrast to what happens between states (**international**) or over them (**supranational**)

The Internet challenged the Great Wall. Should China be open and on-line or closed to the world? Some Chinese citizens and foreigners hoped the Internet would help liberalize China. But Chinese authorities wanted to maintain mind controls at the same time they worked toward modernization. Across China in 2001 police shut off access to the Web for some 6,000 Internet cafes. Less than 10 percent of Beijing's 2,500 Internet cafes had permission to operate. In June a fire in one cafe killed two dozen students and left a dozen hospitalized. The cafe's owners had locked its doors to keep out authorities. Mayor Liu Qi immediately shut down all Internet cafes and said that no further licenses would be issued. In July, Beijing authorities allowed thirty cafes to reopen after they pledged to follow fire codes, keep records of computer use for sixty days, and install filters to keep out pornography and politically subversive messages.

World affairs are shaped not just by states but also by **nonstate actors**—IR actors that are not states. At Level 1, these players are key individuals. On Level 2, they include substate actors such as ethnic groups and economic interests. On Level 3, there are IGOs such as the United Nations. But Level 4 consists only of nonstate actors, from Islam to General Motors to the Mafia. We may think of these various actors as agents operating within the overall structure of IR. On Level 5, discussed below, is another kind of nonstate actor—the biosphere, the life support system for these many agents.

Level 4 is where **globalization** takes place—the transnational movement of people, goods (books, CDs, weapons, drugs), ideas and information, and money and credit, as well as epidemics and pandemics. Some people, ideas, and goods move across borders openly; others are smuggled.[3]

Modern technology gives unprecedented speed and force to the processes of globalization. But political, commercial, and religious movements have operated for millennia across borders and oceans. British trading companies, for example, dominated India before diplomats and troops made it the jewel of the British Empire. Investment capital moves across borders in response to the push and pull of markets. But missionaries and terrorists go for other reasons.

Transnational organizations and movements come in many shapes and sizes.[4] Religions unite millions of believers across borders. Mafias, terrorists, and drug traffickers are powerful transnational players. The biggest **transnational corporations** (TNCs), such as General Motors

3. Robert K. Schaeffer, *Understanding Globalization: The Social Consequences of Political, Economic, and Environmental Change* (Lanham, Md.: Rowman & Littlefield, 1997).

4. Richard J. Barnet and John Cavanagh, *Global Dreams: Imperial Corporations and the New World Order* (New York: Simon & Schuster, 1994); Kenichi Ohmae, *The Borderless World: Power and Strategy in the Interlinked Economy* (New York: HarperBusiness, 1990).

Another side of globalization is its capacity for enlightenment. In China, as happened earlier in the U.S., the Internet began in the 1990s to serve as a platform for a wide spectrum of viewpoints as well as a source of scientific and business information. Despite government controls, Internet use steadily grew in China. Estimates in 2002 suggested that nearly 50 million Chinese regularly logged on, making China the number three user of the Internet in the world. Chinese dissidents in the U.S. often used the Internet to funnel news and views to China not readily available there. But the Internet also gave an outlet to Chinese who pressed their leaders to do more against U.S. policies in many parts of the world.

and Ford, have revenues larger than many states. Thanks to the Internet, however, small businesses can also offer their services worldwide. Music, tastes, and fashions shape life across borders, as do economic practices such as **Fordism** (mass production techniques plus mass consumption). Even brand names such as Coke can move people. In post-Communist Albania, for example, many people viewed their first Coca-Cola plant as a sign of a good life to come. Cricket may unite the Commonwealth (erstwhile British Empire) more than any speeches. The Beatles and Coke may well have done more to subvert the Soviet realm than did the CIA. As Map 1.1 suggests, soccer spread from Europe to the world, while American fast food and Hollywood films swept the globe. The French and German governments subsidize the study of their languages worldwide, but English spreads like wildfire—transforming or destroying other tongues in its wake.

Some transnational actors are backed by governments. During the Cold War (ca. 1946–1989) Moscow and Washington dueled with a variety of "front" organizations of women, trade unions, and student groups funded by the USSR Committee of State Security (KGB) and the CIA. **Nongovernmental organizations (NGOs)** such as Greenpeace operate quite independently of any government.[5] Some transnational organizations even work against governments.

Globalization has positive and negative results. The importance of states declines as TNCs leap political frontiers. General Motors is based in Detroit, but it has offices and plants around the globe. TNC managers

5. Craig Warkentin, *Reshaping World Politics: NGOs, the Internet, and Global Civil Society* (Lanham, Md.: Rowman & Littlefield, 2001).

Map 1.1 Globalization: First soccer, then Hollywood, then McDonald's, and then . . . ?

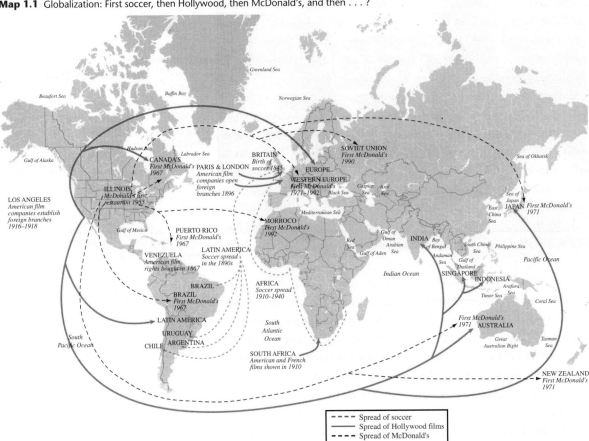

look worldwide for settings that promise lower costs and higher profits. If their global outlook calls for a move to greener pastures, local workers and governments can be left high and dry. Computer programmers in India may get jobs lost in Silicon Valley. Electronic money transfers go on twenty-four hours a day from Hong Kong to London to New York, eluding government controls. Drug dealers and others escape taxes by laundering profits via offshore banks, for example, on several Caribbean islands. Governments that still seek to control the minds and tastes of their citizens (as in China) wage an uphill battle as exotic sights and sounds bounce from satellites to local TV screens.

In the late 20th century, Osama bin Laden and his associates organized **al-Qaeda** (in Arabic, "the base"), a global network of Islamic activists striving to destroy U.S. and other Western institutions and cultures. Since this "base" represented no state and was moveable, al-Qaeda's policies were not so much "foreign" as "global." If driven from Afghanistan, al-Qaeda's cells could operate from Pakistan, Indonesia, or even the United Kingdom.

Cultures may also be transnational. If they spread far and develop strong foundations, cultures give rise to a **civilization**, the most generalized form of culture. There have been dozens of great civilizations in world history. In the 21st century there are at least seven—maybe a dozen—including Western Christianity and Islam. Nearly every civilization is rooted in a religion or system of ethics. The global pattern is shown in Map 1.2.

Apart from categories such as state and transnational, we may also classify IR actors as belonging to North and South; East and West; or the First, Second, Third, or Fourth Worlds (see Table 1.1). The idea of a Third World developed during the Cold War to distinguish those countries that were neither part of the First (or Free) World nor part of the Second (or Communist) World. In fact, most nonaligned countries were in the South. Unlike the **First World**, led by Washington, or the **Second World**, led by Moscow, most **Third World** countries were non-white, non-Christian, and industrially undeveloped. However, each grouping contained enormous diversity. For example, the First World contained both Greece and New Zealand. The Second World embraced not just the USSR and Poland, but also China and Cuba. The Third World included India, Yugoslavia, and Guyana. Some analysts even spoke of a **Fourth World**, made from the very poorest ranks of the Third. Thus, reality is far more variegated than our categories—mere starting points for analysis.

Level 5: The Biosphere or Ecosphere

Level 5 is the broadest arena for IR action and analysis. The biosphere is the envelope of life on this planet—a thin membrane of stone, soil, water, fauna, flora, and atmosphere. Population pressures and resource shortages remind us that IR, like all human activity, depends upon this sphere of life. Both international and transnational action can strengthen or harm the biosphere. If humans preserve their forests and coral reefs, they enhance the globe's capacity for life. If they despoil the planet with open-pit mines, carbon wastes, or the weapons of war, they undermine it. We focus on Level 5 in Chapter 13, but it forms the background to every theme in this book.

Two NGOs cooperated across borders to press for an end to all nuclear testing. In 1989–1990, the Nevada-Semipalatinsk Movement (NSM) linked those who wanted to stop underground tests (permitted by the 1963 limited test ban) in Nevada and at Semipalatinsk in Soviet Kazakstan. American Indians and others in Nevada found themselves to be interdependent with Kazaks living in villages and towns; they were joined by French Polynesians and Japanese and others who suffered from nuclear radiation. The NSM worked with International Physicians for the Prevention of Nuclear War (IPPNW), winner of the 1985 Nobel Peace Prize. Here the president of the Kazak branch of the IPPNW signs a petition calling for a halt to nuclear testing.

Map 1.2 Religions of the World

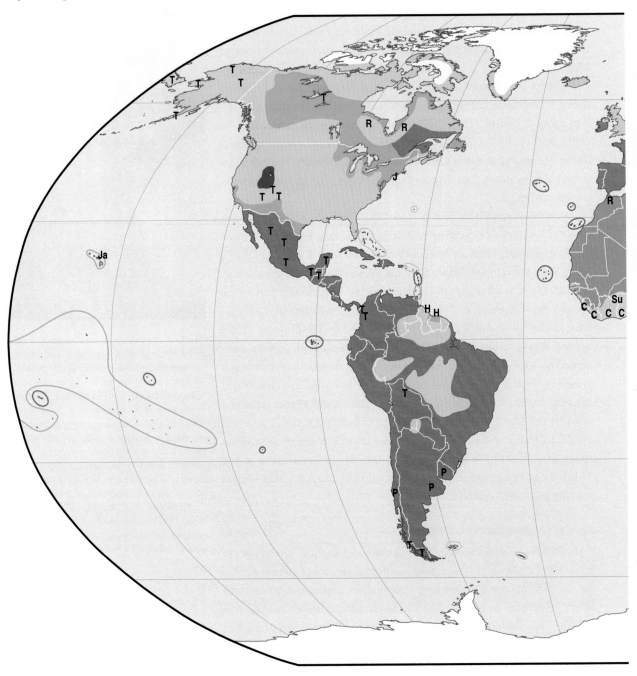

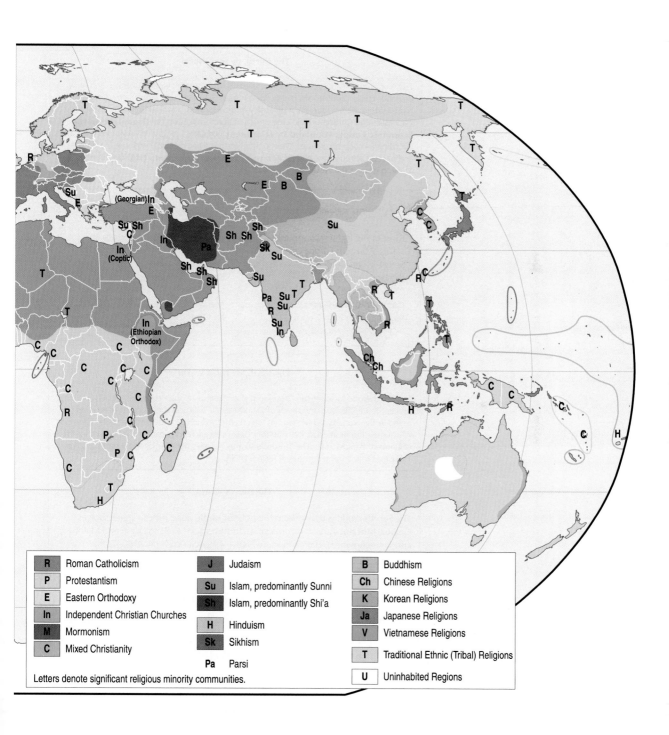

R	Roman Catholicism	**J**	Judaism	**B**	Buddhism

Legend:

R Roman Catholicism
P Protestantism
E Eastern Orthodoxy
In Independent Christian Churches
M Mormonism
C Mixed Christianity

J Judaism
Su Islam, predominantly Sunni
Sh Islam, predominantly Shi'a
H Hinduism
Sk Sikhism
Pa Parsi

B Buddhism
Ch Chinese Religions
K Korean Religions
Ja Japanese Religions
V Vietnamese Religions
T Traditional Ethnic (Tribal) Religions
U Uninhabited Regions

Letters denote significant religious minority communities.

Table 1.1 North and South

The North, or First World

The North consists of Western Europe, the U.S. and Canada, Japan, Australia, and New Zealand. These countries are highly "developed," economically industrialized, capitalist, high-income, democratic, located largely in the Northern Hemisphere, and primarily Caucasian and Christian. This "club of rich nations" makes up the **Organization for Economic Cooperation and Development (OECD)**, founded in 1960 to discuss and coordinate economic policies. Most of the North is allied militarily with the U.S. in bilateral pacts or through the **North Atlantic Treaty Organization (NATO)**, founded in 1949 to protect the West from Soviet attack.

? **The Second World** ?	**Newly Industrializing Countries (NICs)**
Most of the former Communist states of Eastern Europe and the Soviet Union have been striving since the late 1980s to join the First World. Cuba and North Korea are still Communist. China and Vietnam have a foot in each world.	Many countries in the South are acquiring a "northern" status. They include the four Asian "Little Tigers" of Singapore, Hong Kong, Taiwan, and South Korea. Other NICs include Chile, Malaysia, Thailand, Argentina, Brazil, and Indonesia.

The South, or Third World

The Third World includes the "developing" or "less developed countries" (LDCs) of Asia, Africa, the Middle East, and much of Latin America. Many of these countries have adhered to the Nonaligned Movement which emerged in the mid-1950s, and the Group of 77 (numbering more than 125 member states), a caucus on economic affairs within the UN since the mid-1960s. The Third World also includes the Central Asian states (such as Tajikistan) that emerged from the former USSR.

The Fourth World

The Fourth World is drawn from the poorest of the poor: African states such as Guinea, Mozambique, and Somalia; Asian states such as Bangladesh and Maldives; and in the Americas, Haiti and some Native American communities.

The Level-of-Analysis Problem and Agent–Structure Interaction

   With so many players and arenas to explore, students of IR face the **level-of-analysis problem**: Which level(s) must we study to understand a given issue? Which level(s), if any, can be neglected? How do "agents" (such as individuals) interact with "structures"? Which is more weighty—the micro or the macro? Answers may hinge on time and place. Surely the many levels interact, as we shall see in the Cuban missile crisis, analyzed in Chapter 3 below. Knowledge from many disciplines must be integrated to comprehend agent–structure interactions. Ultimately, we should pursue what E. O.

Wilson calls **consilience**—from the Latin for "jumping together"—a unity of knowledge achieved by fusing science, history, ethics, and policy.[6]

THROUGH WHAT LENS SHOULD YOU VIEW IR?

To understand IR we need a good lens—a theoretical perspective that helps us to explain the past, describe the present, anticipate alternative futures, and provide sound guidelines for policy making. Two opposing perspectives have long dominated IR—**realism** and **idealism**. A third view, focused on interdependence, emerged in the last decades of the 20th century. Let us look through each lens in turn.

Image 1: Realism—IR as a Struggle for Power

The Growth of Realism. Realists see IR as a struggle for power—especially material assets—and influence. More than four centuries before Christ, the realist's bottom line was clearly stated by an Athenian general: "The strong do what they have the power to do and the weak accept what they have to accept." The Athenian officer demanded that the people of Melos, an island in the Cretan Sea, fight with Athens against Sparta. But the Melians wanted to remain neutral and appealed to an ideal: "It is to the general good of all men" to uphold the principles of "fair play and just dealing." Impatient with idealistic talk, the Athenians seized Melos, slaughtering or enslaving its people.[7] Our major source for this "Melian debate" is Thucydides, an Athenian general turned historian. The deepest reason for the Peloponnesian War, he said, was the growth of Athenian power and the anxiety this produced in Sparta. A cause and effect of this growth was **hubris**—overweening pride, which led Athenians to overreach.

The tactics of realism were elaborated by Niccolò Machiavelli, a government official exiled from 16th-century Florence. Giving advice to a hypothetical ruler, Machiavelli advised the statesman to be both the lion and the fox—powerful and clever: "Let a prince win and maintain the state—the means will always be judged honorable and praised by everyone."[8]

Living during England's 17th-century civil war, the writer Thomas Hobbes focused on what realists see as the structural cause of the struggle for power: **anarchy**—the absence of government. In a "state of nature" without government, Hobbes argued, every person would do whatever seemed necessary to survive, unleashing a "war of all against all" where life is "nasty, brutish, and short." To escape this turmoil, Hobbes wrote, people contract to obey a supreme political authority. This government provides security within the state.[9]

6. Edward O. Wilson, *Consilience: The Unity of Knowledge* (New York: Knopf, 1998), where he links biology, social science, ethics, and environmental policy. Wilson also seeks to integrate insights from aesthetics.

7. Thucydides, *The Peloponnesian War* (New York: Penguin Books, 1956), Book 5, chap. 7.

8. Niccolò Machiavelli, *The Prince* (Prospect Heights, Ill.: Waveland Press, 1980), 109. For his ties with Leonardo da Vinci, see Roger D. Masters, *Machiavelli, Leonardo, and the Science of Power* (Notre Dame, Ill.: University of Notre Dame Press, 1996). For applications, see Harvey C. Mansfield, Jr., *Taming the Prince: The Ambivalence of Modern Executive Power* (New York: Free Press, 1989).

9. Thomas Hobbes, *Leviathan* (New York: Penguin, 1981 [1651]), 185–188; chaps. 14–17.

For Hobbes, a student of Thucydides' work, IR is a state of nature.[10] Among diverse societies and states, there is anarchy—no overarching government to define and impose rules. Hence, each society must depend on its own strengths and cunning—what today's realists call self-help—to survive. The only way to check others' tyranny is to amass power, either alone or with allies.

There are various kinds of realists. The ultrarealist—a follower of Machiavelli or Hobbes—is a hard-liner who assumes that conflict is inevitable. The ultra goes all out to defeat rivals, treating war as just another tool of policy. The founder of the Soviet state in 1917, Vladimir Lenin, endorsed a kind of ultrarealism for Communists. He taught that politics is "*kto kovo*" (who [conquers] whom). Lenin endorsed any and all means likely to promote a Communist dictatorship worldwide.

Moderate realists do not see IR as a game of "winner-take-all." They are more interested in compromise and stability than expansion. Thus, German Chancellor Otto von Bismarck relied on force to unify Germany and defeat France in 1870 and 1871, but then practiced a skillful *realpolitik*—realist diplomacy—that for twenty years kept an aggrieved France from aligning with Russia against Germany. Bismarck, like other German leaders in the 20th century, used Germany's wealth to generate economic inducements that shaped Russia's foreign policies.[11]

American foreign policy has often been guided by a moderate realism. But it has also engaged in imperial expansion, crusades to end evil, and policies of "anything goes" when fighting bad guys. Moderate realists are not pacifists, but they do not seek war. Thus, presidents Theodore Roosevelt and William Howard Taft as well as Woodrow Wilson wanted strong webs of international law to promote long-term stability. But World War II taught Americans that aggressors must be stopped, by force if necessary. In 1946–1947 President Harry Truman initiated a strategy for containing Soviet expansion.

As the Cold War developed with the USSR, Americans learned moderate realism from former diplomat George F. Kennan, theologian Reinhold Niebuhr, geographer Nicholas Spykman, and IR scholars such as professor Hans J. Morgenthau.[12] These authors set out six axioms of realism:

1. *Human nature:* Humans are self-centered, greedy, and often aggressive.

2. *State centrism:* The state is now the primary actor in world politics. The United Nations is an instrument of states.

3. *Power as interest:* The basic interest of each state is to increase its power. Politics is a struggle for power. At home, states build military and

10. Hobbes's first published work was his 1628 translation of Thucydides' *Peloponnesian War.*

11. Randall Newnham, *Deutsche Mark Diplomacy: Positive Economic Sanctions in German–Russian Relations* (University Park: Pennsylvania State University Press, 2002).

12. Hans J. Morgenthau, *Politics Among Nations: The Struggle for Power and Peace* (New York: Knopf, 1948), updated and revised by Kenneth W. Thompson (New York: McGraw-Hill, 1993). For realist views in the 1990s, see John Mersheimer, "The False Premises of International Institutions," *International Security* 19, no. 3 (winter 1994–1995): 5–49, and others' essays in the same volume called *GET REAL.* For critical evaluations, see Randall L. Schweller and David Priess, "A Tale of Two Realisms: Expanding the Institutions Debate," *Mershon International Studies Review* 41, suppl. 1 (May 1997): 1–32.

▲▲ Can Realists Favor International Institutions?

Moderate realists are often institutionalists—proponents of international law and organization. They see a constructive role for international institutions, though they are reluctant to surrender power to them. They welcome institutions that reduce anarchy, believing that law can benefit the strong as well as the weak, because rules make cheating on treaties and sneak attacks less likely. Institutions can make IR more predictable and reduce the cost of transactions across borders.

In 1919, the Republican-controlled U.S. Senate did not approve President Woodrow Wilson's plan for the League of Nations. Wilson wanted to end power politics. Republican leaders expected it to continue, but most Republican senators were not isolationist; most were conservative internationalists in the moderate realist traditions of former presidents Theodore Roosevelt and William Howard Taft. Taft himself served as president of the League to Enforce the Peace (founded in 1915), which endorsed collective security though it said nothing about economic reform or national self-determination. Moderate Republicans engineered the 1922 Washington Naval Treaty to limit battleships and heavy cruisers, and backed other internationalist policies such as the 1932 Stimson Doctrine (see Chapter 15).

In the 1990s, ultrarealists, including some U.S. senators and congressional leaders, wanted to dissolve the United Nations. Moderate realists saw a constructive role for international institutions.

economic strength; externally, they form alliances against others. Power is an end in itself, but it is also a tool. It is a means, fungible like gold or money, toward many ends.

4. *Rationality:* Governments calculate rationally how to maximize state power. Knowing this, we can read between the lines of flowery messages that one foreign minister sends to another.

5. *Amorality:* There is no common moral code among states. Individual morality stops at the border. As Morgenthau put it, "Realism refuses to identify the moral aspirations of a particular nation with the moral laws that govern the universe."

6. *History over science:* A wise reading of history is the best guide to understanding IR—not mathematical models.

U.S. containment policy, based on these axioms, proved relatively effective from the late 1940s to the mid-1960s. In the late 1960s and 1970s, however, the American superpower foundered in Vietnam and then reeled in the face of sharp increases in the price of oil demanded by the **Organization of Petroleum Exporting Countries (OPEC)**. What had gone wrong? Critics assailed each axiom of realism:

1. *Human nature:* Human behavior is not uniform. Some leaders and followers are more aggressive than others. Individuals can change; so can societies. Life across borders can be improved.

2. *State centrism:* States are not the only important players on the world stage. The TV evening news, antiwar folk singer Joan Baez, and OPEC all challenged U.S. "super power" in different ways.

3. *Power as interest:* Military-political power is no longer fungible. The heavily armed United States was being eclipsed by "trading states" such as Japan and West Germany.[13] To understand IR, critics advised, study **international political economy (IPE)**—how politics and economics combine to shape world affairs.[14]

4. *Rationality:* Governments do not always act rationally. They often foul up due to fatigue, misperception, partisan politics, and bureaucratic rigidity.

5. *Morality:* There is a growing worldwide consensus on morality—for example, on human rights—making morality a weighty factor in IR.

6. *Science:* Analysts of IR go astray when they trust their instincts and make generalizations based upon a few incidents. A scientific approach is necessary to understand IR. Otherwise, bias takes over.

Dissatisfaction with traditional realism led scholars to seek ways to improve the scientific rigor of IR and pay more attention to political economy. Two offshoots of realism developed in the last decades of the 20th century.

Neorealism or Structural Realism. Adapting Thomas Hobbes, professor **Kenneth N. Waltz** explained IR by one key variable: the underlying structure of the international system—its anarchy and the distribution of power. For Waltz and other **neorealists**, wars happen because there is nothing to prevent them—no government over states. IR is less a struggle for power than for security. When push comes to shove, states respond to the power structure in which they operate, regardless of leaders' personalities or form of government.[15] Level 3 is decisive.

World-Systems (Dependency) Theory. Lenin, as noted above, was an ultrarealist as well as a kind of Marxist. Marxism and Leninism lost favor in the late 20th century. But Marxism lived on in **world-systems theory**. This approach, also known as dependency theory, posits that for centuries there has been a world system divided into a core of rich capitalist states, a dependent periphery of poor states, and a semiperiphery between the core and outer circle. What Waltz calls anarchy, world-systems theorists say is really the structural dependency of the periphery on the core. They charge that Waltz and other non-Marxists ignore dynamic forces such as the class struggle pushing toward a revolutionary transformation of the world system.[16] Level 2 is decisive in that it determines Level 3.

Both neorealists and dependency theorists are too deterministic. They downplay the role of individuals, of culture, and other factors and cases that challenge their theories. Over and over we shall see that policy choices are conditioned—not decided—by the structures of power. Let

13. Richard Rosecrance, *The Rise of the Trading State* (New York: Basic Books, 1986).

14. See Robert Gilpin, *Global Political Economy: Understanding the International Economic Order* (Princeton, N.J.: Princeton University Press, 2001); Charles Wolf, Jr., *Straddling Economics and Politics: Cross-Cutting Issues in Asia, the United States, and the Global Economy* (Santa Monica, Calif.: RAND, 2002). For a literature review, see Dennis J. Gayle, Robert A. Denemark, and Kendall W. Stiles, "International Political Economy: Evolution and Prospects," *International Studies Notes* 16, no. 3, and 17, no. 1 (fall–winter 1991–1992): 64–68.

15. Kenneth N. Waltz, *Theory of International Politics* (New York: McGraw-Hill, 1979). See also Waltz, *Man, the State, and War: A Theoretical Analysis* (New York: Columbia University Press, 1959).

16. See, for example, Immanuel Wallerstein, *The Rise and Future Demise of the World Capitalist System* (New York: Cambridge University Press, 1979); Wallerstein, *Geopolitics and Geoculture: Essays on the Changing World-System* (New York: Cambridge University Press, 1991); Robert W. Cox, "Social Forces, States and World Orders: Beyond International Relations Theory," *Millennium: A Journal of International Studies* 10 (summer 1981): 126–155; and "The South in the New World (Dis) Order," *Third World Quarterly* 15, no. 1 (March 1994).

us turn now to idealism, the major alternative to realism for more than two thousand years.

Image 2: Idealism—IR as a Quest for Harmony, Law, and Morality

The Growth of Idealism and Liberalism. Many idealists and liberals expect all peoples to live in harmony thanks to nature, law, or morality. Realists anticipate conflict and war; idealists, cooperation and peace. Realists focus on what is good for the state; idealists think more about the good of humanity.

Idealism is also ancient. The Melians, as we saw, called on the Athenians to practice "fair play and just dealing." But realists, like the Athenian commander, treat rules as nothing more than dictates of the strong. Idealists, in contrast, view legal and moral norms as sacred—built into IR by God or Nature or social contract.

Idealists trust in reason to reform the world and bring peace; realists doubt that social science can subdue greed. Idealists hope for the best; realists fear the worst. These and other differences are summarized in Table 1.2.

Table 1.2 Three Images of IR: Diverse Assumptions

	Realism	Idealism	Interdependence
Focus	the means (power); the possible	the moral objective; the desirable	the means and ends
Nature of IR	anarchy; often win–lose; self-help	harmony (win–win)	potential for mutual gain or pain
Human Nature	egotistical, aggressive, greedy	good	malleable, variable
Values at Stake in IR	survival and influence	peace, justice, welfare, the biosphere	survival, influence, and quality of life
Source of Most IR Conflicts	struggle for power	misperception	struggle for power and misperception
How to Plan	learn from the past	visualize the future	learn from the past and visualize the future
What to Study	history	social sciences, law	all relevant knowledge
Outlook	pessimism, caution	optimism, hope	cautious hope
Key IR Actors	states and systems of states	international and transnational actors	both state and nonstate actors
International Law	undependable—a weak reed to rely on	an independent force for cooperation	weak but growing—an "emergent property"
Human Rights and Morality	irrelevant to IR	central to IR	increasingly relevant
Criterion for Action	national interest	humane ideals	enlightened self-interest and humanism
How to Negotiate	claim values and seek gains relative to your rivals'	seek absolute gains for all parties	greatest possible gains for self and others

Like realists, idealists fall into many camps. Philosophical idealists, like Plato, believe that ideal forms underlie the imperfect, material bodies we see. They agree with St. John: "In the beginning was the Word. . . ." Utopians like Sir Thomas More sketch models of ideal worlds to stimulate thought and action. Grotians (named for Hugo Grotius, 1583–1645, a father of international law) seek to codify the norms imbedded in nature or wise practice. Liberals (dating from John Locke, 1632–1704) want to eliminate anarchy, but they stress liberty and the sovereignty of the individual. Utilitarians (followers of Jeremy Bentham) believe that public policy should seek the greatest utility for the most people. Their 20th-century offshoots favor welfare programs for the dispossessed. Commercial pacifist liberals (followers of Adam Smith and Joseph Schumpeter) hold that free trade contributes not only to wealth but to peace. Liberal pacifists (followers of Immanuel Kant) believe that representative democracy leads to peace and international codes of behavior.

Global idealists proclaim the equality of all men and women. But there are also narrow idealists who struggle on behalf of the "one true faith" or the "master race." They have often spawned so-called holy wars and campaigns to wipe out other peoples and belief systems. Arguing against such narrow idealisms, Soviet President Mikhail Gorbachev called in the 1980s for the "humanization" of international relations—the placing of universal human needs above those of race, religion, or class. He told the United Nations, as awareness of our common fate grows, "every nation would be genuinely interested in confining itself within the limits of international law."[17]

Idealism in U.S. Policy. American policy has long carried the stamp of strong ideals—its founders' confidence that they were destined to build a New World better than the old, the claim that "all men are created equal," and trust in scientific and social progress.

President Woodrow Wilson became the world's most famous idealist between 1917 and 1919, when he summoned Americans to a crusade to make the world safe for democracy and demanded that a league of nations supplant old-style power politics.

Later, President Franklin Roosevelt championed his "four freedoms" (freedom of speech, freedom of worship, freedom from want, and freedom from fear) and the establishment of the United Nations. Throughout the Cold War, both Democratic and Republican presidents alike spoke up for freedom while also emphasizing the pragmatic containment of communism. More than any other U.S. president, however, Jimmy Carter (served 1977–1981) made human rights the central objective of U.S. policy. But when Iranian ayatollahs and Soviet militarists made Carter look

17. For the evolution of Gorbachev's foreign policy, see Walter C. Clemens, Jr., *Can Russia Change? The USSR Confronts Global Interdependence* (New York: Routledge, 1990), chaps. 7–8.

"soft," U.S. voters swung the other way: starting in 1980 they voted for what became twelve years of Ronald Reagan–George Bush realpolitik.

In 1992 the wheel turned again as U.S. voters rejected Bush in favor of Bill Clinton, who, as a candidate, promised to achieve welfare ideals at home and promote human rights abroad. President Clinton's foreign policy turned out to be more pragmatic than idealistic, but he often dispatched diplomats to mediate as "honest brokers" and soldiers to act as the policemen of the world.

Clinton talked like an idealist on human rights and arms control, but behaved like a pragmatic realist toward North Korea. When Pyongyang moved to go nuclear in the mid-1990s, Clinton threatened war, but then—as we shall see in Chapter 6—offered material inducements for North Korea to abjure nuclear weapons.

President George W. Bush gravitated toward ultrarealism—self-help rooted in vast military power—but he often spoke like an idealist, a tent preacher sure of what is right and wrong. Still, his views dovetailed with those of many neoconservatives shaping policy, led by Deputy Defense Secretary Paul D. Wolfowitz and Defense Policy Board member Richard E. Perle (a former student of Wolfowitz who married his daughter). Many "neocons" claimed to be **"Straussians"**—followers of political philosopher Leo Strauss. Focusing on Aristotle and other classic authors, Strauss and his followers lamented moral relativism, as taught by Machiavelli and Hobbes and as practiced by many Americans.[18]

Though focused on ideals, Strauss saw the need for power: "To make the world safe for Western democracies, one must make the whole globe democratic, each country in itself as well as the society of nations." Further: "The only restraint in which the West can put some confidence is the tyrant's fear of the West's immense military power."

Though Strauss overlapped with IR realist Hans J. Morgenthau in the early postwar decades at the University of Chicago, Morgenthau opposed idealism in IR. He held that each country has its own morality—a fact that makes any universal moral code impossible. Another realist, former diplomat George F. Kennan, in lectures at the University of Chicago in 1950, argued that Washington's tendency to justify its policies by moral and legal principles had often led to disaster.

Kennan's caveat applied to the Bush administration. Its self-righteous hubris created problems similar to those that, Thucydides tells us, sank ancient Athens. For example, instead of continuing the negotiations that Clinton pursued with Pyongyang, Bush branded North Korea part of a putative "axis of evil." This kind of moralism backfired when Pyongyang renounced

18. Strauss held that America's civilization rests on the absolutes of ancient Athens and Jerusalem plus the moral relativism of modernity. He championed Athens and put down Jerusalem, arguing that true philosophy could not be reconciled with theology. See Leo Strauss, *Natural Right and History* (Chicago: University of Chicago Press, 1953). Doubting that the masses were interested in ultimate truths, Strauss wrote on one level for Everyman and on another as a guide for elites. Critics worried that self-proclaimed "Straussians" in or close to the Bush White House were deceiving the public with noble myths—fictions—while doing whatever suited their objectives.

its mid-1990s commitments and claimed to be going nuclear. "Moral clarity" was hard to establish because neither Washington nor Pyongyang had completely fulfilled its agreed obligations. Believing North Korea wrong and America right, the Bush team had difficulty seeing the United States as did Pyongyang's leaders—an aggressive bully. The White House was not prone to look for, as Christ once suggested, any motes in its own eyes. The team split in 2003 on whether to use sticks or carrots to alter North Korea's behavior or just put up with it so long as Pyongyang did not sell plutonium to others. All parties concerned with North Korea would have been better off to affirm their mutual vulnerability and seek mutual gain, starting with conditional cooperation in small ways and moving to larger.

Bush's moralism also backfired with respect to abortion. He cut off funding to the UN Population Fund when conservatives charged that UN funds were helping China carry out forced abortions. But with less money available for family planning, more pregnancies occurred in Africa—and hundreds of thousands more abortions.

The Bush team asserted that secular, Western-style democracy is the best form of government and tried to foster this view in Iraq. Millions of Iraqis, however, had other ideas. As Hans Morgenthau had cautioned, each culture has its own values.

The New Idealists. Just as neorealists have sought to improve on Morgenthau's axioms, neoidealists and neoliberals seek to remedy blind spots in the Wilsonian tradition. Some neoidealists, like neorealists, try to apply scientific methods of analysis to IR. Most neoidealists are more attuned to the IPE than traditional idealists, but reject the material determinism of neorealists. Various forms of neoidealism abound:[19]

Transnationalism. Traditional, Wilsonian idealists still hope that governments (Level 2) and organizations such as the United Nations (Level 3) can generate progressive reforms. But transnational idealists focus on Level 4 and hope transnational social movements can transcend state borders. They count on NGOs and communities of experts and cultural leaders to outflank governments.[20]

Environmentalism. Ecologists focus on the eco- or biosphere (Level 5). They see threats to whales, wolves, coral, insects, and trees as threats to all life. They call for **"green accounting"** (calculating environmental costs along with other production costs) and oppose those who resist any restraints on their quest for power and wealth.[21]

Postmodernism. Political language needs to be deconstructed because all texts have multiple meanings. So-called facts are often propaganda to buttress existing power structures. Read between the lines to get at the real meaning.[22]

19. For broad surveys, see Donald J. Puchala, ed., *Visions of International Relations: Assessing an Academic Field* (Columbia, S.C.: University of South Carolina Press, 2002); and Walter Carlsnaes et al., *Handbook of International Relations* (Thousand Oaks, Calif.: Sage, 2002).

20. Thus, the World Order Models Project sought transnational support for four goals—peace, economic well-being, justice, and environmental protection—and a timetable to achieve them. It sponsored books by scholars from the U.S., African, Indian, Scandinavian, and other political cultures. See Richard A. Falk, *Explorations at the Edge of Time: The Prospects for World Order* (Philadelphia: Temple University Press, 1992). See also works by Ali A. Mazrui, Rajni Kothari, and Johan Galtung. For related efforts, see the Web sites of the Lawyer's Committee on Nuclear Policy and International Physicians for Prevention of Nuclear War.

21. See Web sites of the Sierra Club and Greenpeace, also the sources cited in Chapter 13.

22. See, for example, Francis A. Beer and Robert Hariman, eds., *Post-Realism: The Rhetorical Turn in International Relations* (East Lansing: Michigan State University Press, 1996); and Pauline Marie Rosenau, *Post-Modernism and the Social Sciences: Insights, Inroads, and Intrusions* (Princeton, N.J.: Princeton University Press, 1992).

Postmodernists are correct in seeing ethnic and other identities as more manufactured than organic. But deconstruction can also go too far. It is good to punch holes in empty claims, but not necessary to throw away all faith in language.

Constructivism. This school holds that realists ignore social constructs—the deep beliefs each group of people has about other groups and ways of life. Thus, Americans fear China's nuclear arsenal more than they do Britain's, even though China's is much smaller. Why? Americans have few worries about Britain's intentions but feel great uncertainty about China's.[23]

Feminism. Feminists (both male and female) contend that men and patriarchal political systems have dominated and distorted the practice and the study of IR. Man, the hunter and fighter, has shut out woman, the nurturer and cooperator. The prevailing stereotype in many countries is that women are "soft"—not tough enough for the brutal game of politics. Hence, they should be IR spectators or relegated to "low politics." Feminist scholars deconstruct the language of IR to reveal its gender bias; then they hope to reconstruct IR by putting women back in.[24]

There are many varieties of feminism in IR studies—liberal, essentialist, postmodern, Third World, and others. But most focus on a central question: If women were more influential in the study and process of IR, would the world be different? Would policy makers behave differently? Would there be more or less peace?

As we will see in Chapter 5, the UN Development Programme has devised measures of gender bias to ascertain the extent to which women are deprived economically and shut out politically in countries around the world. In Chapter 12 we will learn that "keeping women down" helps to keep entire countries backward and poor; Chapter 15 details women's rights abuses.

Feminists caution that we cannot infer much from the exceptional cases of Margaret Thatcher and other women who have led countries such as Israel, Britain, Pakistan, Turkey, Bangladesh, India, Ireland, Iceland, and Norway.

In sum, feminism provides a valuable lens when kept in focus.

"Worlding" IR. Not just women, but many groups of humans have been omitted from traditional IR. Ethnic minorities and peoples without states, such as the Kurds, need to be better represented in both the practice and study of IR.

A rounded approach to IR would combine gender with ethnicity and other variables. White women in Scarsdale, New York, for example, differ

23. Alexander Wendt, *Social Theory of International Politics* (Cambridge, U.K.: Cambridge University Press, 1999); Ted Hopf, *Social Construction of International Politics: Identities and Foreign Policies, Moscow, 1955 and 1999* (Ithaca, N.Y.: Cornell University Press, 2002).

24. J. Ann Tickner, *Gendering World Politics: Issues and Approaches in the Post-Cold War Era* (New York: Columbia University Press, 2001); Cynthia Enloe, *Maneuvers: The International Politics of Militarizing Women's Lives* (Berkeley, Calif.: University of California Press, 2000). The aftermath of 9/11 underscored the gender issue in a strange way. The last will of skyjack leader Mohammed Atta contained not only praise of Islam but also displayed an extreme mysogynism. Point 5 of the will, dated April 1996, stated: "I don't want a pregnant woman or a person who is not clean to come and say goodbye to me [at my funeral]. . . ." Point 11 stipulated: "I don't want any women to go to my grave at all during my funeral or on any occasion thereafter." The following year, when the Taliban fled Kabul, many Afghan girls and women celebrated their liberation.

greatly from most black women in a Congolese village. Each group exerts a different kind of influence on IR.[25]

Endism. Since the conflict of ideas drives history, the victory of Western liberalism over Communist ideology has meant the "end of history." Francis Fukuyama predicted the "common marketization" of IR—a humdrum era in which corporations and governments build a more comfortable life for their clients. Boring but peaceful. Critics say that the liberal victory is not a final synthesis. It faces its antitheses in the rise of nationalism, Islamic fundamentalism, and antiglobalization.[26]

Civilizationism. Contrary to Fukuyama, Samuel P. Huntington expected "history" to continue in the clash of civilizations. Today's division between Western Christian and Orthodox states in the Balkans is much the same as that which took shape when the Roman Empire was split between Rome and Byzantium. The end of the Cold War pits "the West against the rest"—Confucian, Muslim, Hindu, and other civilizations.[27] Al-Qaeda's jihad and America's response appeared to some observers to confirm the civilizationist thesis.

But Huntington exaggerates the weight of civilization. What we see as clashes of civilizations usually reflects an underlay of conflicting material interests. North Korea and Pakistan exchange favors for tangible advantages—not because their atheistic and Muslim rulers dislike Western Christianity.

Moreover, civilizations change and may be converging. Most of the nearly 3,000 individuals killed on 9/11 were U.S. citizens, but there were also citizens from 62 other countries. They included some 250 Indians, 200 Pakistanis, 23 Japanese, 200 Britons, and 55 Australians. "American" culture was being modified by many newcomers.

Appraising Realism and Idealism. Each variety of realism and idealism contributes to our understanding of IR. But neither greed nor reason governs the world; few humans are basically evil or basically good. Our vision will be impaired if we assume, as realists do, that no better system can emerge. But we will be disappointed if we believe, as some idealists do, that the future is entirely open-ended.

We need a more complete paradigm, less given to either/or categories. If realism is thesis and idealism its antithesis, where is a productive synthesis?

Image 3: Interdependence—Mutual Vulnerability

A worldview anchored in global interdependence offers a broader lens with fewer distortions than either realism or idealism. The concept of interdependence fits our complex world where high–low politics converge

25. For example, Jan Jindy Pettman, *Worlding Women: A Feminist International Politics* (London: Routledge, 1996);

26. Francis Fukuyama, *The End of History and the Last Man* (New York: Avon, 1992). The long view of history with the rise and fall of various systems gives a different impression: See Barry Buzan and Richard Little, *International Systems in History: Remaking the Study of International Relations* (New York: Oxford University Press, 2000).

27. Samuel P. Huntington, *The Clash of Civilizations and the Remaking of World Order* (New York: Simon & Schuster, 1996).

and domestic–external realms intertwine. This worldview affirms both the difficulties and the possibilities of greater cooperation in IR. It acknowledges the continuing importance of states but also the rising tide of cross-border transactions by nongovernmental actors.

What is interdependence? It signifies mutual dependence—a point on the spectrum between absolute dependence and independence. **Interdependence** means mutual vulnerability. It is a relationship in which the well-being of two or more actors is vulnerable, or at least sensitive, to changes in the condition or policies of the other.[28]

To assess mutual vulnerability, we must first ask: Is it balanced? If dependence is basically one-sided, it is not interdependence. Second, is there vulnerability or mere sensitivity? Two countries share strategic vulnerability if they cannot defend against one another. A country is sensitive if it can be hurt by effects from outside before it takes countermeasures. When the U.S. set limits on wheat exports to the USSR in the 1980s, Soviet importers turned out to be merely sensitive to the limits; they could still buy wheat from Argentina and Australia. Third, does the interdependence apply to one issue or many? Some states share vulnerability in just one or two arenas. Canada and the United States, on the other hand, interdepend on a wide range of issues. Fourth, how is interdependence perceived? Parties may interdepend but not perceive it; alternatively, actors may exaggerate their vulnerability. Fifth, does interdependence occur by choice? Interdependence can result from accidents, choice, or coercion. Hoping to tame Soviet expansionism, Washington in the 1970s sought to enmesh the USSR in a web of security, commercial, and scientific cooperation. Some Soviet leaders resisted this web.

Sources and Limits of Interdependence. Mutual vulnerability arises from many sources, each of which has the capacity to enhance or diminish life. Sources of vulnerability include weaponry—vulnerability to mass destruction can spur cooperation or inspire a surprise attack; commerce—trade ties can bolster peace or generate frictions; communication—shared information can lead to mutual appreciation or disdain; science and culture—shared knowledge enriches our lives but can also endanger individuality; and coevolution—having evolved together, humans have become interdependent with one another and with their shared habitat.

Is interdependence good or bad? Does it engender peace or conflict? Interdependence by itself is neither good nor bad. How humans deal with this condition can generate gain or pain. The impact of interdependence on peace is difficult to assess because multiple factors are at work. Some studies suggest that extensive trade ties inhibit violence.[29] But such ties do not exclude violent conflict. Many peoples have fought one another

28. The argument here follows Robert O. Keohane and Joseph S. Nye, *Power and Interdependence.* 3d ed. (New York: Longman, 2001), chap. 1.

29. Susan M. McMillan, "Interdependence and Conflict," *Mershon International Studies Review* 41, suppl. 1 (May 1997): 33–58.

Fig. 1.2 Visions of the World

Hierarchy of realism and structural neorealism

World-system dependency

One-world idealism

Interdependence

30. The relationship between the United States and Japan shows how interdependence can cut in opposite directions. The two countries bicker over trade and U.S. bases but have been partners in

despite their interlocked economies—for example, Americans during their Civil War and Europeans in 1914.[30]

Is interdependence growing? Experts disagree on the extent of interdependence and what it means for IR. But the overall picture at the onset of another millennium is one of escalating interdependence—on many issues and among many partners—worldwide. As Soviet President Gorbachev put it in the late 1980s, the world is "contradictory but also integral and interdependent." Humans face many "global problems too complex to be resolved by any single country."[31] To deal with these problems requires cooperation by all "worlds"—including both genders, all races, all cultures, all classes, all regions, and all religions.

In the late 20th century, global interdependence coexisted with globalization. The two phenomena are related but distinct. Interdependence—mutual vulnerability—implies the continued existence of states. Globalization—global processes that ignore borders—suggests the weakening or even disappearance of state sovereignty as it was known after 1648.[32] The implications and prospects of globalization are discussed in the last chapters of this book.

Complex Interdependence. Some countries are more than trading partners or allies. They are linked in **complex interdependence**, a relationship with three characteristics:

1. There is a complex agenda with no hierarchy. These countries share many concerns, but no single issue stands out so that, if unresolved, it jeopardizes the entire relationship.

2. Interaction occurs at many levels of government and society. Multiple channels connect these societies—not just the meetings of ministers and presidents.

3. Parties bargain hard and long on various issues, but regard military threats as virtually unthinkable.

Complex interdependence and peaceful cooperation can strengthen one another. Canada and the United States have moved toward complex interdependence since the late 19th century, even though their governments and many basic values have remained distinct. All Western European countries have gravitated toward complex interdependence since the 1950s. Movement toward European unity may snowball or stall or switch directions.

How interdependence theorists view the world compared to other theorists is suggested in Figure 1.2. Traditional and structural realists emphasize the hierarchy of power. World-systems theorists divide the world into

What Is Diplomacy?

The word *diplomacy* comes from the Latin "diploma"— a passport or other official document conferring a privilege. By the 18th century, *diplomatic* referred to the conduct of foreign policy, especially by ambassadors or other official representatives, as well as to IR documents such as treaties.

Diplomacy has become nearly a synonym for foreign policy. Accordingly, diplomacy comes in many forms. There is open and closed diplomacy, conducted openly or in secret. The diplomacy of force (including gunboat diplomacy and atomic diplomacy) depends on military threat or coercion. Yen or dollar diplomacy uses commercial penetration and economic influence. Media diplomacy directs some messages through press and television. Public diplomacy (such as Voice of America radio broadcasts) addresses the publics of other countries.

Cultural diplomacy uses the arts, including film, music, and literature. Sports or ping-pong diplomacy uses athletics to win friends or influence people. All this gives rise to two-track diplomacy—a public track conducted by governments and a private track of citizen and nongovernmental diplomacy. The public and private tracks may harmonize, compete, or conflict.

There is also parliamentary diplomacy (exchanges between parliaments), summit diplomacy (between top leaders), sauna diplomacy (a Russian favorite), shuttle diplomacy (used by U.S. envoys traveling between Israel and Arab capitals), and tin cup diplomacy (asking others to pay for one's own adventures).*

There is also diplomacy of deception, disinformation, and half truths. One story holds: "When a diplomat says 'yes,' he means 'maybe.' When he says 'maybe,' he means 'no.' If he says 'no,' he is not a diplomat." Another saying is that "an ambassador is someone sent abroad to lie for her country."

In this book we argue the case for a diplomacy of truth—at least in peacetime. While secret diplomacy appeals to many governments, it often backfires. Accords reached by open diplomacy are more likely to endure, because they must address the interests of all concerned parties.

*On Bismarck's cigar diplomacy, see *Dictionary of Twentieth-Century World Politics*, compiled by Jay M. Shafritz et al. (New York: Holt, 1993), 217.

concentric circles of power. Idealists visualize one world—united despite differences. The interdependence perspective accepts that units have both divergent and shared interests, and that the units can harm or help one another.

THE ART OF THE DEAL: DIVERGENT AND SHARED INTERESTS

Interdependence is a fact. How to respond to this reality is a question for policy makers. Let us review the basics of negotiation, the tools of the diplomat's trade.

HOW TO NEGOTIATE: CLAIM OR CREATE VALUES?

Negotiate is from Latin for "do business." One way to negotiate is to "bargain," derived from the Old French for *haggle*. Most of us negotiate every day, on everything from house chores to terms for a new car. When you haggle about who washes the dishes, the stakes are minor. In IR, the stakes can be major. Sometimes IR conflicts represent a real clash of

security and commerce since the late 1940s. Japanese and Americans can enrich or diminish one another. If Americans and Japanese did not interact, as was the case during the 18th century, they would not quarrel. Neither would Americans drive Hondas or Japanese play baseball. Without its U.S. ally, Japan would probably arm more and invest less.

31. In the 1960s and 1970s, Soviet representatives asserted that American talk of interdependence masked U.S. ambitions to dominate the world, but they began—even before Gorbachev—to recognize "mutual dependence." See Walter C. Clemens, Jr., *The USSR and Global Interdependence: Alternative Futures* (Washington, D.C.: American Enterprise Institute, 1978), chaps. 3–4; and Clemens, *Can Russia Change?* chaps. 5–6.

32. As we shall see in Chapter 16, globalization could lead to governance without government. For signs that this process has begun, see the Web site of Global Action Network Net. For background, see Wolfgang H. Reinicke, "Global Public Policy," *Foreign Affairs* 76, no. 6 (November–December 1997): 127–139.

interests; sometimes discord results from misperception. Either way, the parties take their differences seriously.

Negotiation is a process by which parties communicate about ways to deal with issues on which they have different viewpoints. Negotiation is a major tool in **diplomacy**—the conduct of foreign policy. "The essence of diplomacy," said U.S. diplomat Lawrence Eagleburger in 1986, "is how you manage the day-to-day business, the confidence you build, the atmosphere you create, so that when the tough times come, you can do business."[33] But diplomats do not always negotiate to reach an agreement. Often they seek side benefits such as scoring propaganda points or keeping an open channel of communication. In December 2002, however, Secretary of State Colin Powell was more upbeat. "At its best," he said, diplomacy is like art: It "extends the realm of the possible."[34]

33. Quoted in *Dictionary of Twentieth-Century World Politics*, compiled by Jay M. Shafritz et al. (New York: Holt, 1993), 216.

34. Powell spoke at a gathering to honor five lifetime achievers in the performing arts. See *The New York Times*, December 9, 2002.

Memo to the President: *You and your team negotiate at home as well as abroad. In Washington you negotiate with the White House and Congress about appointments, budgets, and policy priorities. With the Departments of State and Defense and other agencies you negotiate to dovetail actions. You and they must also negotiate with a host of private actors such as the news media, corporations, and churches. From Belgium to Bangladesh, U.S. representatives negotiate with governmental and nongovernmental organizations on everything from military alliances to currency reforms to disaster relief.*

Pursuing your goals, you may utilize hard or soft power—coercion or persuasion. Negotiators often try to back their words with carrots and sticks. You may reward or penalize, smile or frown, appoint conciliatory "doves" or antagonistic "hawks" to key posts, spend less or more on defense, keep ships at home or "show the flag" abroad. You may welcome, reject, or ignore overtures by others. (Silence, too, can be eloquent.) Your government may also negotiate with force, using war as an instrument of policy. If neither hard nor soft power works, you may give in or withdraw.

Many values or utilities can hinge on negotiations—tangible goods such as land and wealth, and intangibles such as honor and credibility. You seek to advance a range of values—those of your country, your government, your department, your own. If the cost is not exorbitant, you may also wish to help other peoples and make the world a better place. You often face hard trade-offs: more of value x at the expense of value y.

IR actors may try to claim values for themselves or create values jointly with others; in short, they can pursue exploitation or mutual gain. You may choose between three approaches to negotiation:[35]

Approach 1: The Win–Lose Hard-liner. You claim and seek values for your side alone. You want to cut the pie so your side gets the largest possible share from a finite asset. You assume that what one side gains, the other must lose. You reject even a win–win solution unless you gain relatively more than your rivals.

35. See also the works by Raiffa, Fisher and Ury, and Lax and Sebenius cited at the end of this chapter in Recommended Resources, also the *Negotiation Journal.*

Your only rule is to win. A lion and a fox, you blend force and deception. You mask your assets, weaknesses, and goals, and expect others to do the same. You value immediate profits more than a reputation for integrity.

If you can't win alone, you partner with others for joint gains at the expense of third parties, as Hitler and Stalin did in 1939 when they split Poland between them. If weak, you can still follow win–lose logic: you "bandwagon" and join the king of the jungle or play the "jackal," following the lion to pick up what remains.[36]

Approach 2: The Win–Win Cooperator. You want accords—almost for their own sake—trusting that win–win outcomes are always available. You value candor and put all your cards on the table. You focus on absolute gains, not relative benefits. So long as you gain, who cares if others profit more?

Approach 3: The Conditional Cooperator. You try to advance your interests by creating values with other actors for mutual gain. You strive to create values that profit each side and help the deal to endure. If you can expand ("grow") the pie, it will be easier to divide and achieve joint benefit. You seek to replace expectations of win–lose with a shared quest for win–win.

You condition your cooperation on reciprocal action by others. But you take precautions lest the other side feign cooperation while seeking a one-sided victory. To break a spiral of conflict, however, you sometimes initiate exploratory steps to reduce tensions.

You are neither malevolent nor altruistic. You employ leverage gracefully—not with a sledgehammer. Though slightly distrustful, you foster openness. You share information about preferences, beliefs, and even minimum requirements. You cultivate habits of joint problem solving. You nourish conditions where neither party needs to worry if the other side gains marginally more. You honor commitments and demand that others do the same.

You understand that joint gains are possible but not inevitable. You reject the settlement unless it looks better than the alternatives to no deal at all.

WHY COOPERATION IS DIFFICULT

If interdependence is a fact, why do IR actors often act like hard-liners and pursue win–lose outcomes? The realist statesman and hard-line negotiator see many reasons to go it alone. They know that each level of international action generates obstacles to mutual gain solutions, beginning with individual greed. These obstacles are multiplied by parasitism and distrust.

Free Riding: The Logic of Collective Action

Some actors seek to **free ride**. Free riders follow the egotistical **logic of collective action**. This logic appeals to narrow self-interest. It advises the

36. See Randall J. Schweller, "Bandwagoning for Profit: Bringing the Revisionist State Back In," *International Security* 19, no. 1 (summer 1994): 72–107.

actor to exploit the goods that others provide and contribute as little as possible. Far from augmenting mutual gain, free riders undermine it because they act like parasites. Parasitism is often feasible because some actors are willing and able to produce public goods such as clean air and security even if others contribute less than their fair share.[37] Free riders often make just enough of a token payment to keep major contributors in the game.

If parasitism prevails, public goods will be underfinanced.[38] An interested party may pay the lion's share but still fail to do all that is needed. Parasitism can harm even the parasites. It weakens alliances and pollution controls, leaving even the free riders endangered and impoverished. As we shall see in Chapter 4, efforts by Britain and France to "pass the buck" encouraged Hitler to commence World War II. Later, free riding weakened the anti-Soviet alliance.[39] It continues to threaten the biosphere, as we shall see in Chapter 13.

The Security Dilemma

The **security dilemma** is that action by one state to increase its security may actually weaken it. John and Ivan, for example, say they wish to live in peace. However, John decides to raise the walls around his city. John says the walls are purely for defense, but Ivan fears his potential foe may be preparing a surprise attack backed by defenses against a counterattack.

Ivan also faces a dilemma: failing to react to John's improved defenses could increase Ivan's vulnerability. But if Ivan takes countermeasures, they may intensify John's insecurity. Action and reaction may produce an arms race—even a war—that neither wanted. This pattern has recurred throughout history.[40] Many players have followed the slogan, "Best safety lies in fear"—often with tragic consequences.

The Prisoner's Dilemma (PD)

IR negotiations often resemble a game. Game theory outlines four kinds of contests.[41] First, a game is called **zero-sum**, or win–lose, when the winnings of one side equal the other's losses, as in poker. Whatever John wins Ivan loses. Hard-line realists often perceive their contest with rivals as zero-sum. Second, a game is **negative-sum**, or lose–lose, if both sides lose more than they gain—the likely result of a nuclear exchange. Third, if both contestants win (as in a friendly race), a game is **positive-sum**, or win–win.

But neither pure conflict nor 100 percent harmony occurs often in world affairs. The fourth and most common IR game is **variable-sum** or

37. Mancur Olson, *The Logic of Collective Action* (Cambridge, Mass.: Harvard University Press, 1965); see also Olson, *The Rise and Decline of Nations* (New Haven, Conn.: Yale University Press, 1982).

38. The Greek *parasitos* means "someone who dines at another's table"; Latin *parasitus* is "one who lives by amusing the rich." Parasitoid insects eventually kill their hosts.

39. Europe and Japan could assume that Washington, for its own reasons, did not want them to fall under Soviet domination. U.S. allies contributed just enough to keep Americans from turning inward. For most of the Cold War, Americans devoted more than 6 percent of their economic production to defense; Europeans, about 3 percent; Japanese, 1 or 2 percent. The result was that Western forces could never match Soviet forces man-for-man, tank-for-tank. Had the Soviets attacked, Washington might have felt compelled to respond with nuclear weapons.

40. Athens built "defensive" walls over Sparta's objections—adding to mutual enmity. Starting in 1983, Washington's plans to build missile defenses caused a similar problem in its relations with Moscow, as we shall see in Chapter 6.

41. Game theory is a branch of mathematics that analyzes decisions in terms of the stakes and likely outcomes. See Frank C. Zagare, *Game Theory: Concepts and Explanations* (Beverly Hills, Calif.: Sage, 1984); Pierre Allan and Christian Schmidt, eds., *Game Theory and International Relations: Preferences, Information, and Empirical Evidence* (Brookfield, Vt.: Edgar Elgar, 1994); Steven J. Brams, *Biblical Games: Game Theory and the Hebrew Bible* (Cambridge, Mass.: MIT Press, 2003). See also the many articles on IR "games" in the *Journal of Conflict Resolution*.

deal is advantageous. The conditional cooperation approach limits exposure to exploitation while offering a good platform for mutual gains.

Combining the concepts of interdependence and conditional cooperation, this book suggests two guidelines for policy. First, actors are more likely to enhance their objectives if they can frame and implement value-creating strategies aimed at mutual gain than if they pursue value-claiming policies aimed at one-sided gain. Exploitation may yield short-run benefits for one side but tends to boomerang in the long run, so that costs outweigh benefits. Earlier, the long run may have been measured in decades or centuries, but in our world of escalating interdependencies, it becomes ever shorter. Profitable exploitation is difficult to sustain for more than a decade.

Few IR conflicts are mere misunderstandings, but creating values requires informed discussion by all concerned parties at home and abroad. The second guideline suggests that the more all parties communicate, the greater the prospect of finding solutions useful to all sides. The more intelligence estimates are publicly available, the fuller will be the public discussion preceding and accompanying each foreign policy thrust, and the higher the probability it will achieve its objectives.

Mutual gain policies and openness, if reciprocated, can lead IR actors toward a multifaceted, complex interdependence with a strong capacity to diminish discord and sustain peaceful cooperation. As we shall see in Chapter 5, the life sciences as well as social sciences suggest that a society's well-being—its overall fitness—may depend on a capacity to cooperate both within and outside the group. To sustain our common life-support system, humans need to cooperate—not free ride or exploit one another.

Complex interdependence can make its participants stronger than the sum of their parts. Their interlocking relationship is like that of diverse life forms coevolved into an ecosystem. A coral reef, for example, protects its members from the ravages of storms and alien species. The resultant structure of mutual aid may be seen as an "emergent property" or "order for free."[45]

The arguments for mutual gain and openness are hypotheses that must be validated or refined by experience. Consider them as you ponder today's news and the case histories in the chapters that follow. Are the arguments valid? Must they be refined? Under what conditions?

 Key Assets of the Effective Negotiator or Mediator

1. Knowledge of the players and the issues

2. Management skills to coordinate your own team

3. Timing—when to wait, pull back, initiate, persist, and follow through

4. Empathy with all whose interests are at stake

5. Communication skills in speech, writing, and gestures

6. Constructive imagination to identify or create mutual-gain solutions

7. Leverage—carrots or sticks—to motivate an accord

8. Toughness to stand pat, threaten, bluff, or fight

9. Flexibility to accommodate when appropriate

10. Stamina and patience to endure long hours, frustration, and travel

11. Integrity to inspire trust

12. A winning personality, interesting to work with

13. Draftsmanship to produce treaty language that copes with differences either by precision or by creative ambiguity

14. Domestic support from your government and society

15. Internal drive to achieve, plus emotional intelligence

45. An emergent property is a kind of "self-organization." See Roger Lewin, *Complexity: Life at the Edge of Chaos* (New York: Macmillan, 1992); and Stuart A. Kauffman, *At Home in the Universe: The Search for the Laws of Self-Organization and Complexity* (New York: Oxford University Press, 1995).

More radical shifts in IR took place as "regime change" and "preemption" became working premises of U.S. policy. The Bush administration demonstrated in 2003 America's capacity to remove "regimes" it deemed dangerous and to do so without explicit UN authorization—over objections not only from Russia and China but also from NATO allies France and Germany. The White House and Pentagon explained that the United States would "preempt" any effort to strike America with weapons of mass destruction. They accused Iraq of possessing such weapons and colluding with terrorists. In April 2003, the forces of three English-speaking countries—the U.S., UK, and Australia—attacked Iraq and demolished the regime of Saddam Hussein within a few weeks.

Many Iraqis welcomed the end of Saddam's regime but most insisted on Iraq's independence and demanded "coalition forces" promptly depart. Some residents of Baghdad tried to pull down a statue of Saddam but needed help. Tying the statue to a U.S. military vehicle, a Marine—a Chinese-American from Brooklyn—created an image that offended many Arab TV viewers. He briefly placed the Stars and Stripes over the statue's face before replacing it with an Iraqi flag. IR is about symbols and feelings as well as power and rules. Americans were also blamed for not protecting Iraq's National Museum even though Iraqis looted it.

What Do You Tell the President? . . . *What do these nuts and bolts add up to? What approach do you recommend? You brief the president: Our world contains danger and opportunity. After 9/11, much is the same, but much is different. The United States has never been stronger—or more vulnerable. We are no longer shielded by geography. Our open society helps foes to penetrate and harm Americans. National security must include homeland security. But U.S. vulnerability is shared by others—from Europe to Singapore. Though many Americans would prefer to go it alone in world affairs, we have gained much from cooperating with others—the United Nations, governments, NGOs, corporations, and individuals—to thwart terrorist attacks.*

Realists and neorealists are right to stress the hard realities of power. But their materialist views do not explain how dedicated idealists with little material power could inflict such heavy damage on the United States and the world. On the other hand, "civilizational differences" are seldom central. Usually they merely aggravate other irritants. North and South Korea oppose each other despite ties to the same culture. Most IR conflicts are still about raw power. Mayan Indians in Chiapas want land, not the ouster of Spanish Christianity. Colombian drug lords have no problem with civilization; they fight for freedom to make money.

The ultimate reality is that most peoples are linked by networks of global interdependence. What we make of interdependence and globalization is for us to choose. The events of 9/11 underscored that non-state actors as well as states can help or hurt one another. We must use U.S. power to subdue immediate threats, but we should also strive to change the milieux in which these dangers arise. Also, interdependence is asymmetric. In most respects, U.S. assets far outweigh those of potential foes and partners. Positive inducements usually work better than negative sanctions. We can use our advantages to encourage other actors to move in directions we prefer them to go. Carrots are more likely to nudge them than sticks.

Now, as before 9/11, our best course is to approach other actors in the spirit of conditional cooperation. The optimal way to enhance each actor's interests is by cooperating to create values with other actors—not by playing winner-take-all or bullying others to accept our dictates. If our ways of life or policies harm others or give offense, we should consider whether they could be altered to mutual advantage.

Openness at home and abroad is another key to success. Effective policies are likely to flow from strategies oriented toward mutual gain, incubated and nourished by relatively open dialogue at home and across borders. Policy failures, on the other hand, are most likely to arise from zero-sum, exploitative strategies conceived behind closed doors and implemented without meaningful dialogue at home, with partners, or with the target country.

KEY NAMES AND TERMS

actors (in IR)
anarchy
best alternative to a negotiated
    agreement (BATNA)
civilization
civilizationism
complex interdependence
consilience
constructivism
coordination game
diplomacy
endism
environmentalism
European Union (EU)
feminism (in IR)
First World
Fordism
foreign policy
Fourth World
free ride
frontier of possibilities
globalization
green accounting
high politics

hubris
idealism
interdependence
intergovernmental organization
    (IGO)
international
international political economy (IPE)
international relations (IR)
level-of-analysis problem
logic of collective action
low politics
Hans J. Morgenthau
negative-sum
neorealism
newly industrializing countries (NICs)
nongovernmental organization (NGO)
nonstate actor
North Atlantic Treaty Organization
    (NATO)
Organization for Economic Coopera-
    tion and Development (OECD)
Organization of Petroleum Exporting
    Countries (OPEC)
positive-sum

postmodernism
Prisoner's Dilemma (PD)
al-Qaeda
realism
Second World
security dilemma
self-help
sovereignty
state
state-centric
Straussian
supranational
Third World
tit-for-tat (TFT)
transnational
transnationalism
transnational corporations (TNCs)
Treaty of Westphalia
ultrarealist
variable-sum
Kenneth N. Waltz
worlding
world-systems theory
zero-sum

QUESTIONS TO DISCUSS

1. With what lens have you viewed world affairs? Did your viewpoint come from your home, schooling, outside reading, travels, or other experiences? How do your assumptions about IR match those outlined in Table 1.2?

2. What kinds of people have won the Nobel Peace Prize? Compare Ralph Bunche and Martin Luther King, Jr.; Jane Addams and Mother Teresa; Lech Walesa and Elie Wiesel; Jody Williams and Shirin Ebadi.

3. If you were locked in a cell separate from another prisoner charged with the same offense, would you plead guilty to win your freedom? What if your admission meant a jail term for the other accused? Can you be sure that she won't plead guilty and implicate you? What are the prerequisites of trust?

4. Does international cooperation depend on trust or on interest, or both? Give examples of each.

5. From your knowledge of recent events, point to a foreign policy action that can be explained by the structure of the international system. Point to another event better explained by the personality of the decision maker or the society where she or he operates.

6. Do idealists ever win?

7. How does interdependence theory differ from idealism?

8. How does complex interdependence differ from other forms of interdependence?

RECOMMENDED RESOURCES

BOOKS

Baldwin, David A., ed. *Neorealism and Neoliberalism: The Contemporary Debate.* New York: Columbia University Press, 1993.

Recommended Resources (continued)

Dougherty, James E., and Robert L. Pfaltzgraff, Jr. *Contending Theories of International Relations: A Comprehensive Survey.* 5th ed. New York: Longman, 2000.

Doyle, Michael W. *Ways of War and Peace: Realism, Liberalism, Socialism.* New York: Norton, 1997.

Fisher, Roger, and William Ury. *Getting to Yes: Negotiating Agreement Without Giving In.* New York: Penguin, 1985.

Fisher, Roger, et al. *Beyond Machiavelli: Tools for Coping with Conflict.* Cambridge, Mass.: Harvard University Press, 1994.

Friedman, Thomas L. *Lexus and the Olive Tree: Understanding Globalization.* New York: Random House, 2000.

Kegley, Charles W., Jr., ed. *Controversies in International Relations Theory: Realism and the Neoliberal Challenge.* New York: St. Martin's, 1995.

Keohane, Robert O., ed. *Neorealism and Its Critics.* New York: Columbia University Press, 1986.

Keohane, Robert O., and Joseph S. Nye. *Power and Interdependence.* 3rd ed. New York: Longman, 2001.

Keylor, William R. *World of Nations: The International Order Since 1945.* New York: Oxford University Press, 2002.

Knutsen, Torbjörn L. *A History of International Relations Theory.* Manchester and New York: Manchester University Press, 1992.

Lax, David A., and James K. Sebenius. *The Manager as Negotiator: Bargaining for Cooperation and Competitive Gain.* New York: Free Press, 1986.

Luard, Evan, ed. *Basic Texts in International Relations: The Evolution of Ideas About International Society.* New York: St. Martin's, 1992.

Mearsheimer, John J. *The Tragedy of Great Power Politics.* New York: Norton, 2001.

Peters, Michael A. *Poststructuralism, Marxism, and Neoliberalism: Between Theory and Politics.* Lanham, Md.: Rowman & Littlefield, 2001.

Raiffa, Howard. *The Art and Science of Negotiation.* Cambridge, Mass.: Harvard University Press, 1982.

Raiffa, Howard, et al. *Negotiation Analysis: The Science and Art of Collaborative Decision Making.* Cambridge, Mass.: Harvard University Press, 2002.

Stein, Janice Gross, and Louis W. Pauly, eds. *Choosing to Cooperate: How States Avoid Loss.* Baltimore: Johns Hopkins University Press, 1992.

Wendt, Alexander. *Social Theory of International Politics.* Cambridge, UK: Cambridge University Press, 1999.

WEB SITES

Council on Foreign Relations
http://www.cfr.org
Foreign Affairs
http://www.foreignaffairs.org
Foreign Policy Association
http://www.fpa.org
Institute for International Sport
http://internationalsport.com/index.html
International Studies Association
http://www.isanet.org
Online Interactive Prisoner's Dilemma Game
http://serendip.brynmawr.edu/bb/pd.html
U.S. Department of State
http://www.state.gov

INTRODUCTION TO WORLD AND REGIONAL MAPS

Geography, like history, is basic to the study of IR. Maps provide both facts and ideas about geography. Like statistics, maps can deceive—by omission or by distortion. But good maps suggest how the size, shape, climate, endowment, and location of each area condition all that has happened or can happen. Geography "conditions" but does not "determine" what people do. Ancient Egyptians lived next to a river that flooded, but they learned how to harness the Nile to form an "hydraulic civilization." Ingenuity, science, and technology turned a problem into an economic asset. Harnessing the river became a key to political power, for the pharaohs and their advisers knew when the Nile would flood.

A map showing which countries have large oil deposits could easily mislead. Yes, oil should mean wealth. But living standards in most oil-rich countries are not high. Many tend to rely on "petrodollars" and neglect other dimensions of spirit and power.

Our world map shows vast distances between most continents. But technology—sails, steam, jet engines—helps "to shorten distances." As communication links improve, we become more aware of shared vulnerabilities, for example, the pneumonia-like SARS epidemic reaching outwards from south China in 2002–2003.

Interdependence between regions deepens but is not new. Intrepid merchants and warriors sailed up and down the Mediterranean and through the straits into the Black Sea. The empire builders of Rome generated a Pax Romana. The Roman peace gave way to other dominions—Pax Mongolica, Pax Britannica, Pax Sovetica, and—possibly—a Pax Americana.

Maps can emphasize what separates people or brings them together. Map 1.1 shows how soccer, McDonald's, and Hollywood films have traveled the globe. In chapter 4 we see maps of military invasions and retreats, for example, the paths taken by North Korean and UN forces in 1950–1951. A photo shows Baltic military officers examining a map of invasion routes Russian armies could take in the 21st century.

Other maps show regions—each pulsing with unique energies but also linked to other locations near and far, small and large. Geography sets limits but does not tell all. It does not say whether the World Trade Organization will break down barriers to international trade or entities such as the European Union and NAFTA will concentrate trade within regions.

North and South America appear to be and are close to one another, but many parts of the Americas deal more with Europe or Asia than with each other. Still, some Mexicans lament they are "so far from God and so close to the United States."

Later we shall see (Map 12.1 on p. 441) how the many ways that maps "project" reality can emphasize—sometimes overemphasize—the importance of income, population, land mass, or location. For example, maps made in the USA often put the Americas at the center of the world. A map based on population would render Canada a sliver of the United States. For a very different perspective—how the planet Earth looks from outer space, or how the cosmos looks from Earth—see NASA's website for a new image every day at http://antwrp.gsfc.nasa.gov/apod/astropix.html.

Flying in an IranAir Airbus from Tehran to Amsterdam in 1998, a new perspective hit me, one seen on this book's cover. A unified chain of mountains stretches from the Himalayas, the Pamirs, the Hindu Kush, and Iran's Zagros, through the Caucasus and Balkans to the Alps, and seas ranging from the Aral, Caspian, Azov, Black, Aegean, and Adriatic out into the Mediterranean. An Iranian geologist on the same flight explained we were seeing what happened when the tectonic plates of India, Arabia, and Africa slammed into the Eurasian plate. Mountains and plains, seas and canals then formed the milieux where civilizations rose and died, where hatreds seethed and wars unfolded, but also where great prophets walked and preached—from Zoroaster to Mohammed, leaving messages that could unite or divide humanity. This domain, like the entire planet, contained multitudes. It housed potentials to enlarge or shut down freedom and well-being.

For unnamed Carribean Countries see North America Map

Abbreviations:

ALB.	Albania	LITH.	Lithuania
BELG.	Belgium	LUX.	Luxembourg
BOS.	Bosnia & Herzegovina	MAC.	Macedonia
CR.	Croatia	MOL.	Moldova
CZECH.	Czech Republic	NETH.	Netherlands
DEN.	Denmark	PORT.	Portugal
D.P.R.K.	Democratic People's	SER.	Serbia & Montenegro
	Republic of Korea	SL.	Slovenia
HUN.	Hungary	SLOV.	Slovakia
GER.	Germany	U.A.E.	United Arab Emirates
LAT.	Latvia	U.K.	United Kingdom

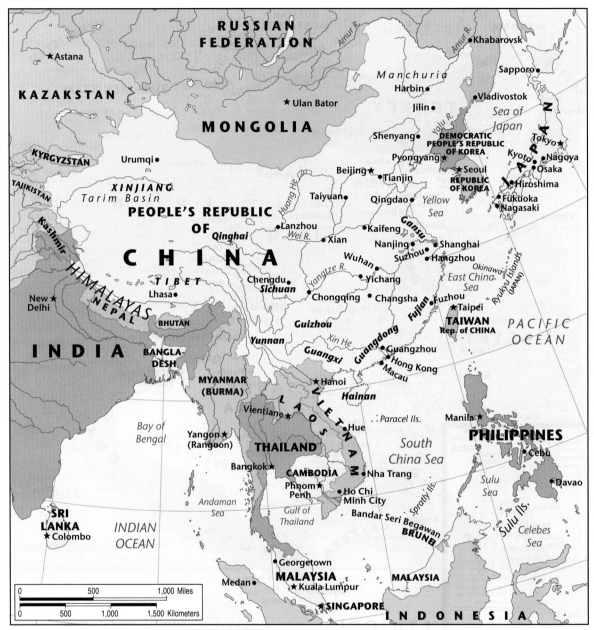

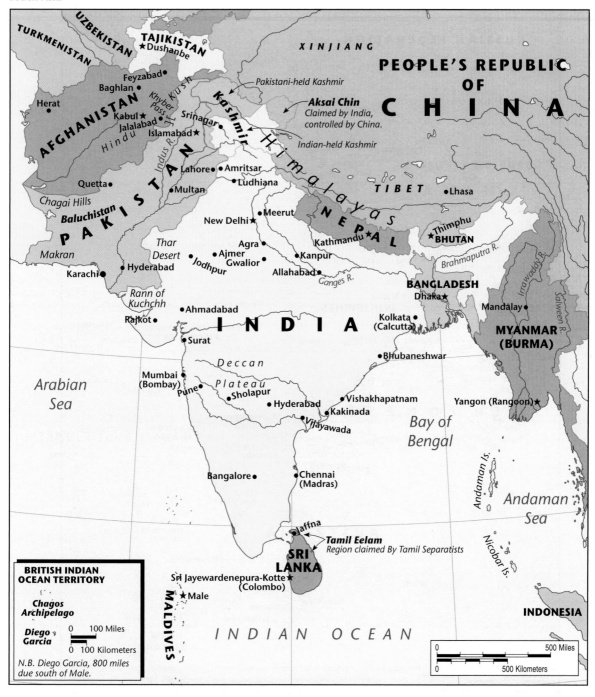

TURKMENISTAN
UZBEKISTAN
TAJIKISTAN
★Dushanbe

XINJIANG

PEOPLE'S REPUBLIC
OF
CHINA

Feyzabad•
Baghlan•
Herat •
AFGHANISTAN
Kabul ★
Jalalabad•
Islamabad ★
Hindu
Khyber Pass
Hindu Kush
Srinagar•
Kashmir

Pakistani-held Kashmir

Aksai Chin
Claimed by India,
controlled by China.

Indian-held Kashmir

Himalayas

Quetta•
Chagai Hills
Baluchistan
PAKISTAN
Makran
Indus R.

Lahore•
•Amritsar
•Ludhiana
•Multan

TIBET
•Lhasa

New Delhi ★
•Meerut
NEPAL
Thimphu
★ ★BHUTAN
Kathmandu★

Thar
Desert
Jodhpur•
•Ajmer
Agra•
Gwalior•
•Kanpur
Allahabad•
Ganges R.
Brahmaputra R.

BANGLADESH
Dhaka★

Karachi•
•Hyderabad
Rann of
Kuchchh
Rajkot•
•Ahmadabad
INDIA
Kolkata
(Calcutta)
Mandalay•
MYANMAR
(BURMA)
Irrawaddy R.
Salween R.

•Surat
Deccan
•Bhubaneshwar

Arabian
Sea
Mumbai•
(Bombay)
Pune•
Plateau
•Sholapur
•Hyderabad
•Vishakhapatnam
•Kakinada
Vijayawada•

Bay of
Bengal

Yangon (Rangoon)★

Bangalore•
•Chennai
(Madras)

Andaman Is.
Andaman
Sea

Nicobar Is.

•Jaffna
Tamil Eelam
Region claimed By Tamil Separatists

SRI
LANKA

Sri Jayewardenepura-Kotte★
(Colombo)
★Male
MALDIVES

INDONESIA

INDIAN OCEAN

**BRITISH INDIAN
OCEAN TERRITORY**

*Chagos
Archipelago*

*Diego
Garcia*

0   100 Miles

0   100 Kilometers

N.B. Diego Garcia, 800 miles
due south of Male.

0   500 Miles

0   500 Kilometers

The Pacific Rim

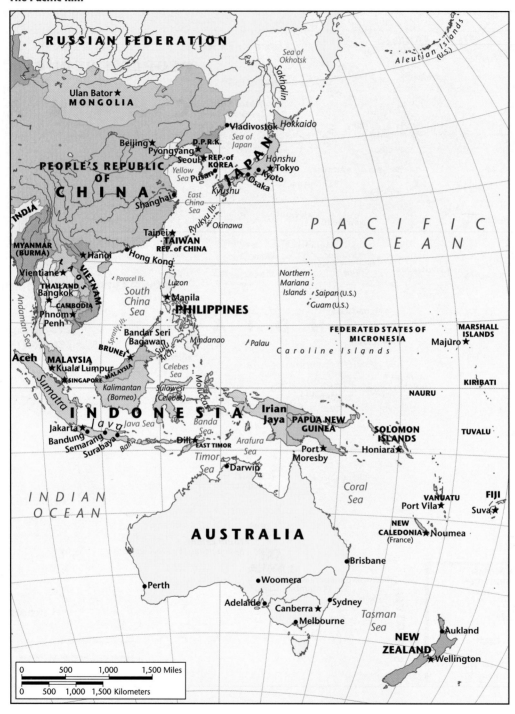

Abbreviations:

Belg.: Belgium
Bosnia: Bosnia and Herzegovina
Cr.: Croatia
Czech Rep.: Czech Republic
Kal.: Kaliningrad (Russian Fed.)
L.: Liechtenstein

Lux.: Luxembourg
Neth.: Netherlands
Mac.: Macedonia
Serbia: Serbia and Montenegro
Sl.: Slovenia
Switz.: Switzerland

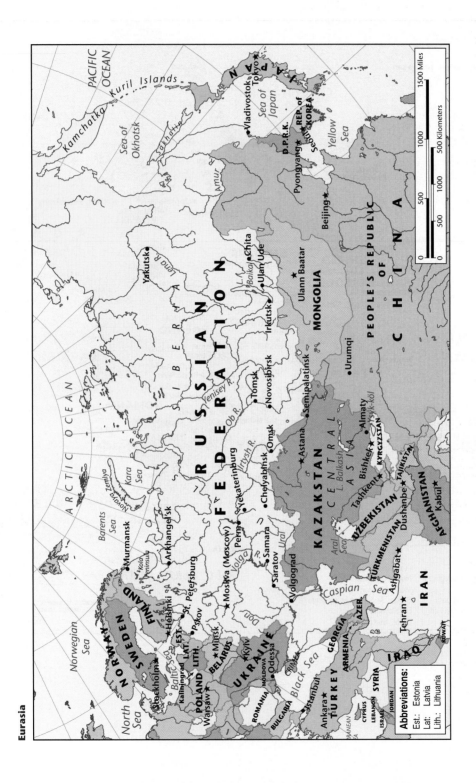

Eurasia

North America, Central America, and the Carribbean

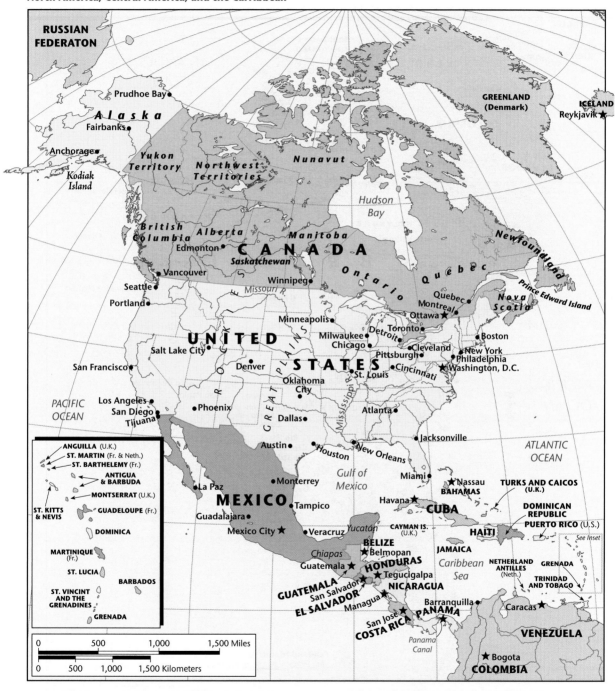

RUSSIAN FEDERATON

Prudhoe Bay•

Alaska
Fairbanks•

Anchorage•

Kodiak Island

Yukon Territory   *Northwest Territories*   *Nunavut*

GREENLAND (Denmark)

ICELAND
Reykjavik ★

Hudson Bay

British Columbia   *Alberta*   *Manitoba*   C A N A D A

Edmonton•

Saskatchewan   *Ontario*   *Quebec*   *Newfoundland*

Vancouver•

Seattle•

Portland•

Winnipeg•   Quebec•   *Nova Scotia*

Prince Edward Island

Montreal•   Ottawa★

Missouri R.   Minneapolis•   Toronto•   •Boston

U N I T E D   Milwaukee•   Detroit•   •Cleveland   New York•

Salt Lake City•   Chicago•   Pittsburgh•   •Philadelphia

San Francisco•   S T A T E S   St. Louis•   Cincinnati•   ★Washington, D.C.

Denver•

Oklahoma City•

Los Angeles•   *GREAT PLAINS*   Atlanta•

San Diego•   •Phoenix   Dallas•

Tijuana•

PACIFIC OCEAN

Austin•   Jacksonville•

Houston•   New Orleans•

ATLANTIC OCEAN

La Paz•   Monterrey•   Gulf of Mexico   Miami•

MEXICO   Tampico•   Havana★   Nassau★   TURKS AND CAICOS (U.K.)

Guadalajara•   BAHAMAS

Mexico City★   Veracruz•   *Yucatán*   CUBA   DOMINICAN REPUBLIC

CAYMAN IS. (U.K.)   PUERTO RICO (U.S.)

Chiapas   BELIZE   HAITI

★Belmopan   JAMAICA   *See Inset*

Guatemala★   HONDURAS   NETHERLAND ANTILLES (Neth.)   GRENADA

GUATEMALA   Tegucigalpa★   Caribbean Sea   TRINIDAD AND TOBAGO

San Salvador★   NICARAGUA

EL SALVADOR   Managua★   Barranquilla•   Caracas★

San José★   PANAMA

COSTA RICA   ★   VENEZUELA

Panama Canal

★Bogota

COLOMBIA

ANGUILLA (U.K.)
ST. MARTIN (Fr. & Neth.)
ST. BARTHELEMY (Fr.)
ANTIGUA & BARBUDA
MONTSERRAT (U.K.)
ST. KITTS & NEVIS   GUADELOUPE (Fr.)
DOMINICA
MARTINIQUE (Fr.)
ST. LUCIA
BARBADOS
ST. VINCENT AND THE GRENADINES
GRENADA

| 0 | 500 | 1,000 | 1,500 Miles |

| 0 | 500 | 1,000 | 1,500 Kilometers |

Caribbean Sea

NICARAGUA
COSTA
RICA
PANAMA

Panama
Canal

Barranquilla
Cartagena

Valencia ★ Caracas

TRINIDAD
AND TOBAGO

VENEZUELA

Orinoco R.

Georgetown
Paramaribo

GUYANA SURINAME FRENCH GUIANA

● Medellin

★ Bogota

Cali ●

COLOMBIA

Magdelena R.

G U I A N A
H I G H L A N D S

Roraima

Quito ★

ECUADOR

Guayaquil ●

Japura R.

Amazon R.

Manaus ● Santarem ●

● Belem

● Sao Luis
● Fortaleza

Maranon R.

Ucayali R.

Jurua R.

Madeira R.

Tapajos R.

Xingu R.

Tocantins R.

Pernambuco

A
N
D
E
S

P E R U

Amazonas

Porto Velho ●

B R A Z I L

Callao ●
Lima ★

Cuzco ●
L. Titicaca

Trinidad ●

★ La Paz

BOLIVIA

★ Sucre

Charcas

Mato
Grosso

Cerrado

Rio Grande

BRAZILIAN HIGHLANDS

Bahia

Salvador (Bahia)

★ Brasilia

PACIFIC
OCEAN

GRAN CHACO

PARAGUAY

Asuncion ★

Parana R.

Parana

Itaipu Dam

Santa
Catarina

Rio
Grande
Do Sul

Rio de Janeiro

Sao Paulo

SOUTH
ATLANTIC
OCEAN

● Porto Alegre

Santiago ★

C
H
I
L
E

A
N
D
E
S

A R G E N T I N A

PAMPAS

Rosario ●

URUGUAY

Buenos Aires ●

★ Montevideo

Rio de la Plata

Concepcion ●

P A T A G O N I A

Falkland Islands (U.K.)
Claimed by Argentina as Malvinas

Tierra del
Fuego

Cape Horn

Drake Passage

ATLANTIC
OCEAN

| 0 | | 500 | | 1,000 | | 1,500 Miles |
| 0 | 500 | 1,000 | 1,500 Kilometers |

CHAPTER TWO

HOW TO WIN AT PEACE: CREATING NEW WORLD ORDERS

THE BIG QUESTIONS IN CHAPTER 2

- When you win at war, how can you win at peace?

- What is the best way to deal with a defeated foe and build a new world order?

- What is collective security? Could it replace power politics?

- Why did the post–World War I settlement last only twenty years?

- Why, in contrast, did the post–World War II settlements in Western Europe and Japan lead to a wide trading and security community of like-minded nations?

- Why did Soviet policies in Eastern Europe backfire?

- What were the fruits of go-it-alone exploitation and of cooperation for mutual gain? What is the "boomerang effect"?

- Is it possible to negotiate major international agreements using open diplomacy?

- What do the peace settlements of the 20th century say about the merits of realism, idealism, and interdependence?

- What about rebuilding Russia? Bosnia? Kosovo? Afghanistan? Iraq? Can history shed light on the problems of today and tomorrow?

After Victory, What? ... *The President again asks your advice on a deep problem. "The West won the Cold War when the Soviet empire collapsed in 1991. We have used force to change the ruling regimes in Bosnia, Kosovo, Afghanistan, and Iraq. If we win in a hot or cold war, how do we win at peace? Shall we try to repress our defeated foes? Forgive and forget? Or seek a partnership for mutual gain?"*

You recall the words of a previous National Security Adviser (who later became Secretary of State): "The rise and fall of previous world orders . . . is the only experience on which one can draw in trying to understand the challenges facing contemporary statesmen." The study of history, however, "offers no manual of instructions that can be applied automatically." History teaches by analogy between comparable situations.[1] But there is no set of master templates. When diplomatic constellations recur, they do so with important differences. Diplomats exaggerate when they say, "c'est la même chose."

You decide to review other attempts at forging a new world order after major wars. You find that one challenge has been to blend tough and conciliatory measures to build a stable peace based on mutual gain. Another has been to distinguish what is desirable from what is practicable.

---

1. Henry Kissinger, *Diplomacy* (New York: Simon & Schuster, 1994), 26. For a symposium on diplomatic history, IR theory, and statecraft, see *International Security* 22, no. 1 (summer 1997).

Memories of the Marshall Plan did not ensure that Europeans would forever go along with U.S. policies. In 2002–2003 many Europeans, as well as Americans and people elsewhere, protested U.S. policies—especially in the Middle East. Some French were hyper mad at the hyperpower and depicted George W. Bush and Israeli leader Ariel Sharon as terrorists who guaranteed the revival of Fascism.

CONTENDING CONCEPTS AND EXPLANATIONS

WHAT IS A WORLD ORDER? WHAT IS PEACE?

Nothing is constant. International life contains both stability and turmoil. Where stability prevails, there is some kind of order. Each **world order** embodies a hierarchy of power with rules dictated by the most influential actors. Often a new order emerges after a previous one has been destroyed by war, after which the victors establish rules that favor them. They try to hold on to power and privilege by manipulating the structures and rules they created while strong.

Order implies peace—within societies and across borders. **Negative peace** is the absence of war. **Positive peace** is more—it is a harmony based on positive associations and satisfaction with things as they are.[2]

A cold, negative peace can be built upon any of six principles: (1) the **hegemony** ("leadership" in Greek) of one major power that, as the George W. Bush administration made clear, may utilize preventive war to put down a rival before it can overthrow the balance of power or a preemptive strike to disarm a rival before it strikes; (2) the **condominium** (shared domination) of two or more powers, as in the U.S.–Soviet Cold War; (3) an **alliance** uniting several states against others; (4) **collective security**, a system of "one for all and all for one," requiring each partner to reply to an attack on another member as an attack on itself; or (5) **deterrence**, restraint achieved by fear of retribution. A negative peace may coexist with structural violence—structures that repress and exploit, and that breed rebellion. The absence of war is not a stable or positive peace, especially if it depends upon fear. If the power to intimidate erodes, negative peace can become war.

A positive and stable peace can emerge not from deterrence but from a value-creating order that generates mutual gain. Peace would be rooted in widely shared perceptions of prosperity, social justice, and environmental well-being. It would be buttressed but not guaranteed by complex interdependence (see Chapter 1). Parties to a positive peace do not see war as a legitimate or likely recourse; instead, they foster extensive forms of dispute avoidance and conflict resolution.

Does external peace among governments require internal peace and harmony within individuals and societies? Can a tormented individual lead the way to peace?[3] Can a repressive dictatorship cooperate peacefully with other countries? Tormented leaders and conflicted societies may take part in a negative peace, but positive peace is far more likely between

2. Kenneth E. Boulding, *Stable Peace* (Austin: University of Texas Press, 1978). Each civilization has a distinctive vision of peace. See Johan Galtung, "Peace," in *The Oxford Companion to Politics of the World*, ed. Joel Krieger, 2d ed. (New York: Oxford University Press, 2001), 640–641.

3. Some teachers hold that peace must begin within a person and radiate outward to other people, groups, and all living things. A Sioux medicine man labored to integrate his personal hoop as a condition for helping his tribe rebuild its hoop. Ultimately he wanted the hoops of all nations to interact in harmony. See Black Elk, as told to John G. Neihardt, *Black Elk Speaks* (Lincoln: University of Nebraska Press, 1961).

The Berlin Wall fell in 1989 and Moscow agreed to the unification of East and West Germany. Germany had been divided after World War II into four zones of occupation, and then, after 1949, into two separate states, West Germany and East Germany—formally called the Federal Republic of Germany (FRG) and the German Democratic Republic (GDR). West Germans made Bonn their capital, while East Germans used their part of Berlin (also divided into Western and Soviet sectors). West Germany and West Berlin prospered in the 1950s and later, while the Communist East languished. So many East Germans migrated to the West that the Communist regime in 1961 erected a wall to keep them in. It separated not just West and East Berlin but the entire FRG and GDR—sometimes dividing villages. Armed guards stood near the wall and often shot to death those who tried to escape to the West.

Barbed wire or other barriers created an "Iron Curtain" to cut off the Communist states from the West. As Communist rule collapsed in Hungary, its border to Austria opened, whereupon East Germans traveled to Hungary and then into Austria. This exodus spelled the collapse of Communist rule in the GDR, and its citizens tore down the wall with their own hands and hammers.

Tearing down the wall proved easier than building up what lay behind. The FRG poured huge sums of money into the former East Germany, but results were slow and spotty. Why did a modest inflow of U.S. aid help West Germany to soar in the 1950s while a much bigger transfer of FRG funds east in the 1990s achieved much less? Part of the answer is that, as this chapter argues, the Marshall Plan was based on mutuality; the FRG aid was more like that of a rich uncle to a poor, backward cousin, of whom little was expected. Other relevant factors are discussed in Chapters 11 and 12.

internally peaceful actors than when one or more parties is deeply conflicted. As we shall see in Chapter 10, authoritarian regimes—most of them led by egomaniacal dictators—started most major wars of the 20th century and ruled two of what President George W. Bush called the axis of evil countries—North Korea and Iraq.

Hopes arose in the early 1990s for a new world order more positive than the mutual deterrence practiced during the Cold War. But these hopes proved short-lived. As the 21st century began, there were new world disorders.[4] To cope with them, let us first examine the failures and successes of previous efforts to build a lasting peace.

THREE WAYS TO MAKE PEACE AND BUILD A NEW ORDER

Each negotiating type outlined in Chapter 1 takes a distinct approach to building a new order. Each approach can be illustrated by important cases.

Approach 1: Carthage

The win–lose hard-liner favors repression to prevent the vanquished from upsetting the victor's new order. If successful, repression can produce a negative peace. The hard line worked fairly well when ancient Rome subdued its longtime rival Carthage (located in today's Tunisia) in 146 B.C. The term Carthaginian peace symbolizes not just defeat but all-out destruction of the vanquished. Rome razed Carthage, killed or

4. Stanley Hoffmann, *World Disorders: Troubled Peace in the Post–Cold War Era* (Lanham, Md.: Rowman & Littlefield, 2000).

How France and Prussia Enraged Each Other

Napoleon defeated Prussia in 1807 and forced its king to sign the **Treaty of Tilsit.** The treaty compelled Prussia to cede territory to France and pay indemnities so vast that they consumed nearly all Prussian government revenues for several years. The treaty limited Prussia to only 42,000 troops, but Prussia evaded this limit and, when Napoleon weakened, denounced the treaty and declared war on France in 1813.

All this was reversed after Prussia and other German states defeated France in 1870; then it became Berlin's turn to dictate terms. The 1871 Treaty of Frankfurt compelled France to pay Germany heavy indemnities and accept German occupation until these debts were paid (which was accomplished in two years). France ceded two border regions, **Alsace and Lorraine**, to Germany. Adding insult to injury, the king of Prussia had himself crowned kaiser (emperor) of the Second German Reich (empire) at the Versailles Palace outside Paris. The French swore *revanche* (revenge). They took it, as we shall see, in 1919, in the same Versailles Palace.

enslaved its people, and salted its fields. Victory over Carthage permitted Rome to establish a *pax Romana* ("peace of Rome") from North Africa to the British Isles. Still, Rome needed Carthage and later rebuilt it to become a granary of the Roman Empire and capital of its province, "Africa."

Total victory requires total defeat. Such outcomes are rare. Usually the victor inflicts halfway measures that permit the other side to survive, determined some day to strike back. Absolute subjugation is seldom practical. A punitive peace requires the victors, drained by their wartime exertions, to hold down a defeated country and its partners, determined to overthrow the settlement.[5]

Repression can hurt both victor and vanquished. It stifles production and creativity. If mines and fields are to be exploited, subject peoples must have the will and strength to work. If the vanquished die or flee, workers must be imported.

In many wars, the winner takes booty—"to the victor go the spoils." Sometimes the victor claims financial indemnities or other **reparations** (from *repair*) as compensation for damages caused by the other side. But compensation can be difficult to extract. The defeated country may have no more gold; its money may be worthless. Goods taken as reparations, such as factory parts, may not be usable elsewhere. For a country to pay reparations, it must recover economically. The victor cannot repress the defeated and simultaneously get substantial reparations from current production.

Approach 2: Appomattox

The win–win negotiator does not punish the vanquished but trusts in conciliation ("bringing together") to restore harmony. An idealist is more likely to seek a "time to heal and to build" than an ultrarealist. But a moderate realist might agree that "no lasting settlement can be made in a spirit of revenge."[6]

A magnanimous settlement—the opposite of a Carthaginian peace—was initiated at Virginia's Appomattox courthouse in 1865, ending the Civil War between the U.S. North and South. **Appomattox** stands for a generous, forgiving approach to the defeated. When Union General Ulysses S. Grant accepted the surrender of Confederate General Robert E. Lee at Appomattox, Grant was not vindictive. He required Lee's troops to disarm but allowed them to take their horses and mules home to work their farms. Lee said this concession "will do much toward conciliating our people."

President Abraham Lincoln and his successor, Andrew Johnson, wanted to heal wounds and rebuild the Union. But few among the Southern elites

---

5. Kissinger, *Diplomacy*, 81.

6. This was what the Spartans told the Athenians when the latter had the upper hand. Thucydides, *The Peloponnesian War* (New York: Penguin Books, 1956), Book 4, chap. 1.

The Big Four peacemakers at the Paris Peace Conference in 1919: David Lloyd George of England, Baron Sidney Sonnino of Italy, Georges Clemenceau of France, and Woodrow Wilson of the U.S. The clash between European realism and Wilsonian idealism did not lead to conditional cooperation but produced rather a patchwork peace heavily colored by vindictiveness.

felt gratitude or obligation. Many exploited Johnson's forbearance and moved to reestablish the prewar planter aristocracy. A French newspaper reporter, Georges Clemenceau, who later became the French premier, opined that the North was letting itself "be tricked out of what it had spent so much trouble and perseverance to win."

After the Civil War, neither the North nor the South found the right mix of firmness and generosity. The approach begun at Appomattox failed because most Southern planters would not change their ways without pressure. Northern liberality gave way to severity. In 1867, Congress put most of the defeated South under a military administration that lasted for nearly a decade. When troops were withdrawn, resentful whites in the "solid South" defied Washington and repressed blacks again. North–South animosities lingered for generations.

Thus, a peace based on indulgence can also fail. If the victor offers a friendly hand, the vanquished may feign cooperation for a time but then defect when the erstwhile victor eases its grip.

Approach 3: Congress of Vienna

The conditional cooperator assumes that most cross-border relationships are variable-sum. This negotiator blends tough and conciliatory

In Paris in 1919, the idealist Woodrow Wilson had to negotiate with an archrealist—French Premier Georges Clemenceau, the same reporter who had questioned the North's indulgence toward the South in 1865. Clemenceau returned to France and climbed to the summit in French politics. Known as the Tiger, he pressed for a tough line toward Germany. But Wilson had far different memories of the U.S. Civil War than did Clemenceau. At age seven, Wilson watched wounded Confederate soldiers die inside his father's church in Augusta, Georgia. Later he saw Confederate President Jefferson Davis paraded under Union guard. Wilson recalled that he once looked up into the face of General Robert E. Lee. Perhaps these childhood memories helped President Wilson—fifty-four years later—to oppose a vindictive peace. As Wilson once observed, "A boy never gets over his boyhood, and never can change those subtle influences which have become a part of him."

measures to establish three conditions: a power structure that prevents another war; a system of shared values that removes any wish for violent change; and a web of interdependence that rewards cooperation and punishes defection. The more these conditions are met, the easier it should be to replace hostility with partnership.

The victors over Napoleon combined firmness with healing at the Congress of Vienna in 1815. The victors—led by Britain, Austria, Russia, and Prussia—could not ignore that France had ravaged Europe for twenty-five years, but they opted to reintegrate France quickly into the new order. The victors sent Napoleon into exile, stripped France of territories it had seized since 1790, exacted heavy reparations (more than 700 million francs), and occupied France until reparations were paid. But they also restored the French monarchy, admitted France to the Congress, and, in 1818, enlarged the four-power alliance of Europe's major powers to make a seat for France.

The Congress of Vienna set the stage for a century of relative peace. Why the long peace? The new order met the three conditions for enduring peace. No state had the means or, for many decades, the desire to challenge the balance of power.[7] The five great European powers inaugurated what became known as the Concert of Europe, a precursor to the UN Security Council. Austria, Prussia, England, Russia, and France maintained peace by concerted diplomatic action and by periodic meetings to deal with threats to stability. The 1815 order began to falter in the 1850s, but Europe was spared another system-wide war until 1914.

COMPARING THEORY AND REALITY: REBUILDING AFTER EACH WORLD WAR

The long peace ended in the most devastating war yet known. World War I began in 1914, sucked in the United States in 1917, halted in 1918, and served as a prelude to World War II. The reasons for both world wars are discussed in Chapter 4. Here we focus on the victors' attempts after each war to build a new world order.

THE NEW ORDER AFTER WORLD WAR I: THE VERSAILLES SYSTEM

The post–World War I order was planned by the victors and imposed on Germany at the Versailles Palace outside Paris in 1919.[8] The so-called Versailles system was stamped by the divergent views and personalities of U.S. President Woodrow Wilson and French Premier Georges

---

7. This term has many meanings, however, as we shall see in Chapter 4.

8. Other settlements were imposed on Austria-Hungary, Bulgaria, and Turkey.

Clemenceau. Had the victor states been led by other individuals, the new order might have been quite different.

Wilson vs. Clemenceau: Idealism's Compromise with "Realism"

Somewhat like President Lincoln in 1865, Wilson in early 1918 proposed a lenient peace—a peace without indemnities or territorial annexations. Wilson wanted to replace realpolitik with collective security. He called for an international organization to guarantee the independence and territorial integrity of all countries large and small. This dream, inspired by many sources, became the League of Nations.[9]

Exhausted but not yet defeated in late 1918, Germany sought soft peace terms like those Wilson had proposed. The parties agreed to an armistice on November 7, 1918. The twenty-seven victor governments then met in Paris to decide the precise content of the peace treaty while the vanquished waited offstage.

The peacemakers confronted unprecedented loss of life and property. Some 40 million soldiers and civilians had been killed by fighting, hunger, or disease; another 20 to 30 million people had been maimed. Some French leaders hoped that the U.S. would finance reconstruction, but Americans had already contributed one-fourth of their economic product to the war effort in 1917 and 1918 and were in no mood to keep lending or giving. Indeed, Wilson insisted in 1919 that London and Paris repay the huge sums that the United States had loaned them during the war. Many Europeans thought that the United States, having profited from the war, should write off its loans. But Americans leaned toward the view later expressed by President Calvin Coolidge: "They hired the money, didn't they?"

Rebuffed by Washington, French leaders looked to Germany. France had paid indemnities in 1815 and again in 1871. Now Paris wanted Germany to pay for the damage it had caused. This goal, however, contradicted another French objective: to keep Germany down. With only half Germany's population, France feared German economic and military growth. But how could Germany pay reparations unless it revived economically?

British Prime Minister David Lloyd George also claimed reparations—not for physical damage but to pay pensions for Britain's widows, orphans, and the disabled. He explained: "I could not face my people and say that human life was of less value than a chimney."

Wilson regarded Clemenceau and Lloyd George as shortsighted and greedy. But the idealist compromised with the realists: He approved their demands for reparations since they agreed to his priority, a league of nations.[10]

9. Thomas J. Knock, *To End All Wars: Woodrow Wilson and the Quest for a New World Order* (New York: Oxford University Press, 1992).

10. President Franklin D. Roosevelt made a similar trade-off in February 1945: He approved many British and Soviet demands for the postwar world so long as they approved his concept of a United Nations.

Table 2.1 How Victors Treated Losers in 1807, 1815, 1871, and 1919

Peace Settlement	1807 (Tilsit)	1815 (Vienna)	1871 (Frankfurt)	1919 (Versailles)
Loser	Prussia	France	France	Germany
Defeated in battle?	Yes	Yes	Yes	No
Occupied?	Yes	Yes	Yes	Yes
Formally accused of responsibility for war?	No	Yes	No	Yes
Deprived of territory?	Yes	Yes	Yes	Yes
Indemnities (payments to victors) required?	Yes	Yes	Yes	Yes
Leaders condemned?	No	Yes	Yes	Yes
Compelled to disarm?	Yes	No	No	Yes
Assisted economically?	No	No	No	No
How long before reintegrated into the international community?	Not excluded	1 to 3 years	Not excluded	3 to 7 years
Mechanism for assuring peace	French army	Concert of Europe	Concert, then alliances	League of Nations

Wilson also abandoned his earlier opposition to secret diplomacy. In January 1918, Wilson had insisted on "open covenants openly arrived at." In 1919, however, most of the treaty terms were decided behind closed doors by Wilson, Clemenceau, and Lloyd George. Other victors—even Italy and Japan—had little say. The major players treated China as a passive object and did not even invite Soviet Russia. The German delegation was also excluded from the deliberations and kept under house arrest. Finally, the Germans were shown the treaty and told to sign it—or else. Thus, in 1919 "open diplomacy" meant only that the final text of agreements would be published.

The treaty imposed on Germany was signed on June 28, 1919, in the same Versailles Palace where in 1871 the Second German Empire had been proclaimed.[11] Was the 1919 treaty harsh, lax, or a blend? It contained 361 articles—some severe, others not. The 1919 treaty was no tougher than the Treaty of Tilsit that Napoleon forced on Prussia in 1807, the treaty that Germany imposed on France in 1871, or the Brest-Litovsk Treaty that imperial Germany inflicted on Soviet Russia in March 1918. But the 1919 treaty was far more vindictive than the 1815 Congress of Vienna settlement. The terms of all four treaties are compared in Table 2.1.

The 1919 compromise between idealism and realism was a patchwork that satisfied nobody. The Versailles system was too harsh to conciliate Germany and too weak to keep Germans down. Versailles was not so

11. The signing took place precisely five years after the event that triggered World War I: the assassination of Austria's Archduke Franz Ferdinand as he visited Bosnia.

extreme as Carthage or Appomattox, but neither was it wisely balanced like the 1815 Vienna settlement.

The 1919 settlement compelled Germany to return Alsace-Lorraine to France and give up other lands in Europe and abroad. Parts of Germany would be occupied for fifteen years. As in 1807, Germany was restricted to a low level of armaments. Germany had to pay extensive reparations— 52 percent for France. In an unprecedented move, the treaty demanded that the German kaiser be tried for war crimes.

Why Did the Versailles System Fail?

The Versailles system—peace treaties, financial settlements, the League of Nations—collapsed like a deck of cards in the 1930s as Tokyo, Rome, Berlin, and Moscow embarked on wars of conquest. Many factors combined to undermine the Versailles peace:

German Revisionism. France and other victors tried to uphold the new order based on the Versailles treaty; Germany worked to revise it. Many German leaders resented the territorial losses and reparations imposed on Germany, the "war guilt" clause (see the sidebar on page 70), one-sided disarmament, and Germany's exclusion from the League of Nations.[12]

Instead of complying with Versailles, key German leaders schemed to cast off Germany's obligations. To evade the arms limitations established at Versailles, the German military in the 1920s secretly developed modern weapons on Soviet territory. In 1935 Germany began openly to rearm. In 1936 it remilitarized the left bank of the Rhine and denounced what Hitler called the "war-guilt lie." It annexed Austria in 1938, and dismembered Czechoslovakia and invaded Poland in 1938 and 1939, respectively.

Nations Without States. Four multinational realms disappeared during the war—the German, Austro-Hungarian, Russian, and Ottoman empires. Failure to meet expectations for self-determination led disgruntled minorities such as German speakers and Slovaks in Czechoslovakia looking to Nazi Germany for support.[13]

A Power Vacuum in Eastern Europe. The structure of power no longer contained but rather encouraged German expansionism. In 1914, Germany was hemmed in by the Russian and Austro-Hungarian empires. By 1919, these barriers were gone. Once Germany recovered, Berlin wanted to regain its former eastern domains.

Economic Nationalism. Between the two world wars most countries hoarded gold and discouraged imports.[14] German leaders managed to

The Communist Vision of a New Order

Like Wilson, Russian Communist leader Vladimir Lenin also denounced power politics, secret treaties, and imperialism. But Lenin had a Communist agenda—a global revolution to destroy the capitalist class and capitalist states responsible for imperialism and war. In their place he proposed a Communist-led "dictatorship of the working class." Disdaining law and religion, Lenin championed class warfare; Wilson believed in sacred covenants and a natural harmony among all humans.

Despite their opposing visions of a new world order, Lenin in 1919 expressed an interest in coming to terms with the victors at Versailles. But Britain and France, joined by the United States and Japan, chose to intervene militarily in the Russian Civil War against the Communists. By 1921 it was clear that the West could not soon unseat the Communists and that the Soviets could not soon ignite a revolution in the West. But each side gave the other grounds for long-lasting distrust.

12. Speech by the president of the German delegation, May 29, 1919, in *The Treaty of Versailles and After: Annotations on the Text of the Treaty* (Washington, D.C.: Government Printing Office, 1947), 39–44.

13. For more on "minorities at risk," see Chapters 8 and 9.

14. When Germany paid reparations in gold, France and Britain used little of this wealth to buy German goods. The 1920s differed from the 1870s, when Germany recycled French indemnities, contributing to prosperity in both Germany and France.

The "War Guilt" Clause: Misperception or Propaganda?

German officials passionately denounced what they called the "war guilt" clause—Article 231 of the Versailles treaty. The German delegation saw guilt where it was not mentioned. From the victors' standpoint, Article 231 merely explained why Germany should pay reparations. It required Germany to accept responsibility for damages to the "Allies and their Associated Governments and their nationals" caused by Germany's aggression. Article 232, moreover, sharply limited Germany's obligations. It required Germany to pay only for damage done to the Allies' civilian populations and properties—not to their military establishments. Nonetheless, Article 231 was a burr in the German consciousness. Hitler later used it to whip up resentment against the Versailles system.

delay, reduce, and eventually halt payments both on reparations and on loans from U.S. banks. Borrowers made lenders their prisoners.[15] Generations later, U.S. creditors were still holding the bag.[16] National egotism yielded economic chaos and mutual impoverishment, which helped spawn militarism in Japan and Germany.

No Collective Security. Wilson wanted the League of Nations to ensure peace by means of collective security. Such a system would require that, if a League member were attacked, all other members would come to its aid. But the U.S. Senate did not approve U.S. membership in the League. The League of Nations Covenant required each member to carry out economic sanctions against an aggressor, but permitted members to choose whether to join in military sanctions. Such loopholes worried France and buoyed aggressors.[17]

U.S. isolationism made it even more imperative for the other victors to reintegrate Germany into a new world order (as the Congress of Vienna did France in 1815). Instead, they treated Germany as an outcast for much of the 1920s. When there was still hope to accommodate Germany, Paris and London were too tough. After 1933, when they confronted a Hitler hell bent on conquest, French and British leaders were too soft. They tried to appease the Nazi beast by letting it feed on other countries. Their concessions gave appeasement a bad name.

Is collective security an impossible dream? It did not get a fair test in the 1920s and 1930s, because the U.S. never joined the League of Nations and other key players—Germany, the USSR, Japan, and Italy—were absent for years. We shall see later (in Chapters 4 and 14) that collective security fared better under the United Nations with strong U.S. leadership.

Zero-Sum Perspectives. All of these challenges to the post–World War I order stemmed from a value-claiming approach: The key actors behaved like egotists in the Prisoner's Dilemma. The painful rewards for such myopia are summarized in Table 2.2.

AFTER WORLD WAR II: CONFLICT AND MUTUAL GAIN

The Big Four victors—Britain, France, the United States, and the USSR—agreed in 1945 to each occupy a zone of Germany and a sector of Berlin. They also agreed to carry out a policy of the four Ds: they would democratize, de-nazify, demilitarize, and deindustrialize Germany. De-nazification began at once. A special court set up at Nuremberg tried twenty-two Nazi leaders for war crimes and crimes

15. Germany devoted about one-fourth of its exports to reparations in the 1920s, but only 5 to 7 percent of its national income—less than the 5 to 11 percent of French income that Paris paid to Berlin in 1871–1873. Stephen A. Schuker, *American "Reparations" to Germany, 1919–1933; Implications for the Third-World Debt Crisis* (Princeton, N.J.: Princeton Studies in International Finance No. 61, July 1988), 56; see also Steven B. Webb, *Hyperinflation and Stabilization in Weimar Germany* (New York: Oxford University Press, 1989).

16. In the 1970s, West Germany paid back the principal on Germany's 1920s debts to foreign bond holders. In 1995, a reunified Germany issued new bonds to pay off the interest due (at 3 percent) by 2010. Caveat junk bonds investor!

17. Inis L. Claude, Jr., *Swords into Plowshares: The Problems and Progress of International Organization*, 4th ed. (New York: Random House, 1984), chap. 12.

Table 2.2 The Results of Value-Claiming Policies, 1919–1939

Going It Alone	Results
1919–1931: U.S. insists on repayment of its wartime loans to Europe	Deepens financial pressures on France and Britain
1919–1932: France and Britain require Germany to pay reparations	Antagonizes Germans and strains international banking
1920s–1930s: High tariffs and protectionist policies in Europe and U.S.	Limits trade, growth, and jobs
1920s–1930s: U.S. spurns the League of Nations	Aborts collective security
1930s: Japan, Italy, and Germany embark on militarist expansion	Leads to World War II and their complete defeat
1930s: Britain, France, and U.S. pass the buck, doing little to contain the aggressors	Opens the way to war and makes defeat of the aggressors more costly

against humanity.[18] The court condemned twelve of the accused to death, jailed seven, and acquitted three. The Allies purged and excluded from public office more than 400,000 people charged with contributing to German militarism. Critics said the trials and purges went too far; others, not far enough. Defenders maintained that they were both just and necessary.

Demilitarization also proceeded quickly. Unlike in 1918, German forces in 1945 were defeated on German soil. The Big Four occupied all of Germany and disbanded its armed forces. (The Soviet occupiers of East Germany, however, formed a heavily armed "People's Police." West Germany did not rearm until 1955.)

U.S. policy emphasized the first D, democratization, and soon replaced deindustrialization with what amounted to a fifth and quite different D—economic development. The Americans wanted Germans to feed and support themselves. Washington believed that Germany and the rest of Europe had to be rebuilt together.

The Marshall Plan/European Recovery Program

The winter of 1946–1947 was harsh in Europe, giving urgency to three forces—power politics, idealism, and interdependence—that pushed the Truman administration to develop a strategy to boost European recovery.

Power Politics. The wartime alliance fell apart. In 1946, Winston Churchill warned that an "Iron Curtain" had descended to divide Europe. Most Americans regarded Soviet communism not just as immoral but also as dangerous. Washington decided in 1946–1947 to contain

18. The importance of these developments for human rights law is analyzed in Chapter 15.

Unlike the Versailles system after World War I, the Marshall Plan provided for the rebuilding of both victors and losers after World War II. Here, West Berlin's biggest concert hall and cultural center is repaired with the help of U.S. funds. Many voices called for another "Marshall Plan" to help the former Soviet countries in the 1990s and to aid Afghanistan and Iraq in 2002–2003. But this was a dream. The First World had become stingy and doubted that great largesse would do much good where conditions were not ripe. In the final analysis, Europeans and Japanese had pulled themselves up by their own bootstraps, encouraged and aided by America. In the 21st century, Afghanistan and Iraq would have to do the same—starting from a much weaker base than the World War II losers.

and, if possible, undermine the Soviet empire. In March 1947, the Truman Doctrine proclaimed U.S. readiness to help Greece and Turkey defend their independence against communism. Later that month, U.S. Secretary of State George C. Marshall went to Moscow and proposed a Big Four alliance to keep Germany demilitarized, but left Moscow feeling rebuffed.

Idealism. Washington wanted to relieve human suffering. The United States delivered some $10 billion in food and other relief supplies to Western Europe in the years 1945 to 1947. Emergency aid reduced misery but did not put Europeans on their feet. Marshall saw firsthand in March 1947 the shortages of food and coal that left France hungry and cold nearly two years after the war. Washington also sought to halt domestic unrest in France and Italy that could help Communist parties, assisted perhaps by Soviet tanks, to seize power.

Interdependence. Washington sought to build powerful economies able to buy U.S. goods. When pent-up demand from the war years waned, the U.S. economy would need foreign markets. Washington also wanted Europe to drop protectionism and embrace free trade.

These interlocked motives gave birth to the European Recovery Program (ERP), or Marshall Plan, named for Secretary of State George C. Marshall. Outlining what became the ERP on June 4, 1947, Marshall presented no master plan; rather, he urged European governments to spell out their needs so that U.S. aid could be integrated into a long-term cure for Europe's economic ills. However, the job could not be done by the United States alone. "The program should be a joint one, agreed to by a number of, if not all, European nations."[19]

Marshall invited participation by the USSR and the states of Eastern Europe as well as Western Europe. Washington feared that Stalin would try to sabotage the ERP, but gambled that Moscow would rebuff the plan. In late June 1947, Soviet Foreign Minister Viacheslav M. Molotov traveled to a meeting in Paris to look this gift horse in the mouth, but he soon pronounced it unfit and returned to Moscow. When Molotov said *nyet*, Western officials breathed a sigh of relief.

Why did the war-ravaged USSR reject economic aid? The Kremlin rejected any notion of mutual dependence with the capitalist world. Molotov asserted that the U.S. plan would enslave European states and destroy their independence. The whole scheme, he said, was designed to save the American economy.[20] Probably the Kremlin wanted to hide Soviet weaknesses and guard against any intrusion that could diminish Soviet domination of Eastern Europe. Pressured by Moscow, Czechoslovakia and Poland also kept away from the ERP.[21] The Kremlin imposed a harsh, "all-roads-lead-to-Moscow" imperial rule wherever the Red Army had driven back German or Japanese forces.[22]

Sixteen Western European states promptly met to coordinate a response to the U.S. offer.[23] They estimated each country's likely budget deficit and proposed a four-year recovery program. Then came the billion-dollar question: Would the Republican-controlled U.S. Congress foot the bill for foreign aid endorsed by a Democratic administration? Would the Republicans scuttle Truman's ERP as they had Wilson's League of Nations?

But the Democrats had learned from Wilson's mistakes. They did not exclude Republicans from foreign policy making in the 1940s as they did in 1919. Instead, they cultivated a bipartisan policy in which Republican–Democrat rivalries stopped at the water's edge. For example, the four-power alliance that Marshall proposed to the Soviets in March 1947 was the brainchild of Republican Senator Arthur Vandenberg.

Whereas U.S. policy in 1919 bore Wilson's personal seal, the ERP was very much a team effort, conceived by leading economists and some of

19. The occasion was a commencement speech at Harvard University, where honorary degrees were given to Marshall, poet T. S. Eliot, and J. Robert Oppenheimer ("father" of the atomic bomb). For the speech, analysis, and many references, see "The Marshall Plan and Its Legacy," *Foreign Affairs* 76, no. 3 (May–June 1997): 157–221.

20. V. M. Molotov, *Problems of Foreign Policy* (Moscow: Foreign Language Publishing House, 1949), 466; see also Scott D. Parrish and Mikhail M. Narinsky, "New Evidence on the Soviet Rejection of the Marshall Plan, 1947: Two Reports," Working Paper No. 9, Cold War International History Project (Washington, D.C.: Woodrow Wilson International Center for Scholars, March 1994).

21. What Czech sources told the U.S. ambassador in Prague is reported in Laurence Steinhardt to George C. Marshall, July 10, 1947, in *Foreign Relations of the United States: 1947*, vol. 3 (Washington, D.C.: Government Printing Office, 1972), 319–320. For Molotov's recollections on this point, see *Sto sorok besed c Molotovym: Iz dnevnika F. Chueva* (Moscow: Terra, 1991), 88–89.

22. *Kremlin* means "citadel" or "walled city." The Moscow Kremlin, dating from the 14th century, has housed the government of tsarist, Soviet, and post-Communist Russia.

23. All Western European countries (even neutral Switzerland) and Turkey took part, with the exceptions of Portugal and Spain, both of which were under the sway of a dictator.

▲▲ Powerful Economies Can
🌐 Bolster Free Trade

British Foreign Minister Ernest Bevin compared the U.S. economic position after World War II with Britain's after the Napoleonic wars. In 1815, Great Britain had 30 percent of the world's wealth; in the late 1940s, the U.S. had 50 percent. After the Napoleonic wars, the British practically gave away their exports for eighteen years, said Bevin, but this had contributed to stability and peace for a century.

This course also held hazards. Some economists believed that Great Britain in the 19th century undermined its economic strength by practicing free trade while its competitors hid behind protectionist barriers. These economists argued that the U.S. after World War II risked following Britain's route to self-destruction; others claimed the two situations defied comparison.

24. See Michael J. Hogan, *The Marshall Plan: America, Britain, and the Reconstruction of Western Europe, 1947–1952* (New York: Cambridge University Press, 1987), 432; and Immanuel Wexler, *The Marshall Plan Revisited: The European Recovery Program in Economic Perspective* (Westport, Conn.: Greenwood, 1983), 251; see also Charles S. Maier, "The Two Postwar Eras and the Conditions for Stability in Twentieth-Century Western Europe," with comments by Stephen A. Schuker and Charles P. Kindleberger, in *American Historical Review* 86 (April 1981): 327–67. For a political science perspective, see Hadley Arkes, *Bureaucracy, the Marshall Plan, and the National Interest* (Princeton, N.J.: Princeton University Press, 1972); and Charles P. Kindleberger, *Marshall Plan Days* (Boston: Unwin Hyman, 1987), 246.

25. Confirmed by the author's surveys noted in the introduction and by numerous publications on the fortieth and fiftieth anniversaries of Marshall's 1947 proposal.

America's most experienced diplomats, including George F. Kennan and Dean Acheson. Its first administrator was a Republican industrialist, Paul G. Hoffman. Truman had the plan named for Marshall, a luminary widely viewed as above party politics.

The Marshall Plan operated from 1948 through 1951. It was both a burden and a boon for the U.S. economy. How large was the burden? Under the ERP, the United States dispensed $13.2 billion in grants and loans (mostly grants)—nearly $100 billion if measured in early 21st-century dollars. ERP transfers initially amounted to 2.3 percent of U.S. gross national product (GNP), but over four years averaged 1.2 percent. (In the 1990s, in contrast, U.S. developmental aid was less than one-tenth of 1 percent of U.S. GNP, spread over the globe instead of concentrated in one region.) But the U.S. economy also gained. Many ERP dollars quickly came home because Europe bought two-thirds of its imports from the United States. Thus, European and U.S. well-being became entwined.

The ERP became a model of mutuality in planning, inputs, and perceived gains. The United States proposed and subsidized the ERP, but Europeans helped plan and implement it. Americans catalyzed Europeans' energies and pressured them to cooperate with the United States and one another—France with Germany, Belgium and the Netherlands with France. U.S. aid was probably a necessary though not a sufficient condition for Europe's recovery.[24] With financial reserves provided by Washington, Europeans did not need to pursue self-sufficiency (their fantasy between the world wars). Instead they could trade with each other and make purchases abroad. Total U.S. grants and loans amounted only to 10 to 20 percent of total investments in Europe in 1948 and 1949, but they sparked a multiplier effect. They facilitated essential imports, eased bottlenecks, encouraged capital formation by Europeans, and curtailed inflation. The ERP could wind down in 1951 because it was no longer needed.

Historians and statesmen from many countries viewed the Marshall Plan as the outstanding success of U.S. foreign policy in the 20th century— perhaps ever.[25] The ERP helped build a transatlantic community of like-minded democracies for economic development and security. None of these countries fought each other again after 1945. The ERP inaugurated an era of peace and prosperity more durable than any other in modern European history. At the onset of the 21st century there was still no "United States of Europe," but the ERP had laid the foundation for a dynamic and expanding European Union.

General MacArthur and Postwar Japan

U.S. policy to Japan also converted a vanquished foe into a partner. Unlike U.S. policy in Europe, however, Washington dealt with Japan and other Asian countries one-on-one instead of multilaterally. And Washington saw no reason to coordinate its Asia policy with the USSR, even though Soviet troops attacked the Japanese in the last days of the war.[26]

Another difference was that U.S. policy in Japan depended heavily upon one person—General Douglas A. MacArthur, commander of the occupation forces. MacArthur believed that U.S. occupation of Japan should express America's influence "in terms of essential liberalism"—not "in an imperialistic manner or for the sole purpose of commercial advantage." Though known for his huge ego, MacArthur developed a good working relationship with the emperor and Prime Minister Yoshida Sigeru. MacArthur gave orders and the Japanese government implemented them. This approach provided a low-cost way to meet U.S. goals while helping to maintain Japan's bureaucratic system and pride.[27]

Having received initial directives from Washington, MacArthur, on August 30, 1945, summarized his tasks in Japan:

First, destroy the military power. Punish war criminals. Build the structure of representative government. Modernize the constitution. Hold free elections. Enfranchise the women. Release the political prisoners. Liberate the farmers. Establish a free labor movement. Encourage a free economy. Abolish police oppression. Develop a free and responsible press. Liberalize education. Decentralize political power. Separate church from state.

By the time MacArthur left in 1951, most of these tasks had been accomplished.

As in Germany, suspected Japanese war criminals were tried. Twenty-five were condemned to die (more than in Germany). Another 200,000 Japanese were excluded from public office (far less than in Germany). The Americans did not indict the emperor, despite his role in initiating and prolonging the war. Kid glove treatment of Hirohito facilitated U.S. occupation, but also helped the Japanese to avoid confronting the past. Many Japanese felt that the war had been a disaster and that their government had misled them, but few were penitent.[28] Many claimed there had been no surrender—only an end to the war. The U.S. position was that Japan had surrendered unconditionally, but MacArthur seldom pressed the issue.

In 1946 the U.S. closed down all production of military goods, stripped Japanese factories of equipment to provide reparations for China and the Philippines, and tried to break up Japan's industrial conglomerates. But such policies made U.S. occupation of Japan expensive. By 1947 the victor was subsidizing the vanquished to the tune of $400 million a year. In

Is Aid Good or Bad? The Cases of Germany and Japan

Is aid useful? The two countries that received relatively little U.S. aid after World War II, Japan and Germany, grew faster than those that collected more. Germany got only $8.50 per capita in 1949; the UK, $24.03; and France, $23.96. The Japanese got even less than the Germans (as did Italy, at $7 per capita).* Does this mean that "the less aid, the better growth"? Probably not. Even Japan and Germany needed a boost. As we will see in Chapters 11 and 12, many factors shape economic growth.

*See analysis and data in A. F. K. Organski and Jacek Kugler. *The War Ledger* (Chicago: University of Chicago Press, 1980), esp. chap. 3 and app. 2.

26. U.S. and British authorities excluded Soviets from the occupation of Italy, and the Soviets excluded Westerners from the countries they had conquered or liberated, such as Bulgaria. The rule seemed to be: Only the state that pays in blood may occupy another.

27. The following draws largely from Richard B. Finn, *Winners in Peace: MacArthur, Yoshida, and Postwar Japan* (Berkeley: University of California Press, 1992); see also Daikichi Irokawa, *The Age of Hirohito: In Search of Modern Japan* (New York: Free Press, 1995).

28. Japan's Ministry of Education made sure that Japanese textbooks excused the attack on Pearl Harbor and Japanese atrocities in China, Korea, the Philippines, Indonesia, and elsewhere. Not until 1995 did the Japanese prime minister offer even personal regret for Japan's wartime treatment of British prisoners.

1949 Washington reversed course and ordered that all Japanese industrial facilities be used for economic recovery. As in Germany, deindustrialization gave way to development.

MacArthur's staff drafted a new constitution for Japan, which was adopted by the Japanese legislature in 1946. Article 9 disavowed war as an instrument of policy and pledged Japan not to maintain armed forces for offensive purposes.

U.S. occupation formally ended in 1951 with the signing of a Japanese–U.S. peace treaty. Unlike Tilsit or Versailles, the 1951 treaty was not punitive. It placed no restrictions on Japan's peacetime activity and made no provision for reparations. The treaty recognized Japan's right to self-defense. Japan and the U.S. also signed an alliance in 1951 (renewed with modifications into the 21st century)—a mutual security treaty that permitted U.S. troops to be stationed in Japan. Over time, Japan's self-defense forces steadily improved, but Washington often urged Japan to do more. The Americans feared not Japan; but Communist China, North Korea, and the USSR.

How did U.S. occupation policies affect Japan? The country's economic attainments were built upon efficient work habits. But the United States gave Japan "an indispensable push" toward prosperity and democracy. Both Japan and the United States won. Japan's longtime prime minister reflected: "The Americans came into our country as our enemies, but after an occupation lasting a little less than seven years, an understanding grew up between the two peoples which is remarkable in the history of the modern world."[29] By the 1960s, Japan was joining North America and Western Europe in a trilateral community—the world's fulcrum of economic development and democracy.

Unlike the Americans, the Soviets hung tough with Japan: Moscow spurned Tokyo's demand for return of Japan's northern islands, annexed by Stalin in 1945. In the early 21st century there was still no peace treaty between Japan and Russia, even though both countries could gain from closer ties.

The Soviet Empire: Exploitation and Dependency

Sharing the tasks of reconstruction could have united Communist and non-Communist Europe. Instead, the ERP sharpened East–West differences. Stalin claimed and extracted values from Moscow's subjects instead of creating values with them and the West. From 1945 to 1956 the Kremlin's policy toward Eastern Europe was far more harsh than the 1919 Versailles system had been to Germany.

29. Finn, *Winners*, 316. In April 1951, President Truman sacked MacArthur because he had exceeded orders in Korea, but Japanese–U.S. relations were not harmed. Indeed, Japan got a lesson in how a civilian government should handle an insubordinate general. At age eighty-six, Yoshida traveled to Virginia in 1964 to attend MacArthur's funeral.

In the years 1945 to 1956, the USSR extracted from Eastern Europe goods valued at $14 to 20 billion—more than the $13.2 billion the United States transferred to Western Europe under the ERP. Like Clemenceau in 1919, Stalin in 1945 felt that the aggressor should pay. The Soviets carted off machinery and factories from the former enemy countries—East Germany, Hungary, and Romania. But even in "liberated" countries such as Czechoslovakia, the Kremlin set up joint stock companies to divert East European output to the USSR. Moscow paid less than world market prices for Eastern Europe's commercial exports. A Polish joke conveyed the bitter truth: "Moscow sells Poland coal-mining machinery at higher than world prices so Poles can dig coal and sell it to Russia for less than world prices." Table 2.3 compares the post-1945 settlements in Europe and Japan with the Versailles system after World War I.

The Iron Curtain dividing Eastern from Western Europe had many elements—not just barbed wire and minefields. Countering Marshall's initiative, Soviet ideologists declared in 1947–1948 that "two camps" faced each other on the world stage. In 1949, Moscow sponsored what

Table 2.3 How Victors Treated Losers After 1919 and 1945

Peace Settlement	1919 Versailles	1945 Settlements		
		U.S., UK, French Occupation	U.S. Occupation	Soviet Occupation
Loser	Germany	West Germany	Japan	East Germany
Defeated in battle?	No	Yes	Yes	Yes
Occupied?	Yes	Yes	Yes	Yes
Formally accused of responsibility for war?	Yes	Yes	Yes	Yes
Deprived of territory?	Yes	Yes	Yes	Yes
Reparations?	Heavy	Light	Light	Heavy
Leaders condemned?	Yes	Yes	Yes, but emperor spared	Yes
Compelled to disarm?	Yes	Yes	Yes	Yes
Assisted economically?	No	Yes	Yes	No
How long before reintegrated into the international community?	3 to 7 years	3 years	6 years	4 to 28 years
Mechanism for assuring peace	League of Nations	Occupation armies; NATO after 1949	U.S. Army; after 1951, the U.S.–Japan Mutual Security Treaty	Soviet Army; Communist parties; bilateral alliances and 1955 Warsaw Pact

some called the Molotov Plan—the Council for Mutual Economic Assistance (COMECON) to promote economic integration of Eastern Europe and the USSR. In practice, however, COMECON cultivated bilateral ties that kept each East European country dependent on the USSR. All roads, it seemed, led to Moscow. Cut off from Western ideas and competition, Eastern Europe stagnated.

The Cold War intensified. In 1949 the Western powers merged their occupation zones and formed a new state, the Federal Republic of Germany (West Germany), and established the North Atlantic Treaty Organization (NATO). Later that year the USSR countered by setting up the German Democratic Republic in East Germany.[30]

The boomerang returned, however, as Soviet exploitation generated uprisings in East Germany in 1953 and Hungary in 1956. After suppressing these revolts with Soviet tanks, Moscow reversed gears. After 1956 the Kremlin sought to stabilize its empire by subsidies—selling Soviet oil to Communist regimes in Eastern Europe at far less than world prices. Over time, however, Moscow's grip loosened, and in 1989 its empire dissolved. In the early 21st century, more than half a century after Stalin ordered his satellites to abjure the Marshall Plan, Eastern European states were integrating economically with the EU.

A balance sheet of cooperation versus zero-sum politics in the decade after World War II is outlined in Table 2.4. Some events in the table are discussed in later chapters, but we note them here to sketch the big picture. Most of the cooperative practices (first column) continued to operate into the 1990s because they generated ongoing mutual advantage. Most value-claiming practices (third column) were short-lived because they benefited only one side.

WHAT PROPOSITIONS HOLD? WHAT QUESTIONS REMAIN?

REPRESSION, LENIENCY, INTEGRATION

What lessons flow from the past? Past efforts to create new global orders suggest that integrative, mutual-gain policies work better than either brutal repression or hope-for-the-best indulgence.

Relations between the strong and the weak can help or harm each side. As a wise Athenian put it: The basis for the security of an empire lies in "good administration"—not harsh repression. The right way to deal with free but dependent people is not to punish but to "take tremendous care of them."[31] Updating this insight, we can say that alliances and empires

30. The Kremlin did not form its own Warsaw Pact alliance until 1955, a riposte to West Germany's entry into NATO that year. East Germany and its borders were not recognized by the West until the early 1970s. East and West Germany joined the UN as separate states in 1973.

31. Diodotus, quoted in Thucydides, *Peloponnesian War*, Book 3.

Table 2.4 Mutual Gain vs. Zero-Sum Politics, 1945–1956

Cooperate	Results	Claim Values	Results
United Nations formed in 1945	Limited but unprecedented achievements	Many Soviet vetoes at UN	Debilitates UN Security Council
World Bank and International Monetary Fund begin operations in 1946	Helps economic reconstruction and growth	USSR subjugates and pillages Eastern Europe	Improverishes the Second World
U.S. relief aid to Europe and Japan after the war	Allays suffering	USSR fosters bilateral trade with Communist states	Isolates the Second World
General Agreement on Tariffs and Trade (GATT) begins in 1948	Helps liberalize trade		
Marshall Plan, 1948–1951	A community for peace and security linking North America, Europe, and Japan—a compromise between old-style alliances and universal collective security	USSR spurns Marshall Plan and organizes COMECON in 1949	Isolates the Second World
NATO forms in 1949		USSR demands bases and joint stock companies in China in 1950	USSR alienates Communist China
"Police action" taken by UN in Korea in 1950			
U.S.–Japanese security treaty signed in 1951	Enduring alliance		
European Coal and Steel Community formed in 1952	A start toward European Union	Soviet tanks crush East German revolt in 1953 and Hungarian uprising in 1956	Deepens animosities between Soviet hegemon and Eastern Europe
West Germany joins NATO in 1955	Enduring alliance		

resemble businesses where "competitive advantage grows fundamentally out of the value a firm is able to create for its buyers."[32]

Repression generates a boomerang effect. The ultrarealist victor who exacts a harsh peace risks rebellion. Zero-sum policies backfired after 1919, as they had after 1807 and 1871. France wanted to keep Germany pinned to the mat after World War I, but Germany rose up for another onslaught.

Similarly, Moscow's heavy hand alienated East Europeans after World War II. The Kremlin repressed its vassals, and in so doing undermined its own power; violated Marxist ideals; and obstructed the growing interdependence that Karl Marx described as early as 1848 in his *Communist Manifesto*. The East Europeans might have become genuine partners of the USSR. Instead, they labored as disgruntled serfs until they could break free.

Forbearance also failed. It was abused by Southern planters after the U.S. Civil War and by German officials pleading for revision of the Versailles treaty in the 1920s and 1930s.

A wiser course was set by the moderate realists who dominated the 1815 Congress of Vienna. They dealt firmly with France but then welcomed their former foe into the Concert of Europe.

32. See Michael E. Porter, *Competitive Advantage: Creating and Sustaining Superior Performance* (New York: Free Press, 1985), xvi.

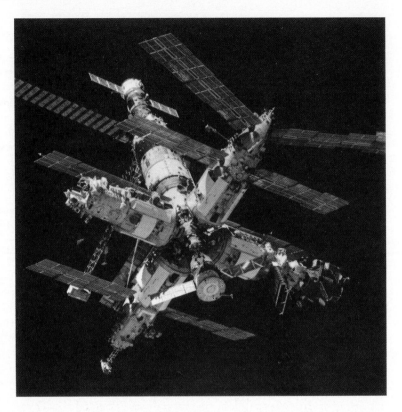

International cooperation in space can benefit from shared expertise, equipment, and financing. It should also reduce prospects of an arms race in outer space. U.S. astronauts and other foreign crew members joined Russian cosmonauts aboard the Russian space station *Mir* in 1996–1997. By 2003, however, international cooperation was troubled by Russia's problems in financing its own programs and by the crash of a U.S. space shuttle, generating major questions about safety and reliability.

Power, idealism, and interdependence converged in the U.S. quest for a new order after World War II. Americans defanged militarists in Germany and Japan but then made partners of their former foes. These policies were realistic—firm but conciliatory and idealistic—based on vision and empathy and imbued by a search for mutual gain.

In the early 21st century, the United States seeks to nurture political, economic, and cultural freedoms in post-Communist Russia, post-Milošević Serbia, and post-Taliban Afghanistan. Some in Washington even hope to shake and rebuild the foundations of political and economic power in the Middle East. But such hopes should be coupled with a realistic appreciation of the deep problems these societies face as they try to shed the burdens of their recent and distant pasts. What is desirable may not be attainable in the near or even the intermediate future.

THE USES OF OPEN DIPLOMACY

Closed diplomacy undermined peace efforts after World War I. The Versailles treaty was drafted behind closed doors and presented as an accomplished fact. Germans were expected to comply with the treaty, and

Republican senators in Washington were supposed to approve the pact even though they had played no role in its writing. Had the views of all concerned parties been heard, the new order might have been more viable.

By contrast, the Marshall Plan represented a triumph of openness. U.S. planners conceived the program in their Washington offices, but it was proposed, negotiated, and implemented in a relatively open setting. The ERP was widely debated by each concerned society—except in Eastern Europe and the USSR, where Moscow dictated a party line for all Communists.

U.S. officials, however, doubted the ability of the American public to respond to arguments based on the economic interdependence of Europe and the United States. As a result, officials gave a heavy anti-communist spin to the Marshall Plan, emphasizing its role in stopping communism. Thus, Americans supported the ERP, but without grasping all the reasons to do so.

To sum up, the U.S. achievements in Europe and Japan flowed from a strategy oriented toward mutual gain and rooted in a relatively open dialogue at home and internationally. The failures of Soviet policy toward Eastern Europe derived from an exploitative approach imposed with no meaningful discussion at home or with target countries.

What Do You Tell the President? .... *The world has become more complicated in the wake of 9/11, but you summarize your thoughts for the President.*

The reconstruction of Western Europe and Japan after 1945 showed that mutual gain policies can be both useful and feasible. Washington extended incentives to cooperate while establishing safeguards against defection. U.S. policies spawned an enduring security and trading community embracing North America, Western Europe, and Japan. Governments sometimes learn the right lessons.

These lessons can guide us as we strive for a new world order in which deeply damaged societies recover from dictatorship, harsh imperial rule, civil strife, and war. But conditions were far more conducive to peaceful reconstruction in postwar Germany and Japan than in any of the societies where, in recent years, the old system collapsed (the Soviet empire and Yugoslavia) or where we have changed the regime (Afghanistan and Iraq).[33] Germany and Japan were industrial, modern societies before World War II. Each experienced democracy in the 1920s. Our aid got them moving again, but the Germans and Japanese relied mainly on their own efforts, capital, and skills to rebuild. The foundations for democracy and a market economy were much weaker in most former Soviet republics, Afghanistan, and Iraq.[34]

33. See also Anthony Lake et al., *After the Wars: Reconstruction in Afghanistan, Indochina, Central America, Southern Africa, and the Horn of Africa* (Washington, D.C.: Overseas Development Council, 1990).

34. Estonia, Latvia, and Lithuania were less wounded by Communist rule than the other former Soviet republics. They had been independent, free-market countries from 1920 to 1940, when they were annexed by the USSR. In 1992, Estonia linked its currency to the German Mark. By 2002, the World Economic Forum judged it to be the most competitive of all post-Communist states.

As the U.S. and UN marshaled their forces in 1990–1991 to drive Iraq from Kuwait, President George Bush (the 41st president) voiced hope for a "new world order." Even as he spoke, however, Yugoslavia was splintering. Soon, many ethnic groups there were fighting one another. Bosnian Muslims suffered the most deaths—filling graveyards like this one near Sarajevo, chosen to bury the dead because it was beyond the range of Serbian artillery. When the UN Security Council failed to take decisive action, the U.S. and other NATO powers intervened—leading to serious confrontations with Russia. Meanwhile, neither the West nor anyone else intervened to stop large-scale massacres in Africa.

Our recent policies, however, have been penny-wise and pound-foolish. We spent billions to drive the Taliban from Afghanistan, but then skimped on aid to restore order and promote reconstruction. For the cost of just one "smart bomb" we could help Afghans to build and run a few schools. Our priorities have become skewed. In the early 21st century we have spent even more on defense—5 or 6 percent of gross domestic product, and even less on foreign aid—about one-tenth of 1 percent. Of course, we do not want to shower money on a regime that wastes it. But if the government we have installed in Kabul lacks vital resources, it will also lack credibility and staying power. If America raises expectations that we will help rebuild a wasted land and then fails, U.S. credibility also suffers.

Post-Taliban Afghanistan needed external aid more than the post-Soviet or former Yugoslav states. Nearly 2 million Afghans returned from exile in 2002 only to find that, when they tried to resume farming, they lacked water (after four years of drought), tools, seed, and fertilizer. Less than half the arable land was cultivated in 2002. Ravaged by decades of war, the country bristled with mines that endangered farmers and children. In 2002–2003, our appointed leader Hamad Karzai was little more than the mayor of Kabul. Neither he nor we provided security outside the capital. Beyond Kabul, many Afghans depended on some intrepid foreign non-governmental organizations, local warlords, or local drug lords.

Most of the failed or defeated states with new regimes are riven by ethnic differences deeper than any social divisions in Germany and Japan. Neither Afghanistan nor Iraq has ever experienced democratic governance open to all classes, all ethnic groups, and both sexes. Afghans speak diverse tongues, and most identify with a village or a charismatic leader more than with "Afghanistan." Many still believe women should wear burkas and not work outside the home. Outsiders may encourage acceptance of cultural diversity but cannot impose it.

In 2003, Shi'a leaders told the coalition to leave and let Iraqis set up their own government. But all signs suggested that Iraqis were not ready to practice self-rule. Ethnic and religious divisions in Iraq are probably deeper than in Afghanistan. Iraqis may be the most educated of Arab peoples, but many display a mean spirit—tougher at times even than Yemeni tribes.[35] One returned Shi'a prelate was hacked to death by his rivals in April 2003. Some Iraqis had so little respect for public goods that they looted not just office buildings but hospitals, even stealing respirators. Others smashed some of Iraq's twelve Steinway pianos.[36]

Americans and Brits in 2003 needed to make good on their commitments to transfer the country's governance and oil wealth to Iraqis.[37] As in the 1920s, however, the new liberators/conquerors of Mesopotamia felt that they had to handpick the country's new government. With whom should the foreigners negotiate? U.S. and UK generals and colonels were pictured in April 2003 seated in one of Saddam Hussein's palaces with nobody across the table. Who would be their interlocutors? The retired U.S. general assigned by the Pentagon to supervise Iraq's reconstruction sought to select an interim government led by Iraqis recently returned from exile in the UK or United States. But many Iraqis distrusted the exiles from the West. Many welcomed Shi'a leaders who had recently returned from Iran. An interim governing council hand-picked by the "occupying power" represented many Iraqi factions but lacked legitimacy as well as power.

The U.S. defense secretary and his Straussian entourage claimed to have all the answers but consented in May 2003 to letting a retired ambassador supervise reconstruction—reporting to the Pentagon rather than to the State Department. The United States denied the UN any but the slightest supervisory role. America blocked even the UN arms inspectors from returning, saying the United States could do the job. Washington did, however, ask the UN to approve its plan for the U.S.–UK "authority" to take charge of Iraq's oil exports and cash flows. As troubles mounted, in October 2003 security adviser Rice tried to redirect authority from the Pentagon to the NSC.

---

35. Iraqis are "devoid of any national consciousness or sense of unity, imbued with religious traditions and absurdities, receptive to evil, prone to anarchy, and always willing to rise against the government"—King Faisal, Hashemite prince installed by the British in 1920 to govern the country they carved out of the Ottoman Empire, as quoted by Lawrence of Arabia. See Martin Walker, "The Making of Modern Iraq," *Wilson Quarterly* (spring 2003), 29–40 at 33. See also two other articles on Iraq—its past glories and troubled present—in this issue.

36. Before the U.S. bombs began to drop, the country's father figure, Saddam Hussein, sent a note to the Central Bank ordering it to hand over nearly $1 billion in cash to his second son and appointed successor, Qusay. The note arrived on March 18, 2002, at 4 A.M., when few bank employees could witness one of the largest heists in history. It took two hours to load the bills—a quarter of the Central Bank's hard currency reserves—into three tractor-trailers. Other looters stole at least $400 million from Iraqi banks.

37. Lawrence of Arabia denounced the British government in the 1920s for reneging on big promises it had made in order to gain Arab support against the Ottomans.

And what about the past? New evidence emerged of the brutality with which Saddam and his associates terrorized their subjects—from mass burial grounds to the torture chambers inside the headquarters of Iraq's Olympic Committee. Soccer players told how they had been beaten there for missing a penalty kick!

Rebuilding may require restitution. Who should be punished for crimes against humanity? By whom? And why—to what end? The options included:

- *Ad hoc international tribunals like those set up after World War II and the Yugoslav and Rwandan conflicts*
- *Iraq's own courts*
- *The permanent International Criminal Court (otherwise rejected by the U.S.)*
- *A truth and reconciliation commission like that set up in post-apartheid South Africa to hear confessions and testimonies*
- *Opening files of the secret police to identify collaborators and document those persecuted by the regime*

Devoting time and resources to rebuilding Afghanistan and Iraq did not come readily to a president who in 2000 expressed his disdain for "nation building." Nor did his deputies stump the country, as Truman officials did in 1946–1948, explaining to chambers of commerce and other groups why foreign aid could benefit America.

If we are to obtain popular support for enlightened diplomacy, foreign affairs specialists and the public must educate one another and communicate openly about the facts and values at stake. Honest dialogue and wise planning require us to elevate foreign affairs beyond party politics and vested interests.[38]

Looking ahead, if Americans are to build peace and thwart would-be attackers, they must do as Voltaire advised, "Get out of our grooves and study the rest of the globe." Not only must many Americans know where Yemen intersects with Djibouti, some must master the languages spoken there.[39]

---

38. Complaints emerged in April to May 2003 that the Pentagon had given major construction contracts in Iraq to Bechtel, Halliburton, and other firms with close ties to the Bush team without open public bidding. Not just Canadian and French firms but rivals in Texas to Halliburton said they had been cold-shouldered.

39. The U.S. ambassador to Yemen slipped away from the capital in 2002 to negotiate directly with tribal leaders who, for a price, told him the travel plans of an al-Qaeda leader whose automobile was soon demolished by a missile fired from a Predator flying robot.

KEY NAMES AND TERMS

alliance	Council for Mutual Economic	negative peace
Alsace and Lorraine	Assistance (COMECON)	North Atlantic Treaty Organization
Appomattox	deterrence	(NATO)
Carthaginian peace	hegemony	positive peace
Georges Clemenceau	Iron Curtain	reparations
collective security	Douglas A. MacArthur	Treaty of Tilsit
Concert of Europe	Marshall Plan/European Recovery	Versailles system
condominium	Program (ERP)	world order
Congress of Vienna	Viacheslav M. Molotov	

QUESTIONS TO DISCUSS

1. Why would a Western leader in the early 21st century care about the outcomes of earlier wars? To what extent does history repeat itself? Why?

2. How open was the diplomacy that produced the Versailles system? The Marshall Plan? Soviet policy to Eastern Europe?

3. Why did General MacArthur work with Japanese officials instead of dictating policy?

4. Compare U.S. policies toward Germany and Japan after 1945.

5. Why did Republicans spurn President Wilson's plans for the postwar world but accept Truman's?

6. Compare the pros and cons, financial and political, of the ERP and the Soviet treatment of Eastern Europe after 1945.

7. Had Stalin asked you to recommend an overall strategy toward Eastern Europe in 1945, what guidelines would you have endorsed?

8. What factors make it difficult to adopt a mutual-gain approach with defeated foes?

9. What are the pros and cons of open diplomacy? When is it feasible? Desirable?

10. What kinds of peace settlement would a realist pursue in post–Communist Russia ? In post–Milošević Serbia? In post–Taliban Afghanistan? In post–Saddam Hussein Iraq? Would the realists' policies differ from country to country? How? Why?

11. Compare the realists' preferred policies in these situations with those espoused by a Wilsonian idealist.

12. If a peace planner accepted the paradigm of interdependence, how would his or her policies agree with or differ from those of the realist and the idealist?

RECOMMENDED RESOURCES

Acheson, Dean. *Present at the Creation: My Years in the State Department.* New York: W. W. Norton, 1987.

Albrecht-Carrié, René. *A Diplomatic History of Europe Since the Congress of Vienna.* Rev. ed. New York: Harper & Row, 1973.

Asmus, Ronald, and Lord Robertson. *Opening NATO's Door: How the Alliance Remade Itself for a New Era.* New York: Columbia University Press, 2002.

Clemens, Walter C., Jr. *Can Russia Change? The USSR Confronts Global Interdependence.* New York: Routledge, 1990.

Craig, Gordon A., and Felix Gilbert, eds. *The Diplomats, 1919–1939.* Princeton, N.J.: Princeton University Press, 1994.

Craig, Gordon A., and Francis A. Lowenheim, eds. *The Diplomats, 1939–1979.* Princeton, N.J.: Princeton University Press, 1994.

Cray, Ed. *General of the Army: George C. Marshall, Soldier and Statesman.* Lanham, Md.: Rowman & Littlefield, 2000.

Fromkin, David. *In the Time of the Americans: FDR, Truman, Eisenhower, Marshall, MacArthur—The Generation That Changed America's Role in the World.* New York: Knopf, 1995.

Gaddis, John Lewis. *We Now Know: Rethinking Cold War History.* New York: Oxford University Press, 1997.

Hoffmann, Stanley. *World Disorders: Troubled Peace in the Post–Cold War Era.* Lanham, Md.: Rowman & Littlefield, 1998.

Hughes, Matthew, and Matthew S. Seligmann. *Does Peace Lead to War? Peace Settlements and Conflicts in the Modern Age.* Stroud, U.K.: Sutton, 2002.

Kennedy, Paul. *The Rise and Fall of the Great Powers: Economic Change and Military Conflict from 1500 to 2000.* New York: Random House, 1987.

Kissinger, Henry A. *Diplomacy.* New York: Simon & Schuster, 1994.

Leffler, Melvyn P. *A Preponderance of Power: National Security, the Truman Administration, and the Cold War.* Stanford, Calif.: Stanford University Press, 1992.

Mastny, Vojtech. *The Cold War and Soviet Insecurity.* New York: Oxford University Press, 1996.

Mayers, David A. *Wars and Peace: The Future Americans Envisioned, 1861–1991.* New York: St. Martin's, 1998.

Rinjiro, Sodei, and John Junkerman, eds. *Dear General MacArthur: Letters from the Japanese During the American Occupation.* Lanham, Md.: Rowman & Littlefield, 2001.

Towle, Philip. *Democracy and Peacemaking: Negotiations and Debates, 1815–1973.* New York: Routledge, 2002.

Zubok, Vladislav, and Constantine Pleshakov. *Inside the Kremlin's Cold War: From Stalin to Khrushchev.* Cambridge, Mass.: Harvard University Press, 1996.

WEB SITES

Afghanistan
    http://www.pbs.org/newshour/bb/asia/afghanistan/
Appomattox
    http://www.ibiscom.com/appomatx.htm
The Congress of Vienna
    http://www.mcps.k12.md.us/schools/churchillhs/
    departments/ss/apeuro/carroll/2unitpage.html
General Military History
    http://www.army.mil/cmh-pg/ (follow links to "online
    bookshelves")

League of Nations Speech by Woodrow Wilson
    http://www.tamu.edu/scom/pres/speeches/wwleague.html
Versailles Treaty
    http://www.lib.byu.edu/~rdh/
World War I
    http://www.worldwar1.com/
World War II
    http://www.bbc.co.uk/history/war/wwtwo/

C H A P T E R   T H R E E

FOREIGN POLICY DECISION MAKING: DO INDIVIDUALS COUNT?

"We Don't Make Mistakes." . . . . The White House asks you,

"How did it come about—humanity's closest brush with a thermonuclear exchange? Could the Cuban missile crisis of 1962 have been avoided? How can we avoid getting into such collision courses in the future? If we find ourselves heading for a collision, how can we avert disaster? How can we improve decision making?"

Review what happened: Both Soviet and U.S. leaders played IR as zero-sum poker. Stakes were high. Bluffs and bullying overshadowed sweet talk. Secrecy aggravated suspicion.

President John F. Kennedy met Soviet leader Nikita S. Khrushchev for two days in Vienna, June 3 and 4, 1961. JFK warned Khrushchev that the consequences would be horrific if "our two countries should miscalculate."

Khrushchev retorted, "We don't make mistakes. We will not make war by mistake." He exploded: "All I ever hear from your people . . . is that damned word 'miscalculation'." Moscow would defend its vital interests whether the U.S. called it 'miscalculation' or not. "You ought to take that word and bury it in cold storage and never use it again," said Khrushchev.

Kennedy reminded Khrushchev that Europeans had earlier misjudged Hitler. During the Korean War, the U.S. (in 1950) had "failed to foresee what the Chinese would do." JFK admitted that he too had made "certain misjudgments." Kennedy wanted to introduce "precision in judgments of the two sides and to obtain a clearer understanding of where we are going."[1]

Despite Kennedy's warnings, both Washington and Moscow misread each other in 1962. That year, the Soviets attempted to secretly deploy nuclear-tipped missiles in Cuba just ninety miles from Florida. Discovering the operation as it neared completion, Washington offered the Kremlin either war or mutual concessions. Moscow chose the latter. Like teenage drivers playing "Chicken," JFK and Khrushchev found themselves on a collision course. Fortunately for the planet, they veered to avoid a crash. Sobered by their brush with disaster, both sides found that they were locked in mutual vulnerability—their very

1. Interpreter's notes, cited in Michael R. Beschloss, *The Crisis Years: Kennedy and Khrushchev, 1960–1963* (New York: HarperCollins, 1991), 196–197.

survival hostage to each other's restraint. In 1963 they took steps to improve communications and promote mutual gain. Having risked disaster by value-claiming, both sides turned to value-creating.

What lessons can you derive for the president? You begin by reviewing what psychologists and social scientists say about perception and decision making.

CONTENDING CONCEPTS AND EXPLANATIONS: IS ANYBODY IN CHARGE? HOW ACTION LEVELS INTERACT

Who or what produced the key decisions in the Cuban missile crisis? Let us look for answers on the first three levels of IR action. We will examine the fourth and fifth levels (transnational and environmental factors) in later chapters.

LEVEL 1: INDIVIDUALS AND HUMAN NATURE

Do individuals count? Proponents of **determinism** say that individuals are the puppets of great forces such as divine will, fate, economics, and eros. The neorealists (discussed in Chapter 1) are also determinists: They hold that the structure of power leaves little role for individuals or social systems. If impersonal forces control our lives, it makes little difference who occupies the White House. Against determinists, voluntarists argue that IR is the product of individuals exercising their free will.

This book contends that individuals are conditioned—not determined—by nature and nurture. Genes and life experiences make each person unique. Each responds differently to the demands of time and place. Whenever we look closely at world-shaking events, one sees the imprint of individuals.[2]

How Personal Characteristics Can Shape Political Outcomes

Many leaders fail despite trumps, while others make the most of a weak hand. As we see in the sidebar on page 90, U.S. president Woodrow Wilson was the most influential person in the world in 1919, but he failed

2. Many political scientists say that individual personalities should be left to historians and psychohistorians. An exception is John G. Stoessinger. See his *Crusaders and Pragmatists: Movers of Modern American Foreign Policy* (New York: Norton, 1979). On the pros and cons of psychohistory, see Saul Friedlaender, *History and Psychoanalysis: An Inquiry into the Possibilities and Limits of Psychohistory* (New York: Holmes & Meier, 1978); and David E. Stannard, *Shrinking History: On Freud and the Failure of Psychohistory* (New York: Oxford University Press, 1980). On the physical burdens of leadership, see Robert E. Gilbert, *The Mortal Presidency: Illness and Anguish in the White House* (New York: Basic Books, 1992).

Why Did the Strong Lose and the Weak Prevail?

President Wilson's personal style and behavior toward opponents practically assured Senate rejection of the League of Nations Covenant, which Wilson embodied in the Versailles peace treaty to make it harder for the Senate to turn down. Senate Republicans demanded modification in the treaty language. But Wilson, as in previous similar situations, refused to compromise. Insecure since childhood, Wilson demanded unquestioning support. His health often failed under pressure and he suffered a stroke as he whistle-stopped the U.S. seeking public backing for the League.* Insisting that the Senate vote on the treaty "as is," Wilson lost, and the U.S. never joined the League.

The personality of Vladimir Lenin, in contrast, helped his Communist Party to hold on to power in Russia despite civil war and foreign military intervention. Like Wilson, Lenin came from a cultivated, middle-class family. Unlike Wilson, the future Communist leader had no self-doubt.** When his Soviet regime was threatened by a German advance in 1918, some of Lenin's comrades refused to compromise with Berlin. But Lenin advised them to trade space for time. The Soviet government finally approved the Treaty of Brest–Litovsk, giving Germany an enormous swath of Russia's territory in exchange for peace. Expediency paid off. Six months later the kaiser fled Germany and the Soviets tore up the pact. Lenin got what he wanted; Wilson did not. Both men died in January 1924.

*On Wilson's psyche, see Juliette L. George and Alexander George, *Woodrow Wilson and Colonel House: A Personality Study* (New York: Dover, 1964); on Wilson's physical frailties, see Edwin A. Weinstein, *Woodrow Wilson: A Medical and Psychological Biography* (Princeton, N.J.: Princeton University Press, 1981); for George and George's comments on Weinstein, see *Political Science Quarterly* 96, no. 4 (winter 1981–82): 642–65. Several Wilson biographies published in the late 1980s downplayed any psychological explanations of Wilson's behavior.

**This portrait is gathered from reminiscences by family members and others who knew Lenin.

to bring his country into the League of Nations. Vladimir Lenin, leader of an upstart party besieged on all sides, helped it to retain power.

To be effective a leader's personality must fit the situation.[3] Very different personality types can win political power in different times and places.[4] President Franklin D. Roosevelt's pragmatism and charm, combined with his wife's idealism, helped him transform the country. While Eleanor Roosevelt thought about what should be done, Franklin focused on what could be done. Crippled by polio at age thirty-nine, FDR was frailer than Wilson, but he remained upbeat to his last day.[5]

Politics may help insecure persons such as Wilson overcome self-doubt; for self-confident persons like Lenin, politics offers a way to impose their will and vision. Still other leaders seek power for its own sake, to acquire personal wealth, or to win acclaim. Idealists as well as realists may seethe with anger over personal grievances that they elevate to matters of principle.

Why Do Decision Makers Sometimes Misjudge?

Rationality in politics means making decisions by calculating probable gains and losses from alternative courses of action and choosing the course most likely to maximize values. Such thinking is not morality or even wisdom, for evil and unwise goals may be pursued rationally.

3. William Howard Taft, for example, made a fine chief justice but a clumsy president—at least in the circumstances he faced. Alexander L. George, *Presidential Decisionmaking in Foreign Policy: The Effective Use of Information and Advice* (Boulder, Colo.: Westview, 1980), 7.

4. For contrasting views, see James David Barber, *The Presidential Character: Predicting Performance in the White House*, 3d ed. (Englewood Cliffs, N.J.: Prentice Hall, 1985); and Theodore Lowi, *The Personal President: Power Invested, Promise Unfulfilled* (Ithaca, N.Y.: Cornell University Press, 1985).

5. David Fromkin, *In the Time of the Americans* (New York: Knopf, 1995); Doris Kearns Goodwin, *No Ordinary Time: Franklin and Eleanor Roosevelt: The Home Front in World War II* (New York: Simon & Schuster, 1994).

But single-minded, rational pursuit of one goal is rare. Most of us—even presidents—"satisfice" rather than maximize: we settle for enough of one value (for example, wealth) to meet our needs while pursuing another value (such as leisure). When a president juggles conflicting goals, such as "guns and butter," the resulting policy mix may appear far from rational.

Foreign policy is also affected by **bounded rationality**—limits on time, intellect, and information that can keep decision makers from fully weighing their values and options. The sheer number and complexity of problems may outstrip their capacity to cope. Pressure to act under a deadline can bring on stress and fatigue that fog the brain. Signals are often ambiguous. Is the other side offering to shake hands to improve relations or to break your wrist?

How can a decision maker keep an open mind and remain alert to change without being drowned in streams of conflicting alarms? She may take shortcuts. But each entails risk. Instead of looking for all relevant data, she may halt the search when she seems to possess sufficient information. But if she stops the quest too early, she may lack the ingredients for a wise decision. Other dangers are outlined in the sidebar on page 92.

Still, not everyone performs worse under stress. Many students find that exams clear away the cobwebs. Richard Nixon claimed to function better under pressure. He described crises as "mountaintop experiences" in which his performance peaked. But even Nixon met a threshhold: He broke after Watergate. Andrei Gromyko, Soviet foreign minister for three decades, seemed to put dogma aside and focus on practical solutions during crises.

LEVEL 2: DOMESTIC FACTORS—STATE AND SOCIETY

A Unified Rational Actor vs. Political Rivalries and SOPs

The **rational actor model** posits that entire governments—indeed, whole countries—are monoliths that calculate how to maximize their collective interests. But states and societies are rarely single-minded calculators. Most are divided by gender, age, ethnic ties, economic interests, education, region, and religion. Each group may push for a different policy at home and abroad. Splits within governments and society also undermine the rational consistency of government policies. Governments are split by partisan and by bureaucratic politics. Rival parties chase their own visions, and sometimes they put their own interests above the country's.

Warning: What You See May Not Be What You Get

Memo to Foreign Ministers: Beware of these pitfalls as you make decisions under pressure and uncertainty.*

1. *Reduced capacity:* Your ability to cope with, and learn during, a crisis is hindered by fatigue and the same factors that led the challenger to misjudge your resolve in the first place.

2. *Selective attention:* You pay more attention to news that seems to affect you immediately.

3. *Stereotyping and simplification:* You pay less attention to facts that contradict your previous views; you are reluctant to throw out the old and build anew.

4. *Self-righteousness:* You fail to empathize with the other side and are blind to change.

5. *Source bias:* You pay more attention to news from familiar, trusted sources.

6. *False postulates:* You leap to sweeping conclusions from a few statistics or anecdotes. You forget, ignore, or confuse facts. As a professor, Woodrow Wilson understood that the president must work with Congress; as president, however, Wilson disdained the Senate in 1919.

7. *Overgeneralization:* You overrate your past successes and trust "tried-and-true" policies. You may depend upon what you think is a sound operational code—beliefs and decision rules on how to respond to challenges.** But rules that work in one context may fail in another. Neither Lenin's prediction of

class warfare nor Wilson's trust in global harmony was a sound guide to all settings.

8. *False analogies:* Past experiences may not fit today's problems. Americans learned from the 1938 Munich deal not to appease aggressors. This lesson worked well enough in Korea in the 1950s but went awry in Vietnam.***

9. *Attention space:* You pay more attention to facts that you will have to act upon and neglect others.

10. *Saliency:* As events become more important, they crowd out others and reduce the number of events on which you can focus.

11. *Momentum:* You pay more attention to facts bearing on actions in which you are already involved.

12. *Utility:* You pay attention to news if it may prove useful. You are less likely to react to warnings unless you also perceive remedies.

*See Ithiel de Sola Pool and Allen Kessler, "The Kaiser, the Tsar, and the Computer: Information Processing in a Crisis," in *International Politics and Foreign Policy—A Reader in Research and Theory,* rev. ed., James N. Rosenau (New York: Free Press, 1969), 664–78; Robert Jervis, "Hypotheses on Misperception," in ibid., 239–54; and Richard Ned Lebow, *Between Peace and War: The Nature of International Crisis* (Baltimore: Johns Hopkins University Press, 1981), 272.

**Alexander L. George, "The `Operational Code': A Neglected Approach to the Study of Political Leaders and Decision making," *International Studies Quarterly* 13 (1969): 190–222.

***Richard E. Neustadt and Ernest R. May, *Thinking in Time: The Uses of History for Decision Makers* (New York: Free Press, 1986).

Rational consistency also suffers because each bureaucracy has its own interests and routines.[6] Each department's **standard operating procedures (SOPs)** aim at effciency but often yield rigidity and mutual contradiction as each unit follows its own drummer. Thus, the Pentagon tested nuclear weapons in 1990 just as the White House sought to arrange a cordial setting for Gorbachev's visit to Washington. Did the Americans conspire to intimidate the Soviet president? Or were the weapons laboratories just "doing their own thing"?

LEVEL 3: THE INTERNATIONAL STATE SYSTEM

The international system, as we saw in Chapter 1, consists of states and the organizations they establish, such as the United Nations. The existing system is anarchic, for it lacks an overarching government, but is not

6. See Graham T. Allison and Philip Zelikow, *Essence of Decision: Explaining the Cuban Missile Crisis,* 2d ed. (New York: Longman, 1999). A Marxist would offer still another explanation: Each government represents the economic interests of the ruling class. There is also a cybernetic model—government as a steering mechanism that responds quickly or slowly to signals, for example, from public opinion or the stock market.

chaotic. The system is defined by its key actors, their interaction, the hierarchies of power and influence among them, and how the system permits, encourages, or limits certain behaviors.

How did each level impact the 1962 missile crisis?

COMPARING THEORY AND REALITY: THE CUBAN MISSILE CRISIS

The 1962 confrontation had deep roots. Arriving in the Caribbean in 1492, Spaniards exterminated most Native Americans and replaced them with slaves from Africa and settlers from Spain. Chafing under Old World rule, most of Latin America obtained independence by 1826. But Cuba and Puerto Rico remained under the rule of Spain. Cubans launched wars for independence in 1868 and again in 1895.

In 1823 U.S. President James Monroe warned that Washington would view as "unfriendly" any effort by Europe to regain colonies in the New World. Monroe worried about Spain, France, and Russia, still expanding down America's northwest coast. The **Monroe Doctrine**, as it was later called, combined isolationism with latent interventionism. It pledged the United States not to meddle in the Old World or in Europe's existing colonies. But the doctrine also set the stage for the United States not just to guard but to dominate the Caribbean and Latin America.

In 1898, U.S. forces helped Cuba gain independence from Spain. But Cuba then came under heavy U.S. influence. Washington's paternalism and U.S. exploitation set the stage for an anti-Yankee revolt. In 1959, rebels led by Fidel Castro overthrew the local dictator, long supported by U.S. commercial interests, and took power.

Could revolutionary Cuba and the United States achieve a working relationship? Castro visited the United States and Latin American countries in spring 1959. He enjoyed rousing welcomes at Harvard University (where his application for admission had been rejected a decade before) and at Princeton, but got a cooler reception at Yale. In Washington, however, he was not received by President Dwight Eisenhower but did meet Vice President Richard Nixon, who concluded that the United States should oust the new Cuban leader (as it had the leftist leader of Guatemala five years before).

Fidel Castro valued his independence. The Soviets saw him more as a "bourgeois nationalist" than a Communist. But Fidel's brother Raúl and their colleague Ernesto ("Che") Guevara were Communists. They pushed for leftist reforms and close contacts with the USSR even as Fidel, Cuba's

Recollections of Intelligence Officer Vadim Orlov on Soviet Submarine B-59

"The anti-submarine forces of the opponent . . . were ready for an encounter with us . . . we could not have expected this kind of counterreaction." Fourteen U.S. ships were tracking the sub. "The Americans were not dilettantes . . . they [began] dropping depth charges. They exploded right next to the hull. It felt like you were sitting in a metal barrel, which somebody is constantly blasting with a sledgehammer." The men aboard were passing out from lack of fresh air—"falling like dominoes. But we were still holding on, trying to escape." The commander was exhausted and furious because he was unable to establish a connection with the General Staff. He ordered that the nuclear torpedo be made ready to fire. Since war may already have begun, he screamed: "We're going to blast them now. We will die, but we will sink them all—we will not disgrace our Navy!" But he relented, did not fire the torpedo, and signaled that the submarine was coming to the surface, whereupon "our pursuers slowed down." Published in Moscow in 2002 and translated for the National Security Archive, George Washington University.

prime minister, sought U.S. economic aid. Receiving none, Cuba, in May 1959 nationalized much land that had been owned by U.S. interests. Washington responded by reducing the amount of sugar Cuba could sell to the United States. In September, Khrushchev exploited the Cuban–U.S. rift by approving the secret sale of Polish arms to Cuba. Soon there was a major Soviet presence in the Western hemisphere, undercutting the Monroe Doctrine.[7] What started as an irritant to Washington became a threat to world peace.

THE UNFOLDING OF THE CUBAN MISSILE CRISIS

The chain of events between 1960 and 1962 that led to the Cuban missile crisis is detailed in the time line on page 97. For Americans, the crisis began on October 14, 1962, when a U.S. spy plane brought back evidence of the missile deployment. The White House did not immediately broadcast this information. Instead, it used the time before the missiles could be made operational to plan an effective response. How could Kennedy get the best advice? How could he avoid both raucus discord and **group think** conformity? Some presidents had asked advisers to play "devil's advocate" for unpopular views. President Eisenhower often requested a list of formal options with pros and cons.[8] Kennedy favored a less formal approach. He set up a working group, later called the **ExCom** (Executive Committee), comprised of some fourteen to twenty officials from various branches of government. Each was to think like a generalist—not as champion of some bureaucratic niche. Sometimes the president stayed away so ExCom members could debate more freely.

A psychologist's study concluded that the ExCom approach minimized group think.[9] But in fact, the group paid little attention to noncoercive options. The ExCom rejected any course that allowed the Soviets to stall while they made the missiles operational. National Security Assistant McGeorge Bundy later branded those who favored a nonmilitary solution as **doves**, in contrast to **hawks**, who demanded tough, unilateral measures. Among the doves, Bundy said, was Adlai Stevenson, U.S. ambassador to the UN, who attended several ExCom meetings. These caricatures persisted in U.S. politics, making it difficult for political figures to propose anything less than a fully macho approach to Vietnam and other conflicts. Perhaps policy makers should strive to be owls, not hawks or doves.

The ExCom focused on six options: (1) do nothing and accept Soviet missiles in Cuba; (2) mend fences with Castro; (3) use diplomacy to squeeze or buy them out; (4) invade Cuba with conventional forces, eliminating the missiles and Castro; (5) take out the missiles with a surgical

7. Gaddis Smith, *The Last Years of the Monroe Doctrine, 1945–1993* (New York: Hill and Wang, 1994), 95–103.

8. Another approach would be "multiple advocacy." See George, *Presidential Decisionmaking*, chaps. 11 and 12.

9. I. L. Janis, *Victims of Group think* (Boston: Houghton Mifflin, 1972).

Fig. 3.1 "Chicken"

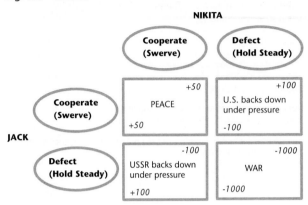

the Soviets did not budge, the United States could still have used force. U.S. military forces stayed on high alert through November 1962.[17] There was no sign, however, that Washington ever contemplated a first strike on the Soviet homeland.

"We were eyeball to eyeball," Rusk observed, and "the other side just blinked." But the reality was more complex. Each side gave the other time and space to avoid a collision. Neither backed the other into a corner from which it could exit only by fighting. To be sure, the United States gained the most—it had compelled Moscow to back down. But Khrushchev could claim that he had won major U.S. concessions. And while Castro felt betrayed by the Soviet retreat, he gained a qualified U.S. pledge not to invade Cuba. All three countries survived intact.

Kennedy did not rub salt in Soviet wounds or crow over the Soviet retreat. Rather, as we will see in Chapters 6 and 7, both U.S. and Soviet leaders in 1963 and, in later years, looked for ways to prevent confrontations and improve relations.

But the 1962 U.S.–Soviet understandings were left hanging. Fuming that he had not even been consulted, Castro refused UN inspection of Cuban territory. Moscow and Washington then devised an alternative: Soviet missiles were lashed to the decks of Soviet ships, where they could be observed and photographed by U.S. planes. But there was no on-site inspection to verify withdrawal of nuclear warheads. And no "suitable safeguards" were established against future weapons deliveries. Lacking these assurances, the United States gave no formal promise that it would not attack Cuba. Indeed, the White House continued to sponsor sabotage in Cuba and assassination plots against Castro. Only in 1970, when Moscow asked Washington for a confirmation, did the

The Game of Chicken

The Cuban confrontation resembled what game theorists call **Chicken**: Two rivals drive straight at each other. The first to swerve is deemed "chicken"—she or he loses "face" but not life (see Figure 3.1). The unflinching rival wins applause. If both swerve at the same time, neither wins but both survive. If both hold a steady course, neither survives. In game theory terms, to swerve is to cooperate while to hold a steady course is to defect.

Chicken differs from the Prisoner's Dilemma (see Chapter 1) in that both sides share a deep interest in avoiding mutual defection—catastrophe. In Chicken, being exploited is not as bad as a head-on crash. Still, each driver will try to look firm so the other swerves. Players like Kennedy or Khrushchev may demonstrate commitment by fixing the wheel, feigning insanity, or appearing not to understand the dangers. If one plays Chicken with a committed player, it pays to back down. A sensible actor would avoid such games altogether! A minor player (like Castro), if rational, would avoid getting caught between two juggernauts.

17. Defense Minister Rodion Malinovskii reported to the Central Committee, Soviet Communist Party, on November 17, 1962, on the status of U.S. forces worldwide. He said that 75 B-52 flights took place each day and that 178 B-47s were based in Europe and 36 in Asia along with two B-52s. Five U.S. missile-firing submarines were on patrol off Norway, while two were at their base in Scotland and one in Charleston. Soviet reconnaissance was not so bad either! See *Diplomaticheskii vestnik* 19–20 (October 15–31, 1992): 62–63.

Table 3.1 How the Deal Served Both Sides, Though Unequally

What Khrushchev Could Say	What Kennedy Could Say
We avoided war.	We avoided war.
The imbalance of forces is no worse and I can confide to my critics in Moscow that Kennedy agreed to pull back U.S. missiles from Turkey.	The balance of power is unchanged. We got a Soviet retreat in exchange for our redundant missiles in Turkey—a swap that Moscow has agreed not to publicize.
Castro is angry, but we got a U.S. pledge not to invade Cuba. We worsened U.S. ties with Turkey.	We pledged not to invade Cuba contingent on an inspection that Castro has prevented, which leaves us with a free hand.
My leadership looks weaker, but we avoided disaster and I can claim victory.	Our domestic and international position is much stronger. We can now try to improve relations with the USSR.

White House confirm privately that the 1962 understanding was "still in full force."[18] How the outcome of the crisis benefited each side is suggested in Table 3.1.

WHY DID THE CRISIS TAKE PLACE?

We are now in a better position to understand how and why the confrontation began. The likely perceptions of each side are outlined in Table 3.2 and elucidated in the text that follows.

Why Did Khrushchev Gamble?

The Balance of Strategic Power. Khrushchev sought to obtain a quick fix—a cheap and ready way to restore Soviet bargaining power. From 1957 until 1961, Khrushchev had enjoyed what the broad public saw as a "missile gap." He claimed that the USSR was turning out missiles "like sausages." Washington did little to rebut Khrushchev in public, but U.S.

18. Henry Kissinger, *The White House Years* (Boston: Little, Brown, 1979), chap. 16.

Table 3.2 How Each Side Saw the Other Before October 1962

How Moscow Saw Washington	How Washington Saw Moscow
We can equalize the balance of power by putting MRBMs in Cuba. We can slip the missiles in and Washington will have to accept a new situation.	The Soviets would not dare confront us in our own backyard. They have never conducted large operations far from their own territory.
Our MRBMs will balance U.S. missiles in Turkey.	Our missiles in Turkey are for defense of the West.
We can protect an outpost of revolution from U.S. aggression.	We don't intend to invade Cuba so the Soviets have no need to protect Castro.
Kennedy is weak and Americans are degenerate. They were irresolute at the Bay of Pigs, the Vienna Summit, on Berlin, and on other issues.	Khrushchev is impetuous. Perhaps we looked weak to him before, but we've made it clear we will not abide offensive missiles in Cuba.
We can and should teach Washington to fall back before our power.	We must stop Soviet expansion. The Kremlin has no right to intrude in the Caribbean.

spy planes (from 1956 to May 1960) and satellites (after August 1960) revealed that the USSR produced and deployed very few intercontinental ballistic missiles (ICBMs).[19] Khrushchev had delayed mass production until an improved model could be perfected.

Taking office in 1961, the Kennedy team did not know precisely how many missiles the USSR possessed, but Pentagon officials began to tell the public that the missile gap favored the United States. Khrushchev's bluff was exposed. Moreover, the Kennedy administration stepped up U.S. missile production, aiming to deploy more than 1,000 intercontinental ballistic missiles (ICBMs). Looking back, we know that in 1962 the U.S. already had 200 nuclear-tipped ICBMs plus thousands of additional nuclear weapons on bombers, aircraft carriers, and submarines able to strike the USSR. The Soviet Union then had only about 20 ICBMs—all liquid-fueled, difficult to launch; no nuclear-tipped missiles in submarines; no intercontinental bombers; and no aircraft carriers.

What Moscow had in spades was medium-range ballistic missiles (MRBMs) and intermediate-range ballistic missiles (IRBMs) that could reach many U.S. targets if deployed in Cuba. Khrushchev planned to deploy these missiles secretly in October 1962 and reveal their existence after the U.S. midterm elections in November. Kennedy would then have to accept them as accomplished facts and give way to Moscow on such issues as West Berlin.[20] Thus, Khrushchev's primary motive was probably to redress the strategic balance of power.

Second, Khrushchev wanted equal treatment. If the USSR had to live with U.S. missiles in Turkey, Americans should also agonize over missiles close to their homeland.[21]

Third, Khrushchev probably hoped to deter a U.S. invasion of Cuba.[22] Some analysts believe this was Khrushchev's main reason for deploying missiles to Cuba. They say that the aging Soviet leader seemed to gain new life from Castro and his revolution and wanted to protect Cuba. But when push came to shove, Khrushchev put Soviet security above all else.

Individuals: The High-Stakes Risk Taker. How could Khrushchev bolster Soviet power and preserve his own rule while avoiding nuclear war?[23] Khrushchev's personal make-up generated a bold, idiosyncratic solution. Khrushchev was sure he could deceive and then bully the pampered millionaire, twenty-three years his junior.

Khrushchev was born in 1894 to a coal miner's family.[24] He once boasted to Western diplomats: "You all went to great schools. I went about barefoot and in rags. When you were in the nursery, I was herding cows. And yet here we are, and I can run rings around you all."

19. See sample photos and documents in Kevin C. Ruffner, ed., *CORONA: America's First Satellite Program* (Washington, D.C.: Center for the Study of Intelligence, Central Intelligence Agency, 1995); on "learning to live with transparency," see John Lewis Gaddis, *The Long Peace: Inquiries into the History of the Cold War* (New York: Oxford University Press, 1987), chap. 7.

20. Anastas Mikoyan, discussion with Castro on November 3, 1962. *Diplomaticheskii vestnik* 19–20 (October 15–31, 1992): 58–62 at 62. Once the crisis began, however, Berlin remained calm, and afterward Moscow never again threatened West Berlin directly.

21. U.S. intelligence agencies concluded in 1958 that Moscow would not use force in response to U.S. deployment of IRBMs on the Soviet periphery, because the USSR could depend on its own ICBM capability. "Probable Sino–Soviet Reactions to U.S. Deployment of IRBMs on the Soviet Bloc Periphery," *National Intelligence Estimate*, no. 100-4-58, April 15, 1958, in *Selected Estimates on the Soviet Union, 1958–1959*, ed. Scott A. Koch (Washington, D.C.: Center for the Study of Intelligence, Central Intelligence Agency, 1993), 271–279.

22. How Castro felt in 1962 we do not know, but decades later he stated that the idea for the nuclear missile deployment came from Moscow. Castro said he approved the scheme because he wanted Cuba to do its part in "defending socialism." To protect Cuba against a U.S. invasion, he added, could have been achieved merely by using better conventional forces. For an interpretation that probably overstates Khrushchev's commitment to Cuba, see John Lewis Gaddis, *We Now Know: Rethinking Cold War History* (New York: Oxford University Press, 1997), 260–280.

23. Similar uncertainties confronted President George Bush and Iraqi leader Saddam Hussein as they faced one another over Kuwait. For how to do "psychology at a distance," see Stanley A. Renshon, ed., *The Political Psychology of the Gulf War: Leaders, Publics, and the Process of Conflict* (Pittsburgh: University of Pittsburgh Press, 1993), published in Persian in Tehran in 1997.

24. Also in 1894, Nicholas II became tsar, Lenin published his first political tract, and Stalin entered a seminary.

CIA psychiatrists called Khrushchev "a gambler . . . expert in calculated bluffing." Khrushchev often moved with bold strokes, burning bridges without considering how to retreat. A different Soviet leader might have reasoned: "Why gamble? The Soviet nuclear arsenal is already sufficient to frighten the Americans. Let Castro save his own skin."

Few if any other Soviet leaders would have risked the Cuban venture. Lenin, in 1918, took "one step backward" when he faced overwhelming German force. Even Josef Stalin had been cautious about projecting military forces, but Khrushchev departed from Soviet tradition—and got the bureaucracy to go along.

Soviet Politics. Khrushchev hoped that a dazzling success in the Caribbean would silence his critics—Soviet officers displeased with his 1960 plan to cut the armed forces by one-third, party officials opposed to his radical reorganizations, others who blamed Khrushchev for the flagging Soviet economy, and anti-Western hardliners (backed by Chinese leaders) who argued that Khrushchev was soft on Western imperialism.[25]

Khrushchev's bold style fed on the compliant Soviet political system—too obedient to thwart its risk-prone leader. Khrushchev surrounded himself with yes-men he had known since the 1940s. He went through the motions of consulting, but ignored any dissident voices.[26] To make matters worse, the KGB fed Khrushchev unreliable reports, for example, that Soviet tests of giant hydrogen bombs in 1961 had deterred an American nuclear first strike on the USSR. (Had Washington considered attacking, the tests would have provided good cause to get on with it.) To understand Kennedy's plans during the missile crisis, the KGB depended heavily on a hot tip from an émigré bartender in Washington who overheard the best guesses of two U.S. journalists.

Khrushchev's gambit was irrational in the sense that it contained a high risk of disaster for goals not crucial to Soviet life. Still, the Soviet system was organized to behave like a rational monolith in pursuit of Kremlin objectives. The system's output, however, did not look like the work of a rational monolith. If there were a master plan, some parts did not dovetail, as we see in Table 3.3.[27] Soviet habits of secrecy kept one hand from knowing what the other was doing.

Why Did Washington Doze?

Why, given a host of cues and clues, was the Soviet deployment not discovered earlier? Why were Americans again dozing, as before Pearl Harbor?[28] We begin with the hubris of Kennedy and his top men.

25. But Beijing commentators, afterward hit Khrushchev going and coming: To send missiles to Cuba, they said, was "adventurism"; to pull them out, "capitalationism." Concurrent with the missile crisis, Khrushchev had sided with New Delhi as India and China skirmished in the Himalayas.

26. First Deputy Minister Mikoyan predicted Castro would refuse the missiles; Foreign Minister Gromyko warned that the Americans would discover them early and respond vigorously. But Khrushchev got Castro's OK and ignored Gromyko. Khrushchev discussed the missile venture with a handful of high officials, including Defense Minister Malinovskii and rocket specialist S. S. Biriuzov, in late May or early June. Then he briefed the entire Communist Party Presidium. Mikoyan, Gromyko, and Presidium member Otto Kuusinen expressed deep reservations, but others kept their doubts to themselves.

27. Soviet military personnel were disguised in civilian slacks and sport shirts when they stepped onto Cuban shores, but they then lined up by fours and moved out in truck convoys. Missiles protruded from some trucks carried along Cuban roads. The commanding officer, an Army general, lacked experience with missiles.

28. See Roberta Wohlstetter, *Pearl Harbor: Warning and Decision* (Stanford, Calif.: Stanford University Press, 1962); and Gordon W. Prange, *At Dawn We Slept: The Untold Story of Pearl Harbor* (New York: Penguin Books, 1981).

Table 3.3 A Unified Soviet Policy vs. What Actually Happened

A Fully Unified Policy	What Actually Happened
1. Prepare surface-to-air missiles (SAMs) and make them operational before MRBM deployment begins.	1. The SAMs were deployed but not authorized to fire on U.S. reconnaissance planes until *after* MRBM deployment began.
2. To avoid detection, deploy MRBMs at night and camouflage the work by day.	2. No camouflage was used at the missile sites until *after* detection by the U.S.
3. Avoid deployment patterns (such as those used in the USSR) that could alert U.S. observers.	3. The SAM, MRBM, and IRBM sites were laid out in the same patterns used in the USSR—familiar to U.S. intelligence.

The Pragmatic Liberal vs. the Communist Gambler. The Soviet leader was inquisitive but had been trained mainly in the school of hard knocks; Kennedy, at prep school and Harvard. Khrushchev's father was a coal miner; Kennedy's, a multimillionaire and U.S. ambassador to England. Khrushchev spoke in peasant proverbs; Kennedy's senior thesis became a book, *Why England Slept,* its foreword written by the publisher of Time-Life. Khrushchev had been a propaganda commissar in the Red Army; Kennedy was an authentic war hero whose wounds never fully healed. (He had many ailments and was often in great, constant pain despite taking a bevy of strong drugs.[29]) Kennedy, his aide Ted Sorensen wrote, had "limitless curiosity about nearly everything," read constantly and rapidly, and grew and profited from experience. He combined tough politics and reckless womanizing.[30]

Kennedy called himself a pragmatic liberal. Where Khrushchev was ideological, Kennedy was uneasy with the idealism of some of his fellow Democrats. But Cuba stirred Kennedy's emotions: Castro symbolized Khrushchev's claim that communism was on the march and reminded Kennedy of his 1961 failure at the **Bay of Pigs**.[31]

The self-assured Kennedy sought out the best and brightest—men he had never met—as top aides to head the Departments of Defense, State, and Treasury. But most of these luminaries had little empathy for others. Blinded by self-righteousness, they believed it proper for the West to encircle the USSR with rockets but wrong for the Soviets to have a base in Cuba.

The Americans noted every Soviet move that might threaten West Berlin, but they ignored how U.S. training exercises known as Quick Kick and Whip Lash in April and May 1962 might look to Havana and Moscow. McNamara later insisted that the Whie House had not decided to invade Cuba and presumed that America's foes would interpret U.S. maneuvers as mere contingency planning.

29. See Robert Dallek, "The Medical Ordeals of JFK," *Atlantic Monthly* 290, no. 5 (December 2002).

30. His affairs included a possible Nazi agent in 1942, a Mafia courtesan in 1960–1962, and a possible East German–Soviet agent in 1963. Beschloss, *Crisis Years,* 141, 613–617.

31. Dean Rusk was surprised that "this man with ice water in his veins" was so "emotional" about Castro. However, McNamara recalled that they were all "hysterical" about Castro. Beschloss, *Crisis Years,* 375.

Bureaucratic Logjam. U.S. intelligence failed Kennedy repeatedly on Cuba. In 1961 the CIA assured him that Cuban exiles could overthrow Castro, but they were stopped on the beach at the Bay of Pigs. On September 19, 1962, the U.S. Intelligence Board concluded that the USSR would not introduce offensive missiles into Cuba.[32] Surely the Soviets would not challenge the Americans in their own backyard.

U.S. officials gathered relevant information from many sources—shipping reports, agents in Cuba, refugees, and sporadic aerial reconnaissance. One report had Castro's private pilot boasting that Cubans had "everything, including atomic weapons." There was evidence of SAM sites, missile patrol boats, and Il-28 bombers, but not of offensive missiles.

Much of this data was as yet undigested when the U.S. Intelligence Board made its report on September 19. SOPs required methodical collecting and sifting of information, much of which was inconclusive. Neither planes nor satellites surveyed every inch of Soviet territory, and U.S. satellites did not target Cuba.

Adding to the uncertainty, the West's ace spy in Moscow was silent. For two years, beginning in August 1960, **Oleg V. Penkovsky**, a colonel in Soviet military intelligence, transmitted to British and U.S. agents more than 10,000 pages of military information on 111 rolls of film—from Soviet war plans to diagrams of missiles. This information explained the pattern ("footprint") of deployed missiles discovered on October 14 and told how many days' grace before the MRBMs would be operational. But no word came from Penkovsky after August 1962; he was arrested by Soviet agents in Moscow on October 24, just as the missile crisis neared its climax.[33]

The president's Foreign Intelligence Advisory Board concluded later that before October 14 the intelligence community lacked the "focused sense of urgency or alarm which might well have stimulated a greater effort."[34] Flights by U-2 spy planes over Cuba were risky and provocative. They took place at fixed intervals and could not cover all of Cuba with one sweep.[35] Increasingly alarmed about reports of missile activity, the CIA on October 4 got high-level approval for a U-2 flight over Cuba, but the flight was delayed ten days by a dispute within the bureaucracy: Would the U-2 be operated by the CIA or by an Air Force pilot in uniform?

When the October 14 flight brought evidence of MRBM deployment, the fragments of gathered information fell into place. The White House had been deceived by Moscow and misled by the CIA.

32. By August 1962, CIA Director John McCone, a conservative Republican businessman, believed a Soviet missile deployment likely. But his was a lonely voice and he departed for Europe on his honeymoon.

33. In 1963, Penkovsky was tried for treason, found guilty, and shot. See Jerrold L. Schecter and Peter S. Deriabin, *The Spy Who Saved the World: How a Soviet Colonel Changed the Course of the Cold War* (New York: Scribner's, 1992).

34. Top secret memorandum for the president, February 4, 1963, in Mary S. McAuliffe, ed., *CIA Documents on the Cuban Missile Crisis 1962* (Washington, D.C.: Central Intelligence Agency, 1992), 362–71.

35. CIA Director McCone said later that his order in late August for daily overflights of Cuba had been cancelled by McNamara and Rusk, who feared "a hell of a mess" if a plane were shot down. Schecter and Deriabin, *The Spy*, 332.

After exiting government service, former U.S. Defense Secretary Robert S. McNamara wanted to know: "What went wrong in Cuba and Vietnam and how can we avoid such mistakes again?" Here he sits across from Cuban President Castro and Vice President José Ramon Fernandez at an October 2002 conference gathered to analyze what happened forty years earlier. For years, no serious study investigated how the crisis was shaped by the personalities of men such as McNamara and Castro. In 2003, however, a detailed portrait, *Khrushchev: The Man and His Era* by William Truman (New York: W. W. Norton) assigned major weight to Nikita's propensity for high-risk, quick-fix remedies to complex problems. He gambled on solving a bevy of worries—a missile gap, the security of a Soviet ally, and mounting domestic opposition—with one bold move.

Republicans and Democrats. Before October 14 the evidence of a Soviet missile deployment was ambiguous. Partisan bias conduced to divergent interpretations. Some Republicans charged that Kennedy was ignoring danger in Cuba. Indeed, the president could not afford to look soft before November's midterm elections. If the Soviets dared send missiles to Cuba, this implied that the president appeared weak to Moscow and was less discerning than Republicans. Once proof of the Soviet missiles existed, partisan politics pushed Kennedy to make a strong response. Why did he risk Armageddon over a few dozen missiles? Kennedy claimed later that, had he done nothing, he would have been impeached.

WHAT PROPOSITIONS HOLD?
WHAT QUESTIONS REMAIN?

INTERTWINING THE LEVELS OF ANALYSIS

Are individual humans mere puppets pulled by the structure of power, as neorealists say? The key roles played by Khrushchev and Kennedy—and by other leaders such as Lenin and Wilson—belie any view that humans are marionettes of great forces. The shifting distribution of nuclear missiles was the stage; the U.S. and Soviet political systems established key parameters; but the origins of the missile crisis and how it played out depended on the personal qualities of Khrushchev and Kennedy.

Political leaders are often like captains on the high seas. In the maelstrom of world politics, the helmsman can make or break the voyage. He is often more important than the crew, the ship, the sea, or the weather. If the helmsman ignores the portents, falls asleep at the wheel, or provokes a mutiny, the ship may never reach harbor. A skillful captain, on the other hand, will steer the ship safely whatever the conditions. If the wind is slack, he will use the time to rest and make repairs. If a head wind lashes the vessel, the captain tightens the sail or tacks. Braced by a strong wind from aft, the helmsman unfurls the sails and advances. At all times the skilled helmsman attends both crew and ship, preparing them for the perils ahead.

Neither Soviet nor U.S. policy was determined inexorably by the strategic balance. So-called American policy was imprinted by Kennedy's beliefs and style. He and his top advisers helped provoke the crisis by their bluster toward Castro and their rapid missile buildup. Former President Eisenhower, for one, thought that a more gradual buildup of U.S. strategic forces would suffice against the slowly emerging Soviet threat.

Once the Soviet missiles were discovered, Kennedy again put his personal stamp on U.S. policy. Had Adlai Stevenson been president and not UN ambassador at the time, he probably would have placed less emphasis on force. Had Lyndon Johnson been president and not vice president, he might have acted without deliberating for a week. Had Eisenhower still been president, he probably would have left more authority with local commanders—a riskier approach than Kennedy's micromanagement.

To be sure, no person is a completely free agent. Personal inclinations are tempered by the logic of situations. As dangers become more visible, reality can dispel wishful thinking. Under pressure, Kennedy became more pragmatic.[36] He objected to rewarding Soviet duplicity, but—reluctant to play at Chicken—privately agreed to pull back U.S. missiles from Turkey.

What role did domestic factors (Level 2) play in 1962? Both Khrushchev and Kennedy were energized and constrained by state and society. "Russian" and "American" political values helped to shape Soviet and U.S. actions in 1962, but "political culture" and "civilization" do not predict how individuals will behave—particularly under stress. If political culture determined behavior, all Soviet and U.S. leaders would have responded identically to the problems they faced in 1962.

The impact of individuals is greatest at times of crisis. At critical moments, decision makers must choose which fork to take and at what speed. The inertia and routines of bureaucracies carry most weight in normal times, but each leader—Khrushchev and Kennedy—bent the bureaucracy to become his servant in October 1962.

Individuals at all levels can act like wild cards to disrupt all calculations. In 1962, for example, Western intelligence benefited from the unprecedented revelations of Colonel Penkovsky. Other individuals could have easily brought on disaster, for example, the Soviet commanding officer in Cuba able to fire tactical nuclear weapons if Americans invaded, with or without authorization from Moscow. As it happened, this same officer gave the order to the Soviet SAM unit that shot down the U-2 on October 27, an act that Khrushchev feared might unhinge his deal with Washington.[37]

We face a knowledge gap. Few leaders are ready to bare their souls or share their medical records with foreign analysts. Even when leaders have been intensively scrutinized, as was Wilson, experts disagree about what made them tick. CIA psychiatrists knew much about Khrushchev but could not predict his behavior in specific situations. Individuals count, but are often unpredictable.

WHAT THE CRISIS IMPLIES FOR MUTUAL GAIN AND OPEN DIPLOMACY

How can the Marshall Plan and Washington's handling of the missile crisis both be regarded as major achievements of U.S. foreign policy? Some

36. Lenin became more realistic and persuaded most of his comrades to modify their dreams as the kaiser's armies drew closer. Wilson, on the other hand, refused to compromise despite warnings that the Senate would otherwise turn down the League.

37. See Khrushchev–Castro letters in Blight et al., *Cuba on the Brink*, 482–484, and many references indexed as U-2 shootdown.

differences were stark. The Marshall Plan was characterized by open planning for mutual gain with Europe. By contrast, the Kennedy team saw the missile crisis as a contest like Chicken. The Marshall Plan was launched with "carrots"; the Cuban blockade, with "sticks"—prepared in secret. Kennedy masked the U-2 discovery while preparing a firm response.

Yet there were also similarities. Both the ERP and Cuban crisis emerged from a bipolar structure of power with intense competition. U.S. diplomacy in each case was bolstered by support from Western Europe (unlike the 2003 war against Saddam Hussein). Both in 1947 and in 1962, U.S. policy was well planned by experts with diverse skills—another difference from 2003, when the Pentagon sought to manage postwar Iraq without Arabists or development specialists from the State Department.

The ERP was a coordination game—a problem of coordinating convergent interests. The missile crisis looked more like Chicken. Still, both Washington and Moscow converted their confrontation into a coordination game. Each avoided backing the other into a corner. Having made a deal, they found ways to implement it. Thus, when Castro refused to permit UN verification that the missiles were gone, Moscow and Washington cooperated on shipboard inspection from the air. Sobered by their trip to the brink, Kennedy and Khrushchev embarked on a strategy to reduce tensions (analyzed in Chapters 6 and 7).

The near catastrophe of October 1962 confirms the warning that zero-sum politics and deception are inferior to joint strategies of mutual gain and open diplomacy. Khrushchev worked for a one-sided triumph. His deception—of the Soviet people, of world public opinion, of the White House, and even of Fidel Castro—was integral to the missile crisis.

Secrecy and deceit bore bad fruit. Had the Kremlin publicly announced a missile deployment in Cuba (as Castro suggested), Washington would have had few grounds on which to protest. No law barred a Soviet presence. The Monroe Doctrine was never international law.

Moscow manipulated Cuba and embarrassed Castro. Trying to assuage Castro's hurt feelings after the crisis, Soviet First Deputy Prime Minister Anastos Mikoyan told him: "It's all right to deceive enemies." With friends, however, "sincerity and openness" are necessary to "resolve differences and reach a consensus. With enemies things are different." But then Mikoyan lied to Castro as well, implying that Moscow's only goal had been to protect Cuba.[38]

Castro later said that if he had known that the Soviets were thinking of how to improve the balance of power, and how few missiles they had in 1962, he would have "advised them to be more prudent."[39]

38. "*S vragami, drugoe delo, ikh mozhno i obmanut'*" (Meeting on November 3, 1962), *Diplomaticheskii vestnik* 19–20 (October 15–31, 1992): 58–62 at 61.

39. Quoted in Blight et al., *Cuba on the Brink*, 203.

U.S. policy before the crisis would have been on far sounder footing had the public been better informed. Few Americans understood how U.S. policy since 1898 had bred anti-U.S. feelings in Cuba. Americans knew very little about U.S. missile superiority or U.S. schemes against Castro. Ignorance kept Americans from anticipating Soviet or Cuban anxieties. For decades after the crisis, Americans did not know that Kennedy had promised Moscow to pull back U.S. missiles from Turkey (a pledge fulfilled in 1963).

Memo to the President: How to Improve Decision Making . . .

Cuba reminds us that nothing is preordained. The underlying structure in 1962 could have contributed to peace or war. We are not free to do whatever we please, but neither are we helpless victims of fate. Humans provoked the crisis and humans avoided war.

How can we avoid another collision course? How should we deal with such crises if they arise? Here are ten guidelines that must be adapted to evolving conditions:

*1. **Pursue mutual gain and openness.** Even with strong rivals, explore conditional cooperation buttressed with safeguards against defection. Better to compromise and create joint values than retreat or march toward war.*

*2. **Blend firmness and flexibility, potential punishment and reward.** Be sure that your strength is evident and credible, but do not bluster needlessly. Consider what the changing balance of power means for potential foes as well as for ourselves. Be aware of how hard it is to communicate. A Khrushchev may read conciliatory gestures as weakness and ignore stern warnings. Only when Kennedy blockaded Cuba did Khrushchev get the message.*

*3. **Strive to see ourselves as others see us.** Had the Kennedy team seen itself through Khrushchev's eyes—as materially strong but irresolute—Washington might have anticipated Khrushchev's gamble.*

*4. **Expect surprise.** Beat down preconceptions and wishful thinking. Investigate how worst-case and least likely scenarios might unfold. Ask whether rationality and value for the other side may differ from your definition.*

*5. **Expect duplicity—certainly from foes who endorse any means to their ends—but try to prevent it.** Lying was part of the Soviet operational code. Do not trust assurances, especially those with ambiguous terms such as "offensive" weapons.*

*6. **Do not stereotype others.** Allow that they may change. Khrushchev became a sober statesman as the crisis evolved. Had Kennedy typed Khrushchev once and forever as a cheat, give-and-take negotiations would have been unthinkable.*

*7. **Things often go wrong.** Do not assume that crises can be readily managed. Luck, as well as skill, avoided a catastrophe in 1962. Do not count on good fortune.*

8. Distance major foreign policy issues from partisan politics. Republicans and Democrats joined forces to organize the United Nations, the Marshall Plan, and NATO; their rivalry helped kill the League of Nations in 1919 and set the stage for the 1962 crisis.

9. Learn. Do not make the same mistakes twice. But do not learn the wrong lessons. Review assumptions and SOPs to cope with change. Decide beforehand what evidence would count for or against your expectations. Weigh competing hypotheses. Integrate new data methodically with your existing beliefs. If an event comes as a surprise, reevaluate your expectations. Discuss misjudgments internally and perhaps with the other side.

10. Do not merely adapt to circumstances but seek deep learning and new solutions. It is easier to adjust tactics than to make substantive changes. After the Cuban crisis, both sides adapted because they wanted to avoid more collisions. But Soviet leaders also pledged: "Never again"—never again would they have to back down before overwhelming U.S. power. The Kremlin "learned" to intensify its arms buildup—a major reason for the eventual collapse of the Soviet empire.

You need confidence but not hubris; willingness to use force but only when needed; tolerance for ambiguity but ability to act under uncertainty; ability to get advice without producing paralyzing splits within your team. You need both memory and openness. Without memory, you are driftwood in the streams of life; without openness, a bullet fired on an unchangeable path.

Our experiences in 1962 are relevant to India and Pakistan, each armed with small but lethal nuclear arsenals. India is larger and more powerful, but Pakistan's nuclear force is a great equalizer. India's government operates under greater democratic restraint than the authoritarian regime of Pakistan. Nationalist and religious emotions often run high in each country, but both governments are dominated by well-educated moderates. They would profit from applying all the lessons of October 1962.

Tomorrow's crises for the United States will probably come from countries even farther from Western values and more desperate than the USSR in 1962. A confrontation with China could arise over another island— Taiwan. The United States would be stronger than China, but Beijing could nonetheless deter Americans with its missiles. After Mao Zedong's death, Chinese leaders were usually more pragmatic than was Khrushchev. Still, if their regime tottered, they could also gamble for high stakes. To win popular support they might again rattle their missiles at Taiwan.

Given the lethality and long reach of modern weapons, we need a strategy of preventive diplomacy. Crisis prevention beats crisis management. We should strive to ameliorate underlying problems so confrontations do not arise. With China, for example, this could be a compromise that keeps Taiwan free while salving China's pride.

A confrontation between the United States and an "axis of evil" state or a nonstate terrorist group would have a different structure from the JFK–Khrushchev faceoff. If North Korea possessed weapons of mass destruction (WMD), their range and effectiveness would probably be uncertain. Hence, Pyongyang's deterrent would have less credibility than Moscow's in 1962 or China's in the 21st century. Still, even Pyongyang's formidable conventional forces would pose a deadly menace to South Korea. If U.S. forces intervened in North Korea,

C H A P T E R   F O U R

WHY WAGE WAR? DOES IT PAY TO FIGHT?

"He calls it Reason, but uses it only to act more beastly than any animal—*er nennt's Vernunft und braucht's allein, nur tierischer als jedes Tier zu sein.*"

—Mephistopheles to the Lord in Goethe's *Faust* (l, 285–286)

T H E   B I G   Q U E S T I O N S   I N   C H A P T E R   4

- Was/is war inevitable? If so, why? Is war merely another tool to conduct policy and negotiate? Or does it represent a malfunction—something wrong within individuals, societies, the state or transnational systems, or even the biosphere?

- Can war be a rational means to an end? Can war be "just"? Can it be rational or just in the nuclear era?

- Are wars increasing in frequency? In the havoc they wreak? Are there any patterns over time?

- What caused the major wars of the past century? Are there any similarities in the factors that brought on World Wars I and II, the interventions in Korea and the Persian Gulf, the U.S. campaign in Vietnam, and the Soviet campaign in Afghanistan?

- Who gained and who lost from these conflicts?

- If you want peace, should you prepare for war? Or do war preparations lead to war?

- What has changed since "9/11"? What remains the same? Is asymmetrical warfare really so new? Or just more of the same?

- Given all this, what should the United States do about "rogue states" such as "Koraq" and "Irkor"? And what about potential U.S. rivals such as China, Europe, and Russia?

Is It Time to Attack "Koraq" and/or "Irkor"?.... The
*United States and its partners face two mean adversaries—Koraq and Irkor. Each has been
called a rogue state—wild like a rogue elephant. The rulers of each country have treated
their own subjects brutally and, what concerns us more, have attacked their neighbors (who
are also our allies) in recent years. Each invasion was repulsed by UN action led by the
United States. Koraq and Irkor are unstable, tempting their leaders to lash out against
neighbors and, if they could reach us, the United States. If war erupts, the best intelligence
estimates a "high likelihood" that Koraq may utilize some of its 5,000 tons of biological and
chemical agents, including nerve gas. Both Koraq and Irkor have sought to buy, steal, or
build nuclear weapons. Koraq mines its own uranium and has been enriching it, contrary
to agreements with the international community. Irkor has no uranium mines, but may
have bought or stolen uranium from Russia's stockpiles. Israelis destroyed Irkor's nuclear
weapon facilities several years ago, but these have probably been rebuilt and housed deep
underground. If so, Irkor's American-trained engineers could probably construct nuclear
warheads within a few years. Indeed, they may have already done so. Both Koraq and Irkor
definitely have short-range missiles capable of striking their neighbors. We know each country has spent large sums trying to purchase or purloin missile technology, but we are unsure
of how quickly either will be able to deploy medium-range or intercontinental rockets. So
far as we know, neither has married nuclear warheads with missiles—yet.*

*As National Security Adviser to the White House, it is your job to counsel the President:
Should your forces strike before either Koraq or Irkor becomes even stronger? Should you
do so whether or not the UN gives its blessing? Odds favor a U.S. victory, but the costs
could be high.*

*At the same time you consider these immediate issues, the President wants a grand de-
sign for U.S. force planning. "If we focus on Koraq and Irkor," she asks, "how should we
think about larger powers such as China, Europe, and Russia? Will they just sit still while
we engage lesser powers? What are our priorities for national and international security?"*

*The Commander in Chief (so designated by the Constitution) also wants your views
on several more general questions: "The Kennedy team," she recalls, "avoided war with*

Moscow over Cuba, but U.S. forces have taken part in two world wars and many smaller ones. Why have Americans fought in distant places when few of us have any desire to conquer foreign lands?

"Haven't weapons become so destructive that war is now outmoded—like dueling and slavery? Why do we and other states keep large nuclear arsenals if nuclear war is unwinnable?"

You need time to reply. You tell the President that you will assess the major viewpoints on the causes and outcomes of war. You will review for her how the 20th century's major wars began and why the United States became involved. You expect to find that, despite its likely horrors, war is still thinkable—even likely. So you must wrestle with conflicting recommendations from the Navy, Army, and Air Force about the proper size and structure of U.S. forces. And you must assess the pros and cons of a preventive war against rogue states versus containment by a blend of the three D's—defense, deterrence, and diplomacy.

CONTENDING CONCEPTS AND EXPLANATIONS

WAR—CREATOR, DESTROYER, REFORMER

War is overt, organized violence of one community against another. It is a means to hold or seize territory, wealth, resources, prestige, and influence—the ultimate tool for value-claiming and resolving conflict. War can be an adventure—a stage for heroism and glory. For most participants and bystanders, however, it is hell.

War destroys and creates. It can make, break, or reform a state.[1] Wars have made states more powerful. Europe's princes used war to expand their realms and form a "body politic" from disparate peoples. War audits the efficiency of the state and can spur reforms meant to improve fighting capacity. Wars encourage governments to expand and streamline their bureaucracies, raise taxes, put more people into government service; reduce social barriers based on race, class, region, or religion; and promote literacy and training. But war can also dissolve a state and devour its human and material resources.

1. Bruce D. Porter, *War and the Rise of the State: The Military Foundations of Modern Politics* (New York: Free Press, 1994).

War as Glory, War as Hell

Pinned down by the Russian winter and the Red Army in 1943, a German officer sent home a letter on the last flight to Berlin from Stalingrad: "You must tell my parents [to] remember me with happy hearts," The officer wrote that he planned to face God not as an angel, but as a "soldier, with the free, proud soul of a cavalryman, as a *Herr* [noble gentleman]!"

Most Germans entrapped at Stalingrad had lost any romantic feelings about war. One wrote home: "You were supposed to die heroically," but what was death at Stalingrad? "Here [our soldiers] croak, starve . . . freeze to death. . . . They drop like flies; nobody cares and nobody buries them. Without arms or legs and without eyes, with bellies torn open, they lie around everywhere. . . . It is a death fit for beasts."

These, and thousands of other letters from Stalingrad were never delivered. Nazi analysts screened them to learn about morale. Only 2 percent had a positive attitude toward Germany's leadership; 61 percent were negative or actively opposed.*

*See *Last Letters from Stalingrad* (Westport, Conn.: Greenwood, 1974). For rather different perspectives, see Frank Gibney, ed., *Senso: The Japanese Remember the Pacific War* (Armonk, N.Y.: M. E. Sharpe, 1995).

THE PATTERNS OF WAR

The Scale and Frequency of War

World Wars I and II were the most destructive in history. As we see from Figure 4.1, however, there has been no clear trend in the frequency, size, or destructiveness of war.

Nor is there evidence that a series of smaller wars means that a larger war is about to erupt—like tremors before a major earthquake. To be sure, several lesser wars took place in the decade before each world war, but the many small- and medium-sized wars since 1945— from roughly twenty to forty each year—have not (as yet) been followed by World War III.

War can be more or less destructive thanks to changes in technology and politics. From the end of the Thirty Years War in 1648 until the French Revolution in 1789, Europe's wars usually spared civilians and workshops. Europe's princes fought with relatively small armies, often mercenaries. The French Revolution, however, gave birth to the "nation in arms" and much larger armies. Soon, the Industrial Revolution turned people and factories into prime targets. The U.S. Civil War (1861–65) was the first great war of industrial civilization. Union forces struck at the economic foundations of the South's armed might and sought to break civilian morale.

Technology has expanded the might and reach of weapons, while changes in political organization have turned entire populations into key participants in war. Many countries have lost over 10 percent of their population in a single war. War turns millions into refugees.

The total number of battle and civilian deaths listed in Figure 4.1 is less than 40 million for the 20th century. If we add the deaths in civil wars listed later in this chapter, the global total is still less than 50 million. But these numbers are probably too low. Thus, Figure 4.1 puts World War II battle deaths at 15 million and gives no estimate for civilian deaths. Estimates for total deaths—combat and civilian—in World War II for just one country, the USSR, range from 20 to 40 million. As we shall see in Chapter 5, some serious analysts put the number of war deaths in the 20th century at between 120 million and 191 million—three to four times the estimates in Figure 4.1. Whether the low or the high estimates are closer to reality, they remind us that humans have been cruel to one another. Mephistophles, quoted at the outset, was at least partly correct. Union General William T. Sherman summed it up. What is war? "Hell." And very different from the sanitized fireworks displays some people enjoy on TV!

Fig. 4.1 Dimensions of Major Wars, 1775–2000

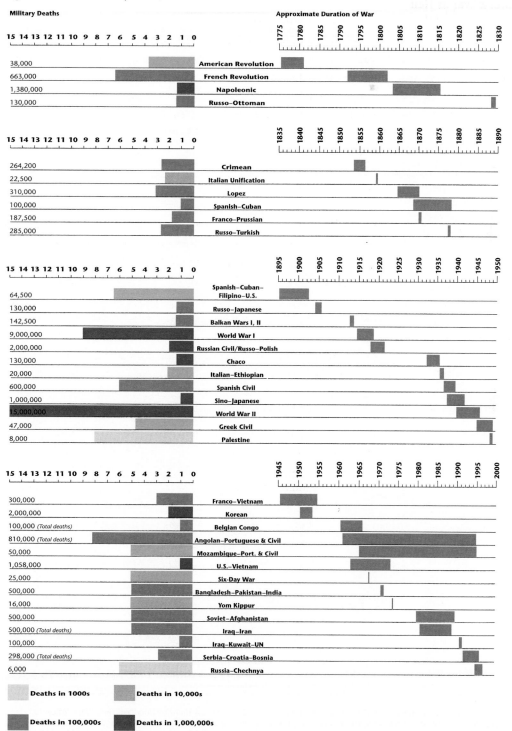

Deaths in 1000s   Deaths in 10,000s

Deaths in 100,000s   Deaths in 1,000,000s

(continued)

Fig. 4.1 *(continued)*

Name of War	Duration	Number of Primary Participants	Battle Deaths	Total Deaths (Military and Civilian)
American Revolution	1775–1781	3	38,000 (Levy)	n.a.
French Revolution	1792–1802	6	663,000 (Levy)	n.a.
Napoleonic	1803–1815	6	1,380,000 (Sivard)	2,380,000 (Sivard)
Russo–Ottoman	1828–1829	2	130,000	191,000 (Sivard)
Crimean	1853–1856	5	264,200	n.a.
Italian Unification	1859	4	22,500	40,000 (Sivard)
Lopez (War of the Triple Alliance)	1864–1870	4	310,000 (Sivard)	600,000 (Sivard)
Spanish–Cuban	1868–1878	2	100,000	200,000 (Sivard)
Franco–Prussian	1870–1871	5	187,500	250,000 (Sivard)
Russo–Turkish	1877–1878	3	285,000	n.a.
Spanish–Cuban, Spanish–Cuban–Filipino–U.S., Filipino–U.S.	1895–1898, 1898, 1899–1902	2, 4, and 2	50,000, 10,000 and 4,500	300,000 200,000, and 12,000 (Sivard)
Russo–Japanese	1904–1905	2	130,000	n.a.
Balkan War I and Balkan War II	1912–1913	5	142,500	n.a.
World War I	1914–1918	15	9,000,000	n.a.
Russian Civil/Russo–Polish	1917–1921	12 or more	2,000,000 (Somin)	9,000,000 (Somin)
Chaco (Bolivia–Paraguay)	1932–1935	2	130,000	200,000 (Sivard)
Italian–Ethiopian	1935–1936	2	20,000	n.a.

SOURCES: Data drawn from J. David Singer and Melvin Small, *The Wages of War, 1816–1965: A Statistical Handbook* (New York: Wiley, 1972), unless otherwise specified. Additional sources include Ruth Leger Sivard, *World Military and Social Expenditure* (Washington, D.C.: World Priorities, 1988 and 1997); Jack S. Levy, *War in the Modern Great Power System, 1495–1975* (Lexington: University Press of Kentucky, 1983); and Ilya Somin, *Stillborn Crusade: The Tragic Failure of Western Intervention in the Russian Civil War* (New Brunswick, N.J.: Transaction, 1996). The data are updated and reclassified in Meredith Reid Sarkees, Frank Whelon Wayman, and J. David Singer, "Inter-State, Intra-State, and Extra-State Wars: A Comprehensive Look at Their Distribution over Time, 1816–1997," *International Studies Quarterly* 47, no. 1 (March 2003): 40–70.

Fig. 4.1 *(continued)*

Name of War	Duration	Number of Primary Participants	Battle Deaths	Total Deaths (Military and Civilian)
Spanish Civil	1936–1939	5 or more	600,00 *(Sivard)*	1,200,000
Sino–Japanese	1937–1941	2	1,000,000	2,150,000 *(Singer and Small, Sivard)*
World War II	1939–1945	29	15,000,000[a]	n.a.
Greek Civil	1945–1949	5 or more	47,000	160,000 *(Sivard)*
Franco–Vietnam	1945–1954	2	300,000 *(Sivard)*	600,000 *(Sivard)*
Palestine	1948–1949	6	8,000	n.a.
Korean	1950–1953	16	2,000,000	2,889,000 *(Sivard)*
Belgian Congo	1960–1965	5 or more	n.a.	100,000 *(Sivard)*
Angolan–Portuguese and Civil	1961–1975; 1975–1995	7	n.a.	810,000 *(Sivard)*
Mozambique– Portuguese and Civil	1965–1975 1975–1995	6	50,000	1,080,000 *(Sivard)*
U.S.–Vietnam	1963–1973	5 or more	1,058,000 *(Sivard)*	2,058,000 *(Sivard)*
Six-Day War (Arab–Israeli)	1967	4	25,000	75,000 *(Sivard)*
Bangladesh– Pakistan–India	1971	3	500,000 *(Sivard)*	1,000,000 *(Sivard)*
Yom Kippur (Arab–Israeli)	1973	5	16,000	n.a.
Soviet–Afganistan	1979–1989	6	500,000 *(Sivard)*	1,500,000 *(Sivard)*
Iraq–Iran	1980–1988	2	n.a.	500,000
Iraq–Kuwait-U.N.	1990–1991 (Desert Storm lasted 6 weeks)	21	100,000	200,000 *(Sivard)*
Serbia–Croatia–Bosnia	1991–1995	3	n.a.	298,000 *(Sivard)*
Russia–Chechnya	1994–1996	2	6,000	35,000 *(Sivard)*
Russia–Chechnya	1999–	2	n.a.	More than in 1994–1996
Sri Lanka	1983–	2 + 1	n.a.	64,000 (BBC)

[a]Figure represents extremely low estimates.

A Note on War Statistics

The raw numbers in Figure 4.1 require interpretation. First, some data are missing. Second, these data do not show severity—deaths per capita. A million deaths in 1945 represented a much smaller share of the population than in 1815 or 1915, when populations were smaller. Third, total deaths rose in the 20th century as more countries fought in a single war. Finally, death rates in industrialized countries were restrained by better health care for the wounded; technologies that put fewer troops on the front lines; and by a shift of the fighting from Europe to Asia, the Middle East, and Africa. Table 4.1 shows how U.S. military deaths decreased per 1,000 soldiers from the 1860s through the 1990s.

For estimates of coalition and Iraqi casualties in 2003, see http://www.antiwar.com/.

Modern technology can kill more people, but it can also pinpoint destruction. Many countries participated in the 1990–1991 Persian Gulf War, but its duration was brief and relatively few military personnel or civilians were killed. In the years that followed, however, Iraqi civilians suffered greatly from damage to the country's infrastructure, economic sanctions imposed by the victors, and Saddam Hussein's preference for building palaces and bombs rather than caring for his subjects. Relatively few soldiers died when forces from the North Atlantic Treaty Organization (NATO) attacked Serbia in 1999, but many civilians perished—estimates ranged from 500 to 5,000 Serbs. The highest toll, however, was among Albanian speakers who lived in Kosovo—as many as 10,000 died—some from Serbia's efforts to eliminate them, some in the fog of war. A similar pattern occurred when U.S. and UK forces attacked the Taliban regime in Afghanistan in 2001–2002. Many more Afghan civilians died than combatants—attackers or Taliban. Less than 200 coalition forces died in the 2003 invasion of Iraq, but thousands of Iraqi soldiers and civilians perished.

Cold statistics, of course, mask the pain suffered by those killed or wounded, their families and friends. And while we can estimate the number of babies not conceived, we can never know what those killed or wounded would otherwise have contributed to happiness, culture, or prosperity.

U.S. losses in war, compared to many other countries, have been small in scale. Table 4.1 shows total U.S. battle deaths since 1775. Some estimates range much higher, placing total battle deaths over some 250 years

Table 4.1 U.S. Military Casualties, 1775–1991

	American Revolution (1775–1781)	War of 1812 (1812–1815)	Mexican War (1846–1848)	Civil War (1861–1865)[a]	Spanish–American War (1898)	WWI (1917–1918)	WWII (1941–1945)	Korea (1950–1953)	Vietnam (1963–1973)	Gulf War (1990–1991)
Total military personnel during the war	ca. 217,000	286,730	78,718	2,213,363	306,760	4,734,991	16,112,566	5,720,000	8,744,000 worldwide; 3,385,000 in Southeast Asia	2,029,600; 467,539 in Gulf region
Battle deaths	6,800	2,280	1,733	140,414	385	53,402	291,557	33,746	47,369	148
Other deaths	18,500	n.a.	11,550	224,097	2,061	63,114	113,842	20,617	10,799	145
Wounded but survived	6,188	4,505	4,152	281,881	1,662	204,002	670,846	103,284	303,648	467
Annual death rate per 1,000	n.a.	n.a.	n.a.	104.4	36.6	35.5	11.6	5.5	n.a.	n.a.

SOURCES: U.S. Department of Commerce, *Historical Statistics of the United States: Colonial Times to 1970*. Two parts (Washington, D.C.: Government Printing Office, 1975), Pt. 2, 1140; Congressional Reference Service, *U.S. Military Personnel and Casualties in Principal U.S. Wars* (Washington, D.C.: Government Printing Office, 1973). Updated by the author using Department of Defense sources.

Battle and other deaths in the first column are from *The American Revolution, 1775–1783: An Encyclopedia*, 2 vols. (New York: Garland, 1993), 1, 272. U.S. official sources give battle deaths as 4,435 in the Revolutionary War but no estimate of other deaths.

NOTE: n.a.= not available.

[a] Figures are for Union forces only. Confederate troops suffered at least 133,821 deaths, of which 74,524 were in battle.

at about 1.3 million—nearly half of them during the Civil War. By comparison, the Soviet Union suffered between 25 and 40 million deaths—military and civilian—during World War II.

The indirect consequences of war—disease and epidemics—have often been more lethal than the fighting. Civilian deaths have often been at least twice those suffered by military forces in most wars since 1789. Spared by geography, few U.S. civilians have been killed as a result of war, except in the Civil War and in the global influenza epidemic (more than 20 million deaths worldwide) following World War I.[2] This situation will change overnight if a weapon of mass destruction hits the United States thanks to a mad or careless Russian or Chinese, a rogue state, or—most likely—a nonstate terrorist cell.

The civilian share of war deaths increased in the 1970s and 1980s to 75 percent or more in Angola, Mozambique, and elsewhere where land mines killed without discrimination, and where even children became soldiers.[3] Indeed, some 2 million children died from wars between 1985 and 1995, while another 10 to 15 million were maimed physically or psychologically. On 9/11, nineteen combatants killed some 3,000 persons, nearly a quarter of them from other countries.

Internal War

Civil wars are bitter and bloody as neighbor turns against neighbor, and even brother against brother. Table 4.2 shows some minimum

2. William H. McNeill, *Plagues and People* (New York: Anchor, 1977), 255.

3. Civilian casualties are estimated in Ruth Leger Sivard, *World Military and Social Expenditures* (Leesburg, Va.: World Priorities, 1988 and 1997).

Table 4.2 Losses in Major Internal Wars

Country	Dates	Number of Fatalities
China	1945–1990	2,605,000
Sudan	1963–1972	500,000
Sudan	1983–	2 million plus
Cambodia	1975–1993	1,121,000
Congo (former Zaire)	intermittent	many millions
Nigeria	1967–1984	1,006,000
Colombia	1949–1962	300,000
	1980s–	more
Guatemala	1970s–1996	150,000
Algeria	1954–1963	102,000
Lebanon	1975–1990	100,000
Nicaragua	1978–1988	80,000
Peru	1981–1995	30,000

estimates of the most deadly of them in the second half of the 20th century.[4] On a per capita basis, Cambodia and Sudan probably topped the list.

Accurate numbers are hard to come by. Thus, estimates of deaths caused by Sri Lanka's internal fighting between 1983 and 2002 ranged from 20,000, to more than 60,000. Estimates of deaths from fighting in Chechnya, Colombia, the Ivory Coast, Sierra Leone, East Timor, the Philippines, and the Democratic Republic of Congo had an equal range of uncertainty. Causality is often uncertain. We know that many thousands of Kosovars were killed in the late 1990s. But did they die from Serbian actions or from NATO bombs? If from Serbian actions, did they occur before or after NATO attacks began? Numbers of the dead in Israeli–Palestinian fighting are better known, thanks to heavy media coverage. But the numbers are misleading, because they seem low. Relative to the populations engaged, they are high.

Besides their human toll, wars cost money. Outlays for four civil wars ranged from $20 billion to $30 billion: Colombia (1963–); Turkish government vs. Kurds (1984–2000); Indonesia vs. East Timorese (1975–1999); Myanmar vs. ethnic minorities (1985–). The annual bill for fighting often approached $1.5 billion in at least seven cases: Colombia (1963–), Algeria (1992–), Croatia (1991–1995), Russia vs. Chechnya (1994–), Turkey

4. International Institute for Strategic Studies, The 2002 Chart of Armed Conflict, supplement to *The Military Balance, 2002–2003* (London: Oxford University Press, 2002); *Oxford Companion to Politics of the World,* ed. Joel Krieger, 2d ed. (New York: Oxford University Press, 2001); and press reports. The IISS Armed Conflict Data Base relies heavily on Sivard (see note to Figure 4.1), but includes additional conflicts.

NATO in 1999 hoped its air power would rapidly compel Yugoslav leader Slobodan Milošević to withdraw Serbian forces from Kosovo. NATO found, however, that ten weeks of aerial bombardment of Yugoslav tanks, bridges, and even the capital Belgrade did not break his resistance. Only when Milošević saw that NATO would launch a ground attack and that Russia would not actively assist Yugoslavia did he agree to withdraw and accept NATO occupation of Kosovo. Soon, 22,000 heavily armed NATO peacekeepers poured in. Here we see British forces landing near the Kosovo–Macedonian border in June 1999.

(1984–2000), Indonesia (1975–2001), and Myanmar (1985–).[5] The economic losses from the ravages of war and potential investors' reluctance to risk capital in unsettled conditions cannot be measured.

Civil and combined civil–international wars have outnumbered international wars since 1945.[6] In the 20th century, many international wars acquired a strong internal component and many "civil" wars (within one state or society) involved outside intervention. For example, the Spanish Civil War (1936–1939) drew in "volunteers" from many countries (as depicted in Ernest Hemingway's *For Whom the Bell Tolls*).

The Arab–Israeli, Korean, Vietnamese, Afghan, and 1990s Balkan and Congolese wars all began as internal conflicts that soon attracted foreign

5. International Institute for Strategic Studies database as of 2002. This source says that annual costs for Mexico vs. Chiapas, 1994–2001, ran to $1.3 billion, but this estimate seems much too high.

6. See surveys reported by Roy Licklider, ed., *Stopping the Killing: How Civil Wars End* (New York: New York University Press, 1993), 6.

intervention. Each became an internal–international war kept within local borders. For Saddam Hussein, even the Persian Gulf War began as a civil war, for he viewed Kuwait as part of Iraq.

From the 17th until the late 20th century, most wars were waged by governments. In the 1990s, however, a "new world disorder" erupted in which war often became a private enterprise. In former Yugoslavia and elsewhere, much of the fighting was conducted by bands of irregulars who served out of personal loyalty, hope for booty, or lust for revenge.[7] They were often joined by volunteers and mercenaries from near and far. Volunteers from many countries joined the Taliban and the anti-Russian forces in Chechnya.

For their parts, the United States and other Western governments increasingly "privatized" security. They hired specialists to defend, train, and kill—sometimes in operations never discussed, much less approved, by legislatures or publics. The U.S. armed forces in the 1990s began to do less fighting and more peacekeeping, for example, in Bosnia. The Pentagon even adopted a new acronym: MOOTW—Military Operations Other Than War. It covered everything from peacekeeping to disaster relief to intimidation. In 2001 the George W. Bush administration tried to reduce America's role in what critics called "social work" abroad. But this proved easier to promise than to do. Where U.S. forces were already committed, as in the Balkans, withdrawing them could be highly destabilizing.[8] Installed with U.S. support in 2002, the new government of Afghanistan had little authority beyond Kabul. It even depended on U.S. bodyguards to protect President Hamid Karzai.[9]

THE SPECTRUM OF VIOLENCE

The gradient of hostility begins with tension, scowls, and curses and continues toward annihilation. What follows are some stages in the spectrum of violence.

Cold War

Cold war is a multifaceted struggle to defeat the other side without overt ("hot") war between the major adversaries. It may include economic warfare (trade restrictions, economic blockades), psychological warfare (propaganda to subvert the enemy and rally supporters), espionage and sabotage, and even proxy wars—hot war by clients.

Cold war may entail military threats to compel or deter certain behavior by others. From 1945 into the 1990s, both Moscow and Washington used "force without war" hundreds of times. Soviet/Russian forces often practiced tank maneuvers to intimidate their neighbors. The U.S. Navy often "showed the flag" to remind others of American power.[10] This kind

7. In the twenty recognized states and eleven unrecognized mini-states that replaced Yugoslavia and the USSR, there were at least twelve party or movement militias, eight armed criminal groups, and six warlord units operating within official armies. Charles H. Fairbanks, Jr., "The Postcommunist Wars," *Journal of Democracy* 6, no. 4 (October 1995): 23.

8. What the Pentagon called "contingency operations" cost $44 billion over and above the basic defense budget from February 1991 (after the Gulf War ended) into fiscal year 2001. These operations included enforcement of no-fly zones over Iraq, peace enforcement operations in the Balkans, and humanitarian assistance.

9. Opponents of the new order killed members of Karzai's cabinet in 2002. Still others burned or shot rockets into four girls' schools near Kabul. The arsonists' note called "on all the countrymen to save their clean sisters and daughters from this infidel net. Stop carrying out the plans of the Americans, or you will face further deadly attacks. Signed: The hero Mujahideen of Afghanistan."

10. Barry M. Blechman and Stephen S. Kaplan, *Force Without War: U.S. Armed Forces as a Political Instrument* (Washington, D.C.: Brookings Institution, 1978); and Stephen S. Kaplan, *Diplomacy of Power: Soviet Armed Forces as a Political Instrument* (Washington, D.C.: Brookings Institution, 1981).

of competition between Moscow and Washington nearly disappeared when the Soviet Union collapsed in 1991, but surfaced from time to time in U.S. relations with Beijing. When China practiced firing missiles into the sea near Taiwan in 1996, two U.S. aircraft carrier groups arrived. These actions conveyed two messages: Beijing warned Taipei not to declare its independence, while Washington warned it would stand by Taiwan. The U.S.–Chinese competition, however, was neither so multi-faceted nor so intense as the U.S.–Soviet rivalry had been.

Unconventional War

Unconventional war encompasses assassination of notables, terrorism (taking hostages, blowing up airplanes and buildings, spewing gas into subways, poisoning reservoirs), and guerrilla warfare (hit-and-run strikes by irregular forces). Such methods are often favored by stateless peoples such as the Kurds and by rogue states (seen as berserk or unprincipled by others).[11] Some actors have accused the U.S. of state terror—intimidation by overwhelming might. But the availability of high-tech weapons helps to even the playing field. In the 1980s and 1990s, for example, many irregular armies acquired antiaircraft missiles and cannons. Chechen rebels shot down Russian helicopters in 2002, some of them carrying more than 100 soldiers. Tomorrow's terrorists may carry "suitcase" nuclear bombs. On 9/11 they did great damage just by skyjacking civilian airliners.

Conventional War

Conventional war employs regular forces such as tanks, planes, and missiles but avoids nuclear weapons, poison gas, and germ warfare. It may be local (restricted to a specific locale) or global. It may be limited or unlimited in terms of weapons and targets.

Nuclear War

Nuclear weapons have been detonated in war only in August 1945—at Hiroshima and Nagasaki. Since 1945 they have been used mainly for de-terrence—dissuasion by terror. The threat that nuclear weapons would be used to retaliate is supposed to deter any country from launching a first strike. Nuclear weapons may have helped prevent World War III, so far, but they have not averted scores of other wars. New questions arise in an era of suicide–homicide: Are all actors on the world stage deterrable? What if the end is near and their regime is falling? What if they expect bliss in the next life? What if their reading of holy scripture leads them to expect and seek an Armageddon to trigger a Second Coming? The note left by a disgruntled student in Arizona who killed three of his teachers

11. A rogue elephant is a vicious, solitary animal, separated from the herd. *Berserk* probably comes from the Old Norse for a warrior who wore bear [*bera*] hides for a shirt [*serkr*], became frenzied in battle, howled, and foamed at the mouth. *American Heritage Dictionary of the English Language*, 4th ed. (Boston: Houghton Mifflin, 2000), 171.

Fig. 4.2 Which Ladder to Climb—Toward War or Cooperation?

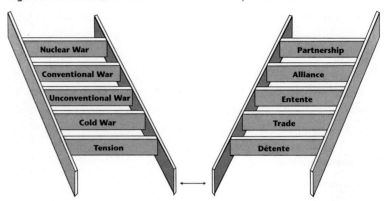

and then himself in October 2002, advised psychologists not to blame his upbringing. He was simply unhappy with how things are!

Inexorable Rise or Escalation Ladder?

Conflict need not move inexorably from cold to hot war. Tensions can escalate or diminish. Actors can move up or down on two ladders, as suggested in Figure 4.2. To deescalate from conflict, actors must climb down the escalation ladder on the left, and move up the ladder on the right toward détente and cooperation. In theory, each rung on each ladder marks an interval—a pause on the path toward violence or cooperation. In practice, however, actors may race up or slide down each ladder, skipping rungs, as we shall see in Chapter 7.

CAN WAR BE RATIONAL?

Realists say that war is just another arrow in the quiver of a rational foreign policy. The realists' bible, *On War*, was written by the Prussian officer Carl von Clausewitz in the early 19th century. Clausewitz defined war as the "continuation of policy by other (violent) means." War should be a "light, handy rapier," not a campaign for all-out destruction, unless policy seeks to eliminate the other side entirely.[12] Battle tactics must be subordinated to strategy. There can be no "purely military" decision except in details such as when and where to patrol.

Clausewitz prescribed model behavior. But today's "rational choice" analysts claim to describe actual behavior. Some contend that governments decide on war as if they seek rationally to maximize gains and minimize losses. Expected utility is key. The theory says that most

12. Carl von Clausewitz, *On War*, rev. ed. (Princeton, N.J.: Princeton University Press, 1984), 604–610; see also Peter Paret, "Clausewitz," in *Makers of Modern Strategy: From Machiavelli to the Nuclear Age*, ed. Paret (Princeton, N.J.: Princeton University Press, 1986), 186–213.

Though Estonians, Latvians, and Lithuanians regained their independence in 1991 by a "Singing Revolution," they did not entrust their futures to nonviolent resistance. Their governments sought membership in NATO and military assistance—equipment, money, training, English-language classes, and moral support. Western governments responded by establishing the Baltic Defence College in Tartu, Estonia, headed initially by a Danish officer. Here we see college staff and cadets in a field exercise near Klaipeda, Lithuania, examining a map that anticipates a Russian attack westward. For background, see Walter C. Clemens, Jr., *The Baltic Transformed: Complexity Theory and European Security* (Lanham, Md.: Rowman & Littlefield, 2001).

governments act in a rational manner: They calculate the war potential of each side, including that of the home front.[13]

The classic realists, however, did not believe that war outcomes could be dependably predicted. "The longer a war lasts," Thucydides warned, "the more things tend to depend on accidents." For his part, Niccolò Machiavelli stressed the role of *fortuna* (luck). Even Clausewitz warned of "friction"—all that can go wrong in war. For example, reinforcements expected in three hours arrive in ten, because rain turned roads to mud.

Other analysts deny that war is inevitable or rational. They see war as a malfunction, a mistake, or a madness that can and should be cured. Humans, they say (or hope), can rise above violence.

CAN WAR BE JUST?

If might makes right, the morality of war is a nonissue. But some idealists distinguish just and unjust wars. A war's justice hinges on three factors: (1) Motive—is the cause just? Most people accept self-defense as a justifiable motive, but some political and spiritual leaders initiate what they call just wars or holy wars (crusades, jihads) to promote their ostensibly spiritual goals. (2) Consequences—are the evils the war seeks to remedy greater than the evils the fighting is likely to produce? (3) Legality—is the war lawful within the framework of international law and the belligerent country's constitution? Nuclear weapons raise new questions: Can any cause justify mass destruction and probable suicide?[14] Nuclear weapons may be good to deter war, but bad if used to wage war.

13. Bruce Bueno de Mesquita, *The War Trap* (New Haven, Conn.: Yale University Press, 1981). If country A experiences widespread domestic resistance to war, its leaders may launch a war anyway lest country B try to take advantage of A's weak home front. Bruce Bueno de Mesquita and David Lalman, *War and Reason: Domestic and International Imperatives* (New Haven, Conn.: Yale University Press, 1992).

14. Joseph S. Nye, Jr., *Nuclear Ethics* (New York: Free Press, 1986); see also *Ethics and International Affairs,* published annually by the Carnegie Council on Ethics and International Affairs.

<table>
<tr><td>

Could Nonviolence Win If Preplanned?

Could a civilian-based system of **nonviolent sanctions** and defense replace armed force? Against a ruthless occupier, nonviolent action risks violent reprisals. But nonviolent resistance helped India (1947) and Poland (1980s) to regain independence. A blend of nonviolent and violent action helped U.S. and South African Blacks resist racial discrimination.

Nonviolent methods include: protest—mass demonstrations, symbolic funerals, renouncing honors, walkouts; noncooperation—civil disobedience, strikes, tax withholding, providing sanctuary, resignations; and intervention—sit-ins, creating parallel institutions, guerrilla theater, exposure of who did what.* These methods aim to make a subject people virtually ungovernable, but they require mass training and discipline of civilians—quite unlike the quick-fix promised by professional soldiers with high-tech weapons.

*Peter Ackerman and Christopher Krueger, *Strategic Nonviolent Conflict. The Dynamics of People Power in the Twentieth Century* (Westport, Conn.: Praeger, 1994).

</td><td>

NONVIOLENCE AS AN ALTERNATIVE

Pacifists reject war as a policy option. They say war is irrational or unjust or both. Some contend that no cause can justify violent means. Others are pragmatists: They hold that nonviolent methods, properly funded and organized, can be as effective as armed struggle while causing less suffering. If they are right, millions of lives could be saved, along with billions of dollars, yen, and rupees. Improvising, the peoples of Estonia, Latvia, and Lithuania conducted a "Singing Revolution" in the late 1980s that helped them regain independence and split apart the Soviet "Union."[15]

WHY WAR? INPUTS AT EACH LEVEL OF IR ACTION

At each level of IR action we find numerous factors that can promote war. Some factors act as long-term, underlying conditions; others, as proximate factors emerging in the five or so years before warfare erupts; still others as catalysts—sparks that ignite the combustible material. Causation presents many puzzles: Does a factor really "cause" war or merely precede it? Mere correlation is not causation. Are any factors both necessary and sufficient to produce a war?[16] Following is a list of factors at each level that often encourage war:

Level 1: Individuals and Human Nature

1. Aggressive tendencies—innate or induced by upbringing and living conditions
2. Belief in personal superiority
3. Misperceptions, miscalculations, hubris, wishful thinking

Level 2: War-Prone States and Societies

4. A culture of violence and assertive value-claiming
5. "Us vs. them" mentality
6. Dictatorship
7. A unifying cause, a distraction
8. Realpolitik that sees war as a useful tool of policy
9. Estimate that victory is likely
10. War-prone military doctrine and technology
11. "Just war" doctrines
12. Economic pressures (surplus people, capital, or goods)[17]
13. A military-industrial complex of makers and merchants of arms and a warrior caste
14. Imperialism vs. national liberation

</td></tr>
</table>

15. Walter C. Clemens, Jr., *The Baltic Transformed: Complexity Theory and European Security* (Lanham, Md.: Rowman & Littlefield, 2001), chap. 3.

16. See Jack S. Levy, "The Causes of War: A Review of Theories and Evidence," in *Behavior, Society, and Nuclear War,* ed. Philip E. Tetlock et al. 3 vols., (New York: Oxford University Press, 1989), 1: 247–251.

17. Lenin thought that war between capitalist countries was inevitable as they struggled to gain secure investment opportunities in less-developed countries. See V. I. Lenin, *Imperialism—The Highest Stage of Capitalism* (1916) (New York: International Publishers, 1933). But Western economists such as Joseph Schumpeter and Kenneth Boulding argued that the profit motive favors peace and civilian industry. Only small sectors of capitalist economies benefit from war, arms competition, or imperialist expansion.

Level 3: The Interstate System—Anarchy and Self-help

15. Absence of a supranational government to keep the peace

16. Territorial or other claims in dispute

17. Altered threat perception (provoking alarm or complacency)

18. The "security dilemma" (one state's "defensive measures" may prod rivals into countermeasures)

19. A shifting balance of power (or new weapon) generates incentives for war

Level 4: Transnational Competition

20. Profit drive of transnational corporations

21. Militant political and religious movements

Level 5: Environmental Pressures

22. Resource scarcities

DOES THE "BALANCE OF POWER" SPELL WAR OR PEACE?

Everyone agrees that the **balance of power** is important, but analysts use the term in many ways. It can be a description, a prescription, or a prediction. As a description, it can refer to any distribution of power assets—equality of assets (for example, 500 tanks on each side), or superiority of one side (for example, 1,000 tanks vs. 500), as shown in Figure 4.3. As a prescription, it suggests: "Maintain a balance of power so that no rival gains an advantage." As a prediction, it anticipates that states will attempt to balance their power in certain ways. Some analysts limit "power" to hard assets such as oil wells and tanks, while others include intangible assets such as morale. A careful writer will specify what sense is intended.

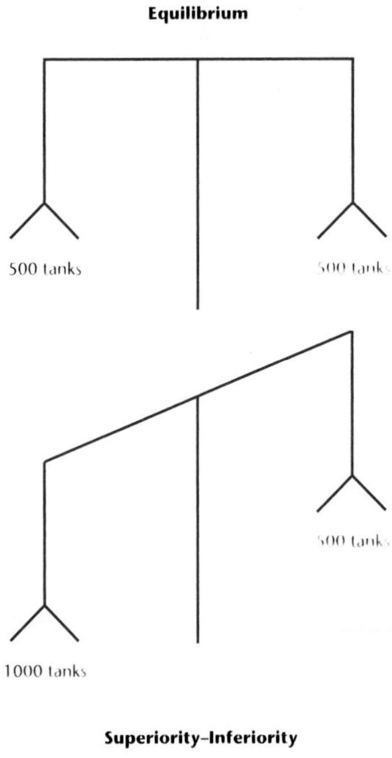

Woodrow Wilson blamed World War I on "balance of power" politics. By contrast, realists and neorealists contend that war may be prevented— or at least postponed—by maintaining the "balance of power." Unfortunately, these analysts do not agree which power balance—which kind of **polarity**—is most stable. Following are five contenders:

1. Unipolarity—power is concentrated in one center that maintains order, such as imperial Rome.

2. Bipolarity—two poles of power balance each other, as in the Cold War.

3. Tripolarity—a third center, perhaps China, balances two main rivals.

4. Multipolarity—five or more major actors align so that no country can dominate others, as in 19th-century Europe.

Fig. 4.3 Two Balances

Equilibrium

500 tanks   500 tanks

1000 tanks   500 tanks

Superiority–Inferiority

How Power Transitions May Spur Preventive and Preemptive Wars

A preventive war is one launched by the weakening party before the challenger can consolidate power in the months or years ahead. Thus, some U.S. leaders suggested **preventive war** against the USSR in the late 1940s before the Kremlin acquired nuclear weapons. A **preemptive strike**, in contrast, seeks to disarm the enemy's forces just minutes, hours, or days before they are launched. Fearing an imminent Egyptian attack in 1967, Israel struck first and destroyed Egypt's air force on the ground. Most governments, however, "wait and see" rather than risk bold actions.

The Bush administration declared in 2002 that the U.S. could no longer afford to wait and watch as America's foes acquired weapons of mass destruction. America would have to preempt their use by timely military action—with or without UN approval. Various "talking heads" on TV then debated the precedents and merits of "preemptive" war, but the issue was really preventive war against a possible future threat—not a war to preempt an imminent strike. Washington had conflated immediate threats from nonstate actors such as al-Qaeda, with long-term weapons development in North Korea, Iraq, and Iran.

18. The underlying reason for the Peloponnesian War, Thucydides wrote, "was the growth of Athenian power and the fear that this caused in Sparta." *The Peloponnesian War* (New York: Penguin Books, 1956), Book 1, 25. For a rebuttal, see Donald Kagan, *The Outbreak of the Peloponnesian War* (Ithaca, N.Y.: Cornell University Press, 1969), 345–346.

19. But the Seven Weeks War, fought only by Austria and some German states in 1866, transformed the entire system by vastly increasing Germany's power. Mesquita and Lalman, *War and Reason*, chap. 7.

5. Unit veto—each government is so strong it can block actions by others (perhaps by threatening the use of nuclear weapons).

Sooner or later, the strong get weaker. Power transition theory holds that a shifting balance of power induces hegemonic war—a war either to uphold or overthrow the existing hegemon ("leader"). If the hegemon is slipping, it may try to beat down challengers.[18] Alternatively, rising powers may seek to topple the faltering hegemon. Hegemonic wars often suck in all actors in the system.[19] A new hegemon generates a new international order with new rules and distributions of wealth.

Are any of these theories true? For better or worse, we shall see that no mechanical distribution of power assured either war or peace in the 20th century. Even a negative peace requires more than a certain balance of power; a positive peace, far more. Power transition theory, our cases show, explains few of the century's major wars.

COMPARING THEORY AND REALITY: GLOBAL AND LOCALIZED WARS

Let us now turn from theory to cases. We examine two global wars that transformed the IR system; two localized conflicts that merely restored the territorial status quo; and two superpower interventions, one of which helped bring down the Soviet empire and destroy the Second World.

TWO GLOBAL WARS

The Riddle of World War I

The Concert of Europe after 1815 gave way in the late 19th and early 20th century to a confrontation between two rival coalitions: the Triple Alliance of Germany, Austria-Hungary, and Italy against the Triple Entente of France, Russia, and Great Britain. Now comes a riddle: Realists say that World War I resulted from the challenge of a rising Germany to the declining hegemon, Great Britain. But the immediate catalyst was a political murder in Bosnia—an incident affecting not the principals but their allies. Would the German–British competition have led to a major war absent the Bosnian catalyst? We cannot know.

Germany was dangerous because it was strong; Austria-Hungary, because it was weak. Unable to cope with the ethnic minorities it already ruled, the Austrian court tried to take over still more land and diverse peoples. Thus, Austria-Hungary annexed Bosnia-Herzegovina in 1908. Adjacent Serbia asked Russia to prevent the annexation, but St. Petersburg felt

Table 4.3 World War I: Action Levels and Likely Causes

Individuals	Incompetent leaders at the top; aggressive ministers and generals in Vienna, Berlin, and St. Petersburg
State and society	Febrile nationalism throughout Europe and Japan; authoritarian regimes in Germany, Austria-Hungary, and Russia; cult of the offensive (see page 136)
International system	Loose bipolar confrontation of two alliances; U.S. initially neutral
Underlying factors	Germany challenges Britain; Ottoman Empire is dying; Concert of Europe declines and anarchy gains
Proximate causes	Russia swears "never again" to abide Austro-Hungarian expansion after Vienna annexes Bosnia-Herzegovina
Catalysts	Assassination in Sarajevo → German "blank check" to Austria → mobilizations → chain-ganging (see page 137)

too weak to intervene. The Russian court then swore "never again" to back down before Austrian expansion.

How and why World War I began is summarized on the time line and in Table 4.3. Why did Europe leap into darkness while Kennedy and Khrushchev stepped back from the abyss?

Level 1: Incompetence at the Top. Unlike Kennedy and Khrushchev in 1962, Europe's leaders in 1914 lacked the skill and determination to veer from disaster. German Kaiser Wilhelm II, for example, focused on himself and his Second German Empire. He once declared: "There is no balance of power in Europe but me—me and my twenty-five army corps," and tagged God as the "ancient Ally of my house." He looked down on Slavs and other non-Germans.[20] By 1914, he imagined a Russian–English–French conspiracy to encircle and destroy Germany. Wilhelm rejected information disputing his hope that Russia would just watch while Austria-Hungary triumphed over Serbia.

Poor judgment became worse under stress. Like Wilhelm, most of Europe's leaders ignored or denied facts that contradicted their existing convictions. Most were self-righteous and treated their own actions as justified. Each was fatalistic. Resignation to war's inevitability made it more likely.

Level 2: Expansionist Forces in State and Society. A coalition of generals, shipbuilders, munitions makers, and others in quest of glory or profit energized Germany's expansion. These lobbies shaped policy much more than the Soviet or U.S. military–industrial complexes of the Cold War era.

Top leaders in Berlin, Vienna, and St. Petersburg were manipulated by aggressive war ministers, generals, and foreign ministers. After authorizing

HOW WORLD WAR I UNFOLDED

1914

6/28
Serbian nationalists assassinate Austrian Archduke Franz Ferdinand in Sarajevo, capital of Bosnia-Herzegovina.

7/15
German Kaiser Wilhelm II offers Austria-Hungary a virtual blank check to punish Serbia but then goes on vacation.

7/23
Vienna issues a ten-point ultimatum: Within 48 hours Serbia must agree to wipe out agitation against the Austro-Hungarian Empire.

7/25
Hoping to avoid war, Serbia accepts all Austrian demands except one: it will not permit Austro-Hungarian officials to take part in a "judicial inquiry against those implicated" in the assassination.

7/28
Austria-Hungary declares war on Serbia but takes no major action.

7/29–30
Russian Tsar Nicholas II orders a partial, then a general, mobilization of Russian forces—an order that he cancels and then reinstates.

7/31
Germany sends a twelve-hour ultimatum to Russia demanding that it demobilize, to which Russia does not reply.

8/1–23
Declarations of war: Germany on Russia and France; Britain on Germany; Austria-Hungary on Russia; Britain and France on Austria; Japan on Germany.

The Ottoman Empire and Bulgaria eventually join Germany and Austria-Hungary; Italy and Romania, however, switch and join the other side.

20. Barbara W. Tuchman, *The Proud Tower: A Portrait of the World Before the War, 1890–1914* (New York: Bantam, 1972), 280.

troop trains to move toward Belgium in 1914, Wilhelm panicked and tried to halt them. Germany's chief of staff told the kaiser that it would be impossible to mobilize German troops only for the Russian front. This advice—a lie—made sure that Germany would fight France as well as Russia.

U.S. capitalists and Soviet Communists in 1962 believed their own system superior, but few Americans or Soviets were fanatic nationalists. Neither country had major territorial claims against the other; neither nursed old wounds caused by the other. Many Europeans in 1914, however, were ardent nationalists. When war was declared, many people cheered; parliaments voted credits to finance the war; most Socialists voted for war, even though it meant killing working-class comrades. Even bankers went along, despite the risk to their foreign holdings.

Level 3: The System—Loose vs. Tight Bipolarity. The tight bipolar balance of power in 1962 helped keep the missile crisis in check. By contrast, the two opposing alliances in 1914 constituted a loose bipolarity. The 1914 system was precarious because it had neither the discipline of tight bipolarity nor the flexibility of multipolar balancing.

Furthermore, there were no superpowers in 1914. Germany dominated the Triple Alliance but had fewer ships than Britain and fewer soldiers than Russia. The Triple Entente had no clear leader. Britain was strong at sea; Russia, on land.

For a coalition to deter attack, it must inspire fear. But no one could be sure if the Triple Alliance and Triple Entente would hold in time of war. Many of their terms were kept secret. Imperial Germany, however, feared it was being encircled while Austria-Hungary feared it might dissolve from within. Both Berlin and Vienna thought that the best way to meet these dangers was by war.

An **entente** is a mere understanding. Britain refused to enter a formal alliance with Russia or France. France and Russia had a "military convention" that specified how many troops each would field in the common defense, but Britain made no such promises. British officers discussed with French officers where British troops would land if they joined a war on the Continent, but it was never clear if Britain's government would send them. Indeed, British leaders held back from declaring war in 1914 until Germany attacked Belgium, whose neutrality London had sworn to uphold.

Europeans in 1914 did not fear war as Americans and Soviets did in 1962. Europe's strategists in 1914 saw war as another tool of a rational policy. With Germans as the strongest believers, most European generals embraced a **cult of the offensive**, a belief that wars could be fought and won in short order, with victory going to the army that struck first, troops charging with fixed bayonets.

Good logistics would be crucial: Germany had the best train system and could mobilize its entire army within two weeks; Russia had more troops, but needed forty days to fully mobilize. German generals were so confident that they planned to hit France first and then shift troops eastward to meet the late-arriving Russians.

Strategic doctrine and different mobilization capacities pressured each set of partners to move quickly and together—chain-ganging, as it were—their fates inseparable. If war seemed imminent, each side wanted to start mobilizing, even though this would compel the rival alliance to do the same. Here was the security dilemma in action. If any country started to mobilize, even for its own defense, its rival saw this as a threat to be countered. The 1914 situation was far more incendiary than that of 1962, because neither Kennedy nor Khrushchev had much incentive to strike first.

All parties in 1914 counted on a quick victory. They did not reckon with Clausewitzian "friction"—all that can go wrong, will. The generals' faith in the offensive proved to be misplaced. Germany's advance into France stalled in mid-September 1914. Machine guns minced advancing infantry and forced their replacements into trenches. Soon Germany faced a stalemate on two fronts. A long war of attrition began, wearing down Germany's initial advantages.

Germany had not counted on having to fight America. Berlin hoped that the United States would not join the Entente or, if it did, could not mobilize in time to make a difference. For its part, the United States tried to remain neutral. But when German submarines resumed unrestricted attacks on U.S. ships delivering supplies to Britain and France on credit, Congress declared war in April 1917.

Europe stumbled into a war that none had sought. Europe's leaders did not appreciate the dangers they faced in 1914. "Reason" told each party that "not to fight" was a worse option than "to fight." Looking back, we see that almost any choice would have served the protagonists better than war.

While many factors made the conflict likely, none made it inevitable. Nothing compelled Austria to attack Serbia, or Germany to issue Austria a blank check, or Germany to mobilize as soon as Russia began its slow mobilization. World War I ended the West's faith in progress and set the stage for an even more bloody collision.

World War II: Similar but Different

The Versailles system lasted less than twenty years. In retrospect, the two world wars look like one long effort by Germany to dominate the world. But there were differences as well as similarities between 1914 and 1939. Compare Table 4.4 with Table 4.3. Let us look more closely at each factor.

What Is Strategic?

Strategic doctrine, a theory on how and when to wage war, can make states more or less likely to fight. *Strategic* comes from *strategos*, Greek for "general," the commander of a *stratos* (army). **Strategy** is a military plan or any long-range design to achieve a major goal, while **tactics** are means to an end, often quite flexible. Tactics may include one or more stratagems—tricks to deceive the other side, such as presenting a Trojan Horse. Indeed, some authors use *strategic* as a euphemism for *deceitful*.

Strategic Arms Reduction Talks in the 1980s treated as **strategic weapons** those arms able to strike deeply into the other side's homeland—in contrast to "battlefield" or "tactical" weapons. Strategic bombing aims at key industries or population centers in an effort to force surrender; strategic goods are those needed for war, for example, oil.

Strategic logic is full of paradox: A good road may be bad, because it is well guarded; a bad road may be good, because it is not.

Table 4.4 World War II: Action Levels and Likely Causes

Individuals	Egomaniacs in Rome, Berlin and Moscow; militarists in Tokyo
State and society	Totalitarian dictatorships in Japan, Italy, Germany, and USSR; irresolute democracies in France, UK, and U.S.; cult of the defensive faces Blitzkrieg
International system	Multipolarity, with uncertainty about Soviet and U.S. power and intentions
Underlying factors	Japan, Italy, and Germany challenge the Versailles order; collective security fails as U.S. stays aloof and Britain and France pass the buck; economic nationalism and the Great Depression
Proximate causes	Japan invades China; Italy conquers Ethiopia; Britain and France appease Hitler as Germany rearms, annexes Austria, and takes Czechoslovakia
Catalysts	Germany and USSR invade Poland after their August 1939 pact to divide Eastern Europe

Level 1: Aggressive Egomaniacs vs. Appeasers. Weak leaders in England and France faced aggressive egomaniacs in Rome, Berlin, and Moscow. Politics for Benito Mussolini, Adolf Hitler, and Josef Stalin gave meaning to lives that in childhood and young manhood were filled with hurt feelings and disappointment. Mussolini and Hitler dreamed of recreating mythic empires run by a master race. Stalin imagined himself another tsar and wished to restore Russia's borders to their pre-1905 configuration. Similar in some ways, Stalin bonded with Hitler between 1939 and 1941.[21] Japan's leaders were driven more by a shared nationalism than by personal pathologies.

Level 2: Totalitarian Dictatorships vs. Irresolute Democracies. Contrary to Woodrow Wilson's hopes, democracy did not flourish after 1919. Dictatorship took hold in the USSR, Italy, Japan, and Germany. Each dictatorship mobilized nationalist feelings to acquire more resources and land (*Lebensraum*—living space). Traumatized by World War I and internally divided, France and Britain favored peace at any price and tried to appease Hitler.

Level 3: Multipolarity + Cult of Defensive + Egotism = Buck Passing. The interwar balance of power was even more ambiguous than that preceding World War I. The cohesion of Britain, France, and Russia (USSR) was weaker in the 1930s than it had been in 1914. The aggressors met little opposition as they dismantled the Versailles system. The League of Nations was too weak to provide collective security. There was no Concert of Europe, no loose or tight bipolarity as in 1914 and 1962, and no unit veto or deterrence based on terror.

The defenders of the status quo did not chain-gang; instead, they passed the buck. Buck passing is to let another actor take responsibility.[22] Why did

21. Alan Bullock, *Hitler and Stalin: Parallel Lives* (New York: Knopf, 1992).

22. "Buck" is for the "buckhorn" knife formerly used to designate the next dealer in poker. To pass the buck was to transfer responsibility to the next player.

check. Both houses endorsed the **Gulf of Tonkin Resolution**, authorizing "the President, as Commander-in-Chief, to take all necessary measures" to combat North Vietnamese aggression.[32] In February 1965, U.S. planes began large-scale bombings of the North. In March, the first U.S. combat troops arrived. By the end of 1965, U.S. forces in Vietnam numbered over 184,000; in February 1969 they peaked at 542,000.

Vast U.S. military and economic assets did not derail Hanoi. High-tech weapons did not staunch the streams of Communist guerrillas heading south on jungle trails. U.S. ignorance of the local language, culture, and values made it difficult to "win hearts and minds" for Saigon.

President Johnson never escalated sufficiently to win the war, because that would have required even more troops or crueler weapons. He wanted to avoid provoking another large-scale Chinese intervention, which, he feared, could trigger a nuclear war. Instead, he increased U.S. forces only enough to forestall a Communist victory. Johnson feared a rerun of the havoc wreaked on the Truman administration by Republican charges that Truman "lost" China to communism in 1949. But the U.S. home front crumbled in 1968 and Johnson withdrew from politics, setting the stage for a Republican to become president.

Richard M. Nixon was sworn in as president in 1969. He and National Security Assistant Henry Kissinger sought a face-saving retreat. They wanted to "Vietnamize" the war—make South Vietnam capable of fighting its own military and political battles against the North. The U.S. intensified its bombing of the North to "buy the time needed to make our ally self-sufficient." Seeking to destroy a North Vietnamese sanctuary, U.S. forces entered Cambodia in 1970, triggering a civil war in which nearly a third of the population perished.

In January 1973, Kissinger and Hanoi negotiator Le Duc Tho signed a truce establishing a cease-fire throughout Vietnam. It provided that all U.S. fighting forces would depart, but North Vietnamese troops could remain where they were. Hanoi soon broke the truce and took all the South in April 1975. Within months, Vietnamese Communists overthrew a pro-U.S. regime in Cambodia and a non-Communist one in Laos. But Thailand, Burma, and Indonesia did not become Communist, one after another, as the falling dominoes theory predicted.

The Vietnam War was probably the greatest U.S. foreign policy failure in the 20th century—perhaps ever.[33] U.S. costs included 58,721 American dead and 519,000 disabled veterans.[34] War-induced inflation derailed U.S. economic growth. Washington's ability to lead the First World declined. Political cohesion plunged within the United States while racial, ideological, and generational conflicts soared.

32. The previously drafted resolution was sent to Congress immediately after skirmishes—whether real or imagined—between U.S. destroyers and North Vietnamese torpedo boats in the Gulf of Tonkin at a time when South Vietnamese commandos were raiding the North.

33. This was the opinion of most experts polled in surveys conducted by the author at the Woodrow Wilson International Center for Scholars in 1976 and 1987 and at the Harvard Center for Science and International Affairs in 1987. There was little disagreement among the U.S. and foreign observers, or the academics and diplomats polled.

34. Estimates of dead and wounded vary, depending on the source. Compare, for example, figures in Table 4.1. Many of the more than 2 million veterans alive in the early 21st century were haunted by nightmares of blood and jungles. The U.S.'s direct expenditures and aid to Saigon made up a large share of the federal budget, from 1965 to 1973, but they were dwarfed by the billions that would later go to veterans' benefits.

Some three decades after helping steer America into the Vietnam War, former defense secretary Robert S. McNamara published his book *In Retrospect: The Tragedy and Lessons of Vietnam* (New York: Random House, 1995). He stated that "[We] acted according to what we thought were the principles and traditions of this nation . . . . Yet we were wrong, terribly wrong. We owe it to future generations to explain why." McNamara also tried to discuss what went wrong with Communist officials in Hanoi but found them uncommunicative. He promoted dialogue with former Russian and Cuban officials to understand the 1962 missile crisis. He later collaborated with psychologist James G. Blight in writing *Wilson's Ghost: Reducing the Risk of Conflict, Killing, and Catastrophe in the 21st Century* (New York: Public Affairs, 2001). But none of this helped those who were killed or wounded in Vietnam.

You've seen the war. Now read the book.

WE WERE WRONG

VIETNAM VETERAN

McNAMARA MEMOIR

DANZIGER

The Christian Science Monitor

Some supporters of the war blamed the U.S. defeat on self-imposed restraint. Critics said that Vietnam was the wrong war in the wrong place waged for the wrong reasons. Washington should have backed Vietnamese nationalists, even if they were Communists, against French imperialists, and kept Hanoi from dependency on Moscow or Beijing.[35] In the 1970s the United States lost its drive to resist Communist advances around the globe. When Soviet troops invaded Afghanistan in 1979, however, Americans awoke.

Moscow's "Vietnam"—Afghanistan

Afghanistan is a landlocked country with some 15.5 million people divided by religion (85 percent **Sunni** and 14 percent **Shi'a** Muslim), by language, and by way of life (urban vs. rural). Of educated Afghans, some have looked to the West, others to Moscow, and still others to Pakistan, Iran, or Egypt for cultural and political cues.

Unlike the United States in Vietnam, Russia had long been concerned with Afghanistan. Both superpowers gave economic aid to Afghanistan in the 1950s, but Washington cut back its involvement in the 1960s. The USSR aided Afghanistan but took out natural gas and minerals at cut-rate prices. "Aid" became a tool for Soviet exploitation.

Afghanistan's feudal monarchy ended in 1973 when the king's cousin, Daud Khan, proclaimed himself president. In April 1978, Daud was killed by military officers who handed power to the Communists—the People's

35. See *The New York Times*, March 24 and April 17 and 30, 1985; David Fromkin and James Chace, "What Are the Lessons of Vietnam?" *Foreign Affairs* (spring 1985); George McT. Kahin, *Intervention: How America Became Involved in Vietnam* (New York: Knopf, 1986); George K. Osborn et al., eds., *Democracy, Strategy, and Vietnam: Implications for American Policymaking* (Lexington, Mass.: Lexington Books, 1987).

Democratic Party of Afghanistan (PDPA). But Afghanistan's Communists feuded among themselves. The "Banner" faction of the PDPA drew from the lower ranks of the Persian-speaking elite in the capital, Kabul; the "Masses" wing appealed to some newly educated persons from rural backgrounds. Masses leader Nur Mohammed Taraki took power in April 1978 and embarked on a revolution by decree and terror. His land reforms and antireligious policies drove traditional Afghans into armed rebellion, supported by Pakistan and Iran. Taraki solicited Soviet aid but Moscow was cool. Soviet generals feared another "Vietnam" if the USSR intervened heavily in Afghanistan.[36]

In September 1979, Taraki was killed by his rival within the Masses leadership, Hafizullah Amin. From Moscow's perspective, Amin was even worse than Taraki. Top Soviet leaders concluded that Amin was "insincere and two-faced": He planned to purge rivals and continue policies that would strengthen the counterrevolution; but he also flirted with conservative Muslim leaders and even with the West. On the other hand, Amin begged Moscow to send special troops to protect him. These and other factors set the stage for Soviet intervention—as outlined in Table 4.7.

Moscow, like Washington, worried about falling dominoes. In 1979, the Kremlin came to fear that unless Soviet forces intervened, Moscow would lose a client state—the first time that an established Communist regime had been overthrown. If Afghanistan fell, what might follow? In early December, the Politburo decided to act. It airlifted special forces to Kabul on December 25, 1979. Instead of shielding Amin, the Soviets

Table 4.7 The Soviet War in Afghanistan: Action Levels and Likely Causes

Individuals	Blood feuds in Kabul: Taraki kills Daud and Amin kills Taraki; Soviet President Brezhnev becomes senile; President Carter appears irresolute
State and society	Afghan society split between traditionalists and modernizers as well as between many ethnic groups; Communist policies of Taraki and Amin spur armed resistance
International system	Bipolar IR, but the USSR and Iran seem to be gaining at the expense of the United States.
Underlying factors	Long-standing Russian interest in dominating Afghanistan and Iran; Soviet advances throughout the Third World in late 1970s unchallenged by United States.
Proximate causes	Soviet worries that Communist regime in Kabul will fall to anti-Communists backed by Iran, Pakistan, and the West
Catalysts	Afghan Communists seek Soviet aid; Soviets intervene militarily in December 1979

36. The following account is based on "top secret" Soviet documents from the period January–December 1979, published in *Journal of South Asian and Middle Eastern Studies* 17, no. 2 (winter 1994). The documents appear to be authentic but incomplete. See also Henry S. Bradsher, *Afghanistan and the Soviet Union*, rev. ed. (Durham, N.C.: Duke University Press, 1985).

killed and replaced him with Babrak Karmal—a man Moscow hoped would obey its directives.

What the Soviets at first called a "limited contingent" quickly grew to 120,000 men (more than twice the size of the Afghan government's forces) and remained for nine years. Signs multiplied that Moscow wanted also to use Afghanistan as a springboard to move south, east, and west. A Sovietized Afghanistan could bully Iran, Pakistan, and the Arab oil producers.

Stirred from its post-Vietnam slumbers, the United States acted to oppose the Soviet intervention in many ways. The CIA helped arm the Afghan resistance with the cooperation of Pakistan, Saudi Arabia, Egypt, and China.

A stalemate developed in which Soviet and local Communist forces controlled Afghanistan's major cities while the anti-Communist mujahideen ("holy warriors")[37] dominated the countryside. Unlike Vietnamese Communists, the mujahideen had little cohesion. Still they too were determined to evict alien trespassers. Soviet hopes in Afghanistan were already flagging when the United States began to supply "Stinger" missiles to the mujahideen in late 1986. This shoulder-braced weapon permitted the Afghan tribesmen to shoot down an average of one Soviet plane or helicopter a day. Stinger hard power combined with mujahideen willpower snapped Soviet overall power.

Soviet casualties mounted. By the mid-1980s Moscow could no longer hide the horrors of the Afghan war from Soviet citizens. Draft-age men began to injure themselves or pay bribes to avoid military service in Afghanistan. While most Soviet citizens initially supported the Afghan expedition, by 1987 many actively opposed it.[38]

In 1988, the Kremlin announced it would withdraw all Soviet troops from Afghanistan within one year. At the same time Pakistan agreed to end interference in Afghan internal affairs and the United States promised to terminate support to the mujahideen in tandem with the halting of Soviet aid to the Communists in Kabul.

As in Vietnam, there were many losers and no clear winners in Afghanistan. The war killed more than a million Afghans—mostly civilians—and produced the world's largest refugee problem: Two million Afghans were uprooted while another 5 million sought refuge in Pakistan or Iran. At least 13,000 Soviet troops—perhaps as many as 50,000—died. Drug addiction multiplied and morale fell within the Soviet armed forces. Overreaching, Moscow undermined its entire empire.

Each superpower allowed itself to be sucked into a conflict where it had few deep interests and where victory would be hard to achieve.[39] The

37. More precisely, a *mujahid* (plural, *mujahideen*) is a fighter in a holy war for the faith, a jihad. In other contexts, Western governments opposed Muslim jihads. Ralph H. Magnus and Eden Naby, *Afghanistan: Mullah, Marx, and Mujahid* (Boulder, Colo.: Westview, 1997).

38. Based on interviews with Soviet citizens traveling in Europe. "The Soviet Public and the War in Afghanistan: Discontent Reaches Critical Levels," Radio Free Europe/Radio Liberty, May 1988.

39. Neither U.S. nor Soviet officials admitted their mistakes until too late. In 1989, however, the Soviet foreign minister told his parliament that Soviet intervention in Afghanistan had been "immoral." No top U.S. leaders issued a mea culpa until Robert S. McNamara's book *In Retrospect: The Tragedy and Lessons of Vietnam* (New York: Times Books) appeared in 1995.

reality was that factional strife in Vietnam and in Afghanistan prevented either superpower from forming a cohesive regime there. No client obeyed its paymaster.[40]

After the Soviet withdrawal, land mines littered Afghan roads and farmlands. Soon, the mujahideen factions turned their knives on one another. Pakistan backed the most radical Muslim fundamentalists, and Moscow labored to keep religious and factional struggles from penetrating the Central Asian fringes of the Russian Federation. The United States lost interest in Afghanistan until it learned that many Muslims, radicalized by or in Afghanistan, had turned their wrath against the United States.

The Persian Gulf, 1990–

Iraqi President Saddam Hussein faced many foes in 1990, both at home and abroad. He wanted to restore to Iraq the glory and power of ancient Babylon. As in North Korea, personal and family lust for power and wealth also underlay a cruel dictatorship.

Unlike Koreans, Iraqis are not one people. Sunni Muslims rule Iraq but make up just 20 percent of the population. Some 60 percent of Iraqis are Shi'a Muslims (as are most Iranians). Some 20 to 25 percent of Iraq's population are Kurds—Muslims with their own customs and language.

How action levels and likely causes interlaced to spur the Gulf War is suggested in Table 4.8.

Repeating its 1950 Korean error, Washington failed to warn Iraq that the United States would resist a takeover of the country's southern neighbor. U.S. diplomats curried favor in Baghdad, trying to use Iraq against Iran, which Washington saw as the greater evil. (On one occasion, U.S. officials even apologized to Iraq for a Voice of America broadcast on the evils of police states!) On July 25, 1990—eight days before Iraq invaded Kuwait—President Hussein summoned U.S. Ambassador April C. Glaspie. He told her that his problem with Kuwait was an inter-Arab dispute. Iraq would negotiate with Kuwait, "but if we are unable to find a solution, then it will be natural that Iraq will not accept death." He warned Americans: "We too can harm you. We cannot come all the way to the United States, but individual Arabs may reach you." Following what she thought were her orders, Glaspie indicated to Hussein that the United States would take no side in this border dispute between neighbors, though it could never "excuse" any settlement by force.[41] If Iraq did invade Kuwait, many U.S. specialists expected Hussein to take only disputed borderlands and islands.

Saddam Hussein: A Psychological Portrait

A megalomaniac like Hitler and Kim Il-sung, Saddam Hussein also became a dictator who brought his country into costly struggles that led nowhere. Hussein's father, a landless peasant, died before he was born. Hussein was brought up by his mother's uncle, an army officer who taught the youth to hate British colonialism. Once in power, he surrounded himself with docile ministers—many of them his own relatives, often from his own community. Hussein compared himself with Nebuchadnezzar II, who destroyed Jerusalem in the 6th century B.C., and with Saladin, the Muslim warrior who drove back Christian crusaders in the 12th century. Still, Saddam Hussein—like Hitler and Stalin—could also talk like a reasonable man who had legitimate grievances.*

*See Stanley A. Renshon, ed., *The Political Psychology of the Gulf War: Leaders, Publics, and the Process of Conflict* (Pittsburgh: University of Pittsburgh Press, 1993); see also Judith Miller and Laurie Mylroie, *Saddam Hussein and the Crisis in the Gulf* (New York: Times Books/Random House, 1990); also Efraim Karsh, "In Baghdad, Politics Is a Lethal Game," *New York Times Magazine*, September 30, 1990, 39 ff.

---

40. The Americans urged the anti-Communist regime in Saigon to carry out land reform to win favor among poor peasants, while the Soviets pressed the Kabul Communists to go easy on their land reforms, which alienated rich landlords.

41. Lawrence Freedman and Efraim Karsh, *The Gulf Conflict, 1990–1991: Diplomacy and War in the New World Order* (Princeton, N.J.: Princeton University Press, 1993), 52–55.

HOW THE 1991 GULF WAR UNFOLDED

1980–1988

Iraq fights Iran.

1981

Israeli bombs destroy Iraqi nuclear plant.

1990

July

Iraq accuses Kuwait and United Arab Emirates of conspiring with "imperialists" and "Zionists" to keep oil prices low.

7/23–25

Iraq masses troops on Kuwait border.

7/25

U.S. Ambassador April Glaspie conciliates Hussein.

8/2–3

Iraq occupies Kuwait and oil prices double.

8/6

UN Security Council imposes sanctions on Iraq.

11/29

UN Security Council authorizes UN coalition forces in the Persian Gulf to use "all necessary means" to expel Iraq from Kuwait.

1991

1/12

U.S. Congress authorizes "all means necessary" to expel Iraq.

1/17

Coalition air attacks begin on Baghdad and on Iraqi troops.

2/24

Coalition forces advance on the ground.

2/27

Washington orders a cease-fire, to start the following day.

42. What is now Iraq had been three provinces of the Ottoman Empire until 1920, and then a British mandate under the League of Nations until Iraq became independent in 1932. Kuwait formally belonged to the Ottoman Empire too, but—at the request of the ruling family—became a British protectorate from 1897 until 1961. Iraq then tried to annex newly independent Kuwait but was prevented by British troops.

Table 4.8 The 1991 Gulf War: Action Levels and Likely Causes

Individuals	Egomaniac in Baghdad (Saddam Hussein) faces effective team leader in Washington (George Bush)
State and society	Dictatorship in Iraq faces feudal dynasty in Kuwait and presidential democracy in United States.
International system	World becomes unipolar with decline of USSR → UN no longer polarized → collective security becomes feasible
Underlying factors	Bristling with Soviet arms, Iraq challenges Kuwait's independence and covets its borders, oil, and wealth
Proximate causes	Kuwait pumps oil beyond OPEC quotas and demands that Iraq repay loans; United States appeases Iraq
Catalysts	Iraq invades and annexes Kuwait and refuses to withdraw despite UN resolutions and U.S.-led military buildup

Hussein had five complaints. First, he maintained that, since Ottoman times, Kuwait was part of Iraq.[42] Second, Kuwait pumped oil from wells in Iraqi territory. Third, Kuwait refused to give Iraq two islands thereby blocking its access to the Persian Gulf. Fourth, Kuwait exceeded the oil production quotas set by OPEC (Organization of Petroleum Exporting Countries) and thus lowered the world price of oil. Fifth, Kuwait refused to cancel its loans to Iraq during the 1980s war that Hussein had waged against the common Arab foe—Iran.

Iraq's forces quickly took Kuwait in August 1990. Some of U.S. President George Bush's advisers urged acceptance of this as an accomplished fact. Like Truman in 1950, however, Bush wanted to prevent one state from extinguishing another. He saw Hussein as "another Hitler" and did not want Iraq to control half, or even a quarter, of the world's oil. If Hussein conquered Kuwait and Saudi Arabia, Iraq would control nearly half of the world's known oil deposits (Iraq, 12.5 percent; Kuwait, 12.2 percent; Saudi Arabia, 21 percent).

In 1990, Iraq's armed forces were the largest and best equipped in the Middle East. But Iraq did not yet have nuclear weapons and would face practical difficulties in using its germ and poison gas weapons. Had Baghdad possessed a credible weapon of mass destruction, the United Nations might have been less likely to drive Iraq from Kuwait.

As in 1950, the UN Security Council endorsed actions favored by the United States. In 1990–1991, however, the USSR was never absent and voted with the majority on every issue. Only Albania and Cuba opposed the majority; China sometimes abstained.

As detailed in Chapter 14, the UN Security Council immediately denounced Baghdad's action and imposed sanctions against Iraq to cut off

Map 4.3 The 1991 Gulf War

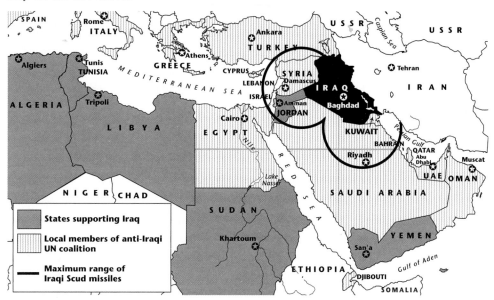

its oil revenues. Iraq did not budge. After the Security Council and U.S. Congress authorized "all necessary measures" to expel Iraq, a U.S.-led coalition attacked Iraqi forces in January and February 1991. Allied planes waged an air war for five weeks before launching a ground attack.[43] Advised that Iraq had been driven from Kuwait, President Bush ordered an end to the ground war after just 100 hours. Retreating Iraqis set 600 Kuwaiti oil wells ablaze, wasting a valuable asset and devastating the fragile Persian Gulf environment.[44] The military operations are outlined in Map 4.3.

Expecting Hussein to soon fall from power, Secretary of State James Baker wanted to include a post-Hussein Iraq in efforts to construct a more stable region. Baker's vision for the Middle East resembled the U.S. policies that integrated Western Europe after World War II. But Arab states backed away, and President Bush opposed any scheme to finance Iraq's reconstruction.[45]

The 1991 Gulf War campaign represented another qualified victory for collective security. As in Korea, however, the egomaniacal dictator remained. His troops massed again near Kuwait in 1994, and pulled back only after the United States again sent a large force to the region. Hussein complied with many UN demands, but not all. The UN Security Council blocked Iraq from selling oil so long as it concealed facilities for making weapons of mass destruction. Without oil revenues, Iraq could not import

43. The number of Iraqi soldiers killed was probably about 1,500 and no more than 10,000; Iraqi civilian deaths, about 1,000. John G. Heidenrich, "The Gulf War: How Many Iraqis Died?" *Foreign Policy* 90 (spring 1993): 108–125.

44. The Chairman of the Joint Chiefs of Staff, General Colin Powell, had never favored the war and jumped at an excuse to suspend operations. See Michael R. Gordon and Bernard E. Trainor, *The Generals' War* (Boston: Little, Brown, 1995). For essays on "After the Gulf War," see *International Journal* 49, no. 2 (spring 1994).

45. James A. Baker, III, *The Politics of Diplomacy: Revolution. War & Peace. 1989–1992* (New York: G. P. Putnam's, 1995), 411–415.

food and medicines. This meant malnutrition and disease for the masses while Hussein's entourage got richer by manipulating the black market.

The UN eventually permitted Iraq to sell limited quantities of oil to generate money for food and medicine, but Saddam Hussein wanted all sanctions lifted. Here was grist for another "just war" debate: Was it right—or *just*—to keep pressure on a brutal dictator if the principal victims were his hapless subjects?

WARS OF THE EARLY 21ST CENTURY

The Russian Federation and Chechnya

History did not end when communism expired in the late 1980s and early 1990s. National memories surged and expressed themselves in demands for liberation from alien oppressors. All fifteen "union-republics" of the former USSR became independent—from Estonia and Ukraine to Kyrgyzstan. But Russian President Boris Yeltsin insisted that all other units (more than eighty) remain with the Russian Federation (RF). One of these was the "Autonomous Chechen-Ingush Republic."

Chechens had suffered greatly under Russian (tsarist and then Soviet) rule since the mid-19th century. In late 1991, Chechens elected a retired Soviet Air Force officer their president and he declared Chechnya independent. The Chechens' ethnic cousins, the Ingush, preferred to remain within the RF.

Yeltsin opposed independence for Chechnya. Located in the north Caucasus, it straddled oil pipelines leading from Azerbaijan to Russia and could buffer Russia proper from Georgia. If Chechnya seceded, Yeltsin thought, other RF borderlands might follow. The Kremlin negotiated treaty-like arrangements with other units of the Russian Federation—even giving "sovereignty" to Tatarstan. But Yeltsin refused to allow Chechnya to break completely. Having learned nothing from nine years of futile fighting in Afghanistan, in 1994 he sent Russia's armed forces to crush Chechen resistance. Two years later, both sides were exhausted and accepted a peace that left Chechnya's status unresolved. Russia resumed the war in 1999, and Yeltsin's handpicked successor, Vladimir Putin, sailed to victory in the 2000 presidential elections by promising to crush the Chechen rebels quickly.

By 2002, Chechnya lay in ruins but Chechen guerrillas kept fighting, relying mainly on weapons taken or purchased from Russian soldiers. Desperate, some Chechens accepted help from outsiders, including al-Qaeda. In October 2002, a faction of young Chechens—women as well as men—took more than 700 hostages in a Moscow theater—an ordeal that ended

Map 4.4 The War in Iraq, March–April, 2003

From the south: Invading Iraq from Kuwait, the U.S. 3rd Infantry division advanced west of the Euphrates River and then across the river into Baghdad. The U.S. 1st Marine Expeditionary Force moved along the Tigris River and into Baghdad while British Royal Marine Commandos and an Air Assault Brigade secured A1 Basra.

In the west: Near Jordan, U.S. forces landed and took A1 Rutbah and, close to Syria, A1 Qaim, to ensure that no missiles could be fired from this area of Israel, as happened in 1991.

In the north: Advancing from Kurdish-controlled areas long protected by the no-fly zone, Kurdish militias and the U.S. 173rd Airborne took Kirkuk and Mosul and secured the oil infrastructure.

In Baghdad: U.S. missiles and airplanes attacked government and military sites for two weeks. When U.S. forces entered the capital, they met little resistance.

North of Baghdad: U.S. Marines took Tikrit, home to Saddam Hussein, also with little resistance.

On the Gulf: the port of Umm Qasr began receiving merchant ships with food and other humanitarian aid.

- *The war will trigger more terrorist attacks against the United States.* Recruitment of would-be martyrs soared around the world, but produced no immediate attacks.
- *Jordan, Pakistan, and Egypt will explode.* Sobriety superseded emotion in many quarters as the utter depravity of Saddam's regime was revealed. Many Arabs turned against their newspapers and TV, even al-Jazeera, that disinformed them before and during the war.
- *Iraq will quickly become a democracy and corrupt regimes will fall, like dominoes, in neighboring countries.* This forecast might prove accurate, but only in the long run. Lacking democratic experience or institutions, a smooth transition to self-rule and power sharing among diverse groups looked unlikely in Iraq. Meanwhile, governments in neighboring countries battened down the hatches.

What next? Ever since the collapse of the USSR, the Pentagon sought forces able to fight two-and-one-half regional wars simultaneously, without allies if need be. The "two" referred to North Korea and Iraq or Iran; the "one-half" to a humanitarian or peacekeeping mission. Having ousted Saddam, the United States still faced potential conflicts with Pyongyang and/or Tehran.

Both Secretary of State Powell, a former general, and Defense Secretary Rumsfeld had strong views on military planning. Powell was the more traditional. The Powell Doctrine stipulated that the United States should fight only for clear goals, using overwhelming force and having a clear exit strategy. The Rumsfeld Doctrine called for smaller, more mobile, and more lethal forces. Rumsfeld wanted to cut spending in traditional assets and invest in transforming the U.S. war machine.

The war in Iraq vindicated some, but not all, of each doctrine. Powell could say: The coalition deployed 250,000 troops against Saddam and needed even more to safeguard supply lines and maintain security in occupied cities. Yes, twice that number were used against Iraq in 1991, but Iraqi forces had shriveled drastically since then. Rumsfeld could reply: Special operations forces proved highly effective. They scouted the land before the bombing began, secured oil wells, and rescued prisoners. New technologies proved their value. In 1991 most coalition weapons were still "dumb;" in 2003 most were "smart"—precision guided. New sensors and real-time battle management systems (part of "network-centric warfare") made it possible to detect enemy targets and quickly destroy them.

In 1991, by contrast, the coalition often failed to attack Iraq's Scud missile launchers in the ten minutes between the time they were pulled from hiding, fired, and returned to a concealed position. In 2003 there were fewer deaths from friendly fire than in 1991 and less collateral harm to civilians. But the biggest battlefield change since 1991 bypassed both the Powell and the Rumsfeld Doctrines: In 2003 coalition ground forces advanced simultaneously with the onset of heavy bombing. Also, air, ground, and naval forces functioned as an integrated whole as never before.

Powell believed in nation-building and wanted a major role for the UN. He preferred "jaw, jaw" to "war, war" with Damascus, Pyongyang, Tehran, or Beijing. If Rumsfeld had his way, the United States would not waste resources in nation-building but would use its muscle to dictate terms to Syria, North Korea, and Iran, and prepare someday to fight "peer rival" China.

Plus ça change, plus c'ést la même chose. Despite the achievements and promise of highly trained forces equipped with advanced technology, the United States would still need most of its current thirteen divisions (ten Army and three Marine)—two divisions in Iraq, and six to eight if war erupted in Korea, plus one brigade in Afghanistan and another in the Balkans. If war erupted in Korea, the United States would need six to eight divisions there.

With Saddam's regime put down, the United States opted to move most of its forces from Saudi Arabia, leaving only a "training" mission there. Some U.S. forces would shift to Qatar and other Gulf Cooperation Council (GCC) states. (Formed in 1981, the GCC included Saudi Arabia, Kuwait, Qatar, Bahrain, Oman, and the United Arab Emirates.) Deploying some forces at sea and some on land—in a changing mix, the United States hoped to keep terrorists off balance and reduce pressures on friendly Arab governments. Forces in Kuwait might be halved, but the United States would retain a base for live-fire exercises in the desert.

The United States continued to deploy forces against terrorist activity worldwide—from Afghanistan to the Philippines and Indonesia. It deployed troops in parts of former Soviet Central Asia and in Georgia. It brought three former Soviet republics—Estonia, Latvia, and Lithuania—into NATO. The Russians didn't like this but, for the present, had to lump it.

Did any of the aggressors we have studied behave like a rational monolith bent on maximizing power? Again, the answer is no—with one possible exception. If the attackers calculated, they generally miscalculated. Most of those that initiated war lost. A possible exception was the United States in 2003. The Bush administration called its war "preemptive" but it attacked Iraq without provocation and acted as though it planned to maximize U.S. economic and geopolitical interests.

Contrary to what neorealists expect, neither the decision to fight nor the outcome of war can be dependably predicted. Yes, the U.S.-led victories over Iraq in 1991 and 2003 could be interpreted as the outcomes of huge power imbalances, but America lost in Vietnam and the USSR lost in Afghanistan, despite similar asymmetries. The structure of power does not foretell who will fight or who will win. It does not forecast skill or morale or the role of accidents, luck, and friction.

JFK looked for ways to avoid going to war in 1962 and offered Khrushchev several incentives to pull back WMD from Cuba. By contrast, Bush seemed to want war. Washington offered Saddam Hussein little reason to cooperate with the UN except to avoid a U.S. attack. Washington never promised to suspend economic sanctions or its overflights of northern and southern Iraq if Baghdad fulfilled specific demands. There was no offer: "If Iraq does x, we will do y." These and other comparisons between 1962 and 2003 are outlined in Table 4.9.

Table 4.9 Dealing with Risk and Uncertainty: Cuba 1962 and Iraq 2003

The Issues	Cuban Crisis 1962	Iraq and United States in 2003
A danger of war with WMD?	Soviet deployment and possible U.S. response set stage for nuclear war.	Iraq may use WMD *if* it has them *and* is attacked. In that case, U.S. and Israel may respond with WMD.
How much consideration of policy options?	Khrushchev decides without debate. JFK and ExCom deliberate multiple options.	Saddam faced little or no opposition to his WMD programs. Bush tends to close doors and focus on the war option.
Role of intelligence	CIA does not anticipate or detect Soviet missiles until nearly operational.	The White House suppresses CIA doubts about Iraqi WMD.
Does other side know it is a target?	Yes. Castro knows the U.S. will try to overthrow or assassinate him.	Yes. Saddam knows the U.S. wants him out but does little to dissuade the U.S. or resist.
Time pressures	JFK wants to neuter Soviet missiles before they become operational.	Bush says the threat can only get worse. Others ask: What's the hurry?
November elections midway in president's first term	Some in CIA want to knock out Castro in October. Khrushchev plans to present fait accompli after the elections. JFK tells ExCom to ignore elections.	Democrats accuse Bush of trying to distract voters from Enron and the economy, but most vote to give the president a blank check on Iraq.
Incentives	JFK expresses hope for a new beginning in U.S.–Soviet relations. Offers a no-invasion pledge and a Turkish pullback. Détente in 1963.	No U.S. offer to lift sanctions or give other incentives to Saddam—only demands for disarmament, proactive cooperation with inspectors, and regime change.
Secrecy vs. openness	The Soviets mask their deployment, and U.S., its discovery. U.S. insists its move in Turkey be kept secret.	Saddam hides some weapons programs. Bush presents many reasons to attack Iraq but may conceal deepest motives.
Does U.S. consider preemptive or preventive war?	Yes—to preempt operational readiness of Soviet missiles and prevent additional deployments.	Bush opts for preventive war. Absent an imminent Iraqi threat, there is nothing to preempt.
Risk taking	Khrushchev ignores risks and focuses on possible gains in Cuba. JFK and McNamara cautiously search for ways to avoid war.	Like Khrushchev, Saddam is a risk taker. Bush defies world opinion and opens a Pandora's Box by attacking Iraq. He says that inaction would be riskier.

WHAT PROPOSITIONS HOLD?
WHAT QUESTIONS REMAIN?

IS WAR A RATIONAL TOOL OF FOREIGN POLICY?
CAN IT BE RATIONAL OR JUST IN AN AGE OF WMD?

Did war serve as a rational tool of foreign policy in the cases we have studied? The answer is seldom, if ever.[49] No war that we have examined was launched after a systematic study of the alternatives, along with their likely gains and losses. To be sure, the top leaders and their advisers talked as though they had analyzed everything, but their analysis was usually slanted to favor a decision already made—often for reasons extraneous to the war.[50]

Has it been wise to resist aggression? In some cases, yes; in others, the answer is not so clear. We must weigh the cost of submitting to a conqueror versus the cost of resisting. Those who resisted Germany in World Wars I and II "won," but for many, the price was dreadfully high. However, submission to Hitler would have been much more horrific than to Wilhelm's Reich. But was it worthwhile for Soviet citizens to drive back Hitler at the price of 25 to 40 million Soviet lives—and then continue to be ruled by Stalin? Poles fought Nazi invaders; Czechs did not. Poles lost far more lives, but gained more self-respect. Which course was better? Both Poles and Czechs soon fell into Stalin's empire.

Only the United States escaped from the world wars with relatively few casualties and a stronger position of power. The United States also gained stature from its role in driving North Korea from the South, and Iraq from Kuwait. But U.S. social cohesion and prestige suffered greatly from the attempt to stop communism in Indochina. America also got little credit among most Muslims for helping their fellow believers in Afghanistan, Kuwait, the Balkans, or Iraq.

The bottom line is that it has generally been more rational, as well as just, to resist than to attack. But expected victory is neither a necessary nor sufficient condition to fight.

HOW DO WARS BEGIN? HOW DO
LEVELS INTERTWINE?

INDIVIDUAL LEADERS: BUNDLES OF MYSTERIES

Has it been rational to fight for national liberation? The U.S. war of independence from Great Britain cost fewer than 26,000 American deaths (more than one in ten of those who served). Almost two centuries later, however, some 3 million Vietnamese died fighting to drive out foreign

49. One possible exception was the 1967 Israeli attack that destroyed any Egyptian capacity to bomb Israel.

50. See, for example, Mao Zedong's telegrams quoted in the appendices to Christensen, *Useful Adversaries.*

forces and unify Vietnam. Hanoi's leaders thought the price worthwhile. But not every struggle for liberation succeeds. Afghans drove out a superpower, but then fell to fighting among themselves.

The bad news is that history, as Edward Gibbon noted, is the record of the follies, crimes, and inhumanities of man to man. The good news is that none of the wars studied in this chapter was inevitable. Each war resulted from zero-sum thinking. The wars begun in 1914, 1939, 1950, and 1990 flowed from the aggressor's myopic greed for more resources, glory, or influence. None explored or rationally pursued its deepest interests. Almost any negotiated revision of existing arrangements—or just maintaining the status quo—would have benefited the challengers more than war. But these propositions probably do not apply to America's wars in 2000–2003. In each case, Washington faced an intransigent opponent unwilling to compromise. The United States achieved at least some of its objectives in Kosovo, Afghanistan, and Iraq at relatively modest cost to America.

As we saw in the 1962 missile crisis, it does matter who is at the helm. Most leaders who authorized or ordered the first shots in the wars we have studied had an ego so large that it blocked the light. Each gave in to wishful thinking, pride, and a lust for power. Each suffered a failure of imagination.[51] Most expected a quick victory and substantial gains at a reasonable price. Few considered the consequences of miscalculation, or the ruin that war could engender. For example, Hitler persuaded his generals to attack the USSR without outfitting the troops for winter weather.

Aggressive tendencies are stronger in some persons than others. Some leaders fight when others keep talking or walk away. Why these differences? How individuals respond to challenges depends heavily upon their personal makeup. Both Hitler and Hussein, for example, seemed to love violence and war. Stalin was sadistic, but cautious about risk taking abroad.

Do the more aggressive personalities seek to compensate for physical or emotional slights? Wilhelm II had a withered arm; Hitler, just one testicle; Stalin, a pockmarked face; Johnson, anxieties about his ability to fill Kennedy's shoes; Saddam Hussein, an abusive stepfather. But real or imagined shortcomings need not produce aggressive behavior. Three U.S. presidents in our cases—Wilson, Roosevelt, and Kennedy—suffered from severe physical disabilities, but each sought to avoid a major war. Individuals are crucial, but their psyches remain a bundle of mysteries.

The State: Aggressive Dictatorships

Wars helped produce modern states but were not needed to sustain them. Still, the most consistent explanation of war proneness is domestic

51. Adapted from Kagan's verdict in *The Outbreak of the Peloponnesian War*, 356.

constitution. Dictatorships started and lost all of the 20th century's major wars. They also committed **democide**—mass murder of their own people (demos). By contrast, as we shall see in Chapter 10, established democracies have seldom, if ever, fought other democracies or exterminated their own citizens. They have, however, often resisted dictatorships and attacked national liberation movements.

The belief that conquest could be achieved quickly and with relative ease inspired Germany in 1914 and again in 1939–1941. It drove North Korea in 1950, and Iraq in 1990. Japan in 1941 did not so much believe as hope it could achieve a quick victory over the United States. *In all these cases the aggressors were too confident, but they were also too fearful.* None of them would have been attacked if they had not started a war. Each had sufficient resources or could have obtained them by trade in a peaceful world. Thus, *the greatest menace to great powers in the 20th century lay "in their own tendency to exaggerate the dangers they face[d], and to respond with counterproductive belligerence* [emphasis added]."[52] This paradox was a result of the security dilemma, combined with undue faith in technologies thought to favor offensive action over the defensive.

Undue fear also pushed the United States into Vietnam in the 1960s and the USSR into Afghanistan in the 1980s. Each great power exaggerated the dangers to its global position if it did not intervene to stop the rot in a client state. On the other hand, neither Washington nor Moscow expected a quick or easy victory against guerrillas on their own turf.

Except for 1914, bureaucracies usually influenced how—not whether— a war was fought. Industrialists never called the shots in the century's wars, even though some pressed for arms buildup.

None of the aggressors we have studied started a war mainly to divert the public from domestic problems.[53] Still, partisan politics often reinforced other motives for war. Thus, Boris Yeltsin attacked Chechnya in 1994 and again in 1999 to buttress his flagging domestic support. Serbian leader Slobodan Milošević found that nationalist policies won him votes, even though they led to war. And the Bush White House felt sure its calls for preemptive war against Iraq would influence the November 2002 elections.

None of our wars resulted from imperialist pressures like those predicted by Vladimir Lenin. Capitalist states did not fight one another for markets. Strategic or ideological concerns far outweighed economic ones in the United States and Soviet forays into Indochina and Afghanistan. The George W. Bush administration, along with France and Russia, however, seemed to covet Iraq's oil. Vice President Dick

52. Steven Van Evera, *Causes of War: Power and the Roots of Conflict* (Ithaca, N.Y.: Cornell University Press, 1999), 192.

53. See Jack S. Levy, "Domestic Politics and War," *Journal of Interdisciplinary History* 18, no. 4 (spring 1988): 653–673.

Cheney's former company, Halliburton, received large Defense Department contracts in 2001 and 2002 and even larger ones in 2003 to rebuild Iraq's oil infrastructure.

Clashes between civilizations have evoked hostility, but they have caused no major wars. Indeed, one culture often fought its supposed soul mates or allied with a rival culture. "Western" France and England allied with "Eastern" Serbia and Russia against "Western" Germany in two world wars. Shinto-Buddhist Japan attacked the West in the 1940s, but after the war allied with the leading Western power. Before 9/11, powerful political interests predicted alignments better than did civilizational unity. After 9/11, however, a large fraction of the world's Muslims and many Christians, especially in the southern United States, seemed to see one another as implacable foes. Still, France and many other non-Muslim actors had their own reasons for disliking the American hyperpower (*puissance*). If Washington became more evenhanded with Israeli–Arab relations, "Islamic" enmity for the United States might well diminish.

The International Balance of Power

No Formula for Stability. Major wars took place in spite of—or perhaps due to—various power balances often touted as keys to peace. Blends of loose bipolarity and multipolarity did not prevent World Wars I or II. Tight Soviet–U.S. bipolarity yielded no world wars but allowed, and perhaps encouraged, localized wars, such as in Korea and Vietnam. Unipolarity did not prevent the Gulf War or the Balkan wars of the 1990s (discussed in Chapters 8 and 9).

Neither equality nor superiority ensures stability. Each order, each balance, will be challenged by expansionist regimes, new weapons and military tactics, new crusading ideologies, intervention of actors outside the system, and the disappearance of smaller states crucial to the balance. The only structure without war has been the unit veto: None of the countries with nuclear arms has yet attacked another, though Pakistan and India went to the brink.

Whatever the balance, war becomes more likely if the status quo states show no capacity or will to curb aggression. In World Wars I and II, Korea, and the Gulf War, the combined defenders were stronger than the challengers. Washington's weight was always decisive, but the United States failed to warn Wilhelm, Hitler, Kim, or Hussein that it would fight aggression. (Mere words, of course, may not suffice: Khrushchev sloughed off U.S. warnings not to deploy offensive weapons in Cuba.)

No foreign policy method can assure peace, but the most promising approach has been conditional cooperation to promote peaceful change. Win–lose hard-liners started four of the century's major wars. Many of those who hoped to avoid the flames—win–win cooperators, stand-patters, and isolationists—were pulled into the fire.

Power Shifts Need Not Produce War. The evidence for power transition theory is weak. World War I started over Austrian greed and Russian honor in the Balkans—not over Germany's drive to overthrow Britain's hegemony. In the late 1930s, however, Hitler hoped to overthrow the existing order before his foes geared up to fight. Similarly, Tokyo in 1941 decided to strike the U.S. fleet before Japanese supplies diminished and the United States became stronger.[54] Washington intervened in Indochina, and Moscow in Afghanistan to prevent expansion by their global rivals.

Power transition theory does not explain the Korean, Gulf, or Balkan wars. Neither Kim Il-sung in 1950, nor Saddam Hussein in 1990, nor Serbian President Slobodan Milošević in the mid-1990s aspired to displace a hegemon. They hoped, rather, to defeat weak targets.

The evidence shows that an improving or worsening power base can lead to a variety of policies—militant expansionism, restraint, or pursuit of collective security, as outlined in Table 4.9.

Where power transition theory could have been truly relevant—the rapid demise of the Soviet empire—it utterly failed: The Second World went down in 1989–1991 not with a bang but with a few whimpers. Thus, there is nothing predetermined about the ways that nations respond to shifts in the balance of power. Leaders have choices.

54. In 1941 Japanese strategists reached a consensus: "Now! The time for war will not come later." Michael A. Barnhart, *Japan Prepares for Total War: The Search for Economic Security, 1919–1941* (Ithaca, N.Y.: Cornell University Press, 1987), 258.

What to Tell the President.... Is war obsolete? Now that you are ready to share your conclusions with the Commander in Chief, you draft the following memo: For thousands of years, war held the potential for profit. It could bring more land for farmers, more glory or wealth for kings. But the Industrial and Information Revolutions changed the calculus. Raw materials can be obtained by trade or replaced more cheaply than by seizing them by war. A growing moral consensus sees occupation of conquered territory as illegitimate. Weapons are unprecedentedly dangerous.[55] Still, such conditions do not guarantee peace: Neither deep vulnerability nor shared values sufficed to prevent the American Civil War or World War I.

---

55. Carl Kaysen, "Is War Obsolete? A Review Essay," *International Security* 14, no. 4 (spring 1990): 42–64. The article reviews John Mueller, *Retreat from Doomsday: The Obsolescence of Major War* (New York: Basic Books, 1989). See also Robert S. McNamara and James G. Blight, *Wilson's Ghost—Reducing the Risk of Conflict, Killing, and Catastrophe in the 21st Century* (New York: Public Affairs, 2001).

Instead, admixtures of emotion laced with calculation or miscalculation seem to trigger one war after another.

Perhaps war should be obsolete, but it is not. Governments may still hope to fight short, decisive wars that win solid gains. Or a crazed leader, expecting defeat, may decide to pull down the roof and evoke universal disaster. War will be harder to eliminate than dueling or slavery. Incentives for war arise from individual personalities, social pressures, uncertain power balances, and shrinking resources. If just one government opts for conquest, the others must resist or submit. For war to disappear, all governments—for all time and with no exceptions—would have to accept that it cannot be profitable. Thus, the ancient Romans captured part of the truth when they said: "If you want peace, prepare for war."

Even when governments prefer peace, nonstate actors may provoke them to fight. Ideological fanatics such as those who led the Communist International (1919–1943) and al-Qaeda are not readily won over by carrots. The United States might placate al-Qaeda by withdrawing from Saudi Arabia and stopping aid to Israel. But it might also have to close down Hollywood and MTV and adopt shar'ia law. Al-Qaeda pressured Muslims everywhere to attack Americans and thereby assured a militant U.S. response.

We should not, like Germany in 1914 or Japan in 1941, exaggerate the dangers we face. We should not attack "Koraq" or "Irkor" to destroy their capacity to field WMD unless we believe they are really on the verge of using such weapons. Otherwise, we should adapt the kinds of policies that sustained us through decades of cold war with the USSR and Communist China.

Conclusion: We continue to need a substantial military establishment. The foundation of our security, however, is not just military strength but overall fitness—a topic addressed in my next memo.

KEY NAMES AND TERMS

balance of power	Gulf Cooperation Council (GCC)	Pyongyang
Blitzkrieg	Gulf of Tonkin Resolution	Rumsfeld Doctrine
buck passing	hegemonic war	Shi'a
chain-ganging	Saddam Hussein	strategic doctrine
Carl von Clausewitz	Kim Il-sung	strategic weapons
cold war	Maginot Line	strategy
conventional war	MOOTW	Sunni
cult of the defensive	nonviolent sanctions	tactics
cult of the offensive	polarity (uni-, bi-, multi-)	Triple Alliance
democide	Powell Doctrine	Triple Entente
détente	power transition theory	unconventional war
economic warfare	preemptive strike	war
entente	preventive war	War Powers Resolution
escalation ladder	proxy wars	
falling dominoes theory	psychological warfare	

QUESTIONS TO DISCUSS

1. Is war rational if it brings destruction to one's own people?
2. If we knew precisely who had what forces, could wars be fought out on computer screens and actual combat be avoided?
3. Which action levels were most important in bringing on World War I and World War II? The wars in Korea, Vietnam, Afghanistan, and the Persian Gulf in 1991 and 2003?
4. Do personal frailties incline leaders toward or away from war?
5. Which balance of power, if any, is most conducive to peace?
6. Can weapons of mass destruction make war obsolete?
7. How did U.S. participation in the Vietnam War resemble Soviet intervention in Afghanistan? How did it differ?
8. Using the framework of Tables 4.2–4.7, outline the possible causes of another war. Which level will be decisive?
9. Was it right to keep sanctions on Iraq if they hurt ordinary people rather than the rulers?
10. From the cases we have studied, is it better to lean toward caution or to take risks in world affairs?
11. Given what you know about U.S. policy in other cases, how should Washington deal with Koraq and Irkor?

RECOMMENDED RESOURCES

BOOKS

Bobbitt, Philip. *The Shield of Achilles: War, Peace, and the Course of History.* New York: A. A. Knopf, 2002.

Boot, Max. *The Savage Wars of Peace: Small Wars and the Rise of American Power.* New York: Perseus, 2002.

Clark, Wesley K. *Waging Modern War: Bosnia, Kosovo, and the Future of Combat.* New York: Public Affairs, 2001.

Clausewitz, Carl von. *On War.* Princeton, N.J.: Princeton University Press, 1984.

Freedman, Lawrence, ed. *War.* New York: Oxford University Press, 1994.

Gilpin, Robert. *War and Change in World Politics.* Cambridge, U.K.: Cambridge University Press, 1981.

The Soviet–Afghan War: How a Superpower Fought and Lost. Translated from Russian and edited by Lester W. Grau and Michael A. Gress. Lawrence: University Press of Kansas, 2002.

Handel, Michael I. *Masters of War: Classical Strategic Thought.* 2d ed. London: Frank Cass, 1996.

Hess, Gary R. *Presidential Decisions for War: Korea, Vietnam, and the Persian Gulf.* Baltimore, Md.: Johns Hopkins University Press, 2001.

Holmes, Robert L., ed. *Nonviolence in Theory and Practice.* Belmont, Calif.: Wadsworth, 1990.

Howard, Michael. *The Causes of War.* 2d ed. Cambridge, Mass.: Harvard University Press, 1989.

———. *The Invention of Peace: Reflections on War and Intentional Order.* New Haven, Conn.: Yale University Press, 2000.

International Institute for Strategic Studies. *The Military Balance.* London [annual].

Levy, Jack S. *War in the Modern Great Power System, 1495–1975.* Lexington: University Press of Kentucky, 1983.

Logevall, Fredrik. *Choosing War: The Lost Chance for Peace and the Escalation of War in Vietnam.* Berkeley: University of California Press, 2001.

Naylor, R. Thomas. *Economic Warfare: Sanctions, Embargo Busting, and Their Human Cost.* Boston: Northeastern University Press, 2001.

Record, Jeffrey. *Making War, Thinking History: Munich, Vietnam, and Presidential Uses of Force from Korea to Kosovo.* Annapolis, Md.: Naval Institute Press, 2002.

Sarkees, Meredith Reid, Frank Whelon Wayman, and J. David Singer. "Inter-State, Intra-State, and Extra-State Wars: A Comprehensive Look at Their Distribution Over Time, 1816–1997," *International Studies Quarterly*, 47, no. 1 (March 2003) 40–70.

Sawyer, Ralph D., trans. *Seven Military Classics of Ancient China.* Boulder Colo.: Westview, 1993.

Schelling, Thomas C. *Arms and Influence.* New Haven, Conn.: Yale University Press, 1966.

Small, Melvin, and J. David Singer. *Resort to Arms: International and Civil Wars, 1816–1980.* Beverly Hills, Calif.: Sage, 1982. (For other studies of the Correlates of War project, check library listings under Singer, J. David.)

Snyder, Jack. *Myths of Empire: Domestic Politics and International Ambition.* Ithaca, N.Y.: Cornell University Press, 1991.

Stockholm International Peace Research Institute. *World Armaments and Disarmament.* Stockholm: annual. (For other studies sponsored by the same organization, see library listings under SIPRI.)

Recommended Resources (continued)

Stoessinger, John G. *Why Nations Go to War.* 7th ed. New York: St. Martin's, 1998.

Stueck, William W. *Rethinking the Korean War: A New Diplomatic and Strategic History.* Princeton, N.J.: Princeton University Press, 2002.

Tilly, Charles. *Coercion, Capital, and European States, AD 900–1990.* Cambridge, Mass.: Basil Blackwell, 1990.

U.S. Department of Defense. *Annual Report by the Secretary of Defense to Congress* (title varies, recent issues available on-line).

Van Evera, Stephen. *Causes of Wars: Power and the Roots of Conflict.* Ithaca, N.Y.: Cornell University Press, 1999.

Vasquez, John A., ed. *What Do We Know About War?* Lanham, Md.: Rowman & Littlefield, 2000.

"Waging a New Kind of War," articles by Jeffrey Boutwell and Michael T. Klare; Richard F. Mollica, Walter C. Clemens, Jr.; and J. David Singer; Neil G. Boothby and Christine M. Knudsen, *Scientific American* 282, no. 6 (June 2000): 46–65.

Waltz, Kenneth N. *Man, the State, and War: A Theoretical Analysis.* New York: Columbia University Press, 1959.

Walzer, Michael. *Just and Unjust Wars: A Moral Argument with Historical Illustrations.* 2d ed. New York: Basic Books, 1992.

WEB SITES

AntiWar.Com, Against a War in Iraq
  http://www.antiwar.com/
The Cold War International History Project
  http://wwics.si.edu/index.cfm?fuseaction=topics.home&topic_id=1409
General Military History
  http://www.army.mil/cmh-pg/ (follow links to "online bookshelves")
The Korean War
  http://www.koreanwar.org/
Operation Desert Storm
  http://www.history.navy.mil/wars/dstorm/ds5.htm
Saddam Hussein's Iraq (from the U.S. State Department)
  http://usinfo.state.gov/regional/nea/iraq/iraq99.htm
The Vietnam War
  http://www.historyplace.com/unitedstates/vietnam/
The War on Terrorism (From the CIA)
  http://www.cia.gov/terrorism/
World War I
  http://www.worldwar1.com/
World War II
  http://www.bbc.co.uk/history/war/wwtwo/

POWER AND INFLUENCE: WHAT WINS?

THE BIG QUESTIONS IN CHAPTER 5

- What makes a country "fit"? What makes an international system fit?

- What is power? Does power assure influence? Does it assure security?

- Is power a reflection of treasure, troops, brains, or something else?

- Which countries are most powerful as another millennium begins?

- Have "trading states" and geonomics left heavily armed states and geopolitics in the dust?

- How should a country allocate its resources to optimize fitness at home and internationally?

"How Should We Use Our Assets?" . . . . *Before her term begins, the President wants a clear view of the big picture. Seeing the rapid changes confronting the nation on every front, the President asks how to balance the many demands upon the country's resources. "How," she asks, "should we allocate our resources to help the country become more fit, more secure, more influential?"*

The President details her concerns: "Great Britain had the world's largest empire. Britain survived World War I but never recovered. The USSR was a superpower, but its empire fell apart after the Afghan campaign. While the superpowers engaged in cold and hot war, Japan surpassed the USSR and became the world's second largest economy. The United States bounced back after defeat in Vietnam, but now faces severe challenges at home and abroad. China is rising. Europe is uniting. Terrorists are gathering."

"U.S. material power is unmatched, but more of our babies die than in most other industrialized countries. Our scientists win a majority of Nobel prizes, but our kids do worse in school than those in Hong Kong or Germany."

"Why do we and other states spend so much money on the tools of death and destruction when we lack funds for better roads and schools? To be influential in world affairs, shouldn't we rely less on military power and more on commerce, science, and diplomacy?"

"Why doesn't our influence better reflect our military and economic power? Our closest partners go their own ways. Even countries we aid spurn our recommendations. We opened our markets to Japan and China, but they block our exports with nontariff barriers. We have helped and even died for Muslim peoples—Kuwaitis, Bosnians, Kosovars, Afghans, Iraqis—but many Muslims hate us."

"To raise America's fitness, must others' well-being decline? Or can all peoples climb together?"

As usual, the President probes deeply. You promise her to survey the debate on what it means to be fit, to analyze how power translates into fitness and influence, and to outline the nature and distribution of power as it shapes up in the first quarter of the 21st century.

CONTENDING CONCEPTS AND EXPLANATIONS

HOW TO BE FIT—RUGGED INDIVIDUALISM OR MUTUAL AID?

You begin by reviewing the concept of **fitness**.[1] The theory of evolution teaches that the fittest organisms and species pass on their genes. By analogy, a fit society is one able to enhance and pass on its way of life. For organisms and societies, fitness may be thought of as an ability to cope with complexity, to survive challenges and make the most of opportunity.

In the late 19th century, Social Darwinists taught that the fittest survive thanks to rugged individualism. Imperialists agreed that strong races should rule the weak: "Might makes right."[2] This view of evolution is challenged by complexity science. It holds that survival depends not just on luck (correspondence between genetic mutations and environmental conditions), but also on a capacity for self-organization and mutual aid.[3] Applied to politics, this view suggests that Social Darwinists and ultrarealists are wrong: Outcomes are not determined by raw power plus cunning. Individuals and groups that cooperate among themselves and harmonize with their habitat have the best prospects to flourish. Egotistical self-seeking (like the logic of collective action, discussed in Chapter 1) can backfire or "blow back."[4] Many societies decline when members fail to pool their strengths for the common good. The two outlooks are summarized in Table 5.1.

A society that does not utilize the potential of all its members weakens its fitness. Discrimination against women, ethnic minorities, regions, or other groupings undermines total capabilities. A society that fails to support its frailest members cannot tap the genius, for example, of a Stephen Hawking, the physically disabled but brilliant holder of Newton's chair at Cambridge University.

A society at peace with itself, whose members believe their society just, is more likely to be fit than one roiled by internal strife or one where

Table 5.1 Who Is Fittest?

View of Human Evolution and IR	Survival Depends On
Social Darwinism and realpolitik	Individual strength in a mutual struggle for survival
Mutual help and interdependence	Ability of group to cooperate and adapt for mutual gain

1. For background, see *International Studies Quarterly* [special issue: "Evolutionary Paradigms in the Social Sciences"] 40, no. 3 (September 1996); for applications and an extensive bibliography, see Joshua M. Epstein and Robert Axtell, *Growing Artificial Societies: Social Science from the Bottom Up* (Cambridge, Mass.: MIT Press, 1996).

2. See Thomas Huxley, "The Struggle for Existence" (1888), and the reply by Petr Kropotkin, "Mutual Aid" (1902), both published in Kropotkin, *Mutual Aid: A Factor of Evolution* (Boston: Extending Horizons Books, 1955); see also Kropotkin, *Ethics, Origin and Development* (New York: Dial Press, 1924).

3. On coevolution and complexity, see Stuart A. Kauffman, *The Origins of Order: Self-Organization and Selection in Evolution* (New York: Oxford University Press, 1993); for applications of complexity theory to IR, see Walter C. Clemens, Jr., *The Baltic Transformed: Complexity Theory and European Security* (Lanham, Md.: Rowman & Littlefield, 2001) and bibliography at pp. 259–261. For a skeptical view of complexity theory, see John Horgan, *The End of Science: Facing the Limits of Knowledge in the Twilight of the Scientific Age* (Reading, Mass.: Addison-Wesley, 1996), chaps. 5–9. For a more balanced appraisal, see "Edge of Chaos" and other relevant entries in Ian Marshall and Danah Zohar, *Who's Afraid of Schrödinger's Cat: All the Science Ideas You Need to Keep Up With the New Thinking* (New York: Morrow, 1997).

4. See Chalmers Johnson, *Blowback: The Costs and Consequences of American Empire* (New York: Henry Holt, 2000).

repression achieves only a negative peace. Positive peace (discussed in Chapter 2) helps fitness.

Internal Fitness

One measure of fitness is **infant mortality**. The fewer babies that die in their first year, the fitter the society. Infant mortality reflects other fitness factors such as education and access to social services. Infant mortality declined worldwide in the late 20th century, but remained far higher in most poor countries than in the rich, as shown in Table 5.2. Health conditions were very problematic in the Commonwealth of Independent States (CIS—the Russian Federation, plus eleven other former Soviet republics). Infant mortality in the Russian Federation was 18 deaths per 1,000 live births in 2000—three times higher than the Organization for Economic Cooperation and Development (OECD) average (6), and six times the Swedish rate (3). In the United States the rate was seven, just above the average for high-income members of the OECD.

A broader indicator of fitness is the **human development index (HDI)** designed by the United Nations Development Programme to measure health, education, and income. Since HDI rankings are often skewed by gender, the UN Development Programme also developed indexes to measure differences between the sexes in HDI and in political participation.[5]

There are many other possible measures of fitness—for example, low crime and inflation rates. Even very fit societies have shortfalls. Most

Table 5.2 Infant Mortality Among Rich and Poor, Selected Years

	1970	2000
Developing countries	108	61
Least developed countries	148	98
Arab states	132	46
East Asia and the Pacific	87	33
Latin America and the Caribbean	86	30
South Asia	128	68
Sub-Saharan Africa	135	107
Central and Eastern Europe and the CIS*	34	20
OECD (First World) countries**	40	12

*Commonwealth of Independent States (former USSR except for Estonia, Latvia, and Lithuania)
**Organization for Economic Cooperation and Development
SOURCE: United Nations Development Programme, *Human Development Report 200* (New York: Oxford University Press, 2002), Table 8 and p. 177.
NOTE: Figures are deaths per 1,000 live births in first year.

5. UN Development Programme, *Human Development Report* (New York: Oxford University Press, annual).

Some Measures of Internal Fitness

GDP—gross domestic product is the value of all goods and services produced in the country, usually stated in U.S. dollars.

GDP per capita—average income (omits discrepancies among classes).

Real GDP per capita—PPP per capita, measured in the purchasing power of the local currency; also expressed in **BMT (Big Mac Time),** the number of minutes the average worker has to work to buy a Big Mac. In 1997, the numbers were as follows: Houston and Tokyo, 9; Hong Kong, 11; Toronto and New York, 12; Montreal and Zurich, 14; Copenhagen and Taipei, 20; Prague, 56; Mexico City, 71; Bombay, 85; Budapest, 91; Jakarta, 103; Moscow, 104; Caracas, 117; Nairobi, 193 (calculations by the Union Bank of Switzerland).

PPP—purchasing power parity is the number of units in a local currency (say, Swiss francs) needed to purchase the same basket of goods and services that a U.S. dollar would purchase in the United States.

The theory of PPP predicts that the exchange rate between two currencies should, in the long run, move toward the rate that equalizes the prices of identical bundles of traded goods and services in each country. The dollar should buy the same amount anywhere. In the short run, however, it does not—as shown by the Big Mac Index. *The Economist,* on April 19, 2001, reported that the average price of a Big Mac in the United States was $2.54. But in China, Malaysia, the Philippines, and South Africa, the price was less than $1.20. Their currencies were undervalued by more than 50 percent. The average price in the European Union (EU) was $2.27 at the prevailing 2001 exchange rate. This meant that the dollar was overvalued relative to the euro. True to the theory, the euro soon rose and surpassed the dollar in value.

But Big Mac Time gets to the consumer's bottom line better than any exchange index. In the late 1990s, the American had to work half as long as the Dane to buy a Big Mac, even if the U.S. currency was overvalued.

HDI—the human development index is based on three measures: life expectancy; educational attainment (adult literacy and combined primary, secondary, and tertiary enrollment); and PPP per capita.

HPI—the human poverty index measures poverty within a country based on percentages of people expected to die before age forty, illiterate adults, people without access to health services and safe water, and underweight children under age five.

GDI—the gender-related development index is the HDI, adjusted for gender.

GEM—the gender empowerment measure shows economic and political participation by gender.

Canadians live well, but many French speakers and Native Americans feel deprived. Japan and Sweden have low homicide but high suicide rates. Thanks to high life expectancy and education, countries such as Costa Rica, Belize, Cuba, and Sri Lanka rank high on the HDI even though their per capita incomes are modest. From limited economic resources they invest heavily in health and education.

Internal fitness also requires a strong life-support system. Harvesting trees on hillsides may produce good income this year but cause serious losses in the future. Environmental accounting, based on satellite surveys, suggests that in many countries the value of wealth lost in the 1990s (for example, topsoil) exceeds that of wealth produced. Quality as well as quantity is at stake: Japanese and Americans replant trees on many hillsides, but the new growth often lacks biodiversity.

Arias received the Nobel Peace Prize in 1987 for his efforts for peace in Nicaragua. He outlined a peace plan ("Esquipulas II") on a napkin in Washington's Mayflower Hotel in 1985, eight months before his election as president. It built on the efforts of the "Contadora" countries—Colombia, Mexico, Panama, and Venezuela—to promote dialogue between the Nicaraguan government and its opposition. Esquipulas II proposed a cease-fire, amnesty for the guerrillas, and a halt to foreign support for the Contra guerrillas. Pressure by Arias helped bring peace to Nicaragua in 1989 and later to El Salvador (1992) and Guatemala (1996). Criticized for his idealism, he replied that politicians have "an obligation to be dreamers . . . Quixotes. It is our obligation to want to change things."

Democratic and demilitarized (with no army since 1948), Costa Rica acquired a high level of fitness relative to most Latin American countries. Under Oscar Arias Sanchez, Costa Rica's president from 1986 to 1990, the country spent twenty times as much on education as on security. Arias renegotiated the country's foreign debt, highest in the world per capita when he took office.

What is key to high human development? Many scholars believe that "culture matters." This view is upheld by Table 5.3. It suggests that high HDI and GDI scores correlate strongly with political freedom and with the cultural traditions of Western civilization. There is less correlation with economic freedom and with "transparency" (honesty and openness) in business. What is most striking is that, except for Japan, all but one of the top twenty countries on the HDI and GDI derive either from the Protestant or Catholic variants of Western civilization. The highest-ranked country from Orthodox Christian traditions is Greece, 24; from Islamic, Brunei at 32; from Buddhist heritage, Thailand at 70; from Africa, Cape Verde at 100. Hindu–Muslim India is 124. Israel, sui generis, is 22. The highest-placed former Communist states are Slovenia at 28, and the Czech Republic, 33. The highest-placed Latin American country is Argentina, 34. In Chapters 10 through 12 we shall investigate further how and why cultural factors shape human development. Literacy and individual freedom, we shall see, have been crucial.

Table 5.3 The Highest-Ranked Countries in "Human Development" and Other Values from Various Civilizations

Country	HDI Rank (*n* = 173)	GDI Rank (*n* = 173)	Freedom Index	Economic Freedom Rank (*n* = 155)	Honesty Rank (*n* = 125)	Competitive Growth Rank 2002 (*n* = 80)	Cultural Tradition
Norway	1	3	Free	27 (MF)	10	9	Protestant
Canada	3	5	Free	18 (MF)	7	8	Catholic
Belgium	4	2	Free	19 (MF)	24	25	Catholic
United States	6	6	Free	6 (F)	16	1	Protestant
Japan	9	11	Free	35 (MF)	1	13	Japanese
Israel	22	22	Free	33 (MF)	16	19	Israeli
Hong Kong	23	23	N.A.	1 (F)	14	17	Mixed
Greece	24	25	Free	56 (MF)	42	38	Orthodox
Korea, Republic of	27	29	Free	52 (MF)	42	21	Mixed
Slovenia	29	27	Free	62 (MF)	34	28	Catholic
Brunei Darussalam	32	31	Not free	N.A.	N.A.	N.A.	Muslim
Argentina	34	33	Partly free	68 (MF)	57	63	Catholic
Estonia	42	N.A.	Free	6 (F)	28	26	Protestant
Cuba	55	N.A.	Not free	155 (RE)	N.A.	N.A.	Catholic
Belarus	56	50	Not free	151 (RE)	N.A.	N.A.	Orthodox
Malaysia	59	54	Partly free	72 (MU)	36	27	Muslim
Thailand	70	60	Free	40 (MF)	61	31	Buddhist
China	96	77	Not free	127 (MU)	57	33	Chinese
Cape Verde	100	82	Free	89 (MU)	N.A.	N.A.	African
South Africa	107	88	Free	44 (MF)	38	32	Mixed
Indonesia	110	91	Partly free	99 (MU)	88	67	Muslim–Hindu
India	124	105	Free	119 (MU)	71	48	Hindu–Muslim
Swaziland	125	103	Not free	72 (MU)	N.A.	N.A.	African

Code: for economic freedom, F = free; MF = mostly free; MU = mostly unfree; RE = repressed.
SOURCES: "HDI" and "GDI" are from UN Development Programme, *Human Development Report 2002* (New York: Oxford University Press, 2002), Tables 1 and 22. "Freedom Index" is from Freedom House at www.freedomhouse.org. "Economic Freedom" is from the Heritage Foundation at www.heritage.org. "Honesty Rank" is from Transparency International at www.transparency.org. Competitive Growth Rank 2002 from World Economic Forum, *Global Competitiveness Report 2002–2003* (New York: Oxford University Press, 2003).
N.A. = not available.

External Fitness

Fitness in foreign relations requires an ability to defend a society against external threats while preserving its way of life. External fitness depends upon internal fitness and vice versa. But there is no set formula for overall fitness. Both Costa Rica and Sweden, for example, demonstrate high domestic fitness. Each country has invested heavily in social welfare and has long avoided foreign wars. Costa Rica, however, spends almost nothing on defense, while Sweden spends heavily for military preparedness. Low defense expenditures do not assure domestic fitness, but neither do high defense outlays preclude it.

International System Fitness

The fitness of an international system can also be evaluated by its capacity to sustain life and help its members fulfill their potential. A world in which many people die needlessly lacks fitness. The world's wars in the 20th century killed at least 40 million people in combat, plus an equal or larger number of civilians (see Figure 4.1 and related statistics in the previous chapter). By some estimates, however, the total killed in the 20th century's armed conflicts was much higher—191 million.[6] Besides deaths caused by war, more than 100 million deaths were caused by authoritarian rule, as we shall see in Chapter 10. Even these tolls were probably surpassed by the damage to public health from underdevelopment, racial and ethnic discrimination, gender bias, and epidemics.[7] In 2002, life expectancy in AIDS-ravaged Zambia declined to thirty-three years—the lowest in the world. Average life expectancy continued to increase worldwide, but the state of the world's public health left much room for improvement. Given the resources available, it amounted to a scandal of global proportions.

The World Health Organization reported in 2002 that war deaths declined to about 310,000 per year in the late 1990s, but that their number was surpassed by suicides (815,000) and homicides (520,000) across the planet. Indeed, deaths from suicide approximated the total for battle deaths and homicide. All these rates, of course, varied sharply by region, country, and district. Colombia and El Salvador led the world in homicides—two or three times higher than third-place Russia. Russia's rate, in turn, was three times higher than the United States. Lithuania, Russia, and Latvia led in suicide. Levels of homicide and suicide, of course, were attributable more to local conditions than to the international system.

No World War III took place after 1945. The number of humans increased and their HDI rankings improved. Political participation became broader, for females as well as males. Every state—nearly 200 by the 1990s—had an equal vote in the UN General Assembly.

The international system early in the 21st century appeared robust but was also quite fragile.[8] Many analysts worried that humans would exhaust their life support system, the biosphere. A fifth of the population in some

6. World Health Organization, (Geneva, 2002), available at: *http://whqlibdoc.who.int/hq/2002/9241545615.pdf*

7. Assuming that the death toll from the 20th-century's wars amounted to 1.2 million lives per year (one-third less than the WHO estimate), Philip Morrison and Kosta Tsipis calculated what would amount to just over 2 percent of the total averaged death rate of 55 million per year. This would cut less than 1.5 years from the present world life expectancy of 65 years. Life expectancy in the U.S., however, grew by more than twenty years in the 20th century, with poor Americans living ten years less than middle and upper income groups, and Blacks living a few years less than Whites. See Morrison and Tsipis, *Reason Enough to Hope: America and the World in the Twenty-first Century* (Cambridge, Mass.: MIT Press, 1998), 26.

8. In November 2002, Israeli tourists found they could not stay in a seaside hotel in Kenya without being bombed or fly home without their plane being attacked by shoulder-held rockets. Once home in Israel, they would again face round after round of bomb attacks by Palestinians.

countries suffered from HIV. Malaria continued to kill more than 1 million persons each year. And if just a fraction of the world's nuclear arms were fired, World War II could look like a garden party. Millions would die and many millions become ill from the effects of radiation and pollution. Nuclear winter might set in.[9]

Coevolution: The Rise and Fall of Fitness Landscapes

What we call evolution is really **coevolution**. Every species and society coevolves with other species and their shared environment. Fitness can be assessed only in relative terms—relative to that of other actors and to a changing life support system. Survival depends upon internal mutation in tandem with a changing environment.

A fit society thrives on complexity, just as marine life teems on the cusp of the steep slope that leads from shallow, warm waters toward the cold currents of the depths. A very fit society can adapt to challenges— from drought and disease to hostile neighbors; a less fit society will cope poorly with domestic and external problems. Fit societies can process information efficiently and create values. These societies take hold and flourish in a life zone between unstable, random movement and an ultra-stable, rigid hierarchy.

A fit society finds resilience in a combination of many strengths coevolved to deal with a changing environment. Like a coral reef, its diverse members benefit from their interdependence. They exist in a symbiosis that nourishes individuals and shields the community from surging currents, extremes of cold and heat, and predators. In this kind of emergent structure, everything is both a means and an end.[10] The society becomes self-organizing—in political terms, it practices self-rule (democracy). Mutual gain produces and benefits from such complexity, as outlined in Figure 5.1.

Like the species coexisting within an ecosystem, human communities—locally or globally—may cultivate a fitness that gives stability to their way of life. Mutual gain may result from each member doing what it does best, as though guided by an "invisible hand."[11] But it can also flow from wise, far-sighted policies. Either way, fitness benefits from cooperation. By this logic, we should not be surprised that the U.S. and Swiss constitutions are among the world's oldest. Less fit systems have come and gone. In political life as in business, long-term fitness and "profit" come from creating value—not from exploitation.

We can picture fitness as a peak rising from a plain.[12] If *A* is a truly fit society, its peak will tower like the Matterhorn; if *B* is an unfit society, its

Fig. 5.1 Exploitation, Mutual Gain, and Fitness: Likely Linkages

9. Using just 299 nuclear warheads in a "counterenergy attack," Russia could cripple U.S. oil supplies and networks and the manufacturing and transportation systems that depend on them. Though the attack focused on energy, 20 million Americans would die. Morrison and Tsipis, *Reason Enough*, 35.

10. Society is more than a mechanical device in which the parts exist only for one another, but is less than an organism in which the parts exist for one another and by means of one another.

11. Adam Smith's term, in *The Wealth of Nations* (1776), discussed in Chapter 11.

12. On the structure of rugged fitness landscapes, see Kauffman, *Origins of Order*, chaps. 2–3.

"peak" will be a low mound. If *B* becomes more fit, its mound will rise. Each actor's peak, however, reflects external security as well as internal health. If *A*'s peak rises in ways threatening to *B*, the latter's fitness may suffer and its peak decline. But if actors cooperate for mutual gain, each of their peaks may rise. Free trade among Mexico, Canada, and the United States seeks to push all three North American peaks upward.[13]

HOW DOES POWER RELATE TO FITNESS AND TO INFLUENCE?

Fitness and power can build upon one another. **Power** includes basic resources, economic strength, political cohesion, military strength, brain power, culture, and alignment with international institutions. If used well, these assets contribute to fitness at home and abroad.

Power is the potential to actualize—to get things done, to claim or create values, to be fit and to influence others.[14] Unless power is used effectively, it will not enhance fitness or influence.

Power assets differ in their **fungibility**—the extent to which they can be interchanged with other assets. For Christopher Columbus, spices and gold were highly fungible; in today's markets, dollars and yen are more useful. One of the most fungible assets is information.

To actualize power—make real its potential—it must pass from the latent stage, through the mobilized or developed stage, and into the kinetic stage. **Kinetic power** is power in motion. Table 5.4 illustrates how different kinds of power transit these three stages.

Power is not the same as **influence**. Power is potential. Power can be a cause. Influence is an effect. To influence others is to sway their minds and affect their behavior. Influence is difficult to measure. A behavioral

13. If a landscape is too smooth or too rugged, its occupants may fail to achieve their full potential. This concept of fitness echoes the theory of Arnold Toynbee: that civilizations rise and fall in response to an optimum or an excessive challenge. See Toynbee, *A Study of History*, 12 vols. (New York: Oxford University Press, 1934–1961).

14. From Latin *poentia* we get "potential," "potent," and "power"—similar to French *pouvoir. Might* in English corresponds to *macht* in German and *moshchnost'* (capability) in Russian. As noted in Chapter 1, note 1, *dynamics*—that which makes something move—probably derives from the Indo-European *deu*, which also gives us us "do".

Table 5.4 Three Stages of Power Realization

Domain	Stage 1: Latent	Stage 2: Developed and Mobilized	Stage 3: Kinetic
Agriculture	Fertile soil	Cultivated fields	Harvested grain being eaten
Minerals	Oil deposits	Oil being pumped and refined	Fuel being converted to energy
Communications	Power lines	PC modems connected to a network	Internet operating on-line
Military	Available recruits	Soldiers trained and ready to move	Soldiers attacking

measure of influence would show the extent to which the United States, for example, can alter the behavior of Mexico and Venezuela. We might review how often these countries voted with the United States at the United Nations. But more study would be needed to learn whether Mexico City and Caracas voted as they did for their own reasons or in response to pressure from Washington—or vice versa.

States and other IR actors try to influence one another using a wide range of instruments and techniques.[15] They negotiate using "hard" and "soft" power. **Hard power** is the ability to coerce others (by force) and command (by threat). Hard power uses mainly tangible assets, such as military, economic, and geographic resources, but can also employ intangibles, such as scarce information. **Soft power** is the ability to inspire consensus (agreement) and to coopt (persuade others to share the same goals). **Conversion power** is the ability to translate hard and soft power into fitness and influence.[16]

A hard-liner seeks influence by coercion and command, often supplemented by deception. Gains from this approach are unstable, however, because exploitation provokes resistance; deception, when discovered, yields a boomerang effect. Both the win–win and the conditional cooperator seek consensus and cooption. If they succeed, cooperation may become a stable, emergent property—a "security community" like that evolved from the Marshall Plan. The conditional cooperator, however, may also use hard power if cooperation fails.

The simplest method to measure power is the **bean count**—summing and comparing assets such as people, rifles, and PCs. The bean count, even if accurate, leaves open many vital questions: What is the quality of the asset being counted? Its availability? Location? Can it be replaced?

Let us analyze some key ingredients of power and examine the debates about how to assess each factor.

Basic Resources. A country's physical setting—its location, climate, size, shape, and resources—provides a foundation for its economic and political life. How physical spaces relate to politics is the focus of political geography.[17]

Is there an ideal physical space? No. Humans can prosper in many settings. Great states have been anchored to rivers (Babylon, Egypt), islands (Crete, Java), deserts (Arabia, the Silk Road), jungles (Yucatán, Cambodia), as well as to temperate climes (Europe, North America). Size is not critical. Small city-states (ancient Athens, medieval Venice, today's Singapore) have achieved power and influence, but so have medium-sized states (Germany) and large empires (Mongolia). Raw materials are not essential if they can be imported or substituted by technology.

Who or What Influenced Whom?

In 1993, Venezuela staked out activist positions in support of Bosnia. Working with Pakistan and several other non-aligned delegations on the UN Security Council, Venezuela pushed through resolutions 819 and 824, establishing "safe areas" in Bosnia. Venezuela also campaigned, unsuccessfully, for lifting the arms embargo against Bosnia. The United States in the next two years became much more active in support of Bosnia. Who or what influenced whom? Did Venezuela influence the United States or did Washington listen to its own drummer?

These questions imply that countries or governments influence one another. We should also look at individuals. Venezuela's permanent representative to the United Nations, Diego Arria, had strong views and a persuasive manner. If another person had represented Venezuela, its UN delegation might have been less supportive of Bosnia.

15. See, for example, Russell J. Leng, "Influence Techniques Among Nations," in *Behavior, Society, and International Conflict*, 3 vols., eds. Philip E. Tetlock et al. (New York: Oxford University Press, 1991–1993), 3: 71–125.

16. Adapted from Joseph S. Nye, Jr., *Bound to Lead: The Changing Nature of American Power* (New York: Basic Books, 1990).

17. See Nurit Kliot and Stanley Waterman, eds., *The Political Geography of Conflict and Peace* (London: Belhaven Press, 1991); Martin Ira Glassner, *Political Geography* (New York: Wiley, 1993); and Saul B. Cohen, *Geography and Politics in a World Divided*, 2d ed. (New York: Oxford University Press, 1973).

Holland, England, and Japan became prosperous without a rich resource base. The same resource can be both an asset and a liability. Thus, China's large population assures a large supply of workers for every task, but they must be fed and housed on limited land.

The IR student and diplomat must not only know political geography, but must also be able to distinguish fact from myth. Today's geopolitical certainty often becomes tomorrow's absurdity. Analysts may lapse into "environmental determinism" by exaggerating the importance of a single factor such as oil or weather. Geopolitical thinking can also be twisted by self-centered ambition. For example, ancient Chinese saw their "Middle Kingdom" as the hub of the universe. Similarly, most U.S. maps show the Americas at the center of the world. Like statistics, maps are selective. They can illuminate or mislead.[18]

How geography conditions IR is sometimes called **geopolitics**. Soviet and U.S. leaders often justified their Cold War policies by reference to political geography—for example, to the importance of controlling the "heartland" or marine "choke points."[19] Both sides viewed the planet as a chessboard where the loss of even the smallest piece could decide the game.

But geopolitics can serve peace as well as war. Its assumptions can rationalize a tough realpolitik, but critical geography in tune with ecology underscores mutual vulnerability and the need for cooperation.

Economic Strength. Economic power undergirds military, cultural, and other forms of power. **Economic statecraft** uses rewards and penalties

18. On postmodern and poststructuralist geography, see John Paul Jones III et al., eds., *Postmodern Contentions: Epochs, Politics, Space* (New York: Guilford, 1993), and other Guilford books on mappings.

19. See Colin S. Gray, *The Geopolitics of the Nuclear Era: Heartland, Rimland, and the Technological Revolution* (New York: Crane, Russak & Co., 1977); Zbigniew Brzezinski, *Game Plan: A Geostrategic Framework for the Conduct of the U.S.–Soviet Contest* (Boston and New York: Atlantic Monthly Press, 1986); and Brzezinski, *The Grand Chessboard: American Primacy and Its Geostrategic Imperatives* (New York: Basic Books, 1997).

Geopolitics: Science, Policy, or Propaganda?

Whether true or false, geopolitical beliefs can shape or rationalize policy. Geopolitics took root in 19th-century universities and helped inspire imperialist expansion. From London to Tokyo, aspiring imperialists drew on theories of geopolitics and Social Darwinism to justify expansionist policies. German professors asserted Germany's need to unify German speakers and give them *Lebensraum* ("living space"). Japanese geopoliticians assayed the raw materials of neighboring countries. British and U.S. advocates of big navies stressed the role of sea power in history.

As the Versailles treaty was debated in 1919, British geographer Sir Halford Mackinder warned his countrymen not to depend upon sea power alone. Whoever controls Eastern Europe, he argued, could dominate the entire Eurasian land mass (or **World Island**):

> Who rules East Europe commands the Heartland:
> Who rules the Heartland commands the World Island:
> Who rules the World Island commands the World.

Similar views were voiced by German geopoliticans in the 1930s as Hitler planned his eastward march and by Kremlin spokesmen in 1968 when Soviet forces invaded Czechoslovakia.

American geographer Nicholas J. Spykman in 1942 provided a rationale for U.S. containment policy: "Who controls the Rimland rules Eurasia, who rules Eurasia controls the destinies of the world." Technology shortened distances, but Washington sought to keep Moscow from dominating the World Island—its heartland or its rimland.

to shape other states' behavior. Positive rewards include lowered tariffs, subsidized trade, aid, and investment guarantees. Negative sanctions may entail boycotts, tariff increases, trade quotas, dumping of surpluses, preclusive buying, freezing of assets, and aid cutoffs.[20]

Geonomics (or "geo-economics")[21] contends that economic factors have replaced geopolitics (understood as geography plus military power) as the material basis for IR. One view is that **trading states**, whose wealth and influence are based on international commerce and not on territorial extent or military might, have supplanted militarized states as influential actors in world affairs.[22] Geoeconomic power, some analysts say, requires the government to foster key industries at home and internationally.[23]

Political Leadership and Cohesion. All other components of power come to naught unless a society has good leadership and the body politic holds together—even under stress. Conversion power also depends on leadership and cohesion.

Leadership is key to the design and implementation of effective policies. Good leadership can work wonders with meager resources; bad management wastes rich resources.

Political cohesion boosts a government's extraction capability—its ability to tax and mobilize assets for public purposes. Extraction capability is part of conversion power. If two societies are equal in GDP and GDP per capita, that with the higher extraction rate can field more resources. But a high extraction capability may merely postpone defeat (as happened to Germany and Japan in World War II) if the other side commands far more resources.[24]

Political cohesion also contributes to **cost tolerance**—a society's ability to endure hardship. The ultimate victor in any competition must be able to persist despite pain and sacrifice. A study of forty wars showed that almost half were won by the party that suffered more than its antagonist.[25]

Do leadership, cohesion, extraction capability, and cost-tolerance develop more readily under authoritarian or democratic rule? There is no formula. Good leadership and strong cohesion—and their opposites—are possible whether a society is ruled from the top down or bottom up.

Military Strength. To prevail in war, it is useful to have every asset—hard, soft, and conversion power. But the optimal blend of military strengths depends upon circumstances—on time and place, the mission, the adversary, the available technology, and other factors as well.

20. See David A. Baldwin, *Economic Statecraft* (Princeton, N.J.: Princeton University Press, 1985), 41–42.

21. In Greek *geo* means "earth," *ekos* means "house" or "habitat," and *nemein* means "management."

22. Richard Rosecrance, *The Rise of the Trading State: Commerce and Conquest in the Modern World* (New York: Basic Books, 1986).

23. See Edward N. Luttwak, *The Endangered American Dream: How to Stop the United States from Becoming a Third-World Country and How to Win the Geo-Economic Struggle for Industrial Supremacy* (New York: Simon & Schuster, 1993). For a different perspective see Jagdish Bhagwati, *The World Trading System at Risk* (Princeton, N.J.: Princeton University Press, 1991). See also below Chapters 11 and 12.

24. Jacek Kugler and William Domke, "Comparing the Strength of Nations," *Comparative Political Studies* 19, no. 1 (April 1986): 39–69 at 51.

25. Steven Rosen, "War and Power and the Willingness to Suffer," in *Peace, War, and Numbers*, ed. Bruce Russett (Beverly Hills, Calif.: Sage, 1972), 166–183 at 175.

Paradoxes: The Bear and the Porcupine

Despite its great mass, the Russian "bear" astride its broad plain has often been attacked. Switzerland, on the other hand, is a prickly porcupine in a mountain fortress; though small and centrally located, Switzerland has not been invaded since Napoleon. Russians are resource-rich but poor; the Swiss have modest resources but are rich. Russians have long been anxious about their place in the world; the Swiss, confident. Russians have often intervened militarily abroad; the Swiss have not threatened others for hundreds of years. The Swiss have converted their power assets far more efficiently than the Russians. How they profited from World War II and the Holocaust, however, is another matter.

If resources are tight, is it wiser to invest in men or machines? There are few guidelines valid for all time. We know that Hitler's "lightning war" skirted French forts but stalled in Russia's frozen vastness. Trying to buttress Soviet cohesion, Stalin assured his subjects that Hitler's surprise attack gave Germany only a transitory advantage. War, said Stalin, pits entire societies against each other, testing all their strengths and weaknesses. Though he implied that people could best machines, Stalin also ordered a crash program to develop atomic bombs.

Lessons from a previous war can mislead. The U.S.'s first computer-guided "smart bombs" failed in Vietnamese jungles, but later versions proved more effective against targets in Iraqi deserts.[26] They were even more effective in the 2001–2002 Afghan campaign. Insights from such wars, however, gave no lessons to policy makers trying to neutralize terrorist cells or restore order to divided societies such as Bosnia.

Brain Power. Brain power is key to unleashing all other power. It includes education (mass and elite), science, technology, information, and communication. Brain power helps societies to avoid both stagnation and chaos while adapting to complexity. The ability to acquire and use information can help actors to adjust and innovate more efficiently than their rivals. An Information Revolution seems to be supplanting the Agricultural and Industrial Revolutions. Information technology depends upon human capital, universities, and a stable supply of electricity.[27]

Education, like a strong economic base, provides the foundation from which other assets may derive. The educated citizen can invent, utilize, repair, and improve the means of production and destruction. As we see in Table 5.5, several countries that ranked high in HDI invested heavily in education but not in defense, for example, Norway and Canada. The United States and Israel invested heavily in both. Greece, Singapore, Russia, Turkey, and Pakistan spent more on defense than on education. Affluent Singapore could afford both books and guns, but the others suffered from the burden of defense.

Users of modern libraries and the Internet are deluged with information. But bits and bytes must be analyzed to become knowledge. And knowledge must be refined—perhaps nurtured by compassion and empathy—to become wisdom.

To develop and apply brain power, a society needs many assets in combination: the leisure and wealth to pursue knowledge + a critical mass of knowledge-seeking individuals and organizations + the means to collect and analyze data + the freedom to reflect on and debate their implications + the wisdom, freedom, and opportunity to apply what has

26. In the Gulf War the kill rate was not "one bomb, one target," as some Pentagon reports claimed. The ratio was more like "four bombs, one target"—still a very high rate.

27. *The Global Competitiveness Report 1997* (Cologny, Switzerland: World Economic Forum, 1997), 59–65.

been learned + mechanisms for corrective feedback. This blend is not easy to attain. Soviet scientists, for example, achieved many scientific and engineering breakthroughs but lacked intellectual freedom and free markets in which to introduce innovations. Indeed, the Soviet government blocked direct-dial telephones and limited fax machines to prevent easy access to the outside world. Such lags are not readily overcome. Ranked by availability of information technology in 1997, Russia and Ukraine placed just above India, Poland, and China.[28]

Computerization is a by-product and probably a source of knowledge and wealth. But modem access does not correlate perfectly with high incomes. In 2000, the OECD countries, on average, had 120 Internet hosts per capita, but the United States had 295; next came Iceland with 144; followed by Norway, Finland, and the Netherlands with 102. But other economic giants—Germany, Singapore, and Japan—had far fewer hosts per capita. Italy, with one of the world's largest GDPs, had fewer Internet hosts (17) than Estonia (28), the most computerized of the former Communist states.[29]

Among people with access to the Internet, men were more likely to use it than women; Internet awareness was lower among women than men in Latin America and southern Europe. The number of Chinese owning PCs shot up at a fast rate in the 1990s from a low base. But in 2000, China had just 0.1 Internet hosts per capita. India, though the city of Bangalore was a world center for computer programming, had even fewer than China.

Some educators believe that the Internet can complement, reinforce, and enhance traditional approaches to learning. Others speculate that it lowers critical abilities and reading skills. Whatever its contribution to education, the Internet opens vast political opportunities—from instant plebiscites to organized resistance to central authority. In the late 1990s, the Web served opposition journalists in Yugoslavia as a vital tool for circumventing the government's monopoly on news. In the 2000 presidential elections, when opposition activists hoped to defeat President Slobodan Milošević at the polls, the Internet became an important organizing tool. The Web site run by radio station B-92 received an average of more than 500,000 visitors a month. The station called itself "the focus of an on-line community concerned with the struggle for democratization." More than 20,000 subscribers signed up for daily e-mail news updates, which were also printed and handed around, helping replace the independent newspapers, burdened by increasing government restrictions. When the Yugoslav army closed

Table 5.5 How HDI Correlates with Education and Defense Expenditures

HDI Ranking and Country	Education as Percentage of GNP	Defense as Percentage of GDP
1. Norway	7.7	1.8
2. Sweden	8.3	2.1
3. Canada	6.9	1.2
6. United States	5.4	3.1
9. Japan	3.6	1.0
13. UK	5.3	2.5
22. Israel	7.6	8.0
24. Greece	3.1	4.9
25. Singapore	3.0	4.8
27. South Korea	3.7	2.8
60. Russia	3.5	4.0
85. Turkey	2.2	4.9
96. China	2.3	2.1
124. India	3.2	2.4
138. Pakistan	2.7	4.5
Low-income average	2.9	
Middle income	3.5	
Low and middle income	3.4	
High income	4.8	

NOTE: Education expenditure data are from 1995–1997. Defense expenditure data are from 2000.
SOURCE: *HDR 2002*, Table 17; World Bank, *World Development Report 2003* (New York: Oxford University Press, 2002), Table 2.1.

28. *Global Competitiveness Report 1997*, 60.
29. UNDP, *HDR 2002*, Table 11.

The CIA collaborated with Peru under a $1.3 billion "Plan Colombia" aimed at staunching drug supplies from Latin America. In April 2001, a Peruvian Air Force jet shot down a Cessna hydroplane carrying American missionaries. The Peruvians mistook the Cessna, one of five civilian craft regularly flying from Iquitos, for a plane used by cocaine smugglers. Having forced the Cessna to crash in the Amazon River, the Peruvians continued their machinegun attack, killing a mother and her baby and wounding the pilot. Villagers in canoes then rescued the pilot and two other survivors.

CIA observers flying nearby in a Citation-5 leased from the Pentagon had monitored the Peruvian jet. "Our role was to simply pass on information," said President Bush. "Our government is involved with helping our friends in South America identify airplanes that might be carrying illegal drugs." The U.S. Embassy in Lima explained, "U.S. radar and aircraft provide tracking information to the Peruvian Air Force on planes suspected of smuggling illegal drugs in the region. U.S. government tracking aircraft . . . are unarmed and do not participate in any way in shooting down suspect planes."

The incident raised questions about American wisdom as well as fitness. Could the war on drugs be won abroad? Would not "victory" require reducing—or ignoring—demand within the United States?

30. U.S. diplomats gained when cryptographers broke Japan's diplomatic code in 1922. Washington and London intercepted and decoded many German and Japanese messages during World War II.

31. In 1990s Washington spookspeak HUMINT stood for "human intelligence"; SIGINT for "signal intelligence"; MASINT for "measurement and signature intelligence," as from acoustic and seismic sensors; RUNINT for rumors; and FUSS for "Fleet Undersea Surveillance System."

32. Allen Welsh Dulles, *The Craft of Intelligence* (1963), analyzed in Thomas Powers, *The Man Who Kept the Secrets: Richard Helms and the CIA* (New York: Knopf, 1979), 342, n. 51; see also Gregory F. Treverton, *Covert Action: The Limits of Intervention in the Postwar World* (New York: Basic Books, 1987), 11.

33. The CIA planned to assassinate dozens of individuals in Guatemala in 1954, but this proved unnecessary. For a review of a memoir and documents relating to such operations, see Theodore Draper, "Is the CIA Necessary?" *New York Review of Books*, August 14, 1997, 18–22.

down B-92's Web site and seized its equipment in 1999, B-92 managed to stay on-line thanks to a Dutch Internet service provider that hosted the Yugoslav site free of charge.

One aspect of brain power is intelligence—information about other IR actors. Good intelligence collection and interpretation can make a weak power strong; faulty intelligence can undercut strength.[30] Useful information may come from spies, open sources such as publications, and machines that watch and listen.[31] "Gentlemen do not open each other's mail," said U.S. Secretary of State Henry Stimson in 1929. But Allen Dulles, for many years director of the Central Intelligence Agency (CIA), later replied: "When the fate of a nation and the lives of its soldiers are at stake, gentlemen do read each other's mail—when they can get their hands on it."[32]

The track record of U.S. intelligence has been mixed. As we saw in Chapter 3, U.S. planners benefited greatly from information provided by reconnaissance flights and from sources within the USSR, such as Colonel Penkovsky. On the other hand, the CIA often misled the White House about Cuba and the USSR. Ostensible CIA successes in overthrowing governments, as in Iran in 1953 and Guatemala in 1954, netted long-term difficulties for all parties.[33] In the 1980s and 1990s, the CIA had so many problems—traitors, "moles," toadies, and whitewashers—that some experts said the United States would have been better off with no intelligence service at all. In the years and months before

September 11, 2001, the CIA and FBI had many signs that terrorists would strike, but they failed to "connect the dots."

The most expensive kind of intelligence comes from satellites and electronic snooping. After the USSR's demise, Americans debated whether they should continue to spend some $28 billion per year to support intelligence gathering and clandestine operations against other states. Should government limit itself to research and halt operations such as coups and other "dirty tricks"? Should all intelligence work, long scattered across the State, Defense, and Commerce Departments and the CIA, be merged? Should the CIA focus on geonomic challenges rather than security issues? If the CIA collects proprietary information, should it be shared with private firms? If so, which firms—and how? Should the United States spy on Japanese or French competitors—risking alliances for commerce? Or should Americans learn what they need from newspapers and trade journals? Virtually all useful information, George F. Kennan wrote, could be gleaned from open sources. Spying is bad for its authors as well as their victims because it produces unlimited cynicism.[34] Given the growth of international crime and terrorism, other observers countered, the United States could not bring its spies in from the cold.[35] After 9/11, many critics said the CIA had become too deskbound and too dependent on machines. It needed agents in the field able to speak the local tongue and penetrate terrorist cells. But the ultimate need was for analysis and wisdom. The United States, like other countries, required analysts and decision makers who could make sense of all the bits and bytes and set out a wise course of action.

Universal Culture. If a country's way of life and values seem legitimate to others, this adds to soft power to persuade and coopt. The United States gained influence in the Cold War competition because its path, charted by Adam Smith and John Locke, had more worldwide appeal than the Communist ways endorsed by Karl Marx and Vladimir Lenin. The United States gained also because Coke, Levis, and Hollywood had greater allure than Stolichnaya vodka, fur hats, or the Bolshoi Ballet. But the appeal of Western culture is often superficial. Devotion to "Magna Macs" does not assure respect for the Magna Carta. A taste for jeans and Marlboros is no endorsement for U.S. views on human rights.

International Institutions. The structure and policies of international institutions are shaped by the dominant actors. The United States gained in the Cold War because the world's major economic institutions—the World Bank, the International Monetary Fund (IMF), and the General Agreement on Tariffs and Trade—harmonized with U.S. preferences for

Navajo Code

Not all codes require expensive machinery. During World War II, Navajos serving with U.S. forces in the Pacific sent messages to one another in their own language—an undecipherable code to the Japanese.

34. George F. Kennan, "Spy & Counterspy," *The New York Times*, May 18, 1997, op-ed.

35. David Fromkin, "Daring Amateurism: The CIA's Social History," *Foreign Affairs* 75, no. 1 (January–February 1996): 165–172.

free markets and free trade. (See Chapters 11 and 12 for discussion of these institutions.) States whose values conflict with prevailing institutions must struggle harder just to survive. The USSR stood apart—isolated and self-isolated—from the World Bank and IMF for most of the Cold War. In the UN Security Council, the USSR cast its veto more often than the other four permanent members because Moscow often was the odd man out. Between 2001 and 2002, however, the Bush administration often took this role for the United States as Washington spurned one international institution after another, for example, the International Criminal Court.

COMPARING THEORY AND REALITY: POWER AND INFLUENCE IN 2000

FROM EMPIRES TO GLOBAL COMPETITORS

Five great empires collapsed in the first two decades of the 20th century—the Chinese, Russian, Ottoman, Austro-Hungarian, and German. The Italian, Nazi, and Japanese empires perished in World War II. Most of the Dutch, French, British, and Portuguese empires had disappeared by the mid-1970s. The Soviet empire perished between 1989 and 1991. The United States controlled several islands but otherwise had no formal empire. Its global influence was indirect, based largely on economic and "soft" power.

In the late 1990s and early 21st century, most of the rich industrial countries grew at about 2.5 percent per year, except for Japan, which stagnated. Many developing countries, led by China, grew at two or three times that rate. Africa, however, grew little faster than its population increase. The former Second World had a negative growth rate after the fall of communism, but entered onto positive ground in the late 1990s.

The world's richest states at century's end did not have large imperial holdings. They competed with one another but were also partners. Their fitness peaks rose in tandem. The most competitive had institutions that cultivated long-term growth in the global economy. Of 80 countries ranked by the World Economic Forum in 2002, the top twenty were the United States, Finland, Taiwan, Singapore, Sweden, Switzerland, Australia, Canada, Norway, Denmark, the UK, Iceland, Japan, Germany, the Netherlands, New Zealand, Hong Kong, Austria, Israel, and—the highest in Latin America—Chile. Of EU states, Greece and Italy were least competitive (38 and 39), ranked just below Trinidad and Tobago (37). Of former Communist countries, Estonia and Slovenia placed highest—26th and 28th, while China placed 33rd and Russia 64th. Poorly governed Zimbabwe and Haiti came last—79th and 80th. Ten countries climbed by four or more places from 2001 to 2002—Taiwan, Sweden, Switzerland, Denmark, Japan, Israel, Chile, Lithuania, India, and Colombia. But many others fell by four or more ranks—New Zealand, Hong Kong, Ireland, Belgium, Italy, Costa Rica, Slovakia, Poland, Jamaica, the Philippines, Argentina, Vietnam, Romania, Venezuela, Turkey, Guatemala, Educador, Honduras, Ukraine, Bolivia, and Zimbabwe.[36]

WHO HAS WHAT: THE PYRAMID OF POWER

The pattern of power at the onset of the 21st century resembled a pyramid, as in Figure 5.2. Each unit in the pyramid can be ranked by military, economic, and cultural power. The United States is preeminent in all three, and therefore stands at the apex. The great powers in the second rung are strong in two kinds of power but preeminent in none.[37]

No other country or coalition could rival the America's combined hard and soft power as the third millennium began. American popular culture influenced tastes the world over, while U.S. space vehicles sent back images from Mars. English was the world's lingua franca for commerce, transportation, and science; it also ruled the Internet. The Internet, like television, spread an American way of looking at the world. In 1997, the Iraqi newspaper *Al-Jumhuriya* denounced the Internet as "the end of civilizations, cultures, interests, and ethics"—as "another American means to enter every house in the world." The paper charged that Americans "want to become the only source for controlling human beings in the new electronic village." Not surprisingly, the Internet was not readily accessible in Iraq.

Table 5.6 traces changes in the parameters of power for the world's major powers from 1776 to the 21st century.[38] It shows the steady advance of the United States in most domains over some 225 years. Other actors rose and fell. The Ottoman Empire was a major actor in 1776 but disappeared after World War I. Great Britain led the world in 1776 but gradually weakened relative to other actors. Germany was ascendant in 1914 and again in 1939. After World War II, however, no single European power could rival the United States or USSR. By 1962, the USSR achieved high or medium strength in many domains, only to disappear in 1991. By 2000, the Russian Federation was still high only in natural resources—minerals and forests—and nuclear missiles. By 2000, Europe as a whole gradually became quite powerful in most respects. Lacking a strong overall government, however, Europe lacked conversion power. Japan seemed to have plateaued, but China was rising. How China, Europe, and the United States may interact in the rest of the 21st century is discussed in Chapter 16.

Fig. 5.2 The Pyramid of Power ca. A.D. 2000

Superpower:
United States

Great Powers:
Japan, China, Germany, Russia

Medium Powers:
UK, France, India, Italy

Potential Great Powers:
EU, Kazakhstan, Ukraine

Regional Powers:
Argentina, Brazil, Egypt, Indonesia, Iran, Iraq, Israel, Pakistan South Africa, South Korea, Taiwan

36. World Economic Forum, *Global Competitiveness Report 2002–2003* (New York: Oxford University Press, 2003).

37. See Brian Nichiporuk, "Pivotal Power: America in the 1990s," MIT Defense and Arms Control Studies Working Paper, Cambridge, Mass., May 1991; for another approach, see Lars-Erik Cederman, "Emergent Polarity: Analyzing State-Formation and Power Politics," *International Studies Quarterly* 38, no. 4 (December 1994): 501–533.

38. The table builds upon the methodology in Joseph S. Nye, Jr., *Bound to Lead: The Changing Nature of American Power* (New York: Basic Books, 1990). The rankings represent the author's (W.C.'s) evaluations of power in each era informed by statistical surveys in *The Statesman's Year-Book* (London, annual), the World Bank, the International Institute for Strategic Studies, and the CIA. For economic history, see Paul Bairoch's works, such as "International Industrialization Levels from 1750 to 1980," *Journal of European Economic History*, 11 (1982) and Paul Kennedy, *The Rise and Fall of the Great Powers: Economic Change and Military Conflict from 1500 to 2000* (New York: Random House, 1987) and its bibliography.

Table 5.6 Parameters of Power, 1776–2000 (H = high strength; M = medium strength; L = low strength)

	Actor	Basic Resources	Economic Power	Political Cohesion	Military Power	Brain Power	International Institutions	Fitness at Home	External Fitness
1776 **U.S. Declaration** **of** **Independence**	U.S.	H	L	M	L	H	L	M	L
	Russia	H	L	L	M	L	M	L	M
	Prussia	M	L	M	M	M	M	M	M
	Britain	M	H	M	H	H	H	M	H
	Japan	L	L	M	L	L	L	L	L
	China	M	L	L	L	L	L	L	L
	Ottoman Empire	H	M	L	M	L	M	L	L
1914 **Eve of** **World War I**	U.S.	H	H	M	L	H	M	M	M
	Russia	H	M	L	M	M	M	L	M
	Germany	M	H	H	H	H	M	H	H
	Britain	M	H	M	H	H	H	M	H
	Japan	L	M	H	M	M	L	M	M
	China	M	L	L	L	L	L	L	L
	Ottoman Empire	M	L	L	M	L	L	L	L
1939 **Eve of** **World War II**	U.S.	H	M	M	M	H	M	M	M
	USSR	H	M	L	M	H	M	M	M
	Germany	M	H	H	H	H	M	H	H
	Britain	M	M	M	M	M	H	M	M
	Japan	M	M	H	M	H	L	M	M
	China	M	L	L	L	M	L	L	L
1962 **Cuban** **missile crisis**	U.S.	H	H	H	H	H	H	H	H
	USSR	H	M	M	H	M	M	M	H
	European Community	M	M	M	M	M	H	M	M
	Japan	L	M	H	L	M	L	M	L
	China	M	L	M	M	L	L	L	L
1976 **After the** **Vietnam War**	U.S.	H	H	M	H	H	H	M	H
	USSR	H	M	M	H	M	L	M	H
	European Community	M	H	M	M	H	H	H	M
	Japan	L	M	H	L	M	M	M	L
	China	M	L	M	M	L	L	L	L

Table 5.6 Parameters of Power, 1776–2000 (H = high strength; M = medium strength; L = low strength) *continued*

	Actor	Basic Resources	Economic Power	Political Cohesion	Military Power	Brain Power	International Institutions	Fitness at Home	External Fitness
1990 **After the** **Afghan War**	U.S.	H	H	M	H	H	H	M	H
	USSR	H	L	L	H	M	M	L	M
	European Community	H	H	M	M	H	H	M	M
	Japan	L	H	H	M	H	M	H	M
	China	M	M	M	M	M	L	L	M
2000 **After the** **Gulf War, the** **dissolution of** **the USSR, and** **the wars in** **Bosnia and** **Kosovo**	U.S.	H	H	M	H	H	H	M	H
	Russian Federation	H	L	L	M	M	M	L	M
	European Union	M	H	M	M	H	H	M	M
	Japan	L	H	H	M	H	M	H	M
	China	M	M	M	M	M	L	L	M

Economic Strength. At the onset of the 21st century, the United States produced more than one-fourth of the world's goods and services—its prevailing share since about 1900, except after World War II when the United States produced nearly half of the world's GDP. As Europe and Japan recovered in the late 1940s and 1950s, the relative weight of the U.S. economy declined but then held steady at 20 to 30 percent of world GDP. In 2000, a country with just 4 percent of the world's population produced and consumed more than one-fourth of its wealth. Its GDP was twice the size of Japan's, four times Germany's, and eight times China's. Despite its slowdown in 2000–2002 and huge stock market losses, the U.S. economy was judged by the World Economic Forum to be the world's most competitive in 2002. America's quality of life, however, did not equal its wealth. The country ranked sixth in HDI.

Let us look more closely at the strong and weak aspects of the U.S. economy.[39] GDP in 2002 was $10.5 trillion—up by half a trillion since 2000. The federal government's expenditures exceeded $2 trillion in 2002—about one-fifth of GDP. In 2000 the government took in $135 billion more than it spent.[40] By late 2002, the surplus had become a deficit of $160 billion—about 1.5 percent of GDP—and galloping toward $300 billion in 2003—before the Iraq bill arrived! Were this gap too small, the president and House Republicans maneuvered in 2003 to cut at least $550 billion from federal taxes—a reduction that, over a few years, would double to $1.1 trillion. Defenders of the White House rejected any

39. The following analysis is drawn from statistics issued in late 2002 on the Web sites of the U.S. Department of the Treasury, the Congressional Budget Office, the Federal Reserve Bank, and the Office of Management and the Budget.

40. Total receipts for fiscal year 2002 were $1.9 trillion—some $858 billion from individual income taxes, $148 billion from corporation income taxes, and $700 billion from Social Security and Medicare receipts.

suggestion that its tax cuts favored the wealthy. True, the cuts would save the chairman of Citicorp about $6 million, but Vice President Dick Cheney would be spared a mere hundred thousand dollars (based on his 2001 return), while the typical American family would pocket all of $217.

In the early 21st century, about three-fifths of federal government spending was "mandatory"—for social security and means-tested entitlements. These outlays were expected to rise from $1 trillion in 2001 to $1.2 trillion in 2004. "Discretionary" spending—for defense and other functions detailed in Table 5.7—was expected to rise from $649 billion in 2001 to $803 billion in 2004. Besides mandatory and discretionary spending, the government had to pay nearly $200 billion in interest on the debt each year.[41] Total U.S. federal debt in late 2002 amounted to more than $7 trillion—nearly three-fourths of GDP for the same year. The share of each citizen in this debt was $22,000.[42]

41. Thus, the fiscal year 2004 budget of $2,195 billion was divided into: discretionary outlays, $803 billion; mandatory, $1200 billion; and interest payments, $191 billion.

42. The Public Debt online.

Table 5.7—U.S. Federal Outlays for Discretionary Programs, 1962–2004 (billions of constant 1996 dollars)

Category and Program	1962	1968	1974	1980	1985	1992	2001	2004 est.
National defense	288.4	380.2	249.1	246.4	331.0	332.0	279.0	334.9
Total nondefense	122.0	165.5	179.6	272.0	234.2	261.0	312.3	354.1
International affairs	35.8	22.9	19.7	25.4	25.8	22.1	20.4	22.0
Science, space and technology	11.2	26.0	12.6	11.6	12.8	18.9	17.9	19.2
Energy	4.3	4.9	2.2	12.2	9.6	6.2	2.7	2.9
Natural resources and environment	14.7	15.8	20.4	30.0	21.9	22.9	23.9	24.7
Agriculture	2.3	3.6	3.1	3.1	3.1	4.8	4.7	4.8
Commerce and housing credit	8.7	9.9	7.7	10.1	5.5	3.0	1.4	−0.1
Community and regional development	2.6	5.9	10.7	17.8	9.3	7.2	11.0	15.4
Education, training, employment and social services	5.3	30.0	31.5	48.1	30.5	37.8	48.4	60.4
Health	6.4	11.6	14.8	16.4	14.0	20.4	30.2	40.8
Medicare	—	1.0	2.1	2.1	2.6	3.3	3.1	3.2
Total Income security	2.6	2.9	8.6	20.1	27.1	31.0	39.9	42.1
Social security	2.1	2.6	2.8	3.0	3.3	2.8	3.4	3.6
Veterans benefits and services	6.0	6.8	10.1	13.3	14.7	16.6	21.1	22.9
Administration of justice	2.8	3.1	7.3	8.9	9.2	16.1	27.0	32.7
General government	8.2	8.9	11.9	10.4	9.9	12.7	12.2	14.0
Total outlays for discretionary programs	**410.4**	**545.6**	**428.8**	**518.5**	**565.2**	**593.0**	**591.3**	**689.0**

SOURCE: *Historical Tables, Budget of the U.S. Government, Fiscal Year 2003*, Table 8.8.

How wisely did the U.S. government allocate its resources? Table 5.7 shows how Washington allocated funds for discretionary programs at critical junctures under nine presidents.[43]

Comparing the first two rows, we see that outlays for defense were more than twice nondefense spending under John F. Kennedy and Lyndon Johnson. Nondefense spending gained under Nixon and exceeded defense under Carter. Under Reagan, however, defense outlays again surpassed nondefense. This ratio did not change in 1992, even though the Cold War had ended. Nondefense came to outweigh defense under Clinton and continued to do so under George W. Bush. Compared to fiscal year 2001, the budget for fiscal year 2004 would add more than $50 billion to defense, but education and health outlays were also to rise—by over $20 billion.

Science and space peaked under LBJ and made a slight recovery under Bush the younger. Energy and natural resource outlays peaked under Carter as the United States wrestled with oil embargos and high prices. When crisis conditions subsided, so did the country's interest in conservation and noncarbon-based energy.

Total outlays for discretionary programs increased by more than one-third from 1962 to 2004. Outlays for community, education, and social services all climbed steeply under Clinton and continued under Bush. These transfers did not make up for declining tax revenues received by states and towns, with the result that many local governments operated in the red, many cutting back what had been considered vital services.

The biggest loser over the years was budget function 150 for International Affairs (detailed in Table 5.8). It declined from $36 billion in 1962 to $20 billion in 1974. It rose under Carter and Reagan and then sank again in the 1990s. Secretary of State Colin Powell requested a nearly 10 percent increase in 2002–2004. Big ticket items included embassy security and military assistance to other countries. Next to outlays for defense, however, those for the State Department and other agencies dealing with foreign affairs were extremely modest.

Imbalances in trade and foreign investment increased. Americans bought more than they sold abroad. The trade deficit rose from $393 billion in 2000 to $433 billion in 2002. This sum, together with the federal budget deficit, amounted to more than 6 percent of GDP.

There was an even larger imbalance in foreign investment. Net foreign investment grew from minus $430 billion in 2000 to minus $498 billion in 2002.

43. JFK, 1962 (just before the Cuban missile crisis); LBJ, 1968 (height of the Vietnam War); Nixon, 1974 (preparing for post–Vietnam); Carter, 1980 (prepared just before the Soviets invaded Afghanistan); Reagan, 1985 (arms buildup); Bush, 1992 (post–Cold War); Clinton, 2001 (Clinton's last year), and Bush, 2004.

Table 5.8 U.S. International Affairs Budget, 2001 Actual and 2004 Estimate (millions of dollars)

	2001 Actual	2004 Estimate
International Development	**$8,205**	**$10,085**
Includes:		
Development assistance and child survival and disease programs	2,124	2,797
Food aid	835	1,210
Multilateral development banks (MDBs)	1,603	1,549
Assistance for the independent states of the former Soviet Union	559	771
Peace Corps	267	362
International narcotics control and law enforcement	417	203
Assistance for Central and Eastern Europe	542	506
International security assistance	**6,368**	**7,103**
Includes:		
Foreign military financing grants and loans	3,568	4,193
Nonproliferation, antiterrorism, demining, and other related programs	311	380
Conduct of foreign affairs	**6,267**	**7,431**
Includes:		
State Department operations	3,331	4,283
Embassy security, construction, and maintenance	1,081	1,336
Foreign information and exchange activities	**878**	**854**
Includes:		
International broadcasting	461	529
Other information and exchange activities	417	313
International financial programs	**900**	**612**
Includes:		
Export/Import Bank	907	610
Total Function 150 (Discretionary Programs)	**$22,618**	**$26,085**

SOURCE: U.S. Department of State, *International Affairs Function 150: Fiscal Year 2003: Analytical Perspectives: Budget of the U.S. Government* (Washington, D.C.: Government Printing Office, 2002).

Most of these statistics had a bright and a dark side related to global interdependence. The fact that the U.S. Treasury could finance U.S. budget deficits by selling interest-bearing securities implied wide confidence in the American political economy. But if that confidence eroded, investors—especially foreigners—might withdraw their funds. This

Japan. Recovering from World War II, Japan became a model trading state, exporting far more than it imported. Japan's economy, education, and social cohesion were strong. Japanese lived longer than most other peoples, even though Japan's consumers received fewer protections than their Western counterparts.[52] Shielded by the U.S. nuclear umbrella, Japan conquered markets rather than foreign territories.[53] Japan invested about 1 percent of GDP on its "Self-Defense Forces" and nearly another 1 percent to support U.S. forces stationed in Japan. Just this sliver of Japan's wealth yielded the world's third- or fourth-largest military budget. In the 1990s, however, Japan's economy stalled and the ruling party lost its grip. Japanese dynamism could wilt if the country's youth refused to work like (and for) the growing numbers of their elders. Despite economic clout, Japan's external influence was curtailed by its inward-looking culture, dependency on the United States, a post-1945 aversion to militarism, and neighbors' fears of revived Japanese imperialism.

China. In the early 21st century, China was medium-strong in hard power but weak in soft. Its troop strength was the world's largest (nearly double that of Russia, India, or the United States). China also boasted a growing nuclear arsenal, including regional and intercontinental ballistic missiles and some missile-firing submarines. China's per capita income was low (less than $1,000 at official exchange rates but over $3,000 PPP). Still, if the trends of the 1990s continued—a set of big "ifs," China's total GDP could overtake Japan's within a few decades. However, China had multiple vulnerabilities: too many people cultivating too little land, environmental degradation, no visible alternative to one-party dictatorship, rampant corruption, resistance to global norms on human rights, and discontent among Tibetans and other minorities. Economic modernization exacted great costs. Unemployment rose as millions left the countryside for cities and privatized factories discharged surplus workers to cut costs. These problems would be aggravated by China's entry into the World Trade Organization, because it opened the Chinese market to foreign firms, goods, and services.

China's influence fluctuated considerably. In 1997, the UK returned Hong Kong to China as a "special administrative region" on the basis of "one country, two systems." If Hong Kong's freedoms were undiminished, it could be an appealing magnet for Taiwan. But neither condition materialized. Hong Kong's freedoms were gradually curtailed, and Taiwanese voters elected a proindependence president. They were not dissuaded by China's missile buildup across the Taiwan Strait.

China, like Russia and South Africa, turned a blind eye to HIV. The PRC did little to prevent the growth of infections or invest in drugs to cope with

52. Japan Tobacco, Inc., owned and operated by the Ministry of Finance, was the largest corporate taxpayer in Japan in 1993. Lung cancer killed 3 out of 100,000 in 1955; 31 of 100,000 in 1991.

53. The sharing of burdens was uneven. The United States spent a much greater share of its GNP on defense than did Japan or Germany. Still, the United States also gained: Japan and Germany aligned with Washington on nearly every security issue of the Cold War.

Absent ties with Washington, Japan and Germany would surely have felt compelled to build a nuclear deterrent. Had this happened, neighboring states—recalling World War II—would probably have been far cooler to their ex-foes.

the disease. All of China's weaknesses converged as the country incubated, concealed, and then tried to cope with SARS, the pneumonia-like epidemic, in 2003.

Russia. Though the USSR appeared in the 1970s to be fit, its foundation proved weak, and the Soviet peak collapsed in the 1980s. Russia emerged as a separate state, along with more than fourteen other states along Russia's borders. The core of the former Soviet Union was still the world's largest country, with vast resources and a huge nuclear arsenal. But Russia's internal fitness plunged in the 1990s. Infant mortality continued to rise while male life expectancy fell to fifty-eight years. Russia's fledgling democracy foundered while corruption and criminality mounted. Russia's leaders in the 1990s tried to raise a new peak, but they wandered in a swampy labyrinth, quarreling over how to get out. One statistic speaks volumes: More than 800,000 scientific workers (from a population of 147 million) emigrated from 1992 to 2002.[54] In 2000, Russian voters endorsed Vladimir Putin as president, welcoming again a strong fist to impose order. Putin then tried to square a circle: He encouraged market freedoms while curbing political.

Germany. Germany was strong in most respects except in military power. Its population and GDP were Europe's largest, but less than one-third those of the United States. Domestic cohesion was strained by the burdens of integrating East and West Germany; discontent over "guest workers" and political refugees; high unemployment; and general belt-tightening to reduce debt and meet the demands of the European Monetary Union.

European Union. Could the EU become a superpower comparable to the United States? Yes. Did its citizens want this to happen? Yes, said two-thirds of Europeans polled in 2002. Would it happen? No.[55]

The EU had a larger population than the United States—379 million to 282 million in 2002. If ten East European countries joined in several years, as expected, this would bring the EU population to 454 million. If Bulgaria, Romania, and Turkey later joined, that would bring the EU populaton to 550 million—nearly twice the U.S. and four times that of the Russian Federation (where deaths far exceeded births). The EU GDP would soon outstrip the American, though per capita incomes would be lower in many EU states. Most EU countries had very high HDI scores but, as we shall see in Chapter 11, most European economies were much less competitive than the United States.

While the U.S. federal budget exceeded $2 trillion in 2003, the EU budget amounted to less than $100 billion—just over 1 percent of GDP. Of course, the national budgets of the EU member states were

54. Andrei Polunin in *Trud*, no. 106, June 24, 2002, p. 2 The article claimed that Russian-speaking software specialists accounted for 30 percent of Microsoft's new products.

55. Timothy Garton Ash, "Could a United States of Europe Rival the United States of America?" Lecture at Boston University, December 2, 2002.

high—indeed, higher as a percentage of GDP than in the United States. But that is just the point: The member states of the EU kept it on a tight leash. The EU's budget would have to rise twentyfold or more before it could rival the scope of the U.S. federal government.

The EU pioneered the "common marketization" of IR—downgrading security–sovereignty issues while cooperating in a single trading bloc. But when the EU tried to achieve a common foreign and defense policy, it failed. Both London and Paris possessed nuclear forces, but neither was willing to share them. Europeans talked much but did little to stop the bloodshed at their Balkan doorstep in the years 1992 to 1995. Europeans labored to create their own force independent of NATO, but it was minuscule and lacked the long reach and modern weapons of U.S. forces.

Europeans chafed at U.S. "hyperpower" and the heavy-handed, outspoken unilateralism practiced by George W. Bush. Some Americans returned the favor, regarding the Europeans as parasites and pansies. In the late 1990s and early 21st century, the UK was closer to the United States on most foreign policy issues than to continental Europe.

Regardless, there would not be a federated United States of Europe in any foreseeable future. Europe's linguistic and cultural diversity prevented the separate states from becoming "one from many." In 2002, the EU had eleven official languages; in the future it could have twenty-two—requiring 432 possible translation matches. The closest thing to a common newspaper was the *Financial Times* and *International Herald Tribune.*

Differences in economic levels and pure greed also impeded unity. The stability pact underlying the European Monetary Union was like a straitjacket. Germany had to break the pact and face large fines in order to take on more debt to stimulate job growth. There was no mechanism to help a country facing a financial liquidity crisis.

Nearly half of the EU budget went to supporting agriculture. Of that $46 billion, most went to German and French farmers, even though others were in greater need. These problems would multiply as new states from Eastern Europe joined the EU. In 2002, the EU planned to provide some $3 billion a year by 2005 to subsidize agriculture in its new members such as Poland.

Europe was ages behind the United States in constructive solutions to minority problems. Thanks to its low birth rate, Europe needed infusions of young workers. Europe's educated youth tended to be internationalist, but older people and factory workers did not readily accept Turks, Croatians, and other foreigners working and trying to settle in Europe. By 2002, there were some 20 million Muslims living in Europe. Europe could not do without them or evict them, but neither could it assimilate them. Both sides—Europeans and potential settlers—resisted integration. The first time the word *European* was used came at the Battle of Tours in 732, when "Europeans" fought Muslims. If Turkey joined the EU, there would be another 65 million Muslims in the EU.

The most significant "other" against which Europeans might mobilize was the United States, but shared values with Americans were too strong to galvanize European unity. Far more united both sides of the Atlantic than divided.

Wild Cards. Apart from these established players, the deck was loaded with wild cards. Some countries make the most of their potential, while others waste their assets. Would oil-rich Saudi Arabia, Azerbaijan, and Kazakstan modernize or remain narrow dictatorships focused on accumulating petro dollars? Would Brazil and Argentina develop or dissipate their human and other resources? The personal qualities of individual leaders—their vision or blindness, heroism or cupidity, energy or sloth—will boost some countries and harm others. Bad luck—an earthquake or drought—will knock some actors to their knees.

Given these trends, what does the future hold? Best- and worst-case scenarios are sketched in Chapter 16.

DID GEONOMICS SUPERSEDE GEOPOLITICS AND MILITARY FORCE?

Did the end of the Cold War mean that hard power—military and geopolitical assets—had become irrelevant? That a strong economy rooted in global trade was the key to fitness and influence? Military power could be a useful backdrop but faced severe limits. Without a Soviet threat, Americans and Europeans saw few reasons to put their troops in harm's way. The world spent much less on defense in the late 1990s than in the late 1980s.

But geonomics and economic statecraft also faced limits. Japan and Germany could focus on trade only because their basic security was still assured by the United States Both Japan and Germany depended on Middle Eastern oil, but neither country could keep sea lanes open or prevent Iraq from seizing Kuwait and its oil. Others could ride piggyback and help pay the bill, but U.S. military power was their last resort.

Reluctant to fight, actors tried economic statecraft. But it produced no miracle cures. Economic carrots and sticks had little impact on states pursuing "vital interests." Thus, Tokyo's financial offers did not spur impoverished Russia to hand back to Japan the northern islands taken by the Red Army in 1945.

OH, ALL RIGHT, WE'LL GO BUY SOME FOOD...

The Christian Science Monitor
Los Angeles Times Syndicate

Iraq's fitness withered under UN sanctions intended to compel the country to permit destruction of its weapons of mass destruction and facilities to produce them. Infant mortality increased and life for most Iraqis became more tenuous. In 1995 and 2001 the UN Security Council relaxed sanctions to permit limited sales of Iraqi oil to purchase food and medical supplies. But Saddam Hussein often seemed reluctant to purchase such supplies. His cronies sold smuggled oil to outsiders and operated a black market within Iraq. His palaces increased in number and splendor.

Washington employed a wide range of economic levers for political ends, often in ways that impaired U.S. business interests. The National Association of Manufacturers identified sixty cases in 1993–1997 in which the United States imposed sanctions against thirty-five countries. Washington targeted not just Cuba and Iran but corporations doing business with them. Other targets included Iran and Libya for terrorism, Colombia and Myanmar for drug trafficking, Pakistan for pursuing a nuclear weapons program, Brazil and Taiwan for environmental violations, Saudi Arabia and Mauritania for abusing workers' rights, and African countries for condoning female circumcision.

Such pressures showed little effect. Fidel Castro and Libya's Colonel Moammar Qaddafi remained in power. So did Saddam Hussein, until dislodged by force. Despite U.S. threats to raise tariffs against China, Beijing's human rights policies changed little. Despite its need for imports, North Korea specialized in defiance—not compliance.

Economic sanctions work best when uniformly backed by many countries.[56] Thus, UN sanctions added to the reasons why South Africa gave up racist policies in 1994 and why Serbia recognized Bosnia in 1995. Economic statecraft also gains from linkage to other carrots and sticks. In 2001, Serbia surrendered its former president, Slobodan Milošević, to the Hague war crimes tribunal because this was the sine qua non for a large package of econonic aid.

56. See Gary Clyde Hufbauer et al., *Economic Sanctions Reconsidered: History and Current Policy*, 2d ed. (Washington, D.C.: Institute for International Economics, 1990); and Lisa L. Martin, *Coercive Cooperation: Explaining Multilateral Economic Sanctions* (Princeton, N.J.: Princeton University Press, 1992).

No asset guarantees clout. Oil and grain offer leverage, but no single supplier controls prices. Oil was a kind of black gold in the 1970s but lost purchasing power in the 1980s and 1990s. Cartels such as the Organization of Petroleum Exporting Countries cannot readily enforce production quotas on their members. Kuwait's bulging purse did not deter aggressors. Neither oil nor money nor air-conditioned classrooms could assure longer life spans, good science, and social cohesion.

WHAT PROPOSITIONS HOLD? WHAT QUESTIONS REMAIN?

POWER DOES NOT ASSURE INFLUENCE OR FITNESS

We see that every power asset faces limits. No single asset guarantees influence or fitness. Fitness requires the capacity to cope with multiple challenges at home and abroad, converting them into opportunities. This capacity is multifaceted and requires many kinds of strength.

Memo to the President: *To meet the challenges of today and tomorrow, the United States must balance means and ends, intangible and tangible assets. We must nurture and make good use of our vast natural endowment and creative people.*

Long-term fitness is more likely to arise from cooperation (as in the Marshall Plan) than from zero-sum politics (as in the Cold War and the Vietnam War). The optimal way to convert power resources to fitness is through value-creating on a broad scale. This requires dialogue. We must hear out our partners, as in the Marshall Plan era—not dictate or tell them "take it or leave it."

The United States enjoys super power but only medium fitness at home. Our influence abroad is in no way commensurate with our material and cultural power. It diminished rapidly when President George W. Bush downgraded multilateralism and embraced unilateralism. America's fitness declined as the Bush team sharply increased military spending, granted hefty tax cuts to a wealthy minority, reduced outlays for social welfare and education, and failed to promote energy efficiency. The results were bitter: The enormous budget surplus built up in the late 1990s quickly became a budget deficit. Meanwhile, the trade deficit also grew and foreigners, led by Arabs, withdrew much of the money they had placed in U.S. accounts.

We do not like to think of ourselves as imperialists, but we have had a vast empire since 1898. We should strive to make our presence and our policies an influence for mutual gain—not exploitation. At times we may be forced to act alone or with a limited "coalition of the willing." If our policies are wise and just, however, we should be able to forge a global consensus.

Like the Bush administration, we may be tempted to follow the advice that Virgil in The Aeneid *gave to imperial Rome: "Make your task to rule nations by your government—these shall be your skills: to impose ordered ways upon a state of peace, to spare those who have submitted, and to subdue the arrogant." Let others shape bronzes and make marble come to life; let others plead their cases in court; let others analyze the heavenly bodies.*

In our times, however, Virgils' advice is not feasible or desirable. Americans can and must lead—not rule. Except in extreme cases, we should persuade and coopt rather than compel or coerce. We should nurture our strengths in the arts, the law, and the sciences—the very domains that Virgil seemed to disdain.

The world is unipolar but interdependent. Americans should act to nudge the world toward mutual gain. Here are six policy guidelines:

1. Increase the country's overall fitness—internal and external.

2. Cultivate a consensus at home and abroad for our policies.

3. To stop rogue aggressors, maintain sufficient strength to command and coerce. Buttress security against nonstate terrorists.

4. Invest more in health, education, and other features of domestic well-being. Not just money but wise choices and leadership are required on all fronts.

5. Promote informed dialogue at home and abroad. Value-creation thrives on openness; value-claiming and misjudgment on secrecy. Greater openness and better communication are needed to make our country and the whole world more fit.

6. Look for solutions that grow our fitness with that of others. We can climb higher with others than we can alone.

KEY NAMES AND TERMS

bean count	gender empowerment measure (GEM)	influence
Big Mac Time (BMT)	gender-related development index	intelligence
C⁴ISR	(GDI)	kinetic power
coevolution	geonomics	power
conversion power	geopolitics	purchasing power parity (PPP)
cost tolerance	gross domestic product (GDP)	real GDP per capita
economic statecraft	hard power	soft power
fitness	human development index (HDI)	trading state
fungibility	human poverty index (HPI)	transparency
GDI per capita	infant mortality	World Island

QUESTIONS TO DISCUSS

1. What country is most fit—by what measure?

2. Select two countries whose influence you believe exceeds their hard power. Point to two other countries whose influence is less than their power might warrant. What is the evidence for your assessment?

3. Can/should the U.S. adopt the Japanese approach to security and economic development?

Questions to Discuss (continued)

4. You must advise the U.S. president about discretionary spending. What outlays will you keep, increase, or reduce?

5. As defense minister of Lithuania, should you build a modern army, train the entire population in civilian resistance, or both? If both, how will you allocate resources?

6. Do you agree with the Pyramid of Power in Figure 5.2? If not, why?

7. Will states such as Brazil, Ukraine, and Kazakstan play the same, a smaller, or a larger role in IR in 2020? What factors and trends must you consider to answer this question?

8. Consider two of the potential great powers. What would it take for them to actualize their potential?

9. Point to a situation where State *A* wishes to change the behavior of State *B*. How could State *A* utilize economic levers to accomplish its objective?

10. How does oil affect peace, security, and economic well-being in the countries bordering the Caspian Sea? The South China Sea? The Caribbean?

RECOMMENDED RESOURCES

BOOKS

Blanchard, Jean-Marc F. F., Edward D. Mansfield, and Norrin M. Ripsman, eds. *Power and the Purse: Economic Statecraft, Interdependence and National Security.* London: Frank Cass, 2000.

Brewer, Thomas L., Gavin Boyd, and Paul A. Brenton, eds. *Globalizing Europe: Deepening Integration, Alliance Capitalism and Structural Statecraft.* Northampton, Mass.: Edward Elgar Publishing, 2002.

Clemens, Walter C., Jr. *The Baltic Transformed: Complexity Theory and European Security.* Lanham, Md.: Rowman & Littlefield, 2001.

Cortright, David, and George A. Lopez, eds. *Smart Sanctions: Targeting Economic Statecraft.* Lanham, Md.: Rowman & Littlefield, 2002.

Demko, George J., and William B. Wood, eds. *Reordering the World: Geopolitical Perspectives on the Twenty-first Century.* Boulder, Colo.: Westview, 1994.

Dizard, Wilson Jr. *Digital Diplomacy: U.S. Foreign Policy in the Information Age.* Westport, Conn.: Praeger, 2001.

Dobson, Alan P. *U.S. Economic Statecraft for Survival, 1933–1991: Of Sanctions, Strategic Embargoes, and Economic Warfare.* New York: Routledge, 2002.

Epstein, Joshua M., and Robert Axtell. *Growing Artificial Societies: Social Science from the Bottom Up.* Cambridge, Mass.: MIT Press, 1996.

Kennedy, Paul. *The Rise and Fall of the Great Powers: Economic and Military Conflict from 1500 to 2000.* New York: Random House, 1987.

Mandelbaum, Michael. *The Ideas That Conquered the World: Peace, Democracy, and Free Markets in the Twenty-first Century.* New York: Public Affairs, 2002.

Mead, Walter Russell. *Special Providence: American Foreign Policy and How It Changed the World.* New York: A. A. Knopf, 2001.

Nye, Joseph S. *The Paradox of American Power: Why the World's Only Superpower Can't Go It Alone.* New York: Oxford University Press, 2002.

Rosecrance, Richard. *The Rise of the Trading State: Commerce and Conquest in the Modern World.* New York: Basic Books, 1986.

Tellis, Ashley J., et al. *Measuring National Power in the Postindustrial Age: Analyst's Handbook.* Santa Monica, Calif.: RAND Corporation, 2001.

World Bank. *World Development Report.* New York: Oxford University Press, annual.

UN Development Programme. *Human Development Report.* New York: Oxford University Press, annual.

WEB SITES

The Electronic Industries Association
   http://www.eia.org
Geopolitics
   http://www.frankcass.com/jnls/gib.htm
Human Development Reports/Index
   http://hdr.undp.org/
The Internet Society
   http://www.isoc.org
Navajo Code Talkers
   http://www.archives.gov/digital_classroom/lessons/code_talkers/code_talkers.html
Organization for Economic Cooperation and Development
   http://www.oecd.org
World Economic Forum
   http://www.weforum.org/

PART 2

From Anarchy, Order?

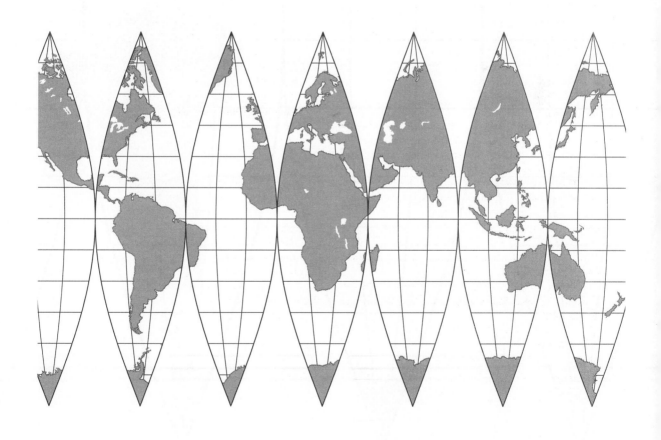

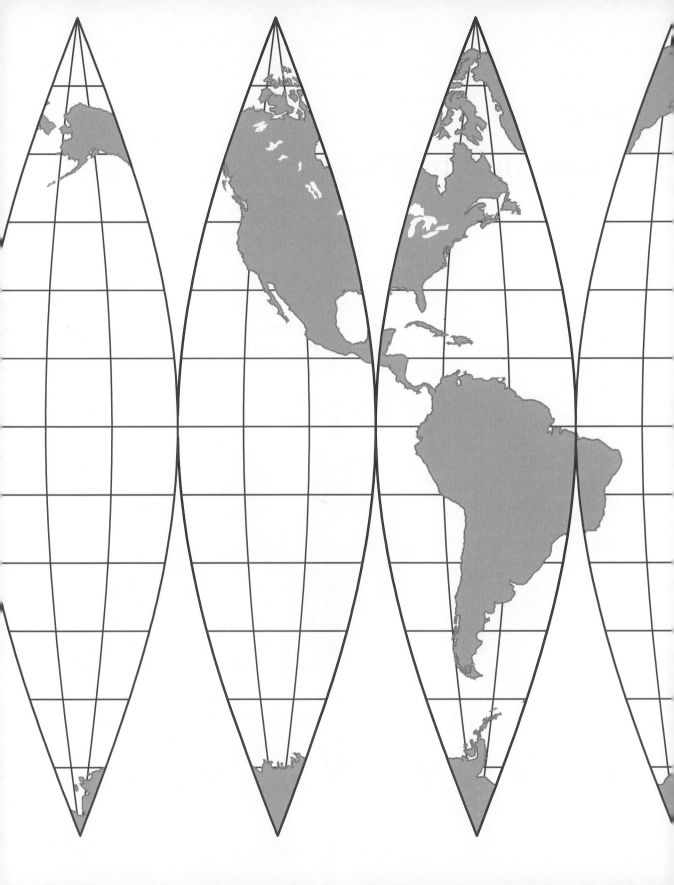

C H A P T E R   S I X

ARMS AND ARMS CONTROL: CAN SWORDS BECOME PLOWSHARES?

The President Asks You to chair a policy review. Participants include analysts from the Defense, State, and Energy Departments; the Defense Intelligence Agency and the CIA; the Office of Homeland Security; plus some of your team from the National Security Council. Your task is to answer three basic questions: First, given the foreseeable threats to the United States and world security, what should be the mission and size of U.S. armed forces? Should we seek to maintain a clear lead over any and all military rivals? Can we retire to a "Fortress America"? Should we commit some forces to an international force under the UN Security Council?

Second, how should we think about disarmament? Can we scrap all nuclear weapons? Are negotiations merely a public relations gimmick to make each side look like a champion of peace? Are arms limits good or bad for our security? For the economy? For our overall fitness?

Having read how Leonardo da Vinci and Niccolò Machiavelli worked on a Florentine project to take away Genoa's water supply by diverting the River Arno, she asks whether we should regard some weapons as beyond the pale.[1] If we reject them, she also wonders, may we be more vulnerable to their use by others?

If we and other major states limit our arms, does this make us more or less vulnerable to attacks by smaller states or nonstate actors that have access to powerful weapons?

Third, what about cheats? How should we respond if we discover that Koraq has been violating its pledge to stop producing weapons of mass destruction (WMD)? And if Irkor masks WMD from UN inspectors, should we forcibly disarm the country?

The President recalls that the Bible has words for and against arms control. The ancients knew that many assets are "dual use": What builds or defends can also attack. The blade of a plow can cut a furrow or kill. Favoring arms reductions, the prophet Isaiah (Isaiah 2:4, KJV) told his people to "beat their swords into plowshares, and their spears into pruning hooks." But Joel (Joel 3:10–21, KJV) voiced the opposite message. He told the Israelites that God ordered them to "beat their plowshares into swords and pruning hooks into spears" to fight their oppressors.

1. Walter D. Masters, *Machiavelli, Leonardo and the Science of Power* (Notre Dame, Ind.: University of Notre Dame Press, 1996).

The Israelites learned the dangers of disarmament. The Philistines imposed on them an arms control regime to make sure the Hebrews did not turn plowshares into swords. The Philistines forbade the Hebrews to forge iron tools and required them to sharpen their plowshares only on Philistine soil. When war came, only two Hebrews had a sword or spear (1 Samuel 13:19–22).

The President suggests that nuclear power is like plowshares. Both are dual use. She asks: "How can we channel nuclear and other modern technologies to build rather than destroy?"

You share this goal but know that the obstacles are enormous. The eagle on the U.S. official seal clutches sharp arrows in one set of talons; in the other, an olive branch. The symbols are clear: Fitness requires a blend of strength and conciliation. But what is the right mix of arms and arms control? You promise the President to review how self-help and mutual aid can be linked to enhance security.

CONTENDING CONCEPTS AND EXPLANATIONS

WHAT IS SECURITY?

Security is freedom from danger. A wise security policy seeks to uphold a country's fitness, its physical survival, and way of life. But absolute security is impossible. Governments must balance their resources between problems at home and problems abroad. Fitness can erode from failure to meet internal or external challenges.

Human security depends upon a favorable environmental support system. Arms buildups and war can do extreme damage to the biosphere. The nuclear powers, trying to achieve external security, poisoned their own wells and peoples, leaving archipelagos of radioactive hot spots across the former USSR, China, and the United States. The Pentagon spends billions each year to clean up many thousands of hazardous sites.

For security, most IR actors depend first of all on their own efforts. But when each actor is vulnerable, security may depend on mutual aid as well as on self-help. Governments say that they arm to be secure, but forces for and against arming spring from every level of IR.

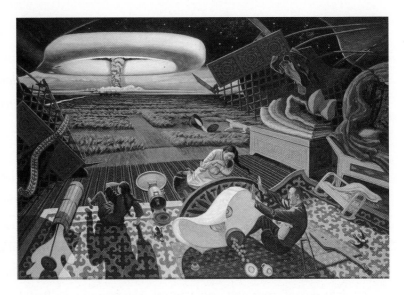

The first Soviet nuclear test took place in 1949—four years after Hiroshima—not far from the city of Semipalatinsk in Soviet Kazakstan. This painting by Kazak artist Amen Khaidarov suggests how a Kazak family in its yurt might have seen and felt the blast. Kazakstan's people, land, and water suffered from the residues of nuclear weapons testing. Having become independent in 1991, Kazakstan, Ukraine, and Belarus bowed to U.S. inducements and pressures, agreeing to give up their Soviet-era nuclear weapons to Russia. Thus, four countries voluntarily engaged in complete nuclear disarmament—these three plus South Africa, while Iraq was forcibly disarmed. North Korea, as we shall see, offered a more complicated case.

HOW LEVELS OF IR GENERATE AND RESTRAIN ARMS COMPETITION

Key Individuals

The man who supervised development of the first atomic bombs, U.S. Secretary of War Henry Stimson, became the first U.S. leader to advocate internationalization of atomic energy. Albert Einstein and many other physicists who had urged creation of nuclear weapons, lest Germany acquire them first, later sought their abolition. Some founded the journal *Bulletin of the Atomic Scientists*, with its famous clock showing the minutes remaining before midnight.

Josef Stalin ordered crash programs to build nuclear and thermonuclear weapons for the USSR. In the 1940s the "father of the Soviet H-bomb," Andrei Sakharov, thought of himself as a soldier in a "new scientific war" to break the U.S. monopoly in advanced weapons. In the 1950s, however, he worried about the health consequences of nuclear testing.[2] Convinced that the two superpowers had achieved a balance of terror in the 1960s, Sakharov devoted his life to arms control and human rights.

Not every weapons scientist becomes an advocate of arms control. Never forgetting the Communist takeover of his native Hungary, the "father of America's H-bomb," Edward Teller, labored for more than fifty years to advance U.S. superiority in weapons.

2. Sakharov urged the Kremlin (often in vain) to move local populations far from the test sites. Sakharov calculated that a one-megaton test would cause 10,000 deaths worldwide from radiation-induced cancers and genetic illnesses. By 1957, the total power of nuclear bombs tested around the world added up to nearly 50 megatons—500,000 casualties by his estimates. Despite Sakharov's pleas, the USSR in 1961 tested an H-bomb that he helped to design. This single explosion had the force of more than 50 megatons—perhaps 100 megatons. When he failed to stop duplicate tests, Sakharov was overcome by "unbearable bitterness" and wept. Andrei D. Sakharov, *Memoirs* (New York: Knopf, 1990), 201–229.

State and Society

Strong forces within society press for and against arms. President Dwight D. Eisenhower in 1961 cautioned Americans against the influence of the "military-industrial complex"—an "immense military establishment and a large arms industry." In democratic countries antimilitarists can become well informed, but they find it hard to mobilize support against those who claim to be fulfilling the "requirements for national security." Still, U.S. public opinion swings up and down on "how much is enough." In dictatorships, however, few people have any knowledge, let alone voice, on such matters.

International Dynamics: The Security Dilemma and Multiple Symmetry

Anarchy leaves each state insecure. As we know, the security dilemma is that the very steps State *A* takes to make itself more secure may goad State *B* into countermeasures that threaten *A*. This problem contributes to a model of **multiple symmetry** that says: Each rival must match or surpass every asset of its adversary or lose the competition. Multiple symmetry must be maintained—in troops, weapons, alliances, and spies.[3] Compelled to anticipate expected growth of State *A*'s forces, its rival *B* tends to overshoot.

Some scholars believe that arms races always end in war.[4] Others disagree. The race may peter out if one or both sides focus on other problems, become friends, or reach exhaustion. Qualitative competition in laboratories is probably safer than quantitative rivalry in the field.

The model of multiple symmetry oversimplifies how states interact. Still, it helps us grasp the anxieties that could drive two parties to a deadlock. In game theory terms, **Deadlock** is continual mutual defection, where D,D is greater than C,D (see Table 6.1). Once either side defects, deadlock continues because neither side has a sufficiently strong incentive to break off the competition.[5]

Another way to understand arms racing is through the parable of the **Stag Hunt**.[6] Imagine five hunters waiting for a stag. If they kill a stag, they can feed their families for a week. But hours pass and no stag appears. Instead, a hare emerges from the bush. One hunter shoots the rabbit even though the noise scares any stag from the area. The single hunter defects from the common cause to get meat sufficient for his stew tonight, ruining prospects for a larger bounty for all. Tomorrow he, like the others, may be hungry.

Table 6.1 Arms Choices and Arms Race Deadlock

		Country B	
		Cooperate	Defect
Country A	Cooperate	C,C	C,D
	Defect	D,C	D,D (deadlock)

3. For this theorem, see Jan F. Triska and David D. Finley, *Soviet Foreign Policy* (New York: Macmillan, 1968), 284–309.

4. Samuel P. Huntington pointed to at least eight arms races that did not end in war, including France vs. England (1840–1866), Argentina vs. Chile (1890–1902), Japan vs. the U.S. (1916–1922), and—as he wrote—the U.S. vs. USSR since 1946. See Huntington, "Arms Races: Prerequisites and Results," *Public Policy* 8 (1958): 41–86.

5. See George W. Downs, David M. Rocke, and Randolph M. Siverson, "Arms Races and Cooperation," *World Politics* 38, no. 1 (October 1985): 118–146, and other articles in this special issue on cooperation under anarchy.

6. This story is adapted from Jean Jacques Rousseau, *A Discourse on the Origin of Inequality* (1754), analyzed in Kenneth N. Waltz, *Man, the State, and War: A Theoretical Analysis* (New York: Columbia University Press, 1959), 167–168.

The Parable of Eagle, Lion, Dragon, and Bear: How Each Wanted the Other to Disarm

Eagle offered a simple solution to arms control: "Let us do away with claws and sharp teeth." Lion called for abolishing fiery breath. Dragon demanded the abolition of talons and speed. Smiling, Bear countered: "Comrades, let us replace all weapons with the great universal embrace."

Each hunter, like a rival state, has a preference order:

1. Cooperate and trap the stag—limit the costs of defense and share the benefits of prosperity.

2. Get the rabbit by yourself—build up arms while others are passive (if this produced a major advantage, it might be the first choice for some states).

3. You and others chase the rabbit—arms race, risk war.

4. Stay in place while others chase the rabbit—remain unarmed while others arm.

The long Cold War confrontation between the United States and USSR resembled a mix of Chicken, Deadlock, and Stag Hunt. Facing a severe security dilemma, Washington and Moscow locked themselves into a costly pattern of action and reaction. As we shall see, it was not a precise tit-for-tat. Neither side sought to match or exceed the other in all fields. Still, a rough parity took shape. Its costs included the price of arming, unrealized gains from cooperation (C,C), and augmented danger of war (D,D). But states, like hunters, may decide that their joint interests require safeguards to prevent defection.

CAN SWORDS BECOME PLOWSHARES?

Security Regimes: Arms Control and Disarmament

A state may seek security by matching or bettering the armed might of its foes. Alternatively, a state may seek security without making adversaries feel threatened. To deal with their security dilemma, Washington and Moscow developed **security regimes**—rules, informal norms, decision-making procedures, and other incentives to cooperate rather than defect.[7] Security regimes are valuable because self-help is costly and dangerous. But they are also difficult to achieve, because foes fear their rivals may cheat.

Arms limitations offer one kind of security regime. There are two main types of arms limitation: **Disarmament** means the reduction or elimination of armaments. Arms control is broader. It includes any regulation of arms. **Arms control** could entail disarmament—fewer arms—but it could also mandate more arms or a freeze at existing levels.

Why Limit Arms—or Talk About It?

Throughout the 20th century, Russia (tsarist as well as Soviet) and the United States took the lead in promoting arms control. Why should two

7. On regimes, see Stephen D. Krasner, ed., *International Regimes* (Ithaca, N.Y.: Cornell University Press, 1983), and many essays appearing in the journal *International Organization*.

of the strongest powers call for arms limitation? Arms control diplomacy can serve many goals:

- *Make war less likely and enhance crisis stability:* Reduce incentives to shoot first. Take steps to prevent accidental war and uncontrolled escalation.
- *Limit damage if war occurs:* Reduce unnecessary destruction. Develop "clean" bombs that destroy military objects and minimize civilian losses. Use smart bombs featuring computerized guidance systems that avoid enemy defenses and zero in on military targets.
- *Shape economic growth:* Convert military resources to civilian uses. Alternatively, intensify arms competition for domestic purposes and to bankrupt the other side.
- *Control the climate of world politics:* Promote détente to raise mutual understanding or mask hostile operations.
- *Shape politics in the rival camp:* Divide foes and support partners.[8]
- *Win political support:* Appear both strong and reasonable.
- *Improve the military balance:* If you are Eagle (see sidebar), try to declaw Lion. If you have no nuclear weapons, call for their abolition. If you have plenty, stop others from acquiring them. So long as each player depends on self-help, each seeks to retain its own strengths and abolish the weapons it lacks.

How to Control Arms

Diplomats, generals, scientists, business entrepreneurs, and peace activists have devised a multitude of ways by which to limit the engines of destruction. Governments have used five main methods:

- *Practice unilateral restraint:* Produce and deploy fewer forces. Make them less threatening. For example, build fewer tanks and more tank traps.
- *Disarm defeated foes:*[9] Examples include Germany in 1919 and again in 1945; Iraq after 1991.
- *Take parallel action:* Sometimes states limit their arms in tandem, with or without an understanding. Soviet leader Nikita Khrushchev in 1963 and 1964 endorsed "disarmament by mutual example."
- *Buy them out:* The First World in the 1990s paid the Second World to disarm—from Russia and Kazakstan to North Korea.
- *Negotiate:* Negotiations to limit arms are difficult if the parties have unequal or different assets. As we shall see, however, skilled diplomats have often parlayed asymmetries into deals that serve both sides.

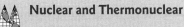 **Nuclear and Thermonuclear**

Nuclear, atomic, fission—each term signifies an "A-bomb" that splits uranium or plutonium atoms. Thermonuclear, hydrogen, fusion—all signify an "H-bomb" that uses a nuclear trigger to detonate hydrogen atoms. But *nuclear* has become shorthand for both A- and H-bombs.

8. Thus, Lenin advised Soviet diplomats in 1922 to do everything possible to strengthen the "pacifist wing" of the bourgeoisie so as to divide Moscow's foes. Ultimately, Lenin wanted to arm the proletariat in capitalist countries and "disarm [*obezoruzhit'*] the bourgeoisie." See Walter C. Clemens, Jr., *Can Russia Change? The USSR Confronts Global Interdependence* (New York: Routledge, 1990), chaps. 3 and 4.

9. The German and Russian languages have two different words for *disarm: entrüsten* and *obezoruzhit'* mean "to disarm by force"; *abrüsten* and *razoruzhit'* mean "to disarm voluntarily."

Scientists have invented ingenious ways to monitor nuclear testing, dismantle arms, and verify arms reductions. Engineers and business entrepreneurs have found ways to neutralize chemical weapons and land mines. Peace activists have generated strong pressure on governments to limit arms.

COMPARING THEORY AND REALITY: CONTROLLING VERTICAL AND HORIZONTAL PROLIFERATION

Could policy makers cap the twin volcanoes of the arms buildup? One volcano expanded upward after 1945 as the major powers piled one new weapon on top of the other; the other volcano expanded sideways as additional countries attempted to acquire nuclear and other arms. The two volcanoes have been linked. As one reached higher, the other broadened. If the first subsides, will the second shrink?

HOW THE VERTICAL VOLCANO GROWS AND SUBSIDES

The Genie Escapes the Baruch Plan

The United States tested the world's first nuclear bomb in New Mexico on July 16, 1945. In August, U.S. planes dropped two atomic bombs— "Little Boy" and "Fat Man"—on Hiroshima and Nagasaki.

With Nazi Germany and Japan defeated, what should the United States do with this new power? Secretary of State James Byrnes advised President Harry Truman to use the U.S. nuclear monopoly as a lever in negotiations with Stalin. But Secretary of War Henry Stimson argued that the bomb was no diplomatic "master card."[10] Stimson advised Truman to internationalize nuclear power in order to avoid a dangerous arms race. It mattered less whether the Soviets mastered the atom in four years or in twenty than that they be peace-loving partners when they did.

Implementing Stimson's suggestion, the Truman administration in 1946 proposed to the United Nations the creation of an International Atomic Development Authority to control all nuclear plants and materials throughout the world. The proposal became known as the **Baruch Plan**, named for Bernard Baruch, a financier chosen by Truman to present the idea. But Baruch loaded the plan with one-sided **jokers**—provisions that virtually assured its rejection by the USSR. For example, the plan's first stage required the Soviets to open their secrets to inspection but permitted the United States to keep its nuclear monopoly so long as it chose.

10. See Daniel Yergin, *Shattered Peace: The Origins of the Cold War and the National Security State* (Boston: Houghton Mifflin, 1977), 123; and James Chace, "Sharing the Atom Bomb," *Foreign Affairs* 75, no. 1 (January/February 1996): 129–144.

The Soviets rejected the Baruch Plan, demanding nuclear disarmament first, inspection later. The United States sought inspection first, disarmament later. Though Soviet diplomats talked tough at the United Nations, Khrushchev later recalled that Stalin "trembled with fear" because the USSR lacked nuclear arms and surrounded Moscow with 100-mm antiaircraft guns.

The USSR soon mastered the nuclear genie. The first Soviet atomic explosion took place on August 29, 1949—little more than four years after the first U.S. test.

Having lost its nuclear monopoly, the Truman administration decided to develop a "super" or thermonuclear bomb. The first U.S. hydrogen bomb was tested in February 1954 and yielded 15 megatons. The Soviets were not far behind. Their first H-bomb explosion occurred in November 1955 and yielded 1.6 megatons.[11]

What could have been seen as a shared Stag Hunt problem turned into an ongoing arms competition expensive to each side. Could it have been avoided? What if professional U.S. diplomats (not a cranky Wall Street speculator) had talked directly to Stalin instead of conducting a public sparring match at the UN? What if, after the Soviets tested their first atomic bomb in 1949, Truman had pledged not to develop a U.S. H-bomb and called on Stalin to exercise similar restraint?

Soviet scientist Sakharov later opined that U.S. moderation would have achieved nothing: Stalin would have pursued a thermonuclear bomb anyway. Had Washington suspended work on the H-bomb, Stalin would have seen this as "a cunning, deceitful maneuver or as evidence of stupidity or weakness." Stalin would have sought "to avoid a possible trap, and to exploit the adversary's folly at the earliest opportunity."[12] We cannot know if Sakharov was correct, but his opinion helped explain why Moscow and Washington deadlocked at D,D.

Similar problems recurred throughout the Cold War. Usually ahead in technology, the White House had to decide: "Shall we try to abort this new weapon with Soviet cooperation or try to stay ahead?" Usually Washington chose the second track, and Moscow played catch-up.

Many realists have claimed that the clash over atomic energy confirmed their view that disarmament diplomacy is cold war by other means.[13] It masks an underlying struggle for hegemony. Distrust causes arms—not vice versa. Significant arms limitations cannot be negotiated between a have and a have-not. Lacking **parity** (rough equality), the only arms accords possible will be cosmetic—for show. Once a weapon has been developed, it will be deployed. The Soviets

11. For other crucial dates, see David Holloway, *The Soviet Union and the Arms Race* (New Haven, Conn.: Yale University Press, 1983), 26.

12. Sakharov, *Memoirs*, 99.

13. The propositions here derive from John W. Spanier and Joseph L. Nogee, *The Politics of Disarmament: Soviet–American Gamesmanship* (New York: Praeger, 1962); Colin S. Gray, "The Purpose and Value of Arms Control Negotiations," in U.S. Senate Committee on Foreign Relations, *Perceptions: Relations Between the United States and the Soviet Union* (Washington, D.C.: Government Printing Office, 1978); and Joseph J. Kruzel, "From Rush–Bagot to START: The Lessons of Arms Control," *Orbis* 30, no. 1 (spring 1986): 193–216.

will never accept on-site inspection. Conclusion: Exploit rather than be exploited. Arm.

Much water would flow over the dam before each side learned that arms controls, if well crafted, can enhance mutual security. It took decades for Moscow and Washington to master conditional cooperation.

How Much Terror for Deterrence?

From the late 1940s into the 1990s the West staked its security upon deterrence—a strategy to paralyze the other side with terror.[14] If the adversary is intimidated, deterrence succeeds. If the foe attacks, deterrence fails.[15]

U.S. strategists said that stability depended on a capacity for "mutual and assured destruction"—MAD. To strike the first blow—with conventional or nuclear arms—would be suicidal if the other side could retaliate with nuclear weapons.

Was MAD crazy? The White House reckoned that the United States had to be able to absorb a first strike and still inflict "unacceptable punishment" on the USSR. Some analysts said that a **minimum deterrent**, small but adequate, might be achieved with a few dozen or perhaps a few hundred nuclear weapons. But the Kennedy team decided to build more than a thousand land-based ICBMs (intercontinental ballistic missiles) and more than thirty submarines armed with many **SLBMs (submarine-launched ballistic missiles)**. Defense Secretary Robert S. McNamara said that U.S. forces must be able to destroy at least one-fifth of the people and one-half of the industry of the USSR to dissuade the Kremlin from striking first. To overcome "all that can go wrong" (what Carl von Clausewitz called "friction"), many warheads would be required.[16]

To obtain a dependable **second-strike** force the Pentagon built a **triad** of long-range bombers, land-based missiles, and SLBMs. Any leg of the triad would have to be able to retaliate if the other two were destroyed. Some U.S. bombers were always aloft to assure they would survive a Soviet attack.[17]

The Soviet deterrent rested far more on land-based missiles than the U.S. deterrent. This was an important asymmetry. Soviet planes and submarines were less dependable than those of the United States. On the other hand, Moscow held all of Europe hostage to its combined nuclear and conventional forces.

Critics said each side engaged in overkill. But military planners replied that large and diverse forces were needed to demonstrate that a first strike could never disarm the victim to the extent that it could not strike back.

14. Deterrence derives from the Latin for "terror." The same root exists in German and Russian: *Abschreckung* and *ustrashenie*. Sometimes Soviet writers used instead *sderzhivanie*, which approximates "containment" (from *derzhat'*—"to restrain"—and *derzhava*—"power"). For Washington, deterrence was part of containment.

15. For more on deterrence, methodology, and simulation, see *International Studies Notes* 22, no. 1 (winter 1997).

16. Some planes, missiles, and warheads would malfunction; some would miss their targets; some would be intercepted; others would be countered by "hardening" of Soviet sites; some would destroy each other ("fratricide").

17. A spoof of the resulting dilemmas was the film *Dr. Strangelove, or How I Stopped Worrying and Learned to Love the Bomb.*

Department lawyers retorted that SDI tests of "subcomponents" (such as lasers and satellites) were permitted so long as actual weapons systems were not deployed. Furthermore, the White House charged that the Soviets were developing their own SDI.[20]

Moscow worried that SDI would produce defenses that undermined the Soviet deterrent. Like a boxer, the USSR feared that if its opponent combined a powerful defense with a long reach, it might seek a knockout; such fears, some U.S. experts worried, could tempt Moscow to strike soon, before U.S. defenses were ready.

The Kremlin did not accept Reagan's assurances that he would share SDI discoveries with the USSR. Moscow beefed up its offensive forces to ensure penetration. For several years, the Kremlin demanded a halt to SDI as a precondition for any arms control. In 1987, however, Moscow relented. Seeing that SDI would not yield any sudden breakthroughs, Soviet President Mikhail Gorbachev signed arms controls with Washington despite continued SDI activity.

Theater Ballistic Missile Defense. United States support for Star Wars waned in the 1990s. A decade of SDI research costing more than $30 billion yielded no signs that an effective country-wide defense would ever be feasible against a large-scale ICBM attack. Russia continued to possess thousands of nuclear weapons able to wipe out the United States in half an hour, but their new masters seemed less hostile since the demise of the USSR.

In the 1990s, the Pentagon put less emphasis on developing a **national missile defense (NMD)** of the entire country. Instead it focused on **theater ballistic missile defense (TBMD)** to protect U.S. forces abroad and allies such as Japan and Israel from short- and intermediate-range missiles, improved versions of the "Scud" missiles deployed by North Korea, Iraq, and other countries.[21] The Pentagon investigated both low- and high-altitude TBMD technologies. Low-altitude systems (such as upgraded "Patriot" missiles) would target short-range (1,000-km or less) ballistic missiles within the earth's atmosphere, while theater high-altitude area defense (THAAD) systems aimed at intermediate-range missiles (approximately 1,000–3,000 km) above the atmosphere.

Arms controllers worried that upper-level defenses could degrade Russia's deterrent and subvert the stability achieved by the ABM treaty. In 1996, the Pentagon bowed to this logic and decided to emphasize low-altitude TBMD, slowing but not stopping work on high-altitude systems.

20. While the USSR seems not to have matched the U.S. research effort, Soviet engineers erected a large radar at Krasnoyarsk that, if switched on and tied to ABM launchers, could have shielded a large swath of Soviet territory. After the U.S. government and some NGOs charged that the Krasnoyarsk installation violated the ABM treaty, the Soviet government dismantled the radar in the late 1980s.

21. Michael Klare, *Rogue States and Nuclear Outlaws* (New York: Hill & Wang, 1995).

Rejecting this logic, the Republican-dominated Congress in 1995 called for deployment of a multisite ABM force to protect the entire United States by 2003. President Bill Clinton vetoed the bill, however, saying it would put the United States on a collision course with Russia and the ABM treaty. Russia's arsenal was getting smaller but also older, and perhaps more accident prone. The Pentagon wanted a hedge against "limited strikes, whatever their source"—which could include Chinese as well as Russian ICBMs. Therefore, the United States continued to investigate technologies useful for NMD or TBMD. At the same time, Washington tried to treat Russia more as a partner than an adversary. The U.S. invested nearly 2 billion dollars in the 1990s to help Russia implement arms control treaties and develop cooperative security programs to promote shared security interests—a waste of money, some critics charged, while supporters called it a brilliant initiative that should be expanded.

China had a small but growing stock of nuclear weapons in the 1990s (about seventeen ICBMs, forty-six IRBMs, and twelve SLBMs on one submarine). Washington assumed that Beijing, like Moscow, was a sober actor not likely to start a nuclear war. Still, some leaders of the People's Republic of China (PRC) threatened in 1996 to nuke Los Angeles if the United States interfered in PRC efforts to incorporate Taiwan. Few PRC leaders shared the cooperative security mentality of their U.S. and Russian counterparts. In late 1997, however, Beijing agreed (more explicitly than before) not to send nuclear equipment to other countries.

Real Disarmament: INF, START 1 and 2, and CFE

INF. As the Cold War melted, many fresh streams bubbled through the ice. Presidents Reagan and Gorbachev in 1987 signed the first major disarmament agreement between Washington and Moscow—the Intermediate-Range Nuclear Forces (INF) Treaty. Reagan demanded and got from Gorbachev a commitment to zero-INF. The INF Treaty obliged Washington and Moscow to destroy all their ground-based missiles, both ballistic and cruise, with a range of 500 to 5,500 km. To reach zero, the Kremlin had to remove over three times as many warheads and destroy more than twice as many missiles as Washington, a process both sides completed in 1991. Skeptics noted, however, that both sides retained other missiles able to do the same work as those destroyed, and that INF warheads and guidance systems could be recycled.

START. In 1991, Gorbachev and U.S. President George Bush signed the first Strategic Arms Reduction Treaty (START), known as START 1. It obliged Washington and Moscow within seven years to cut their forces by more than one-third, to 1,600 strategic delivery vehicles (ICBMs, SLBMs, heavy bombers) and 6,000 warheads. When the USSR dissolved later that year, the Russian Federation (RF) took the Soviet Union's place in START and other arms control regimes. Three other successor states inherited nuclear weapons—Ukraine, Belarus, and Kazakstan—but they agreed to send all nuclear warheads in their territories to Russia. START 1 became legally binding in 1994, and each party began steps to meet the ceilings set for seven years hence—2001.

President Bush and RF President Boris Yeltsin in 1993 signed another treaty, START 2, requiring each side to cut its arsenal by 2003 to no more than 3,500 strategic nuclear warheads. The parties also agreed that ICBMs could have only one warhead each and that no more than half the allowed warheads could be deployed on submarines. START 2 was approved by the U.S. Senate in 1996, but the Russian legislature ratified the treaty conditionally in 2000 and it never entered force.

Confronted by expansion of NATO eastward and by deteriorating Russian conventional forces, many Russian leaders wanted to keep or improve their nuclear arsenal. The Kremlin's military doctrine changed in the mid-1990s to allow Moscow "first use of nuclear arms" even against a conventional attack.

At the turn of the century, many hardheaded analysts argued that it was time to eliminate nuclear weapons altogether because they were unusable and unnecessary, given new varieties of precision-guided conventional weapons. If a nuclear umbrella were needed, a few hundred would suffice. By these measures, as we see in Table 6.2, the United States and Russia possessed many more nuclear weapons than either needed.

Table 6.2 Global Stocks of Strategic and Tactical Nuclear Warheads, 1949–2002

Year	U.S.	Russia	UK	France	China	Total
1949	235	1				236
1953	1,436	120	1			1,557
1962	27,297	3,322	205			30,824
1964	30,751	5,221	310	4	1	36,287
1978	24,243	25,393	350	235	220	50,441
1990	21,211	33,417	300	505	430	55,863
2002	10,600	8,600	200	350	400	20,150

SOURCE: Robert S. Norse and Hans M. Kristensen, "NRDC Nuclear Notebook," *Bulletin of the Atomic Scientists* 58, no. 6 (November/December 2002): 103–104.

Some eleven years after George Bush the elder signed START 1, George W. Bush signed the **Strategic Offensive Reductions Treaty (SORT)** with RF President Vladimir Putin on May 24, 2002. The 43rd U.S. president wanted to reduce U.S. strategic weapons to the level needed for a "credible deterrent," but preferred to do so without a binding treaty. Russia also wanted to cut its forces but demanded a formal contract. Wanting Russia's help against terrorism, Bush agreed to sign a treaty, but it was just three pages long with extremely flexible commitments. START 1, by contrast, ran to more than 700 pages.

SORT required each side to reduce its operationally deployed strategic nuclear warheads to between 1,700 and 2,200 over the next decade—by December 31, 2012. At American insistence, the warheads did not have to be destroyed; they could be stored for possible reassembly. Nor did SORT ban multiple warheads—an option left open since START 2 never became law. SORT established no verification procedures but could piggyback on the START 1 verification regime until December 2009, when the START inspection system was scheduled to close down. SORT provided only for a bilateral commission that would meet twice a year to discuss implementation of the treaty. Each party could withdraw from SORT on just three months' notice.

Putin signed SORT even though Moscow objected to Bush's decision, announced in December 2001, to abrogate the ABM treaty signed thirty years before. The 1972 agreement permitted either side to withdraw from the treaty if it gave six month's notice and stated what "extraordinary events related to the subject matter of this Treaty . . . jeopardized its supreme interests." No extraordinary event had occurred, except that Bush wanted to build a national defense system and Putin could not stop him.

Indeed, to deploy a defense system to protect the United States was surely imprudent as well as costly ($9 billion budgeted for fiscal year 2003). Attempting to deploy such a system was not necessary and could make the United States less secure. This conclusion fairly leapt from the National Intelligence Estimate on the "Foreign Missile Developments and the Ballistic Missile Threat Through 2015."[22] Russia, it said, would be compelled by economic constraints to reduce its forces in the next decade, but an unauthorized or accidental launch of Russian missiles was "highly unlikely." Beijing's desire to protect its deterrent from U.S. defenses would push China to expand its force from about 20 to about 100 warheads able to hit the United States. The "axis of evil" countries could not build an ICBM in the next decade. It was more thinkable that they

22. Unclassified version on the CIA Web site in 2002. The report spoke for the entire "intelligence community," noting disagreements among agencies on some details.

might acquire or develop a cruise missile that could strike the United States from a ship. This kind of missile would not be intercepted by the kind of ABM defense being built in Alaska.

The best and cheapest way for a rogue state to hit Ameica with WMD would be by "using nonmissile means," such as a suitcase or a truck. They would be cheaper than ICBMS; could be covertly deployed; and would be more reliable and accurate than a poorly vetted ICBM, and more effective for disseminating germ weapons than a ballistic missile. Their provenance could be masked so that the United States did not know whom to punish. These conclusions were on the last page of the eighteen-page report.

While the intelligence community implied that a national ABM was a half-baked and pernicious idea, some members of Congress asserted that the president had no legal right to abrogate the ABM treaty by himself. The Constitution does not specify how to terminate a treaty. But Representative Dennis Kucinich (D-Ohio) argued that since a treaty may not be ratified without approval of one or both houses, their consent is also required to end a treaty. He pointed to more than fifty precedents, beginning in 1798, when both houses voted to end two treaties with France, an act then signed by President John Adams.[23] In 2002, Kucinich and other members of the House of Representatives sued to enjoin President Bush from usurping the powers of Congress, but he ignored their complaints, as he did those of several NATO partners as well as Moscow and Beijing. Of other governments, only India endorsed Bush's action.

Many hardheaded analysts thought that nuclear weapons should be reduced to a few hundred or eliminated entirely. But the George W. Bush administration stressed that it wanted to keep deployed at least 2,200 nuclear warheads, with many more in storage. Washington announced its readiness to use nuclears "first"—even in response to a non-nuclear challenge. The most likely targets were Iraq, North Korea, and Iran, but the White House allowed that it might also use nuclears against China or Russia. This first-use doctrine was spelled out in tandem with warnings that the United States might strike first to preempt or prevent a foe's attack plans. In short, Washington put the world on notice of its determination to strike first with nuclear weapons at U.S. discretion.

Would Washington's words and deeds intimidate others or intensify their quest for WMD? Anti-American terrorists would not be swayed. China, India, and Pakistan showed no signs of slowing their nuclear buildups. Some Pakistani and Indian leaders welcomed a climate in which barriers to nuclear war were coming down. North Korea admitted that it was enriching uranium to make bombs.

23. When President Jimmy Carter abrogated the U.S. mutual security treaty with Taiwan in 1978–1979, Senator Barry Goldwater and others in Congress sued him. A district court enjoined the president not to abrogate, but an appeals court said abrogation was a presidential perogative. A divided Supreme Court said this was a political issue on which it could not rule. Justice Powell argued that the reason the Court could not rule was that the Senate had not claimed its rights in a formal resolution. See Walter C. Clemens, Jr., "Who terminates a treaty?" *Bulletin of the Atomic Scientists* 57, no. 6 (November/December 2001), 38–39, 42–43.

The White House called for a "preemptive" strike, but what it really meant was "preventive war." The distinction is crucial. A preemptive strike is launched to disarm a foe preparing to attack in the very near future—perhaps in hours or days. Thus, Israel in 1967 destroyed Egyptian planes on the ground before they could attack. By contrast, a preventive war moves against an enemy before its military buildup can shift the balance of power—a matter of months or years. For example, Berlin and Tokyo started World War II before their foes' rearmament could catch up with head starts by Germany and Japan. Preemption has a stronger basis in morality and law than preventive war. Prior to invading Iraq in 2003, the United States had never launched a major preventive or preemptive war.

As the cartoon suggests, the Bush doctrine on preemption could lead other actors to justify their wars as "preemptive." Either India or Pakistan might say its forces were preempting the other's attack. The doctrine could help multiply the world's disorders.

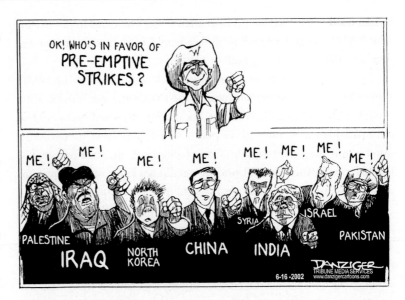

Even after SORT, the risks of nuclear war may have been greater than during the Cold War. The stocks of Russia's nuclear weapons and bomb-making materials were still exposed to misuse or theft. U.S. funding to protect Russia's inventory was still limited; and some Russians balked at exposing any of their arsenal to Americans.

CFE. Western negotiators had sought for decades to cut a deal that would pull down the numerical superiority in conventional forces enjoyed by the Soviet-led Warsaw Pact. They finally got what they wanted in 1990. The 1990 **Conventional Forces in Europe (CFE) Treaty** set equal ceilings for ground and air forces of two groups of states—in effect, NATO and the Warsaw Pact—"from the Atlantic to the Urals." On average, one-third of existing tanks and artillery were destroyed or removed from the designated region. Again, Russia made the largest cuts.

The formal treaty was signed when it was no longer needed. The Warsaw Pact collapsed in 1991 even before the Soviet Union. Quotas for individual countries remained, but East–West parity disappeared because most former Soviet allies and some former Soviet republics gravitated toward NATO. Russia did what it wanted despite the treaty. The Kremlin exceeded its CFE quota on its southern flank, where it had moved large conventional forces to fight in Chechnya and to shape events in Azerbaijan and Georgia. Russia asked for and got adjustments on its "flank" limitations. In the late 1990s, the CFE treaty was revised to abolish bloc-to-bloc limitations; reduce most quotas for individual states; constrain Russia's deployments along its borders; allow existing NATO countries to deploy forces for a time in new NATO countries (such as Poland) within regional limits; and increase transparency.

A Revolution in Arms Control and Disarmament: How Did It Happen?

INF, START, and CFE differed from earlier treaties: First, Moscow and Washington disarmed. They did not merely limit arms—they junked weapons, new and old. Generals winced to see modern missiles and bombers literally sawed in half. Second, cuts were asymmetrical. In each case the Kremlin agreed to make larger cuts than Washington to reach zero or similar force levels. Third, verification of earlier treaties depended on "national means" (mainly satellite reconnaissance). But INF, CFE, and START mandated highly intrusive on-site inspections that would continue for years even after arms reductions had been completed.

Why these breakthroughs? Each side believed that it could gain more from mutual cooperation than from armed rivalry. The real world inhabited by Presidents Reagan and Gorbachev, Bush and Yeltsin, differed sharply from the artificial confines of Prisoner's Dilemma (PD):

• *Direct communications:* Unlike PD's isolated players, Washington and Moscow communicated directly about common problems—even their mutual distrust.

• *Repetition and learning:* Unlike a single round of PD, relations between states go on and on. Americans and Soviets gathered from decades of experience that mutual defection is costly.

• *Limited payoffs:* Unlike the PD structure which posits "catastrophe" for the sucker, Washington and Moscow retained a nuclear deterrent so that, even if one side cheated, it could not dictate terms.

• *Safeguards:* Most Soviet–U.S. agreements were backed by elaborate "verification" systems.

• *Multiple players:* More than two actors played key roles. If Washington or Moscow defected, it would face repercussions in Berlin, Beijing, Tokyo, and New Delhi.

• *Multiple options:* Each player had many options beyond "cooperate" or "defect." Package deals could be worked out with sweeteners.

Beneath all these factors, something more fundamental pushed Moscow toward contingent cooperation with the West: The Soviet system was imploding. The USSR had more arms than it needed or could afford. Gorbachev negotiated away these arms to gain goodwill abroad.

He hoped that reduced military spending and more Western technology would save the Soviet system. But everything was too little and too late. The Soviet empire collapsed. Still, Gorbachev's policies set the stage for continued cooperation between Russia and the West in the 1990s and beyond.[24]

Horizontal Proliferation: How Many Players Should Have the Bomb?

For nearly twenty years the nuclear weapons club was limited to the Big Five. The United States entered first—in 1945, followed by the USSR in 1949; Great Britain, 1952; France, 1960; and China, 1964. The fact that this exclusive club consisted only of permanent members of the Security Council gave its exclusivity some rationale. But a dozen or so nuclear have-nots also pursued the nuclear weapons option. Israel started assembling bombs in the 1960s and had 100 to 200 bombs by the mid-1990s; Israel insisted on keeping its "Samson option" until a stable peace took hold in the Middle East.[25] Several Arab countries and Iran carried out nuclear research and development to produce (some said) an "Islamic bomb." Israeli bombs destroyed Iraq's Osiraq nuclear plant 1981, but Iraq continued its nuclear labors—discovered by outsiders only after Desert Storm.

Can the Genie Be Put Back in the Bottle?

Seeking to freeze the nuclear weapons club, U.S. and Soviet negotiators in 1968 drafted the Nuclear Nonproliferation Treaty (NPT) and asked all states to sign. The pact permitted states with nuclear arms to keep them, but banned other states from acquiring them. Many governments welcomed the idea, but others protested "unfair discrimination" against nuclear weapons have-nots.

Britain backed the NPT, but France and China refused to join unless the United States and USSR began to disarm. Beijing called for abolishing all nuclear weapons (leaving the world's largest manpower supply untouched). Meanwhile, it pledged never to initiate use of nuclear weapons.

Why should have-nots forego nuclear arms? The NPT obligated the nuclear haves to (1) share nuclear technology for peaceful uses with NPT signers; (2) shield signers from nuclear blackmail or nuclear attack; and (3) negotiate "in good faith" to end their own nuclear arms competition.

Some countries found such assurances weak or wanted their own nuclear weapons no matter what. The countries most likely to cross the nuclear threshold—India, Israel, Argentina, Brazil, Pakistan, and

24. He was greeted like a hero by an overflow Harvard University audience on November 11, 2002. Gorbachev conceded that his attempted reforms of the Soviet system had moved too slowly, constrained by conservatives in the Communist Party Politburo.

25. Seymour M. Hersh, *The Samson Option: Israel's Nuclear Arsenal and American Foreign Policy* (New York: Random House, 1991).

South Africa—did not sign the NPT, at least initially. So their nuclear ambitions were unfettered.

But most countries joined the NPT, and it entered into force for them in 1970. Signers included many states that could build nuclear weapons but chose not to—Japan, the two Germanys, Italy, Czechoslovakia, and Sweden. Some other states signed the NPT but acted as though they sought to buy or build the bomb anyway. They were free to continue research and could withdraw from the treaty on just three months' notice.

The NPT worked far better than many analysts expected in the 1970s. Argentina and Brazil renounced their local arms race and joined the NPT in the 1980s. South Africa dismantled its secret arsenal and then joined the NPT in 1991. This reduced the number of nuclear haves from seven to six—the Big Five plus Israel. France and China grudgingly joined the NPT in 1992.

The nuclear club expanded from six to nine when the USSR disappeared in late 1991. Newly independent Ukraine, Kazakstan, and Belarus inherited major parts of the Soviet arsenal, but they too joined the NPT as nuclear have-nots and transferred their nuclear arms to Russia. U.S. economic and diplomatic support tipped the balance against keeping nuclear arms.

That left six countries with deployed nuclear arms. By the mid-1990s eight or nine countries had renounced nuclear weapons after possessing them or approaching the threshold: South Korea, Taiwan, Argentina, Brazil, South Africa, Ukraine, Kazakstan, Belarus, and perhaps North Korea. Two more stopped just short of deployment: India and Pakistan. All these decisions were influenced by U.S. sticks and carrots.[26] If all else failed, those concerned about nuclear spread could destroy incipient nuclear plants, as Israel did in 1981 when it bombed Saddam Hussein's Osiraq nuclear reactor. But Iraq extracted the uranium and followed another route to the bomb.[27] Many nuclear facilities were discovered and destroyed by UN inspectors in the 1990s.

More than 170 states met in 1995 and debated whether to extend the NPT. Many have-nots complained that the Big Five plus Israel still had nuclear arms; Tehran denounced U.S. efforts to block Russian technology sales to Iran. Despite these and other complaints, the conferees voted on May 11, 1995, to extend the NPT without time limits. They concurred that the treaty contributed to a more stable world.

The NPT became the centerpiece of a multifaceted security regime to limit the spread of nuclear and other WMD. Each component of the regime, however, faced serious challenges, as noted in Table 6.3.

26. Mitchell Reiss, *Bridled Ambition: Why Countries Constrain Their Nuclear Capabilities* (Baltimore, Md.: Johns Hopkins University Press, 1995).

27. One account is Khidhir Hamza, *Saddam's Bombmaker: The Terrifying Inside Story of the Iraqi Nuclear and Biological Weapons Agenda* (New York: Scribner, 2000), 128–135. He also discusses the roles of France and Iran.

Table 6.3 Elements of the Nonproliferation Regime

A Growing Infrastructure	Problems
The **International Atomic Energy Agency (IAEA)** was established in 1957 to promote the peaceful uses of nuclear energy. It also monitors NPT (Nuclear Nonproliferation Treaty) compliance and UN restrictions on Iraq.	Too little money, too few staff, and too weak a mandate for its duties. Efforts to expand its mandate to inspect beyond "declared facilities" encountered much resistance in North Korea and elsewhere.
Nuclear test limitations: the 1963 limited nuclear test ban and the 1996 comprehensive ban on all nuclear tests.	Israel, India, and several other key states refused to sign either agreement. The comprehensive ban did not go into effect. The United States did not ratify the comprehensive ban because the Pentagon wanted the option to resume nuclear testing underground.
Nuclear-free zones for Antarctica (1959), Latin America (1967), the South Pacific (1985), Southeast Asia (1995), and Africa (1996).	No agreement was reached on the Middle East, South Asia, or most regions where any of the Big Five operated militarily.
The **NPT** banned further spread of nuclear weapons. Signed in 1968, it entered into force in 1970 and was renewed in 1995 without a time limit.	Not signed by Israel or major threshold states such as India. THE NPT lost credibility because the nuclear powers failed to carry out large-scale nuclear disarmament or even ratify the comprehensive nuclear test ban. Russian and U.S. agreements on strategic warheads did not affect tactical nuclears—easier to steal, transport, and deploy.
The **MTCR** (Missile Technology Control Regime) was established in 1987 to curb the spread of military missiles. By 1997, it had twenty-eight members and three "adherents"—the PRC, Israel, and Ukraine.	The regime had many loopholes. Some of the Big Five exported anti-ship cruise missiles to more than forty countries. China and North Korea transferred ballistic missiles and their components to Pakistan and Middle Eastern buyers.
From 1991 to 1998, the UN Special Commission and IAEA worked to neuter all Iraqi WMD capabilities. Other UN and IAEA inspectors resumed work in Iraq in late 2002 but withdrew before hostilities began in March 2003.	Iraq hid whatever it could from the inspectors. France and Russia wished to relax the pressure. UNSCOM withdrew from Iraq in 1998. Its successor in 2002 was less experienced and had less U.S. support.
The **BWC** (Bacteriological and Toxin Weapons Convention of 1975) banned possession of biological weapons.	Lacked verification procedures. Iraq cheated, and perhaps Russia. Laboratories in the United States and elsewhere opposed intrusive inspection. In 2001, the Bush administration spurned a protocol meant to tighten enforcement and instead stepped up U.S. biodefense research. Washington warned other states not even to discuss a verification protocol in the future (*Arms Control Today*, December 2002, p. 19)!
The **CWC** (Chemical Weapons Convention of 1992) was ratified by the United States and Russia in 1997. It banned production and use of chemical weapons and required their destruction within ten years.	Washington feared that the Russians withheld data. As of 2002, Moscow had barely begun to eliminate its enormous stockpile, but Congress was reluctant to help fund its dismantlement.

The antiproliferation regime cracked in 1974 as India tested a "peaceful" nuclear device. But India then maintained a "can deploy but have not yet done so" posture. When Hindu nationalists took power from the Congress Party, however, India began to test and deploy nuclears in the late 1990s—followed soon by Pakistan. The *known* nuclear club thus expanded from six to eight. By 2002 each country had assembled less than 50 nuclear warheads but had sufficient fissile material to double or triple its arsenal. Israel probably had about 200 warheads.

Is More Better—or Worse?

Why struggle to halt nuclear spread?[28] As we see in Table 6.4, some realists hold that "more is better." Nuclear spread, they argue, would extend

28. Barry R. Schneider, "Nuclear Proliferation and Counter-Proliferation: Policy Issues and Debates," *Mershon International Studies Review* 38, no. 2 (October 1994): 209–234.

deterrence and prevent bullying. Some favor only a selective proliferation to great powers such as Germany and Ukraine. Other neorealists endorse a wide horizontal spread of nuclear weapons to permit each state to block actions it opposes—a unit veto.[29]

Those who believe that "more is worse" do not argue that some peoples are more rational than others. They fear that the more nuclear actors, the more chances of a nuclear strike due to human, mechanical, or system frailty.

They concede that nuclear terror may have contributed to the "long peace" between Moscow and Washington, but add that the Soviet–U.S. standoff benefited from overall power parity, spy satellites that reduced the fear of surprise attack, some tacit "rules of the road," the absence of territorial claims, and lack of historical wounds to avenge.[30] None of these factors eases tensions between North and South Korea; India and Pakistan; or in the Middle East. Absent these factors, nuclear arms could easily inflame rather than stabilize.

How did the situation look in North Korea? Pyongyang signed the NPT in 1985, but the Clinton administration warned the IAEA (see Table 6.2) that North Korea was cheating—diverting sufficient fissile material from its Soviet-made nuclear reactor to make four to six bombs. Pyongyang put off any IAEA inspections until 1992 and refused in 1993 any special inspections of facilities that U.S. intelligence suspected of housing fissile material. Moreover, North Korea was building two larger reactors that could soon enable it to produce thirty nuclear bombs a year. When the UN Security Council in 1993 demanded that North Korea permit "special inspections" of suspected nuclear material storage sites, Pyongyang said it would withdraw from the NPT. We can guess how North Koreans saw their options (see Table 6.5).

Table 6.4 Is Nuclear Spread Inevitable? Is More Better?

Outcomes	How Likely Is Nuclear Spread?	
	Inevitable	Avoidable
Good	More is better.	Individual states should go all out to join the club.
Mixed	The worst dangers can be managed.	Be selective: permit only "stabilizing" proliferation.
Bad	Expect catastrophe and build defenses.	Proliferation can be halted and perhaps reversed.

Table 6.5 The 1994 Debate in North Korea: Should the DPRK Continue Its Nuclear Weapons Development?

Yes	No
We must practice self-help because Moscow and Beijing deserted us for the West.	Our economic plight compels us to join the world economy while preserving our government.
Even a few bombs can deter enemy attack and give us leverage; the U.S. talks big but does little.	If we go nuclear, South Korea and Japan may follow. Better to strike a deal with the U.S. that isolates South Korea.
Our foes will not dare attack us because they do not want a major war. Besides, we can attack Seoul and blow up South Korea's reactors.	Hanging tough is pointless. No one will attack us if we renounce nuclear arms. The U.S. promises us energy assistance.

29. Scott D. Sagan and Kenneth N. Waltz, *The Spread of Nuclear Weapons: A Debate* (New York: Norton, 1995); John J. Mearsheimer, "The Case for a Ukrainian Nuclear Deterrent," *Foreign Affairs* 72, no. 3 (summer 1993): 50–66; and Steven E. Miller, "The Case Against a Ukrainian Nuclear Deterrent," ibid., 67–80.

30. See John Lewis Gaddis, "The Long Peace: Elements of Stability in the Postwar International System," *International Security* 10, no. 4 (spring 1986): 99–142.

The United States prepared to attack the North Korean nuclear facilities in 1993, but North Korean and U.S. diplomats began to talk—details of how and why are in the next chapter. By 1994, they had reached a deal that permitted each side to back away from war. Too distrustful to sign a treaty, the parties accepted an "agreed framework" setting out a schedule of steps each country would take so long as the other did its part. North Korea would remain a full party to the NPT. North Korea would freeze its nuclear activities and dismantle its nuclear facilities. It would permit some IAEA inspections immediately and more later on. In exchange, the United States would arrange to supply North Korea with two light-water reactors (not suited for producing fissile materials) and heavy oil (good for heating but not for tank fuel) to make up for the energy lost by taking its existing reactor off-line. Washington would also reduce barriers to trade and investment and gradually normalize relations with Pyongyang, provided that North Korea reciprocated for example, by curbing its missile exports.

U.S. negotiators got built-in guarantees. The deal delayed most concessions until North Korea implemented key provisions. No oil arrived until the freeze on nuclear facilities began. No significant nuclear component would arrive until IAEA inspectors had accounted for past plutonium production and placed it under safeguards. Doors opened to peace.

Yes, Pyongyang drove a hard bargain. By violating its NPT and IAEA commitments, North Korea extorted pledges of over $4 billion worth of power supplies. South Korea would build the reactors. Seoul and Tokyo would pay for the reactors; the United States, for the oil. Still, $4 billion was trivial next to the costs of war—a bargain price for major arms control.

The Clinton administration also pressed North Korea to stop its development of two- and three-stage ballistic missiles. A deal seemed imminent in 2000, but negotiations were placed on hold until a new president was elected and inaugurated. In 2001, however, the new administration questioned the value of North Korea's word. And in January 2002, President Bush placed North Korea on his "axis of evil" list. When a U.S. emissary visited Pyongyang in October 2002, he presented the North Koreans with evidence that they had been covertly developing nuclear weapons. They replied (in effect): "What do you expect? You place us on the axis of evil list and prepare to attack us. You and your partners are just now starting work on the nuclear reactors promised eight years ago. The 1994 deal is off." The White House agreed and stopped U.S. payments for monthly deliveries of heavy oil to North Korea.

On the Bus

I'M WARNING YOU, COLIN, THIS BETTER **NOT** WORK...

11 18 2002
DANZIGER
TRIBUNE MEDIA www.danzigercartoons.com

Secretary of State Colin Powell persuaded the president to give the UN a try. Perhaps, as the cartoon suggests, the president and his adviser, Dr. Rice, did not want UN inspection to succeed. Yes, if Iraq stiff-armed the inspectors, this could justify a U.S.-led invasion. But in winter 2002–2003 the IAEA and UNMOVIC made enough progress to encourage France and other governments to call for giving the inspectors more time. President Bush and UK PM Tony Blair, however, complained that the inspection process was flawed. They asserted that Iraq was still in material breach of its obligations and needed to be disarmed by force.

While North Korea was far better armed, Bush's major arms control concern was Iraq. Baghdad had obstructed inspections by **UNSCOM (UN Special Commission)** so broadly that UNSCOM inspectors departed Iraq in 1998 and did not return. Bush in 2002 threatened to disarm Iraq or change its regime or both—with or without UN approval. France and Russia did not want the United States to act alone or to obtain an automatic go-ahead from the Security Council. Seven weeks of arm wrestling by U.S., French, and Russian diplomats produced a compromise. The UN Security Council unanimously approved Resolution 1441 on November 8, 2002. It provided for inspection by **UNMOVIC (UN Monitoring, Verification, and Inspection Commission)** and the IAEA to replace the previous system of UNSCOM plus the IAEA.

Washington hawks expected Iraq to dissimulate and give America a reason to attack. Doves hoped Iraq could be disarmed without war. But if Baghdad defied the UN ultimatum, America would enjoy greater support and less opposition if it sought to disarm Iraq by force. The Security Council resolution left it unclear whether or not Washington would be obliged to obtain another UN resolution to justify military action.

The UN gave Iraq seven days to reply. How would Baghdad respond? Four days after the Security Council resolution, Iraq's parliament rejected the UN demands but left the final decision to Iraq's top leaders. On the fifth day, the Foreign Ministry accepted the UN resolution insofar as it harmonized with international law—a potentially crucial qualification.

What the UN Security Council Resolution 1441 required of Iraq

Acting under Chapter VII of the Charter of the United Nations [the Security Council]:

1. Decides that Iraq has been and remains in *material breach* of its obligations. . . through Iraq's failure to cooperate with United Nations inspectors and the IAEA, and to complete the actions required under. . . resolution 687 (1991);

2. Decides. . . [to] afford Iraq. . . a *final opportunity* to comply with its disarmament obligations. . . .

3. Decides that . . . Iraq shall provide to UNMOVIC [UN Monitoring, Verification and Inspection Commission], the IAEA, and the Council, not later than 30 days from the date of this resolution, a *currently accurate, full, and complete declaration* of all aspects of its programmes to develop chemical, biological, and nuclear weapons, ballistic missiles, and other delivery systems such as unmanned aerial vehicles and dispersal systems designed for use on aircraft, including any holdings and precise locations of such weapons, components, sub-components, stocks of agents, and related material and equipment, the locations and work of its research, development and production facilities, as well as all other chemical, biological, and nuclear programmes, including any which it claims are for purposes not related to weapon production or material;

4. Decides that *false statements or omissions* in the declarations submitted by Iraq . . . and failure by Iraq at any time to comply with, and cooperate fully in the implementation of, this resolution shall constitute a *further material breach* of Iraq's obligations and will be reported to the Council for assessment. . . .

5. Decides that Iraq shall provide UNMOVIC and the IAEA immediate, unimpeded, unconditional, and unrestricted access to any and all, including underground areas, facilities, buildings, equipment, records, and means of transport which they wish to inspect, as well as immediate, unimpeded, unrestricted, and private access to all officials and other persons whom UNMOVIC or the IAEA wish to interview . . . [and] further decides that UNMOVIC and the IAEA may at their discretion conduct interviews inside or outside of Iraq, may facilitate the travel of those interviewed and family members outside of Iraq . . . without the presence of observers from the Iraqi government; and instructs UNMOVIC and requests the IAEA *to resume inspections no later than 45 days following adoption of this resolution and to update the Council 60 days thereafter.* . . .

7. . . . UNMOVIC and the IAEA [shall have the following right and facilities]:

. . . to determine the composition of their inspection teams [to secure] . . . the most qualified and experienced experts available;

. . . the privileges . . . provided in the Convention on Privileges and Immunities of the United Nations. . . .

UN inspectors returned to Iraq in late 2002, but they numbered less than 100 and were not so practiced as the earlier inspection teams. Iraq produced a 12,000-page inventory of its weapons and dual-use activities. Iraq denied it had conducted any WMD activities since the previous UN inspections stopped in 1998. Washington and London asserted this was a bald lie and that the long inventory contained many critical omissions.[31] Washington declared that an incomplete inventory constituted a material breach of Iraq's duties under the UN resolution. The weapons inspectors found a few missiles with ranges slightly longer than permitted but little other evidence of WMD.

France, Russia, and some other Security Council members wanted to give the inspectors more time, but President Bush and Prime Minister Blair argued that inspections were going nowhere. Iraq could hide its

31. See *The New York Times*, December 13, 2002, pp. 1, 14–15.

. . . entry into and out of Iraq . . . immediate movement to and from inspection sites, and the right to inspect any sites and buildings, including . . . *Presidential Sites.* . . .

. . . to be provided by Iraq the names of all personnel currently and formerly associated with Iraq's chemical, biological, nuclear, and ballistic missile programmes. . . .

. . . security of UNMOVIC and IAEA facilities . . . ensured by sufficient UN security guards;

. . . to declare, for the purposes of freezing a site to be inspected, exclusion zones, including surrounding areas and transit corridors, in which Iraq will suspend ground and aerial movement so that nothing is changed in or taken out of a site being inspected;

. . . free and unrestricted use and landing of fixed- and rotary-winged aircraft, including manned and unmanned reconnaissance vehicles;

. . . verifiably to remove, destroy, or render harmless all prohibited weapons, subsystems, components, records, materials, and other related items. . . .

. . . free import and use of equipment or materials for inspections and to seize and export any equipment, materials, or documents taken during inspections. . . .

10. Requests all Member States to give full support to UNMOVIC and the IAEA . . . by providing any information related to prohibited programmes or other aspects of their mandates, including on Iraqi attempts since 1998 to acquire prohibited items, and by recommending sites to be inspected, persons to be interviewed, conditions of such interviews, and data to be collected. . . .

11. Directs the Executive Chairman of UNMOVIC and the Director General of the IAEA to report immediately to the Council . . . any failure by Iraq to comply with its disarmament obligations, including its obligations regarding inspections under this resolution;

12. Decides to convene immediately upon receipt of a report . . . to consider the situation and the need for full compliance with all of the relevant Council resolutions in order to secure international peace and security;

13. Recalls [its warnings that Iraq] will face *serious consequences* as a result of its continued violations of its obligations;

14. Decides to remain seized of the matter.

Note: Elisions and emphases made by the author (W. C.).

weapons and intimidate its scientists so they would not reveal WMD secrets. Unable to get a UN resolution authorizing war, the United States and UK chose to invade without UN approval. Having ousted Saddam Hussein's regime in four weeks, the coalition carried out its own searches for WMD. The initial searches by coalition forces discovered only a few trailers that may have served as mobile laboratories to produce biological weapons. They hoped eventually to find stronger evidence to back up the bold claims.

Washington and London hoped that their evident determination to disarm by force a country that U.S. and UK leaders had suspected of producing WMD might dissuade other actors from trying to go nuclear. Pyongyang and Tehran, however, seemed to intensify their quests. Perhaps they judged that even a small nuclear force could deter a U.S.-led attack.

Meanwhile, the nuclear arms volcano grew higher and wider. India and Pakistan fielded nuclear weapons in the late 1990s and, when

Abu Kamara, age fourteen, holds a British rifle in May 2000 as he patrols a village not far from Freetown, capital of Sierra Leone. The gun is nearly so long as he is tall. Child soldiers multiplied in many poor countries in the late 20th and early 21st centuries. They were lured or compelled to take part in struggles for "national liberation" (as in Sri Lanka), against Zionism (in Palestine), or for mineral wealth—diamonds, oil, and precious metals (across Africa). Relative to diamonds, guns were cheap; so were lives and psyches. Children who learned to live by plunder and extortion lacked the education that might be useful in peacetime. British equipment delivered to the Sierra Leone Army to fight rebels could easily wind up in the arms of a child soldier. Tamils in Sri Lanka and Palestinians did not need rifles. Suicidists turned themselves into conventional weapons.

tensions surged in 2001, approached the brink of nuclear war. When India made some moves toward détente in 2003, Pakistan suggested that both sides eliminate their nuclear arsenals. New Delhi, however, worried not only about Pakistan but also about China, which continued its nuclear buildup. Indeed, Beijing warned it would take compensatory measures if the United States built a national missile defense. Here was a chain reaction: United States → PRC → India → Pakistan.

Meanwhile, nuclear threats coming from Pyongyang could provoke Japan to drop its nuclear allergy. If that happened, Beijing would have still another reason to buttress its own arsenal. Here was a potential chain reaction that could strengthen the first: United States → DPRK → Japan → PRC → India → Pakistan.

The failure of the Bush team to take North Korea seriously—either as a negotiating partner or a danger—could have wide repercussions. Proffering few carrots or threats to North Korea, Washington in 2003 indicated it might be satisfied merely to stop Pyongyang's export of weapons grade materials to other countries. Even this weak fallback position would be difficult to sustain, because small amounts of plutonium could be easily concealed.

Meanwhile, in the Middle East, Israel's arsenal continued to help justify efforts by Iran and other Muslim states to acquire their own nuclear weapons.

"Loose Nukes"

The nuclear threats arising from the former Soviet Union were more difficult to control than when the Kremlin ruled its empire with an iron fist. The good news was that tactical nuclear weapons were returned to Russia from the Soviet border republics in 1991–1992 and that Ukraine, Kazakstan, and Belarus foreswore nuclear arms. The bad news was that the former Second World overflowed with nuclear arms and fissile materials. Underpaid Russian scientists and colonels might sell a ball of plutonium or even a warhead from Russia's stockpiles. Nuclear smugglers were arrested in Russia, Germany, and Eastern Europe. One investigator said the Russian Navy guarded its potatoes better than its nuclear fuel.[32]

Russia and the United States agreed in 1992 to a Weapons and Nonproliferation Agreement to control fissile materials.[33] Under the **Cooperative Threat Reduction Program** (funded by the 1991 **Nunn–Lugar Act**), the U.S. Congress allocated $100 to $300 million annually to facilitate denuclearization and demilitarization of Russia, Ukraine, Kazakstan, and Belarus, and to reduce the threat of WMD proliferation.[34] But Russians complained that the United States kept its purse strings tight while some U.S. officials charged that the Russian Ministry of Atomic Energy and the Russian military shielded their secrets and assets from outsiders. In 2002, the United States agreed to invest $10 billion over the next decade to dismantle Russian weapons and prevent nuclear spread. The other advanced industrial nations agreed to match this sum. This would mean $2 billion a year—about one-fourth what the U.S. alone was spending just on antiballistic missile defense in 2003.[35] The genie was out of the bottle. It was not clear how many masters the genie would serve.

CONVENTIONAL ARMS PROLIFERATION

Weapons of mass destruction are comparatively cheap. Most arms spending is for conventional weapons. The world arms trade declined in the late 1980s, but the apparent successes of U.S. smart bombs increased demand for U.S. exports.

Double standards prevailed. Washington called for mutual limits on arms sales, only to step up arms transfers to Israel and other clients. U.S. exports accounted for nearly half the world's arms trade in the early 21st century. U.S. military aerospace exports alone jumped from about $8 billion to $11 billion in 1996. Saudi Arabia, Egypt, and Taiwan were the biggest buyers. Runners-up in arms exports were the UK (19 percent of world trade in 1999), France (18 percent), and Russia (7 percent). Unable to compete with the United States in high performance conventional

32. William C. Potter, "Before the Deluge? Assessing the Threat of Nuclear Leakage from the Post-Soviet States," *Arms Control Today* 25, no. 8 (October 1995): 9–16; see also the U.S. National Academy of Sciences report on excess weapons plutonium, summarized in ibid., 17–20.

33. Moscow and Washington built upon precedents. The NSG (Nuclear Suppliers Group) was established in 1974 to regulate nuclear exports, and the INFCE (International Nuclear Fuel Cycle Evaluation) in 1977 by both suppliers and importers to control nuclear energy.

34. See William S. Cohen, *Report of the Secretary of Defense to the President and Congress* (Washington, D.C.: Government Printing Office, April 1997), 61–67.

35. For a report on what had been done and remained to be done, see Senator Richard G. Lugar, "The Next Steps in U.S. Nonproliferation Policy," *Arms Control Today*, December 2002, 3–7.

arms, China and Russia sold missiles and nuclear equipment to the Islamic world. And tiny Israel exported weapons worth twice as much as China's exports.[36]

Washington explained that U.S. exports helped "maintain the balance of power"—whereas those of Russia and China destabilized it. U.S. and other arms exporters justified exports by the benefits to domestic industry: Without foreign sales, unit costs would be much higher at home. Furthermore, they said: "If we don't sell abroad, our rivals will. How can we keep our technological edge without foreign sales?"

In 1991–1992, the United Nations established the Registry of Conventional Arms. Perhaps transparency would inhibit the arms trade. UN members were supposed to volunteer data on the number of weapons—from tanks to missiles—imported or exported. But voluntary obligations were easily skirted. Officials in Chile reported one thing to the UN, another thing to the IMF, and something else in the national press.[37]

Attempting to increase transparency, more than thirty states adhered to the 1996 "Wassenaar Arrangement"—a voluntary system to coordinate national controls on the export of conventional arms and dual-use technologies by promoting information exchange through a consultative forum. As of 1997, the United States, UK, France, and Russia belonged, but not Israel, China, or any Arab country.

A major threat to life and limb comes from one of the cheapest and most common weapons—land mines. More people have been killed by land mines than by WMD. In the 1990s there were at least 85 million mines beneath the soil of sixty-four countries—from Afghanistan to Cambodia to El Salvador. Mines are easy to plant but difficult to remove. To neutralize a $5 mine can easily cost $1,000. But consider also the cost of mines not cleared: lives lost, bodies maimed, farmlands unplowed; the costs of caring for invalids (such a burden that some were executed by their own families in Afghanistan). Humanitarian agencies sought to persuade all UN members to ban the export of antipersonnel mines. But demand and supply (from forty-eight manufacturing countries) remained high.

Canada and nongovernmental organizations (NGOs) led the fight for a global ban signed in Ottawa by more than 100 countries in 1997—minus the signatures of the United States, Russia, and China. Beijing and others liked land mines cheap and dirty. Washington wanted to ban all but high-tech mines that deactivated after a specified time and insisted on the right to retain mines on the North–South Korea dividing line.

36. International Institute for Strategic Studies, *The Military Balance, 2000–2001* (London: Oxford University Press, 2000), 288 and the 1997 edition, 264–265; *Arms Control Today*, December 2002, 32–34.

37. See Edward J. Laurence et al., *Arms Watch: SIPRI Report on the First Year of the UN Register of Conventional Arms* (New York: Oxford University Press, 1993).

Even "nonlethal" weapons could be lethal. In 2002, Russian special forces used gas to incapacitate terrorists, but the admixture was so strong that it killed many innocent people. The United States and other governments were developing agents that could blind, paralyze, or put to sleep demonstrators, terrorists, soldiers, and—why not?—government decision makers. Pilots on long missions took drugs to stay awake and, later, to sleep. If a technology existed, it might well be used—and abused.

WHAT PROPOSITIONS HOLD? WHAT QUESTIONS REMAIN?

INTERDEPENDENCE, MUTUAL GAIN, AND OPENNESS

If all nations disarm, will there be peace? Not unless human life and institutions are transformed. States arm because they fear and fear because they arm. If all swords become plowshares, some humans will still menace others with slings and clubs. David's "dual-purpose" sling sufficed to kill Goliath.

Mutual vulnerability makes the security dilemma pervasive. As a result, real security must be both mutual and universal.[38] But this insight is difficult to implement. Like the hunter who leaps for the hare, governments often pass up potentially large mutual gains for small, one-sided gains available here and now.

Secrecy often amplifies insecurity. Governments prefer to plan and negotiate armaments behind closed doors. Former Secretary of State Henry Kissinger used "back channels" to Moscow that bypassed Congress and even the official U.S. negotiating team. Not surprisingly, when the White House presented SALT 1 as a done deal, the Senate complained. Secrecy can blind even the secret holders. Had MIRVs been debated more openly, they might have been curbed—to mutual advantage.

The Arms Control Paradox

Here is the paradox: Arms controls are easiest to negotiate when they are not needed—when relations are so cordial that neither party fears the other. Still, the record shows that arms limitations are possible even when tensions run high. Thus, Washington and Moscow negotiated and implemented SALT 1 while the Vietnam War raged; they concluded the INF Treaty while the Reagan White House backed anti-Communist guerrillas worldwide.

38. Both conditions were stressed by Soviet President Gorbachev in the late 1980s. See Clemens, *Can Russia Change?* chaps. 7–8.

Is Parity Necessary for Arms Control?

Must rivals have the same quantity and quality of arms before they can trim forces? The answer is no. Many arms accords have been concluded despite deep asymmetries. Trade-offs may be paid in multiple currencies. Soviet leaders often focused on economic gains from arms control while U.S. leaders sought strategic stability. Contrary to realist doctrine, arms accords often permit mutual but unequal gain.

The "multiple symmetry" model distorts history and offers bad advice. It exaggerates the action–reaction behavior of competing actors. The USSR never tried to match the U.S. Navy, nor did the United States emulate the large Soviet Army. *Sufficiency* is a better guide to policy than matching. Each society should listen to its own drummer—not mechanically mimic others.

Prevention is easier than cure. It is more feasible to ban a weapon before deployment than after. But preventive measures are difficult to adopt during periods of technological ferment. Against terrorists or truly rogue regimes, nothing may work—not even the threat of annihilation.

Does Arms Control Save, Make, or Lose Money?

The economic impacts of defense spending are complicated. Military outlays can pillage wealth. But they can also benefit an economy if they nourish technology, work habits, and infrastructure. The U.S. interstate highway system and the Internet resulted from defense programs. Taiwan, Singapore, and South Korea for decades spent much more of their GDP on defense than Japan did, but they also achieved high growth. North Korea outspent South Korea on military preparedness but stagnated economically.

The hoped-for peace dividend proved difficult to collect. Both Washington and Moscow wanted to keep weapons labs and production lines open. It is difficult to turn swords into plowshares—even more difficult in former Communist economies than in free market economies. Backed with Nunn–Lugar funds, some U.S. firms tried to enlist former Soviet arms builders in civilian enterprises, but the match was often jarring. Should former missile makers now produce soft drinks? Joint ventures with U.S. companies scored some successes but were hobbled by many problems.[39] Former Communist states such as Slovakia found that to make autos instead of tanks would require much retooling and retraining. It was easier to turn out Soviet-designed tanks and planes for Third World markets.

39. Kevin P. O'Prey, *A Farewell to Arms? Russia's Struggles with Defense Conversion* (New York: Twentieth Century Fund, 1995).

Memo to the President:

All countries are vulnerable to nuclear and other forms of terror. The task of hitting a fly in the sky (or a swarm of hornets) remains technologically daunting. Even if antiballistic missile defenses are improved, they will not stop low-flying cruise missiles. Nor will they help against weapons smuggled into a country. A nuclear sword of Damocles can still fall at any moment. What if just one or two missiles penetrate our defenses and strike any city with nuclear, biological, or chemical (NBC) weapons? A single nuclear explosion in the atmosphere can knock out our electric systems. Will survivors, if any, have electricity? Will their computers and cell phones work? Will their charge card and bank records remain? Will their cars find gas? Will their homes have heat? Water?

Every country with nuclear power stations is vulnerable to terrorists. A conventional bomb can open a reactor and spew deadly radioactivity far and wide.

Are Negotiations Good for Arms Control? Is Arms Control Good for Peace?

Arms accords may be steps toward a world where brute force plays a declining role next to soft power, where fitness and well-being are measured not by warheads but by fewer infant deaths and more education. But the net impact of arms control on peace and security is unclear. Significant arms limitations have been negotiated and implemented: Some treaties have probably reduced the danger of war and saved money; arms talks have kept channels open and contributed to détente. But disarmament negotiations and propaganda have also spurred distrust and arms competition. Despite many treaties, the USSR and United States in 1990 possessed 55,000 nuclear warheads (tactical and strategic).

How Much Is Enough?

Americans never collected a substantial peace dividend. In constant dollars, the U.S. defense budget in the late 1990s was still four-fifths its level in the late 1980s. U.S. defense outlays in the late 1990s exceeded the combined military budgets of all other industrialized countries. This disparity widened under President George W. Bush.

The Pentagon requested some $15 billion more in fiscal year 2004 (details in tables 6.6 and 6.7). The four major allocations went to operations and maintenance, 31 percent of the total; military personnel, 26 percent; procurement, 19 percent; research, development, testing, and evaluation, 16 percent. The Navy and the Air Force would each get about $114 billion; the Army, $94 billion. The Missile Defense Agency funds would run to more than $9 billion of these totals, but the cost of war fighting in Iraq was not included.

The indirect burdens of defense were still larger, because the growing budget deficit would scare away foreign investors and raise the cost of borrowing inside the United States. A climate of anxiety would reduce economic activity. Reservists called to active duty would disrupt economic life. Money spent on defense tended to reduce funds for education, culture, and welfare inside the United States as well as American contributions to emergency relief and development in less fortunate countries.

Table 6.6 Fiscal Year 2004 Department of Defense Budget Authority Request, February 3, 2003

National Defense Discretionary Funding ($U.S. billions)

Budget Authority	FY '03	FY '04	FY '05	FY '06	FY '07	FY '08	FY '09	TOTAL FY '04–'09
DoD military	364.6	379.9	399.8	419.8	440.5	461.8	483.6	2,585.4
DoE and other	17.6	19.3	19.8	19.9	19.5	18.6	19.0	116.1
TOTAL	**382.2**	**399.1**	**419.6**	**439.7**	**460.0**	**480.4**	**502.7**	**2,701.5**

*DoE = Department of Energy military program.

Table 6.7 FY '04 Budget Request by Function Increase/Decrease from FY '03 (in $U.S. billions)

Function	FY '03	FY '04 Requested	$ Change	Percentage Change
Military personnel	93.4	98.6	+5.2	+5.6%
Operations and maintenance	113.6	117.0	+3.4	+3.0%
Procurement	70.0	72.7	+2.7	+3.9%
Research, development, testing, and evaluation	56.8	61.8	+5.0	+8.8%
Military construction	6.3	5.0	−1.3	−20.6%
Family housing	4.2	4.0	−0.2	−4.8%
Other DoD programs	17.3	17.9	+0.6	+3.5%
Miscellaneous other	3.1	2.8	−0.3	−9.7%
TOTAL	**364.6**	**379.9**	**+15.3**	**+4.2%**

Twelve Policy Guidelines

Let us be neither hawks nor doves. Better to be wise like owls.[40] Here are twelve guidelines:

1. Americans' willingness to deal with global security threats depends on technologies that keep U.S. casualties low. We should continue to enhance our "system of systems"—coordinated intelligence and precision targeting. But we must also maintain substantial forces quickly transportable over vast distances. We must continue to invest in quantity as well as quality. Cutting military forces and research can save money today but compel sharp increases later. If demobilization invites aggression, peace dividends can evaporate. Compared to fighting, arms at the ready are cheap.

2. Maintain a credible but nonprovocative deterrent, but reduce reliance on nuclear deterrence over the long run. Develop a conventional deterrent to supplant nuclears. It would be imprudent to scrap all nuclear weapons if only because scientists will still know how to make them. But we should encourage Russia to join

40. See also Graham T. Allison, Albert Carnesale, and Joseph S. Nye, Jr., eds., *Hawks, Doves, and Owls: An Agenda for Avoiding Nuclear War* (New York: Norton, 1985).

us in cutting our nuclear weapons to a number well below 1,000 and encourage China to hold to a minimum deterrent.

3. Do more to bring Europe, Russia, China, Japan, and others into cooperative security programs. We could get by with much smaller forces if we had greater confidence that other players would partner with us for mutual gain.

4. Continue to block horizontal proliferation of WMD. Take strong measures with Moscow to control and reduce Russia's stocks of WMD and the materials to make them.

5. Try to eliminate any nuclear threat from Iraq, North Korea, or Iran by a strong blend of carrots and sticks. If they have missiles tipped with WMD, develop and deploy theater defenses to protect against regional threats. Do not build an extensive ABM system that could undermine Russian or Chinese confidence in their present deterrents.

6. Lengthen the fuse. Prevent war by miscalculation or accident. Strengthen intelligence and command and control systems.

7. Prevent and control crises.

8. Pursue conventional as well as WMD arms control. Join with others to tighten verification of bans on biological and chemical weapons.

9. Link arms control analysis and defense planning. Avoid propagandistic and political distractions.

10. Restructure and improve our capacity to resist terrorists, homegrown and foreign, some of whom may have mass destruction weapons.

11. Strengthen the United Nations, the IAEA, and other international security regimes for arms control, verification, and enforcement. Lay the foundation for a permanent UN police force.

12. Most important, reduce the root causes of arms and diffidence, transform relationships.

KEY NAMES AND TERMS

antiballistic missile (ABM)	joker	Strategic Arms Limitation Talks (SALT)
arms control	minimum deterrent	Strategic Arms Reduction Treaty (START)
Baruch Plan	multiple individually targetable reentry vehicles (MIRVs)	Strategic Defense Initiative (SDI)
Conventional Forces in Europe (CFE) Treaty	multiple symmetry	Strategic Offensive Reductions Treaty (SORT)
cooperative security	national missile defense (NMD)	submarine-launched ballistic missile (SLBM)
Cooperative Threat Reduction Program	Nuclear Nonproliferation Treaty (NPT)	theater ballistic missile defense (TBMD)
Deadlock	Nunn–Lugar Act	triad
disarmament	parity	UN Special Commission (UNSCOM)
Intermediate-Range Nuclear Forces (INF) Treaty	second strike	UN Monitoring, Verification, and Inspection Commission (UNMOVIC)
International Atomic Energy Agency (IAEA)	security regime	
	security	
	Stag Hunt	

QUESTIONS TO DISCUSS

1. "Arms limitation efforts have succeeded only when the weapons at stake are obsolete or otherwise redundant." Is this an accurate assessment?

2. "Arms control negotiations have been counterproductive. At best they created an illusion of progress while the tools of war multiplied." Evaluate.

3. "The strongest power, to retain its hegemony, should strive for supremacy in the quality and quantity of arms." Evaluate.

4. How have the nuclear haves sought to limit supply of nuclear arms? How have they sought to reduce demand for them?

5. Advise Moscow: Should the Kremlin seek to maintain parity with the U.S. in the early 21st century?

6. Advise Pyongyang: Should North Korea strive to obtain nuclear arms—either openly or clandestinely?

7. Advise Beijing: Should the PRC condemn, ignore, or support U.S. efforts to build theater ballistic missile defenses?

8. Advise India: Should you accept Pakistan's proposal for complete bilateral nuclear disarmament?

9. Advise Washington: Should you seek to negotiate complete nuclear disarmament, a Russian–U.S. ceiling of 250 nuclear weapons, or maintain the SORT ceiling of 2,200 nuclear weapons? If ceilings are placed on RF and U.S. forces, should you ignore other nuclear powers or seek limits on their forces as well? Do the principles of the 1922 Washington Naval Treaty offer guidance?

10. Advise London: Should you promote alternative approaches to security, such as nonviolent sanctions?

RECOMMENDED RESOURCES

BOOKS

Blacker, Coit D., and Gloria Duffy, eds. *International Arms Control: Issues and Agreements*. 2d ed. Stanford, Calif.: Stanford University Press, 1984.

Bunn, George. *Extending the Non-Proliferation Treaty: Legal Questions Faced by the Parties in 1995*. Washington, D.C.: American Society of International Law, 1994.

Butler, Richard. *Fatal Choice: Nuclear Weapons and the Illusion of Missile Defense*. Boulder, Colo.: Westview, 2001.

Cirincione, Joseph, Miriam Rajkumar, and Jon B. Wolfsthal. *Deadly Arsenals: Tracking Weapons of Mass Destruction*. Washington, D. C.: Carnegie Endowment for International Peace, 2002.

Ellis, Jason D. *Defense by Other Means: The Politics of US–NIS Threat Reduction and Nuclear Security Cooperation*. Westport, Conn.: Greenwood Publishing Group, 2001.

Encyclopedia of Arms Control and Disarmament. 3 vols. New York: Scribner's, 1993.

Garthoff, Raymond L. *Détente and Confrontation: American–Soviet Relations from Nixon to Reagan*. Washington, D.C.: Brookings Institution, 1985.

Goldblat, Jozef. *Arms Control: The New Guide to Negotiations and Agreements with New CD-ROM Supplement*. Thousand Oaks, Calif.: Sage Publications, 2002.

Graham, Thomas Jr. *Disarmament Sketches: Three Decades of Arms Control and International Law*. Seattle: University of Washington Press, 2002.

Harvard Project on Cooperative Denuclearization. *Cooperative Denuclearization*. Harvard University Center for Science and International Affairs, Harvard University, Cambridge, Mass., 1993.

Holloway, David. *Stalin and the Bomb: The Soviet Union and Atomic Energy, 1939–1956*. New Haven, Conn.: Yale University Press, 1994.

Institute for National Strategic Studies. *Strategic Assessment*. Washington, D.C.: Government Printing Office, 1995–. Annual.

Krepon, Michael. *Cooperative Threat Reduction, Missile Defense and the Nuclear Future*. New York: Palgrave, 2002.

Lavoy, Peter R., Scott D. Sagan, and James J. Wirtz. *Planning the Unthinkable: How New Powers Will Use Nuclear, Biological, and Chemical Weapons*. Ithaca, N.Y.: Cornell University Press, 2000.

Lindsay, James M., and Michael E. O'Hanlon. *Defending America, Updated: The Case for Limited National Missile Defense*. Washington D.C.: Brookings Institution Press, 2002.

Rhodes, Richard. *The Making of the Atomic Bomb*. New York: Simon & Schuster, 1986.

Shields, John M., and William C. Potter. *Dismantling the Cold War: U.S. and N.I.S. Perspectives on the Nunn–Lugar Cooperative Threat Reduction Program*. Cambridge, Mass.: MIT Press, 1997.

SIPRI Yearbook [title varies]. Stockholm: Stockholm International Peace Research Institute, 1970–. Annual.

Recommended Resources (continued)

U.S. Arms Control and Disarmament Agency. *Documents on Disarmament* [multiple volumes]. Washington, D.C.: Government Printing Office, 1960–1986.

U.S. Department of State. *Documents on Disarmament, 1945–1959.* 2 vols. Washington, D.C.: Government Printing Office, 1960.

U.S. Senate. Committee on Foreign Relations. *Disarmament and Security: A Collection of Documents, 1919–1955.* Washington, D.C.: Government Printing Office, 1956.

Wright, Susan, ed. *Biological Warfare and Disarmament: New Problems/New Perspectives.* Lanham, Md.: Rowman & Littlefield, 2002.

JOURNALS

Adelphi Papers
Arms Control Today
Bulletin of the Atomic Scientists
Nonproliferation Review
Survival

WEB SITES

The Antiballistic Missile Treaty (full text)
http://www.psr.org/s11/abmfs.html
Arms Trade Database
http://www.cdi.org/issues/armstrade/
Carnegie Endowment for International Peace: Nonproliferation Program
http://www.ceip.org/programs/npp/index.html

Center for Nonproliferation Studies
http://cns.miis.edu/
DFax Disarmament News
http://csf.colorado.edu/dfax/index.htm
Federation of American Scientists Arms Sales Monitoring Project
http://www.fas.org/asmp/
Henry L. Stimson Center
http://www.stimson.org/
Hiroshima Archive (pictures, information, time line)
http://www.lclark.edu/~history/HIROSHIMA
International Atomic Energy Agency
http://www.iaea.or.at/
The Internet and the Bomb
http://www.nrdc.org/nrdcpro/nuguide/guinx.html
Land Mine Campaign
http://www.vvaf.org
SALT 1
http://www.fas.org/nuke/control/salt1/
SALT 2
http://www.state.gov/www/global/arms/treaties/salt2-1.html
SIPRI Chemical and Biological Warfare Project
http://www.sipri.se/projects/chembio.html
Treaty on the Non-Proliferation of Nuclear Weapons (full text)
http://www.unog.ch/disarm/distreat/npt.pdf

NEGOTIATING CONFLICT: HOW CAN FOES BECOME PARTNERS?

THE BIG QUESTIONS IN CHAPTER 7

- What are the options for dealing with conflict?

- How should you blend carrots and sticks to influence others?

- Is it best to "fight fire with fire"?

- When should you be tough? When should you be conciliatory?

- How can you get more of what you want without fighting?

- How can you escape the vicious cycle of distrust when dealing with a strong and determined adversary?

- How can you minimize criticism from domestic foes when making peaceful overtures to adversaries abroad?

- What risks can you take for peace? Can you be sure that foreign foes will not abuse your efforts to move toward peace?

- How can you replace conflict and distrust with a strategy of peace and mutual gain? How turn détente into an entente?

- What kinds of leaders have been the most effective negotiators?

- What strategies work best between and among actors who are at once partners and rivals?

How to Deal with "Koraq" and "Irkor"? .... *Each*

regime has been condemned by Human Rights Watch and Freedom House for repressing its own people. The supreme leader in each country is an enigma—sometimes smiling but usually menacing. You believe that Koraqi agents blew up an Air France and a JAL airliner. Irkor holds dozens of Western and Japanese businesspeople and journalists captive—charged with espionage. Both Koraq and Irkor claim the right to absorb their neighbors as long-lost provinces. Each threatens to harm the United States if America interferes in what each regime sees as its domestic jurisdiction.

You would prefer to resolve differences without war, but you are reluctant to make concessions. You don't want to look soft. Domestic foes may accuse you of cowardice. If you give Koraq an inch, it may try for a mile. Is it even thinkable to cut a deal with Koraq's leader? If not, should you isolate, weaken, and perhaps overthrow him?

Has niceness ever worked in dealing with hard-line foes? You study the precedents: For decades, Washington and Moscow were locked in protracted conflict. So were Washington and Beijing, and Beijing and Moscow. Each bilateral confrontation shaped the other to form a great power triangle. Each conflict heated up and cooled down, leaving embers that still glow. You note that mainland China and "island China"—Taiwan—are torn between conflict and conciliation; this is true of North and South Korea as well. Do the experiences of Beijing, Moscow, Washington, Taipei, and the two Koreas offer any guidelines for coping with Koraq and Irkor?

CONTENDING CONCEPTS AND EXPLANATIONS

WHEN TO BE TOUGH? WHEN TO BE CONCILIATORY? HOW?

States and other IR actors have interests that harmonize or conflict with those of other players. If they harmonize, the parties may collaborate to enhance parallel or shared objectives. If they clash, they confront each other as adversaries. Tensions may escalate from harsh words to threats to open hostilities. Détente (the relaxation of tensions) is also possible. Moving away from confrontation, actors engage in trade, form an alliance, reach an entente (understanding), achieve solidarity, and confederate or unite. A warming trend toward accommodation is a rapprochement. But détente need not produce entente or solidarity; smiles and sweet talk could be tricks intended to get the other side to lower its guard. Détente is often short-lived. If it does not produce an entente, it may give way to renewed tensions.

As we see in Table 7.1, the parties to a conflict may fight or withdraw. They may also try to divide the values at stake, or transform the relationship and create values together. To divide or create values, however, requires cooperation. If you are a conditional cooperator, how can you induce the other side to cooperate? Should you be tough or conciliatory? How should you blend sticks and carrots? Do you begin with a threat or a smile? If the other side frowns, how long do you keep smiling?

Table 7.1 Four Responses to Conflict

	Passive	Active
Negative	Surrender values (retreat)	Claim values (fight)
Positive	Divide values	Create values for mutual gain

Tit-for-Tat

Negotiation implies an exchange—a quid pro quo, something for something. The quid could be different in size or quality from the quo. But tit-for-tat (TFT) requires rough symmetry. It means to pay back in kind. It connotes a vengeful "eye for an eye, tooth for a tooth." But the payback could also be a reward for a positive action.[1]

A strategy based on TFT proved to be the winning strategy in repeated plays of the Prisoner's Dilemma in the computer tournament described in Chapter 1. The strategy was a simple variant of TFT: If you move first, be nice and cooperate. Thereafter match the other player's previous move. Start off nice and never initiate toughness, but be provokable—immediately respond to toughness with toughness. However, you should also be forgiving—return to cooperation as soon as the other side cooperates.

1. Indeed, *tit* may come from *tip*, a reward. But the meaning of the phrase TFT is very much like "this for that" or quid pro quo.

TFT pleases realists. This behavior sends a clear message that you will punish force with force but reward cooperation.[2] The TFT approach will elicit good, cooperative outcomes and minimize poor ones. Both sides learn to forgo immediate gains in favor of long-term rewards.[3] The downside is that if both sides follow TFT, just one tough move puts them on an endless treadmill of mutual defection. Once mutual defection begins, it persists. This explains why the Cold War "conflict spiral" was so hard to break. Washington and Moscow usually matched each other's tough deeds and ignored tentative smiles. The security dilemma aggravated their relationship. One side's defensive steps looked threatening to the other. TFT logic pressed for multiple symmetry or better. Furthermore, U.S. and Soviet TFT was self-righteous. Each side reasoned: "They started it, we're just paying them back in kind."

TFT also took hold at the **demilitarized zone (DMZ),** the no-man's land buffer zone between North and South Korea established by the 1953 armistice.[4] Representatives of the UN Command and North Korea met weekly in a Quonset hut at **Panmunjom** in what became a ritual of mutual acrimony. Each blamed the other for violating the armistice. An atmosphere of mutual distrust and disdain reigned. If a North Korean gave an American a piece of paper with his left hand—a sign of contempt—the American usually accepted it with his left.[5]

How to Reverse a Conflict Spiral: True GRIT

How could the parties shift from "fighting fire with fire" to "enlarging the pie" for mutual gain? An alternative approach suggests that one side make unilateral but contingent concessions. Psychologist Charles E. Osgood in 1962 proposed reversing the conflict spiral by **GRIT—graduated reciprocation in tension reduction.**[6] Either side might initiate the process, but the stronger party could more safely accept the risks that go with taking the first steps.

Before embarking on GRIT, the initiator must make clear to the other side its intent to get off the treadmill. Here is the message it must communicate:

"We are embarking on a strategy to reduce tensions. We will make several unilateral initiatives to demonstrate our goodwill. We shall give you time to show your goodwill. We shall proceed to larger concessions and compromise accords if you reciprocate. But unless tension reducing moves become mutual, we will revert to TFT."

GRIT may face many pitfalls. First of all, a friendly gesture may be misconstrued. Thus, in 1970, a U.S. Army lieutenant in the UN Command

2. When Queen Elizabeth visited San Francisco to see President Reagan in 1983, she observed that the Union Jack was flown upside down. The gaffe may well have been inadvertent. Still, when Reagan visited the queen on her royal yacht *Britannia*, the U.S. flag dangled upside down. If allies teach one another lessons in this manner, foes are even more inclined to do so.

3. Robert Axelrod, *The Evolution of Cooperation* (New York: Basic Books, 1984); and Axelrod, "An Evolutionary Approach to Norms," *American Political Science Review* 80 (1986): 1095–1111.

4. The July 27, 1953, armistice was signed by U.S. General Mark Clark, commander in chief, UN Command; Kim Il-sung, supreme commander, [North] Korean People's Army; and Peng Dehuai, commander, Chinese People's Volunteers. The agreement provided also for a Neutral Nations Supervisory Commission.

5. The UN command reported more than 1,000 armistice violations just in 1968 and 1969, leaving 221 killed among UN personnel, 96 South Korean civilians dead, and over 600 North Korean infiltrators killed south of the DMZ. The North replied by accusing the "U.S. imperialist aggressors" of more than 7,000 violations in 1969.

6. At tense moments in the Cold War, some Westerners called for unilateral disarmament. Their slogan: "Better Red Than Dead." But no Western government seriously considered this option. Charles Osgood hoped to break the impasse. See Osgood, *An Alternative to War or Surrender* (Urbana: University of Illinois Press, 1962); see also Amitai Etzioni, *The Hard Way to Peace: A New Strategy* (New York: Crowell-Collier, 1962).

at Panmunjom decided to improve the climate by smiling at North Korean soldiers in the Quonset hut instead of glaring sternly. When a North Korean indicated that he wanted to pass, the American smiled and made way for him. Shortly thereafter, the American found himself surrounded by several North Koreans who began to jostle him. They interpreted his conciliatory gesture as weakness.[7]

GRIT could not begin with goodwill gestures by a low-level officer. For GRIT to work in this instance, the U.S. president or head of the UN (U.S.) team should have announced a new strategy—and made sure that North Korean leaders and troops got the message.

A second pitfall is that small steps may lead nowhere. To be safe, the initiator usually begins with symbolic gestures. The other side may interpret these as cheap tricks and not reciprocate. Neither side wishes to be fooled.

Third, the initiator may renounce GRIT if the other side takes too long to respond. During this interval, the initiator's leaders are exposed to domestic criticism as well as external risk.

Fourth is the **monkey wrench problem**. Domestic foes or jealous clients can throw a monkey wrench that disrupts the process of tension reduction. Détente is a fragile flower, easily crushed.

Fifth, governments are not monolithic. Bureaucratic inertia and vested interests can throttle GRIT. Purveyors of propaganda and "dirty tricks" may continue their standard operating routines—business as usual.

Finally, momentum may be hard to sustain. The first steps toward conciliation may come cheap, while further moves encounter profound obstacles, as we shall see in each case study.

Triangular Diplomacy

If there are three parties to a conflict, **triangular diplomacy**—the attempt by one party in a dispute to exploit differences between two others—may be useful. When Washington perceived that China and Russia were rivals, several U.S. presidents hoped that a U.S. carrot to China would act like a stick against Russia. Each corner of the triangle was a giant or potential giant. The United States had the world's largest economy; Russia/USSR, the largest territory; and China, the largest population.

Did good relations between two corners of the triangle depend upon tension between the other two? Or could relations have been positive among all three? Realists advised triangulation, believing that "the enemy of my enemy is my partner, at least for now." Idealists prescribed friendship among all three—win–win–win. The interdependence school saw triangular diplomacy as another form of exploitation that might yield

7. Walter C. Clemens, Jr., "GRIT at Panmunjom: Conflict and Cooperation in Divided Korea," *Asian Survey* 13, no. 6 (June 1973): 531–559 at 548.

short-term gains but then backfire. Given their mutual vulnerability, the three great powers were most likely to enhance their long-term objectives if they could cultivate three-sided cooperation. Which school, if any, was right? Let us review some cases that illustrate how varying blends of niceness and toughness shaped IR during and since the Cold War.[8]

COMPARING THEORY AND REALITY: STICKS AND CARROTS

THE GREAT POWER TRIANGLE

The world's power structure was essentially bipolar from 1945 until the late 1980s. The image of bipolarity was strong in the 1950s, when Beijing's leaders publicly followed Moscow's line. But they openly split from the Soviet camp in the 1960s and began to play an independent role.

Soviet power declined in the 1980s, as we saw in Chapter 5, while China grew stronger. By the 1990s the balance was unipolar, leaving China with a potential to challenge the United States or cooperate for mutual gain.

The Spirit of Geneva, 1955

The first summit meeting between Soviet and Western leaders since World War II took place in Geneva in 1955. The summit generated a "Spirit of Geneva"—the first East–West détente in a decade. How did it come about?

After Josef Stalin's death in March 1953, his successors signaled that they wanted better relations with the West. President Dwight D. Eisenhower decided to test Soviet intentions. He instructed his speechwriter: "Let us come out, straight, no double-talk, no slick sophisticated propaganda devices—and say: this is what we'll do—we'll withdraw our armies from there if you'll withdraw yours. . . . The slate is clean—now let's begin."[9] Eisenhower delivered his "Give Peace a Chance" speech on April 16, 1953. He said he would believe in Moscow's desire for peace when that desire turned into deeds, for example, an armistice in Korea and a peace treaty for Austria. Washington, he said, would then be ready to negotiate on German unification and disarmament.

The Soviets liked this new tune so much that they published Eisenhower's full text in the Communist Party newspaper *Pravda*, and the government organ, *Izvestiia*. Within months the Kremlin endorsed the Korean armistice and relaxed its grip on Austria. The new party secretary, Nikita Khrushchev, wanted a GRIT-like approach to East–West differences. He called for peaceful coexistence, seeing it as a way to defeat the capitalist world without war.

8. One book on tension-reducing strategies concluded that niceness won out over harshness. See Joshua S. Goldstein and John R. Freeman, *Three-Way Street: Strategic Reciprocity in World Politics* (Chicago: University of Chicago Press, 1990). Their analysis, however, depends heavily on "event" data banks based on newspaper accounts that are quite incomplete. Thus, journalists did not know until 1963 that Moscow and Beijing had signed a defense technology pact in 1957 and immediately quarreled about its basic terms.

9. Quoted in Deborah Welch Larson, "Crisis Prevention and the Austrian State Treaty," *International Organization* 41, no. 1 (winter 1987): 27–60 at 36. See also Matthew A. Evangelista, "Cooperation Theory and Disarmament Negotiations in the 1950s," *World Politics* 42, no. 4 (July 1990): 502–528.

As we see from the time line, both sides mixed conciliatory moves with harsh ones. Neither Moscow nor Washington gave GRIT a fair chance, because each side sent contradictory messages. Each side behaved as though it was caught in an approach–avoidance syndrome. It wanted, but also did not want, an accommodation. Soviet Foreign Minister Vyacheslav M. Molotov and U.S. Secretary of State John Foster Dulles preferred East–West confrontation. They and other hard-liners undermined the push to extend the Spirit of Geneva.[10]

No corner of the great power triangle pursued a clear line toward the other two. Stalin had bullied the Chinese Communists for decades. After Stalin's death, Khrushchev wanted to put Sino–Soviet relations on a more friendly footing. But Khrushchev and Chinese leader Mao Zedong quickly came to despise one another. One was a miner's son who spoke in peasant proverbs; the other saw himself as a great military strategist and a poet. In 1954, Moscow and Beijing began to compete for the goodwill of Indonesia and other nonaligned countries.

But some elements of GRIT and triangular diplomacy entered into Chinese–U.S. relations. Premier Zhou Enlai began to play China's own peace card. He called in April 1955 for Chinese–U.S. negotiations on Taiwan, then under the protection of the U.S. Navy. In July, Beijing released eleven U.S. airmen imprisoned in China and suggested talks with Washington. Chinese and U.S. ambassadors met in Geneva in August. The ambassadors scored no breakthroughs, but Beijing and Washington developed this format and used it on several occasions before normal relations were established in the 1970s.

For most of 1955, the great power triangle showed a small but uncertain positive sign between Washington and Moscow, a possible shift from minus to plus between Washington and Beijing, and both plus and minus elements between the two Communist giants (see Figure 7.1).

TIME LINE: RISE AND DECLINE OF THE GENEVA SPIRIT IN 1955

3/19
Soviets propose international controls of nuclear disarmament.

5/1
Soviet bombers fly over Red Square to impress Western observers.

5/10
Soviet diplomats endorse West's disarmament principles.

5/14
Soviets create Warsaw Pact alliance.

5/15
Big Four recognize Austria's independence.

7/18–8/23
Big Four hold summit meeting in Geneva.

8/12
Soviets announce 640,000-man troop reduction.

August
Soviets conduct H-bomb tests.

10/27–11/16
Big Four foreign ministers' meeting in Geneva ends in acrimony and Spirit of Geneva wanes.

---

10. The 1955 and 1963 cases described here and in the next section are documented in Lincoln P. Bloomfield, Walter C. Clemens, Jr., and Franklin Griffiths, *Khrushchev and the Arms Race: Soviet Interests in Arms Control and Disarmament, 1954–1964* (Cambridge, Mass.: MIT Press, 1966).

In March 1963 *President John F. Kennedy asks: "How can the U.S. step back from the Cuban precipice and—at the same time—curb China's nuclear weapons program?"*

Kennedy reviews the record—U.S. relations with the USSR have fluctuated between détente and hostility since Stalin's death. The Spirit of Geneva and several later détentes proved short-lived. It seemed that some demon kept inserting a monkey wrench to sabotage the process. In 1956, relations soured due to troubles in Hungary and Egypt; in 1960, a U.S. spy plane was shot down just before a summit meeting.

Fig. 7.1 Détente and Tension in 1955

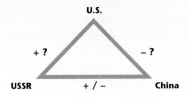

The Spirit of Moscow, 1963

Kennedy decided to break the post-Cuba logjam. On June 10, 1963, Kennedy made a speech at American University in Washington— "Toward a Strategy of Peace."[11] There is no record that Kennedy read Dr. Osgood, but JFK's words and deeds looked almost like textbook GRIT. "Peace," Kennedy said, "is a process, a way of solving problems." It did not require an end to all quarrels, but only a mutual tolerance and submission of disputes to a "just and peaceful settlement." Kennedy altered U.S. perceptions merely by talking about Soviets as fellow human beings. "No government or social system is so evil that its people must be considered as lacking in virtue." He hailed the "Russian people for their many accomplishments." He said that "no nation . . . ever suffered more than the Soviet Union" did in World War II. Kennedy urged attention to "common interests and to the means by which . . . differences can be resolved."

Kennedy announced that test ban negotiations would begin soon in Moscow and that the United States would not conduct further "nuclear tests in the atmosphere so long as other states do not do so."

The message got through. As in April 1953, when *Pravda* and *Izvestiia* printed the full text of Eisenhower's speech, the two Soviet papers published Kennedy's June 10 speech. Suddenly, Soviet jammers let Voice of America broadcasts get through. Khrushchev responded with a conciliatory

11. For the background, see Robert F. Kennedy, foreword to Walter C. Clemens, Jr., ed., *Toward a Strategy of Peace* (Chicago: Rand McNally, 1965), xiii–xv; for the speech text, see ibid., 22–30.

How Better U.S.–Soviet Relations Hurt Sino–Soviet Relations

Even though Khrushchev and Mao did not get along, Moscow and Beijing enjoyed a brief honeymoon in the mid-1950s. It ended for many reasons. Basically, China challenged Soviet leadership and became too aggressive for Moscow's tastes.

Visiting China on his way home from the U.S. in 1959, Khrushchev criticized Beijing for being too belligerent about Taiwan and warned: "We cannot use our fists to test the stability of capitalism." Mao Zedong resented such advice and fumed that "some people have come into our own house to bully us." In 1960, the Kremlin cut off all economic aid to China and withdrew all Soviet technicians.

China feared that Moscow and Washington were negotiating a nuclear test ban to prevent China from developing its own nuclear bomb. Beijing warned Moscow several times

in 1962 and 1963 not to sign an arms agreement with Washington. The Soviets replied that a test ban was not in the cards. On June 9, 1963, Moscow changed its tune. The Kremlin gave Beijing advance notice of what Kennedy announced the very next day: that "high-level discussion will shortly begin in Moscow looking toward early agreement on a . . . test ban treaty." Even so, the Kremlin kept open its options: The Soviets hosted a high-level Chinese delegation that arrived in Moscow ten days before the U.S. and British test ban delegations.

Moscow responded publicly to Chinese charges that the Soviets were "capitulating" to U.S. imperialism. The Soviet Communist Party sent an open letter on July 14, 1963, reminding Beijing that "the nuclear bomb does not adhere to the class principle—it destroys everybody within the range of its devastating force."

Ignorant of the new approach to China, Secretary of State William Rogers and Vice President Spiro Agnew spoke out like broken records from the past. Rogers even stated in April 1971 that a presidential visit to China could not take place until Beijing complied "with the rules of international law." Fortunately for détente, Zhou Enlai listened to Kissinger instead of Rogers.

Kissinger explained that his secret diplomacy and back channels sought to circumvent normal procedures. But for every agency excluded—usually the State Department—he became dependent upon another's facilities—increasingly, the CIA's. Kissinger blamed the State Department for its tendency to circulate every cable throughout its bureaucracy.

After long and secret preparations, Kissinger, on July 9, 1971, flew to Beijing from Pakistan. All went well. On July 15, Nixon told the world about Kissinger's trip and announced that he, too, would visit China. In February 1972, the famed anti-Communist clinked glasses with the world's leading revolutionary, Chairman Mao Zedong. Meanwhile, Kissinger and Zhou drafted the **Shanghai Communiqué**, which defined the framework for normalization.[17]

How did U.S. rapprochement with China in 1972 affect U.S. policies toward the USSR? Washington's new China card probably made the Kremlin—and Hanoi—more anxious to strike their own deals with Washington. Plans were laid for Nixon to visit Moscow in May 1972 and sign major arms accords with Brezhnev. Washington also pressed for a peace treaty with Hanoi. On the eve of his planned summit, Nixon sharply raised the ante by intensifying bomb raids on Hanoi and its port, Haiphong, where Soviet ships were anchored. Nixon gambled and won. Despite U.S. escalation in Vietnam, Brezhnev did not rescind his invitation to Nixon. The Kremlin did not permit an embarrassment in a remote region to prevent accords on arms, trade, and other concerns vital to Soviet interests. And Hanoi soon returned to serious negotiations with U.S. representatives in Paris.

The triangle showed a strong plus between Washington and Moscow, a growing plus between Washington and Beijing, and a very strong negative—deep conflict—between Moscow and Beijing (see Figure 7.3).

Kissinger achieved normalization with Beijing and détente with Moscow. But was so much secrecy necessary or desirable? Probably not. Open diplomacy based on public discussions at home and abroad would probably have yielded the same gains without the associated costs. Improved relations with China met little opposition in the United States, but the rapid reversal of U.S. policy surprised and offended Tokyo and

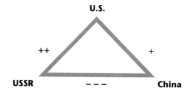

Fig. 7.3 Détente and Tension in 1972

17. Without naming the USSR, the document denounced efforts by any other country to establish "hegemony" or "collude" with other countries to "divide up the world into spheres of interest." In effect, Washington pledged not to cooperate with Moscow against Beijing.

Taiwan was the major sticking point. The communiqué stated Beijing's view that Taiwan is a "province" of China, and Washington's, that Taiwan is "part" of China. The United States favored a "peaceful settlement of the Taiwan question by the Chinese themselves." The United States tried in vain to get a commitment from Beijing not to "liberate" Taiwan by force, but Beijing refused, saying that Taiwan "is China's internal affair."

Tit-for-Tat on Spies

Complaining about Soviet espionage, the U.S. government in 1986 ordered Moscow to curtail sharply the number of personnel in its Washington embassy. Gorbachev responded TFT. He told the Soviet Politburo that the Americans behaved "like bandits. . . . This hostile anti-Soviet action cannot be left unanswered." He ordered Soviet support staff out of the U.S. embassy in Moscow, leaving the Americans empty-handed. Gorbachev did not fear U.S. reprisals, he said, because Soviet–U.S. ties were limited anyway.

Taipei. Japan and Taiwan, each a key U.S. ally, wondered how far they could count on the United States.

The White House played its China card like a club. But was this toughness needed? Probably not. Moscow had its own reasons to pursue arms control plus trade with the United States, while China needed the United States as much as (or even more than) Washington needed Beijing. Seeing both Moscow and Beijing shift toward Washington, Hanoi feared isolation. But neither Moscow nor Beijing exerted much pressure on Hanoi to come to terms with Washington.

Gorbachev GRIT

Moscow's belligerent foreign policy helped bring the United States and China together in the early 1980s. As Washington and Beijing teamed up, the USSR acted like a cornered bear. By late 1984/early 1985, however, the Kremlin again sought détente with the West and, by 1986, with China. Mikhail S. Gorbachev, Communist Party leader after March 1985, talked and acted as though coached by Western exponents of GRIT and interdependence. But whereas Dr. Osgood expected the stronger side to take the first steps, Gorbachev initiated a strategy of tension reduction even as his country was tottering. Gorbachev's policy was manifest and persistent, despite rebuffs abroad and criticism at home.[18]

Gorbachev in 1985–1987 softened previous Communist doctrine on many points. For example, he argued that the needs of all humanity—not the working-class revolution or a state's national interest—should guide policy. All countries are interdependent even though contradictions among them continue. War can no longer be an effective way to pursue policy. Even local wars can escalate. Conflicts must be resolved by dialogue. Soviet–U.S. military parity and nuclear deterrence do not guarantee peace. Military deployments should be guided by "reasonable sufficiency"—adequate for defense but inadequate for attack.

Unlike Nixon and Kissinger, Gorbachev and his aides communicated their new line directly to their colleagues. Gorbachev told his diplomats not to act like "Mr. Nyet." Gorbachev's meetings with Western and Third World intellectuals became front-page news throughout the USSR.

Gorbachev broke from TFT with a series of dramatic moves. As we saw in Chapter 6, Gorbachev accepted several arms accords that trimmed Soviet forces more than Western. Also, the Kremlin held to a unilateral moratorium on nuclear testing for eighteen months and permitted U.S. scientists and seismic equipment near Soviet test sites. Gorbachev unilaterally cut Soviet military personnel by one-tenth and

18. On the Gorbachev revolution, see Walter C. Clemens, Jr., *Can Russia Change? The USSR Confronts Global Interdependence* (New York: Routledge, 1990).

pledged to restructure remaining units in strictly defensive configurations. He withdrew Soviet forces from Afghanistan and supported arrangements to end regional conflict in Cambodia, southern Africa, the Persian Gulf, and the Middle East. Gorbachev also lowered emigration barriers for Soviet citizens and curtailed repression of political dissidents. He moved to make the USSR a participant in world commerce and science.

Not every Gorbachev move inspired confidence. For example, the nuclear test moratorium pushed the White House where it did not wish to go. Gorbachev officially began the Soviet moratorium in 1985 on the 40th anniversary of Hiroshima—August 6. This played well in Japan but not in Washington.

Détente did not proceed in a straight line. As noted in the sidebar, Soviet–U.S. relations were often strained even in the Gorbachev years. For a time, Washington played down Gorbachev's concessions. President Reagan believed in negotiating from strength and continued pressures to force back what he called the "evil empire." When Reagan and Gorbachev met face-to-face, however, they got along well. Reagan came to agree with British Prime Minister Margaret Thatcher that Gorbachev was, at last, a Soviet leader with whom the West could do business.

Gorbachev had no China card, because Beijing's leaders were hostile to Moscow. But Gorbachev employed GRIT-like moves to win Chinese confidence. In 1986 he repudiated "selfish attempts to strengthen [Soviet] security at others' expense" and called for "new and fair relations in Asia and the Pacific." He stressed Moscow's readiness to deepen economic and other ties with China.[19] Far from trying to exclude Washington, as his predecessors had done, Gorbachev affirmed that the U.S. was "a great Pacific power."

Three years of conciliating China paid off. Gorbachev visited Beijing in May 1989—the first summit between Soviet and Chinese leaders in thirty years. In 1989 and 1990, each leg of the triangle was positive for the first time since 1945. It turned out that two positive legs did not require a negative (see Figure 7.4). None of the great powers had to exploit differences between the other two to advance its interests.

How to Blend "Niceness" and "Toughness"

We have seen four cases where niceness helped elicit niceness. In Table 7.2 we consider each case's basic parameters.

In each instance the initiator took risks. Each faced opposition at home and among allies. In these cases, however, initiatives for peace were

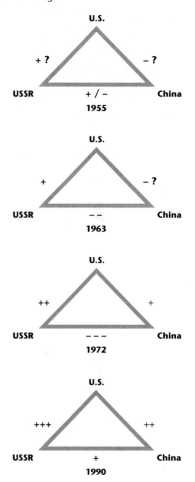

Fig. 7.4 Changing Parameters of the Great Power Triangle

19. Gorbachev also pledged to withdraw significant Soviet forces from Afghanistan before 1986; hoped for normalized relations between Vietnam and China; and promised a "positive reply" to China's request to build a railroad linking its Xinjiang–Uighur region with Soviet Kazakstan. He also offered to cooperate with Beijing in space and to train Chinese cosmonauts.

Table 7.2 Four Cases of Tension-Reducing Initiatives

	1955 (USSR→U.S.)	1963 (U.S.→USSR)	1970–1972 (U.S.→PRC)	1985–1989 (USSR→U.S.)
Initiator	**Khrushchev**	**Kennedy**	**Kissinger**	**Gorbachev**
Lead from strength?	No	Yes	Mixed	No
First steps symbolic or substantive?	Both	Symbolic	Symbolic	Both
Open or covert?	Open	Both	Covert	Open
Did the other side abuse?	No	No	No	No
Use triangle card?	No	No	Yes	No

seldom abused. Usually the first GRIT-like moves elicited a positive response within months. But movement toward reconciliation never developed in a straight line; it moved in zig–zag fashion. Two or three years of probing were usually needed to cultivate a new "spirit." Tricks and stratagems were not needed. It turned out that neither covert nor triangular diplomacy was essential for GRIT to succeed.

CROSS-STRAIT GRIT

GRIT-like policies also helped mainland and island China to moderate their conflict. In 1949 the Communists forced the Nationalists to retreat to Taiwan and a few offshore islands. Still, each side claimed to rule all of China. The Communists called their state the People's Republic of China (PRC); the Nationalists, headquartered in Taipei, called theirs the Republic of China (ROC). The PRC and ROC waged an intense cold war (occasionally hot) across the Taiwan Strait for decades after 1949.

Beijing initiated tension-reducing moves with Taipei in 1979—the same year that Washington shifted U.S. recognition of "China" from the ROC to the PRC. But the ROC leadership did not respond in any positive way to Beijing's overtures until 1986. The smaller, more vulnerable party was suspicious and reluctant to lower its guard. In the 1980s the Communists in Beijing governed nearly a billion people; the Nationalists in Taipei, about 21 million.[20]

As Osgood recommended, it was the larger, stronger party that took the initiative and persisted. The pragmatic American psychologist, however, recommended small steps to begin the process of reconciliation. Instead, Beijing departed from Osgood's prescription by launching initiatives on highly sensitive issues. Thus, the PRC government called for an

20. Jun Zhan, *Ending the Chinese Civil War: Power, Commerce and Conciliation Between Beijing and Taipei* (New York: St. Martin's, 1993).

end to military confrontation with Taiwan and proposed high-level talks on "reunifying the homeland," though Beijing also offered cooperation in other, less sensitive realms—shelter for fishermen, visits to relatives, sports, and science.

Taiwanese businessmen wanted access to the mainland. They got to the PRC market in the 1980s through Hong Kong—still a British colony until 1997. ROC authorities said in 1985 that they would neither "encourage" nor "interfere" with indirect trade between island and mainland China. In 1986, however, ROC President Chiang Ching-kuo hinted that ROC policy to the mainland should also change.

An external event in 1986 spurred the first direct talks between Taipei and Beijing officials. After a defecting Taiwanese pilot flew a cargo plane to the mainland, airline representatives from both sides met in Hong Kong to discuss the plane's return to Taiwan. A few months later—practically on his deathbed—President Chiang lifted Taiwan's martial law and the ban on ROC civilians' visits to the mainland.[21]

In the late 1980s, Taipei took many small steps to improve relations with Beijing. The ROC reduced and then eliminated rewards offered to defecting PRC pilots, lifted restrictions on the import of selected raw materials from the mainland, permitted PRC students studying in the United States to visit Taiwan, and welcomed ROC–PRC–Singapore police cooperation against criminals.

Following a request by the ROC president in May 1990, the PRC president in September announced that Beijing had pulled back all combat troops from Fujian Province opposite Taiwan. In the early 1990s, Taiwanese investment in mainland China soared; so did visits, mail, and telephone calls. In 1993, both sides agreed to regular consultations on issues of common interest. Washington tried to maintain good relations with Beijing while nourishing informal ties with Taipei. Russia and the ROC also reached out to each other. A positive sign linked each player (see Figure 7.5).

Commerce, kinship, and a shared civilization encouraged closer ties between Taiwan and the mainland. Taiwan had technology and capital, while the PRC had the fastest rate of economic growth and an abundance of cheap labor.

But a potential monkey wrench became a Damocles sword in 1995. Beijing had long threatened to fight Taiwan if it declared independence from the rest of China. In the 1990s, however, the ROC began to seek its own seat at the United Nations. When Washington allowed ROC President Lee Teng-hui to make a "private" visit to Cornell University (where

Fig. 7.5 Four-Cornered Cooperation in 1993

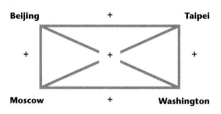

21. Walter C. Clemens, Jr., and Jun Zhan, "Chiang Ching-kuo's Role in the ROC–PRC Reconciliation," *American Asian Review* 12, no. 1 (spring 1994): 140–163.

Tensions over Taiwan often interrupted U.S–PRC détente. The 1979 Taiwan Relations Act committed the United States to supply defensive arms to Taiwan. The act specified that America would "consider any effort to determine the future of Taiwan by other than peaceful means . . . a threat to the peace and security of the Western Pacific area and of grave concern to the United States." In 1982 Washington agreed with Beijing that U.S. arms sales to Taiwan would be reduced, but permitted some "nongovernmental sales" and arms production under license. As the ROC became a democracy in the 1990s, many Americans sympathized with mounting demands within Taiwan for independent statehood. China intensified its military buildup facing the Taiwan Strait—a warning that it might fight to thwart island China's independence. Some Taiwanese thought that better radar and modern weapons would keep them safe. Others believed that a political solution was needed.

Just as the confrontation over a U.S. spy plane forced down on Chinese territory was winding down, the Bush administration in April 2001 announced the largest arms sale to Taiwan in a decade. The deal included eight diesel submarines and four frigates, but lacked other lethal weapons sought by Taipei.

he had earned a Ph.D.) in 1995, Beijing responded vigorously. It suspended official meetings with ROC officials and began launching ballistic missiles into the sea north of Taiwan. A U.S. warship returned to the Taiwan Strait on December 19, 1995—the first time since 1979. The aircraft carrier *Nimitz* passed through, Washington said, because of bad weather elsewhere. Tension, as well as tension reduction, could be fine-tuned.

Cross-strait tensions eased briefly in early 1996. Presidents of forty-three ROC and PRC universities met in Taiwan and called for closer academic cooperation to usher in "the Chinese century." In February and March 1996, however, tensions in the South China Sea worsened. China brought back large military forces to Fujian Province and conducted live-fire training to invade Taiwan. Some PRC officials threatened to "nuke" Los Angeles if the United States stood by Taiwan. But two U.S. aircraft carrier flotillas assembled 200 miles southeast of Taiwan (400 miles from China proper), and the U.S. secretary of defense boasted that the United States had the "best damn navy in the world." Fine-tuning became a shouting match.

A small, vulnerable client state helped trigger the long war between Athens and Sparta and between the two alliances in 1914. Clients in Cairo and Jerusalem nearly brought Moscow and Washington to blows in 1973. Now the fate of Taiwan renewed enmity between the PRC and the U.S.

"Firm containment" or "flexible engagement"? The Clinton administration sought to show firmness even while engaging China in constructive relationships. Meanwhile, every computer-aided-design software package that the United States sold to China increased the PRC's capacity to "nuke Los Angeles."

The return of Hong Kong to China in 1997 ushered in a new phase of PRC–ROC relations. If China kept its word and implemented a policy of "one country, two systems," the Hong Kong model would be more thinkable for Taiwan. By 2001, Hong Kong's government looked increasingly like a Chinese puppet. As a result, more and more Taiwanese demanded a clear break with China and elected a president committed to independence. China fumed and deployed even larger military forces in Fujian. At the same time, however, Taiwanese firms were transferring not only their manufacturing operations to the mainland but also their research and development operations. Most PRC students who studied in the United States remained, but many ROC students returned to Taiwan. Their know-how was then transferred to China. If this process continued, the brains and nerves of American machines and weapons would depend on components and technologies from the PRC. Commerce might tame politics, but there were no guarantees. As we know, highly interdependent Europeans and Russians fought each other in two world wars.

GRIT ACROSS THE DMZ

GRIT can fail—especially sham GRIT, when one side (or both) fakes its desire for reconciliation. South Korea (officially, the Republic of Korea, or ROK) and North Korea (the Democratic People's Republic of Korea, or DPRK) were different from Nationalist and Communist China. Since 1953 the South had become prosperous and confident; the North, an impoverished hermit kingdom under the world's longest-reigning dictator. Still, North Korea in the 1960s and 1970s often proposed steps that could have led to reunification. South Koreans then were reserved. They had not forgotten North Korea's massive attack in 1950 and its many acts of terrorism since.

As in Taiwan, greater prosperity made ROK diplomacy more confident. In the early 1980s, Seoul proposed a summit meeting with Pyongyang and twenty pilot projects to help North and South cooperate. Now it was the North Koreans who balked. They demanded withdrawal of U.S. troops from Korea as a precondition for high-level dialogue.

A pattern emerged: North Korea demanded "all or nothing," while South Korea advocated "step-by-step" reconciliation. This was not GRIT but a propaganda war. Each side put the onus for stalemate on the other. Neither side made concessions to show its sincerity. Each preferred TFT.

First Steps May Lead Nowhere

Table tennis helped break the ice between Beijing and Washington. Could it do the same for the two Koreas? South and North Korea agreed to field a unified table tennis team for the world championships in 1991. But would it train in North or in South Korea? And what would be its official name? Lengthy negotiations produced two compromises: The team would train in Japan; it would be called Korea.

Ping-pong reunited some Koreans. In Japan a DPRK ping-pong official met his sister for the first time in four decades. She had gone south during the Korean War while he remained in the North.

Washington in 1991 welcomed moves to ease North Korea out of its isolation. Recalling how ping-pong helped melt the ice between Washington and Beijing in 1971, the United States offered to send a soccer team to North Korea and invited the joint Korean table tennis team to visit three U.S. cities. But sports diplomacy faltered. Korean sport unity turned out to be a one-shot deal. In September 1991, both North and South Korea joined the United Nations as separate states.

In 1991, things changed. As its Soviet patron expired, North Korea, for the first time, acknowledged the ROK government as a legitimate entity, and together they signed a treaty banning nuclear arms from the Korean peninsula. Seoul affirmed that U.S. nuclear arms had been withdrawn. Both sides agreed to a summit meeting in Seoul.

In the early 1990s, the ROK had poor relations with the DPRK, but positive ties with Beijing, Moscow, and Washington. North Koreans connected positively with no one. Still, Pyongyang had two aces: The DPRK army—much larger than the ROK army—was deployed within easy striking distance of Seoul. Second, the DPRK might "go nuclear."

What to do? North Korea was sealed off—one of the most closed societies in the world. U.S. policy makers wondered how to draw North Korea from its shell and persuade its leaders to forgo nuclear weapons. Should Washington try to conciliate the North by cancelling the annual maneuvers conducted by U.S. and ROK forces? Or stage them again to intimidate the North and please hard-liners in the South? Could U.S. bombers or missiles mount "surgical strikes" to wipe out DPRK nuclear facilities? Even if they hit their target, radiation might spread. North Korea threatened to ignite a firestorm in South Korea.

Amid rising tensions, Kim Il-sung in 1994 met with two U.S. groups making "private" visits to Korea. Evangelist Billy Graham went to Pyongyang with a Columbia University professor of religion who grew up in a missionary family in Korea. Next, Kim Il-sung met with former president Jimmy Carter. These unofficial meetings with North Korea's dictator set the stage for renewed negotiations between DPRK and U.S. diplomats. Neither Graham nor Carter officially represented the United States, but each had close ties with the White House. Private (Track 2) diplomacy opened the way to official (Track 1) diplomacy. Kim Il-sung died soon after the thaw began in U.S.–DPRK relations. His son Kim Jong Il became the paramount leader and continued the contradictory smiles and menaces practiced by his father.

In October 1994, North Korean and U.S. officials approved the "agreed framework"—a schedule of steps to provide nuclear reactors to the DPRK while denying it the capacity for nuclear weaponry (described in Chapter 6). To implement these undertakings, of course, would be complicated.[22] Though isolated and in need, North Korea upped the ante. It tried to exclude South Korea and deal only with the United States. It wanted not just the reactors but also—gratis—the supporting infrastructure and communication links. When Washington stood firm, however, Pyongyang backed down. It agreed that South Korea would supply the reactors.

22. James Goodby and William Drennan, "Koreapolitik," *Strategic Forum* 29 (May 1995): 2.

Like Kissinger and Zhou Enlai in the early 1970s, Washington and Pyongyang tried to sustain the momentum of tension reduction. Small steps might have large consequences. Pyongyang and Washington in January 1995 began to dismantle the trade embargo each had imposed forty-five years before. Each side would now permit direct phone calls and financial transactions. Washington would permit U.S. steelmakers to buy magnesite from North Korea to line their blast furnaces. DPRK and U.S. journalists could now open news bureaus in each others' country. The U.S. State Department said that further relaxation of economic sanctions would depend on progress on the "nuclear issue" and on DPRK restraint in exporting missile technology.

While U.S.–DPRK relations improved somewhat, those between the two Koreas languished. Some U.S. experts suggested arms control measures to build confidence between Seoul and Pyongyang: greater transparency for each side's military forces; constraints on military deployments near the DMZ; a "nonoffensive defense" military posture to replace any capacity for deep penetration across the DMZ, verified by the UN and observers from each side; a direct communications link between the ROK and DPRK defense ministers; reduced military forces (U.S. as well as Korean) on each side of the DMZ; and promises by Washington, Beijing, and Moscow not to circumvent the DPRK–ROK accords.

Even as the October 1994 deal began to be implemented, however, tensions again worsened between the two Koreas. Severe floods and other problems reduced North Korea's harvests and food supplies. The DPRK regime urged its people to get by on two meals a day—one if they could manage. South Korea sent rice, but Pyongyang refused to say thanks. Instead, it arrested some ROK fishermen on charges of spying. Millions of North Koreans faced starvation, but South Korea blocked outside food aid until Pyongyang changed its tune. Even as Pyongyang began to receive more food and other assistance from outside, a North Korean submarine crashed onto the South Korean coast, disgorging a dozen commandos, whom the South Koreans hunted down.

Some ROK officials feared that a dying North Korea might still launch a last-ditch attack. Others feared the DPRK might open its borders and deluge the ROK with millions of refugees. Still others hoped the DPRK would collapse and bequeath its nuclear arsenal to the South.

Pyongyang in 1997 continued to bargain hard. The nongovernmental organization Oxfam (Oxford Committee on Famine Relief, founded in 1942) and UN observers concluded that North Korea was on the brink of

Severe economic problems in North Korea helped condition DPRK foreign policy. Here, a fourteen-year-old girl in Anju City, DPRK, forages for food in April 1997. Some experts believe that 2 million North Koreans died of starvation in 1990s. Though its economic situation improved only marginally, Pyongyang in 2002–2003 ignored threats to suspend food and oil deliveries from outside. Kim Il-sung seemed determined to build nuclear weapons. His envoys said the problem could be resolved by bilateral talks with the United States, but the Bush administration insisted on four-power talks. Nearly isolated, the United States bombed Iraq but refused to talk with Pyongyang one-on-one, even though the DPRK nuclear program was far more advanced than Iraq's.

mass starvation. Two years of flooding had been followed by a prolonged drought. The world mobilized to send food, but Pyongyang still balked at direct talks with South Korea. Even as DPRK diplomats met with U.S., PRC, and ROK negotiators at Columbia University, Pyongyang demanded the withdrawal of U.S. troops from the peninsula and cancellation of U.S.–ROK maneuvers scheduled for late 1997 in Japan. A "German" solution became more thinkable: collapse of the Communist government, leading to the merger of non-Communist and Communist regions, endorsed by the great powers. In the winter of 1997–1998, however, the South Korean economy shuddered, throwing many people out of work and helping to elect a new, more liberal president, Kim Dae Jung.

South Korea's new president initiated a "Sunshine Policy" toward North Korea in 1998. No longer would the South seek to undermine or absorb the North. Instead, the new ROK government fostered Track 2 relationships—trade, tourism, and investment in special economic zones in the North. Pyongyong responded fitfully—alternating smiles with frowns and menacing actions. But Kim Jong Il received Kim Dae Jung in Pyongyang in 2000, and the ROK president received the Nobel Peace Prize. His critics charged that the ROK president had paid Kim Jong Il $100 million for the summit chit-chat.

GRIT across the DMZ zigged and zagged. The North in 2000 established diplomatic relations with Italy and Australia and sought to normalize relations with the United States. The Clinton administration seemed close to a comprehensive understanding with the North—normalized relations and a lifting of U.S. sanctions in return for an end to DPRK nuclear weapon and missile programs. But when George W. Bush came to office in 2001, he scorned the value of talking with Pyongyang. In 2002 he placed the DPRK on the "axis of evil" with Iran and Iraq. Still, Washington did not threaten North Korea with a "preemptive" attack as it did Iraq, in part because Pyongyang had a more credible deterrent than Iraq. Also, all the adjacent countries—Russia, China, and Japan—were striving to stabilize the Korean peninsula.

GRIT BETWEEN CIVILIZATIONS

In 1997 and 1998, Iran's newly elected president, Mohammed Khatami, delivered several conciliatory messages toward the United States. He rejected any idea of an inevitable clash of civilizations and argued that Iran and the West had much to learn from each other. Like other practitioners of GRIT, he had good things to say about the "people" of the other camp. Both Tehran and Washington shared mutual interests in oil and gas. Each was hostile to Saddam Hussein in Iraq. An opportunity for sports

This satellite image taken August, 13, 2002, shows the southern half of nuclear facilities in Yongbyon, DPRK. In 2002 and 2003, North Korea cut IAEA seals and removed or obstructed monitoring equipment at the Yongbyon nuclear reactor and its spent fuel pond, a fuel rod fabrication plant, and a reprocessing facility.

diplomacy arose when Iranian and U.S. soccer teams were matched to play each other in 1998. A monkey wrench intruded, however, when U.S. officials at the Chicago airport insisted on fingerprinting the Iranians. An American professor went to Tehran and lectured on GRIT at a conference on conflict resolution sponsored by the Iranian Foreign Ministry in 1998.[23] But the convergent interests of Iran and the United States faced heated opposition from hard-liners on each side. Even though Iran helped the United States in its Afghan campaign in 2001, Bush placed Iran on his "axis of evil" list in 2002. Khatami continued to plug for more liberal policies but was stymied by the country's Supreme Spiritual Council, which regularly ordered the arrest of those who joined Khatami's calls for a stronger civil society and a dialogue across civilizations. In 2002 and 2003, however, huge student demonstrations pressed for deep liberalization. Washington conducted secret talks with Khatami's representatives in 2003 even as both governments spoke harshly of each other in public. Iraq could help bring the United States and Iran together or divide them even further.

23. Officials at the U.S. State Department encouraged me to accept the invitation, but U.S. sanctions kept them from contributing to the cost. The Iranian mission to the UN gave me a visa, and my expenses in Tehran were covered by a Foreign Ministry think tank, which also helped arrange travel to other cities. A newspaper close to the president gave favorable front-page coverage to my remarks on GRIT, but this paper was closed down some months later by hard-liners. Outside the conference, I found myself on a mountain trail with an Iranian Army colonel urging two privates to give up smoking. All of us enjoyed an activity that transcended any political differences. The think tank, however, did not respond to my efforts to maintain positive exchanges. As usual, one did not know if the failure to respond was deliberate or a botched communication.

GREAT PERSUADERS

Each movement toward détente and each agreement we have studied depended upon conditional cooperation. Individual negotiators dealt with problems and found ways to reach agreements useful to each side. These individuals embodied many of the "key assets of the effective negotiator" (see p. 41). Each seemed to understand GRIT theory intuitively.

Of the major statesmen ranked in Table 7.3, Kissinger was probably the most skilled negotiator, followed closely by Zhou Enlai. Kissinger and Zhou pursued their own versions of GRIT with signals that could not be rebuffed and which, if criticized, could be denied. Both men knew the issues well and could identify ways to bridge differences.

Despite a weak hand, Gorbachev did what he could to save the Soviet system and join the First World in a joint quest for peace and prosperity. He demonstrated how tension reduction could be pursued for years to overcome the other side's distrust.

President Reagan did well in fostering détente with Gorbachev. Though Reagan did not study the issues carefully, he could negotiate from great strength. He enjoyed solid domestic support even as Soviet power steadily declined. He charmed many Soviets as well as Americans.

Table 7.3 Ranking Great Persuaders
Following is a tentative ranking of some statesmen and diplomats active in the great power triangle. Ratings are based on their strengths in the fifteen traits of a strong negotiator outlined in Chapter 1. Kissinger scored highest, followed by Zhou Enlai; Krushchev and Brezhnev ranked at the bottom.

	1	2	3	4	5	6	7	8	9	10	11	12	13	14	15
Kissinger		✓		✓			✓	✓	✓	✓		✓	✓	✓	✓
Zhou Enlai	✓	✓						✓	✓	✓	✓	✓	✓	✓	
Carter		✓			✓	✓			✓		✓	✓	✓	✓	
Gorbachev	✓							✓	✓		✓	✓	✓		✓
Kennedy				✓				✓		✓	✓		✓		
Reagan			✓					✓					✓		
Gromyko	✓	✓								✓					
Khrushchev										✓	✓				✓
Brezhnev										✓	✓				

1: Conversion Power; 2: Knowledge; 3: Domestic Support; 4: Management; 5: Empathy; 6: Integrity; 7: Timing; 8: Communication; 9: Constructive Imagination; 10: Toughness; 11: Flexibility; 12: Stamina; 13: Personality; 14: Draftsmanship; 15: Achievement Drive
SOURCE: Evaluations based on formal ratings by former U.S. ambassador Hermann Eilts; professors Roger Kanet and David Mayers; Dr. Jun Zhan; and the author.

How these negotiators thought about diplomacy and how they graded one another is suggested in the memoirs of Andrei Gromyko, Henry Kissinger, Jimmy Carter, Zbigniew Brzezinski, Cyrus Vance, James Baker, Anatoly Dobrynin, Mikhail Gorbachev, George Shultz, George Bush, and Brent Scowcroft. Rich nuggets may be found by readers of Chinese and Russian in the memoirs of PRC and Soviet interpreters. Works by and about the lead U.S. negotiators with the Balkan states and North Korea, Richard Holbrooke and Robert Galucci, are quite informative. Bill Clinton's personal diplomacy with Boris Yeltsin is detailed in a book by Strobe Talbott, his major adviser on Russia.[24] Glimpses into the minds of Madeleine Albright, Condoleezza Rice, and Colin Powell are available in their writings.

WHAT PROPOSITIONS HOLD?
WHAT QUESTIONS REMAIN?

HOW TO MAKE GOODWILL CREDIBLE

Reconciliation begins when parties decide to "give peace a chance." A strategy of peace is a wager that dangers can be minimized and assets enhanced by détente. This was the bet made both by Moscow and by Washington in 1955, 1963, 1972, and the late 1980s.

Either strength or weakness can motivate efforts to reduce tensions. Beijing leaders initiated tension reduction with Taiwan from a position of growing strength; Taipei did not reciprocate until it felt secure. On the other hand, North Korea maintained its aggressive diplomatic style even after its economy had practically collapsed.

Each party must show that its "niceness" is a strategy—not a stratagem. Except for the two Koreas, however, none of the cases we have studied shows much chicanery. Neither the initiator nor the reciprocator exploited the process of tension reduction to harm the other side. A series of conciliatory moves usually generated a positive response by the other side—often within days or weeks. The long interval between Beijing's initiatives and a positive ROC rejoinder was the exception—not the rule.

Still, niceness without bargaining power might get nowhere. Without some capacity to hurt as well as help, a negotiator's carrots may be devoured and yield nothing in return. Without sticks, conciliation may be fruitless.

The problem in tension reduction has been how to sustain it—not to begin it. Having backed away from confrontation, it is difficult to proceed toward cooperation without being derailed.

Another Obstacle to GRIT: Divergent Memories

Washington listened in 1997 and 1998 to the overtures of Iran's newly elected president, but many U.S. officials continued to harp on the injuries inflicted on the United States by Iran in the 1980s, forgetting why many Iranians still smarted from the U.S.'s pre-1979 policies. Similarly, Washington still resented Fidel Castro's bluster but ignored the reasons why many Cubans disliked the U.S.'s pre-1959 policies. Mutual history lessons might help make a fresh start.* For all these reasons, Track 2 diplomacy might have to precede Track 1.** In 2003, however, the Bush administration moved to ban the cultural and educational tours to Cuba that Washington had tolerated for several years.

*See op-eds by Walter C. Clemens, Jr., "The Lessons of Cuba," *Christian Science Monitor*, April 4, 1974, and October 21, 1993.

**Between Cuba and the United States, however, sports did little to promote détente. A pitcher who defected from Cuba was voted the most valuable player in the 1997 World Series. Though Havana permitted the pitcher's brother to attend the game, the brother, also a pitcher, returned to Cuba but then defected.

24. Strobe Talbott, *The Russia Hand: A Memoir of Personal Diplomacy* (New York: Random House, 2002).

Memo to the President: In dealing with Koraq, we must negotiate from strength. We must be firm but not provocative. If the Koraqis offer a conciliatory gesture, however, we should not abuse it.

Since our overall position is stronger than Koraq's, we can better afford to take risks for peace. But we do not court needless rebuffs. Test the waters quietly to learn whether the time is ripe—whether, despite its tough exterior, Koraq may be ready, for its own reasons, to improve relations with us.

If conditions seem favorable, announce our intention to reduce tensions by a series of steps to move us from confrontation toward cooperation—contingent on reciprocity. Carry out a sequence of unilateral initiatives and give the other side time to respond. Promote open communication—at home and abroad—as circumstances permit. If the other side reciprocates, graduate from symbolic to more substantive initiatives. But respond firmly to rebuffs or defection.

With Koraq the question is how to move from confrontation to détente. With Russia and China we have moved past détente and achieved a kind of entente. Still, there is a danger of renewed confrontation with countries whose power position has quickly shifted and remains in flux. Leaders may seek to regain their country's past clout or exploit its rising influence. With Moscow and Beijing we need no triangular tricks. The West and Japan should cultivate a positive symbiosis that includes both Russia and China—networks of complex interdependence to promote mutual gain and transcend differences. If peaceful engagement fails, however, we must contain and isolate aggressors, preventing coalitions that threaten peaceful states.

KEY NAMES AND TERMS

China card
demilitarized zone (DMZ)
détente
entente
graduated reciprocation in tension-
   reduction (GRIT)

Mohammed Khatami
monkey wrench problem
Panmunjom
ping-pong diplomacy
rapprochement
Shanghai Communiqué

Spirit of Geneva
Sunshine policy
Taiwan Strait
triangular diplomacy
yi yi zhi yi
Zhou Enlai

QUESTIONS TO DISCUSS

1. How does GRIT differ from TFT? What are the pitfalls of each approach? The potential gains?

2. Why and how can a government use triangular diplomacy?

3. Did détente between two of the three great powers depend upon tension between one of them and the third?

4. How did Track 1 and Track 2 diplomacy interact in PRC–ROC and DPRK–ROK relations? How could both tracks be used to foster détente between two other countries?

5. Select a country today that resembles "Koraq." As adviser to the White House, which approaches to conflict and conflict resolution do you recommend?

6. Can GRIT be adapted not just to reduce tensions but to sustain positive ties when tensions develop, for example, between Washington and Moscow?

Questions to Discuss (continued)

7. Compare two leading foreign policy makers today with two analyzed in this chapter. What are their strengths and weaknesses?

8. How do historical memories impede accommodation? What can be done to deal with them?

9. Reflect on your failure or success to "make up" with a friend. Compare similarities and differences between your experience and one of the cases in this chapter. How are personal relations alike or different from those between governments?

RECOMMENDED RESOURCES

BOOKS

Armstrong, Tony. *Breaking the Ice: Rapprochement Between East and West Germany, the United States and China, and Israel and Egypt.* Washington, D.C.: U.S. Institute of Peace, 1993.

Baker, James A., III. *The Politics of Diplomacy: Revolution, War & Peace, 1989–1992.* New York: G. P. Putnam's, 1995.

Bogle, Lori Lyn, ed. *Cold War: National Security Policy Planning from Truman to Reagan and from Stalin to Gorbachev.* London: Taylor & Francis, 2000.

Brzezinski, Zbigniew. *Power and Principle: Memoirs of the National Security Adviser, 1977–1981.* New York: Farrar, Straus, Giroux, 1983.

Burr, William, ed. *The Kissinger Transcripts: The Top Secret talks with Beijing and Moscow.* New York: New Press, 1998.

Chang, Gordon H. *Friends and Enemies: The United States, China, and the Soviet Union, 1948–1972.* Stanford, Calif.: Stanford University Press, 1990.

Christensen, Thomas J. *Useful Adversaries: Grand Strategy, Domestic Mobilization, and Sino–American Conflict, 1947–1958.* Princeton, N.J.: Princeton University Press, 1996.

Clemens, Walter C., Jr. *The Arms Race and Sino–Soviet Relations.* Stanford, Calif.: Hoover Institution, 1968.

DeLuca, Anthony R. *Gandhi, Mao, Mandela, and Gorbachev: Studies in Personality, Power, and Politics.* Westport, Conn.: Greenwood, 2000.

Fischer, Beth A. *The Reagan Reversal: Foreign Policy and the End of the Cold War.* Columbia, Mo.: University of Missouri Press, 2000.

Hamburg David A. *No More Killing Fields: Preventing Deadly Conflict.* Lanham, Md.: Rowman & Littlefield, 2002.

Kissinger, Henry. *The White House Years.* Boston: Little, Brown, 1979.

Long, William J., and Peter Brecke. *War and Reconciliation: Reason and Emotion in Conflict Resolution.* Cambridge, Mass.: MIT Press, 2002.

Mayers, David. *The Ambassadors and America's Soviet Policy.* New York: Oxford University Press, 1995.

McNamara, Robert S., and James G. Blight. *Wilson's Ghost: Reducing the Risk of Conflict, Killing, and Catastrophe in the 21st Century.* New York: Public Affairs, 2001.

Miall, Hugh, Oliver Ramsbotham, and Tom Woodhouse. *Contemporary Conflict Resolution: The Prevention, Management and Transformation of Deadly Conflict.* Oxford, U.K.: Blackwell, 1999.

Osgood, Charles E. *An Alternative to Peace or Surrender.* Urbana: University of Illinois Press, 1962.

Shattan, Joseph. *Architects of Victory: Six Heroes of the Cold War.* Washington D.C.: Heritage Foundation, 2000.

Shultz, George P. *Turmoil and Triumph: My Years as Secretary of State.* New York: Scribner's, 1993.

Watkins, Michael, and Susan Rosegrant. *Breakthrough International Negotiation: How Great Negotiators Transformed the World's Toughest Post–Cold War Conflicts.* New York: Wiley, 2001.

Zelikow, Philip, and Condoleezza Rice. *Germany Unified and Europe Transformed: A Study in Statecraft.* Cambridge, Mass.: Harvard University Press, 1995.

JOURNALS

Asian Survey

Beijing Review

China Daily (Beijing)

Current Digest of the Post-Soviet Press (formerly Current Digest of the Soviet Press)

Far Eastern Economic Review

Free China Journal (Taipei)

International Negotiation

Issues and Studies (Taipei)

Journal of Conflict Resolution

Negotiation Journal

WEB SITES

Deescalating Conflict and GRIT (general strategies): http://www.orst.edu/instruct/comm440-540/transform.htm

Eisenhower's Address on the Spirit of Geneva http://www.nv.cc.va.us/home/nvsageh/Hist122/Part4/IKESpiritGeneva.htm

Web Sites (continued)
International Peacekeeping News
    http://csf.colorado.edu/dfax/ipn/index.htm
Kissinger Recalls Ping-Pong Diplomacy
    http://news.bbc.co.uk/1/hi/world/asia-pacific/1229207.stm
NATO
    http://www.nato.int/

Program on Negotiation, Harvard Law School
    http://www.pon.harvard.edu/
Project Ploughshares, Institute for Peace and Conflict Studies
    http://www.ploughshares.ca/
Stockholm International Peace Research Institute
    http://www.sipri.se/

C H A P T E R   E I G H T

WHAT UNITES AND DIVIDES HUMANITY? NATIONALISM AND FAITH

THE BIG QUESTIONS IN CHAPTER 8

- Why do many people see others in terms of "us vs. them"?

- How do ideas about race, nation, and religion affect IR?

- Is every nation a state? Every state a nation?

- What do minorities want? How do majorities respond?

- Are there ways to give minorities "voice" so they are not over-whelmed by majorities?

- What can we learn from relative successes and failures? Why could many become "one" in the U.S., but not the USSR?

- Why have the Swiss stayed together while the South Slavs split asunder?

- Is there any link between the forces that destroyed Yugoslavia and Islamist fury against America?

- How did "9/11" affect ethnic–nationalist–religious conflicts, as in Singapore and Sri Lanka?

- Can outsiders help? What options stand before the international community?

- Will nationalism be supplanted by other principles of identification? If so, will they be narrower or broader?

The UN Secretary-General requests that you head a panel to study ethnic, nationalist, and religious conflict worldwide. You and your colleagues must draft an action plan to protect peoples at risk. You know that pride in one's own group is a powerful force. So too, for many individuals and groups, are religious beliefs. These forces energize cultures and build states, but they also lay waste. Most wars since 1945 have been internal, fueled in large part by ethnic hatreds, often laced with religion. Their furies have killed millions and turned millions more into refugees. Besides local hatreds, however, we now have a global war between many Muslims and the West. These furies were building before 9/11. Since then, they have ravaged the planet.

Why do so many people think in terms of "us versus them?" Think back to Aristotle's teaching that humans are "political animals." To be fully human, we must associate with a community. But with whom or what should we identify? Family? Clan? Tribe? Fellow believers? City-state? Empire? Race? Class? Profession? Gender? All of humanity? All living things? Beginning in the late 18th century, many have answered: "Our nation." Against this trend, Karl Marx and his successors urged people to think, "Class." Breaking from Marxism, Soviet leader Mikhail Gorbachev, in the late 1980s, declared that the interests of humanity should supersede all others. A decade or so later, however, 9/11 highlighted still another fault line dividing humanity: religion—or what passes for religion.

Can the narrow passions of tribe, sect, or nation be supplanted by a quest for mutual gain? You and your panelists look for lessons in countries that have coped with ethnic and cultural diversity and those torn apart. You consider what each society can do to save itself and what outsiders can do to help. How can we prevent or moderate tension and replace it with—if not affection—order? To make recommendations you must first review both theory and facts.

CONTENDING CONCEPTS AND EXPLANATIONS

THE DOCTRINE OF NATIONAL SELF-DETERMINATION

A doctrine of **national self-determination** took shape in 19th-century Europe and won strong endorsement from Woodrow Wilson in 1917–1919.[1] The doctrine has four articles of faith:

1. Every person belongs to a nation. *Nation* here means "people"—not any people but those among whom one is born, a particular people such as the Japanese.[2]

2. It is good and natural for nations to feel **nationalism**—a sentiment that "my nation is great and warrants my loyalty. We as a nation have had a glorious past and, working together, can build a great future."

3. All nations (or at least the larger ones) deserve political expression in a nation-state.

4. Every nation-state has its "legitimate" and "vital" national interests.

BEFORE NATIONALISM: "US VS. THEM"

Most peoples have been—and many still are—**ethnocentric**: they see themselves at the center of all life.[3] Ethnocentrists define themselves as fully human; outsiders are "barbarians" or "foreign devils." Ethnocentrists view the world as "us vs. them."[4]

Ethnic comes from the Greek word *ethnos*, for "another people"—outsiders who have their own ethos or set of standards and values.[5] From *ethos* (how a people behaves) we get *ethics* (how people should behave). The word history reveals a deep problem: How can there be a common ethical code for all ethnic groups if each plays by its own rules?

Ethnocentrism is old, but nationalism is fairly new. Ancients had their tribes, city-states, and empires, but few if any had nation-states, states celebrating the ethos of one major ethnos. Thus, Athenians and Spartans shared a common language and gods, but each group gave its political allegiance not to Greece but to its own city-state (*polis*).[6] Athenians saw Spartans as a different ethnos with a different ethos.

Rulers of ancient empires, however, were elitist—not nationalist. The rulers of imperial Egypt, Persia, and China esteemed their own **culture**—their ethos—not their nationhood. The ancient polity that most resembled a modern nation-state was Israel—first under King David and later under the Maccabee dynasty. Israel combined the unifying

1. Prussian-born scholar Johann Gottfried Herder in the late 18th century taught that being a citizen was not sufficient. To live with meaning, a person must be part of a nation (*Volk*). Herder contended that every people has its own spirit (*Volksgeist*). Georg Hegel added in the 1820s that every *Volk* needs its own state (*Staat*). "All worth that the human being possesses . . . he possesses only through the State." Herder's nationalism was pacifistic; Hegel's lent itself to violence.

2. French *nation*, Spanish *nación*, and Italian *nazione* all derive from Latin *nasci*—to be born. People, in general, is *peuple*, in French; in German, *Leute*; and in Russian, *liudi*. A particular nation is *nation*, *Volk*, or *narod*, respectively. The German *Volk* is akin to "folk," as in folk songs.

3. The Chinese termed their country the Middle Kingdom. Chinese people are "central country people"—*zong guo ren*, while foreigners are "outside country people"—*wai guo ren*. But both terms share the root *ren* for "people" (represented as resembling the two legs of a human).

4. Language differences set people apart. Terms such as the Greek *barbaroi*, Russian *nemtsy*, and Hebrew *goyim* (non-Jews) all imply human incompleteness, since these persons could not communicate with the in-group of "real persons." John A. Armstrong, *Nations Before Nationalism* (Chapel Hill, N.C.: University of North Carolina Press, 1982), 5.

5. The Greek *demos* means city people—those who live in a polis. *Ethnos* means country people—outsiders. The adjective *ethnikos* means "foreign" and was used in Greek translations of the Bible to render the Hebrew *goyim*. From *ethnikos* comes *ethnic*. To study Native Americans, the U.S. government established the Bureau of Ethnology.

6. The presumed Indo-European root *dem* gave Latin *domus* (home), from which English got "domestic" and "domain." The Greek *demos* probably meant the households in an area—the inhabitants. From this root English took *democracy* and *demography*. Indo-European *pele* probably means a high, fortified place, from which the Greeks got *polis*, from which English took *politics* and *police*.

spirit of "God's Chosen People" with the structure and symbols of a nation-state—a unifying capital, belief system, and laws.

Until the 19th century, most humans identified with the village or land where they lived, hunted, or farmed—not with some abstract "nation."[7] No modern form of nationalism is much more than 500 years old. Nationalism arose in England under Henry VIII and later emerged in Holland, the United States, and France.[8] Napoleon carried the flame of nationalism to Germany, Russia, Spain, and as far as Egypt. Over time, other peoples caught the spark—from Latin America to Africa. Demands for a Jewish homeland arose again at the end of the 19th century. Many of today's nationalisms took shape only after World War II.

IS NATION AN OBJECTIVE OR SUBJECTIVE REALITY? WHAT ABOUT "RACE" AND RELIGION?

Can "nation" be defined in objective terms? Josef Stalin tried to do so. He wrote: "A nation is a historically constituted, stable community of people, formed on the basis of a common language, territory, economic life, and psychological make-up manifested in a common culture."[9] But few nations, if any, fit Stalin's criteria.

Ultimately, nationhood is a subjective reality. A nation is any group of people who believes or feels it is a nation. It is an imagined community because most members can never meet one another personally, yet they choose to emphasize what unites them rather than what separates them.[10] Looking back, nationalists find or imagine a glorious past. If necessary, they invent a new past. Looking ahead, they also sketch the road to a glorious future.

Nationalism is sometimes a secular religion—a belief that each person should feel a deep, perhaps supreme loyalty to the nation. For extreme nationalists, the nation is the tree; the individual, a branch. The tree nourishes the branch but can live without it; the branch can be sacrificed for the tree.

Nationalisms come in all sizes and shapes. Some are comparatively liberal, open, and tolerant; others are more **authoritarian**, closed, and aggressive. Two kinds of nationalism have sparked conflict in the 20th century: **expansionist nationalism**, as in Nazi Germany, seeks to conquer outsiders; **intermingled nationalism**, as in Bosnia, may generate ethnic struggles among close neighbors.

Nationalism is not identical to patriotism—devotion to one's fatherland (*patrie* in French, *patria* in Latin, *Vaterland* in German). Patriotism may—but need not—be nationalist or ethnocentric. A patriot in country *A* need not deny the value of country *B*. Still, both patriotism and

7. Italian nationalists derided *campanilismo*—the world view of persons whose perspective stopped at what they could see from the local bell tower (*campanile*).

8. Liah Greenfeld, *Nationalism: Five Roads to Modernity* (Cambridge, Mass.: Harvard University Press, 1992). Two centuries before Henry VIII, however, English writers discussed an English "nation," while Chaucer in 1386 wrote about someone who, alas, had to travel to a *Barbre nacioun*. For a catalog of national and ethnic stereotypes, see Shakespeare's *Merchant of Venice* (1596). Portia scorns each type but also dislikes a man whose clothes and behavior are from "every where."

9. J. V. Stalin, "Marxism and the National Question" (1913), in Josef Stalin, *Marxism and the National–Colonial Question* (San Francisco: Proletarian Publishers, 1975), 15–99 at 22.

10. Benedict Anderson, *Imagined Communities: Reflections on the Origin and Spread of Nationalism*, rev. ed. (London: Verso, 1991).

ethnocentrism can lead to fear of foreigners, or xenophobia, as well as to racism, chauvinism, and holy wars.[11]

Is race also an imaginary construct? Race in its widest sense can mean all the descendants from the original stock—as in the "human race." But racists construct divisions of humanity on the basis of physical criteria. Racists assert that organic, genetically transmitted differences between human groups are intrinsically linked with the presence or absence of certain socially relevant characteristics, such as intelligence.[12] The idea that humanity is divided into races arose in the 18th and 19th centuries. Raciology—a putative science of racial differences—took shape in the early 20th century, but lost its scientific standing in the second half.[13]

How deep are "racial" differences? Mérième, a ten-year-old Arab girl in Paris, asked her father if she could give blood to Abdou, a black boy in her class. Would that work? "Yes," her father replied. For the human race is one and the variable is in the blood group. The father, the Moroccan-born novelist Tahar Ben Jelloun, reminded Mérième that her Arab mother gave blood to a Vietnamese friend and the donation worked.

The girl asked her father many questions after they attended a street protest against anti-immigrant laws. "What is a law? What is an immigrant? What is discrimination?" When she asked about racism, he replied that being a racist depends largely on one's upbringing, on what someone hears at home or at school. "You are not born a racist, you become one," he told her. "Prejudice is a way of judging others before knowing anything about them. Often we make mistakes. Prejudice can make us afraid."

Racism can also be a pretext. Mérième's cousin blamed her own bad marks in school on teachers who "don't like Arabs." But Mérième knew that the problem lay elsewhere. The cousin didn't do her homework.

Ben Jelloun's answers to his daughter became a best-seller across Europe.[14] Still, a white high school student in Paris reminded him how deep racist passions run. "Have you ever converted a racist?" she asked. The same point was made by a critic who complained that Ben Jalloun's book was "like a Band-Aid on a broken leg."

Is religion—like nation and race—also a product of imagination? A social scientist cannot say, for metaphysics is beyond science. But elementary logic says there cannot be more than one true faith. When a Muslim says that Islam is the final word and that Christians are wrong, or vice versa, at least one side must be wrong. At most, one group is the "Elect".[15] The claims of the others arise from imagination and presumption. Even though they have no basis in fact, exclusivist claims give rise to much strife and misery.

11. *Chauvinism* denotes an aggressive, showy patriotism. The term derives from Nicolas Chauvin, a soldier devoted to Napoleon.

12. Peter Jackson, ed., *Race and Racism: Essays in Social Geography* (London: Allen & Unwin, 1987), Introduction.

13. The term *race* may also be limited to a single line of descent, as in the "race & stocke of Abraham" (first recorded use in 1570); "the British race" (1600); the "Race of Satan" (Milton in 1667). The first reference in English to race as one of several great divisions of mankind was in 1712, as in "the Tartar race." In 1842, another author contrasted the Egyptian and Syro-Arabian races. In 1861, an author distinguished five races—Caucasian, Mongolian, Ethiopian, American, and Malay. In 1883 there was discussion of the "seeds by which the several races of plants are propagated" and of "racial" differences between Manchus and Mongolians. In 1885, an author found racial connections between another people and the Tatar-Mongolians. These citations are from the *Compact Edition of the Oxford English Dictionary* (1971). Its supplement noted a reference in 1924 to raciology—the scientific study of race, but the OED did not mention *racism*.

14. Tahar Ben Jelloun, *Le racisme expliqué a ma fille* (Paris: Seuil, 1999); expanded U.S. edition with essays by American authors: *Racism Explained to My Daughter* (New York: New Press, 1999).

15. Would a wise and benevolent deity give the Light to a subset of humanity and let the other live in Darkness for ages? Some ethnocentrists say "yes."

Nearly three-fourths of humanity belonged to one of four faiths in 2000: Christianity—2 billion worldwide; Islam—1.3 billion in many countries, the greatest number in Indonesia; Hinduism—nearly 800 million, mostly in South Asia; and Buddhism—350 million in 92 countries. There were some 15 million Jews in many countries but concentrated in the U.S., Israel, and Europe. Some 15 percent of the world's population—nearly 900 million—professed no religion, was agnostic, or seemed indifferent. Another 222 million were atheists. Many Chinese accepted Confucianism or Taoism—widely regarded as ethical systems or philosophies more than as religions.

Like it or not, religion meets IR head on. A special issue of *Millennium: Journal of International Studies,* vol. 29, no. 3, published in 2000 at the London School of Economics, included articles on: "The 'Sacred' Dimension of Nationalism," "Forgiveness, Reconciliation, and Justice: A Theological Contribution to a More Peaceful Social Environment," "Taking Religious and Cultural Pluralism Seriously: The Global Resurgence of Religion and the Transformation of International Society," "Writing Sacral IR," "Islam and the West: Muslim Voices of Dialogue," "Does Religion Make a Difference?" and "Toward an International Political Theology." But while the professors counted angels on pinheads in their Ivory Towers, the Taliban was stoning accused fornicators and Hindus were getting ready to burn Muslims in Ahmadabad, long the residence of Mahatma Gandhi, venerable teacher of nonviolence.

Jihad vs. Crusade in the 21st Century

After jihadists attacked America on 9/11, President George W. Bush declared a "crusade" against terrorism. His vocabulary, if not his emotions, reached back nearly 1,000 years to a time when European Christians fought Muslims for the "Holy Land." The White House soon replaced the term *crusade* with *war,* but the damage was done, and many Muslims—rightly or wrongly—saw U.S. policy as a campaign against Islam. "Born again" at age forty, President Bush often denounced evil in the world and called on all persons and countries to take sides. His views were endorsed by the Christian Coalition, many of whom expected Armageddon soon—an apocalyptic battle to be fought near Jerusalem, after which only true believers would be saved.

Many wars have been inspired or justified by religion. The ancient Israelites saw themselves as God's elect, entitled to seize the "Promised Land." Helped by the sword, Islam spread quickly from Arabia to Persia and across North Africa to Iberia. "Jihad" for Muslims may signify a struggle within oneself or against infidels. European and American imperialism usually blended Christianity with commerce and conquest.

Rival interpretations of the same faith can provoke holy wars—as between Catholics and Protestants, Old Believers and Orthodox Russians, Sunni and Shi'a Muslims—and bitter struggles, as between Reformed, Orthodox, and other Jews in Israel. Hindus and Buddhists have fought each other, as in Sri Lanka, and among themselves.

How could any educated and sensitive person believe that her or his group's pigmentation, national culture, or "link to God" entitles them to hold sway over others? Fantastic as such claims may seem, they have guided many—perhaps most people—for millennia, among them, Hitler's "master race" (which modified Christianity to its own ends) and imperial Japan. Such claims have also resonated in a white, Anglo-Saxon, Protestant America and its 21st century expression, the Christian Coalition. While Saddam Hussein and Osama bin Laden made big political and religious claims, neither claimed to represent a master race.

Your panel wonders: "What makes individuals feel bonded in one group? Why do they emphasize what unites them rather than what divides them?" You identify many wellsprings of solidarity—many of which fuse nationalism with religion.

Territory: People often believe their land is sacred—a God-given "Motherland" or "Fatherland."

Mission: Many peoples believe they are "chosen" by God or Fate to do great things; some feel entitled to exploit the nonelect.

Conquest and indoctrination: Diverse peoples have been conquered and molded into a single unit, such as the "United Kingdom of Great Britain and Northern Ireland." Some groups forget their separate origins; others do not.

External threats: Outside pressures help to forge "national" unity. This tempts politicians to manufacture foreign bogeys if they are not visible. If the bogey is an "infidel," mobilizing the public may be easier.

Gender: Men do not want to be "emasculated" or their women to be ravished by outsiders. Many women praise their heroic men.

Fear of extinction: Many groups fear their genes and cultures will be overwhelmed unless they unite and fend off outsiders, including would-be rapists and spreaders of alien genes.

Mobilization: People can be mobilized to feel a common nationalism. Both democracies and dictatorships mobilized nationalist sentiment in World War II.

Leaders: Some leaders genuinely believe in a national cause; others—entrepreneurs of nationalism, many of them scholars,

Why Did Estonians Remain Estonians?

Estonians have lived on the shores of the Baltic Sea for thousands of years. From the 13th century, however, they were ruled by Danes, Germans, Swedes, and then Russians. In the 19th century, most Estonians were still peasants, but modernization buttressed nationalism. The introduction of railroads permitted church choirs from scattered parishes to come together for festivals of traditional Estonian music. Meeting their kinspeople, Estonians celebrated and strengthened their common heritage. Tsarist Russian and, later, Soviet officials tried to throttle Estonian nationalism, but Estonians (as well as neighboring Latvians and Lithuanians) persisted with nationwide music festivals and other symbolic actions. Their drive for independence in the 1980s became a "Singing Revolution." Still, no person has "Estonian" stamped on her or his genes. Today's Estonian way of life derives from an ancient peasant ethos heavily influenced by outside cultures. Even Christianity was an alien import.

Fig. 8.1 Possible Synergies Among Nationalism, Modernization, and Internationalism

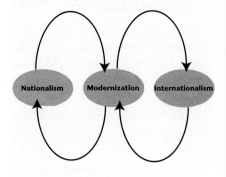

Mobilizing the Disadvantaged for a Sacred Cause

Some analysts say that nationalism has replaced religion, but the two have often worked as partners—as in Catholic Poland, in Buddhist Sri Lanka, and in many Islamic countries. Iran's ayatollahs tapped the alienation of Iran's disadvantaged to support their theocracy. The ayatollahs' regime formed a 3 million-strong volunteer force of Bassiji ("those who are mobilized") to help fight Iraq in the 1980s, often with suicidal mass wave tactics. When that war ended, the Bassiji were directed in 1993 to struggle against the bullets of "cultural corruption" such as lipstick and Western videos that, Commander Ali Reza Afshar said, "make our young impotent to rebuild the nation."*

*One Iranian professor complained that the Bassiji "give fifteen-year-old boys, or unemployed slum dwellers, guns and send them into the streets." They "gain power over the professionals and the élite they believe looks down on them." Chris Hedges, "Mobilizing Against Pop Music and Other Horrors," *The New York Times*, July 21, 1993, A4.

lawyers, and even physicians—*provoke and exploit national sentiments to increase their own influence.*[16]

Modernization: Nationalism nourishes, and is nourished by, modernization—roads, mass communications, industrialization, urbanization, education, and political participation. But modernization can also undermine national identity. The global spread of products—McDonald's, Microsoft, and MTV—fosters a "McWorld" culture threatening the uniqueness of each "nation."[17] *To resist these pressures, some peoples become even more ethnocentric. Figure 8.1*

16. Two historians at Rwanda National University "manufactured doctrines of Hutu ethnic supremacy depicting all Tutsis as a malignant cancer in the nation's history that deserved to be excised once and for all." Michael Chege, "Africa's Murderous Professors," *National Interest*, no. 46 (winter 1996–1997): 32–40.

17. Benjamin R. Barber, *Jihad vs. McWorld* (New York: Ballantine, 1996); Ezra Suleiman, "Is Democratic Supranationalism a Danger?" in *Nationalism and Nationalities in the New Europe*, ed. Charles A. Kupchan (Ithaca, N.Y.: Cornell University Press, 1995), 107–121.

Why Did Colonists Become "Americans"?

In the 17th century England's colonies in North America dealt with the motherland far more than with one another. In the 18th century, however, they were linked ever closer by trade, publications, mail, travel, and the exchange of ideas. As colonists exchanged goods and ideas more with one another and relatively less with the English motherland, they came to feel more "American" and less "English." But external pressures—the taxes and Red Coats of King George III—catalyzed their union. Even then, less than half the colonists were devoted to independence. Even they needed to be mobilized and led.*

*See Richard L. Merritt, "Nation-Building in America: The Colonial Years," in *Nation-Building*, eds. Karl W. Deutsch and William J. Foltz (New York: Atherton, 1966), 56–72.

- Corporate status—recognition as a distinct minority with equal or special rights sought by religious or linguistic groups such as Kurds within Turkey, Iraq, and Iran.

- Change in policy, for example, land reform to benefit Mayan Indians in Mexico.

- Constitutional change in the balance of power, for example, the demand for proportional representation by the Albanian-speaking minority in Macedonia.

- **Autonomy**—self-government, often demanded by **indigenous** peoples such as the Navajo.

- State capture, the goal of Tajiks and other minorities fighting Pashtuns for control of Afghanistan.

- **Secession**, the goal of a minority seeking to join an existing state or to form a new one. As we see in the sidebar, Germans in Czechoslovakia wanted to join Germany in the 1930s, while Slovaks wanted their own state. The Germans were "irredentist." **Irredentism** is a nationalist movement demanding the union of irredenta—a people ruled by an alien government—with kinfolk in their own nation-state.[22]

If the aggrieved minority turns to violence, the intensity and scale of its violence may rise along an escalation ladder:

- Banditry, sporadic terrorism
- Campaigns of terrorism
- Local rebellion—armed attempts to seize power in a locale
- Small-scale guerrilla activity (less than 1,000 armed fighters)
- Large-scale guerrilla activity (more than 1,000 fighters making six or more attacks per year) affecting a wide area
- Protracted civil war

Nonviolent political action by aggrieved minorities more than doubled from 1950 to 1990, while violent action quadrupled. The Communist world was fairly quiet until the late 1980s, when the Soviet and Yugoslav realms began to explode.

Methods of Dealing with Ethnic Minorities

Demands of ethnic minorities have been met by policies drawn from a wide menu of tough and conciliatory measures.[23] Ethnic demands can be met differently in unitary, federal, and confederal systems. A **unitary state** monopolizes power at the center and grants limited power to local communities. A **federation** balances power between the center and the

How Nationalism Made and Split Eurasia's "Heartland"

Czech nationalists (backed by Woodrow Wilson) created Czechoslovakia in 1919 from the Austro-Hungarian Empire. The Czech majority dominated politics. Minorities—Slovaks, Germans, Hungarians, Poles, and Roma—felt slighted. Hitler asserted Germany's right to incorporate all German irredenta. The 1938 Munich agreement authorized Germany to annex Czechoslovakia's largely German-speaking Sudetenland, whereupon 400,000 Czechs moved out. Hungary and Poland then grabbed border regions heavily populated by their irredenta, while Slovakia separated and became a German puppet state. The remaining Czech lands became a German protectorate in 1939. After Hitler's defeat, Czechs returned to the Sudetenland and some 3 million Germans were expelled. Slovakia was reincorporated in a unitary Czechoslovakia in 1945, obtained federal autonomy in 1968, and became independent in 1993. Thus, contending nationalisms created, destroyed, and partitioned Eurasia's "heartland" many times in just over eight decades.

22. The term *irredenta* is from the Italian for "unredeemed"—a reference to Italian speakers under Austrian rule before World War I.

23. See John McGarry and Brendan O'Leary, eds., *The Politics of Ethnic Conflict Regulation: Case Studies of Protracted Ethnic Conflicts* (London: Routledge, 1993), 4.

Some Targets of Ethnic Cleansing

Ethnic cleansing is a euphemism for forced population transfers or genocidal murders. The term was used by Serbs and others in the former Yugoslavia to justify their genocidal massacres, rapes, and forced population transfers of one another in the 1990s. Dispersal and enslavement of conquered peoples have occurred since ancient times.* Ethnic cleansers have targeted:

Muslims and Jews in 15th-century Spain

Huguenots in 16th- and 17th-century France

Native Americans from the 15th through the 19th centuries

Armenians in 19th- and early 20th-century Ottoman Turkey

Jews and Roma in Nazi Germany

Chechens, Crimean Tatars, and others in Stalin's USSR

Germans from the Sudetenland in 1945

East Indians in Uganda in the 1960s

Chinese in Indonesia in the 1960s

Tutsis by Hutus in Burundi and Rwanda in the 1990s.

*See Andrew Bell-Fialkoff, *Ethnic Cleansing* (New York: St. Martin's, 1996). For a review of writings on genocide, see Irving Louis Horowitz in *American Political Science Review* 87, no. 2 (June 1993): 530–531.

states. A **confederation** has a weak center and keeps most power in the local units.

Hard-Line Ways to Eliminate Ethnic Differences. Elimination of ethnic differences is most easily accomplished in unitary systems. Methods include top-down pressures and education to encourage **assimilation** (absorbing minorities into the dominant culture, for example, fusing Bretons and Basques into "French"); **genocide**, the systematic annihilation of whole peoples (Jews and Roma under Hitler); and forced population transfers such as those listed in the sidebar. Other hard-line ways to manage ethnic differences include control by one ethnic group (Whites in the U.S. South before the 1960s) and partition (apartheid in pre-1990s South Africa).

But repression often generates a backlash. Even when an ethnic group has been "cleansed," its remnants may retaliate for many years afterward. Thus, Armenian assassins stalked Turkish diplomats around the globe in the 1990s to revenge alleged Ottoman massacres before and during World War I.

Conciliatory Ways to Manage Ethnic Differences. Methods include integration into a common civic culture that does not obliterate but rather accommodates differences; enlisting ("co-opting") minority elites (attempted in the USSR); affirmative action (the U.S. in the 1970s); mediation by outsiders (the UK in Zimbabwe in 1979); arbitration (the Hopi–Navajo dispute in the 1980s);[24] one person–one vote, but with institutionalized protection for the minority (Zimbabwe, the new South Africa); and **power sharing**—assuring each segment of society a voice in decisions and a share in public resources (Switzerland since 1943, Belgium since 1970, South Africa and Bosnia in the 1990s).

Power sharing (also known as "consociational democracy") and special protection of minorities depart from the winner-take-all stance of **majority rule**. If one ethnic group has more than half the votes, it can pass laws that favor its interests while restricting others. Minorities may reject such democracy. Our case studies will detail how power sharing has worked in Switzerland and failed in Yugoslavia. We shall see that if a minority has "voice" within a system, it is more likely to be loyal and less likely to "exit"—separate from—the system.[25]

Self-Determination vs. World Peace

Demands for self-determination by individuals or groups within existing states can convulse the entire international system. Outsiders—the United Nations and individual states—are torn between two principles: respect for state sovereignty and respect for human rights. The first

24. Mediation and intervention are analyzed in Chapter 9.
25. See Albert O. Hirschman, *Exit, Voice, and Loyalty: Responses to Decline in Firms, Organizations, and States* (Cambridge, Mass.: Harvard University Press, 1970).

principle dictates nonintervention in the affairs of sovereign states and support for existing borders; the second, a need for intervention when human rights are at risk.

Supporters of nonintervention hold that outsiders should let ethnic groups within a state settle their own disputes. The UN and its members should act, if at all, to quash secessionist movements. The UN should not allow minorities to alter boundaries or create new states. Any attempt to change borders will produce greater suffering than that it is meant to address.

Interventionists support the interests of human rights and peace over state sovereignty. Where human rights are abused, peace is at risk. And maintenance of international peace and security is the primary reason for the UN. Civil strife inevitably leads to refugee flows and other dislocations that burden other states.

International law and organization have been erratic in dealing with these issues. The League of Nations Covenant (1919) omitted any mention of national self-determination. Woodrow Wilson and other statesmen at Versailles agreed that it was impossible for each nation to have its own state.[26] Instead, the League labored to promote *minority* rights, especially in the new states of Eastern Europe.

The post-1945 legal order focused on *human* rights—not minority rights. The UN Charter endorsed the principle of national self-determination but did not declare it a legal right. The Charter called on states with "trust territories" (such as Belgium, trustee of Rwanda–Burundi) to promote self-government there. The Charter emphasized self-government of particular territories—not of nations or peoples.

Most UN members backed independence for Europe's colonies such as India, but did little for ethnic minorities or nations within existing states (such as Estonia in the USSR). Without UN support, most secessionist movements failed from 1945 to 1990.[27] When the Second World collapsed in 1991 and 1992, however, UN members quickly recognized most of the new states that emerged from the USSR and Yugoslavia, and also Eritrea (1993), which had struggled to separate from Ethiopia since the 1950s.

The boundary between interstate and intrastate problems became fuzzier. In 1991 and 1992, minority rights again became an international concern. The U.S. State Department demanded that the breakaway republics of Yugoslavia "guarantee ethnic and minority rights" *and* respect the "inviolability of borders." But this was to square the circle: How could each ethnic group enjoy self-determination in a multinational state without changing borders or moving populations?

26. The peacemakers gave some but not all peoples a choice. Communities living along Germany's borders with Denmark and Poland could vote whether to join Germany or its neighbor. But the peacemakers prohibited the German-speaking Austrians from ever joining Germany; they put millions of Germans and Slovaks in one country dominated by Czechs.

The League Covenant consigned some "less advanced" peoples to administration by "advanced nations" under the League of Nations "mandate" system. Thus, South West Africa (a former German colony) became a mandate of South Africa.

27. The United Nations crushed a movement in Katanga province to secede from the former Belgian Congo in 1960. But Singapore left the Federation of Malaysia without a fight in 1965, while Bangladesh—aided by India's military—broke from Pakistan in 1971.

Ethnic ferment encouraged outside intervention. Some top Russian leaders claimed the right to protect 25 million Russians living in former Soviet republics. Moscow also sided in the mid-1990s with Abkhazians wishing to transfer their territory from Georgia to Russia.

Foreign meddling can turn an intrastate problem into one between states. Thus, U.S. leaders and some Russian leaders backed different horses in Yugoslavia and Georgia. U.S.–Russian discord on such matters roiled the entente sought by Presidents Bill Clinton and Boris Yeltsin.

In the late 20th and early 21st centuries, tens of millions of people sought refuge from communal violence—a misery for them and a burden to most host countries already facing heavy unemployment. West Europeans and Australians tightened their border controls, rules on asylum, and procedures for naturalization. Neo-Nazi and nativist movements pressed to exclude or evict foreigners.[28] Do victims of ethnic strife have any legal rights in the countries where they seek asylum? Do rights come only with citizenship? There are no easy answers.

Your panel decides to compare three multiethnic societies that have held together with three that have failed. Was there some recipe for success? For disaster? You hope eventually to carry out many case studies, but you begin with three comparisons—the U.S. and USSR, Singapore and Sri Lanka, and Switzerland and Yugoslavia. You look for lessons—both for individual societies and for outsiders, including the United Nations: How can harmony replace hate?

---

28. The European Court of Justice guaranteed social rights to workers and their families within the European Community regardless of their immigrant status.

France favored immigrants from Poland (part of Western Christendom) over North Africans. But France naturalized more outsiders than Germany, where citizenship depended upon descent (blood), while birth on German soil did not count. Roger Brubaker, *Citizenship and Nationhood in France and Germany* (Cambridge, Mass.: Harvard University Press, 1992); compare Harry Goulbourne, *Ethnicity and Nationalism in Post-Imperial Britain* (New York: Cambridge University Press, 1991). See also *Daedalus* 126, no. 3 (special issue: summer 1997): "A New Europe for the Old?").

29. Walter C. Clemens, Jr., "Who or What Killed the Soviet Union? How Three Davids Undermined Goliath," *Nationalism and Ethnic Politics* 3, no. 1 (spring 1997): 136–158.

COMPARING THEORY AND REALITY: SELF-DETERMINATION AND WORLD ORDER

CASE 1: WHY DID THE U.S. HOLD TOGETHER WHILE TWO RUSSIAN EMPIRES COLLAPSED?

The U.S. expanded and held together from the late 18th into the 21st century, while most other states experienced revolutionary change and/or major territorial losses. Indeed, two Russian empires collapsed—the tsarist in 1917 and the Soviet in 1991. Many features that helped make "one from many" in the U.S. were lacking in the USSR.[29] Some key differences between the two societies are summarized in Table 8.2.

Table 8.2 Comparing U.S. and Soviet Integration (1990)

Variable	U.S.	USSR
Population size	Large (250 million)	Large (291 million)
Civilizations	One, plus others in an evolving synthesis	Several distinct
Major ethnic groups	75 percent Anglophone White; 12 percent Black; 9 percent Hispanic; 4 percent other	51 percent Russian; 15 percent Ukrainian; 6 percent Uzbek; 4 percent Belarus; many others
Languages	One official plus some bilingual education	One countrywide official language plus official languages within each republic
Government	Federal democracy	Authoritarian "union" under Communist dictatorship
How formed?	Mainly voluntarily	Unity imposed by Moscow
Ethnic segmentation by political unit	None, except for Indian reservations	Each union-republic named for an ethnic group (Kazaks, Chechens, and others)
History of ethnic conflict?	Yes, especially Whites against Indians and Blacks	Yes, with genocide in 1930s and 1940s
GDP per capita	Very high	Low to medium

SOURCES: World Bank, *World Development Report* (New York: Oxford University Press, annual); U.S. Department of State, *Country Reports on Human Rights* (Washington, D.C.: Government Printing Office, annual); and U.S. Central Intelligence Agency, *World Factbook* (Washington, D.C.: Government Printing Office, annual).

Civilization

The U.S. was rooted in Western Christianity but moved in the 20th and 21st centuries toward a new way of life enriched by African, Hispanic, Asian, and other influences. Nearly three-fourths of the Soviet population were Slavs rooted in Eastern Orthodox civilization. The many ethnic minorities of the USSR kept their distinct identities far more than did minorities in the United States Russians remained distinct from Lutheran Estonians and Latvians, Catholic Lithuanians, Sunni Muslims of Uzbekistan, Shi'a Muslims of Tajikistan, and Buddhists abutting Mongolia.

In the late 20th century, the U.S. no longer resembled a melting pot so much as a microcosm of humanity—a mosaic in which each stone kept its luster and reflected the brilliance of others. The USSR remained a patchwork quilt of clashing colors. Why did no unified "Soviet nation" emerge despite long efforts to promote "brotherhood" and "convergence"? In brief: repressed nationalism.

Voluntary vs. Coerced Participation

Most of the individuals and new territories joining the U.S. did so voluntarily. There were important exceptions: Native Americans, Africans, Hispanics in annexed Mexican lands, many Hawaiians, and Inuits. By contrast, the Russian state was built and sustained by force—from Lithuania to Vladivostok—though some minorities (such as Georgians and Armenians) had at times welcomed Russian protection against Ottoman Turks.

Segmentation

Countries can be segmented—partitioned, divided—by natural borders (for example, rivers), by ethnicity, or by other criteria. No U.S. "state" represented a single ethnos, though some cities were dominated by German–Americans and other "hyphenated" minorities. By contrast, the structure of the Soviet Union enshrined territorial ethnicity. Not only were its fifteen union-republics named for ethnic groups clustered there (Ukraine, Armenia, Turkmenia), but so were over twenty autonomous republics and regions (Tataria, Yakutia).

Language

The U.S. had essentially one language, which most immigrants wanted to learn.[30] Despite some efforts to make Spanish an official language, many Hispanics opposed bilingual education because it slowed assimilation. By contrast, most Soviet republics were allowed to keep using the local language, though Russian was promoted as the language for communicating countrywide. To be sure, the Kremlin tried to gut minority languages and cultures of local symbols and replace them with "socialist" emblems, but the effect of Moscow's policies was to keep local languages and nationalisms alive in most republics.[31]

Democracy vs. Autocracy

U.S. democracy gave hope to most ethnic minorities that they could improve their lot by working within the system. Majority rule favored the entrenched majority; the largest minority was nearly disenfranchised until the 1960s. A different system such as proportional representation would have assured better representation for minorities but might have been very divisive.[32]

Tsarist Russia and the USSR, by contrast, were ruled by autocrats, secret police, and a rigid bureaucracy. Outside the ruling elite, no group—least of all ethnic minorities—had a voice. Stalin established the façade of a federal system, but real power remained in the Communist Party and its top leader. When the party lost its ability to intimidate, the system collapsed.[33]

The North's victory in the U.S. Civil War in 1865 made clear that no state could secede from the Union. By contrast, the Soviet Constitution allowed the union-republics to secede. When the Communist dictatorship

30. At times, however, foreign languages were the medium of instruction in some U.S. public as well as parochial schools, and bilingual schools became common in the late 20th century. See Lawrence H. Fuchs, *The American Kaleidoscope: Race, Ethnicity, and the Civic Culture* (Hanover, N.H.: University Press of New England, 1990), chap. 24.

31. In the 1920s, it appeared that 192 languages would be treated as official. See Yuri Slezkine, "The USSR as a Communal Apartment, or How a Socialist State Promoted Ethnic Particularism," in *Becoming National: A Reader*, ed. Geoff Eley and Ronald Grigor Suny (New York: Oxford University Press, 1996), 203–238 at 214–216.

32. Proportional representation, as in France, would give a party seats in Congress proportional to the number of votes it receives countrywide (not just in the county or state) and thus foster many parties.

33. On Stalin's "Big Deal" with the privileged sectors of society, see Vera S. Dunham, *In Stalin's Time: Middle Class Values in Soviet Fiction*, rev. ed. (Durham, N.C.: Duke University Press, 1990).

One of the largest peoples without a state is the Kurds—some 20 to 25 million people living as second- or third-class citizens in Iran, Turkey, Iraq, Syria, and the Caucasus. Kurds have no common tongue, though most speak offshoots of Iranian, and no common faith, though most are Sunni. But they are aware of a shared culture that, most of them believe, makes them a nation. The photo shows a Kurdish family that fled Saddam Hussein's rule in 1991, living in difficult conditions in a zone protected by U.S. forces from Iraqi attacks in the years between 1991 and 2003 (see maps 4.3 and 4.4). Following Saddam's ouster in 2003, Kurds hoped to share power in a new Iraqi government, but worried that Turkish troops might try to absorb their lands (and oil wells) into Turkey. Kurds had reason to fear not only Saddam's autocracy but also Iraqi democracy, because they could easily be outvoted.

weakened in the 1980s, Lithuanians and others quoted the USSR Constitution and asserted: "We have the right to secede."

Many—probably most—non-Russians felt exploited by the Russian-dominated center. Many Russians, in turn, disdained non-Russians as ingrates and troublemakers.

Had the USSR been an economic success, national differences might have been subdued, though this is not certain. It was the country's wealthiest republics—Estonia, Latvia, and Lithuania—that led demands for secession, while the poorest regions—those of Central Asia—favored continued union.

Lack of democracy and free expression made the pot boil. Not until 1987 did the Kremlin encourage the Soviet media to address national complaints somewhat openly. By then it was too late: Grievances erupted like a volcano, opening wounds instead of healing them. A Soviet scholar compared the USSR with India. Both contained multiple civilizations and languages; both were segmented. India was much poorer and its central government weaker. Despite decades of communal violence, India held together. Freedom to speak, write, and organize politically acted as safety valves absent in the Soviet system.[34]

Soviet President Mikhail Gorbachev sponsored a more liberal constitution in 1991 offering more autonomy to each union-republic, but by then the Balts and others were putting their laws above those drafted in the Kremlin. To prevent enactment of the new constitution, a handful of hard-liners tried to overthrow Gorbachev in August. In the chaos that

34. India, he thought, was moving toward the Swiss power-sharing model. See A. A. Prazauskas, "Ethnoregional Political Cultures and the Problem of National–State Integration in India and the USSR," *Vostok* 5 (May 1991): 38–51. For a more complex picture, see Salman Rushdie, *The Moor's Last Sigh* (New York: Pantheon, 1995).

The Russian Federation includes many diverse peoples. But only one demanded complete independence from the RF in the 1990s—Chechens, a Muslim people living just north of the Caucasus Mountains. Trying to keep the federation intact and retain control of oil lines traversing Chechnya, Russian troops waged a savage war against Chechens in 1994–1996, renewed it in 1998–1999, and continued it into the 21st century. Many Chechens sought refuge in neighboring Ingushetia, whose people did not try to split from the RF. Here we see a father and son in December 2002 taking down their tent in a refugee camp in Ingushetia. They were bowing to Russian pressures to return to Chechnya, even though fighting continued, most buildings were damaged, and few services operated. Having often proclaimed victory in Chechnya, President Putin wanted to show that normal life was resuming there.

35. Following the Moscow hostage crisis in late 2002, Putin loosened the reins on Russian troops in Chechya. Result: More young Chechen men were rounded up from their villages at night, tortured, butchered, and thrown in garbage dumps. Addressing a European summit in Brussels on November 11, 2002, the former KGB agent declared: "If you want to become a complete Islamic radical, and are ready to undergo circumcision, then I invite you to Moscow. We're a multidenominational country. We have specialists in this question [circumcision] as well. I will recommend that he carry out the operation in such a way that after it nothing else will grow." Though Putin's comments were softened by the interpreter in Belgium, they were later published accurately in Russian newspapers, evoking no comment.

followed, Boris Yeltsin pulled the Russian Republic out of the "Union" and the deck of cards collapsed in December. A decade or so after the Soviet collapse, the major ethnic challenge to the unity of the Russian Federation—Chechyna—helped bring Presidents Putin and Bush together. Putin characterized the Chechens as bandits paid for by al-Qaeda. So he and the U.S. had a common enemy, he claimed.[35] And Bush went along. While Yeltsin and then Putin waged war against Chechens, however, Moscow in the 1990s negotiated autonomy agreements with Tatarstan, Bashkira, and some forty other subunits of the Russian Federation. Still, tensions between the non-Muslim Russian majority and Muslim minorities in the RF smouldered in the early 21st century.

CASE 2: WHY DID SINGAPORE PROSPER AND SRI LANKA IMPLODE?

Just to the south of India is another spinoff from the British Empire with democratic institutions—the island of Sri Lanka, earlier known as Ceylon. In the 1970s, many social scientists regarded Sri Lanka as a model developing country. In 1983, however, Sri Lanka fell apart, torn by one of humanity's oldest ethnic and religious conflicts. Nearby is Singapore, also an island nation of many cultures once tied to the British Empire, but one that has enjoyed social peace and ethnic harmony. After 9/11, however, peace came to Sri Lanka and ethnic and religious tension to Singapore. Why?

Modernizing Nationalism

Like Venice and Hamburg in the Middle Ages, Singapore shows how a commercial city-state can be a major actor in world affairs.[36] Transformed under imperial British rule from a malarial fishing village into a great port, Singapore became independent in 1965. Dominated by ethnic Chinese, the government has used state power to encourage and enforce ethnic harmony. Singapore's authoritarian, unitary form of government has also fostered economic modernization and shared the expanding wealth with its citizens. The government uses English but also accepts Chinese, Tamil, and Malay as official languages.

Singapore has promoted a unifying nationalism based on pride and hope in the island nation's achievements. English, along with skyscrapers and apartment blocks, is an alien import. Unlike the United States, which looks backward with pride and forward with hope, Singapore focuses on the future. It tells its various peoples to bond in a new nationalism. Critics said that Singapore's authoritarian government—a blend of Big Brother and McWorld—stamped out cultural differences and freedom of expression. Others saw the regime as an enlightened despotism. Both admirers and critics agreed that economic and social progress benefited from ethnic calm, while ethnic harmony benefited from prosperity.

How a Model Developing Country Ran Amok

Though much richer than Singapore in natural resources, Sri Lanka remained much poorer—as Table 8.3 makes clear. Having suffered ethnic riots at independence in 1969, Singapore used unitary state power to enforce mutual tolerance. But democracy failed Sri Lanka, because Sinhalese—three-fourths of the population—abused their power. The majority used government to prop up its privileges, language, and religion.

Many Sinhalese are ethnocentric. They consider themselves the "Lion People" and protectors of Buddhism. For the Sinhalese popular mind, a multiracial or multicommunal state is "incomprehensible."[37] Many Sinhalese see themselves as racially and religiously superior to the Tamil minority. Sinhalese are Aryans who migrated from northern India over 2,000 years ago. Tamils are Dravidians, often darker and shorter than Sinhalese. Most Tamils practice Hinduism. Some two-thirds are "Ceylonese Tamils"—offspring of ancient settlers from southern India. The other third are "Estate Tamils"—poorest of the poor, descended from migrants who arrived in the late 19th and early 20th century to work on

36. On Hamburg and the Hanseatic League, see Klaus Friedland, *Die Hanse* (Stuttgart: Kohlhammer, 1991).

37. K. M. de Silva, *A History of Sri Lanka* (Delhi: Oxford University Press, 1981), p. 4. See also Dennis Austin, *Democracy and Violence in India and Sri Lanka* (New York: Council on Foreign Relations, 1995), and essays on South Asia in Joseph V. Montville, ed., *Conflict and Peacemaking in Multiethnic Societies* (New York: Lexington Books, Macmillan, 1991), chaps. 15–19.

Table 8.3 Comparing Singapore and Sri Lanka (1993)

Variable	Singapore	Sri Lanka
Population size	Small (3.2 million)	Small (18 million)
Civilizations	Four	Two, plus Western
Major ethnic groups	78 percent Chinese 14 percent Malay 7 percent Tamil	74 percent Sinhalese 18 percent Tamil 7 percent Moor
Languages	English and three other official	One official; two "national"; English
Government	Authoritarian	Majority-rule democracy
How formed?	Mainly voluntarily	Unity imposed on rivals by European imperialists
Ethnic segmentation by political unit	None	De facto in two, mainly Tamil, provinces
History of ethnic conflict?	Little	Much
GDP per capita	Medium high ($15,730)	Low ($540)

SOURCES: World Bank, *World Development Report*; U.S. Department of State, *Country Reports*; and U.S. Central Intelligence Agency, *World Factbook*.

tea plantations. Imperial Britain imposed order on Ceylon from 1815 until its independence in 1948.

With independence came majority rule and renewed ethnic conflict. The Sinhalese majority cut back the numbers of Tamils in higher education and civil service, where Tamils held more jobs than their share of the population.[38] Like Singapore, Sri Lanka could have adopted English as its official language to transcend local language differences and step into world trade. Instead, the Sinhalese-dominated government made Sinhala the official language in 1956.

Some Tamils tried to work within the system. Others demanded cultural rights or autonomy for Tamil regions. When moderate demands were rebuffed, some called for an independent Tamil state—"Eelam." The Liberation Tigers of Tamil Eelam (LTTE), formed in 1976, suppressed voices of moderation. Its most militant fighters were semieducated rural youths without jobs, spurred on by charismatic leaders. Like Palestinians confronting Israel, young Tamils asked: "What have we got to lose?"

Systematic warfare began in 1983 after Tamil Tigers massacred Sinhalese in remote regions and Sinhalese took revenge against Tamils in the capital.[39] Violence fed violence. Extremists murdered kinsmen who favored ethnic conciliation.

38. British colonial administrators steered U.S. missionary educators toward Tamil communities. The result was that Tamils were better prepared on average for professional life than Sinhalese.

In early 1983, I walked along the Colombo beach with a Tamil, an ex–civil servant forced into early retirement. From memory he recited Shakespearean sonnets and fragments of Ralph Waldo Emerson's essays. He also knew the great Hindu classics. Although the days were balmy, his heart was heavy, fearing a storm to come. Months later, I got a shaky letter from the north; his home in Colombo had been burned and he was on the run.

39. The young Tamils learned guerrilla tactics and fanaticism from a Sinhalese youth group, the People's Liberation Front or JVP, which in 1971 fought Sri Lanka's government for three months with home-made weapons before being brutally repressed. See A. C. Alles, *Insurgency—1971* (Colombo: Colombo Apothecaries' Co., Ltd., 1979); see also de Silva, *A History*, 540–48.

Big smiles and private thoughts as the third round of peace negotiations began in Oslo between LTTE and Sri Lankan government representatives in December 2002. Tamils are on the left, Sri Lankan government officials on the right, with Norwegians in between. Like the 1993 Oslo Accord between the Palestinians and Israel, the LTTE–Sri Lankan talks resulted from multitrack diplomacy. Europeans had practical as well as idealistic motives to get involved: They feared war in the Middle East and a continuing flow of Tamil refugees from Sri Lanka.

"Made in Oslo" was not some magic elixir. In the Middle East, the 1993 accords became nearly a dead letter in less than a decade. In the Indian Ocean, despite a cease-fire supposed to last at least fifteen months, several naval battles took place in March 2003 between LTTE and Sri Lankan vessels. The two sides planned further talks to iron out ambiguities in the rules governing the cease-fire at sea.

Meanwhile, after her party lost the recent parliamentary elections, Sri Lankan President Chandrika Kumaratunga accused her party's rival, Prime Minister Ranil Wickremesinghe, of permitting the Norwegians to violate Sri Lanka's sovereignty. She said her government invited the Norwegians to act as "facilitators"—not to serve as mediators or arbitrators. She complained that a Norwegian was to be the "final arbiter" in interpreting possible violations of the cease-fire. But the PM backed the Norwegians and the cease-fire, also endorsed by the U.S., India, Japan, and the EU.

After an LTTE bomb killed the previous president in 1993, Sri Lankans in 1994 elected a new head of state, President Chandrika Bandaranaike Kumaratunga,[40] who wanted ethnic peace. When her father was prime minister, he was assassinated by Sinhalese extremists in 1959; when her mother was prime minister, Sinhalese Marxists attacked the government in 1971; Kumaratunga's politician husband was killed by Tamils in 1994.[41] Her government offered autonomy to the Tamils in 1995, but the Tigers fought on. Sri Lankan troops captured the Tamils' main city, Jaffna, in 1996, but the Tigers countered by blowing up the Central Bank in Colombo. Besides frightening tourists and foreign investors, the Tigers scared off Australian and West Indian cricket players from taking part in championship matches in Colombo. A Tamil in Jaffna told a visitor: "You see us living in darkness. But some day we will get our freedom." The Tigers' leader relished power and did not wish to share it with anyone. Each side used any lull in the fighting to rearm. Tens of thousands of civilians and troops from each side were killed between 1983 and 2002.

Post-9/11: A Role Reversal

Things changed in 2001 and 2002. The LTTE leaders gave up their demand for an independent Tamil state and sat down with Colombo to negotiate details of an autonomous region within Sri Lanka. Hostilities ceased and people began to travel freely across what had been battle lines. Men and women who had left their families to fight in the 1980s or 1990s came home after ten and fifteen years in the bush.

40. An LTTE woman blew up herself and India's former prime minister, Rajiv Gandhi, in 1991.

41. Hamish McDonald, "Politics by Murder," *Far Eastern Economic Review* 157, no. 44 (November 3, 1994): 14–15.

Why the new climate? The Colombo government had stuck to its line and its guns. Tiger leaders showed signs of battle fatigue. UK authorities classified the LTTE as a terrorist organization and banned donations. Beginning in 2000, Norwegian mediators helped the parties to negotiate.

Meanwhile, Singapore no longer looked like an oasis of calm. In December 2001, even as U.S. bombing in Afghanistan tapered off, Singapore security agents rounded up fifteen members of a terrorist cell planning to bomb the U.S. Embassy and other American installations in Singapore. In August 2002, the Internal Security Department arrested another twenty-one—accused of carrying out reconnaissance for those already in jail. All but one of the thirty-six arrested were citizens of Singapore. Some had been trained in Pakistan and Afghanistan by al-Qaeda.

Observers doubted that many of Singapore's 400,000 Muslims would join a radical terrorist network. Few believed that such a network could function in a small, highly controlled city-state where the police monitor phone calls and e-mails and government censors control the press. But elder statesman Lee Kwan Yew had often warned that Singapore's ethnic harmony was fragile. Ethnic riots had erupted at independence in 1969, though no terrorist acts had occurred since the mid-1970s, when the Japanese Red Army (Communist terrorists) briefly hijacked a ferry.

Were those arrested just the extreme fringe of a basically content Muslim minority or the advance guard of widespread discontent that had lain fermenting but dormant for decades? Had the suffocating calm of Singapore given birth to a new generation unwilling to live "by bread alone"?

CASE 3: WHY DOES SWITZERLAND PROSPER WHILE THE SOUTH SLAVS FIGHT?

Switzerland is the world's oldest democracy and has one of the world's highest incomes. It has experienced no foreign wars and almost no civil strife since the 19th century. Though the Swiss use four different languages and practice two major faiths, most consider themselves members of a single Swiss nation.[42] Yugoslavia—land of the South (*Yugo*) Slavs—was the least repressive Communist state and one of the richest. Yugoslavia split from the Soviet bloc in 1948 and asserted its "nonalignment" with Moscow or the West. Like officially neutral Switzerland, Yugoslavia armed heavily and trained its reserve forces to foster national unity and discourage invaders. Yugoslavia also had a federal structure and power-sharing arrangements similar to Switzerland's. When the 1984 Winter

42. See also Carol L. Schmid, *Conflict and Consensus in Switzerland* (Berkeley: University of California Press, 1981), chaps. 3 and 4; and Jonathan Steinberg, *Why Switzerland?* 2d ed. (Cambridge: Cambridge University Press, 1996).

Table 8.4 Comparing Switzerland and Yugoslavia (1990)

Variable	Switzerland	Yugoslavia
Population size	Small (6.7 million)	Medium (23.9 million)
Civilizations	One	Three
Major ethnic groups	74 percent German 20 percent French 4 percent Italian 1 percent Romansch 49 percent Roman Catholic 48 percent Protestant	36 percent Serbian 20 percent Croatian 9 percent Muslim 8 percent Slovene 8 percent Albanian 6 percent Macedonian 5 percent "Yugoslav"
Languages	Three official plus one national	Four official, plus others
Government	Federal democracy with extensive power sharing	Authoritarian confederation under Communist Party
How formed?	Mainly voluntarily	Unity imposed by Communist dictator
Ethnic segmentation by political unit	De facto in most cantons	Much ethnic intermingling in key republics, but most republics are named for an ethnic group
History of ethnic conflict?	Little	Much
GDP per capita	High ($32,680)	Medium ($3,060)

SOURCES: World Bank, *World Development Report*; U.S. Department of State, *Country Reports*; and U.S. Central Intelligence Agency, *World Factbook*.

The Yugoslav Federation

The six republics of Yugoslavia in 1945 were as follows:

> Slovenia
> Croatia
> Bosnia and Herzegovina
> Montenegro
> Macedonia
> Serbia (including the autonomous provinces of Vojvodina and Kosovo, raised to autonomous republic status in 1971)

Each major Yugoslav republic was named for a cultural-ethnic group that could, and later did, claim state sovereignty. In this respect, Yugoslavia followed the Soviet constitutional model (Ukraine, Armenia, etc.)—a formula for splitting if central power ever faltered. As we see in Map 8.1, Yugoslav unity was the more fragile because each republic except Slovenia had distinct ethnic minorities within its borders. Thus, when Yugoslavia broke up in the early 1990s, many Serbs in Croatia and Bosnia wanted to join Serbia.

Olympics convened in Sarajevo, Yugoslavia looked more "First" than "Second" or "Third World."[43] Why, then, did Yugoslavia disintegrate in 1990? There was no single cause. As Table 8.4 shows, there were both similarities and differences between Switzerland and Yugoslavia.

Unity from Below and from Above

Switzerland began as a defensive alliance of just three cantons (similar to U.S. "states") in 1291. Gradually, other cantons joined to form a confederation. Switzerland still calls itself a confederation, but—like the U.S. after 1787—it became a more centralized federation in the 19th and 20th centuries.

By contrast, Yugoslavia did not emerge from the free choice of the South Slavs. Unity was imposed from above after World Wars I and II— by a king in 1919 and, with more popular support, by the anti-Fascist Partisan leader, Marshal Tito, in 1945. Yugoslavia's unity depended on a strong center; Switzerland's, on strong cantons. Yugoslavia was less than the sum of its parts; Switzerland was more.

43. Appearances can deceive. Los Angeles looked integrated as it hosted the Summer Olympics in 1984. A few years later it was racked by race riots.

Map 8.1 Ethnic Divisions in the Former Yugoslavia, 1991

Civilization

While all Swiss came from a single Western civilization, three civilizations clashed in Yugoslavia: Serbs saw themselves as defenders of Orthodox Christianity against the Islam of Bosnian Muslims and Albanians and the Western Christianity of Croats and Slovenes. The demarcation lines between Western and Orthodox Christians dated from the third and fourth centuries when the Roman Empire and Christianity split into a branch based in Rome and another in Constantinople. Islam entered the scene in the 14th and 15th centuries when Ottoman Turks penetrated the Balkans, conquered Constantinople, and converted Bogomil Christians to Islam. To be sure, the three civilizations coexisted peacefully for long intervals, but entrepreneurs of hate could evoke nationalist passions by invoking past injustices and bloodletting.

Serbs recalled how their ancestors were defeated by Muslim Turks in 1389. Closer to hand, they recalled that, when Croatia became a Nazi puppet state during World War II, its rulers carried out forced conversions to Catholicism and massacres of Orthodox Serbs in border regions. One in six Serbs under Croat rule died in the war—more than 300,000. Had so many Serbs not died then, Serbs might well have been a majority (not a mere plurality) within Yugoslavia—even in Bosnia—in the 1990s.

Racial and physical differences have divided Americans, Soviets, Sri Lankans, and Singaporeans (among others). But they have played little or no role in Switzerland or in differences among Serbs, Croats, and Bosnian Muslims. Most Swiss and South Slavs cannot be distinguished by their appearance. Unlike the Swiss, most South Slavs speak the same language—Serbo-Croatian, though they use different alphabets to write it and have regional dialects. The Yugoslav constitution declared the languages of all the country's nationalities to be equal. Only in the armed forces was the Serbo-Croat language mandatory.

But each ethnic group in Yugoslavia felt exploited by another. Power was centered in Serbia, where Belgrade was the national as well as the republican capital. The two richest republics, Slovenia and Croatia, complained that they were taxed to benefit the center and the poorest republics.[44] Christians feared Bosnian and Albanian Muslims. Ethnic Albanians and Hungarians chafed at Slavic dominance. Serbs felt that Serbia's borders had been shrunk just to make others feel better. All groups feared Serbian imperialism.

Power Sharing

The Swiss practiced power sharing at every level of society. In the federal government and in private organizations such as the National Soccer Association, each ethnic group was assured a voice. The government's executive body, the Federal Council, consists of seven members—usually four German speakers, two or three French, and sometimes an Italian—with its chair (the federal president) rotating each year. The Swiss legislature has two houses. The upper house, like the U.S. Senate, assures two seats for each canton.[45]

44. In Yugoslavia, as in the USSR, the richest republics took the lead in demanding independence. These republics were also those closest to Western Europe: Slovenia and Croatia and the three Baltic republics—Estonia, Latvia, and Lithuania. One of India's richest regions, the Punjab, was most assertive about its rights.

45. The power-sharing approach helps cope with class and religious differences in Austria, Belgium, and the Netherlands, but has had less success in Lebanon, Malaysia, and Cyprus. Power sharing is like "a delicately but securely balanced scale." A rival approach, that of top-down control (as in Israel with its Arab minority), is like "a puppeteer manipulating his stringed puppet." See Kenneth D. McCrae, "Theories of Power-Sharing and Conflict Management," in *Conflict and Peacemaking in Multiethnic Societies*, ed. Montville, 100.

Power sharing of a kind existed also in Yugoslavia—at least on paper. In 1974 President Tito rammed through a new constitution that weakened central power and made Yugoslavia a loose confederation. The executive looked much like Switzerland's Federal Council with the presidency rotating each year. The 1974 constitution took Kosovo and Vojvodina from Serbia and made them autonomous republics—a move that angered nationalist Serbs.

The reality was that Yugoslavia, like the USSR, was dominated by the Communist Party and its top leader. Tito's leadership kept Yugoslavia together. After his death in 1980, each ethnic group became more restive. A new strongman emerged in Serbia—Slobodan Milošević. The longtime Communist became an entrepreneur of Serbian nationalism. "Slobo" became president of Serbia in 1989.

The Breakup

Slovenia and Croatia became separatist, while Serbia was irredentist. If other republics split from Yugoslavia, Milošević warned, Serbia would act to expand its borders and recover its irredenta.[46] Milošević used what had been Yugoslavia's Federal Army (with its mainly Serbian officer corps) to take borderlands, heavily populated by Serbs, from Croatia. Bosnia became the next battleground. Of Bosnia's 4,355,000 people, Muslims made up nearly one-half—1,905,000; Serbs came second (1,364,000); then Croats (752,000). With much higher fertility than the other groups, Muslims could expect one day to make up a clear majority.[47] This worried the Serbs, who feared Islamic fervor. Few Bosnian Muslims practiced Islam with more than routine devotion, but Serb demagogues recalled how some Bosnian Muslims cooperated with Croat Fascists in World War II; they warned that Muslims in Sarajevo wanted to establish an Islamic theocracy linked with Iran and Turkey.[48]

If Bosnia remained part of Yugoslavia, Bosnian Serbs would feel protected from Muslim excesses. But most of Bosnia's Muslims, along with many Croats and some Serbs, wanted to form an independent Bosnia. It would be a secular, multicultural, and multiethnic state. But for power sharing to work in Bosnia, proportional representation would not suffice. Serb leaders demanded a Bosnian state of equal nations—each with a veto on major decisions. If that were impossible, Serbs would separate, partition the country, and drive out Muslims from ethnically mixed areas.

46. Reflecting the unity of civilizations, the Vatican recognized predominantly Catholic Slovenia and Croatia even before the European Union did in January 1992.

47. Most Bosnians had been Christians for more than 1,000 years. Aligned neither with Constantinople nor with Rome, they were persecuted both by Orthodox and Western Christian armies. But in the 15th century many Bosnians converted to Islam—the faith of their Ottoman Turk conquerors. Some Bosnian Muslims became landlords and tax collectors for the Ottomans. Class as well as religion divided them from their Christian neighbors.

48. To be sure, Alija Izetbegović, elected president of Bosnia-Herzegovina in 1992, called for pluralism. But in 1970, he had advocated an Islamic government—from Morocco to Indonesia. Muslims, he wrote, should "destroy the existing non-Islamic power" and "build up a new Islamic one."

Possible Mass Graves
Kasaba/Konjevic Polje Area, Bosnia

Unclassified
Jul 95

Recently disturbed earth
Vehicle revetment

Unclassified

Ethnic cleansing could mean "only" forced population transfer, but it could also mean genocide. Here we see an aerial photo of possible mass graves of Bosnian Muslims murdered by Bosnian Serbs. In March 2003 the remains of some 600 Muslim men and boys from the town of Srebrinica, slaughtered by Bosnian Serbs in July 1995, were reinterred, each in a green-wrapped casket. Between 6,000 and 8,000 males from Srebrinica had been killed in 1995 and placed in mass graves. About 600 had been identified by DNA testing. Despite NATO troops in Bosnia, in 2003 the two main Bosnian Serb leaders indicted for these crimes remained free, protected by bodyguards.

As in Sri Lanka, majority rule in Bosnia sparked open warfare. Bosnia's government in February 1992 organized a referendum—a popular election on whether to secede from Yugoslavia. Most Muslims and Croats voted for Bosnia's independence, but Serbs stayed away, fearing they would be outvoted. Power sharing collapsed. In April 1992, Europe and the U.S. recognized Bosnia's independence, but war had already begun. Bosnian Serbs, armed and staffed by the ex–Federal Army, seized whatever land they could within Bosnia, just as other Serbs had done in Croatia. Ethnic cleansing and genocide commenced.

UN mediators recommended "cantonization" of Bosnia—three cantons: one for Muslims, one for Serbs, and one for Croats, with power sharing in the capital Sarajevo. But a clean-cut partition was impossible without many population transfers (ethnic cleansing). Furthermore, Serbs controlled 70 percent of Bosnian territory in the mid-1970s and were reluctant to give up what they had won. Muslims refused to recognize Serbian conquests or give the Serbs more territory than their population numbers might warrant.

The barbarism practiced by the former Yugoslavs against each other in the 1990s mocked all religions. No group was innocent, but a CIA study concluded that Serbs were responsible for 90 percent of ethnic

NATO Collecting Weapons from Albanian Rebels in Macedonia

HE WAS TURNING IN HIS ARMS
ONE BULLET AT A TIME...

How to persuade dissident minorities to give up their arms? This was a sticking point in Northern Ireland, Sri Lanka, and Kosovo. In the Former Yugoslav Republic of Macedonia, NATO forces labored to persuade the Christian Slavic majority to guarantee political representation and cultural minority for the Muslim, Albanian-speaking minority. But some Albanian speakers (joined by irredentists from Kosovo and Albania proper) believed that they could get their way only by force.

cleansing and genocide. In 1992 alone, Serbs systematically raped more than 40,000 Bosnian Muslims and destroyed every major repository of Bosnian Muslim culture.[49] Some analysts explained that Serbs suffered from a persecution complex. They more than compensated by their massacres of others.

Multicultural cooperation was lived every day in Sarajevo by the staffs of besieged hospitals, the newspaper *Liberation*, and several radio stations. The Bosnian government's seven-man executive body in the mid-1990s included President Izetbegović and two other Muslims, two Croats, and two Serbs—an ethnic balance, as in Switzerland. Worn down as they were by years of siege, however, distrust mounted among the three groups.

In the early 21st century, a decade or so after Yugoslavia broke asunder, much of the area was still torn by ethnic and sectarian differences. Major interventions by NATO and the United Nations, described in the next chapter, generated a negative but sullen peace. The roots of conflict remained. There were few signs that the former Yugoslavs could emulate the Swiss civic culture that accommodated diverse languages and religions.

Minorities as the 21st Century Began: One-sixth of Humanity

As the 21st century began, disadvantaged minorities were active in 116 of the world's 161 larger countries. They made up one-sixth of humanity:

• In Western democracies minority populations made up a small part of the population. A negative peace prevailed in Northern Ireland.

49. Some Croat residents of Switzerland traveled to Bosnia for "rape weekends."

Elsewhere, there was little ethnic violence except for sporadic terrorist actions by Basques in Spain.

• Eastern Europe and the former USSR had many ethnic minorities, but they made up a small proportion of the regional population. In Estonia and Latvia, however, Russian speakers made up a third or more of the population. Few of them knew the local language, and most were not citizens. Still, not one death occurred in the Baltic republics as a result of ethnic violence after they regained their independence in 1991. In the Balkans, by contrast, there was an uneasy, NATO-imposed truce between Serbs and Kosovars, most of whom wanted to split from Serbia, and between the Macedonian government and the Albanian-speaking minority of Macedonia. In the Caucasus, Azerbaijan and Armenia remained at odds over Nagorno-Karabakh.

• China faced sporadic terror attacks by Uighurs and widespread discontent among Tibetans.

• Liberated from Taliban rule in 2002, Afghanistan suffered from ethnic conflict. Many regional warlords fought to maintain local control or capture the central government.

• India faced demands for secession or greater autonomy by Kashmiris, Tripurs, and other minorities. Muslim–Hindu violence flared in Gujarat state.

• In the Middle East, Kurds challenged Turkey, Iraq, and Iran; Palestinians and Israeli Arabs challenged Israel; Shi'i challenged Iraq, Lebanon, and several Gulf states.

• In Africa, the Sudan and Nigeria were rent by war and threats of war between Muslims and Christians. The Congo and many African countries suffered from ethnic rivals fighting for oil, diamonds, and other natural resources. Zimbabwe's treatment of its White farmers changed from peaceful coexistence to expropriation.

• In Latin America, indigenous groups challenged governments in Nicaragua, Mexico, and Ecuador.

Despite many hot spots featured in newspaper headlines, the big picture was that ethnic conflict peaked in 1994–1995 and then declined. By 2002 the trend was clear: There were fewer secessionist wars and less groups taking part in open conflict. Deescalating conflicts far outnumbered those escalating.[50] Thus, open warfare among the South Slavs stopped after NATO forces occupied Bosnia and Kosovo. Tamils and Sinhalese entered a ceasefire. Except for Chechnya, the sprawling Russian Federation was at peace. Hostilities stopped within and between former Soviet republics such as

50. Gurr, *Peoples versus States*, pp. 12, 285–286 and the study published three years later: Monty G. Marshall and Ted Robert Gurr, *Peace and Conflict 2003: A Global Survey of Armed Conflicts. Self-Determination Movements, and Democracy* (College Park, Md.: University of Maryland Center for International Development and Conflict Management, 2003), 26–38.

Georgia, Armenia, and Azerbaijan. East Timor achieved independence in 2002 after a long war and UN (mainly Australian) intervention.

Lessened hostilities resulted in part from intervention by outside powers, regional organizations, or the UN. Battle fatigue also contributed. As in Northern Ireland, armed groups turned to symbolic protest and conventional politics. In Belfast and elsewhere, many parties found that compromise accords offered greater rewards and fewer penalties than zero-sum struggle. This somewhat cheery picture might change in a flash, however. Indeed, it was punctured dramatically in May 2003, when suicidists struck in Israel, Saudi Arabia, and Chechnya—each with far-reaching consequences. For example, the U.S. promptly removed all nonessential diplomatic personnel from Saudi Arabia. And just one bomber can sabotage mediation efforts such as those we shall examine in the next chapter.

WHAT PROPOSITIONS HOLD? WHAT QUESTIONS REMAIN?

Our world is torn between forces that unite and divide humanity. Nationalism—often fused with racial and religious hatred—operates at all levels of international relations. On Level 1 it inspires individuals to create and to destroy; on Level 2 it energizes and tears apart entire countries; on Level 3 the ideal of the nation-state provides the organizing principle of the international system, but it impedes movement toward transnational or supranational organization; on Level 4 irredentist nationalisms generate local conflict, as in the Caucasus; but the most powerful transnational forces are Western-style globalization and its nemesis, radical Islam; on Level 5, indigenous peoples defend their turf while nationalist self-seeking and violence threaten the entire biosphere.

Why Do Some Societies Live in Harmony while others self-destruct? Can *we mitigate if not prevent a clash of civilizations? Your panel sums up its findings in the form of policy recommendations for individual societies and for the international community:*

Guidelines for Dominant Groups in Multiethnic Societies

1. Promote a sense of participation, equal opportunity, and mutual gain among all members of society. Avoid even the perception of a "tyranny of the majority."

2. Accommodate diversity. The U.S., Singapore, and Switzerland offer positive models that contrast with the failed approaches taken in the USSR, Sri Lanka, and Yugoslavia.

3. Remember that prosperity is a result and a tool of ethnic harmony. The three successful societies we have studied were not always rich. Their wealth is more the result than the cause of their successful integration.

4. Bury your hatchets. Do not be haunted by tribal myths of past defeats and glories. Despite the Civil War and racial conflict, Americans elected six Southerners as president between 1913 and 2001 and began to elect Blacks to prominent roles in national and big city politics.

5. Discuss openly what are the deep needs and interests of your society and its parts. Open debate filters out bad ideas and increases the likelihood that decisions will be durable.[51] There is no "national interest" etched in stone.

6. Try to understand minorities within your own society and why they fear exploitation. Support their languages and cultures without spawning separatism. In the U.S., for example, urge or require White Christians and Jews to study the sacred texts, cultures, and histories of others—Native Americans, Africans, Parsis, Shintos, Muslims, Buddhists, Hindus, Sikhs, and pagans.[52]

Guidelines for Ethnic Minorities

1. Uphold your interests but avoid needless provocation of other ethnic groups.

2. Protect and enhance your own culture but do not spurn the dominant one.

3. Do not forget your past but live in the present and look to the future. You can integrate with the world and still maintain your own culture. Many of the world's most affluent and cultured societies speak a language that few others share—Swiss–German, Finnish, Swedish, Danish, Norwegian, Dutch, Flemish.

4. If you face repression, try to mobilize the international community. But recognize that the United Nations and its members have limited will or capacity to intervene. Ultimately most peoples at risk must rely upon their own resources.

Options for the International Community

The United Nations and its member states face a range of options for dealing with peoples at risk.

- *Status Quo Orientations*
    1. Hands off. Let the contenders settle their own problems.
    2. Maintain existing borders. Do not allow minorities to alter boundaries or create new states.
- *Strengthen Preventive Diplomacy*
    3. Develop early warning indicators. Interview refugees. Study satellite images to learn whether fields are planted and harvested on schedule.

---

51. See Robert A. Dahl, *Democracy and Its Critics* (New Haven, Conn.: Yale University Press, 1989).

52. When the University of North Carolina required incoming students to read annotated selections from the *Quran* in 2002, some students withdrew in protest. Some critics said students should have been exposed to the entire book because the selections omitted passages about killing infidels.

4. *Legislate. Revise and alter international law to give more protection and voice to minorities within international organizations.*[53]

5. *Try to transform conflict by promoting economic and social change.*

6. *Monitor. Observe and report on cease-fires, human rights, and elections.*

7. *Mediate. Promote negotiations between disputants and, if negotiations stall, propose solutions.*

• *More Forceful Interventions*

8. *Deftly employ the tools of diplomatic recognition, nonrecognition, and derecognition.*[54]

9. *Utilize conditional economic aid and sanctions.*

10. *Intervene with force to keep peace or make peace.*

Our panel rejects do-nothing options. Why? Ethnic persecution violates international law, spawns refugees, and triggers war—civil and across borders. The panel favors preventive diplomacy (options 3 to 7). More forceful interventions can be dangerous and costly. If used, they require great skill and commitment. Halfway measures may make things worse.

CAN WE MITIGATE, IF NOT PREVENT, A CLASH OF CIVILIZATIONS?

If sectarian differences arise mainly from tensions between economic haves and have-nots, as in Northern Ireland, the remedies are fairly simple. Ways must be found to reduce disparities and make the have-nots feel that they are part of the whole.

But resentments against U.S. power and Western values are widespread in Islamic and other countries. How to cope with these clashes—rooted in moral as well as material differences? Our panel sees merit in two quite different approaches: universality and pluralism.[55] *The first looks for and strives to enhance the values common to various religions and civilizations. The second approach stresses acceptance of and respect for differences. Our panel recommends using both.*

Last but not least: spiritual leaders of all faiths should encourage peace and understanding—never "holy" war or homicidal suicide[56] *They should echo Black Elk's vision that the hoop of his people and the hoops of all peoples can and should interlace in harmony.*[57]

---

53. For suggestions, see Gidon Gotlieb, *Nation Against State: A New Approach to Ethnic Conflicts and the Decline of Sovereignty* (New York: Council on Foreign Relations, 1993).

54. The West gave some moral support to Estonia and other republics trying to break from the USSR but did not recognize their independence until Soviet power collapsed. By contrast, the West jumped to recognize the states wishing to secede from Yugoslavia. Nonrecognition—at least for a time—might have cooled tempers there. Later, the West derecognized Serbia in some ways to punish its aggressions.

55. See Henric Schiegelow, ed., *Preventing the Clash of Civilizations: A Peace Strategy for the Twenty-first Century* (New York: St. Martin's, 1999).

56. Besides their negative effects on everyone's mental and physical well-being, suicide–homicides failed to achieve their ostensible political goals in the Middle East or Sri Lanka.

57. See Chapter 2, note 2. Similar views were expressed by Mohammad Khatami, elected president of the Islamic Republic of Iran in 1997. The very name of the country, however, seemed to exclude full participation by non-Muslims. Some Iranian leaders, followed by some in Nigeria in 2002, called for the death of certain writers who, they said, had insulted the Prophet.

KEY NAMES AND TERMS

assimilation	ethos	nation
authoritarian	expansionist nationalism	nationalism
autonomy	federation	national self-determination
confederation	genocide	power sharing
culture	indigenous	secession
ethnic	intermingled nationalism	unitary state
ethnic cleansing	irredentism	
ethnocentric	majority rule	

QUESTIONS TO DISCUSS

1. What is a nation-state? How common are nation-states in IR?
2. What is the difference between an ethnos, a nation, and a state? Give examples.
3. Name four sources of nationalism. Which were most important in the U.S.? In Russia? In Sri Lanka?
4. Are human rights the same as minority rights?
5. What factors undermined the unity of the USSR, Sri Lanka, and Yugoslavia?
6. What factors helped the unity of the U.S., Singapore, and Switzerland?
7. Can ethnic minorities dominate a country? How?
8. For a realist, which goal would have priority—human rights, minority rights, or national sovereignty?
9. Are multicultural studies good or bad for a country with many ethnic groups?
10. Which options for the international community should be developed? Which avoided?

RECOMMENDED RESOURCES

BOOKS

Anderson, Benedict. *Imagined Communities: Reflections on the Origin and Spread of* Nationalism. Rev. ed. London: Verso, 1991.

Cobban, Alfred. *The Nation-State and National Self-determination.* Rev. ed. New York: Thomas Y. Crowell, 1970.

Deutsch, Karl W. *Nationalism and Its Alternatives.* New York: A. A. Knopf, 1969.

Deutscher, Irwin. *Accommodating Diversity: National Policies That Prevent Ethnic Conflict.* Lanham, Md: Lexington Books, 2002.

Diamond, Larry, and Marc F. Plattner, eds. *Nationalism, Ethnic Conflict, and Democracy.* Baltimore: Johns Hopkins University Press, 1994.

Fox, Jonathan, *Ethnoreligious Conflict in the Late Twentieth Century: A General Theory.* Lanham, Md.: Lexington Books, 2002.

Gellner, Ernest. *Nations and Nationalism.* Ithaca, N.Y.: Cornell University Press, 1983.

Gould, Carol C., and Pasquale Paquino, eds. *Cultural Identity and the Nation-State.* Lanham, Md. Rowman & Littlefield, 2001.

Greenfeld, Liah. *Nationalism: Five Roads to Modernity.* Cambridge, Mass.: Harvard University Press, 1992.

Gurr, Ted Robert. *Peoples vs. States: Minorities at Risk in the New Century.* Washington, D.C.: United States Institute of Peace, 2000.

Gurr, Ted Robert, et al. *Minorities at Risk: A Global View of Ethnopolitical Conflicts.* Washington, D.C.: United States Institute of Peace, 1993.

Halperin, Morton H., et al. *Self-Determination in the New World Order.* Washington, D.C.: Carnegie Endowment for International Peace, 1992.

Hedetoft, Ulf, and Mette Hjort. *Postnational Self: Belonging and Identity.* Minneapolis: University of Minnesota Press, 2002.

Horowitz, Donald L. *Ethnic Groups in Conflict.* Berkeley: University of California Press, 1985.

Hutchinson, John, and Anthony D. Smith, eds. *Nationalism.* New York: Oxford University Press, 1994.

Juergensmeyer, Mark. *The New Cold War? Religious Nationalism Confronts the Secular State.* Berkeley: University of California Press, 1993.

Kivisto, Peter. *Multiculturalism in a Global Society.* Oxford, U.K.: Blackwell Publishers, 2002.

Malesevic, Sinisa, and Mark Haugaard. *Making Sense of Collectivity.* London: Pluto Press, 2002.

Recommended Resources (continued)

Mortimer, Edward, and Robert Fine. *People, Nation and State: The Meaning of Ethnicity and Nationalism.* London: I. B. Tauris & Company, 1999.

Petersen, Roger D. *Understanding Ethnic Violence: Fear, Hatred, and Resentment in Twentieth-Century Eastern Europe.* Cambridge, U.K.: Cambridge University Press, 2002.

Power, Samantha. *"A Problem from Hell": America and the Age of Genocide.* New York Basic Books, 2002.

Skrentny, John D. *Minority Rights Revolution.* Cambridge, Mass: Harvard University Press, 2002.

Snyder, Jack L. *From Voting to Violence: Democratization and Nationalist Conflict.* New York: W. W. Norton, 2000.

Spiegelman, Art. *Maus: A Survivor's Tale.* 2 vols. New York: Pantheon, 1986, 1991.

Szporluk, Roman, ed. *National Identity and Ethnicity in Russia and the New States of Eurasia.* Armonk, N.Y.: M. E. Sharpe, 1994.

Wiebe, Robert H. *Who We Are: A History of Popular Nationalism.* Princeton, N.J.: Princeton University Press, 2002.

JOURNALS

Nationalism and Ethnic Politics
Nationalities Papers
Nations and Nationalism
Third World Quarterly

WEB SITES

The Campaign to End Genocide
http://www.endgenocide.org/

Genocide in the 20th Century (information on all seminal cases)
http://www.historyplace.com/worldhistory/genocide/

French Nationalism, the National Front Party, Jean-Marie Le Pen
http://news.bbc.co.uk/1/hi/world/europe/1943193.stm

The John Birch Society
http://www.jbs.org/

Minorities at Risk Project (monitors the persecution and movement of ethnic groups worldwide)
http://www.cidem.umd.edu/inscr/mar/

Operation Joint Endeavor (the UN operation in Bosnia)
http://www.nato.int/ifor/ifor.htm

Yugoslavia, A Country Study
http://memory.loc.gov/frd/cs/yutoc.html

C H A P T E R N I N E

INTERVENTION AND MEDIATION: HOW CAN OUTSIDERS HELP?

The UN Secretary-General asks you and your panel to probe deeper. You have reviewed why peoples are at risk and suggested how ethnic groups can reduce conflict and create values together. But what if there is an impasse? Bloodshed? All-out war? How can outsiders—"third parties"—help? The secretary-general now wants you to spell out the principles and techniques by which the United Nations and its members can intervene to curtail conflict—within and between states.

The secretary-general wants you to consider many forms of intervention—from mediation by private citizens and professional diplomats to peace enforcement by soldiers. He wants you to consider not only actions authorized by the UN Security Council but by member states without a formal UN mandate.

Quickly you recall the many efforts by UN representatives and those of other countries to prevent or end conflicts around the globe. For example, UN official Ralph Bunche in 1950 and Canadian diplomat Lester B. Pearson in 1957 won the Nobel Peace Prize for their contributions to peace in the Middle East. Jimmy Carter won the prize in 2002 for his mediating the Camp David Accords in 1978, and for his subsequent contributions to peace as a private citizen. But the overall record is mixed. Some interventions have eased bitter conflicts; others have achieved little or backfired. What have been the ingredients of success and failure?

You promise the secretary-general to review the patterns of third-party interventions and distill lessons that may guide the United Nations and its members.

CONTENDING CONCEPTS AND EXPLANATIONS

WHAT CAN OUTSIDERS DO THAT DISPUTANTS CAN'T DO FOR THEMSELVES?

Imagine that John and Regina decide to separate. How should they divide their shared property? John walks to work and listens to music at home. Regina drives and goes to concerts. Reasonably, they agree that John may take the compact disk player and CDs; Regina, the family car. But John also demands custody of the dog, because the sound equipment is worth less than the car.

A month after the split, John and Regina solicit help from a "Post-Settlement Embellishment Service." If the mediator knows the true preferences of each side, she or he may suggest improvements on deals struck by two antagonists. The intervenor learns that John now sees the dog as a nuisance and that Regina deeply misses her pet. The intervenor suggests that John transfer Fido to Regina. Each party is better off, including Fido.[1]

If a third party could help each side *after* their initial settlement, why not invite a mediator at an earlier stage? A related question: If knowledge of each party's preferences can promote mutual benefit, should negotiators mask their objectives or explain them candidly?

Why mediate? Mediators can win influence, access, glory, material rewards, personal satisfaction, and insight. Sometimes they do good. The century's most dedicated mediator, former president **Jimmy Carter**, explained that his Christian "faith *demands* that I do whatever I can" wherever and whenever.[2]

But mediators often suffer ridicule or worse. Some peacemakers have been assassinated, for example, UN Middle East mediator Folke Bernadotte in 1948. UN Secretary-General Dag Hammarskjöld died in a plane crash as he supervised UN intervention in the former Belgian Congo in 1961. Other such cases will be noted.

PEACEFUL SETTLEMENT OF DISPUTES AND PEACEFUL CHANGE

An ounce of prevention is worth a pound of cure. The UN Charter (Chapter VI) calls for diplomacy to prevent disputes from erupting into war. It obliges parties to a dispute to "seek a solution by negotiation . . . mediation . . . arbitration, judicial settlement, resort to regional agencies

1. Howard Raiffa, "Post-Settlement," *Negotiation Journal* 1, no. 1 (January 1985): 9–12.
2. Jim Wooten, "The Conciliator," *New York Times Magazine*, January 29, 1995, 28.

How Does Arbitration Differ from Judicial Settlement?

Arbitration is adjudication of a dispute by one or more arbitrators who are selected by the disputants and whose decision the disputants agree in advance to accept as binding. Like a judge, an arbitration tribunal decides cases. But unlike the parties before a court who cannot choose the judge, the actors who agree to arbitration choose who is to adjudicate their case. Often three arbitrators are chosen to assure a swing vote. A panel of arbitrators was set up by the 1899 Hague Convention for the Pacific Settlement of Disputes, but it is not a permanent court—only a list of arbitrators from whom disputants may choose. By contrast, a *permanent* world court consisting of fifteen judges was established in 1920 under the League of Nations to hear cases brought to it by states and international organizations. Its successor, the **International Court of Justice** became a basic organ of the United Nations in 1945 and continues to hear cases at The Hague.*

What Is Wrong with This Advice? A former U.S. diplomat warns that arbitration allows a third party to determine your country's destiny. "Arbitrate only if you manifestly have principle on your side but are so weak that you must call on others to enforce it."**

This is poor advice on two counts: first, the strong as well as the weak may benefit from arbitration because it offers a way to resolve a dispute short of war, second, regardless of the decision, you can hardly count on "others to enforce it." Article 94 (2) of the UN Charter provides that if a party refuses to carry out the obligations incumbent in an International Court decision, the other party may appeal to the UN Security Council, which may make recommendations or take action to give effect to the judgment. The Security Council has never acted on this authority.

*The work of these bodies is reviewed regularly in the *American Journal of International Law.*
**Charles W. Freeman, Jr., *The Diplomat's Dictionary*, rev. ed. (Washington, D.C.: United States Institute of Peace, 1997), 28.

How an Objective or Even Random Standard Can "Mediate"

Archeologists from three countries were invited to Egypt in 1902 to study the three pyramids at Giza. George A. Reisner, the head of the U.S. team, recalled: "Everyone wanted a portion of the Great Western Cemetery." Seated on the hotel veranda, the three teams discussed how to allocate the cemetery. They divided it into three strips, put into a hat bits of paper marked 1, 2, and 3, and allowed Reisner's wife to draw out the papers. She then "presented them to each of us. The southern strip fell to the Italians; the middle to the Germans; and the northern strip to me. Then we proceeded to divide the pyramids." (Notes by Reisner at the Boston Museum of Fine Arts.)

or arrangements, or other peaceful means of their own choice." Chapter VI authorizes the Security Council to *recommend* "procedures or methods" to resolve disputes. If the Security Council investigates and finds that the dispute may endanger peace, it may even *recommend* (not decide) the terms of settlement.

The parties to a dispute may prefer to sort out their own problems. But if their direct talks fail, they may accept mediation or arbitration. In 1871, for example, London and Washington submitted to international arbitration a U.S. claim for damages incurred during the U.S. Civil War. The panel awarded damages to the U.S., saving each side from a prolonged contest.

THE SPECTRUM OF INTERVENTION—PASSIVE AND ACTIVE

Third parties may intervene in others' disputes in many ways. The spectrum of intervention runs from smiles, handshakes, and suggestions to bribes, aid packages, jeeps, armored cars, and tanks. Outsiders may try to exacerbate a dispute or resolve it. They may tilt to one side or seek mutual gain.

Mediation is a third-party intervention to help disputants accommodate differences they may wish to resolve but have difficulty resolving by themselves. It is one tool of peacemaking—the management of disputes

A Master Mediator: Teddy Roosevelt

President Theodore Roosevelt convened and mediated the 1905 Portsmouth (New Hampshire) Conference that ended the Russo–Japanese War and the 1906 Algeciras (Spain) Conference that calmed tension between France and Germany over Morocco. Roosevelt gradually expanded his role from facilitator to formulator and manipulator. He made no threats and promised rewards to no one. "TR" did not even attend the Portsmouth or Algeciras meetings. He kept abreast by telephone, telegram, mail, and visits from U.S. and foreign participants. He nudged the negotiators from afar.

In 1905, TR persuaded Kaiser Wilhelm to urge Tsar Nicholas to make concessions to Japan. A year later, however, it was Wilhelm who spurned compromise with France. But the kaiser capitulated when TR threatened in a private message to publicize a letter from the German ambassador (a sports partner of TR) committing Berlin to accept whatever deal Roosevelt thought reasonable.

When news came that Russian and Japanese negotiators had agreed to peace terms, TR exclaimed: "This is magnificent. It's a mighty good thing for Russia, and a mighty good thing for Japan. And," he added, thumping his chest, "a mighty good thing for me too!" Roosevelt's efforts helped maintain an Asian balance of power favorable to U.S. interests and commerce. In 1905, he wanted to curb Japanese expansion; in 1906, German. He also won the thanks of millions and a Nobel Peace Prize.

SOURCE: Eugene P. Trani, *The Treaty of Portsmouth: An Adventure in American Diplomacy* (Lexington: University of Kentucky Press, 1969), 141.

---

without war. It differs from peacekeeping—the interposition of lightly armed forces between consenting disputants to deter fighting or monitor a cease-fire. Unlike peacemaking and peacekeeping, peace enforcement implies the use of well-armed forces to restore or impose peace. Assuming that fighting has stopped, it may be time for peace building—structural measures to prevent violence and generate a positive peace. All these techniques are potential instruments of conflict resolution—removal of the causes and manifestations of conflict.

Mediation is usually less threatening than arbitration or a court proceeding. The mediator does not judge the disputants but helps them decide for themselves how to manage their differences. Governments usually shun judicial proceedings if vital interests are concerned, especially if the judge might rule against them. They may believe that the existing legal order is unjust or passé and hope that the mediator may help generate new rules.

The mediator may use her or his good offices—the unbiased use of one's formal position—to facilitate communications between the contestants. The initial steps are called prenegotiation. In this stage, the facilitator may help to set the agenda, propose meeting sites and procedures, generate a constructive ambience, and sponsor a fact-finding inquiry to collect and analyze relevant information (also buying time during which tempers may cool). After prenegotiation comes negotiation and, if a deal is struck, implementation, verification, and follow-on steps.

Between a Rock and a Hard Place: Negotiation, Judicial Decision, or Mediation?

Greece in 1996 planted its flag on an islet close to the Turkish coast. The islet was inhabited only by goats, but Greece claimed that international law (treaties of 1932 and 1947) gave it the right to these rocks and the mineral wealth around them. Turkey disagreed and mobilized forces to expel the Greeks. Athens proposed to Ankara that they submit the case to the International Court of Justice. Ankara refused. Turkey thought the existing law unfair and, confident of its greater strength, suggested bilateral negotiations. A U.S. mediator persuaded each side (nominal allies in NATO) to pull back its forces, leaving the claims unresolved.

Not Every Third-Party Intervention Is Beneficent

Self-appointed British and French mediators gave Czechoslovakia's Sudetenland to Hitler in September 1938. Prague did not request this intervention; Czech representatives were not even allowed into the meeting. Betrayed by their allies, the Czech authorities pulled their troops from the Sudeten forts, giving Hitler easy access to the entire country.

A more activist mediator may go on to formulate solutions and even encourage, manipulate, or bully the parties to accept a settlement. The mediator may also serve as catalyst, educator, translator, definer of standards, expander of resources, bearer of bad news, agent of reality, or scapegoat.

WHAT ARE THE INGREDIENTS OF A SUCCESSFUL MEDIATION?

For mediation to work, the dispute must be **ripe**. The disputants may welcome mediation if their dispute is long and complex, their own negotiations have stalled, and/or the costs of continued conflict are painful. Each side hopes the mediator will help resolve their dispute, but they may also hope for "side payments" (perhaps an aid package or diplomatic recognition contingent on a peace accord).

From ancient times to the early 21st century, mediators have wrestled with countless international disputes. Table 9.1 lists many of the 20th century's major efforts. It notes the main resources used and whether the mediation achieved "success"—defined as three years or more of negative peace.[3] Several other interventions are discussed in this chapter—Kosovo, Macedonia, Sri Lanka—where some positive results were achieved but the long-term outlook remained unclear. Besides the cases listed in Table 9.1 or discussed in this chapter, other international

3. Updated from Walter C. Clemens, Jr., "Can Outsiders Help? Lessons for Third-Party Intervention in Bosnia," *International Journal* 48, 4 (autumn 1993), 687–719.

Timing: When Can a Third Party Intervene in the Cycle of Conflict?

What Level of Violence?	How Many Entry Points?	What Barriers to Entry?	Opportunity for Procedural Control?
Low	Many. Attitudes have not hardened.	Low-medium. Parties are open to consultation.	Low. Parties ready to fight if this is a better alternative to negotiated settlement.
Rising	Declining as attitudes harden.	Medium-high as parties see risks to negotiation and worry about status.	Low. Parties ready to escalate.
High	Few. "We–they" images have hardened.	High. Parties are locked in continuing struggle.	Moderate-high as hurting stalemate leads parties to welcome alternatives to war.
Declining after peace settlement	Rising if attitudes soften.	Low-medium.	Moderate-high if parties are more willing to sustain the negotiating process.

SOURCE: Adapted from Chester A. Crocker, Fen Osler-Hampson, Pamela Aall, eds., *Herding Cats: Multiparty Mediation in a Complex World* (Washington, D.C.: United States Institute of Peace Press, 1999), 28.

Table 9.1 The Track Record of 20th-Century Mediation: No Recipe for Success

Dates	Disputants	Mediator	Good Offices	Formulate Solutions	Manipulate	Help Elections	Economic Sanctions	Economic Controls	Peacekeepers	Enforce Peace	Military Threats	Military Action	Success(S)/Fail(F)
1905	Japan–Russia	U.S.	X	X	X								S
1906	France–Germany	U.S.	X	X	X								S
1938	Germany–Czechoslovakia	UK, France, Italy		X	X								F
1948	Arabs–Israel	UN	X	X	X								F
1966	Pakistan–India	USSR	X										F
1970–90s	Hopis–Navajos	U.S.	X	X	X			X					F
1977–78	Ethiopia–Somalia	USSR	X	X	X			X			X		F
1978–84	Chile–Argentina	Vatican	X	X	X								S
1978	Egypt–Israel	U.S.	X	X	X			X	X				S
1979	Rhodesian factions	UK	X	X	X	X		X	X				S
1982	UK–Argentina	U.S.	X		X								F
1987–90	Tamils–Sinhalese (Sri Lanka)	India		X	X				X	X	X	X	F
1988	Namibia–South Africa	U.S. and others	X	X	X	X		X	X				S
1988–90s	Nagorno–Karabakh	USSR/Russia		X	X						X	X	?
1990–91	Iraq–UN	USSR, Jordan		X	X								F
1990s	Cambodians	UN	X	X	X	X		X	X				?
1992	Haitians	UN, U.S., Carter	X	X	X	X	X	X	X	X	X		?
1992–94	Somalis	UN, U.S.	X	X	X			X	X	X	X	X	F
1993	Israel–PLO	Norway	X										S
1993–94	Estonia–Russia	U.S.			X			X					S
1993–94	Ukraine–Russia	U.S.		X	X			X					S
1993	Israel–Syria	U.S.	X	X	X			X	X				?
1993	Ireland, UK, Northern Ireland	U.S.	X		X			X					?
1994	Macedonia–Greece	U.S.	X	X	X			X	X				S
1991–94	Southern Slavs	UN, EU	X	X	X		X		X		X	X	F
1995	Southern Slavs	U.S., EU	X	X	X	X	X	X	X	X	X	X	?

mediations in the 1990s dealt with the South China Sea, Rwanda, Burundi, Tajikistan, Mozambique, Cambodia, El Salvador, Ecuador and Peru, Ethiopia and Eritrea, the Aral Sea, Abkhazia and Georgia.[4] Of these, Eduador and Peru seemed to net the most stable outcome.

What succeeds? Economic and military levers are sometimes useful, but the mediator depends heavily upon personal qualities. They include "the patience of Job . . . the wit of the Irish . . . the broken-field dodging abilities of a halfback . . . the hide of a rhinoceros." To these we may add the insights of a psychiatrist; faith in free choice rather than dictation; trust in human potential, with its strengths and frailties; plus the ability to distinguish the available from the desirable.[5] Let us convert these concepts into operational guidelines and then examine their validity in major cases.[6]

THE MEDIATOR'S HANDBOOK: HOW TO BRIDGE DIFFERENCES

Your Qualifications

1. Knowledge: Know the issues, the personalities, their interests, and their domestic setting.

2. Timing: Present your initiatives when conditions are ripe, for example, when key players are tired and no longer trust in self-help. If you enter early, before the conflict escalates, the parties may not listen. If you wait until the disputants beg for outside help, you may gain influence, but only after much destruction.

3. Trust: Cultivate the confidence of each side, but make the most of any bias imputed to you.

4. Endurance: You may need to travel far and work around the clock.

The Disputants

5. Participants: Limit the number of parties represented but include all those essential for success.

6. Negotiators: Encourage the parties to assign negotiators with the authority and skills conducive to productive negotiations. For highly sensitive issues, bring top officials into the negotiation.

7. Empathy: Help each side to "walk in the other's shoes." For example, have each side write down what it thinks are the interests of the other party and then have members of the opposite delegations discuss their papers one-on-one.

8. Cultural sensitivity: Reduce misunderstandings rooted in cultural differences.[7]

4. See the case studies in Chester A. Crocker et al., eds., *Herding Cats: Multiparty Mediation in a Complex World* (Washington, D.C.: United States Institute of Peace Press, 1999); and Melanie C. Greenberg et al., eds., *Words Over War: Mediation and Arbitration to Prevent Deadly Conflict* (Lanham, Md.: Rowman & Littlefield, 2000). Compare Table 9.1 here with the analysis of intervention success in *Words Over War*, 348.

5. William E. Simkin, *Mediation and the Dynamics of Collective Bargaining* (Washington, D.C.: Bureau of National Affairs, 1971), 53.

6. These principles derive from works by Fisher, Princen, Zartman, and others cited in the Recommended Resources at the end of the chapter. The principles also distill the "art of the deal" (see Chapter 1) and the techniques used to reconcile victors and vanquished (Chapter 2), moderate rivalries (Chapters 3, 6, 7), and identify trade-offs in trade and environmental disputes (Chapters 11 and 14).

7. Some theorists argue that professional diplomats acquire a language of their own that transcends their origins. But Raymond Cohen, *Negotiating Across Cultures: Communication Obstacles in International Diplomacy* Rev. ed. (Washington, D.C.: United States Institute of Peace Press, 1997), provides ample evidence of culturally related obstacles to understanding among diplomats. Furthermore, few heads of state or of independence movements are professional diplomats.

Table 9.2 An Example of Positions vs. Interests

Disputants	Positions	Interests
Sinhalese majority	Sri Lanka must remain a unified state dominated by Sinhalese values and people.	Territorial integrity and sovereignty; noninterference from India; secure access to all ports and territory; prosperity; freedom from terrorists; free practice of Buddhist religion and use of the Sinhala language; allegiance of all peoples to the Sri Lankan state.
Tamil separatists	Tamils must have a separate state in the north and east of the island.	Equal treatment in schools, jobs, resources, language, religion; political representation in Colombo plus local self-government; prosperity; freedom from terrorists; free practice of the Hindu religion and use of the Tamil language; confidence in democratic processes.

Techniques for Crafting an Accord

9. Agenda: Establish an agenda and setting (public or private) conducive to "business" rather than to propaganda.

10. Generate constructive ideas: Get the parties to brainstorm before asking them to commit. Distinguish the contours of a possible deal from a formal commitment.

11. **Positions vs. interests**: Focus on interests—not positions. (For examples, see Table 9.2.)

12. **Reservation price (RP)**: Learn the RP or walk-away price of each disputant—its minimum acceptable terms. Help disputants to set responsible RPs and weigh the costs of no agreement.

13. Openness: Encourage candor about interests, RP, and other considerations shaping each side's negotiating position.

14. Packaging: "Fractionate" the issues into smaller, more negotiable parts or "link" them into a comprehensive settlement.

15. Integrative bargaining: Expand the available goods; avoid "distributive" haggling on how to split an existing pie.

16. Creative trade-offs: Overcome asymmetries in assets by creative trade-offs, for example, "land for land" or "land for peace." Discourage demands for equality (for example, 100 acres or planes for each side).

17. Problem-solving rules: Generate objective criteria by which to solve problems, for example, scientific information.

18. Best alternative to a negotiated agreement (BATNA): Show each party it can gain more through accommodation than from its BATNA. Underscore the long-term costs of violence if the negotiations fail. Deflate unreasonable expectations and loosen commitments.

19. **Single negotiating text (SNT)**: Rather than debate rival proposals, develop and refine an SNT to clarify where the parties agree and disagree.

20. "Dance of packages": Lead the disputants toward the efficient frontier for joint gains. (Up to that frontier, sketched in Figure 1.5, page 40, both sides may gain; beyond it, only one party gains.) An initial package might favor A; the second package, B; as preferences are discussed and revealed, a third or fourth package may yield values for both sides.

21. **Leverage**: Utilize sticks and carrots—penalties and rewards. Offer sweeteners to compensate parties for concessions. Pressure them with deadlines. If necessary, threaten to break off the talks, mount an economic blockade, suspend aid, or launch a military intervention.

22. Buttress Track 1 mediation with Track 2: While official mediators deal with officials, private individuals and NGOs can try to mobilize concerned interest groups to exert constructive pressures on the official negotiators to reach an accord. Each has its advantages at different stages of the conflict cycle.

Multiparty mediation, however, can confuse and diffuse the negotiating effort. In the Balkans, we shall see, neither the EU nor the UN nor individuals such as Jimmy Carter had sufficient clout to negotiate and impose a settlement. Things changed only in August 1995, when the U.S. intervened and employed nearly every kind of leverage (listed in the sidebar).

Sustaining the Accord

23. Publicity: Advertise the agreement and its contribution to mutual gain.

24. Protection: Make sure that other concerned parties "get onboard" or at least do not sabotage the deal. Insulate the accord from crises elsewhere that could torpedo the deal.

25. Implementation: Help to implement the accord and verify compliance with personnel, forces, or funds from individual states, the UN, or a regional organization such as the Organization of American States.

26. Transcend differences: Foster a web of positive ties.

Let us see whether these guidelines are supported by experience. What factors contributed to mediating success or failure?

COMPARING THEORY AND REALITY: LESSONS OF THIRD-PARTY INTERVENTIONS

CAN THE HOLY LAND BE MADE WHOLE?

President Jimmy Carter did the "impossible" when he brokered peace between Israel and Egypt in 1978. But Norwegians facilitated in 1993 an even more "impossible" accord between Israel and the Palestinian Liberation

---

◢◣ What Kinds of Leverage Can a Third-Party Muster?*

1. Reward power: side payments if the disputants change their behavior.

2. Coercive power: sanctions if they fail to change their behavior.

3. Expert power: insights from the mediator's knowledge, experience, and imagination.

4. Legitimate power: rights and authority under international law.

5. Referent power: desire of the parties to maintain a valued relationship with the mediator.

6. Informational power based on content of information conveyed by the go-between message carrier.

7. Reputational power: leverage based on the mediator's reputation.

*States can reward and sanction, but private individuals, UN, and NGO mediators may have the other kinds of leverage. See work by Jeffrey Rubin and others discussed in Crocker et al., *Herding Cats*, 29.

Organization (PLO). How could tiny Norway match the achievement of a superpower?

The United Nations became active in the Middle East in 1947 when a special committee appointed by the General Assembly recommended that Palestine (since 1920 under British administration) be partitioned into two states—one for Arabs and one for Jews. Arabs—inside and outside Palestine—favored a unitary state and rejected partition. When British forces departed in 1948, Israel proclaimed its statehood—immediately recognized by the USSR and the U.S. and soon by most UN members. Egypt and other Arab states, however, tried to destroy Israel but were driven back. Indeed, the area controlled by Israel expanded. The UN sent Swedish soldier-diplomat Folke Bernadotte to mediate, but he was assassinated by Israelis determined to scupper any UN plan to internationalize Jerusalem. UN official Ralph Bunche (see box) then became the chief UN mediator. He persuaded Egypt and Israel to sign an armistice in 1949, followed by similar accords between Israel and Jordan, Lebanon, and Syria. For this achievement, Bunche received the Nobel Peace Prize in 1950.

The First African American to Win the Nobel Peace Prize

Ralph Bunche mediated all his life (1904–1971). He mediated between Black and White Americans, between radical and moderate Blacks, and between governments and peoples.

Bunche's political and diplomatic career was grounded in knowledge and concern about "race" issues at home and in the world. He contributed to one of the first major studies of Black–White relations in the United States, Gunnar Myrdal's *An American Dilemma;* wrote his Harvard Ph.D. dissertation on French administration of two League of Nations "mandates" in Africa; and—as Italy invaded Ethiopia—wrote *A World View of Race* (1936). In World War II, he advised U.S. intelligence and the State Department on Africa. As a U.S. delegate to the 1945 conference where the UN Charter was adopted, Bunche drafted many of the provisions on the Trusteeship Council.

Bunche was a master at drafting agreements that bridged differences. But he also had a human touch. Trying to get Egyptians and Israelis to sign an armistice in 1949, he invited both delegations to his hotel bedroom and met them wearing his bathrobe. He pulled out beautiful commemorative plates each diplomat would receive if they signed the cease-fire. Otherwise, he joked, he would personally break a plate over each man's head. Soon, they signed.

Despite harassment by Senator Joe McCarthy and a hectic life at the UN, where he rose to under secretary-general, Bunche also served in 1953–1954 as President of the American Political Science Association. In the 1950s he received more honorary degrees than any other American. Bunche's 1951 appeal for enlightened self-interest (quoted above next to the table of contents) sums up the main thrust of this book. All the while there were personal issues: How to "mediate" between one's family, "group," profession, country, and humanity?

For more on this remarkable person, see Brian Urquart, *Ralph Bunche, An American Life* (New York: W. W. Norton, 1993) and Charles P. Henry, *Ralph Bunche: Model Negro or American Other* (New York: New York University Press, 1999). The award winning PBS documentary *Ralph Bunche: An American Odyssey* is available from William Greaves Productions, Inc., *www.williamgreaves.com.*

The UN Truce Supervision Organization was established to monitor the 1949 armistices, and the UN Relief and Works Agency (UNRWA) was established to assist Palestinian refugees. The UNRWA continued into the 21st century, along with several UN and other international contingents that monitored and policed Israel's borders. The UNRWA was serving some 4 million Palestinian refugees—one-third of them living in some sixty camps. These organizatons cost little compared to war but imposed heavy burdens on UN finances. Also, UNRWA programs relieved pressure on Jordan, Israel, and other countries to settle the refugee problem.[8]

Interventions and monitoring missions by the United Nations and other third parties purchased some respite from war but left basic disputes and wounds in place. More than half a century after the 1949 armistices, the problems between Israel and its neighbors continued to fester. The same was true of tensions between Pakistan and India. Cyrpus—divided between Greeks and Turks—presented another long-lived problem.

The UN can do little more than its members are willing to support. Should the UN secretary-general be proactive or bow to the sovereign wishes of member states? When secretaries-general Trygvie Lie and, later, Dag Hammarskjöld played active roles, they were denounced by the USSR as Western agents. But when Egypt demanded withdrawal of the UN troops policing Egypt's border with Israel in 1967, UN Secretary-General U Thant bowed to Cairo's wishes and abruptly withdrew them. This led Israel to launch a preemptive strike against Egypt. Had the secretary-general found some reason to dig in his heels and delay the withdrawal, the 1967 Six-Day War might well have been avoided.

Both the Arab states and Israel have disliked many UN actions and judged the body too partial to the other side. Following the Six-Day War in 1967, however, the UN Security Council unanimously approved a well-balanced Resolution 242. It asked the parties to trade land for peace—"withdrawal of Israeli armed forces from territories occupied in the recent conflict"[9] in exchange for an end to the "states of belligerency" between the Arab states and Israel. Arabs would have to acknowledge the "independence of every State in the area," but Israelis would have to arrange "a just settlement of the refugee problem."

However, Resolution 242 was not implemented, and Arab–Israeli relations remained tense. Egypt and Syria attacked Israel in 1973 but were driven back. The parties then accepted a cease-fire mediated by U.S. Secretary of State Henry Kissinger and later approved by the UN Security Council. Kissinger's subsequent "shuttle diplomacy" between Israel,

8. Milton J. Esman, "A Survey of Interventions," in Esman and Shibley Telhami, eds., *International Organizations and Ethnic Conflict* (Ithaca, N.Y.: Cornell University Press, 1995), 21–47 at 26–30.

9. Despite Arab and Soviet protests, Israeli and U.S. negotiators kept the resolution from specifying withdrawal from "all" or even "the" territories—thus leaving a loophole for Israel to retain some territories, for example, East Jerusalem. The equally authoritative French version of the resolution, also does not specify "the" territories.

Egyptian President Anwar Sadat (*left*), U.S. President Jimmy Carter (*center*), and Israeli PM Menachem Begin clasp hands on the north lawn of the White House on March 26, 1979, after Sadat and Begin signed a peace treaty between Egypt and Israel. Sadat and Begin received the Nobel Peace Prize that year; Jimmy Carter, in 2002.

Egypt, and Syria produced several agreements for partial disengagement of Israeli and Arab forces.

The parties looked to the U.S. for help in managing their conflict. Israel did not trust the UN majority or any other country except the United States. Egyptian President **Anwar Sadat** and some other Arab leaders thought they could count on Washington to play the honest broker. Sadat regarded U.S. Ambassador Hermann Eilts and President Jimmy Carter as real friends.

Following the 1973 war, Sadat sought peace. To break the diplomatic logjam, he embarked on GRIT-like gestures.[10] In November 1977, Sadat invited himself to Jerusalem and told the Israeli parliament that he wanted to remove the "psychological barrier" between Arabs and Jews. Sadat endorsed UN Resolution 242 but also demanded "self-determination" for Palestinians.

Peace negotiations in the Middle East are far more complicated than those in 1905 between Russia and Japan (see the upper sidebar on page 313). President Roosevelt faced only two main disputants. Mediators in the Middle East have faced *dozens*. No single actor can make peace among Arabs and Israelis, but any can *brake* and even *break* movement toward peace. Hard-liners in Israel, Syria, Iraq, Saudi Arabia, and the USSR sometimes acted as spoilers.

Jimmy Carter and Camp David, 1978

Sadat's 1977 visit to Jerusalem sparked several rounds of Egyptian–Israeli talks, but Israeli and Egyptian negotiators soon hit a dead end. At

10. As we saw in Chapter 7, GRIT stands for graduated reciprocation in tension reduction.

Three Negotiating Styles at Camp David

Of the three Camp David protagonists, Carter ranked first in the fifteen traits of an effective negotiator (see Chapter 1).* He was strong in every respect except rapport with the home front. Begin placed second. He ranked very high in knowledge, toughness, stamina, ability to leverage assets, and competitive spirit. He was a stickler for detail. In contrast, Sadat focused on general principles. Sadat ranked high in "nice" qualities such as flexibility, empathy, and tolerance. Begin lacked the winning personality of Sadat; he showed little flexibility or capacity to identify mutually useful solutions. The Israeli leader bargained from material weakness, but got what he wanted.

*Rankings are by Hermann Fr. Eilts, U.S. ambassador to Cairo during the Camp David era, and by professors Roger Kanet, David Mayers, and the author (W. C.).

that point President Carter invited President Sadat and Israeli Prime Minister Menachem Begin to join him at Camp David, the presidential retreat in Maryland. Each leader, with advisers in tow, arrived there in September 1978. They expected to stay just a few days but remained for thirteen in cramped quarters pervaded by "cabin fever."

The dispute was ripe for a settlement but many problems remained. Carter saved the day by skillful use of mediating techniques, by the leverage he brought to bear, and by his personality and persistence.[11] Since Sadat and Begin drew sparks, Carter met with each separately. The U.S. team prepared twenty-three versions of a single negotiating text.[12] The SNT pressured each side to say "yes" or, if it said "no," to offer a constructive alternative and to disclose its reservation price.

Carter drew heavily on trust and legitimacy. He began as a facilitator but soon became a formulator and manipulator. He used superpower leverage to clinch the deal. In the end, Carter, Begin, and Sadat "agreed to agree." They signed one document committing Israel and Egypt to enter a peace treaty within three months. The treaty, concluded in March 1979, offered "land for peace" (the basic quid pro quo when Israel dealt with other neighbors into the 21st century). Israel got peace with Egypt but had to withdraw from the Sinai desert, captured in 1967. Egypt had to demilitarize most of the Sinai and permit a multinational force and observers to be deployed there, a force that included both U.S. and Soviet personnel.[13]

Both worn down and elated, Sadat accepted a package far short of his original goals. Camp David left Palestinians in limbo. Sadat also failed to obtain any mention in the treaty of East Jerusalem, which Israel regarded as part of its capital—a unified Jerusalem. Many Arabs treated Sadat as a traitor, and some Arab governments severed ties with Cairo for a decade. Sadat was assassinated in 1981.

Norway and the 1993 Oslo Accord

Camp David left Palestinians worse off than before. Peace with Egypt gave Israel a freer hand to deal with Palestinians in the Israeli occupied territories. They suffered from sweep arrests, deportations, and confiscation of land by Israeli forces. Based now in Tunis, PLO leader Yasser Arafat renounced terrorism and called for separate Palestinian and Israeli states in Palestine. But Israel refused to talk with the PLO.

By 1991 there were some 5.5 million Palestinians—nearly half of them under Israeli rule. The Palestinian–Israeli confrontation became riper after the 1991 Gulf War. Many Israelis saw that their security

11. William B. Quandt, *Camp David: Peacemaking and Politics* (Washington, D.C.: Brookings Institution, 1986); Jimmy Carter, *Keeping Faith: Memoirs of a President* (New York: Bantam, 1983), esp. 322–344; and William B. Quandt, *Peace Process: American Diplomacy and the Arab–Israeli Conflict Since 1967* (Washington, D.C.: Brookings Institution, 1993).

12. Carter, *Keeping Faith*, 322, 340–344.

13. This and many other relevant documents are in *The Middle East*, 7th ed. (Washington, D.C.: Congressional Quarterly, 1991), 302 ff.

required cooperation with all their neighbors, including the Palestinians. Iraq's defeat led Arafat to grope for improved ties with the West.

Enter the Norwegians. Starting with personal contacts by a Norwegian social scientist and his diplomat wife, the Norwegian Foreign Ministry used its good offices to help PLO representatives and Israelis to meet in Oslo without public knowledge.[14] Roughly twenty meetings were held, from January to August 1993. Sometimes the Norwegians sat in on the PLO–Israeli exchanges; sometimes not. Often they were briefed afterward. Having heard each side's version, the Norwegians sometimes suggested ways to bridge differences.[15]

In August 1993, Israel and the PLO stunned the world by announcing their "Oslo Accord"—the joint Declaration of Principles (DOP) providing for an interim period of limited Palestinian self-rule and a commitment to reach a final settlement within five years. Like Camp David in 1978, the DOP was fuzzy—another "agreement to agree". It left major questions unanswered and displeased hard-liners on each side, but optimists hoped it would serve as a step toward a larger settlement. For the present, it brought mutual recognition for Israel and the PLO. Each pledged to live next to each other in peace. Israel surrendered very little to the Palestinians, as we see in Map 9.1, but any reduction in territory could be critical for a country just one or two dozen miles wide in places.

The parties thought secrecy was needed to negotiate the DOP in Olso. But the announcement of the **Oslo Accord** as an accomplished fact shocked many Palestinians and Israelis. Failure to inform the home front about the course of negotiations probably cost PLO and Israeli officials much domestic support.

The Oslo Accord showed that U.S. carrots and sticks were not essential for an Israeli–Palestinian agreement. But the parties wanted—and got—Washington's official endorsement. The DOP had been "initialed" in Oslo, but in September it was formally signed at the White House by the Israeli foreign minister and a PLO negotiator—"witnessed" by the U.S. secretary of state and the Russian foreign minister.

In October 1993 Norway began to chair an international donors group that promptly raised $2.4 billion in grants and loans for the Palestinians, but distribution got off to a slow start. Corruption and inefficiency by Palestinian officials handling these funds worried donors and angered many Palestinians.

Seeking to implement the Oslo Accord over five years, Israeli and Palestinian negotiators in 1994 signed the Cairo Agreement, providing

14. Jane Corbin, *Gaza First: The Secret Norway Channel to Peace between Israel and the PLO* (London: Bloomsbury, 1994); and David Makovsky, *Making Peace with the PLO: The Rabin Government's Road to the Oslo Accord* (Boulder, Colo.: Westview, 1996), with documents and references to other key writings. For an account by the chief Israeli negotiator, see Uri Savir, *The Process! 1,100 Days That Changed the World* (New York: Random House, 1998).

15. Like Carter in 1978, Johan Holst, the Norwegian foreign minister, gave generously of himself. Worn down by many long meetings and travels, Holst died in January 1994 at age 56. "The moment he entered the peace process, it was in the center of his life until his last breath," said Shimon Peres. Yasser Arafat called Holst "a great peacemaker."

Map 9.1 The Oslo Accord

Under full Palestinian control from May 1994

Under full Palestinian control from 1995

Under Palestinian administrative control from 1995

■   Jewish settlements in occupied territories

········   East Jerusalem

– – – –   Boundary of the West Bank

Scale of miles
20 km

10 mi

for Palestinian self-rule in Gaza and Jericho. The Palestinian Authority was set up, chaired by Arafat. A Palestinian police force was established and funded by an international task force headed by Norway.

In 1995 an interim ageement, or "Oslo 2," extended Palestinian self-rule on the West Bank. In 1997, Israeli troops were "redeployed" from Hebron, the largest and most conflict-ridden town on the West Bank. The situation was monitored by a six-nation observer group headed by Norway.

Goodwill and effective international mediation can be sabotaged. Some Palestinians never gave up their determination to drive Israelis into the sea and take back what they saw as Arab land. Some Israelis were determined

The Peace Destroyer's Handbook: How to School a Suicide Bomber

Martyrs are made, not born. Trainers from the Islamic Resistance Movement in the 1990s knew the steps to take to mobilize a young man to detonate the land mine attached to his leg in order to kill Israelis and thwart the peace process between Israel and the PLO:

1. Find a likely candidate. He is single, aged eighteen to twenty-four, with a relative wounded, jailed, or killed by Israelis. He is often despondent and angry. He is unemployed and has had trouble finding a bride. He believes that this life is nothing, while a wonderful paradise awaits martyrs. He sees Israelis as monsters and remembers his grandparents' tales about life before Israelis took their land in 1948—"how no butter ever tasted so sweet, no grapes were ever so juicy." He believes that a martyr's family will be honored and subsidized for decades.

2. Cultivate and deepen these convictions.

3. A week before the bombing is planned, show him how to explode the bomb.

4. In the days before the mission, sit him with a mullah and chant relevant scriptures.

5. On the prescribed day, send him off with assurances that his mission is sacred even though the *Quran* forbids suicide and the murder of innocent civilians.

to retain and settle whatever lands they believed were given them by God or were a strategic necessity. Israel's Labor Party generally favored an accommodation with the Palestinians. The other major party, Likud, and the smaller ultra-Orthodox religious parties did not. In November 1995, an Israeli assassinated Labor's prime minister Yitzhak Rabin. Following political murders by Israelis and Palestinians, Likud leader Benjamin Netanyahu was elected prime minister in June 1996. He backed away from Olso and backed Jewish settlements in areas that Palestians saw as theirs. After more political murders, the deeply divided Israeli electorate in May 1999 made Labor leader and former general Ehud Barak the country's prime minister.

From Camp David to the Temple Mount

Striving to rescue a faltering peace process, U.S. President Clinton invited Arafat and Barak to Camp David in July 2000. There, and in December 2001–January 2002, Barak offered the Palestinians the best terms ever tendered by Israel. They included return of over 90 percent of the West Bank and Gaza, "functional sovereignty" over the Muslim and Christian quarters of Jerusalem's walled city, and repatriation of some 20,000 Palestinian refugees. But Arafat turned down the offer. Had he accepted, he confided to one American, he would have been assassinated. Other Americans agreed with Israeli diplomat Abba Eban that Arafat never missed an opportunity to miss an opportunity.

Clinton's interventions were praised and disparaged. Like Carter in 1978, he was persistent and offered detailed proposals to resolve even such contentious issues as the fate of Jerusalem. Critics said all this was premature. Clinton wanted a deal to beautify his presidency but the time was not ripe. Soon, antagonisms worsened on both sides.

With Oslo a virtual dead letter, Palestinians became angrier and more desperate in 2002. In the Palestinian diaspora as well as on the West Bank and in Gaza, young women offered their lives for the cause. Here we see a Palestinian woman in Beirut, Lebanon, dressed as a suicide bomber in April 2002. This version of "women's lib" had already been pioneered by Tamil Tiger Women.

Many Israelis began to lose hope in the peace process. In September 2000, accompanied by armed guards, Likud party leader Ariel Sharon—despised by Palestinians for his role in a 1982 massacre—visited the Temple Mount.[16] Sharon explained that he wished to demonstrate the right of Israelis to visit a site sacred to Jews as well as Muslims. As Sharon may have expected, his actions provoked the "Second Intifada." His bravado persuaded Israelis to elect him in February 2001—just one month after George W. Bush's inauguration. Both Sharon and Bush stepped back and demanded an end to Palestinian violence as the precondition for resuming negotiations with the Palestinians. Bush sent Colin Powell and other U.S. officials to the Middle East but they lacked a strong mandate to nudge either side.

Why did a constructive peace process become derailed in 2000–2002? Hard-liners on both sides spoiled any GRIT-like movement toward compromise. Some Arabs were determined to wipe out Israel and refused any deal implying Israeli's right to survive. Sharon was pushed toward even tougher measures by his Likud rival Netanyahu and by the religious parties whose support Likud needed in parliament. Israelis complained they had no one to negotiate with—even as they leveled Arafat's headquarters, talked of expelling him, and killed some of his security guards. What Israelis called "defensive" or "preemptive" measures looked like "offensive" measures to Palestinians.

Peacemakers among Palestinians and Israelis tried to deflect both sides from their tit-for-tat death cycles, but moderate voices were muffled

16. The Temple Mount is also the location of the Haram al Sharif, a sacred site for Muslims. Violence was apparently encouraged by the organization Fatah Tanzim. Violence escalated rapidly from rock throwing to machine-gun and mortar fire, suicide bombings and lethal road ambushes, including some incidents instigated by settlers against Palestinians.

Mr. Powell Finally Gets to the West Bank...

The Bush administration tried at first to stay detached from the Arab–Israeli conflict. By the time it allowed Secretary of State Powell to visit Israel, Ariel Sharon's government had leveled Palestinian residences suspected of harboring terrorists and was demolishing parts of Yasser Arafat's headquarters. While Jimmy Carter had been willing to sup with the devil to make peace, the Bush team refused to talk with Arafat and insisted on his departure as a condition for constructive intervention. Most Arabs saw this stance as giving Sharon a free hand and added to their hatred for U.S. policies in the region.

by Israeli jets and Hamas suicides. A moment of hope came and went in March 2002, when Saudi Prince Abdullah offered a peace proposal: Israel should withdraw from occupied territories in return for Arab recognition. Even this suggestion was drowned out by rising violence.

Meanwhile, President Bush insisted on regime change not just in Iraq but in the Palestinian Authority. He demanded that the authority be reformed and its current leadership (Arafat) be replaced. Bowing to U.S. and domestic pressure, Arafat in May 2002 signed a "Basic Law" for the Palestinian Authority that had been sitting on his desk for five years. It guaranteed basic rights to Palestinians so long as they accorded with "public morality." All Palestinian legislation, the Basic Law said, must conform with Islam's *shar'ia* principles.

The pain for Israelis and Palestinians was almost too much to endure but not enough to drive them to radical measures to end the pain. Things changed after the U.S.–UK liberation/occupation of Iraq. President Bush intervened personally to forge peace between Israel and Palestinians who, Bush insisted, had to have their own state. By mid-2003 it appeared that this could be another case (see Table 5.9) where, if Washington committed its great power, it could exert a positive influence.

FROM CIVIL WAR TO MAJORITY RULE IN SOUTHERN AFRICA

The obstacles to conflict resolution in southern Africa rivaled those in the Middle East. Many wars racked Africa in the late 20th and early 21st centuries. Still, Blacks and Whites there managed to avoid all-out war between races. A keystone in the broader peace was peace in Rhodesia—after 1980, Zimbabwe.

Rhodesia in the late 1970s was the last African colony tied to Europe. Though the country's population of 6 million was 98 percent Black, a White minority ruled. In 1965, this minority government declared Rhodesia's independence from Great Britain. London refused to permit Rhodesia's independence without assurances of majority (Black) rule. The UN Security Council imposed mandatory economic sanctions on Rhodesia (the first time the UN had taken such action). Meanwhile, Black guerrillas fought government forces.

Lord Carrington at Lancaster House

Margaret Thatcher became British prime minister in May 1979 and authorized her foreign secretary, Lord Carrington, to work out a settlement granting Rhodesia independence under majority rule. Carrington convened the principal Rhodesian players for talks at Lancaster House in London.

Why did Carrington succeed when earlier mediation efforts by the previous Labour government and by U.S. Secretaries of State Henry Kissinger and Cyrus Vance had failed? A number of reasons may be cited:

• Prospects of a quick victory on the battlefield had dimmed for each party in Rhodesia's civil war. The hurting stalemate made a mediated settlement more attractive.

• Carrington simplified negotiations by persuading the antigovernment Blacks (divided along ethnic lines) to form a single team facing the Whites and their new prime minister, a Black bishop.

• Economic squeeze: Rhodesia's economy increasingly suffered from war, UN sanctions, and White flight.

• Minority protection: The new constitution assured political representation for Whites and protection for their property. It could not be altered for at least seven years.

• Like Carter in 1978, Carrington was persistent and creative. The talks started in September 1979 and continued until all parties signed a settlement in late December. It was Carrington and his team—not the immediate parties to the conflict—"who were constantly looking under the rocks, trying to find a solution, and suggesting alternative routes." It took the weight of Thatcher's government to conceive, negotiate, impose, and implement a settlement. British policy toward Rhodesia and Zimbabwe in 1979 and 1980 was so even-handed that no

Another monkey wrench stalled the peace process in October 2002, when an IRA spy ring was found with information it might exploit in another terror campaign. Having consulted with Irish Premier Bertie Ahern, PM Tony Blair reimposed direct rule of Northern Ireland from London. Blair and Ahern agreed that "paramilitarism" must end for power sharing to function.

The Republican extremists in Northern Ireland, somewhat like the Palestinian bombers, could not see and act on a good deal when they had one. A sense of deprivation—unfairness—mixed with religious fervor led to a blind reliance on terror over politics. Add Northern Ireland to the list of places where terror netted no real political gains.

Somalia, Haiti, Cambodia

The 1980s and 1990s saw the emergence on every continent of **failed states**—places where the central government broke down, leaving various factions to struggle for power. They included Somalia, Haiti, Cambodia, Liberia, Bosnia, Afghanistan, and Zaire-Congo. Other countries teetering on the brink of failure were Macedonia, Rwanda, Colombia, Tajikistan, and perhaps even Pakistan. The reasons for "failure" were diverse in each case. They ranged from ethnic discord to the withdrawal of superpower money, from aged dictators to population–economic–environmental squeeze.

Somalia in the 1980s became the exemplar of a failed state. One out of eight Somalis was dying from starvation or clan warfare. At the request of the UN Security Council, the U.S. in 1992 led a multinational force into Somalia to assure food deliveries. Soon, "mission creep" began as U.S. forces sought to arrest one clan leader and impose order. After more than a dozen U.S. soldiers were killed, U.S. forces withdrew in 1993. A second UN force tried to keep the peace in 1993–1995, but it had fewer resources and a larger territory to cover. Here was another case where the Security Council issued big orders without establishing the means to carry them out.

Again authorized by the Security Council, a multinational force led by the U.S. intervened in Haiti to oust a military junta and reinstate the country's elected president. As noted later in this chapter, nothing happened until Jimmy Carter met with the junta and U.S. forces were airborne. The junta then agreed to depart, but chaos soon returned. UN observers plus troops and police from various countries tried to put Haiti on the road to democracy and economic development, but this was not easy after two centuries of repressive dictatorships.

By far the biggest and most expensive UN intervention was in Cambodia. In 1991 UN representatives negotiated a truce between factions that had fought one another since 1970. With Security Council approval, the

UN secretary-general arranged an election, held in 1993. Just three military advisers remained to assist the secretary-general's representative,[23] but development funds flowed in. From 1991 to 1997 the United Nations, the World Bank, the U.S., Australia, and other individual countries sank more than $4 billion into Cambodia to promote peace, self-government, and prosperity.

Positive outcomes were sparse. In 1997 Hun Sen—the same dictator who ruled Cambodia in the 1980s—evicted or killed his opponents and regained supreme power. In Hun Sen, a Communist passion for total control exploited a Cambodian tradition of god–king autocracy.

By the late 1990s, political violence in Cambodia gave way to the more humdrum problems of corruption, drug trafficking, and refugees. The UN resident coordinator—a sort of ambassador—supervised an array of UN development programs. Hun Sen's Cambodian People's Party maintained its domination in the 2002 local elections. About twenty people were killed before the poll, including eight opposition candidates, but local and foreign observers deemed the elections essentially fair. However, the UN gave up trying to establish a special tribunal to try Khmer Rouge members suspected of war crimes, and the Cambodian government pledged that its courts would do the job. A saying in the Caribbean seemed relevant: "If better can't be done, let the worse continue."

Can outsiders change countries such as Somalia, Haiti, and Cambodia? Consider this precedent: Following the U.S. Civil War, federal troops from the North occupied the former Confederacy for twelve years. When the troops withdrew, much of the old order re-emerged. The federal troops, however, were relatively stronger than any "Blue Berets" on loan from member states to the United Nations. As the 21st century began, the UN could muster small numbers of peacekeepers but not an army of peace enforcers. How, then, was peace imposed and maintained in the Balkans? Mainly, we shall see, by U.S.-led NATO forces plus the OSCE.

SOFT AND HARD POWER IN THE BALKANS

Why did UN representative Cyrus Vance and European Union (EU) mediator Lord David Owen fail to halt "ethnic cleansing" among the South Slavs in the early 1990s? Why did U.S. mediators do better in the mid-1990s? Here is a mystery with many parts: Was not the South Slav dispute "ripe" for settlement years before the U.S. intervened? Were not the UN and EU mediators experienced diplomats who had done well in previous mediating endeavors?[24] Were not the UN and EU peace plans similar in many essentials to the U.S.-designed agreement accepted by the

23. For history and documents, see *The United Nations and Cambodia, 1991–1995* (N.Y.: UN Department of Public Information, 1995).

24. Former UK foreign secretaries Lord Carrington and Lord Owen represented the EU in the former Yugoslavia; Vance, U.S. secretary of state for President Carter, represented the UN. Other experienced mediators such as Norway's Thorwald Stoltenberg and Sweden's Carl Bildt, took a turn, but none got very far with the South Slavs. Private citizen Jimmy Carter also flew in for a few days and arranged a short-lived cease-fire.

South Slavs in Dayton, Ohio, in November 1995? Did not this agreement "reward aggression" and split Bosnia along ethnic lines?[25]

Why Intervention Faltered in the Early 1990s

The problem was not misunderstanding. Neither language nor cultural misunderstandings obstructed peace in the Balkans. Bosnians, Serbs, and Croats all spoke Serbo–Croat. Most of their leaders—historians, poets, lawyers, and physicians—were also fluent in English.

Many problems undermined mediation efforts in the early 1990s. First, there were too many cooks in the Balkan kitchen—and none with the means to do the job. Each cook was following a different recipe or no recipe at all. Before the U.S. intervention in 1995, no would-be mediator in the Balkans spoke for a strong, unified political entity. Both the UN and the EU were internally divided. The U.S. tilted toward Bosnia; Russia and France favored Serbia; Germany backed Croatia; China preferred nonaction. Besides the major actors shown in Figure 9.1, there were many domestic factions and other bit players.

There was no unified "UN" force in the Balkans. The main units came from France and Britain, but other "Blue Helmets" arrived from countries as small as Estonia and as large as Russia. Coordination was a nightmare. Some units played favorites. Finances were muddled. Some "UN" forces were paid for by their own countries, others from the UN peacekeeping budget; some got side payments from black marketeering.

The UN chain of command resembled a dog chasing its tail. The local commander (usually British or French) could not use military force without the approval of the UN secretary-general or his local representative, Yasushi Akashi. But Akashi often vetoed military actions favored by Western governments or approved the moves too late for them to succeed.

UN forces in the Balkans also suffered from "mission creep." At first their job was to protect food convoys; next they were tasked to preserve certain towns as "safe havens"; later, they were told to destroy Serb mortars and artillery menacing Sarajevo. When the UN authorized NATO planes to attack Bosnian Serb installations in May 1995, the Serbs grabbed UN peacekeepers and held them as human shields to deter more NATO raids.

What Produced a Breakthrough in 1995?

The U.S. sat on the sidelines in the early 1990s, cheering or sniping as UN and EU mediators pursued peace in the Balkans.[26] In August 1995, however, President Bill Clinton decided that the U.S. should intervene

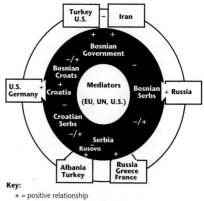

Fig. 9.1 Too Many Cooks, Too Many Ingredients in the Balkan Broth in 1995

Key:
+ = positive relationship
– = conflicted relationship
–/+ = mixed relationship

25. The Vance–Owen Plan would have divided Bosnia into ten cantons. This plan offended the ideal of multicultural internationalism and the legal principle of territorial integrity. For a defense of the plan, see David Owen, *Balkan Odyssey* (New York: Harcourt Brace, 1996).

26. The U.S. ambassador to Denmark told me in 1992: "We are waiting for the Europeans to realize that they can't do the job."

Terms of the Dayton Accord, November 21, 1995

The **Dayton Peace Accord** preserved the fiction of an integral Bosnian state but divided Bosnia into the Croat–Muslim Federation and the Bosnian Serb Republic. The central government with a rotating presidency would remain in Sarajevo. Each faction—Muslims, Croats, and Serbs— would retain its own army. A side deal authorized the U.S. to train and equip the Croat–Muslim federation so that it could hold its own against Bosnian Serbs.

The Bosnian Serb Republic got 49 percent of the land— roughly where the armies stood in late 1995. All refugees got the legal right to return home. Persons indicted by the International War Crimes Tribunal in The Hague could not hold elected office. Dayton promised Serbia that UN economic sanctions would be lifted but denied Belgrade access to World Bank loans until Serbs showed compliance with the peace accord.

Dayton replaced lightly armed UN peacekeepers with more than 60,000 heavily armed NATO forces—one-third of them Americans. Their mandate was much clearer than that given earlier to the UN "Blue Helmets." NATO troops were to supervise the peace and, if necessary, impose peace. The NATO forces were commanded by a U.S. general not subject to the UN. A side agreement continued a peacekeeping role for Russian forces, commanded indirectly by the U.S.

energetically, and sent Assistant Secretary of State Richard E. Holbrooke to mediate a Balkan peace. Holbrooke had long sought power, fame, and a place in history.[27] He quickly became the most forceful mediator of the 20th century.

Why did Clinton decide to act? Two reasons were uppermost. First, power politics: The longer the Balkan conflict dragged on, the more it exposed differences within NATO. It also had the effect, repugnant to Washington, of raising Iran's international stature, as Iranian volunteers trained and armed Bosnians. Second, moral outrage: In August 1995, TV viewers from Karachi to the White House saw images of children in Sarajevo mangled by a Serb mortar attack and of frozen human limbs protruding from a mass grave near Srebrenica, a UN "safe area" where an estimated 6,000 to 8,000 Muslim men were murdered.[28]

Holbrooke's mission began with tragedy. Three of his fellow diplomats died when their armored car slipped off the mountain road to Sarajevo, a route they took because Bosnian Serbs refused to guarantee their safe passage by air. Holbrooke accompanied their coffins back to Washington but soon returned to the Balkans, determined that his colleagues would not have died in vain. (What role is there for luck? If no U.S. diplomats had died, would Holbrooke have been so tenacious? If Holbrooke's vehicle had overturned, would his successors have been so effective?)

Why were the disputants more ready to accept a mediated settlement in fall 1995? One reason was that seekers of ethnic purity had been partially gratified by massacres or conquest. Another was that the Croats and Muslims had gained the upper hand, compelling the Serbs of Bosnia and

27. Michael Kelly, "The Negotiator," *New Yorker*, November 6, 1995, 81 ff.

28. Lightly armed Dutch peacekeepers did nothing to stop the murder. They had called for air strikes, but the French general commanding "UN" forces refused. When he finally did act, it was too little too late.

of Croatia to retreat. The Serbs outside Serbia, meanwhile, had lost the support of Serbian President Slobodan Milošević, now tired of the war he had fomented. In 1995 Milošević was seeking an end to the UN economic sanctions that hamstrung Serbia. Bosnian Serbs agreed to let Milošević represent them in late 1995 negotiations, but later complained that he had betrayed them.[29]

Holbrooke's resources were far superior to those of the EU and UN mediators. Carl Bildt, the EU representative in 1995, had to use a calling card to make phone calls; Holbrooke had mobile phones linked to the full communications machinery of the U.S. government. A comparative unknown, Bildt once depended on Holbrooke to liberate him from interrogation by UN (French) peacekeepers at the Sarajevo airport.

Both lion and fox, Holbrooke met Croat, Bosnian, and Serb leaders in their offices, palaces, and hunting lodges. He mixed walks in the woods and jokes over plum brandy with intense pressure and manipulation. Earlier, Holbrooke gave a green light to Croats to retake the Krajina region. Now he ordered them and their Bosnian allies not to take Banja Luka, the main Serb town in Bosnia, even though it had been the site of much ethnic cleansing. Why? An outflow of Bosnian Serb refugees into Serbia proper might lead Milošević to scupper the evolving deal.

When the Bosnian Muslims refused a cease-fire in October 1995, Holbrooke introduced a U.S. general with intelligence reports ("invented," some say) showing that Bosnia's position was precarious. The message: "Get a cease-fire now before the Serbs counterattack."

All parties submitted to a cease-fire in October. Holbrooke then summoned them to a Dayton, Ohio, Air Force base (not too comfortable and a vivid reminder of U.S. hard power) for talks that ended only when an accord was reached—a process that lasted twenty-one days. When the delegates bickered, Holbrooke presented them the three widows and six fatherless children of the U.S. diplomats who died near Sarajevo. The message: "You owe them peace as a memorial." Bosnia's PM Haris Silajdžić said he was overwhelmed.[30]

Bosnian Serbs had reasons to oppose and to accept the Dayton Accords, as outlined in Table 9.4.[31] But the Dayton arrangements resembled those proposed by Bosnian Serb President Radovan Karadžić a year before. The Serbian Republic of Bosnia, *(Republika Srpska)* achieved a high degree of autonomy within the Bosnian republic along with half its land.

As we see in Map 9.2, *Republika Srpska* encircled the rest of Bosnia and Herzegovina, known as the Croat–Muslim Federation. After Dayton, however, Bosnian Serbs bickered among themselves while Bosnia's

Table 9.4 Hard Choices for Bosnian Serbs

Losses If We Agree to the Dayton Accord	Gains If We Reject the Dayton Accord
We must forsake the cause of Greater Serbia.	We remain loyal to the Serbian and Orthodox cause.
We cannot win more territory and must give up some we now control.	We may be able to hold on to our present territory and gain more.
Many Muslims and Croats may return to our villages and towns.	We can keep our territory ethnically clean.
We permit foreigners to dictate what we do.	We defy NATO, the Croats, and Muslims. Russia and Serbia may help us.
The War Crimes Tribunal may arrest our leaders.	The War Crimes Tribunal cannot reach us.

Gains If We Accept the Dayton Accord	Risks If We Reject the Dayton Accord
Peace.	The war goes on.
An opportunity, and perhaps funds, to rebuild.	Little chance to rebuild.
Promises that we can return to lands lost.	We could be driven from our present territory.
Trade and other exchanges with Serbia and others outside the Balkans.	Isolation. Belgrade may further reduce our supplies.
Little threat to our religion.	Possible Muslim–Catholic conquest.

29. For Holbrooke's account, see his *To End a War* (New York: Random House, 1998). For another view from the State Department, see Daniel Serwer, "A Bosnian Federation Memoir," in Crocker et al., *Herding Cats*, 547–586. For a perspective from the National Security Council, see Ivo H. Daalder, *Getting to Dayton: The Making of America's Bosnia Policy* (Washington, D.C.: Brookings Institution, 2000).

30. Roger Cohen, "Taming the Bullies of Bosnia," *New York Times Magazine*, December 17, 1995, 58 ff; see also Joe Klein, "Setting the Table," *Newsweek*, October 16, 1995, 68 ff.

31. Compare with the Bosnian Serb outlook in 1993 in Roger Fisher et al., *Beyond Machiavelli: Tools for Coping with Conflict* (Cambridge, Mass.: Harvard University Press, 1994), 65.

Map 9.2 Bosnia and Herzegovina After the Dayton Accords

The port town of Brčko, shown on the map as a disputed territory, was administered by a commission headed by a U.S. diplomat for four years after Dayton. In 1999 it became a "District" of Bosnia and Herzegovina with its own local government and international financing that promoted business as well as ethnic harmony. By law it became a demilitarized condominium where the Serbian Republic and Bosnian–Croat Federation overlap. For details on this comparatively positive story, see www.ohr.int/ohroffices/brcko/

Croat–Muslim Federation became more cohesive and, thanks to U.S. military trainers and equipment, stronger.[32]

Holbrooke soon acted as fireman. He met with Bosnian, Croat, and Serbian leaders in February 1996 and in August 1997 and got them to reaffirm their Dayton commitments. NATO gunships flew overhead in 1996 as NATO ground troops demanded that Bosnian Serbs permit a check of their equipment. NATO's hard power provided serious leverage, but for how long would it work? How long would Western publics be willing to invest money and risk lives to keep the Balkans quiet? Would the South Slavs revert to their old ways when the outsiders left?

Albania, Kosovo, and Macedonia

"Balkanization"—carving new units out of existing structures—did not end with the Dayton Accord. Albanian speakers, most of them Muslims, chafed under Serb domination in Kosovo, officially a province of Serbia, and in Macedonia, a sovereign state independent of Serbia since 1991–1992.[33] Two-thirds of Macedonians were Slavs who spoke a

32. Leonard J. Cohen, "Bosnia and Herzegovina: Fragile Peace in a Segmented State," *Current History* 95, no. 599 (March 1996): 103–112, and related articles in that issue. See also the report by Enis Dzanić and Norman Erik in *Jane's Intelligence Review* (December 1997).

33. Admitted into the UN in 1993 as the "Former Yugoslav Republic of Macedonia" to ease worries in Athens about any conceivable claims from the "FYRM" on Greek territory.

language similar to Serbian. Like Serbs, they were Orthodox Christians. So one element in both Kosovo and Macedonia was a faceoff between Muslim Albanian speakers and Christian Slavs.[34] Some Albanian nationalists wanted to expand Albania proper into a "Greater Albania," redeeming the Albanian irredenta in Kosovo and Macedonia. But Albania proper was the basket case of Europe, and most Albanian speakers in Kosovo and Macedonia looked down on their less developed cousins in Albania.

In the 1990s, Albanian speakers in Kovovo outnumbered Serbs by more than 10 to 1 but felt persecuted by the Milošević regime in Belgrade and its local Serb enforcers. So the Albanian-speaking Kosovars wanted their own state independent of Serbia. Albanian speakers in Macedonia, however, made up only about one-fourth of Macedonia's population. Since most of them lived just across the border from Kosovo, they could conceivably join a "Greater Kosovo," if one existed. But their most likely prospect was more rights within Macedonia.

After losing Bosnia, Milošević intensified ethnic cleansing in Kosovo. If Albanian speakers moved elsewhere, Serbs could more easily settle and dominate a region ruled by Serb kings before the Ottomans moved northward. Albanian speakers responded to Milošević in three ways. Some moved elsewhere. Some, led by Ibrahim Rugova, practiced nonviolent resistance. They created a parallel system of schools, health care, and local administration paid for by unofficial taxes and remittances from abroad. Impatient, still others joined or backed the Kosovo Liberation Army (KLA) waging guerrilla war against Serbs with weapons from Albania proper or purchased with donations from abroad.

In 1998 Holbrooke persuaded Milošević to stop repression of Albanian-speaking Kosovars and admit Western observers to Kosovo. But violence by Serbs and the KLA continued. In early 1999 Holbrooke conveyed a NATO ultimatum to Milošević, which he rejected. NATO then launched an air war against Serbia that went on for three months. When Serbia did not quickly capitulate, NATO bombed not just Serbian military targets but civilian infrastructure—even bridges on the Danube, far from Kosovo. Indeed, some observers accused NATO of war crimes, though this charge was dismissed by the International Criminal Tribunal for the Former Yugoslavia. Belgrade said that 5,000 Serb civilians were killed; others said just 500. At least 10,000 Albanians perished in the melee. But Milošević agreed to withdraw Serbian forces from Kosovo and permit NATO forces to occupy what was still officially a part of Serbia for an indefinite future.

Meanwhile, Albanian speakers in Macedonia voiced their grievances. Some joined guerrilla groups based along the border with Kosovo and

34. Albanian is an Indo-European language but very different from any Slavic language. The Macedonian language straddles Serbian and Bulgarian. Its grammar was worked out by Harvard Slavicist Horace Lunt after World War II who, for his troubles, was denounced by the Tito government as a CIA agent seeking to disrupt Yugoslav unity.

Individuals Who Made a Difference

• Elie Wiesel, the Romanian-born American professor who helped persuade Bill Clinton that the U.S. should intervene to prevent the kind of genocide against Bosnians that Hitler conducted against Jews. He sat with Clinton as the Holocaust Museum opened in Washington.

• Richard Holbrooke, the roving ambassador who went all out to achieve policy goals he believed in and, at the same time, boost his chances of becoming secretary of state. When Al Gore lost the presidential race in 2000, Holbrooke returned to Wall Street.

• Yugoslav leader "Slobo" Milošević, "the sleaziest person you've ever met" and armed with an IQ of 160, according to a Western diplomat. When Milošević lost the presidency in the elections, Serbia's new government sent him to The Hague for war crimes. It thus met the remaining condition for Western economic aid.

• Secretary of State Madeleine Albright, an inveterate anti-Communist, more hawkish than most Clinton appointees and able to explain U.S. policies in Serbian by radio addresses beamed to Belgrade.

• Ibrahim Rugova, a proponent of Kosovar rights by nonviolent methods; he was displaced for a time by Kosovar militants, but prevailed in the 2001 elections.

• Viktor Chernomyrdin, a former Russian PM dispatched by Russian Federation president Boris Yeltsin to mediate the NATO–Serbian conflict over Kosovo. He brought about Serbia's capitulation by warning Milošević that Russia would not act to stop an invasion by NATO ground forces.

• Bernard Kouchner, the French founder of Doctors Without Borders and chief of the UN Interim Administration Mission in Kosovo, proved to be a weak administrator whose refusal to get tough with local Albanians exacerbated the plight of Serbs in Kosovo. In 2001 he was replaced by a former Danish defense minister, Hans Haekkerup.

waged hit-and-run attacks against government forces. In Macedonia, however, the West favored the status quo. Western diplomats persuaded both sides to accept guarantees of cultural autonomy for Albanians and power-sharing arrangements in government.

Starting in 1991–1992, the West intruded more and more forcefully, attempting to stabilize the former Yugoslavia and promote human rights. A decade later, Bosnia and Kosovo were virtual protectorates managed by NATO, the EU, and the OSCE—with the reluctant blessing of the UN. Here, in summary form, was the pattern of escalation:

• Diplomatic recognition of breakaway Slovenia, Croatia, Bosnia, and Macedonia

• Intrusion of UN and European mediators and peacekeepers in Bosnia

• Arming Croatia and acquiescing in its removal of ethnic Serbs to Serbia

• NATO attacks on Serbian artillery and tanks threatening Bosnia

• All the carrots and sticks used by Holbrooke to get the parties to sign the Dayton Accords

• Dispatch of NATO troops to supervise the Dayton Accords

• Demands for regime change in Serbia

• Demands that Serbia accept Western human rights monitors in Kosovo

• Air war by NATO against Serbia to force its withdrawal from Kosovo

• NATO, UN, and OSCE administration of Kosovo

• Heavy pressure on Serbia to deliver Milošević to The Hague tribunal

• Heavy pressure on Macedonia to share power with the Albanian minority

The U.S. and other Western governments supported contradictory principles. They still paid lip service to state sovereignty and territorial

Was the West Right to Intervene Forcefully in the Balkans?

Realism: Intervention Was Wrong

The West went too far and did more harm than good. Bosnia remained tense. Despite Western pressures, nationalist parties prevailed over reformist and multiethnic parties in Bosnia's October 2002 elections. The same three parties that led Bosnia into war in 1992 won most of the votes. The Croatian Democratic Union, the Serbian Democratic Party, and Democatic Action (Muslim) took all the seats for the joint presidency. Muslim hard-liners made the biggest gains. Nearly half the electorate stayed home—many displeased by the failure of the departing moderate coalition to improve living conditions.

After 1999 Kosovo was in limbo—legally still part of Serbia but now dominated by Albanian speakers, some of whom sought revenge against Serbs and Roma. Most Serbs fled to Serbia after 1999 and were afraid to return.

The West should have permitted the former Yugoslav republics to deal with their internal problems without outside interference. Yes, the strong would have tried to impose their will and the oppressed would have fought back. But the Balkans have been this way for centuries and will be in the future, despite the West's meddling. Nothing in the Balkans was so bad as Chinese repression of Tibet or Russian genocide in Chechnya.

U.S. policies in the Balkans provoked major tensions with Beijing and Moscow. NATO "social work" reduced the West's capacity to deal with larger problems.

Idealism: Intervention Was Right

Western interventions stopped bloodshed and gave peace a chance. The West was forging a new order in which human rights trumped state sovereignty. Bosnians lived in ethnic harmony before and can do so again. The West forced Serbian forces to withdraw, at least temporarily, from Kosovo, freeing Albanian speakers there from Belgrade's repression. Time is needed to heal wounds—again.

Western intervention in Macedonia prevented major violence and persuaded both sides to accept power-sharing arrangements.

Building on this momentum, the EU in 2002 convinced Montenegro to remain part of a union with Serbia albeit with its own economic system and a separate currency.

The West pioneered new institutions. For example, UN police in Kosovo used electronic surveillance to fight drug trafficking.

The Kosovo War provided lessons that served U.S. and UK forces well in Afghanistan in 2001 and 2002. Though the U.S. and UK intervened there mainly to rout out the Taliban, they achieved another liberation promoting human rights and helping traditional Muslims deal with the modern world.

The West could not protect Tibetans and Chechens because China and Russia were too strong to challenge. But in 2001 and 2002 both Beijing and Moscow were ready to ignore Western actions in the Balkans. They focused more on the need to maintain and strengthen solid economic ties with the West.

The U.S. and its allies should do for Palestinians what they did for Bosnians and Kosovars. They should pressure Israel to withdraw from occupied territories and agree to share power in Jerusalem. If a truncated Israel was more vulnerable, Western forces should protect Israel as they did Bosnia and Kosovo.

integrity, but soon subordinated these goals to protection of human rights. They also violated the principle of Big Five unanimity as the precondition for action affecting peace and security. They treated the Balkans as an issue that Western governments could and should handle on their own—thereby avoiding a Russian or Chinese veto at the Security Council. Was this a wise course? As we see in the box "Individuals Who Made a Difference", both realists and idealists muster strong arguments.

MEDIATIONS WITH SOFT POWER

Many persons won Nobel Peace Prizes for peace work without economic or military levers. Among Americans so honored were Theodore Roosevelt, for his 1905 and 1906 mediations; Ralph Bunche, for brokering an Arab–Israeli cease-fire; Martin Luther King, Jr., for nonviolent actions to reduce racial discrimination; and Elie Wiesel, for remembering the Holocaust and protesting genocide.

The century's leading freelance mediator was Jimmy Carter. In May 1994 he affirmed a democratic election in Panama. In June he met with Kim Il-sung and set the stage for official U.S.–DPRK negotiations. In September he persuaded Haiti's generals to step aside. In December 1994 Carter arranged a short-lived cease-fire in Bosnia.

Carter's personality and negotiating techniques were often effective. Still, behind the private envoy loomed enormous hard power. While Carter talked to Kim Il-sung, for example, the Pentagon was actively preparing for another war on the Korean peninsula.[35] And Haiti's junta gave in only after a U.S. invasion force was in the air. Carter's team (which included Senator Sam Nunn and retired General Colin Powell) had persisted beyond the deadline set by the White House. Carter was unorthodox but often effective.

Religious leaders can provoke or restrain violence. Quakers helped promote peace talks between the Nigerian government and secessionist Biafra in 1970. The Vatican in 1978–1984 mediated a dispute between Chile and Argentina over the Beagle Channel.[36] Bishop Samuel Luiz Garcia in the mid-1990s brokered a cease-fire and negotiations between Mayan Indians and the Mexican government. In the Balkans, some South Slav priests and mullahs promoted hate but others worked for reconciliation.

Norwegian NGOs and officials were active worldwide, from Burundi to Colombia. The private sector worked with the Norwegian government to provide executive airplanes, remote country houses, constitutional lawyers, university-based expertise, and discretionary funds ("venture

35. Carter phoned the White House as President Clinton discussed possible military action against North Korea. Asked whether the terms that Carter had discussed with Kim Il-sung were satisfactory, Clinton stipulated additional North Korean concessions before he would send U.S. negotiators to meet with North Koreans in Geneva—concessions that Carter secured.

36. This and many other cases are detailed in Thomas E. Princen, *Intermediaries in International Conflict* (Princeton, N.J.: Princeton University Press, 1992).

Nobel Peace Prize Laureates from the United States

1906: Roosevelt, Theodore, U.S. president who mediated the 1905 Treaty of Portsmouth ending the Russo–Japanese War.

1913: Root, Elihu, former secretary of state and initiator of several arbitration agreements.

1920: Wilson, Thomas W., USA, U.S. president and a founder of the League of Nations.

1926: Chamberlain, Sir (Joseph) Austen, British foreign secretary and a negotiator of the Locarno Treaty and **Dawes, Charles Gates,** U.S. vice president, chairman of the Allied Reparation Commission and originator of the Dawes Plan.

1930: Kellogg, Frank Billings, former secretary of state who negotiated the Briand–Kellogg Pact to outlaw war.

1931: Addams, Jane, international president of the Women's International League for Peace and Freedom; and **Butler, Nicholas Murray,** president of Columbia University and promoter of the Briand–Kellogg Pact.

1945: Hull, Cordell, former secretary of state and an initiator of the United Nations.

1946: Balch, Emily Greene, former professor of history and sociology. International president of the Women's International League for Peace and Freedom; and **Mott, John Raleigh,** chairman of the first International Missionary Council in 1910, president of the World Alliance of Young Men's Christian Associations.

1947: the Friends Service Council, London (founded in 1647) and **the American Friends Service Committee (the Quakers),** Washington (first meeting in 1672).

1950: Bunche, Ralph, director of the UN Division of Trusteeship, mediator in Palestine in 1948.

1953: Marshall, George C., former secretary of state and of defense, and originator of the Marshall Plan.

1964: King, Martin Luther, Jr., leader of the Southern Christian Leadership Conference and campaigner for civil rights.

1970: Borlaug, Norman Ernest, led research at the International Maize and Wheat Improvement Center, Mexico City.

1973: Kissinger, Henry A., secretary of state and **Le Duc Tho,** North Vietnam (who declined the prize), for jointly negotiating the Vietnam peace accord.

1985: International Physicians for the Prevention of Nuclear War, Cambridge, Massachusetts, and Moscow.

1986: Wiesel, Elie, author and humanitarian.

1997: International Campaign to Ban Land-Mines (ICBL), and **Jody Williams.**

2002: Jimmy Carter, former U.S. president and mediator of the Camp David Accord and many others.

capital for peace"). The Foreign Ministry established two organizations to tap and coordinate the energies of both government and NGOs: the Norwegian Emergency Preparedness System and the Norwegian Resource Bank for Democracy and Human Rights. Their combined resources permitted the Norwegians to act quickly and flexibly. For example,

• Norway initiated a peace process between the government and rebels in Guatemala that began in Oslo in 1990 and led to a cease-fire signed in Oslo in 1996. Norway worked with UN mediators and a "Group of Friends"—Colombia, Mexico, Spain, and the United States. Shielded by the morally unchallenged NGO known as Norwegian Church Aid, Norway funded conference participation by the bankrupt (but still potent) guerrillas as well as exchange programs between the Guatemalan and Norwegian military.

Can Educators Help?

Informal exchanges, brainstorming, and simulations can clear the way for formal understandings. Psychology professor Herbert Kelman arranged many informal talks between Greek and Turkish Cypriots; law professor Roger Fisher did so between Georgians and South Ossetians; Israeli professors explored possible terms with PLO officials before and after Oslo. Elementary school teachers brought Israeli and Palestinian children together to paint and discuss their images of peace. In Chapter 14, we shall read of plans to organize a University of the Middle East, with campuses in many countries.

• In the Caucasus, a Norwegian-funded NGO facilitated talks between the Georgian government and separatists on refugee exchanges and telecommunication links.

• Starting in 1995, the Sri Lankan government and Tamil Tigers asked Norwegians to facilitate two cease-fire panels. Seven years later, after many breakdowns in the negotiations and many returns to violence, the two sides made peace under Norwegian auspices. As noted in the previous chapter, Sri Lanka's president and prime minister feuded in 2003 over whether the Norwegians were exceeding or meeting their mandate.

The Netherlands, Sweden, and other small states also played constructive roles in promoting peace and reconciliation. "Small" can be flexible and creative. Rich countries with high taxes could afford to do something constructive for the less fortunate.[37] Besides, some of their citizens wanted to curb the flow of asylum seekers from zones of chaos.

WHAT PROPOSITIONS HOLD? WHAT QUESTIONS REMAIN?

Outsiders can help to manage, if not resolve, conflicts. Intermediaries can help antagonists shift from mutual pain to mutual gain. If the settlement offers mutual gain, the parties may grow to transcend their conflicts. But clumsy, half-hearted interventions can make things worse.

INGREDIENTS FOR EFFECTIVE MEDIATION

For disputants to reach an accord, conditions must be ripe. But disputants often spurn a possible deal even though conditions seem ripe. A skilled mediator can help the disputants to see that a negotiated settlement is their best alternative.

History reveals no correlation between the kinds of leverage used and mediation success. Mediation that used only soft power succeeded in 1905 to end the Russo–Japanese War and in 1993 to initiate peace between Israel and the PLO. Blends of tangible and intangible power fostered Egyptian–Israeli peace in 1978 and peace the next year in Zimbabwe. Washington's mix of economic sweeteners and diplomatic pressures helped persuade Ukraine, Kazakstan, Belarus, and (with serious qualifications) North Korea to renounce nuclear arms.

When dealing with tough customers, hard power may also be required. Holbrooke used every kind of stick and carrot to nail down the Dayton Accords and sustain it. Hard power alone, however, has never sufficed to bring about a lasting peace. Hard power backfired for India in Sri Lanka (1987–1990), achieved for Russia very tenuous cease-fires in the

37. The Dutch once had a large overseas empire—a source for some of their present wealth. They owe humanity—but so do other ex-imperial giants such as Portugal and Belgium, who did very little to compensate for ravaging less developed countries. Norway had no colonies. It was for centuries ruled by Sweden.

Caucasus and Central Asia (mid-1990s), and failed for the U.S. in Lebanon (1982–1983) and in Somalia (1992–1993).

The personal qualities of individual mediators can be decisive. "The Mediator's Handbook" outlined earlier in this chapter offers useful guidelines, but they must be adapted to time and place. The Norwegians did little except to facilitate settings conducive to fruitful negotiation. A skilled mediator such as Carter can convert a partially ripe situation into a settlement, for example, by using an SNT. A clumsy mediator such as Alexander Haig or Rajiv Gandhi may botch the opportunity. But some mediators may fail even though they use textbook techniques and great levers.

A mediator resembles a salesman. A word or gesture can make or break a sale. Teddy Roosevelt clinched the Moroccan deal by a threat. He warned the kaiser that he would publish an embarrassing letter if Berlin spurned the terms worked out at Algeciras.

Effective mediators come in many shapes and colors: Roosevelt and Holbrooke were as gruff as Vance and Carter were polite. Vance refused "tricks" and bullying, but ultimately failed in the Balkans. Holbrooke had no such scruples. He pushed and pulled the South Slavs to the table. Lords Carrington and Owen were somewhat formal; most Americans, informal. Norwegians ranged between these poles.

Successful intervention usually requires a major commitment of time, energy, and other resources—the kind invested at Camp David, Lancaster House, and Dayton. Mediators like Carter, Carrington, and Holbrooke sink their teeth into the problem and do not let go until a deal is reached. Clinton emulated Carter at Camp David in 2000, however, and failed. Even the best mediation can fail if one or both sides is intransigent. Mediation diplomacy can risk both the health and political fortunes of its participants; many in search of peace have died for their pains.

SHOULD A MEDIATOR SUP WITH THE DEVIL?

Many mediators felt uneasy dealing with suspected genocidists but did so as part of the job. Still, Lord Owen (trained as a physician) could not bring himself to discuss medicine with Bosnian Serb leader Radovan Karadžić, a former psychiatrist but also an accused war criminal. Owen's partner, Cyrus Vance, thought that a mediator should not see anyone as evil incarnate. But he conceded that compromise with persons as evil as Hitler is impossible.[38]

Carter said that judgments about others should be left outside the meeting room. The mediator should focus the disputants on whether an agreement can advance their interests. "People in conflict have to be willing to talk about ending it, or at least changing it, and there has to be

38. Vance thought, however, that with Saddam Hussein "we probably should have given talks more time." Leslie H. Gelb, "Vance: A Nobel Life," *The New York Times*, March 2, 1992, A15.

someone willing to talk to them, however odious they are—and that's where I come in."[39]

A related question concerned war crimes. Could there be peace without justice? Some observers answered no. They demanded that NATO troops in Bosnia arrest any persons indicted by the International Criminal Tribunal for the Former Yugoslavia. Others argued that stability was more important than bringing accused war criminals to trial. For their part, NATO troops did not wish to pick a fight and, for several years, looked the other way when an indicted offender drove by.[40] In 1997, however, some UK troops arrested a few mid-level Bosnian Serbs suspected of war crimes and sent them to the tribunal at The Hague. Croatia, hoping for more U.S. aid, dispatched a few of its accused war criminals to The Hague. In 2001 a big fish arrived there—Slobodan Milošević, defeated in the October 2000 elections for the Yugoslav presidency. The new president, Vojislav Koštunica, opposed extraditing Milošević but finally did so to get Western aid. The next year, however, a local Mafia assassinated Koštunica.

39. Wooten, "The Conciliator."
40. Theodor Meron, "Answering for War Crimes: Lessons from the Balkans," *Foreign Affairs* 76, no. 1 (January/February 1997): 2–9.

Memo to the UN Secretary-General: The UN and its members have a vested interest in preventive diplomacy and, when necessary, effective peace enforcement. Mediation and peace enforcement are far cheaper than war.

But the UN has no resources unless member states provide them—no funds, no troops. The UN Secretariat can do little to help peoples at risk without the support or acquiescence of the permanent members of the Security Council. This situation has not paralyzed the UN. Even during the Cold War the UN dispatched mediators, observers, and peacekeepers to trouble spots around the world. Still, the most effective mediations have taken place outside the UN framework.

Americans conducted much of the 20th-century's mediation work. But no single country can be expected to resolve the many conflicts around the globe. A Camp David or Dayton-type mediation places enormous demands on top officials with other duties.

Why have private individuals and governments usually mediated more effectively than international organizations? UN mediators are circumscribed. They cannot operate out of the public eye (like the Norwegians with the PLO and Israelis). They have few carrots or sticks. They depend upon a fragile consensus in the Security Council.

Despite these problems, we should do whatever we can to make mediation by UN representatives more frequent and more effective. One way is to tighten the links between the UN and its member states. Thus, we have engaged as mediators two former U.S. secretaries of state and an ex–prime minister of Sweden. We should do more to strengthen our overall capacity for preventive diplomacy. Most mediation has been ad hoc—an improvised response to a specific challenge. When there are signs of trouble, we should have ample means and clear authority to send observers, monitors, and mediators. The United Nations needs an established procedure for providing mediators to global hot spots. Let us establish a panel of mediators, like the list of arbitrators kept at The Hague—a list from which you, the Security Council, and disputants could choose mediators. Let us have stand-by forces in every major country earmarked for UN service.

Are we our brothers' and sisters' keepers? Yes. Let us help humanity to develop stronger means of preventive diplomacy.

Upon seeing this memo, the U.S. Ambassador to the UN decides to forward a copy to the Secretary of State, adding his own postscript.

P.S. To the Secretary of State:

These are good ideas. The U.S. cannot pull all other peoples' chestnuts from the fire. To support the Secretary-General, let us pay our own bills to the UN on time. Let's share more intelligence for early warning. Let's commit to submit all our disputes to the International Court of Justice or to a mediator. Also, for your eyes only, I find it embarrassing here to call for bringing war criminals to The Hague while defending U.S. opposition to the International Criminal Court. This is a mindless inconsistency. While we try to strengthen the UN, however, we must be ready to intervene with mediators like Holbrooke or the Marines—or both.

KEY NAMES AND TERMS

Yasser Arafat	Richard E. Holbrooke	peacemaking
arbitration	International Court	positions vs. interests
Ralph Bunche	of Justice	prenegotiation
Jimmy Carter	leverage	reservation price (RP)
conflict resolution	mediation	ripeness
Dayton Peace Accord	Oslo Accord	Anwar Sadat
failed state	peace building	single negotiating text (SNT)
Rajiv Gandhi	peace enforcement	spectrum of intervention
good offices	peacekeeping	third-party intervention

QUESTIONS TO DISCUSS

1. Consider a dispute to which you or your group is a participant. Could an outside mediator advance your interests? How?
2. Why should the U.S. (Canada, Mexico, or any other country) invest time, energy, and other resources in mediating others' disputes?
3. Why do some interventions succeed and others fail? What are the ingredients of an effective mediation?
4. When, and to what extent, does effective mediation require the use of carrots and sticks?
5. Are the mediator's personal characteristics important? If so, give examples.
6. What can we learn from mediation efforts in the Middle East and the Balkans? Why did Carter, Holst, and Holbrooke succeed where others failed?
7. Why has it been easier for individuals and governments to mediate effectively than for the international community to do so?
8. What can be done to reduce buck passing and strengthen the UN capacity for effective mediation?
9. Imagine that you, representing country X, are the mediator between countries Y and Z. Write down their interests and principles. Formulate two ways that they might be reconciled. Outline the techniques and pressures you can use to achieve a peaceful settlement.

Questions to Discuss (continued)

10. Imagine that you have this same task but that you represent the UN secretary-general, who has been authorized by the Security Council to undertake this mediation. Formulate how the two parties might be reconciled and what techniques and pressures you can mobilize.

RECOMMENDED RESOURCES

BOOKS

Bercovitch, Jacob, and Jeffrey Z. Rubin, eds. *Mediation in International Relations: Multiple Approaches to Conflict Management.* New York: St. Martin's, 1992.

Bishara, Marwan. *Palestine/Israel: Peace or Apartheid: Prospects for Resolving the Conflict.* London: Zed Books, 2001.

Brams, Steven J. *Negotiation Games: Applying Game Theory to Bargaining and Arbitration.* New York: Routledge, 1990.

Central Intelligence Agency. *Balkan Battlegrounds: A Military History of the Yugoslav Conflict, 1990–1995.* Washington, D.C.: CIA Office of Public Affairs, 2002.

Cousens, Elizabeth M., and Charles K. Cater. *Toward Peace in Bosnia: Implementing the Dayton Accords.* Boulder, Colo.: Lynne Rienner, 2000.

Crocker, Chester A., et al., eds., *Herding Cats: Multiparty Mediation in a Complex World.* Washington, D.C.: United States Institute of Peace, 1999.

Damrosch, Lori Fisler, ed. *Enforcing Restraint: Collective Intervention in Internal Conflicts.* New York: Council on Foreign Relations, 1993.

Darby, John. *Effects of Violence on Peace Processes.* Washington, D.C.: United States Institute of Peace, 2001.

Fisher, Roger, et al. *Beyond Machiavelli: Tools for Coping with Conflict.* Cambridge, Mass.: Harvard University Press, 1994.

Gidron, Benjamin, et al., eds. *Mobilizing for Peace: Conflict Resolution in Northern Ireland, Israel/Palestine, and South Africa.* Oxford, U.K.: Oxford University Press, 2002.

Greenberg, Melanie C., et al., eds. *Words Over War: Mediation and Arbitration to Prevent Deadly Conflict.* Lanham, Md.: Rowman & Littlefield, 2000.

Holbrooke, Richard. *To End a War.* New York: Random House, 1999.

McInnes, Colin, and Nicholas J. Wheeler, eds. *Dimensions of Western Military Intervention.* London: Frank Cass, 2002.

Mitchell, Christopher. *Gestures of Conciliation: Factors Contributing to Successful Olive Branches.* New York: St. Martin's Press, 2000.

Princen, Thomas E. *Intermediaries in International Conflict.* Princeton, N.J.: Princeton University Press, 1992.

Record, Jeffrey. *Making War, Thinking History: Munich, Vietnam, and Presidential Uses of Force from Korea to Kosovo.* Annapolis, Md.: Naval Institute Press, 2002.

Shawcross, William. *Deliver Us from Evil: Peacekeepers, Warlords, and a World of Endless Conflict.* New York: Simon & Schuster, 2001.

Stein, Janice Gross, ed. *Getting to the Table: The Processes of International Prenegotiation.* Baltimore, Md.: Johns Hopkins University Press, 1989.

Telhami, Shibley. *The Stakes: America and the Middle East.* Boulder, Colo.: Westview, 2002.

Whittaker, David J. *Conflict and Reconciliation in the Contemporary World.* London: Routledge, 1999.

Zartman, I. William, and J. Lewis Rasmussen, eds. *Peacemaking in International Conflict: Methods and Techniques.* Washington, D.C.: United States Institute of Peace, 1997.

For listings of more than 100 publications relevant to peacemaking, look under "United States Institute of Peace" in library and book catalogues.

JOURNALS AND JOURNAL ARTICLES

Ethics & International Affairs (special issue: "Intervention") 9 (1995).

"Flexibility in International Negotiation and Mediation." *Annals of the American Academy of Political and Social Science,* no. 542 (November 1995).

International Journal (special issue: "Intervention") 48, no. 4 (autumn 1993).

Journal of Conflict Resolution

Journal of Peace Research

Negotiation Journal

"Resolving Regional Conflicts: International Perspectives." *Annals of the American Academy of Political and Social Science,* no. 518 (November 1991).

"Rethinking Peacekeeping (three essays)" *Washington Quarterly* 18, no. 3 (summer 1995): 49–90.

WEB SITES

The Camp David Accords
http://www.mfa.gov.il/mfa/go.asp?MFAH00ie0

Conflict in Northern Ireland, from the BBC
http://news.bbc.co.uk/hi/english/static/northern_ireland/understanding/default.stm

The General Framework Agreement
http://www.nato.int/ifor/gfa/gfa-home.htm

Rhodesia–Zimbabwe Civil War
http://www.onwar.com/aced/data/romeo/rhodesia1971.htm

Theodore Roosevelt, including information on the Portsmouth Conference
http://www.theodoreroosevelt.org/

PART 3

International Political Economy

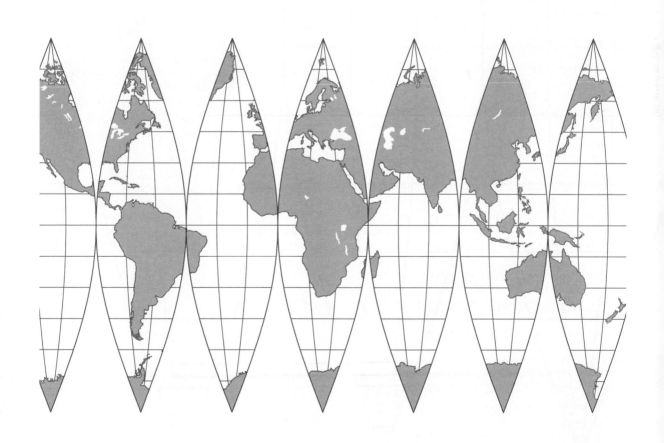

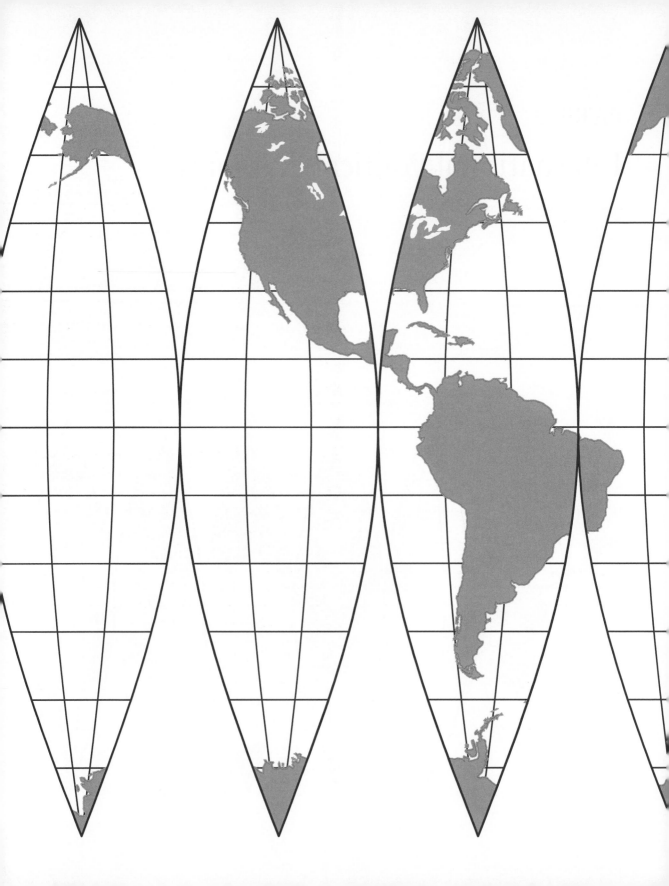

DEMOCRACY AND AUTHORITARIANISM: WHAT IMPACT ON INTERNATIONAL PEACE AND PROSPERITY?

THE BIG QUESTIONS IN CHAPTER 10

- What is democracy? How does it differ from authoritarianism?

- Would you expect a democracy or a dictatorship to be more successful in foreign policy?

- How do your expectations fit with 20th- and 21st-century history?

- Who usually wins when democracies fight authoritarian regimes?

- Do democracies fight democracies?

- Do authoritarian regimes help their societies to become more fit and affluent?

- Is democracy waxing or waning?

- Would India benefit from a tighter grip at the top?

- Does it matter to India whether Pakistan and China are authoritarian?

- Does it matter to the U.S. whether other countries become democratic?

"Is a Firmer Hand Needed?" . . . . *The President of India is deeply troubled. The world's largest democracy has fallen behind China and other neighbors in economic growth, mass education, and health care. Religious and ethnic strife have risen, leading the President to think about invoking emergency powers to govern directly.*

The President asks you, a lawyer, and a university professor in Mumbai, to come to New Delhi and review the situation: Is a firmer hand needed to rule India? Is democracy a luxury of the rich? Does India need a more authoritarian government to improve life within the country and wrestle with China and Pakistan? Is it time to change India's constitution? Should we make it clear that India is a Hindu state or keep up our attempt at secularism?

India's political elite envies Singapore's paternalistic government, which guided that country to riches and stability. If just four ethnic groups living in tiny Singapore benefited from a strong hand at the top, might India—one of the world's most populous and heterogeneous countries—also profit from top-down, centralized governance?

Meanwhile, India's ambassador to Washington discusses these and related questions with her old friend, the U.S. Secretary of State. Is not order better than chaos? Would not Somalia and Haiti also benefit from a strong, authoritarian government? The ambassador, a student of U.S. history, recalls the question posed by Abraham Lincoln on July 4, 1861: "Must a government . . . be too strong for the liberties of its own people, or too weak to maintain its own existence?"

The Secretary of State notes that many Americans are indifferent to the ways in which others are governed. A common attitude is: "It's their business—not ours." But other Americans feel a duty to spread good government. Some even believe that U.S. security and prosperity depend upon the spread of political and economic liberty. Assuming they are right, however, the question looms: What, if anything, can outsiders do to promote democracy where it is weak?

minimize global political violence." Rummel added that democracy has another advantage over authoritarian regimes: "The citizens of democracies are the least likely to be murdered by their own governments; the citizens of totalitarian, especially Marxist systems, the most likely."[9] We shall also compare Rummel's theory with reality.

STRENGTHS AND WEAKNESSES OF AUTHORITARIANISM

Decisiveness

Authoritarians claim to mobilize human and other resources better than democracies. For government to function, disputes must be resolved by one alone—"*uno solo*," as Florentine political analyst Niccolò Machiavelli put it.[10] Authoritarians can indoctrinate and command, tax as they please, keep secrets, and intervene abroad with whatever forces are needed—when they are needed. If they wish, they can redistribute the wealth to promote equality.

For English philosopher Thomas Hobbes, only a strong sovereign could assure safety, otherwise there would be a "war of all against all." Authoritarian rule keeps the lid on ethnic and nationalist conflict. Whereas India faces constant ethnic and religious turmoil, China's strong central government keeps its minority peoples under firm control. The Soviet empire repressed the bickering of Central Asians, Caucasians, and East Europeans. The breakup of central control unleashed chaos where there had been a *pax sovetica*.

When the Kremlin cracked down on Hungarian insurgents in 1956, it did so decisively. When the Kennedy administration sought to overthrow Fidel Castro in 1961, it did so halfheartedly. The Soviet regime was manned by professional politicians schooled in *kto kovo* (who, whom); the U.S. government, by political amateurs.

However, the weaknesses of the Soviet system could be more disruptive than those of U.S. democracy. Dictatorship generated tensions with other social forces and institutions. Still, both the Soviet and U.S. systems had great staying power. Brzezinski and Huntington expected the two systems to change but not converge. They predicted "parallel evolution."

Information Blockage

Authoritarian regimes suffer from information blockage. Messengers fear telling the bad news. If the boss gets bad news, she or he may not share or discuss it with others. We saw in Chapter 3 how *uno solo* (Khrushchev) initiated the Cuban missile gambit—a policy that could

9. Rudolph J. Rummel, *Lethal Politics: Soviet Genocide and Mass Murder Since 1917* (New Brunswick, N.J.: Transaction, 1996), xi. Rummel documents these hypotheses in more than a dozen books. His summation is *Power Kills: Democracy as a Method of Nonviolence* (New Brunswick, N.J.: Transaction, 1997).

10. Harvey C. Mansfield, Jr., *Taming the Prince: The Ambivalence of Modern Executive Power* (New York: Free Press, 1989), 83.

have destroyed the world. In Chapter 5, we noted how the Soviet regime resisted installing touch-tone telephones.

Abuse of Power

The more unchallenged the government, the more it is likely to abuse power. As English historian Lord Acton put it (in 1887): "Power tends to corrupt and absolute power corrupts absolutely." But even Lord Acton might have been taken aback by the accuracy of his prediction. As we have seen, 20th-century dictators murdered their own people by the millions.

COMPARING THEORY WITH REALITY: TRACK RECORDS OF AUTHORITARIANISM AND DEMOCRACY

DEMOCRACIES USUALLY DEFEAT AUTHORITARIAN REGIMES IN WAR

While authoritarian regimes started most of the major wars of the 20th century, they also lost them—usually to democracies.[11] Authoritarian Germany, Austria-Hungary, and the Ottoman Empire were defeated by Western democracies in World War I.[12] The dictators of Italy, Germany, and Japan launched World War II, but they were defeated by a coalition that included the authoritarian USSR as well as the Western democracies. When authoritarian Arab states and democratic Israel made war, Israel always prevailed. Authoritarian Pakistan was defeated or stalemated several times by India.[13] Democratic Britain defeated the Argentine junta in 1982. The First World prevailed over the Soviet empire in cold war.

Why did democracies fight more effectively than de Tocqueville predicted? Authoritarian regimes can reach decisions more quickly than democracies, but often these decisions are unwise. Thus, Germany twice waged a two-front war, and then, compounding its follies, took on the world's economic colossus in 1917 and again in 1941.

Authoritarians can indoctrinate and mobilize their people to obey, but they often inhibit creativity and leadership, also important in war.

Since World War II, democracies have usually lost when they fought against national liberation movements. Thus, the Dutch were driven from Indonesia (1949), the French from Vietnam (1954) and Algeria (1962), the U.S. from Vietnam (1973), and the Portuguese from Africa (1975). Why? Many in the West doubted that the cause was just or worth fighting for.

11. A survey of all wars between democracies and autocracies, 1816 to 1988, finds that democracies won four out of five. See David A. Lake, "Powerful Pacifists: Democratic States and War," *American Political Science Review* 86, no. 1 (March 1992): 24–37 at 31–33.

12. Authoritarian Russia was defeated by authoritarian Japan in 1905 and by authoritarian Germany in 1917.

13. However, China bested India when they faced off in 1962 over disputed territory high in the Himalayas, deepening India's resolve to become a modern military power.

DEMOCRACIES BAND TOGETHER AND RARELY, IF EVER, FIGHT EACH OTHER

Liberal peace theory holds that stable, sovereign democracies seldom, if ever, wage war against other stable, sovereign democracies. For a time this theory was seen as being as near to an empirical "law" as exists in IR.[14] It appeared to be valid across the seventy or more interstate wars that have taken place since 1815 involving at least 270 states.[15] Far from fighting each other, democracies tended to band together in war. The theory states: "seldom, if ever." There are possible exceptions, for example, the War of 1812, the U.S. Civil War, the Boer War, and the many European and U.S. battles with national liberation movements. But even these possible deviations disappear if we define four terms precisely:

War means an armed conflict that kills at least 1,000 persons in battle.

Democracy requires free elections in which "practically all adults" have the right to vote. Many countries met this standard in the late 20th century. For earlier times, the theory lowers the bar and counts as democratic countries in which at least 30 percent of adult males could vote. Not until the 1850s could most white males vote in the U.S., while women gained suffrage only in 1920; most U.S. blacks found it hard to vote until 1965. It was not until 1971 that the voting age was lowered to eighteen in the United States. Most other countries were much slower to broaden the voting franchise. Female suffrage existed in very few countries until after World War I. If the women's vote had any pacifying effect, it would have had little effect until the 1920s or later.[16]

Stable means established and functioning as a democracy for at least three years.

Sovereign means "recognized as independent by the international community."

Applying these standards, we see that none of the candidate conflicts constituted a war between stable, sovereign democracies: The War of 1812 between the U.S. and Great Britain took place when neither side had wide suffrage; the U.S. Civil War (1861–1865) took place between a democracy and a landed aristocracy that was neither stable nor sovereign; both the Boer War (1899) and the Second Philippine War (1899–1902) pitted democracies (Britain and the U.S.) against liberation movements that were neither settled nor sovereign.

Democracies have rarely, if ever, fought other democracies. But democracies have often wielded a big stick. The U.S. has threatened force on hundreds of occasions. Of course, a threat is not a war unless many die.

14. Jack S. Levy, "The Causes of War: A Review of the Theories and Evidence," in *Behavior, Society, and Nuclear War*, 3 vols., ed. Philip E. Tetlock et al. (New York: Oxford University Press), 1: 209–333.

15. Bruce Russett et al., *Grasping the Democratic Peace: Principles for a Post–Cold War World* (Princeton, N.J.: Princeton University Press, 1993), 9–20. See also Michael W. Doyle, "Liberalism and World Politics," *American Political Science Review* 80, no. 4 (December 1986): 1151–1169, and his two related articles in *Philosophy and Public Affairs* 12, no. 3 (1983): 205–235 and 12, no. 4 (1983): 323–353; for other references, see Cecelia Lynch, "Kant, the Republican Peace, and Moral Guidance in International Law," *Ethics & International Affairs* 8 (1994): 39–58.

16. In Great Britain, a majority of adult males could not vote in secret elections until 1872; even then, some 40 percent of adult males remained disenfranchised. Women did not gain suffrage in France, Italy, and Japan until the 1940s; in Switzerland, until 1971.

France and Belgium have intervened often in Africa. Besides the major wars waged in Korea, Vietnam, and the Persian Gulf, U.S. military forces openly intervened in the Dominican Republic (1965), Grenada (1983), Panama (1989),[17] Kosovo (1999), Afghanistan (2001–2002), and Iraq (2003). The CIA used covert action to unseat leftist governments in Iran (1953), Guatemala (1954), and Chile (1973). None of these covert actions amounted to a "war" with 1,000 or more combat deaths, though more than that number died in subsequent repression by U.S.-backed dictators. Neither were these covert operations approved in advance by Congress; in fact, some were later condemned by Congress.[18]

Why was there fighting between the states emerging from Yugoslavia (for example, Croatia and Bosnia) and the former Soviet Union (for example, Armenia and Azerbaijan)? Since most of these states claimed to be democratic and devoted to free markets, did their behavior contradict the assumptions of liberal peace theory?

Some analysts observed that all states in transition are war-prone, but they disagreed on which direction is more dangerous—toward democracy or toward authoritarian rule (Germany's path in the 1930s).[19] Jack Snyder wrestled with this question in his book *From Voting to Violence: Democratization and Nationalist Conflict.*[20] Using democratization as the independent variable, Snyder assessed the consequences for war and peace in ex-Communist states where democratization was successful, nonexistent, or partial. Where successful (as in Slovenia, Estonia, and Hungary), democratization helped ensure peace. Where nonexistent (as in Kazakstan and Turkmenistan), authoritarian governments imposed peace. Between these extremes, partial democratization conduced to war, as between Armenians and Azeris, and Abkhazians and Georgians. Thus, unresolved transitions were perilous.

Snyder's approach offered a helpful heuristic—a tool to drive and refine research. But his findings did not really challenge or even refine liberal peace theory. Partial democratization is surely not the same as "stable" democracy functioning for at least three years.

And Snyder erred in saying that authoritarian regimes were able to impose peace. The former Soviet republic of Tajikistan experienced a long and deadly civil war in the 1990s. Serbia was basically authoritarian under Milošević. He provoked war with Serbia's neighbors, with Kosovars, and finally with NATO.

Applying any of these theories to post-Soviet Russia is difficult because the country's status was unclear. If democratization has been only partial, the consequences can cut in opposite directions. President Boris Yeltsin sent Russian troops into Chechnya in 1994 hoping to rebuild his popularity by

17. In Grenada, U.S. forces organized new and free elections; in Panama, they installed a president already chosen in free elections.

18. For details, see Chalmers Johnson, *Blowback: The Costs and Consequences of American Empire* (New York: Henry Holt, 2000) and, from different perspectives, Michael Hardt and Antonio Negri, *Empire* (Cambridge, Mass.: Harvard University Press, 2000) and Andrew J. Bacevich, *American Empire: The Realities and Consequences of U.S. Diplomacy* (Cambridge, Mass.: Harvard University Press, 2002).

19. Edward D. Mansfield and Jack Snyder, "Democratization and the Danger of War," *International Security* 20, no. 1 (summer 1995): 5–38, reprinted in *Debating the Democratic Peace: An International Security Reader*, ed. Michael E. Brown et al. (Cambridge, Mass.: MIT Press, 1996), with related articles.

20. Jack Snyder, *From Voting to Violence: Democratization and Nationalist Conflict.* New York: W. W. Norton, 2000. See also Bear F. Braumoeller, "Deadly Doves: Liberal Nationalism and the Democratic Peace in the Soviet Successor States," *International Studies Quarterly* 3, no. 41 (September 1997): 375–402.

appealing to nationalist sentiment. But then partially democratized Russians objected to this campaign and pressed the Kremlin to end it.[21] In 1999 and 2000, however, these same partially democratized Russians voted for Vlaimir Putin as the strong fist to beat down the Chechens. One or two years later, most Russians were tired of this struggle but had few levers to influence their elected president. Thus, Snyder's analysis tends toward the tautology: "Successful democracy is where there is no ethnic conflict." The independent variable is the same as the dependent.

But elaborate explanations are not needed. The new states of the 1990s, such as Armenia and Croatia, were more authoritarian than democratic; they were not "stable." Even their independence was in doubt, because foreign influences (Russia's and Serbia's) were so strong. If, and when, they and their neighbors become stable, settled democracies, they may well find other ways to resolve their disputes.

Another challenge to liberal peace theory comes from a series of "near misses"—cases when democracies came close to war. Liberal peace theorists reply that most close calls took place in the 19th century between incipient democracies with limited suffrage. In the last decades of the 20th century there were near misses between Greece and Turkey, when democracy in one or both countries had been replaced or threatened by military rule.[22]

Democracy and market orientation, of course, are not the only factors that bear on war and peace. This book contends that the capacity to deal with ethnic and other problems can be more fully explained by the concept of social fitness, which subsumes but goes beyond democratization. Fitness, as discussed in Chapter 5, is the capacity to cope with complex challenges and opportunities. The best way to acquire such fitness is by self-organization—avoiding the extremes of rigid hierarchy (as in authoritarian Kazakstan) or social chaos (as in Georgia). Social development as well as social peace thrive on self-organization. History shows that societies based on self-rule are geared to mutual gain. Democratic societies have created the highest living standards in history. Authoritarian regimes usually seek power and/or wealth for their rulers. They are too rigid to respond to the challenges and opportunities of the computer age. They are a menace to themselves and others, as we see in North Korea and Iraq.

Why Don't Democracies Fight One Another?

Too Few to Fight. Some critics of liberal peace theory say that the sample is too small to form any empirical "law" of IR. The universe of democratic dyads able to fight one another has been small. Thus, most of the 270 states involved in interstate wars since 1815 were not democracies. There were few

21. Snyder observed: "Thus, Russia's fragile democratic institutions could be mobilized in crisis against imperial excesses, but they were less effective in scrutinizing nationalist mythmaking on a day-to-day basis." *From Voting*, 236–237.

22. For background, see Graham T. Allison and Kalypso Nicolaidis, eds., *The Greek Paradox: Promise vs. Performance* (Cambridge, Mass.: MIT Press, 1997).

democracies until the 20th century, and many are too remote to fight one another, for example, Chile and France. With few potential belligerents, it is not surprising that few democracies have fought each other. But statistics do not explain the existential transformation occurring since 1945: War has become virtually unthinkable between some countries that fought in past wars. Germany and France are still adjacent. So why is war now out of the question?

Common Interests. Democratic or not, the industrial powers of North America, Western Europe, and Japan shared many common interests that have motivated them to band together and not fight one another. All were exhausted by World War II. All feared nuclear war. All feared the USSR and Communist expansionism. All profited from trade. The U.S. hegemon maintained order within the First World.

But common interests and trade ties do not assure peace. They did not prevent Europeans from fighting each other in two world wars. Exhaustion and fear of nuclear weapons did not prevent a long cold war between the USSR and the West. Soviet hegemony did not prevent uprisings in Eastern Europe or border wars with China.

Kant's Synergy. It is difficult to prove why something has *not* happened. But there are good reasons to believe that democracy and peace reinforce each other. The inner logic between self-rule and peace was set out in Kant's essay "On Perpetual Peace" (1795–1796). Kant pointed to the combined impact of representative government, the federation of nations, international law, the spirit of trade, and the growth of a common, enlightened culture.[23]

The key to peace, Kant argued, is *representative* government (which Kant called a *republic* to distinguish it from the direct democracy convulsing revolutionized France after 1789). Kant gave six reasons. First, where "the consent of the citizenry is required . . . to determine whether there will be war, it is natural that they consider all its calamities before they enter so risky a game." By contrast, authoritarian rulers can simply declare war and leave it to diplomats to concoct justifications.

Second, Kant predicted that free, self-governing peoples will tend to form federations to preserve peace and their rights. If a powerful and enlightened people forms a representative government, "it will provide a focal point for a federal association among other nations that will join it in order to guarantee a state of peace among nations . . . and through several associations of this sort such a federation can extend further and further."

Third, since these representative governments will not accept any other government over them, they will have to accept an enlarged body of international law that will "finally include all the people of the earth." As community prevails among the earth's peoples, "a transgression in one place in the world is felt *everywhere* . . . [emphasis in original]."[24]

23. Text in Immanuel Kant, *Perpetual Peace and Other Essays* (Indianapolis: Hackett, 1983), 107–143.

24. On the Kantian tradition in international law, see David R. Mapel and Terry Nardin, "Convergence and Divergence in International Ethics," in *Traditions of International Ethics*, eds. Mapel and Nardin (Cambridge, U.K.: Cambridge University Press, 1992), p. 297–322. For a skeptical view, see Jens Bartelson, "The Trial of Judgment: A Note on Kant and the Paradoxes of Internationalism," *International Studies Quarterly* 39, no. 2 (June 1995): 255–279.

Fourth, representative government and law are linked with commerce. The "*spirit of trade* cannot coexist with war, and sooner or later this spirit dominates every people [emphasis in original]." Those with the most to lose economically will exert every effort to head off war by mediation.[25]

Fifth, common institutions should lead to mutual respect. Language and religion divide men, but "the growth of culture and men's gradual progress toward greater agreement regarding their [common] principles lead to mutual understanding and peace." The "right to visit, to associate [with other peoples], belongs to all men by virtue of their common ownership of the earth's surface. . . ." An alien has a right to hospitality; he should not be treated as an enemy upon his arrival in another's country so long as he behaves peaceably.

Sixth, as the number of representative governments expands, the bases for peace will become global and perpetual. There must be justice and peace *among* states for it to exist *within* a single state. Civil society cannot flourish in fear of external attack.[26] Kant urged governments to remember that if their policies attempt to do what is morally right, peace and other good results will follow. If each state behaves morally, the space between them can become an extension of the rational political community or "civil society" achieved within each state. The international arena then could be dominated not by amoral anarchy but by "pure practical reason and its righteousness."[27]

Kant also realized, however, that the system he outlined would be vulnerable to the wild streak in human nature that could tear down the rule of reason. He cautioned that "from the crooked timber of humanity no straight thing can ever be made." But he hoped that each individual, reaching upward like a tree for air and sun, would grow straight under the canopy of civil society.[28]

Why the Liberal Peace?

Institutional Limits on the Government's Power to Make War. Kant's first point is the least persuasive. "Peoples" sometimes rise to the idea of a good war. Public opinion and the public's representatives have done little to constrain presidents and prime ministers from using military force.

The Perception of Shared Norms. Kant's fifth point is his weightiest. Peoples that perceive one another as democratic have not fought each other. Indeed, they tend to band together against authoritarians. As Britain became more democratic in the late 19th century, tensions between London and Washington diminished. In the late 19th century, the U.S. and Britain committed themselves to third-party arbitration of disputes they could not resolve bilaterally. Instead of struggle between

25. Kant lived in Königsberg, once a thriving participant in the Hanseatic League of city-states on the Baltic Sea and the Atlantic shores of northern Europe. Subject in 1795 to the King of Prussia, Kant wrote when there were very few representative democracies in the world, but he may have been inspired by the spirit of the "Hansas." He was certainly familiar with British and French writings on democracy and many of the peace plans proposed by other authors.

26. See also the essays in *Kant: Political Writings*, 2d ed., ed. Hans Reiss (Cambridge: Cambridge University Press, 1991).

27. See also Lynch, "Kant, the Republican Peace, and Moral Guidance," 57.

28. See the fifth of Kant's nine theses in "Idea for a Universal History with a Cosmopolitan Intent" (1784), in *Perpetual Peace and Other Essays*, 15–39 at 33.

the imperial hegemon and the challenger, a "special relationship" developed between them.

Perceptions Are Crucial. France invaded Germany in 1923 to collect war reparations, but few Frenchmen thought of Germany then as democratic, though it had been for four years. Lacking mutual respect, Greece and Turkey have experienced many "close calls."

The Spirit of Trade. Kant did not treat commerce as a cure for war. He avoided the simplistic view of the "Manchester School"—economists who, in the 19th century, promised that "the free flow of goods across national boundaries" would erase misunderstandings and ensure peace. Unlike them, Kant insisted that peace depended upon a combination of factors—representative democracy, law, commerce, and mutual respect.

A Social Field. Taken together, Kant's six points read like a description of the European Union and, by extension, the "security community" that links Europe, Canada, the U.S., and Japan. Rummel says that all these factors interact to form a "social field"—an exchange society with a habit of problem solving by negotiation and accommodation.

If we broaden the concept of representative government to include not just democracy (self-rule by the many) but oligarchy (self-rule by the few), Kant's formula may also explain long periods of peace in premodern times, for example, among the Hanseatic city-states, the Swiss forest cantons, and the nations of the Iroquois confederation.[29] Hanseatic city-states such as Lübeck, Königsberg (where Kant later lived), and Riga were governed by town councils elected by leading merchants. Their towns took shape in the 12th and 13th centuries and flourished for 400 to 500 years. The German-speaking Hansas lived in peace with each other and prospered from trading along routes that extended from Novgorod to London and even to Lisbon. The Hansas' values were so similar that other Hanseatic towns simply copied the laws of leading city-states such as Lübeck. When challenged by Denmark, the Hansas put together a navy and replaced the Danish king. In the 17th century, however, the Hanseatic city-states were absorbed by expanding nation-states such as Prussia and Poland. Unlike the peaceful Hansas, these new states were ruled by kings who treated war as a royal sport and prerogative—a behavior that helped inspire Kant's treatise on peace.

DEMOCRATIC STATES ARE THE MOST PROSPEROUS IN HISTORY

29. Spencer R. Waert, *Never at War: Why Democracies Will Not Fight One Another* (New Haven, Conn.: Yale University Press, 1998).

Democratic societies have created for their members the highest living standards in history. They are geared to mutual gain and value-creation rather than toward exploitation, at least within their borders. The top twenty countries on the Human Development Index (HDI) for 2002 were all democracies.

Authoritarian regimes tend to be exploitative. They seek power and/or wealth for the rulers and the "state" rather than the common people. Most Communist dictators lived in luxury while their subjects scraped by and often starved. Exploitation of the many by the few benefited the regime for a while, but boomeranged in the long run. The authoritarian USSR achieved the world's second largest economy, but it focused on steel and cement—not consumer goods. The USSR was more fit for war than for peace. Its longtime core, Russia, placed 60th in HDI rankings for 2000.

The highest-placed authoritarian country in HDI rankings for 2002 was Singapore—number 25. Of former Communist countries, now democratic Slovenia and the Czech Republic scored highest at 29 and 33, respectively. The highest-ranking Muslim countries were the authoritarian oil producers Brunei and Bahrain at 32 and 39; China ranked 96th; oil-rich Indonesia, 110; and Egypt, 115.

Basically democratic Sri Lanka and India, however, placed 89th and 124th, while authoritarian Pakistan ranked even lower—at 138. Thus, neither democratic nor authoritarian rule assures a good life. More is needed—overall fitness, discussed in Chapter 5 and examined in more detail in Chapters 11 and 12.

THE COSTS OF AUTHORITARIAN RULE

The ultimate reason to reject authoritarian rule is that it endangers life. Many authoritarian governments have practiced democide—mass murder of people (*demos*)—at home and abroad. Democide includes genocide (destruction of a particular people) and other forms of mass murder. It also includes politicide—the extermination of political foes.[30] As used here, it excludes casualties of war.

From 1900 to the late 1980s, governments probably murdered about 170 million people, of which some 107 million were killed by Communist regimes. The megamurderers were the USSR (62 million), Communist China (35 million—perhaps more), Nazi Germany (21 million), and nationalist China in 1928–1949 (10 million). By comparison, total military and civilian deaths from all international and internal wars of the 20th century numbered from 40 to 191 million.

The most lethal regime (defined by the percentage of its own people killed in a short time) was Cambodia under the Khmer Rouge

30. The following analysis and statistics are from Rudolph J. Rummel, *Death by Government* (New Brunswick, N.J.: Transaction, 1996), and Rummel, *Power Kills*. Rummel's estimates of democide usually take a middle ground between others' high and low estimates. Russian, Kazak, and Chinese scholars have produced much higher estimates than Rummel for some events in their countries.

Ordinary people can be mobilized to carry out genocide. This happened in Rwanda in April 1994 when a small group of Hutu political and military leaders ignited 100 days of massacres that killed half a million Tutsis, mostly by machetes, along with thousands of Hutu political rivals and ten Belgian peacekeepers. Tutsis made up about 10 percent of Rwanda's population and were widely resented by Hutus, because the Belgian colonial administration (terminated in 1962) had given Tutsis many favors. The photo shows victims' skulls on display in the Ntarama Genocide Memorial, located in a church seventeen miles from Kigali, where even those who sought refuge were massacred. Like other genocidists, mobilizers of the Rwanda's massacres dehumanized their victims and met little opposition from outside the country. Belgium and the U.S. weakly protested early massacres, while France backed the Hutu regime before and after the genocide. The UN Security Council, influenced by Washington, refused requests from the commander of the UN peacekeeping mission in Rwanda for reinforcements and a stronger mandate. The Clinton administration feared another debacle like that it suffered in Somalia the year before. Later, the UN Security Council set up an international criminal tribunal to prosecute those accused of genocide and crimes against humanity in Rwanda in 1994. In the early 21st century, the judges struggled with huge case loads and limited resources.

(1975–1979). Croatia under Ustashi (Fascist) rule in World War II and Mexico in 1900–1920 also ranked among the most lethal regimes of the century.

Individual leaders were crucial. The century's bloodiest are listed in Table 10.2.

How could a regime do such things? Table 10.3 breaks down Soviet democide beginning in 1917. Nearly 62 million people died, some 55 million of these Soviet citizens—killed on orders of the "dictatorship of

Table 10.2 Leading Democidists of the 20th Century

Leader	Ideology	Country	Democidal Years	Millions Murdered
Stalin	Communist	USSR	1929–1953	43.0
Mao Zedong	Communist	China	1923–1976	38.0
Hitler	Fascist	Germany	1933–1945	21.0
Chiang Kai-shek	Militarist–fascist	China	1921–1948	10.0
Lenin	Communist	USSR	1917–1924	4.0
Tojo Hideki	Militarist–fascist	Japan	1941–1945	4.0
Pol Pot	Militarist	Cambodia	1968–1987	2.4
Yahya Khan	Militarist	Pakistan	1971	1.5

SOURCE: Adapted from Rudolph J. Rummel, *Death by Government* (New Brunswick, N.J.: Transaction, 1996), 8.

Mr. Bush Explains to the Chinese Why Certain Nations Are on the Axis-of-Evil List

President Bush assigned only Iran, Iraq, and North Korea to the "axis of evil," but the Communist dictatorship in China also met some of the relevant criteria. For nine months in 2001 Bush treated China as a potential rival rather than as a possible strategic partner. After 9/11, however, Bush sought to collaborate with China against terrorism. The White House then said little about human rights in China. Critics observed that the Bush administration also came to power without a popular mandate and menaced other states, even threatening the use of nuclear arms. Did it belong on the same axis?

the proletariat" seated in the Kremlin. Lenin began these policies; Stalin and his aides continued them. In Rudolph Rummel's words, the persons killed were "not combatants in civil war or rebellions and they were not criminals. Indeed, nearly all were guilty of . . . nothing." They were from the wrong class or nation or race or political faction, or relatives of the above. Some were conquered, like Balts; some were believers in God; some were potential oppositionists, for example, teachers or

Table 10.3 Soviet Democide Compared to Battle Deaths

Period	Years	Democide	Battle Deaths
Civil War	1917–1921	3,284,000	1,410,000
New Economic Policy (NEP)	1921–1928	2,200,000	n.a.
Collectivization	1929–1935	11,440,000	200
Great Terror	1936–1938	4,345,000	1,200
Pre–World War II	1939–1941	5,104,000	256,000
World War II	1941–1945	13,053,000	19,625,000
Post–World War II	1946–1953	15,613,000	90,000
Post-Stalin	1954–1991	6,872,000	22,000
TOTAL	74 years	61,911,000	21,404,400

SOURCE: Adapted from Rudolph J. Rummel, *Lethal Politics: Soviet Genocide and Mass Murder Since 1917* (New Brunswick, N.J.: Transaction, 1996), 6.
NOTE: n.a. = not available.

even Communist leaders. Many were killed just to fill a quota. Very high percentages of those killed were Ukrainians and Kazaks—starved in the 1930s and after World War II.[31] One-third of all Chechens perished when Stalin ordered that they be moved during World War II.

The biggest single mass murder took place during China's Great Leap Forward (1958–1962), when 30 to 40 million Chinese starved to death. Mao Zedong refused to admit that his economic experiment could be so disastrous. He kept himself and his "People's Liberation Army" well nourished but did nothing to relieve mass famine.[32]

Many dictatorships have presided over democide by famine—in the USSR, China, Ethiopia, and elsewhere. But democracy has nearly eliminated famine. Famine in the 20th century was usually a consequence of poor distribution, not an absolute shortage of food. Food was available—usually within the country—but only at a price that the poor could not pay. Democratic governments develop contingency plans to cope with food shortages or simply pay whatever is required to purchase food at market prices. Indians experienced many famines under imperial British rule but rarely under self-rule.[33]

Given this kind of brutality, what can be said in support of authoritarian rule? It has produced democide on every continent—including the Americas, where Mexico had one of the most lethal regimes of the century. The death toll in Latin America was not so high on a global scale, but the dictators and military juntas of numerous Latin American countries also produced democide, sometimes, as in Guatemala, under the watchful eyes of U.S. agents. The best that can be said for the Latin American and Iberian dictators is that they generally stayed at home, killing their own people but few foreigners.

Democracies have also committed mass murder—of Native Americans, Australian aborigines, New Zealand Maoris, and the Irish. All the imperialist countries committed democide as they expanded into Siberia, Africa, Asia, and the Americas. Most of these events took place before the 20th century, directed against persons viewed as alien—a situation quite different from Cambodia, where Communist dictators killed one-third of their own citizens. The U.S., Canadian, Australian, and New Zealand governments have taken some steps toward restitution. John Donne wrote: "Any man's death diminishes me." Who is not diminished by the murder of 170 millions (more than the entire population of today's Russia)? An International Criminal Court that could deal with crimes against humanity was approved by most UN members in 1998, but the U.S. voted "nay," as we shall see in Chapter 16.

31. Rummel, *Lethal Politics.* Similar estimates result from a study of Soviet archives by Alexander N. Yakovlev, *A Century of Violence in Soviet Russia* (New Haven, Conn.: Yale University Press, 2002).

32. Jasper Becker, *Hungry Ghosts: Mao's Secret Famine* (New York: Free Press, 1996); Dali L. Yang, *Calamity and Reform in China: State, Rural Society, and Institutional Change Since the Great Leap Famine* (Stanford, Calif.: Stanford University Press, 1996); Tu Wei-ming, "Destructive Will and Ideological Holocaust: Maoism as a Source of Social Suffering in China," *Daedalus* 125, no. 1 (winter 1996): 149 ff.; and Arthur Waldron, "'Eat People'—A Chinese Reckoning (History of Cannibalism in Communist Chinese History)," *Commentary* 104, no. 1 (July 1997): 28 ff.

33. Jean Dreze et al., *The Political Economy of Hunger: Selected Essays* (New York: Oxford University Press, 1995); Amartya Sen, "Food and Freedom," *World Development* 17, no. 6 (June 1989): 769 ff.; Frances D'Souza, "Democracy as a Cure for Famine," *Journal of Peace Research* 31, no. 4 (November 1994): 369 ff.; David Hardiman, "Usury, Dearth, and Famine in Western India," *Past & Present,* no. 152 (August 1996): 113 ff. and Sugata Bose, "Starvation Amidst Plenty: The Making of Famine in Bengal, Honan and Tonkin, 1942–1945," *Modern Asian Studies* 24, no. 4 (October 1990): 699 ff.

DEMOCRACY IS SPREADING

Democracy has replaced authoritarianism across much of the planet. Democracy is becoming the global rule rather than the exception. A majority of the world's inhabitants expect to vote for political leaders in free and fair elections.

The number of democratic states has increased in what Samuel P. Huntington portrays as three large waves, interrupted by two *reverse waves* in which authoritarian regimes displaced democratic. A third riptide tugged at the democratic shoreline in the 1990s:[34]

Long wave of democratization (1828–1926)—led by the U.S. and Great Britain, this wave culminated in new states after World War I such as Czechoslovakia and Estonia.

Short reverse wave (1922–1942)—led by Italy, Japan, and Germany.

Short wave of democratization (1943–1962)—led by Italy, Japan, West Germany, Greece, Turkey, India, and Israel.

Short reverse wave (1958–1975)—led by Peru, Brazil, Argentina, Pakistan, Indonesia, and India (under emergency rule 1975–1977).

Third wave of democratization (1974–)—led by Portugal, Spain, Ecuador, Peru, Brazil, India, Cape Verde, Taiwan, Namibia, followed after 1989 by the Czech Republic, Estonia, Slovenia, and other formerly Communist states.

Reverse wave (1990–)—involved Sudan, Suriname, Serbia, and many ex-Soviet republics such as Belarus, Turkmenistan, and Tajikistan.

The Polity IV project at the University of Maryland and annual surveys by Freedom House, a nonprofit foundation in New York, pointed to trends similar to those highlighted by Huntington. The Polity IV project identifies not only democracies and autocracies (similar to what this book calls "authoritarian" regimes) but also transitional polities moving toward or away from self-rule, which it terms "anocracies." Their growth is traced in Figure 10.1. It shows that Huntington's third wave continued and picked up momentum after the mid-1980s so that eighty-three states were democracies by 2002; autocracies fell to twenty-eight by that year, while anocracies plateaued—leaving forty-seven in 2002.

While the global trend toward democratization was clear, there was great diversity within and between regions:

• *Europe:* The democratic line jumped up in the mid-1970s, when Portugal and Spain threw off autocracy. The line rose sharply in the late 1980s and early 1990s, when autocracy gave way to democracy in much of Eastern Europe and Russia.

34. Samuel P. Huntington, *The Third Wave: Democratization in the Late Twentieth Century* (Norman: University of Oklahoma Press, 1991).

Fig. 10.1 Global Regimes by Type, 1946–2001

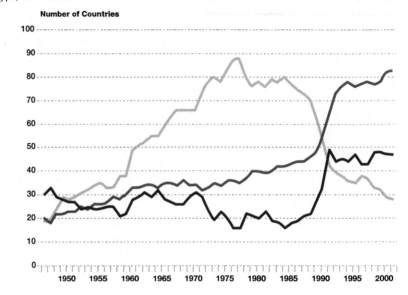

- *South and Central America:* The democratic line began to rise in the late 1970s and continued in the 1980s, when it leveled off. By 2002 the Americas had only one clear autocracy, Castro's Cuba, and one anocracy, Haiti.

- *Asia and Sub-Saharan Africa:* The number of democracies rose in the late 1980s and early 1990s—coincident with the collapse of Soviet communism and South African apartheid.

- *Middle East:* By 2002 this was the world's least democratic region, where there were three times as many autocracies as democracies. The number of transitional polities such as Jordan, however, was rising.

Freedom House analyzes not just "democracy" but also political and civic liberties. Its yearly surveys rank each country's liberties from 1 to 7, based on answers to two sets of questions (see Table 10.1). In 2003 Freedom House found 89 countries that were basically "free," along with 55 "partly free" (similar in some ways to Polity IV "anocracies"). Another 48 were judged "not free" (similar to Polity IV "autocracies"). All "free" and most of the "partly free" societies were electoral democracies—a total of 121 in 2003. The global pattern is depicted in Map 10.1.

The number and percentage of "free" people increased, as shown in Table 10.4. In 2003, "free" countries contained 2.7 billion people—44 percent of the world's population; "partly free," 1.3 billion people—21 percent; "not free," 2.2 billion people—35 percent. The 48 "not free"

Table 10.4 Number and Percentage of People Living in Free, Partly Free, and Not Free Countries (population in billions)

Year	Free	Partly Free	Not Free	World Population
1973	1.3 (35.05%)	.7 (17.65%)	1.8 (47.30%)	3.8
1983	1.7 (36.32%)	.9 (20.04%)	2.0 (43.64%)	4.6
1993	1.4 (24.83%)	2.4 (44.11%)	1.7 (31.06%)	5.4
1994	1.0 (19.00%)	2.2 (40.41%)	2.2 (40.59%)	5.5
1995	1.1 (19.97%)	2.2 (40.01%)	2.2 (40.02%)	5.6
1996	1.1 (19.55%)	2.4 (41.49%)	2.2 (38.96%)	5.7
1997	1.3 (21.67%)	2.3 (39.16%)	2.3 (39.17%)	5.8
1998	1.3 (21.71%)	2.3 (39.12%)	2.3 (39.17%)	5.8
1999	2.4 (39.84%)	1.6 (26.59%)	2.0 (33.58%)	5.9
2000	2.3 (38.90%)	1.5 (25.58%)	2.1 (35.51%)	6.0
2001	2.5 (40.69%)	1.4 (23.70%)	2.2 (35.61%)	6.1
2002	2.5 (40.79%)	1.5 (23.86%)	2.2 (35.35%)	6.1
2003	2.7 (43.85%)	1.1 (20.87%)	2.2 (35.28%)	6.2

SOURCE: www.freedomhouse.org

countries in 2002 included Burma, Cuba, North Korea, some African dictatorships, and 27 predominantly Muslim countries (including Libya, Saudi Arabia, Syria, and Sudan). The territories of Tibet and Chechnya got the lowest grades possible for political and civil liberties.

Seismic political events lay beneath these numbers. Large numbers of East Europeans moved from "not free" to "partly free" in 1989–1992. Balts, Ukrainians, and Russians made the same move in the early 1990s after the dissolution of the USSR. But electoral and ethnic violence pushed India from the "free" to the "partly free" column in 1991–1992. In the 1990s the three Baltic republics and several East European countries became "free," but the large shift in 1998–1999 was due to India's change back from "party free" to "free." China, home to more than a billion people, remained "not free." But in 2002 four countries joined the ranks of the free: Brazil, Serbia, Lesotho, and Senegal. Bahrain and Kenya moved from not free to partly free.

CAN THE THIRD WAVE HOLD? CAN IT EXTEND FURTHER?

War made the state and the state made war. Government enriched the ruling class. How then did it happen that the privileged few shared power

Map 10.1 Freedom in the World

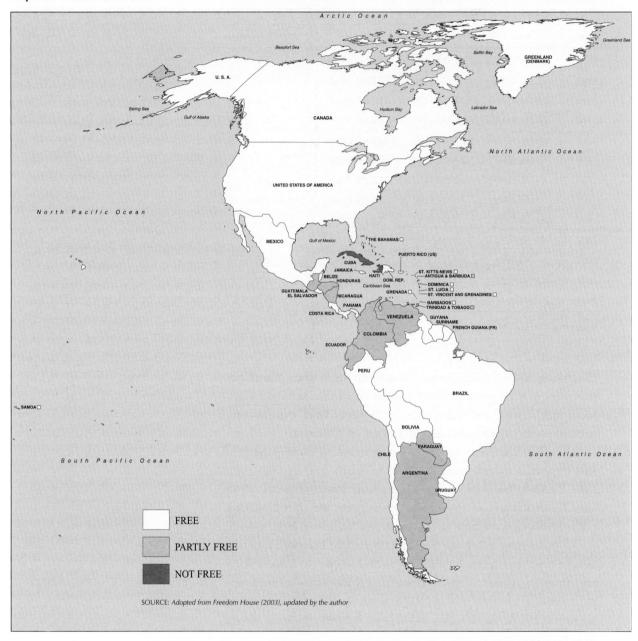

FREE

PARTLY FREE

NOT FREE

SOURCE: *Adopted from Freedom House (2003), updated by the author*

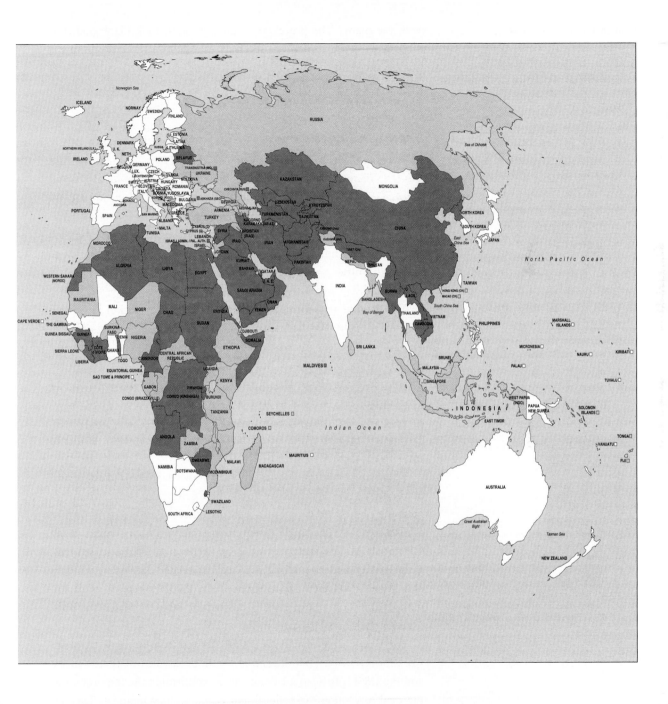

with the many? The process of democratization took place gradually, with many detours and even reversals. It rested on three conditions: a democratic political culture, an institutionalized market economy, and independence from foreign coercion. Can these conditions be maintained where they exist? Can they be fostered worldwide?

Three Prerequisites of Democracy

Political Culture of Mutual Gain and Mutual Respect. In Europe and the U.S., democracy originated in a view that each individual is equal before God and humanity. Democrats distrusted authority and hierarchy. Their ideas drew strength from religious reformers who argued that every individual could and should read and interpret Holy Scripture for her or himself. Individualism grew in tandem with a print revolution as Bibles and other works were published in tongues commoners could understand.[35]

The Protestant Reformation unleashed a dual revolution in literacy and free thought. For the first time in Christian history, leading religious and political leaders argued that all people should read God's Word and interpret it for themselves.[36] But when German peasants rose up against their lords in the 1520s, Martin Luther tried to retract freedoms he had proclaimed. Too late, for he had opened a Pandora's box. The tides of literacy and freethinking ebbed and flowed, but gradually swept over Europe and into North America. The Reformation became the mother of modern democracy.[37]

This twin revolution boosted the West above the rest—materially and culturally. As the 21st century began, nineteen of the twenty countries with the highest HDI rankings were in Western Europe or in former British colonies. The single exception was Japan, which adapted many but not all Western ways. All of the top twenty in HDI also scored relatively well in gender equality (GDI—gender-related development index) and honesty (business "transparency"). With the exception of Japan, with its Shinto–Buddhist heritage, all had the Bible translated and published in their own languages by the end of the 16th century.

The West's achievements, of course, derived from multiple factors at work for centuries.[38] But the end of Communist rule in Eastern Europe and the USSR provided a laboratory test confirming the importance of the dual revolution for political and economic development. The evidence is presented in Table 10.5 and Figure 10.2. The table ranks the former Communist states by HDI and other values. The figure shows the

35. The first Bible was published in 1455—in Latin. But soon the scriptures became "user friendly." Between 1466 and 1526, the Bible (or much of it) was printed in German, Italian, French, and English. More Europeans began to read—and think—for themselves.

36. Long before Christ, Jews valued the Book and trained boys and sometimes girls to read and discuss it. Jews' dedication to literacy and free thought helped them to survive recurrent persecutions and, in the 20th century, make the desert bloom in Israel.

37. Benson Bobrick, *Wide as the Waters: The Story of the English Bible and the Revolution It Inspired* (New York: Simon & Schuster, 2001), 268.

38. These factors included a moderate climate; scientific and industrial skills; an acquired immunity to diseases that wiped out others, such as Native Americans; plus imperial momentum. See Jared Diamond, *Guns, Germs, and Steel: The Fates of Human Societies* (New York: W. W. Norton, 1997).

Table 10.5 Former Communist Countries Ranked by HDI and Other Values

Country	HDI Rank	GDI Rank	Freedom Index	Economic Freedom	Honesty Rank
Slovenia	29	27	Free	79 (MU)	27
Czech Republic	33	32	Free	32 (MF)	52
Hungary	35	35	Free	32 (MF)	33
Slovakia	36	34	Free	60 (MF)	52
Poland	37	36	Free	45 (MF)	45
Estonia	42	n.a.	Free	4 (F)	29
Croatia	48	43	Free	108 (MU)	51
Lithuania	49	42	Free	29 (MF)	36
Latvia	53	46	Free	38 (MF)	52
Belarus	56	50	Not free	148 (RE)	n.a.
Russian Federation	60	52	Partly free	131 (MU)	71
Bulgaria	62	53	Free	108 (MU)	45
Romania	63	55	Free	131 (MU)	77
Macedonia	65	n.a.	Partly free	97 (MU)	n.a.
Armenia	76	62	Partly free	45 (MF)	n.a.
Kazakstan	79	n.a.	Not free	125 (MU)	88
Ukraine	80	66	Partly free	137 (MU)	85
Georgia	81	n.a.	Partly free	108 (MU)	85
Azerbaijan	88	n.a.	Partly free	118 (MU)	95
Moldova	105	86	Partly free	105 (MU)	93

CODE: Economic freedom: f = free; MF = mostly free; MU = mostly unfree; RE = repressed.
SOURCES: For "HDI" and "GDI," see United Nations Development Programme [2002]; for Freedom Index, see Freedom House, 2001; for Economic Freedom, see Heritage Foundation, 2002; for Honesty, see Corruption Perceptions Index, Transparency International, 2002.

correlation between HDI and the date each society had the Bible published in the vernacular. What we see is that the highest-ranked countries in HDI and freedom, such as the Czech Republic and Slovenia, had the Bible in their own language in the 15th or 16th centuries. They belonged to Western Christianity. Catholic France and Italy at first resisted the dual revolution, but were swept along by it. The lowest-ranked countries in HDI and freedom in Figure 10.2 did not have the Bible in their vernacular until the 19th or even the 20th century. Most did not achieve mass literacy until after World War II. The Orthodox Church did not welcome Bibles in

Fig. 10.2 Date the Bible Published in the Vernacular vs. HDI Rank of Ex-Communist Countries in 2002

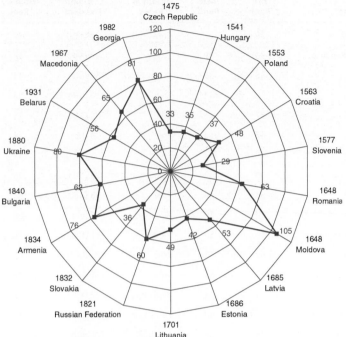

The dual revolution began early for Czechs and Hungarians but started much later in Orthodox countries such as Macedonia and Georgia. The Bible was published in Czech in 1475 but not in modern Georgia until 1982. The Czech Republic placed 33rd on the HDI in 2002; Georgia placed 81st.

SOURCES: United Bible Societies, September 3, 2002.
http://www.worldscriptures.org/index2.html.
United Nations Development Programme, *Human Development Report 2002* (New York: Oxford University Press, 2002).

the vernacular and was ambivalent about mass literacy.[39] The Communists who displaced Orthodox kings and tsars promoted mass literacy but opposed free thought. They imposed a new orthodoxy—the party line.

Most major religions—or sects thereof—have at times buttressed intolerant, authoritarian political systems. In societies where there is only one acceptable religious belief, there is usually but one correct political line. But cultures change. Many Protestant societies were intolerant theocracies but evolved into tolerant democracies. The Catholic countries of Iberia and Latin America seemed for centuries to be bulwarks of authoritarianism, but most democratized in the last quarter of the 20th century.

There are many kinds of democratic political cultures. The U.S. was settled by dissenters—the "Protestants of Protestantism." U.S. democracy originated in individual self-reliance and fear of big government—unlike Canada and some European democracies, where people rely more heavily on government. Yet all are democracies. Even more variation exists in non-Western societies.

39. The sole exception was Romania, which published both the New and Old Testaments in the 17th century. What is now Romania had closer ties to the West than most Orthodox countries, but soon was absorbed into the Ottoman Empire.

An Iraqi uses his bloody thumbprint to mark the "yes" box as he casts his ballot in the October 2002 referendum to reelect President Saddam Hussein to another term. When U.S.–UK forces first entered Iraq in 2003, they received a cool reception. Three weeks later, when Hussein's regime had collapsed, many Iraqis welcomed Americans and Brits as liberators and tore down statues and pictures of their once feared dictator. Having won the war, the U.S.-led "coalition" faced the even more complex challenges of building peace. For a cautionary note, see Douglas Porch, "Occupational Hazards: Myths of 1945 and U.S. Iraq Policy," *National Interest* 72 (summer 2003): 35–47.

Before World War II it seemed that Confucian societies defied democratization. In the late 20th century, however, Japan, South Korea, and Taiwan moved toward democracy. China's Communists keep power by totalitarian controls, not by Confucianism, which Mao Zedong tried to obliterate. There are ardent democrats in Hindu India; in Buddhist Burma, Cambodia, Sri Lanka, and Thailand; and in multiethnic, multifaith South Africa.

The biggest question is Islam. The traditionally Muslim regions of the former USSR are not shown on Figure 10.2. But their HDI and freedom scores are much lower even than traditionally Orthodox Belarus and Russia. They came to mass literacy even later and received almost no official support for independent thinking.

No state with a Muslim majority was ranked as "free" by Freedom House. About a dozen were "partly free"—Bangladesh, Albania, Jordan, Kyrgyzstan, Malaysia, Pakistan, Turkey, Bosnia, and a few more. The others—more than two dozen—were "not free." Not just Iraq (in 2002), but two U.S. "partners," Egypt and Saudi Arabia, were among the least free. Was it an accident that they gave birth to the "9/11" killers?

As the 21st century began, most Muslims lived under authoritarian regimes. Most were poor. Comparatively few were literate. Fewer still had been taught to question and debate dogma. Unlike Jews or modern Christians, few if any Islamic societies encouraged mass literacy and individual interpretation of sacred texts. In religious schools, memorization and recitation of the *Quran* is far more important than discussion. For non-Arabs there is an additional problem: Unlike the Christian Bible, the language in which the *Quran* was first written is regarded by Muslims as sacred—the only truly accurate way to express God's message. Educated Egyptians and Saudis can read the classical Arabic in which the *Quran* was written. But few Bosnians, Azeris, or Central Asians can read classical Arabic.[40] For the Muslims of many countries, the *Quran* was rendered in their languages mainly in the form of paraphrase and commentary. Bosnians, however, got a complete version in 1875, translated into Serbo-Croat.[41]

Turkey is the only Islamic country to have experienced long intervals of relatively stable democracy, but even Turkey, for decades, repressed the language as well as the culture of its Kurdish minority. Pakistan has been democratic but only for brief intervals between periods of authoritarian rule. Even when signing the UN conventions on human rights, Libya and Iraq added a qualifier: "Islamic law" takes precedence over treaty law.

But Islam is not intrinsically opposed to democracy. The Sufi sect has celebrated individual freedom for many centuries. Chechen intellectuals in 1997 told a seminar audience at Harvard University about freedom as a value shared by Chechens and Westerners. **Mohammad Khatami**, a senior cleric elected president of Iran in 1997, praised the West for upholding the "idea of 'liberty' or 'freedom,' the most cherished values of all mankind." He noted that the West has cast aside the "regressive thinking that had been imposed on the masses in the name of religion," and "broken down subjugation to autocratic rule." He warned against dogmatic Muslims who would trample religious and intellectual freedom. "If we step on freedom, we will have caused a great catastrophe." Many of Khatami's backers were women and young people, who, at age fifteen, could vote. A public opinion survey in 2002 showed that two-thirds of Iranians favored talks with the United States. In reply, hard-liners charged that the poll was fabricated; shut down the polling institute and another, similar organization; accused the directors of each institute of espionage; and locked them in solitary confinement.[42]

Outlooks and conditions evolve. At the time of the Crusades, the Islamic world was more enlightened and tolerant than Christian Europe. In 2002, however, a team of Arab scholars concluded that the steps toward liberalization taken in some Arab countries had been highly regulated and not open to all citizens. Women held only 3.5 percent of seats in parliaments of Arab countries—a much lower percentage than in most developing regions. Transfer of power through

40. An Azeri engineer in Moscow showed me his family's *Quran*, which, he explained, none of them could read, because it was in Arabic.

41. Translations into Malay were so bad, says professor Merlin Swartz, Boston University Department of Religion (2002) that one would almost have needed to know Arabic to understand them.

42. The deputy speaker of the Iranian parliament said he favored talks with Americans but cautioned that U.S. pressure hurt reformers. Nazila Fathi, "Iranian Lawmaker Opens Door to American Talks," *The New York Times*, December 16, 2002.

Women as well as men in the U.S. armed forces risked their lives to protect or liberate Middle Eastern dictatorships rich in oil but dominated by beliefs about women and women's rights very different from those prevailing in the West. An African-American woman was one of the first POWs taken by Iraq in 2003.

the ballot box was "not a common phenomenon in the Arab world." When faced with dissent, Arab governments often mobilized street demonstrations or proclaimed a state of emergency to suspend the constitution. On a more positive note, civil associations were revived in recent years in some Arab countries, but they were often hemmed in by bureaucratic constraints.[43]

Markets and Middle Class. Democracy thrives on middle-class prosperity that can be achieved only by a market economy. Neither guarantees the other, but each nurtures the other. Some authoritarian regimes have initiated economic growth; none but Singapore has generated high levels of consumer abundance.[44]

"Liberty through the market; no liberty without."[45] Capitalism creates an opportunity for civil society—a social space in which individuals, groups, and institutions can develop, free of state control. Without this freedom, innovation is less likely in economics, science, culture, or politics.

Socialist systems, even the most humane, tend toward authoritarian control. Socialism makes affluence less likely because it inhibits freedom in all spheres. Authoritarian regimes tend to horde resources and production for their own use. They choke private enterprise by making property rights and contracts hinge on the whims of autocrats.[46]

Transitions to democracy are most likely in countries emerging from poverty to middle levels of economic development. In the 1980s, this

43. UN Development Programme, *Arab Human Development Report 2002* (New York: UNDP Regional Bureau of Arab States, 2002), 108–109.

44. See Peter L. Berger, "The Uncertain Triumph of Democratic Capitalism," in *Capitalism, Socialism, and Democracy Revisited*, eds. Diamond and Plattner, 1–10, and other essays in this collection.

45. The quote is from Friedrich A. Hayek in 1944. For this and related references, see Raymond M. Duch, "Tolerating Market Reform: Popular Support for Transition to a Free Market in the Former Soviet Union," *American Political Science Review* 87, no. 3 (September 1993): 590–608 at 594.

46. Mancur Olson, "Dictatorship, Democracy, and Development," *American Political Science Review* 87, no. 3 (September 1993): 567–576.

meant per capita incomes of $4,000 to $6,000 per year, distributed so as to have a large middle class. The class must feel that its earnings are safe from inflation or confiscation. Individuals and families must see opportunity for social and economic advancement.

Democracy is both a cause and effect of prosperity.[47] As in 19th-century Germany and Japan, the economic takeoff of South Korea, Taiwan, and Singapore in the 1960s took place under authoritarian capitalism.[48] In the 1980s, however, both South Korea and Taiwan moved from authoritarianism toward democracy. The authoritarian state fostered a large middle class and was then transformed by it. The growing middle class demanded a voice. Low-level prosperity and rapid economic growth may be possible without democracy, but not middle- or high-income prosperity. The collapse of many Asian economies in 1997 was blamed on authoritarian cronyism. Beijing's rulers hoped that China would follow the Singaporean route and not be diverted down the Taiwan–South Korean road.

Independence. Self-rule is impossible while a society labors under foreign oppression. Americans could not be self-ruling when ruled by English laws and Redcoats. Nor could East Europeans while they lived in the shadow of Moscow's Red Army. Bulgarians looked at Moscow and remembered the watchwords acquired during centuries under Ottoman rule: "Bend your neck"—in effect, "Don't raise your head, lest someone cut it off." Many East Europeans wanted self-rule, but none threw off Communist hegemony until the meltdown of Soviet power in 1989–1991. With independence achieved, however, most East Europeans found it hard to exorcise the authoritarian strains buried in their political cultures. The good news was that most governments were formally independent at the end of the 20th century. For most, there was no external force compelling them to accept one or another form of government.

The Next Reverse Wave—How Strong?

Disgust with Politics as Usual. The democratic system does not promise successful government, but only a way to change governments peacefully if the public wants a change. If democratically elected governments perform poorly, malcontents may demand an iron fist.

In the early 1990s, demagogic leaders appeared on every continent—Ross Perot in the U.S., Alberto Fujimori in Peru, Vladimir Zhirinovsky in Russia, **Silvio Berlusconi** in Italy. Europe's authoritarians and racists gathered steam from unemployment and fears that political

47. Kyung-won Kim, "Marx, Schumpeter, and the East Asian Experience," in *Capitalism, Socialism, and Democracy Revisited*, eds. Diamond and Plattner, 11–25.

48. But the economic success of Asia's "Little Dragons" did not hinge on their authoritarian regimes. Rather, each followed an export-oriented trade strategy and benefited from high literacy and the Japanese model. See Jagdish Bhagwati, "Democracy and Development," in *Capitalism, Socialism, and Democracy Revisited*, eds. Diamond and Plattner, 31–38 at 35–37.

refugees and "guest workers" drained resources and took jobs from locals. "Skinheads" attacked foreigners. In 1995–1997, however, many authoritarians were bypassed or repudiated—including Perot, Fujimori, Zhirinovsky, and Berlusconi. In Russia, however, former KGB operative Vladimir Putin became president in 2000. Berlusconi bounced back in 2001 and again became Italy's prime minister. Prospects for democracy in Burma, Cambodia, and many African countries continued to look grim. Pakistan was again ruled by a general. As for India, the Hindu nationalist Bharatiya Janata Party won a clear parliamentary majority in 1999 and held it, despite, or because of, Hindu–Muslim communal bloodshed.

Can Free Markets Destroy Democracy? A more insidious threat to democracy may be posed by the market itself and the power of mass media technology.[49] What if the forces that control the media in effect brainwash humanity? In that case, a reverse wave would start not in fledgling democracies such as the Kyrgyz republic but where markets and modern media are already strong, as in Italy, where Berlusconi's personal media empire included three TV networks.

Democracies value the individual; markets treat individuals as tools to make money. Democracies value equality; markets foster inequality. Democracies depend on compromise; markets encourage competition. Democracies need a stable, settled electorate; markets and modern technology promote a nomadic lifestyle. Democracies require majority rule with respect for minorities; markets reward self-seeking. Markets and modern technology praise the ephemeral—today's fashion, the price differential, sensation. Today's market economy requires big money for election campaigns. Television means sound bites and expensive advertising, paid for by lobbies seeking favors. Market elites may win out over democratic elites. Religious fanatics may get the most votes.

If market masters also commandeer cloning, the vision of **Aldous Huxley**, depicted in *Brave New World*, may be near.[50] Optimists hope that technology will liberate humans. Pessimists fear the opposite. They worry about the response to 9/11 in Washington, where Defense Secretary Donald Rumsfeld installed a sort of information tsar in the Pentagon, retired Admiral John Poindexter, a self-confessed perjurer during the Reagan years, whose task was to collect and collate every bit of information about everyone—from medical records to e-mail transcripts to credit card bills. A sign, "Knowledge Is Power" (in Latin) hung behind Poindexter's desk. Rumsfeld also wanted to guide "information operations" to shape what other peoples thought of the U.S.—not just

49. Jacques Attali, "The Crash of Western Civilization: The Limits of the Market and Democracy," *Foreign Policy* 107 (summer 1997): 54–64; see also Claude Moisy, "Myths of the Global Information Village," ibid., 78–87.

50. Published in 1932, before full-fledged Stalinism or Nazism, *Brave New World* depicts a hellish dystopia in the 25th century.

Saved by the Web

In late 1996, Serbians in Belgrade staged antigovernment demonstrations to protest President Slobodan Milošević's annulment of municipal elections won by his opposition. Milošević attempted to thwart the protests by forcing Radio B-92—the main independent source of Serbian news—off the air, leaving government-controlled media a clear path to influencing the public in his favor.

But the path was not so clear. Students, professors, journalists, and others simply connected to Radio B-92's World Wide Web site, where they could listen to the station's digital broadcasts in Serbo-Croat and English over audio Internet links. Government officials in Europe, humanitarian agencies, journalists, and supporters continued to receive reports of the protests and, then of the station closure. With their help, an international Internet campaign pressured Milošević to relent, and Radio B-92 was back on the air just two days after it had been shut down. In addition, the government eased its reactions to the protests and indicated a possible reconsideration of the election annulment.

SOURCE: Chris Hedges, "Serbs' Answer to Tyranny? Get on the Web," *The New York Times*, December 8, 1996, 1, 20.

Iraqis—but also Germans. In May 2003, the French ambassador complained that the Pentagon was planting lies about France in the *Washington Times* and other U.S. news media. Poindexter left office in 2003 after another of his brainstorms—betting on terrorist attacks as a way to anticipate them—sparked a firestorm of criticism.

Can Outside Influences Promote Democratization?

Political and economic changes result primarily from developments within each society, but outside influences can help at the margins.

The Power of Example. Good models surpass sermons. Chinese demonstrators in 1989 erected a large "Goddess of Democracy" resembling the Statue of Liberty. (Within a few years, however, their god was mammon.)

Teaching. U.S. educators tried to teach self-government: after 1898 to Cubans, Puerto Ricans, and Filipinos; after 1945 to Italians, Germans, and Japanese; and after 1991 to ex-Soviets and East Europeans. In the 1990s, Harvard's John F. Kennedy School of Government offered classes in democratic civil–military relations to Russian and PRC officers. The Soros Foundation provided funds to rewrite Russian history books to foster a civil society ("Money down the drain," some critics said).

Advocacy. U.S. ambassadors encouraged democrats in South Korea, Portugal, Uruguay, the Philippines, and many Latin American countries. But Washington coddled some anti-Communist dictators, spoke softly to Communist regimes when it sought détente, and seldom challenged oil sheikdoms (even after 9/11).

Economic Pressures. UN-sponsored economic boycotts of Rhodesia and South Africa added to pressures on them to become multiracial democracies. Western aid-givers sought to condition aid to other African countries based on the dismantling of authoritarian rule. Beginning in 1974, the U.S. Congress conditioned foreign aid, investment, and even trade on the human rights performance of other countries. West Germany's major political parties subsidized their colleagues trying to democratize Spain and Portugal in the 1970s. Washington subsidized third-wave democratization in Portugal, Poland, and Nicaragua.

Openness. If PCs, Xerox, and the Internet are there, free thought and political competition cannot be far behind. China's great wall cracked. Beijing banned opposition political parties and free trade unions but permitted some Chinese to deal directly with foreign traders and tourists, to travel and study abroad, and to communicate with foreigners on modems.[51]

U.S. Achievements and Failures. What was America's track record in promoting democracy? The record is difficult to assess, because U.S.

51. See Edward Friedman and Barrett L. McCormick, eds., *What If China Doesn't Democratize? Implications for War and Peace* (Armonk, N.Y.: M. E. Sharpe, 2000).

Freed from France by a slave revolution in 1804, but long ruled by dictators and their death squads, Haitians danced for joy when the military junta was forced out by U.S. and UN pressures in December 1994, allowing Jean-Bertrand Aristide, elected president in 1990, to return from exile in the United States. But could self-rule become a reality where a wealthy few guarded their privileges against impoverished, often illiterate masses? After a colleague served as president in 1996–2000, Aristide was again elected president. But his administration did little for the country. Some former supporters accused Aristide and friends of betraying the public trust.

interventions often aimed more at security or economic goals than at building democracy. Still, it seems clear that the U.S. contributed greatly to building solid democracies in Germany, Italy, and Japan. It also fostered democracy in Taiwan, South Korea, and the Philippines. Interventions helped stabilize the Dominican Republic after 1965, Grenada after 1983, and Panama after 1989. A series of interventions in Cuba, Haiti, Nicaragua, Iran, Vietnam, and Cambodia left each country with right-wing dictators who eventually were overthrown by leftist regimes. In 2003 the jury was still out on Bosnia, Kosovo, Afghanistan, and Iraq. But each presented challenges that were absent in post–World War II Germany, Japan, Italy, Taiwan, and South Korea. Each of these successful cases had just one major ethnic group and language. The first three had a strong state capacity for self-governance. Each could absorb and make good use of economic assistance and foreign investment. Elite and popular interests soon converged with American. Only in Japan did a U.S. general administer the country for years. By contrast, Iraq in 2003 looked like a Tower of Babel, which once rose there.[52]

Security. Security threats from within or without can destabilize democratic institutions. President George Bush used military force to protect the Aquino government in the Philippines and President Guillermo Endara in Panama from right-wing assaults; President Bill Clinton deployed troops to support democracy in Haiti and Bosnia. U.S. and UK forces drove the Taliban from Afghanistan and installed a rather democratic regime in Kabul. They drove Baathists from Iraq.

52. For an even more pessimistic analysis, see Minxin Pei and Sara Kasper, "*Lessons from the Past: The American Record in Nation-Building,*" Washington, D.C.: Carnegie Endowment for International Peace, 2003.

WHAT PROPOSITIONS HOLD?
WHAT QUESTIONS REMAIN?

Churchill and Nehru claimed too little. Experience shows that democracy, in most cases, performs far better than authoritarian systems. Democracy has contributed to domestic and external fitness far more than authoritarianism.

Democracy's achievements suggest it may be a superior form of government. Shared democracy is probably the most dependable basis we know for peace. All countries with high domestic fitness (high HDI ratings) are democracies with mixed economies. By contrast, many authoritarian governments have been lethal to their own subjects and to outsiders. If peace benefits from democracy and democracy from a market economy, then peace also benefits from a market economy. Mutual respect and trade permit a positive peace, not just the absence of war.

Memo to the President of India:

More democracy rather than repression will help India cope with its many problems. As in China, India's economy develops not because of central controls but because these controls are being loosened.

Many of our troubles result from illiteracy—not from democracy. Only one-third of our females and just two-thirds of our males are literate. Our democracy should be able to widen literacy and provide health care. Democratic Sri Lanka fulfills these tasks far better than authoritarian China and Pakistan but also better than democratic India. One party held power for too long in India. It permitted corruption to grow and tolerated a low level of government efficiency and social services. Permitting Muslims special privileges (for example, the right to have more than one wife) has aggravated sectarian differences. A truly sectarian state would not exempt any sect from its basic laws.

Our federal union has held together because of democracy—not in spite of it. Our ethnic, linguistic, and religious variety is unmatched anywhere—Hindi and fourteen other official languages plus English (an "associate" tongue). A free press and the right to assembly have permitted each group to express its sentiments openly. The USSR, by contrast, kept a lid on its ethnic grievances. Ultimately the lid blew off and the Soviet empire collapsed.

Top-down direction is feasible in Singapore because its 3 million people are all crowded into a small city-state. By contrast, India is large—equal in area to one-third of the United States. Managing our lands on the Singapore model is simply not possible. Dependent upon grassroots development, we need to strengthen our democracy—not weaken it.

Nor can our diversity be compared with China's, where less than 10 percent of the population is non-Han. Even so, China has trouble controlling its Uighur and Tibetan minorities.

Where we have used strong-arm tactics—in Kashmir, the Punjab, and elsewhere—we have created deep, festering wounds. When Prime Minister Indira Gandhi imposed emergency rule in 1975–1977, she resolved nothing.

One of India's greatest achievements is that famine has taken few lives since independence. China, by contrast, has lost more than 30 million to famine. The number of deaths resulting from communal strife in India is large, but pales next to the millions executed or imprisoned for political reasons in China.[53]

We need to consolidate democracy and to promote it in Pakistan and China. Were all three countries thriving democracies, tensions would decline and trade increase. We could begin to develop complex interdependence, spend less on arms, and join in nuclear disarmament. We could shape Pakistan's internal politics by taking steps to solve the Kashmir problem, by agreeing to limit or reduce our nuclear weapons capabilities, and by promoting better Hindu–Muslim relations. With Pakistan and China, we could do more to promote educational and cultural exchange. We should emulate the ways that French and Germans have learned to replace enmity with mutual respect and amity.

Having discussed these matters with the Indian ambassador and considered worldwide trends, the U.S. Secretary of State sends a brief memo to the White House.

Memo to the President of the United States:

It is in U.S. interest to cultivate democracy and market economies everywhere. We have no guarantees that one democracy will not fight another, but the spread of democracy may be our best protection against war.

We also know that political and economic freedom boost one another. Market democracies are good for peace, trade, and prosperity.

The U.S. should invest more resources to help spread and consolidate democracy. To begin with, of course, we should try to improve our own. The costs of improving our own democratic institutions and fostering them abroad are minuscule next to the costs of war or preparing for war.

KEY NAMES AND TERMS

authoritarian	dictatorship	political culture of authoritarianism
Silvio Berlusconi	Adolf Hitler	political culture of democracy
civil society	Aldous Huxley	politicide
constitutionalism	Immanuel Kant	reverse wave
demagogue	Mohammad Khatami	Josef Stalin
democide	liberal peace theory	third wave
democracy	Benito Mussolini	totalitarian dictatorship

---

53. This historic experience was altered, however, in 2002, when authorities in the southern state of Tamil Nadu refused to dispense wheat stocks to the poor for fear of driving down prices. This was something new in India as it shifted from socialism to capitalism under the Bharatiya Janta Party.

QUESTIONS TO DISCUSS

1. Does it make any difference for a country's domestic and foreign policy whether its government is authoritarian or democratic?
2. Does domestic policy shape foreign policy or vice versa?
3. Do authoritarian regimes need war? Are they more aggressive than democracies? If so, why?
4. Why do authoritarian regimes have lower living standards than democracies?
5. Why did authoritarian regimes last so long in Eastern Europe?
6. Can a political culture derived from a non-Protestant tradition become democratic? Consider the political impact of other religions such as Roman Catholicism, Orthodoxy, Sunni Islam, Shi'a Islam, Buddhism, and so forth.
7. Are free markets and democracy compatible?
8. Can democracy be fostered from outside? How?
9. How can market forces threaten democracy?
10. Can democratization be reversed? Where is the third reverse wave most likely? Why?

RECOMMENDED RESOURCES

BOOKS

Arato, Andrew *Civil Society, Constitution and Legitimacy* Lanham, Md.: Rowman & Littlefield, 2000.

Barkawi, Tarak, and Mark Laffey, eds. *Democracy, Liberalism, and War: Rethinking the Democratic Peace Debate.* Boulder, Colo.: Lynne Rienner, 2001.

Brown, Michael E., et al., eds. *Debating the Democratic Peace: An International Security Reader.* Cambridge, Mass.: MIT Press, 1996.

Dahl, Robert A. *On Democracy.* New Haven, Conn.: Yale University Press, 1998.

Dalpino, Catharin. *Deferring Democracy: Promoting Openness in Authoritarian Regimes.* Washington, D.C.: Brookings Institution, 1998.

Diamond, Larry J., and Marc F. Plattner, eds. *The Global Divergence of Democracies.* Baltimore, Md.: John Hopkins University Press, 2001.

Dreze, Jean, and Amartya Sen. *India: Development and Participation.* 2d ed. New York: Oxford University Press, 2002.

Gilbert, Alan. *Must Global Politics Constrain Democracy? Great-Power Realism, Democratic Peace, and Democratic Internationalism.* Princeton, N.J.: Princeton University Press, 1999.

Gourevitch, Philip. *We Wish to Inform You That Tomorrow We Will Be Killed with Our Families: Stories from Rwanda.* New York: Picador USA, 1999.

Levy, Jack S. "The Causes of War: A Review of the Theories and Evidence," in *Behavior, Society, and Nuclear War,* ed. Philip E. Tetlock, et al. of 3 vols. New York: Oxford University Press, 1989–1993, vol. 1, pp. 209–333.

Lijphart, Arend. *Patterns of Democracy: Government Forms and Performance in Thirty-six Countries.* New Haven, Conn.: Yale University Press, 1999.

Linz, Juan J., and Alfred Stepan. *Problems of Democratic Transition and Consolidation: Southern Europe, South America, and Post-Communist Europe.* Baltimore: Johns Hopkins University Press, 1996.

Mandelbaum, Michael. *The Ideas That Conquered the World: Peace, Democracy, and Free Markets in the Twenty-first Century.* New York: Public Affairs, 2002.

Moore, Barrington. *Social Origins of Dictatorship and Democracy: Lord and Peasant in the Making of the Modern World.* Boston: Beacon Press, 1993.

Putnam, Robert D., et al. *Making Democracy Work: Civic Traditions in Modern Italy.* Princeton, N.J.: Princeton University Press, 1993.

Ray, James Lee. *Democracy and International Conflict: An Evaluation of the Democratic Peace Proposition.* Columbia: University of South Carolina Press, 1995.

Rosenbaum, Alan S., ed. *Is the Holocaust Unique? Perspectives on Comparative Genocide.* Boulder, Colo.: Westview, 1997.

Rummel, Rudolph J. *Statistics of Democide: Genocide and Mass Murder Since 1900.* Piscataway, N.J.: Transaction, 1998.

Russett, Bruce, et al. *Grasping the Democratic Peace: Principles for a Post–Cold War World.* Princeton, N.J.: Princeton University Press, 1993.

Schultz, Kenneth A. *Democracy and Coercive Diplomacy.* New York: Cambridge University Press, 2001.

Sen, Amartya. *Development as Freedom.* New York: Anchor Books, 2000.

Shlapentokh, Vladimir. *A Normal Totalitarian Society: How the Soviet Union Functioned and How It Collapsed.* Armonk, N. Y.: M. E. Sharpe, 2001.

Recommended Resources (continued)

Soroush, Abdolkarim. *Reason, Freedom, and Democracy in Islam: The Essential Writings of Abdolkarim Soroush.* Ahmad Sadri and Mahmoud Sadri, eds. New York: Oxford University Press, 2000.

World Bank. *The State in a Changing World: World Development Report 1997.* New York: Oxford University Press, 1997.

WEB SITES

Adolph Hitler
http://auschwitz.dk/Hitler.htm

Comparative Democratization Project (understanding global transitions to democracy)
http://democracy.stanford.edu/

Machiavelli's *The Prince,* in full text
http://www.ilt.columbia.edu/publications/machiavelli.html

Mohammed Khatami
http://persia.org/khatami/

The Stalin Reference Archive
http://www.marxists.org/reference/archive/stalin/

"What Is Fascism," by Benito Mussolini
http://www.fordham.edu/halsall/mod/mussolinifascism.html

CHAPTER ELEVEN

THE WEALTH OF NATIONS: TOP-DOWN OR BOTTOM-UP?

- In what ways did the First World become first—how does the liberal thesis fit?

- If Japan rivals the rest of the First World, does that mean that government guidance and protection work better than the "invisible hand" of free enterprise?

- Does Washington seek to square the circle when it promotes both free trade and strategic trade?

- Do political or economic concerns play the heavier role as Ottawa, Mexico City, and Washington evaluate their North American Free Trade Agreement?

- Why do some liberals who say they like free trade oppose the World Trade Organization (WTO)?

- Do the problems of First World economies stem from the inability to compete abroad or from inefficiencies at home?

- Should First World governments tilt toward neoliberalism, neomercantilism, a blend, or none of the above?

"What Is Wealth? How Best to Attain It?....Do we
Europeans need more government or less—more guidance and help from above or more
creativity from below? Is 'Europe' too big or too small? What can we Europeans learn
from the United States? What can they learn from us?" These are the questions the Euro-
pean Commission in Brussels wants you, a distinguished German economist, to answer.
Back home in Berlin, both Social Democrats and Christian Democrats ask you similar
questions. Yes, Germany is the largest country in the European Union—both in popula-
tion and total wealth. By the early 21st century, however, Germans and most Europeans
seem to have lost their former dynamism. Unemployment is up. Creativity is down. Eu-
ropeans are winning fewer industrial patents than Americans, Japanese, or Koreans.
Have Europeans given too large a role to government? Have we protected both our in-
dustrialists and our workers too much? Is there too much organization and too many
rules—or too little?

Should we Europeans really seek a globalized economy or try to beat the Americans, the
Chinese, and the Japanese in what can be a zero-sum competition? If Boeing wins a con-
tract in Saudi Arabia, Airbus does not. If the Chinese permit Mercedes to set up a factory
but then "adapt" the technology, we lose in the long run.

Should we honor free trade in practice or just with lip service? The Americans say
they want free trade, but we find their government interfering in world trade and
protecting U.S. industries. The Americans say they believe in law but often ignore it.
When the World Trade Organization rules against them, they drag their feet in com-
plying. They block us from trading with countries they don't like—Libya, Iran, Cuba,
and others. They pressure us to buy bananas from Central America, where they own
the plantations, rather than from the British West Indies or Africa, where we have
historic ties.

The Industrial Revolution began in Europe. Should we continue to worship at the altar
of GDP? Should we Europeans lead the world to a way of life that does more to nurture
the human spirit and enhance our shared habitat, the biosphere?

You retreat to your cottage on the North Sea to think again about the wealth of nations. You must evaluate a basic issue of IPE: Should government guide economic development or merely facilitate it? Did government help or hinder the steps by which Europeans, North Americans, and Japanese became the richest peoples in history? You decide to review the wisdom of Adam Smith, Karl Marx, John Maynard Keynes, and other economic thinkers, but you begin by rereading Charles Dickens's David Copperfield.

CONTENDING CONCEPTS AND EXPLANATIONS

QUALITY OF LIFE

The brutality of England's Industrial Revolution struck Charles Dickens as well as Karl Marx. Dickens recorded how David Copperfield, age ten, worked in a riverfront warehouse overrun by rats. He washed empty wine bottles and pasted labels on new ones for a London wine merchant whose goods were shipped to the East and West Indies. It was the early 1820s and David owed his job to foreign trade, but he would have preferred to stay in school.

The Industrial Revolution began in England about 1780. Before that time, living standards for most Europeans were no better than for most Chinese or subjects of the Ottoman Empire. Famine and plague visited Europe regularly. In the 17th and 18th centuries, most Europeans subsisted on bread, often in short supply.[1]

But incomes in England doubled in the sixty years after 1780, and millions moved from the countryside into London and other cities in search of jobs and a better life—a pattern followed in many developing countries in the late 20th century.

London in the early 19th century bore some resemblance to Third World cities of the late 20th century. Not far from the genteel streets where Dickens wrote and where Karl Marx studied at the British Museum, jerry-built rookeries stood back-to-back without drainage.[2] The river Thames was an open sewer whose waters were dumped, untreated, into the cisterns of London householders. Poor people were fortunate if they could use a standing pump turned on briefly once each week. Others

1. In 18th-century France, bread was the staple food for three-quarters of the population and it consumed half their income. Bread prices doubled in the year before the 1789 revolution. See Simon Schama, *Citizens: A Chronicle of the French Revolution* (New York: Knopf, 1989), 306; and Nathan Rosenberg and L. E. Birdzell, Jr., *How the West Became Rich: The Economic Transformation of the Industrial World* (New York: Basic Books, 1986), 172.

2. A building inspector reported in 1847: Excrement was "lying scattered about the rooms, vaults, cellars, areas and yards, so thick, and so deep, that it was hardly possible to move for it." A public health reformer wrote that these people lived like cattle— "swarms to whom personal cleanliness is utterly unknown." Peter Ackroyd, *Dickens* (New York: HarperCollins, 1990), 381–382.

Map 11.1 High, Low and Middle Incomes: GNI per Capita across the World (2001)

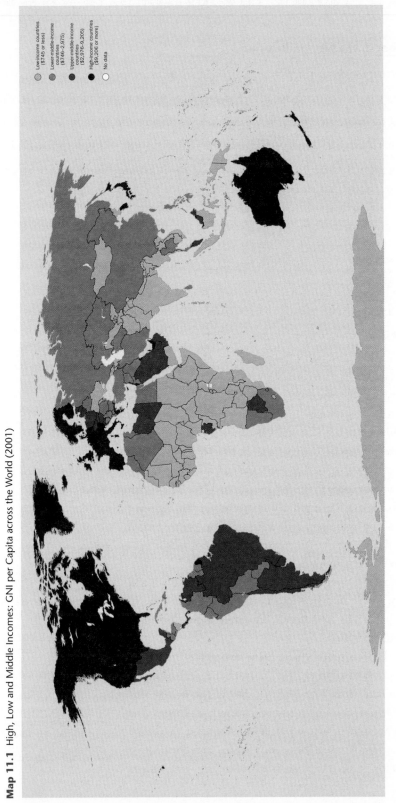

Low-income countries
($745 or less)

Lower-middle-income
countries
($746–2,975)

Upper-middle-income
countries
($2,976–9,205)

High-income countries
($9,206 or more)

No data

SOURCE: *World Bank Atlas*

and 1940s. In 1944 they were also incorporated into the international monetary system drawn up at a conference in Bretton Woods, New Hampshire. Mindful of cross-border economic interdependence, Keynes argued at Bretton Woods the need for global collective action to protect against market failures. Cutbacks in imports by one country, for whatever reason, could hurt other countries' economies. The Bretton Woods system extended the idea of aggregate demand management from the national to the international arena. The system sought to establish a climate favorable to expansion of international trade and investment in which individual countries could also pursue "full employment" at home.

The Bretton Woods system and other institutions created in the late 1940s opened the way to more than a half century of economic expansion. The system rested on three pillars. First was the U.S. dollar, convertible into gold at $35 per ounce. Second, the International Monetary Fund (IMF) was to help countries deal with short-term liquidity problems and maintain full employment by financing public works they might otherwise be unable to afford. Third, the International Bank for Reconstruction and Development, or "World Bank," was to extend long-term loans for reconstruction and development. The first pillar collapsed in 1971, when President Richard Nixon cut loose the dollar from gold and let it float freely against other currencies. The other two pillars were still standing in the early 21st century, battered by critics in many quarters still evolving.

A fourth institution worked in tandem with the Bretton Woods institutions. The General Agreement on Tariffs and Trade, or "GATT," was established in 1947 to promote reciprocal reduction of tariffs and foster free trade by multilateral concessions. A key GATT principle was that a rule-based trading regime is preferable to quantitative targets. The main rule was equal treatment—MFN. Another important rule was a requirement for transparency—publication of all relevant regulations governing imports.

Initially, twenty-three states adhered to GATT; by the early 1990s, 125 countries took part in its last negotiating "round." GATT acquired a reputation as the "General Agreement to Talk and Talk," but its efforts paid off. GATT helped industrial countries to reduce tariffs on industrial products averaging 40 percent of product value in 1947 to just 5 percent in the early 1990s. During that time, trade in manufactured goods increased at three times the rate of world production.[8]

Starting in 1965, the industrialized countries offered some concessions to developing countries, exempting them from some duties of reciprocity.

8. Joseph A. McKinney, "The World Trade Regime: Past Successes and Future Challenges," *International Journal* 49, no. 3 (summer 1994): 445–471 at 447.

However, as developing countries became major exporters of textiles and clothing, they faced demands by the U.S. and Europe for **voluntary export restraints (VERs)**—in effect, quotas.

GATT's successes helped in the 1970s and 1980s to foster their antithesis: neomercantilist policies that utilized **nontariff barriers (NTBs)** to keep out foreign imports. NTBs include government subsidies and procurement policies ("buy national"), health and safety regulations, safety and quality standards, and even customs procedures (long delays at the dock). Environmental protection policies ("no imports of endangered species or their body parts") can also serve as NTBs.

Desperate to cope with Japan's export power and frustrated by Japan's maze of NTBs, the U.S. departed from the GATT principle of rule-based trade and sought quantitative commitments, for example, a Japanese pledge to import a certain number of auto exhausts, and VERs to constrain Japanese exporters.

GATT's final round of negotiation, the "Uruguay Round," began in 1986 and continued until 1993, when conferees agreed to replace GATT with a stronger body to coordinate world trade (discussed later).[9]

Neoliberalism adapts classic economic liberalism to an age when industrialized and developing countries are locked in global interdependence. Neoliberals believe in freer trade rather than free trade, because they see a need for government to shield the domestic economy (including jobs) from radical external challenge. Neoliberals respect the "invisible hand" but believe it must be assisted by an enlightened WTO, World Bank, and IMF.[10]

How Countries and Firms Acquire Competitive Advantage

The concepts of absolute and comparative advantage explain why the U.S. exports wheat. They do not explain why Japan, with few resources, makes autos so efficiently that they can be sold in Michigan. Technology and management can help firms and entire countries circumvent scarcity. Japan and other countries reduced the U.S.'s comparative advantage in resource endowment by cultivating **competitive advantage**—greater productivity based on better or more factor inputs. Skilled labor and a developed infrastructure were once a U.S. monopoly. No more.

IPE theory has progressed from Smith's absolute advantage to Ricardo's comparative advantage to contemporary ideas of competitive advantage. As we shall see later in the chapter, economists have constructed indexes of international competitiveness using factors that include:[11]

1. Resources (human and physical, capital, infrastructure)
2. Demand (domestic and foreign buyer requirements)

9. For an official summary of the Uruguay Round results, see *Focus: GATT Newsletter*, no. 104 (December 1993).

10. For a critique of recent IMF policies, see Joseph E. Stieglitz, *Globalization and Its Discontents* (New York: W. W. Norton, 2002).

11. Michael E. Porter, *The Competitive Advantage of Nations* (New York: Free Press, 1990), chap. 3.

3. Proximity of related industries (especially those that are themselves competitive internationally)

4. Firm strategy, structure, and rivalry (how companies are created and managed)

5. Government policies (see four types outlined in the sidebar).

6. Discontinuities and chance (inventions, for example, in biotechnology; changing input costs such as oil shocks; surges of demand; stock market crashes)

Looking back, we can see that some of these factors help explain why high-quality leather goods have been produced in Florence for hundreds of years. Florence benefited from its combination of human resources, local tastes, and location. In the age of jumbo jets and e-mail, however, proximity counts for less than in Renaissance Florence. World-class firms now team with distant partners in pursuit of excellence. Networking across borders stimulates learning. Powerful connections open doors.[12]

What is the bottom line for policy makers? Is there an ideal mix of bottom-up and top-down economics? Does the U.S. need the same mix as Japan? Does Europe need its own blend? Let us enrich theory with practice.

COMPARING THEORY AND REALITY: BOTTOM-UP AND TOP-DOWN DEVELOPMENT

How did the West become rich? The thesis of classical liberalism holds that political and economic freedom, cultivated in England, unleashed human creativity that produced mutual gain in most of the Western world. But the liberal thesis seems to meet its antithesis in a "Japan, Inc." that advanced at a rapid clip for much of late 19th and 20th centuries. Neomercantilists say that Japan advanced rapidly thanks in large part to government direction and protection. Does Japan's rapid rise mean that a top-down, government-backed "industrial policy" works even better than the bottom-up process esteemed by liberals? In this chapter and the next, we examine efforts by the U.S. and other governments to find a *synthesis* that supersedes both the bottom-up and top-down models.

THE LIBERAL THESIS OF ECONOMIC AUTONOMY: IS IT ADEQUATE?

The liberal thesis explains the global ascendancy of the West since 1500 by decentralization of authority, experiment, and responsibility. In contrast, the centralized regimes of the East—Russia, the Ottoman Empire,

Four Ways Government Can Shape a Country's Competitive Advantage

• Macroeconomic policy to accumulate factors of production, smooth market operations, and protect the environment. Policy instruments include fiscal and monetary regulations to encourage savings and investment; support for education, research, and development; and penalties for pollution and rewards for the use of "clean" fuels.

• Compensatory policy to assist those injured or left behind by time and social change, for example, retraining workers.

• Industrial policy to protect and promote selected industries such as those vital to security or high employment. Industrial policy may subsidize R&D. It may defend local industry by tariffs or by quantitative limits such as voluntary export restraints accepted by others.

• Strategic (or "managed") trade policy to promote exports and gain market share abroad in selected industries.

12. Rosabeth Moss Kanter, *World Class: Thriving Locally in the Global Economy* (New York: Simon & Schuster, 1995), 88. This idea is embodied in the reorganized format of the journal *Foreign Policy* that appeared in summer 1997 (no. 107).

Should You Buy an International Mutual Fund Now?

Are prediction and prescription complicated? Here were just some of the contradictory messages you can find in one issue of a financial newspaper:

Buy! The International Monetary Fund predicts stronger growth for the world's economies in the year ahead, fueled by the engine of U.S. growth.

No! Faster growth will lead U.S. central banks to raise interest rates to curb inflation. Higher interest rates will curb the growth in private investment in emerging markets.

Buy! European finance ministers are trimming their deficits so their countries remain within the limits imposed by the European Monetary Union.

No! Pressure for lower deficits will curb any movement to create more jobs and reduce Europe's high levels of unemployment.

Buy! The dollar may fall again against foreign currencies. When you travel abroad, it will cost you less if you draw on the fund.

No! When you sell your foreign funds, valued in Swiss francs, you will get fewer dollars back. Also, Europeans will buy less from the U.S.

Buy! Russia's stock market is booming.

No! Russia's stocks depend heavily on oil exports. When Iraq pumps oil full speed, oil prices will collapse.

Buy! Japan's economy will rise again.

No! If Japan's economy rebounds, the yen will gain against the dollar, wiping out your profits in Japanese securities.

Caveat emptor.

China, Japan—enforced an official belief system—even on commerce and weapons development. Lacking any supreme authority, Europe's rival states searched constantly for competitive advantage. Competition sorted out the useful applications of science from the nonuseful. Military improvements interacted with technological and commercial advances. A spiral of growth and innovation helped the competitive Western states and their corporations dominate the globe.[13]

The West grew rich by allowing its economic sector the autonomy to experiment in developing new products, in methods of manufacture, in modes of enterprise organization, in transport and communication, and in capital–labor relations. New market institutions made it possible for innovators to earn high rewards and threaten noninnovators with extinction. Europe's traders jolted consumer tastes with exotic products. Some manufacturers found ways to mass produce and sell goods more cheaply than guilds.[14] New businesses took many forms. Some were small, some

13. Rosenberg and Birdzell, *How the West Grew Rich*; and Paul Kennedy, *The Rise and Fall of the Great Powers: Economic Change and Military Conflict from 1500 to 2000* (New York: Random House, 1987).

14. Josiah Wedgwood sold decorated porcelain to the Russian court, but his earthenware pottery transformed the kitchens of the working class in the Industrial Revolution. Wedgwood and a dozen other scientist-inventors belonged to the Lunar Society (so-named because they could ride on wretched roads to meetings held near the full moon). Most were Puritans or Unitarians who believed that the good life is *more* than material decency; it must be *based* on material decency. J. Bronowski, *The Ascent of Man* (Boston: Little, Brown, 1973), 274–279.

large. Inventors and entrepreneurs needed funding to develop and market their ideas. They were financed in many ways, usually from private sources. They embodied the "self-organization" intrinsic to "fit" social systems.

In the West, the market served as an experiment linking technology and human welfare. Laissez-faire advanced each of the three variables more effectively than could centralized planning. Figure 11.1 shows how each corner of the triangle boosted the other two. Spurred by the Reformation and the printing press, the spread of literacy was crucial to the growth of democracy, industrialization, and women's liberation. Sweden, probably the first country to achieve mass literacy for both sexes, ranked at or near the top in gender equality as well as personal income at the turn of the 20th century.[15]

What does the liberal thesis omit? Many factors other than economic liberalism contributed to the rise of the West—the slow accretion of knowledge and capital over centuries, including science and technology derived from the Islamic and Chinese civilizations; mercantilist and state-sponsored exploration of the New World and its riches; slavery (a source of capital for industry and cheap cotton for textile mills);[16] a strong foundation in agriculture and animal husbandry; protectionist support for infant industries in Britain, the U.S., and Germany; government-sponsored infrastructure development such as the American canals and railroads; government subsidy of agriculture, shipping, and airplane manufacture; and government support for military research and development (R&D) with spillover benefits for the civilian economy.

Many critics challenge the liberal claim that free trade made the West prosperous after World War II. One school holds that free trade was an illusion, because GATT-sponsored tariff reductions did not stop governments from protecting their native industries and farmers with NTBs and subsidies. An opposing school holds that trade liberalization did occur, but that it harmed British and U.S. industry. Free trade, linked to fixed currency exchanges, paralyzed the hegemons while their rivals ascended.

IS JAPAN THE ANTITHESIS OR A VARIANT?

Does East Asia play by rules different from the West? Beginning in the late 19th century, Japan industrialized far more quickly than any Western country. In the 1980s, Japan surpassed the USSR as the world's second-largest economy, while its per capita income (measured by currency exchanges)

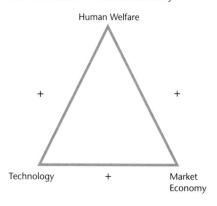

Fig. 11.1 Technology to Meet Human Needs Can Be Profitable in a Market Economy

Human Welfare

Technology   Market Economy

15. Sweden's state church decreed in 1686 that everyone—including children, farmhands, and maidservants—should "learn to read and see with their own eyes what God bids and commands in His Holy Word." Most Swedes learned to read within their own families, for there were few schools. By 1740 nearly all Swedes, male and female, could read (but not write)—almost 160 years before general literacy was achieved in England. Egil Johansson, "The History of Literacy in Sweden," in *Literacy and Social Development in the West: A Reader*, ed. Harvey J. Graff (Cambridge, U.K.: Cambridge University Press, 1981), 151–182 at 157, 180. In 1992, women in Sweden's workforce received wages that averaged 90 percent of men's (compared with a 67 percent average in the Organization for Economic Cooperation and Development).

16. Eric Williams, *Capitalism and Slavery* (Chapel Hill: University of North Carolina Press, 1944); also, a book inspired by Williams: Hugh Thomas, *The Slave Trade: The Story of the Atlantic Slave Trade, 1440–1870* (New York: Simon & Schuster, 1997).

Literacy and Economic Growth

Which came first—literacy or wealth? Commoners started to read in Europe in the 15th and 16th centuries. Printing presses turned out newspapers and books. Protestant regions such as Sweden and Holland became the most literate and, allowing for resource differentials, more affluent than Catholic regions.

More than half of English men could read by 1760 on the eve of the Industrial Revolution, but New England exceeded Europe in average literacy because it was settled by literate Europeans. The American rebels in the 1770s could read and think for themselves. Their commerce and cohesion increased with publication of the first newspaper to circulate through the colonies, published by a former printer's apprentice, Benjamin Franklin.

The correlation between literacy, wealth, and democracy could be mapped by 1900: The least literate parts of Europe and Russia were among the poorest—and also the least democratic. Authoritarians preferred that their subjects not think for themselves.* For better or worse, literacy also spurred nationalism.

* Michael Stubbs, *The Social Context of Literacy* (London: Routledge & Kegan Paul, 1986), 82–90, 211–216; and Sidney Pollard, *Peaceful Conquest: The Industrialization of Europe, 1760–1970* (New York: Oxford University Press, 1982), 222, 249, 252.

---

exceeded the United State's. Japan accumulated trade surpluses throughout the 1980s, while the U.S. trade balance turned negative in 1983 and stayed negative into the early 21st century.

Any evaluation of Japanese industrial policy must take into account the fact that Japanese officials saw the economy not just as a means to prosperity but as a platform for national security. Before World War II, Japan's ideology drew upon both mercantilism and militarism. Its slogan was "Rich Nation, Strong Army." After 1945, Japan renounced war but still believed it must master advanced technology, diffuse it, and nurture it. Defense capabilities were embedded in the civilian economy. Japan's post-1945 approach might be called "rich nation, strong technology." Japanese firms became world leaders in dual-use (military and civilian) materials and components such as opto-electronics. U.S. science and technology were the stepchildren of the military; in Japan they were its godparents. Japan generated a single, integrated economy.[17]

Japan cultivated a strategy of export-led development—producing manufactures that win market share abroad and reinvesting the proceeds to cultivate still more economic strength at home. Japan combined industrial policy and strategic trade policy to make its manufactures competitive. This strategy benefited for many years from currency exchange rates that made Japanese products relatively cheaper than U.S. or European.

Critics say that "Japan, Inc." abused free trade—that Japan's Finance Ministry and Ministry of International Trade and Industry (MITI)

17. Richard J. Samuels, *"Rich Nation, Strong Army": National Security and the Technological Transformation of Japan* (Ithaca, N.Y.: Cornell University Press, 1996), 319–321.

protected Japanese industries and promoted exports to gain control of entire product lines, such as semiconductors. Thus, Japan bought two supercomputers from the leading U.S. manufacturer in 1980 and then resisted more purchases while Japanese makers developed their own supercomputers. In 1987, the Nippon Electric Company (NEC) offered a supercomputer to the Massachusetts Institute of Technology for one-third the prevailing price. Amid charges that Japan was "dumping" its products at below cost, MIT declined the deal, but the NEC was now ready to penetrate foreign markets.[18]

How Important to Japan Was Its Industrial Policy? How Useful?

Neoliberals deny that industrial policy was important or useful for Japan. The country played by much the same rules as the West. When the Tokyo government did back some industry (see "Four Tests of Industrial Policy Success"), it had only limited success. Had capital been allowed to flow freely to Japan's true strengths, even higher profits might have been realized. One of Japan's great success stories was Honda, run by a maverick who insisted on making autos for export against the advice of MITI.

Neoliberals hold that the main contribution of the Japanese government was macroeconomic—support for education, savings, and investment. For decades the government treated Japan's as a "shortage economy" and rationed both foreign exchange and credit. The government compensated those hurt by social change and retrained displaced workers. As we see in Table 11.1, Japan devoted a far higher percentage of its GDP to investment than did two other rich countries, the U.S. and Switzerland, but China invested a much larger share of its wealth than

18. In 1997, the U.S. Commerce Department ruled that the NEC had sold its Vector supercomputer at unfair value to the U.S. National Center for Atmospheric Research. The Department imposed antidumping duties of 454 percent on the Vector, and duties of 173 percent on Fujitsu supercomputers, and more than 300 percent on all other Japanese supercomputers. NEC spokesmen charged that the U.S. government was closing off its market to outsiders. The NEC claimed that its supercomputer needed only eight days to carry out tasks that required one month on a U.S. Cray/C90 machine.

Table 11.1 How Important Are Investment and Exports to Overall Economic Strength?

Country	Gross National Income per Capita $ in 2001	PPP per Capita Dollars in 2001	Gross Domestic Investment as % of GDP in 1999	Exports of Goods and Services as % of GDP in 1999
United States	$34,800	$34,800	19%	12%
Switzerland	$36,900	$31,300	20%	40%
Japan	$35, 900	$27,400	29%	11%
Hong Kong	$25,900	$26,000	25%	132%*
Mexico	$5,500	$8,800	24%	31%
China	$890	$4,300	40%	22%
India	$460	$2,500	24%	11%

SOURCE: *World Development Report 2003*, Table 1; *WDR 2000/2001*, Table 13
*Hong Kong exports include trans-shipments from China.

Japan. A high rate of investment, of course, does not ensure economic success if other fundamentals are lacking, as in India.

Japanese exports in the 1950s and 1960s sold because they were cheap; later they sold because they were superior. Neither price nor quality resulted primarily from government support. Japanese autos and transistor radios acquired their reputation for dependability without any help from MITI. As we also see in Table 11.1, however, in the mid-1990s Japan's gross domestic product (GDP) depended no more on exports than the United State's. Hong Kong, by contrast, prospered on exports, most of them from the rest of China. Mexico also exported a great deal, aided by its free trade relationship with the United States. Lacking any such privileged ties, Switzerland's GDP depended heavily on exports.

Table 11.2 shows that Japan was much more egalitarian than the high-income U.S., Switzerland, and Hong Kong; medium-income Mexico; or low-income China and India. Indeed, the World Bank reported in 2003 that the only other countries to match Japan's egalitarian division of wealth were the four high-income states of Denmark, Finland, Norway, and Sweden. But former Communist states, Belarus and Slovakia, placed even lower than Japan on the Gini Index, a measure of income equality which treats absolute equality as 0 and absolute inequality as 100. Belarus scored 22; the Central African Republic, 61.

Did Japan Retrace the U.S. Pattern?

Japan's industrialization was mandated from above, but—as in the West—it arose from a decentralized system of landholding and power

Table 11.2 How Is Wealth Divided in Rich and Developing Economies?

Country	Gross National Income per Capita Dollars in 2001	Percentage Share of Income— Lowest 10%	Percentage Share of Income— Highest 10%	Gini Index and Year of Survey
United States	$34,800	1.8%	30.5%	40.8 (1997)
Switzerland	$36,900	2.6%	25.2%	33.1 (1992)
Japan	$35,900	4.8%	21.7%	24.9 (1993)
Hong Kong	$25,900	1.8%	43.5%	52.2 (1996)
Mexico	$5,500	1.3%	41.7%	53.1 (1998)
China	$890	2.4%	30.4%	40.3 (1998)
India	$460	3.5%	33.5%	37.8 (1997)

SOURCE: *World Development Report 2003*, Tables 1 and 2.

sharing. Some leading entrepreneurs in Japan had been samurai warriors. Their behavior in business resembled that of the U.S. "robber barons."

The "catch-up" factor helped Japan. The country that starts from a lower base can shoot up more easily than the leader. A latecomer to industrialization, Japan was like a cross-country skier that follows in another's track. Japan did not take the same risks or invest in untried ideas as Europe and the U.S. had done. Just as U.S. manufacturers improved processes developed in Europe, so Japan improved on those begun in the U.S.

Like the U.S. in the 19th century, Japan gained on the front-runner in the 20th. Both Americans and Japanese advanced on others thanks to their greater efficiency, attention to quality and detail, quick response to new technology, and reinvestment of profits in equipment and plants.[19] Americans visiting Japan in the 1970s and 1980s were struck by the highly motivated workforce. Similarly, a British parliamentary study in 1868 noted the clean workplaces in the U.S., "the care universally bestowed on the comfort of the work people," and workers who "readily produce a new article; understand everything you say to them [and] help the employer by their own acuteness and intelligence."

Lacking comparative advantage in natural endowment, Japan compensated by cultivating its competitive advantage. By 1996 all but one of the world's fifteen largest companies were U.S. or Japanese.[20] Just as the Japanese model began to look superior, however, the Japanese economy froze and fell into negative growth lasting into the 21st century. The very technique said to ensure its superiority over the U.S. approach proved

19. Innovation takes nerve and money. In 1878, the British journal *Engineering* ridiculed Thomas Edison's ideas for an incandescent light for their "most airy ignorance of the fundamental principles both of electricity and dynamics." Edison's ideas, it said, were not for "practical or scientific men."

Andrew Carnegie was then becoming the world's leading steel producer. His secret: high-volume, low-cost manufacturing that exploited the newest technology and sought market share rather than large profits per sale. Smug British steel makers criticized Carnegie's "hard driving" and "scrap and build" policies as wasteful. Carnegie replied: "It is because you keep . . . used-up machinery that the United States is making you a back number."

Like some Japanese producers a century later, Carnegie did not have to answer to investors or even to banks. He held more than 50 percent of a limited partnership and was prepared to invest for the long haul. Jean Strouse, "How Economic Empires Are Born," *The New York Times*, February 25, 1992, A21.

20. Only one was European, Royal Dutch Shell, which placed sixth in size and first in profits. The five largest were General Motors, Ford, Mitsui, Mitsubishi, and Itochi; the others were Marubeni, Exxon, Sumitomo, Toyota, Wal-Mart Stores, General Electric, Nissho Iwai, Nippon Telegraph & Telephone, and IBM.

Why the Competitiveness Obsession?

Did governments worry excessively about the "competitive advantage of nations"?* Perhaps the U.S. and Japan were not like Coke and Pepsi—fighting for market share. No major country was like a firm that might "go under." A trade deficit could be interpreted as a sign of strength. If the U.S. trade deficit widened with Japan, it might narrow elsewhere. In any event, the U.S. trade deficit was small compared to GDP and virtually invisible next to assets.

Imports from Japan could benefit Western consumers and provide lessons for European and U.S. manufacturers. An industry survey in 1997 revealed that British automakers using Japanese methods had become far more efficient than German or other continental manufacturers.

* Paul Krugman, "Competitiveness: A Dangerous Obsession," *Foreign Affairs* 73, no. 2 (March/April 1994): 28–44; for criticism and Krugman's reply, see *Foreign Affairs* 73, no. 4 (July/August 1994): 186–203.

fatal. American firms had to worry about short-term results because their finances depended on investors glued to quarterly profit statements. The "long-term" perspective of Japanese industry that permitted them to carry out R&D indifferent to short-term profits grew from collusion with banks that loaned them money on easy terms. In the 1990s, however, it emerged that Japanese banks held many bad loans. Japanese businesses had used ready credit not only for R&D but also to buy high-priced Tokyo real estate and entire Hollywood studios. Decades of rapid economic growth in Japan gave way to prolonged stagnation. The doldrums were prolonged by a government slow to "prime the pump" with public works and by cautious Japanese consumers reluctant to binge on credit like Americans.

THE NEOLIBERAL QUEST FOR SYNTHESIS: THE U.S. IN THE WORLD ECONOMY

Seeking to build U.S. economic strength at home and abroad, President Bill Clinton developed a brew that mixed three parts neoliberalism with one part neomercantilism. He promoted free trade in tandem with industrial policy and strategic trade. Clinton's "global engagement" also sought to promote development in LDCs, address environmental degradation, and encourage market economics in the former Soviet empire.

Free trade can harm not just dolphins and turtles but also public health. Even as state and federal authorities sought to curtail smoking in the U.S., tobacco interests such as those close to Senator Jesse Helms promoted tobacco sales abroad. They even objected to antismuggling rules to facilitate tax collection by foreign governments. Meanwhile, a public health catastrophe awaited China and other countries as young women joined men in a habit made accessible by rising affluence and promoted by the Marlboro cowboy.

US Government Pushes Asian Nations to Accept Tobacco Exports

DON'T THINK OF IT AS A DEADLY DRUG... ...THINK OF IT AS FREE TRADE.

SENATOR HELMS

DANZIGER
The Christian Science Monitor
Los Angeles Times Syndicate

The Clinton Technology Policy

The Clinton administration endorsed an industrial policy that it called "technology policy." It aimed to compensate for "market failure" when private firms do not conduct sufficient research and development. It backed dual-use technologies applicable to commercial as well as military products. Clinton wanted to orient government investment in defense, space, health, and education to strengthen the country's technological base. The Clinton team encouraged private firms to enlarge the information highway within the U.S. and worldwide.

International Trade and Growth: Win–Win

International trade has been an engine of growth. World exports grew at better than 6 percent per year from 1960 through 1995, while world output grew by only 3.8 percent yearly. Trade allowed countries to gain from their comparative or competitive advantage. As we see in Figure 11.2, trade and economic output grew together and fell together from 1996 to 2001, in the U.S., Japan, and Europe.

The Clinton White House embraced "export activism," portraying free trade as a win–win strategy for the U.S. and its partners. The Clinton team claimed that exports led the U.S. economic revival, accounting for nearly four-fifths of the total increase in domestic manufacturing between 1987 and 1993.[21] In August 1997, Clinton said that one-quarter of the country's economic growth in the previous four years came from foreign trade.

As we see in Figure 11.2, however, U.S. imports came to exceed its exports. The imbalances in trade with Japan, China, and the EU were huge. Why? Japan and Europe imported less as their own economic growth slowed, but China did not have this excuse, for its economy (not shown in the figure) continued to grow at a rapid pace. American trade negotiators complained that China as well as Japan kept out U.S. goods by use of unfair NTBs.

There was also an imbalance in foreign direct investment (FDI). Foreigners invested more in the U.S. than vice versa, Japanese investments in the U.S. exceeded American in Japan by 3 to 1.21. FDI offers a useful way to take advantage of lower wages abroad and gain access to foreign markets and skirt tariffs, VERs, and NTBs. By producing in Ohio or Tennessee, Japanese manufacturers could offer their autos directly to U.S. customers. FDI produced nearly 5 million U.S. jobs.[22] It also brought new technology and management techniques while outgoing FDI helped U.S. firms to operate abroad. Outgoing FDI cost U.S. workers some low-pay jobs but stimulated other, high-wage jobs at home and abroad.

21. The share of manufactured goods in U.S. exports steadily climbed, while those of agriculture, forestry, and mining declined. Aircraft, computers, and office equipment dominated U.S. high technology exports, which totaled $138 billion in 1995. U.S. imports of high technology (mostly electronic products from Asia) amounted to $125 billion in 1995. U.S. Bureau of the Census, *Statistical Abstract of the United States 1996* (Washington, D.C.: Government Printing Office, 1996), Tables 1303 and 1304.

22. *Statistical Abstract 1996*, Tables 1288 and 1290.

Fig. 11.2 Trade and output decline synchronously in major markets, 1996–2001 (Percentage change on a year-to-year basis)

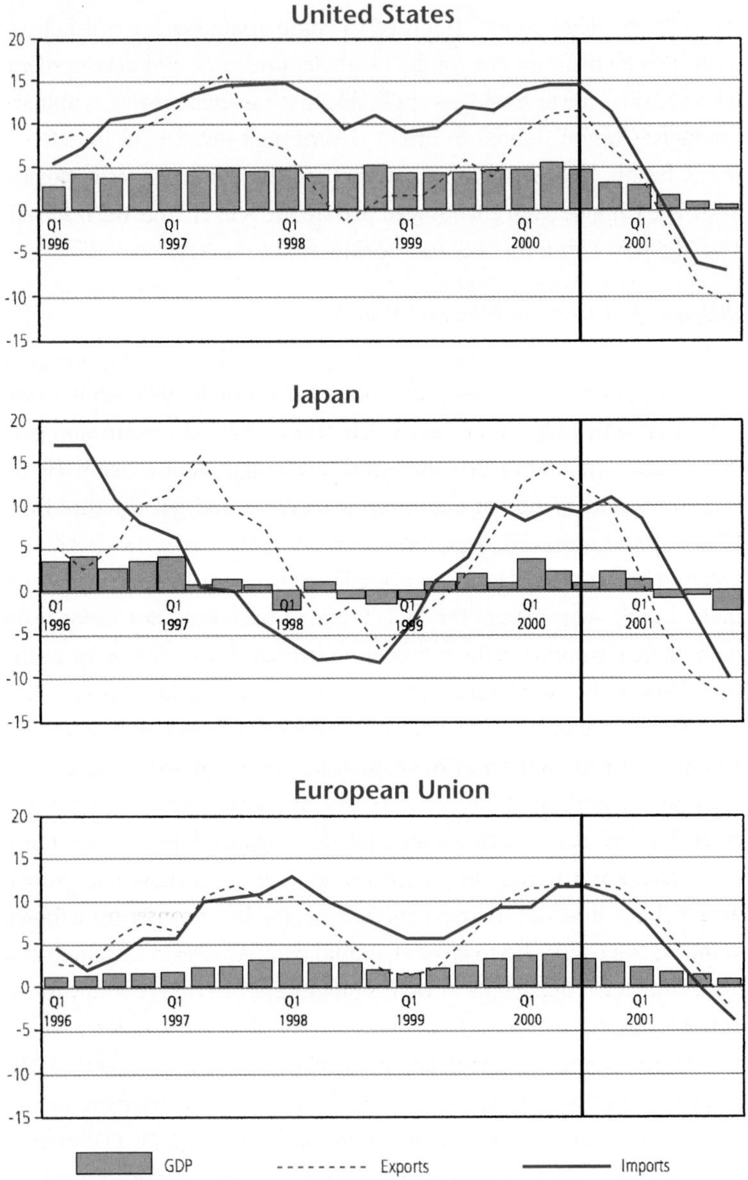

United States

Japan

European Union

GDP   - - - - - - Exports   —— Imports

SOURCE: World Trade Organization, *Annual Report 2002.*

Strategic Trade: Clinton's National Export Strategy

Clinton developed a national export strategy that reduced controls on high-technology products such as computers.[23] The president became "CEO, USA" or "Uncle Sam, salesman," taking credit for persuading Saudi Arabia to buy Boeing planes and an AT&T phone system rather

23. AT&T could now bid for $40 billion in phone equipment orders from China.

than European models. Europeans complained that Washington used political muscle to exclude economic competitors.[24] Some critics argued that Clinton could not have it both ways—free trade and strategic trade.

A truly strategic trade policy would seek to enhance long-range strategic interests—not business profits. Professor Henry Nau argued that Clinton gave minimal attention to democratic reforms in the former Second World and to halting the spread of dangerous technologies. Instead, the president focused on economic security, defined as high-wage jobs and access to foreign markets for U.S. firms. But which was more strategic—access to Japanese car markets or close partnership with Tokyo to deal with North Korea?[25]

Multilateral Trade: GATT and the World Trade Organization

As noted earlier, the General Agreement on Tariffs and Trade was established after World War II to reduce barriers to international trade. By the early 1990s, GATT participants (125 countries) generated 85 percent of world trade. But the U.S. and many other governments wanted a stronger forum. They agreed in 1993 to replace GATT with the World Trade Organization (WTO), Formalized in 1995, the WTO became a full-fledged international governmental organization, not a mere coordinating secretariat. The WTO's top decision-making forum is a semiannual ministerial meeting intended to give it more political clout than GATT. The WTO had stronger, clearer rules than GATT that applied not just to manufactures but also to agricultural commodities and some services such as accountancy.[26] These rules would be enforced by a semijudicial disputes procedure. Departing from GATT practice, reports by independent panels would be automatically adopted by the WTO unless a consensus opposed them. Countries that have had complaints lodged against them may appeal to an appellate body, but its verdict is binding. Thus, WTO members cannot block adverse findings, as they could under GATT. If offenders did not comply with panel recommendations, trading partners could claim compensation or, as a last resort, impose tit-for-tat sanctions.

Many members of Congress opposed the WTO because, they said, it challenged U.S. sovereignty, would raise the U.S. deficit by eliminating tariff revenues, forbid subsidies important to U.S. farmers, and do little to protect intellectual property or promote free trade in services. Environmentalists worried that the U.S. would have to lower its protective standards (for example, barriers to imported tuna caught by methods that trapped dolphins) because the WTO might regard them as obstacles to free trade.

The Clinton administration, and later the administration of George W. Bush, discounted any threat posed by the WTO to U.S. sovereignty.

24. In May 1994, Saudi Arabia gave a $4 billion contract—the biggest telecommunications contract in history—to AT&T after visits to Riyadh by Clinton's secretary of state and secretary of commerce, and a Clinton letter to King Fahd. A Canadian and a Swedish firm claimed to have underbid AT&T.

25. Henry R. Nau, *Trade and Security: U.S. Policy at Cross-Purposes* (Washington, D.C.: AEI Press, 1995).

26. Robert B. Reich, *The Work of Nations: Preparing Ourselves for 21st-Century Capitalism* (New York: Knopf, 1991).

The George W. Bush Economic Agenda

The George W Bush administration called for freer trade with the countries of the Middle East as well as with those of Latin America. When U.S. producers asked for help, however, the Bush team defied WTO rules and raised tariffs on imported steel (except from Mexico and Canada). When Europeans said they did not want bioengineered foods, Washington asked the WTO to declare their rules illegal. Other governments complained of massive subsidies to U.S. agriculture, for example, sugar and dairy products, and export credits.

The main economic priority of the Bush team, however, was tax breaks, mainly for top income brackets, presented as a panacea for whatever ailed the economy. As the U.S. federal debt mounted, foreign investors lost confidence and drove down the value of the dollar. A second Bush priority was oil. The administration threw away previous restraints to open wild places to mining, drilling, and lumbering. It propagated voluntary action as the best way to cope with environmental issues and industrial safety. Confirming the expectations of geoeconomists and Marxists, the Bush team projected U.S. military forces to oil-rich regions such as the Caspian Sea and Persian Gulf while neglecting areas without oil, even the rife-with-tension Korean peninsula. Meanwhile, the Bush team made sure that friends and donors got multimillion-dollar contracts to rebuild Iraq.

Each country retains the right to make and implement its policy regardless of WTO rulings.[27] They expected that liberalized trade under the WTO would generate more income for the U.S. and the world. More trade would mean higher revenues from tax income—not tariffs. DRI/McGraw-Hill estimated in the mid-1990s that trade liberalization would generate 1.4 million jobs (most of them well paid) over ten years.

Mexico, Canada, and the U.S.: Are Free Trade and FDI Win–Win?

Arguments for and against free trade were tested after the North American Free Trade Agreement (NAFTA) entered force in 1994. NAFTA established a free-trade area linking the U.S. with Canada and Mexico, its first- and third-largest trading partners, respectively. The theory held that each partner would benefit by reason of its comparative advantage. U.S. wages in manufacturing exceeded Mexican by 7 to 1, but U.S. productivity led Mexico's by 8 to 1. The exact productivity–compensation balance differed by industry, but so would the cost of moving U.S. factories to Mexico. With or without NAFTA, the U.S. would "export" many low-skill jobs.

Before NAFTA, Mexican trade barriers averaged 11 percent on imports, compared to the U.S. average of 4 percent. Reducing these barriers could generate more jobs in both countries. Mexicans bought 80 percent of their total imports from the U.S. As more Mexicans received higher wages, they could be expected to buy more U.S. manufactures. Mexico, like Canada, needed the secure access to the U.S. markets that a free trade agreement could provide.[28]

But political considerations rivaled economic considerations. Mexican reformers (many with U.S. business degrees) hoped to push–pull Mexico

27. The future looked dim. The National Association of Manufacturers reported that 30 percent of companies said they could not reorganize work because employees could not learn new jobs; another 25 percent said that they could not upgrade products because employees could not learn the necessary skills. Louis V. Gerstner, Jr., "Our Schools Are Failing, Do We Care?" *New York Times*, May 27, 1994, A27.

28. Gilbert R. Winham, "NAFTA and the Trade Policy Revolution of the 1980s: A Canadian Perspective," *International Journal* 49, no. 3 (summer 1994): 472–508 at 478 ff.

from the Third World into the First. NAFTA could help them succeed with little risk to U.S. interests.[29] Perhaps NAFTA would contribute to democracy as well as to greater prosperity in Mexico. Yet the very day that NAFTA entered force, January 1, 1994, an insurrection broke out in the state of Chiapas, triggering demands throughout all of Mexico for political and economic reform. Hopes for better governance in Mexico were dashed in the mid-1990s by high-level political assassinations and involvement in drug-trafficking and a massacre of Mayan Indians in Chiapas.

All calculations as to NAFTA's economic effect were thrown off by a financial crisis in Mexico in January 1995, following a steep devaluation of the peso in December 1994. Mexico's output fell 7 percent in 1995, but the Clinton administration arranged a $50 billion rescue plan with the IMF that quickly stabilized the peso.

The U.S.–Mexican border region flourished as a kind of "fourth member of NAFTA." With 20 million inhabitants and $100 billion in cross-border trade, the area in 1996 witnessed 225 million legal frontier crossings each way—mostly Mexican shoppers who spent $22 billion in the U.S. some Mexicans reexamined their national identity, while more Mexican women joined the labor force, usually at low wages.[30] There were winners and losers, but Mexico seemed to be NAFTA's major beneficiary. From 1993 through 2002, U.S. trade with Canada increased 80 percent, but U.S. trade with Mexico nearly tripled. What had been a $2 billion U.S. trade surplus with Mexico turned into a $30 billion deficit.[31]

U.S. workers lost their jobs to Mexicans in the textile and clothing industries; also in electronics, transport equipment, metal products, and industrial machinery. Overall, however, U.S. jobs in manufacturing remained stable, and wages rose until the economic downturn in 2001–2003. Still, NAFTA-related job losses hit some communities very hard, for example, El Paso, Texas, and Gaston County, North Carolina, where 7,400 people lost jobs from a total population of 191,000. In 2001, the U.S. Labor Department gave NAFTA-related aid to 21,000 displaced workers—one-third more than in 2000.

What Mexico gained it began to lose in the early 21st century as many U.S. companies shifted production from *maquiladora* plants close to the U.S. border to China. For example, a maker of golf club shafts based near San Diego closed two of its three plants in nearby Tijuana and increased production in China. Why? To lower labor costs in a very competititive business. Again Mexicans lamented their location— "so far from God, so close to the United States."

NAFTA had both positive and negative effects on the environmemt. The good news was that there were few signs of a "race to the bottom" as

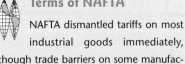

Terms of NAFTA

NAFTA dismantled tariffs on most industrial goods immediately, though trade barriers on some manufactures and agricultural commodities would remain for five to fifteen years. NAFTA included special agreements on services, investment, and intellectual property rights. One effect was that U.S. investors could own and operate firms on the same basis as Mexicans in Mexico and Canadians in Canada. Washington won side agreements to improve environmental protection and labor conditions in Mexico and to deal with possible import surges: If explosive trade growth threatens a domestic industry, a special committee can recommend treaty revisions.

29. Paul Krugman, "The Uncomfortable Truth About NAFTA: It's Foreign Policy, Stupid," *Foreign Affairs* 72, no. 5 (November/December 1993): 13–19.

30. Timothy C. Brown, "The Fourth Member of NAFTA: The U.S.–Mexico Border," *Annals of the American Academy of Political and Social Science* 550 (March 1997): 105 ff.; Isidro Morales Moreno, "Mexico's National Identity After NAFTA," *American Behavioral Scientist* 40, no. 7 (June/July 1997); and Ann K. Nauman, "The Integration of Women into the Mexican Labor Force Since NAFTA," ibid.; also David R. D'avila Villers, ed., *NAFTA, The First Year: A View from Mexico* (Lanham, Md.: University Press of America, 1996).

31. *Kiplinger Business Forecasts* (Washington, D.C.), No. 0712, July 10, 2002.

The Complex Interface of Business, Politics, Law, and the Environment

S. D. Myers, Inc. based in Tallmadge, Ohio, recycled polychlorinated biphenyl (PCB) wastes. The firm entered purchase orders for more than CND$50 million to treat PCBs from Canadian schools, hospitals, and municipal utilities. When the Canadian government banned the export of PCB waste, the Ohio company lost its Canadian business. S. D. Myers sued for damages before a NAFTA arbitration tribunal. The tribunal ruled that Canada's export ban violated two NAFTA obligations. The tribunal said the ban aimed to protect Canadian processors of PCB waste and discriminated unfairly against a U.S. firm, which charged less than its Canadian rivals. The tribunal awarded S. D. Myers $8.2 million for damages incurred in 1994–1997, when Canada withdrew its export ban. The award was far less than the value of the business lost, but the S. D. Myers attorney said the decision showed NAFTA worked for small as well as large firms.

NAFTA tribunals had ruled against Canada in every case brought against it, Canadian NewsWire Ltd. reported on October 21, 2002. By contrast, the U.S. had won every case brought against it, and Mexico had prevailed in a majority of cases brought against it.

manufacturers moved to where environmental controls were weakest. But some communities along the U.S.–Canadian and U.S.–Mexican borders suffered more air pollution due to rising rail and road freight traffic. There was also more pollution from industries producing petroleum products, base metals, and transportation equipment.[32] One Canadian newspaper observed, however, that Canada's environment improved when the country had to meet U.S. standards.

Did NAFTA register any political fallout? Mexican–U.S. dialogue and cooperation improved in many fields. Mexico's PRI party lost the presidential election for the first time in 2000. The new president, **Vicente Fox**, had a good relationship with George W. Bush. After his inauguration, Bush made his first presidential trip abroad to Mexico, where he pledged to reform immigration procedures for Mexicans. After 9/11, however, Bush focused on terrorism even as Fox wrestled with a legislature dominated by the PRI old guard. But Fox stood by Mexico's NAFTA commitment to lower tariffs for U.S. food products in 2003, despite demonstrations by worried Mexican farmers. He also went all-out to wipe out drug traffickers and their government patrons.

Regionalization vs. globalization? George W. Bush wanted to extend free trade southward. Congress in October 2002 granted the president a freer hand to negotiate trade deals. The White House immediately established a free trade regime with Chile. Costa Rica and other Central American governments wanted similar treatment. If this movement continued, NAFTA could extend nearly from the North to the South Pole. The leaders of Venezuela and some other Latin countries, however, seemed in the early 21st century to be more interested in demagogic promises than in trade deals.

With or without the rest of Latin America, the region from Canada to Chile constituted a formidable economic region of 432 million people (15 million in Chile, 32 m. in Canada, 103 m. in Mexico, and 282 m. in the U.S.). An enlarged EU, however, could contain more than 600 million—half the size of India or China! Would the future see a face-off between the Americas and the trade blocs of Europe and Asia? Would regionalization torpedo globalization? Our next case study suggests that rumors about the death of globalization were vastly exaggerated.

The Airplane Industry—National Prize or Transatlantic Interdependence?

As the 21st century began, two airplane manufacturers, the Boeing Corporation and Airbus Industrie, stood toe-to-toe in what could be a zero-sum competition (*concurrence* in French) between America's single

32. Report by the Trilateral Commission for Environmental Cooperation (CEC) issued December 15, 2002, at www.ced.org. For background, see Bryan W. Husted, "The Impact of NAFTA on Mexico's Environmental Policy," *Growth and Change* 28, no. 1 (winter 1997): 24 ff.; Anthony DePalma, "NAFTA Environmental Lags May Delay Free Trade Expansion," *The New York Times*, May 21, 1997, A4.

biggest exporter and a rapidly growing rival. Twenty percent of Airbus was owned by BAe Systems in England, and 80 percent was owned by the European Aeronautics Defence and Space Company—"EADS," formed in 2000 by the merger of French, German, and Spanish defense contractors. The civil aircraft industry is heavily politicized and closely tied to the defense industry. Without export of civilian and military airplanes, America's trade imbalance would be much larger. Competition between U.S. and European plane makers takes place in the framework of a huge transatlantic trade regulated by bilateral and multilateral agreements. A trade war over aircraft could damage other businesses and consumers not connected to either Airbus or Boeing.

Each side accused the other of unfair practices. The Americans said that Airbus took off only thanks to billions of direct subsidies by European governments. Europeans replied that Boeing and other U.S. aviation giants benefited from military contracts in two world wars, the Cold War, and the post–Cold War. Washington subsidized R&D and mass production of advanced war planes—many sold overseas as well as to the Pentagon. Military R&D and assembly techniques transferred readily to civilian aircraft manufacture.

Unlike Europeans, U.S. manufacturers could count on a huge home market. Boeing and Lockheed had worked closely with U.S. carriers such as Pan American and TWA, which had pioneered world routes. The Americans often acted before others and then held on to their **first mover advantages (FMAs)**. Added to all this, Congress gave U.S. airlines a $15 billion bailout after 9/11—what Europeans called a Marshall Plan for Boeing.

Of course it takes more than subsidies to succeed. Dynamic risk-taking entrepreneurs had played a vital role in U.S. aviation.[33] Despite government funding, the USSR never produced world-class civilian planes. Soviet engineers built interceptors, satellites, and missiles but lacked any drive to please civilian consumers. Their forte was rugged machinery for hard power. Soviet planes were purchased mainly by Soviet allies and clients.

Air frames are a strategic industry. Any country that buys its aircraft from one supplier is hostage to it for spare parts and improved models. China bought its first Boeing 707s in 1972, immediately after President Nixon's visit to Mao Zedong. Unwilling then to count on U.S. goodwill, Beijing purchased extra planes to cannibalize for parts. By the 1990s, mutual trust had deepened so that Boeing operated one of its three largest overseas centers for spare parts at the Beijing Capital Airport, and stationed field representatives in eighteen cities throughout China. Leery

Early critics of NAFTA feared a "loud sucking sound" as Canadian and U.S. jobs moved south. Supporters hoped free trade would boost employment in all three countries. Some U.S. firms established *maquiladora* operations just inside the Mexican border—export-processing plants that took advantage of low-wage labor (often female) and proximity to the U.S. market. Despite difficult working conditions, many Mexicans welcomed the regular wages of the *maquiladora* plants. They lamented the "loud sucking sound" when many of these jobs moved to China.

33. William E. Boeing built his first seaplane next to a lake in Seattle just ten years after the Wright Brothers' first flight.

Anti-globalizationist wrath mixed with antiwar, anticapitalist, and anti-American feelings when the European Social Forum met in Florence, Italy, in November 2002. In early 2003, as U.S. and UK forces fought their way into Iraq, many Europeans spurned U.S. brands.

of dependency, however, China and other countries bought Airbus as well as Boeing products.

European aircraft producers found it hard to catch up with the United States. They had less money than Americans to invest in the 1950s and 1960s. Each European government favored its own manufacturers and its own flag carrier, such as Air France. Still, the UK and French governments decided to bolster a strategic industry by coproducing a supersonic transport (SST), the Concorde. Since the U.S. Congress refused to subsidize a similar plane, Britain and France found a niche. Rather than invest in an SST, Boeing built a jumbo jet, the 747. The Concorde was glamorous but costly. It consumed three times as much fuel per passenger mile as a Boeing 747. Because any SST generates sonic boom, the Concorde won few overland routes.

France and Britain, later joined by Germany and Spain, targeted another niche: They would coproduce a wide-bodied "Airbus" for shorter hauls. The idea was sound but the organization poor. A consortium assigned tasks by quota: France's Aérospatiale and British Aerospace got the largest jobs because their governments each owned 30 percent of the business; Germany's Daimler-Benz Aerospace and Spain's CASA received fewer jobs—20 percent and 10 percent, respectively.[34]

Asserting that government subsidies for Airbus were unfair, the White House in 1978 threatened to impose antidumping duties on Airbus aircraft ordered by Eastern Airlines. To ward off such action, the Europeans agreed in the 1979 GATT treaty to ban uneconomic pricing for airliners.

34. For reportage and analysis, see *The Economist, Aviation Week & Space Technology,* and *Europe.* For background, see Lynn Matthew, *Birds of Prey: Boeing vs. Airbus, A Battle for the Skies,* rev. ed. (New York: Four Walls Eight Windows, 1997).

The place of the Commission in the overall structure of the European Union is discussed in Chapter 15.

As Airbus gained still more market share, an EU–U.S. agreement in 1992 restricted "launch aid"—the money invested in new models–to one-third of total development costs and required that this sum plus interest be repaid within seventeen years.

The 1992 EU–U.S. agreement ended most disputes over existing aircraft but left open the question of who would build the next generation plane—a super-jumbo jet capable of flying 550 to 800 passengers over oceans. Boeing proposed joint development with Airbus. By 1995, however, the two sides concluded they could not work together on this project. Airbus decided to proceed with its own plans for a super-jumbo; Boeing opted merely to improve is existing planes. In 1997, as we see in the box "EU vs. Boeing," Europeans tried to prevent Boeing from merging with McDonnell Douglas Corporation.

The EU vs. Boeing + MDC

Boeing wanted to merge with the McDonnell Douglas Corporation (MDC) in 1997. EU Commissioner for Competition Karel Van Miert opted to fight the merger, though this action risked a trade war with the U.S. on many fronts. Van Miert said he was defending "competition," but most observers saw his action as strategic industrial policy writ large. He argued that a Boeing–MDC merger would give Boeing the benefit of extensive R&D at MDC paid for by the U.S. Defense Department. He complained also that recently signed exclusivity deals between Boeing and three U.S. airlines would keep Airbus from offering them its super-jumbo for the next twenty years.

How could the EU stop two U.S. firms from merging? In 1989 the EU declared its approval necessary for any merger of companies with a combined worldwide turnover of 2.5 billion European Currency Units (ecus)—worth about $2.7 billion—and a combined European turnover of 100 million ecus. Regardless where the firms were based, the EU could block their merger if it is not "compatible with the common market." How? By its own rules the EU could fine Boeing 10 percent of its worldwide earnings, beginning with any Boeing assets in Europe. President Clinton hinted in July 1997 that the U.S. might reply in kind—perhaps confiscating any Airbus properties in the U.S.

Both the EU and the U.S. claimed to support free trade and to oppose monopolies. In the 1990s the EU usually allowed the U.S. Federal Trade Commission to decide U.S. merger cases and vice versa. So it was unusual but not unprecedented for the EU to protest the Boeing–MDC merger because it had already been approved by the FTC. Earlier, however, the FTC had imposed tough conditions on the merger of two Swiss pharmaceutical companies.

Van Miert grudgingly gave EU approval to the Boeing–MDC merger after Boeing agreed not to enforce its exclusivity contracts and pledged to license any patents derived from MDC defense contracts.

French leaders said Boeing's concessions to the EU were merely cosmetic and demanded that the EU monitor Boeing's compliance carefully. Meanwhile, Airbus signed up more than twice as many new orders as Boeing at the 1997 Paris Air Show.

Major European firms—Rolls-Royce, GEC–Marconi, Smiths Industries, Messier–Dowty—supplied components to Boeing. Europeans could benefit when Boeing licensed the results of military research done by MDC. Both German and Japanese firms had used licenses to co-produce as strategic ladders to advance their technology. Japanese firms succeeded without really flying. They mastered design and integration skills as well as materials to produce major components for U.S. and European aircraft. They often applied the knowledge they had learned from one foreign partner when working with another. Thus, Kawasaki Heavy Industries developed a tool for Airbus from its commercial experiences with Boeing, enabling Airbus to perform tasks it had previously been unable to perform.

When Saudi Arabia thought of buying planes from Europe, Clinton reminded King Fahd of who saved his country from Iraq and Iran. The phone call was worth $6 billion in orders for Boeing and MDC. In this same spirit, President Jacques Chirac persuaded China to buy Airbus products, if only because France muffled Western complaints about human rights in China.

By the early 21st century, Boeing plants in Seattle were still turning out more planes, but Airbus—with main assembly lines in Tolouse, France—was winning more orders. The struggle for market share pushed both firms to trim prices. Competition intensified after "9/11" because most carriers cut back orders of new planes.

Boeing lost two major deals in 2001–2002—one to Airbus, the other to another U.S. firm, Lockheed-Martin. In 2002, Airbus won a $12 billion order from the no-frills British airline easyJet for 120 planes. Boeing had hoped to win at least half the order but got nothing. Boeing was losing its erstwhile FMA against latecomers. The more planes Airbus produced, the more it achieved economies of scale like those long enjoyed by Boeing.

Boeing lost a much larger contract in 2001, when the Pentagon picked Lockheed-Martin to build an all-purpose Joint Strike Fighter (JSF) for U.S. and UK forces, and was expected to buy more than 3,000 planes for more than $200 billion. This sum would be 10 to 20 times larger than the likely Airbus–easyJet deal; four times greater than Boeing's total revenues in 2002 ($58 billion); and eight times the 2002 revenues at Airbus.

A British collaborator provided the technology that helped Lockheed win the JSF contract—the shaft-driven lift fan provided by Rolls Royce/Allison Defence. The fan was for the short take-off and vertical landing (STOVL) capability required by the U.S. Marines and the Royal Navy. Part of the JSF would be assembled in Lancashire, England. Vision Systems International, an Israeli firm cooperating with Kaiser Electronics, would also contribute to the JSF. Lockheed also expected to cooperate with firms in Italy, the Netherlands, Turkey, Canada, Denmark, and Norway.[35]

Meanwhile, the Bush administration encouraged Boeing, prime contractor for missile defense systems, to bring European firms into missile defense projects. In July 2002, Boeing announced partnerships to create products for a global missile defense with England's BAe, the pan-European EADS, and the Italian firm Alenia. London's *Daily Telegraph* claimed that only BAe had the kinds of technology and expertise the Americans wanted, and that the other deals were politically motivated—to reduce European resistance to U.S. missile defense. Thus, what could

35. In 2000, Lockheed-Martin and Airbus, agreed to cooperate on a number of aeronautical initiatives including support systems for the JSF and a 50–50 collaboration to build a support plane for U.S. and European armies. Lockeed considered but then backed away from contributing to the proposed Airbus super-jumbo. By 2002, Airbus was boasting it would produce a transport plane to supersede the Lockheed Galaxy and Boeing Super Guppy.

have been a bitterly nationalist competition was heavily interlaced with transatlantic cooperation. Earlier, a U.S. firm provided the computer-aided design and manufacturing programs for Airbus, while a French company provided the same software for Boeing. Some Airbus planes used General Electric engines. Indeed, Boeing and EADS were collaborating in various ways. In 2001, they cohosted two global forums to educate suppliers and airlines about using bar codes on parts for commercial airplanes and military logistics. Together, Boeing and EADS set out International Standard Organization (ISO) technical specifications, as sought by U.S. and other NATO procurement agencies.

Emboldened by the growing market share of Airbus, EADS set up a lobbying and business office near the White House and began to seek U.S. defense contracts. It planned to begin small and then strive for larger contracts. Some Americans regarded the European intrusion as impudent, especially after 9/11, but the Pentagon encouraged EADS and other European firms to bid.

In short, relations between airplane and defense industries were not zero-sum. Instead, they were components in a complex interdependence uniting both sides of the Atlantic and some other countries. To be sure, the business was highly competitive. McDonnell Douglas, once an innovator, became known in the 21st century for its name on toy models sold on the Internet. Looking ahead, the prospects of both Boeing and Airbus were uncertain. Airbus planned to manufacture its A380, a 550-passenger jet by 2006, and claimed to have 80 percent of the orders needed to make it profitable. But the super-jumbo's success hinged not only on the state of global business but also on efforts to curb terrorism. If the two companies had worked together to produce a super-jumbo, there might have been mutual benefit. If only one tried, it alone assumed the risks and possible gains.

The Boeing–Airbus competition was good for airlines in China, Japan, and other countries because it encouraged each company to improve the quality of its products and contain prices. But plane makers outside Europe and the U.S. could build nothing rivaling a jumbo passenger plane.[36] China bought Russian military planes but purchased civilian airliners in the U.S. or France. In 2002, the U.S. State Department accused Hughes Electronics Corporation and Boeing Satellite Systems of illegally transferring sensitive technology to China that would improve its missiles. If the charges were upheld by a federal judge and higher State Department authorities, the firms could be fined $60 million and barred for three years from selling controlled technologies abroad.

36. However, both European and U.S. manufacturers sought to collaborate with aerospace firms abroad. In 1997, Airbus planned a new 100-seat regional airplane with Chinese and Singaporean aircraft companies. SeaLaunch, a project to launch commercial satellites at sea, combined Norwegian platforms and Ukrainian boosters with Boeing's integrative planning. The first element of the International Space Station was built by a Russian firm under subcontract to Boeing. Boeing was collaborating with other Russian firms to conduct supersonic flights and develop new titanium alloys. By 1997, China had supplied major parts for 2,000 Boeing planes and helped design the 737–700 empennage. Know-how, risks, and potential profits were being shared.

Is win–win possible? It requires an act of faith to trust that an invisible hand will guide all actors to greater prosperity if each pursues its private good and practices free trade. If Saudi Arabia buys a 737 or 747 rather than an Airbus, the near-term and long-term benefits accrue to Boeing, Washington, and U.S. taxpayers. Saudi Arabia may become locked into its Boeing connection, depriving Europe of markets and capital for future R&D.[37]

The Boeing–Airbus case highlights the importance of strategic, knowledge-based industries in economic transformation and infuence in world affairs. It suggests that the ideals of free trade and free competition without government intervention are unattainable in certain industries.

Sources of Competitive Strength

In 2002, the European Union committed itself to take in ten new members. The Euro reached parity and more against the dollar. Airbus, at the same time, seemed to pull ahead of Boeing. How competitive were the world's economies? The World Economic Forum assessed competitiveness by means of the Growth Competitiveness Index (GCI)[38] and Microeconomic Competiveness Index (MICI). The two indexes overlapped, but the GCI anticipated strengths over the next six to eight years, while the MICI asked how well a country used its present stock of resources.[39] The country where Boeing was based placed first on both indexes in 2002, while Finland ranked second (reversing their positions in 2001). But no country in the Airbus consortium placed in the top ten on the GCI, though the UK placed 11th. Both the UK and Germany placed among the top ten on the MICD. France was 30th on the GCI and 15th on the MICI; Spain, 22nd and 25th on the two indexes. If the World Economic Forum was correct, the success of Airbus did not tell the whole story.

Many small economies did better on the future-oriented GCI than the MICI. Thus, Taiwan was 3rd in growth competitiveness but only 16th in microeconomic assets. Similarly, Singapore was 4th on the GCI but 9th on the MICI. In the same vein, the top-ranked ex-Communist country on the GCI was Estonia—26th, which placed only 30th on the MICI. Slovenia, however, was nearly the same on each index—28th on the GCI and 27th on the MICI.

We also see major discrepancies between the GCI and HDI rankings (juxtaposed in Table 11.3). Most of the top countries in GCI lagged in HDI—the U.S., Finland, Singapore, Switzerland, Denmark, Hong Kong,

37. When I flew to Tehran in 1998, the Iranian carriers used a European Airbus, while U.S.-made military planes, acquired before the 1979 revolution, could still be seen at Iranian airports.

38. The GCI focused on three assets: (1) technology—innovation, information, communication; (2) public institutions—stability of law and contracts, lack of corruption; and (3) macroeconomic stability—rates of inflation, savings, exchange, credit, and government expenditures. For its part, the MICI measured the sophistication of company operations and the national business environment—the set of institutions, market structures, and economic policies supportive of high current levels of prosperity. The GCI was heavily influenced by Jeffrey D. Sachs and others at the Harvard University Institute for International Development; the MICI by Michael E. Porter and others at the Harvard Business School. See Peter Cornelius et al., eds., *Global Competitiveness Report 2002–2003* (New York: Oxford University Press, 2003). In 2002, Sachs moved to Columbia University's Earth Institute and the UN World Health Organization.

39. The EU's fifteen member states are consulted on merger regulation but have no formal say in the final Commission decision. The member states presented a united front though individual states wavered, fearing a knockdown effect on other industries if a trade war erupted. Philip Lawrence and other academic specialists from the UK, Italy, and Germany urged the Commission to block the merger. See "Europe Must Fight US Air Threat," *The Independent*, July 18, 1997.

Estonia's capital kept its medieval walls and Gothic churches even as McDonald's and modern hotels encircled the Old Town in the center of Tallinin. While most other former Soviet republics remained authoritarian and statist, democratic Estonia became a more free market than any major European country. Some observers warned that joining the European Union with its thousands of rules would gut Estonia's dynamism. But each country has its own character and needs. Slovenia was another star of the ex-Communist realm. Unlike Estonia, however, much of its economy remained state protected and regulated.

and Chile. The top countries in HDI—Norway, Sweden, and Canada—lagged in GCI, as did others, such as Australia, Iceland, Japan, and the Netherlands. Reasons for the discrepancies differ from case to case, but some of the most competitive states lacked the welfare benefits that boosted HDI rankings. Compare, for example, the U.S. and Canada. When looking at countries ranked lower than 30, the comparisons lose meaning because the GCI omits about half of the states with HDI rankings.

Less-developed countries can become competitive by importing technology from abroad and putting it to good use. Highly developed

Table 11.3 Growth Competitiveness Rank vs. HDR

Country	Growth Competitiveness Ranking, 2002	Human Development Ranking, 2002
United States	1	6
Finland	2	10
Taiwan	3	—
Singapore	4	25
Sweden	5	2
Switzerland	6	11
Australia	7	5
Canada	8	3
Norway	9	1
Denmark	10	14
United Kingdom	11	13
Iceland	12	7
Japan	13	9
Germany	14	17
Netherlands	15	8
New Zealand	16	19
Hong Kong SAR	17	23
Austria	18	15
Israel	19	22
Chile	20	38
Korea	21	27
Spain	22	21
Portugal	23	28
Ireland	24	18
Belgium	25	4
Estonia	26	42
Malaysia	27	59
Slovenia	28	29
Hungary	29	35
France	30	12
Thailand	31	70
South Africa	32	107
China	33	96
Tunisia	34	97
Mauritius	35	67
Lithuania	36	49
Trinidad and Tobago	37	50
Greece	38	24
Italy	39	20
Czech Republic	40	33
Botswana	41	126
Uruguay	42	40

Table 11.3 Growth Competitiveness Rank vs. HDR (*continued*)

Country	Growth Competitiveness Ranking, 2002	Human Development Ranking, 2002
Costa Rica	43	43
Latvia	44	53
Mexico	45	54
Brazil	46	73
Jordan	47	99
India	48	124
Slovak Republic	49	36
Panama	50	57
Poland	51	37
Dominican Republic	52	94
Namibia	53	122
Peru	54	82
Morocco	55	123
Colombia	56	68
El Salvador	57	104
Croatia	58	48
Sri Lanka	59	89
Jamaica	60	86
Philippines	61	77
Bulgaria	62	62
Argentina	63	34
Russian Federation	64	60
Vietnam	65	109
Romania	66	63
Indonesia	67	110
Venezuela	68	69
Turkey	69	85
Guatemala	70	120
Nigeria	71	148
Paraguay	72	90
Ecuador	73	93
Bangladesh	74	145
Nicaragua	75	118
Honduras	76	116
Ukraine	77	80
Bolivia	78	114
Zimbabwe	79	128
Haiti	80	146

SOURCES: World Economic Forum, *Global Competitiveness Report 2002–2003* (New York: Oxford University Press, 2003), and United Nations Development Programme, *Human Development Report 2002* (New York: Oxford University Press, 2002).

Is Capitalism Doomed?

Communism has expired, but will Lenin have the last laugh? He predicted that capitalism will destroy itself. First, by exporting capital to less developed countries, capitalists will give them the means to rival the West. Second, Western capitalists will eventually fight one another over market share. Lenin did not think, as Kant did, that representative democracy would promote trade and stem war.

Lenin's first point gained plausibility with the spread of technology. Many technological breakthroughs occurred in North America, but Japanese, Chinese, and other Asians quickly mastered the know-how and used it to generate a competitive advantage.

Some critics suggest that capitalism is doomed because economic imperatives conflict with realpolitik. Capitalism thrives on free flows of labor, technology, and money. But each state wants greater wealth and power; each wants to sell, grow, and possess more. Unless the U.S. stands head and shoulders above all rivals combined, movement toward global integration will be reversed. But this kind of hegemony cannot last. Sooner or later, others—perhaps Europe, Japan, or China—will challenge the hegemon.

countries must be innovative just to stay ahead. The World Economic Forum identified twenty four core-innovators—countries that patented at least fifteen U.S. utility patents per million population in 2001. The remaining fifty or so countries studied were defined as non-core innovators. Core-innovators are also better at adapting foreign technology and tend to license more foreign technology than do non-core innovators.

The U.S. scored high in technology and macroeconomic stability (just before the federal budget surplus disappeared) but only 16th in stability of public institutions (as Enron and other frauds surfaced in 2002). Finland, by contrast, ranked high in honesty as well as technology but did less well in macroeconomic environment. Taiwan scored high on technology; Singapore, in macroeconomic strengths.

Change in the rankings can speak volumes. From 2001 to 2002, China rose from 39th to 33rd on the GCI, despite worries about bank solvency, while India rose from 57th to 48th. Russia was virtually unchanged at 63/64, but Argentina fell from 49th to 63rd. Turkey went from 54th to 69th. Both Argentina and Turkey did moderately well on technology but poorly in public institutions and macroeconomic stability. The GCI placed Tunisia at 34th and Botswana at 41st, taking note of their moderately strong public institutions and the macreconomic environment.

The MICI for 2002 dovetailed with the GCI in many cases. Where it did not, there was a story to tell. The UK ranked only 11th on the GCI but 3rd on the MICI—up from 7th in 2001. The improvement was due to greater venture capital availability, intellectual property rights protection, effectiveness of antitrust policy, and buyer sophistication. By contrast, the Netherlands's place on the MICI fell from 3rd in 2001 to 7th in 2002. This reflected declining sophistication in Dutch financial markets, firm strategy, public administration, and marketing. Malaysia scored the biggest jump on the MICI—from 37th to 26th in 2002, thanks to greater cluster vitality and stronger rules governing competition, value chain presence, and branding. However, the Philippines, Indonesia, Argentina, and Turkey all suffered significant declines on the MICI.

The World Economic Forum in 2002 argued that market economies offered the best prospects for economic growth. But it also noted the backlash against liberalization caused by the Enron and other business scandals in the U.S., and financial crises in countries such as Argentina. Also, many businesses lowered their commitment to globalization after 9/11. They became more cognizant of the risks in cross-border activities. Threats of terrorist activity underlined their vulnerability to forces beyond their control.

WHAT PROPOSITIONS HOLD? WHAT QUESTIONS REMAIN?

ROADS TO WEALTH

Adam Smith was correct. The material wealth of nations lies in their productive capacity rather than their gold hoard. The most productive nations have followed the path laid out by Smith and Ricardo—modified by Keynes. No system has met human needs better than the mixed market–welfare states pioneered in the West. They score higher in measures such as GDP, PPP, and the Human Development Index (HDI). The average First World citizen lives not "like a king," but better and longer than royalty of past centuries, with central heating, plumbing, a diversified diet, easy access to information and communication, and good health care. Three roads to wealth dominated IPE analysis as the 21st century began. The assumptions of each school are summarized in Table 11.4. The fourth alternative, state socialism, had few government backers except in Havana and Pyongyang.

Is there an ideal admixture of government intervention with the market? No formula fits all times and places. Japan's industrial policy and Germany's welfare state may have been useful for a time, but the less regulated American system seems to have worked better in the long run. A true comparison is impossible given America's natural endowment, its ethnic composition, and military hegemony since World War II.

Neoliberals concede that government intervention might be needed in some domains, for example, air traffic control or health care. In most economic spheres, they say, government meddling is not needed and may

Table 11.4 Why Economies Stagnate, Prosper, or Decline: Three Perspectives

Trend	Top-Down Neomercantilism	Bottom-Up Laissez-Faire and Free Trade	Neoliberal Synthesis
Stagnation	Weak government, poor resources	Excessive government obstructs comparative advantage	Failure to develop competitive advantage
Prosperity	Value-claiming by a strong, "can-do" government that uses industrial policy and strategic trade to limit FDI and achieve a favorable trade balance	Minimalist government that gives a free hand to free enterprise and free trade, in cooperation with WTO, to achieve a high rate of GDP growth	Competitive advantage by wise macroeconomic and technology policies; support for freer trade, combined with NTBs and VERs, conduce to economic growth, competitiveness, and high HDI
Decline	Exhaustion of raw materials or other key inputs; excessive foreign ownership; low barriers to dumping and cheap foreign products, permitting trade deficit and loss of market share	Excessive value-claiming and emphasis on profits, aggravated by excessive defense spending, leads to a low rate of GDP growth	Failure to maintain competitive advantage by effective macro-economic, technology, and trade policies reduces economic growth, market share, and HDI

do more harm than good. MITI played at best a supporting role in Japan's economic ascent. More important were cultural values—dedication to education, discipline, a perfectionist work ethic—combined with high rates of saving and investment.

What about strategic trade? As we saw when discussing the frontier of possibilities (Figures 1.3–1.5), trade can be win–win but one side may gain more than the other. Neomercantilists see states with trade surpluses as winners; those with trade deficits, as losers. Taiwan, with the world's largest currency reserves per capita in the 1990s, had more options than Argentina, heavily in debt. But neoliberals counter that a favorable trade balance does not necessarily mean that a country "wins." Ordinary Japanese would have a higher living standard if they had access to more foreign products, less costly than homegrown. If Japanese markets were more open, Tokyo would have less friction with Washington.

In business, as in diplomacy, Americans often insist: "Do it our way." To crack the Japanese market, more Americans need to learn the Japanese language and adapt. (It took years before U.S. auto exporters put steering columns on the righthand side for Japanese drivers.) If Americans became more truly global, their trade balance would take care of itself. The neoliberal holds that economic success comes not from claiming, hoarding, or redistributing wealth, but from creating values useful to others. In IPE, as in IR generally, the same principle applies: mutual gain policies, if followed by each party, enhance the interests of each better than exploitative value-claiming.

Memo to the EU Commission:

We need to redefine wealth. It is not a goal but a means. A means to what? The UN Development Programme provides a one-word answer: choice. This is the ultimate standard by which the Human Development Index measures the progress of each national political economy. The point of political life should be to open choices—to permit people to become all that they can be and wish to be, provided they do not harm others' choices. We can adapt this standard to measure the vitality of Europe and every other region—indeed, of the entire IPE system.

Choice rests upon the three variables that go into the HDI—health, education, and income—qualified by their availability to each gender (measured by the indexes of Gender Development and Empowerment). If we look more closely, we see that each ingredient in the HDI depends upon intellectual, political, cultural, and other freedoms. Choice as "output" requires choice as "input." If humans may choose how to study, think, and live, they are more likely to achieve the heatlh, education, and income that generate freedom of choice.

Looked at another way, the HDI measures social fitness—the ability of each society to cope with complex challenge and opportunities. This kind of fitness is found in the midrange of a spectrum between rigid hierarchy and chaos. The inhabitants of a fit society will enjoy high standards of health, education, and income. But they will also be flexible—able and ready to adapt.

More, they will be public spirited. They will value public goods such as clean air and water, security, and a spirit of brotherhood and sisterhood. They will eschew the parasitic logic of taking what they can for themselves—community be damned. Their public spirit will extend beyond their village to their state, region, and to the planet. Each will feel, with John Donne, that "no man [or woman] is an island; every person's death diminishes me."

Members of a fit society will value freedom and self-reliance while recognizing the need for a social safety net for the weak, ill, or aged. They will balance individualism and community. If Americans gravitate toward individualism, and Europeans, toward community, perhaps both should move to a Golden Mean suited to the time and place. Viewing wealth as a means to choice, we will do far more to protect our biosphere. One auto or even 1,000 autos in a given space may enhance individual choice. Ten thousand autos in the same space may not. If the 10,000 autos poison the air, that also reduces human choice. If autos are left to rust, we have still less room to move about. The U.S. and Europe have pioneered a lifestyle of material abundance. We must now pioneer a lifestyle that is more sustainable as well as gratifying.

Europe is the world's largest market of well-educated, affluent persons. Europeans can compete in nearly any domain. For example, several European firms beat out U.S. competitors to build turbines for China's Three Gorges Dam. Airbus is now winning more contracts than Boeing. But Europeans must cooperate more with each other. They should learn at least one of several common tongues (perhaps English, French, and German). Perhaps we should speak less of competitiveness and more of creativity. We Europeans would be better off if we focused less on beating the U.S. and more on unleashing our human potential.

We are tempted to protect whatever wealth-producing industries we have from foreign competition. But history confirms that Adam Smith's Invisible Hand works better than central guidance. Deregulation, on the other hand, invites abuse and chaos. Fitness requires a middle ground between order and disorder. Still, bottom-up development is superior to top down—both as a way of life and for its results.

KEY NAMES AND TERMS

absolute advantage	Gini Index	nontariff barriers (NTBs)
Bretton Woods system	gross national income (GNI)	North American Free Trade
capitalism	industrial policy	Agreement (NAFTA)
comparative advantage	International Monetary Fund	productivity–compensation
competitive advantage	(IMF)	balance
economic liberalism	laissez-faire	rule-based trading regime
export-led development	less developed country (LDC)	Adam Smith
first-mover advantage (FMA)	mercantilism	socialism
foreign direct investment (FDI)	Ministry of International Trade and	strategic trade
Vicente Fox	Industry (MITI)	voluntary export restraints (VERs)
free trade	most-favored nation (MFN)	World Bank
General Agreement on Tariffs and	neoliberalism	World Trade Organization
Trade (GATT)	neomercantilism	(WTO)

QUESTIONS TO DISCUSS

1. How adequately does the liberal thesis account for the rise of the First World? How important were resources extracted from the New World and capital derived from the slave trade?

2. What benefits did Josiah Wedgwood and Benjamin Franklin enjoy that might not have existed for a pragmatic scientist in 18th-century China? Mao Zedong's China? China in the 1990s?

3. If government subsidies helped McDonnell Douglas and Boeing, why didn't they get better results in the USSR?

4. If female literacy and liberation helped Sweden, why do so many women stay at home in equally prosperous Japan and Switzerland?

5. Study Table 11.1. Does domestic investment correlate with overall economic strength? Explain your answer. Do high levels of foreign trade correlate with overall economic strength? Explain your answer.

6. Is wealth more polarized in high-income countries than in low-income countries? Explain your answer.

7. Is NAFTA good for Mexicans? If yes, why? Is it good for Canadians?

8. Are regional trade organizations good or bad for world trade?

9. Does the rivalry of Airbus and Boeing differ from that of Portugal and Holland in the Age of Exploration?

10. Should governments trust in an "invisible hand"? Should they worry about the country's trade balance?

11. Should anyone care where an idea or product originated if we are all part of one global village?

RECOMMENDED RESOURCES

BOOKS

Bhagwati, Jagdish. *Free Trade Today*. Princeton, N.J.: Princeton University Press, 2002.

Campbell, John L, and Ove K. Pedersen, eds. *The Rise of Neoliberalism and Institutional Analysis*. Princeton, N.J.: Princeton University Press, 2001.

Chomsky, Noam, and Robert W. McChensney. *Profit over People: Neoliberalism and Global Order*. New York: Seven Stories Press, 1998.

Crane, George T., and Abla Amawi, eds. *The Theoretical Evolution of International Political Economy: A Reader*. 2d ed. New York: Oxford University Press, 1996.

Crosby, Alfred W. *Ecological Imperialism: The Biological Expansion of Europe, 900–1900*. Cambridge, U.K.: Cambridge University Press, 1986.

Diamond, Jared M. *Guns, Germs, and Steel: The Fates of Human Societies*. New York: W. W. Norton, 1999.

Dobson, Alan P. *Flying in the Face of Competition: the Policies and Diplomacy of Airline Regulatory Reform in Britain, the USA, and the European Community, 1968–1994*. Brookfield, Vt.: Ashgate, 1995.

Gilpin, Robert. *The Political Economy of International Relations*. Princeton, N.J.: Princeton University Press, 1987.

Gilpin, Robert, and Jean M. Gilpin. *Global Political Economy: Understanding the International Economic Order*. Princeton, N.J.: Princeton University Press, 2001.

Hardt, Michael, and Antonio Negri. *Empire*. Cambridge, Mass.: Harvard University Press, 2000.

Irwin, Douglas A. *Free Trade Under Fire*. Princeton, NJ.: Princeton University Press, 2002.

Mayer, Frederick. *Interpreting NAFTA*. New York: Columbia University Press, 1998.

O'Brien, Robert., et al. *Contesting Global Governance: Multilateral Economic Institutions and Global Social Movements*. Cambridge, UK: Cambridge University Press, 2000.

Schwartz, Herman M. *States Versus Markets: History, Geography, and the Development of the International Political Economy*. New York: St. Martin's, 1994.

Singer, Peter. *One World: The Ethics of Globalization*. New Haven: Conn.: Yale University Press, 2002.

Smith, Adam. *The Wealth of Nations*. New York: Modern Library, 1937 [1776].

Soros, George. *George Soros on Globalization*. New York: Public Affairs, 2002.

Veltmeyer, Henry, and James F. Petras. *Globalization Unmasked: Imperialism in the 21st Century*. London: Zed Books, 2001.

WEB SITES

Adam Smith's *The Wealth of Nations* (full text)
http://www.bibliomania.com/2/1/65/112/frameset.html

Article in *Time* by Karl Van Miert
http://www.time.com/time/magazine/1998/int/980706/business.profile.determi41.html

Comments on Japan's Industrial Policy
http://www.ncpa.org/ea/easo93/easo93h.html

Web Sites (continued)

The International Forum of Globalization (analysis of the
WTO, IMF, World Bank, etc.)
http://www.ifg.org/

NAFTA
http://www.nafta-sec-alena.org/english/index.htm

United States Trade Representative
www.ustr.gov

The World Bank (includes information on the economics of
developing countries)
http://www.worldbank.org/

World Bank
http://www.worldbank.org

World Trade Organization
http://www.wto.org

CHALLENGES OF DEVELOPMENT: SOUTH MEETS NORTH

THE BIG QUESTIONS IN CHAPTER 12

- How poor is poor? What share of humanity lives in poverty? Where are they?

- Why are the poor poor? Do the reasons lie abroad or at home?

- To stimulate economic growth, is it more useful to raise the incomes of men or women?

- Why are 100 million women missing in Asia?

- Is there such a thing as the "happy native," content without industry?

- Isn't it better to be self-sufficient than to depend on trade with others?

- Was there an East Asian miracle? How could Asia's "little Tigers" develop so rapidly despite their poor resource base?

- Does the Tiger model offer lessons for South Asia or Africa?

- Was it wise for Malaysia to press for an end to currency trading?

- What is the most cost-effective spur to economic development?

- How can outsiders help Third World development?

East Meets East: Why Do India and Egypt Lag Behind China?

East Meets East: Why Do India and Egypt Lag Behind China? . . . . *The Indian and Egyptian ambassadors to the United Nations meet at a diplomatic reception in New York. They have known each other since university years at the London School of Economics. Their top leaders have just addressed the General Assembly. India's Prime Minister has denounced Pakistan for stirring unrest in Kashmir; Egypt's president has criticized Israel for oppressing Palestinians. But the two ambassadors are concerned about something else: Why does China's economy grow at nearly 10 percent a year—twice, three, or even four times the rate of India's and Egypt's? Why has China's population nearly stabilized while India's and Egypt's continue to multiply at a rapid rate? Does the Communist regime in Beijing do more for its subjects than the democratic system in India?*

Why do some parts of the East lag behind others? India and Egypt, no less than China, have evolved from ancient civilizations that once were engines of science and the arts. In recent centuries, however, each country was dominated by Westerners and Russians. Each now supports a large population living in a fragile environment.

"Put aside Pakistan and Israel," says the Indian. " What about our own people? How can we help them to live better?"

"A group of Arab intellectuals writes that our own politics and culture are the problem," the Egyptian replies. That is the basic conclusion of the Arab Human Development Report.

The Indian recalls a similar study, Human Development in South Asia, *assembled by a Pakistani economist, Mahhub ul Haq. "This was a great man," says the Indian. "He helped shape the UNDP Human Development Index. But he went back to Pakistan from New York, determined to spur his country and mine, plus our neighbors, to the needs of the times. His report should have been a wake-up call, but we are still asleep at the wheel.*

A man of action, the Egyptian offers a plan: "Let's review the Millennium Development Goals adopted by the UN General Assembly. In 2000, as you know, the General

Assembly spelled out a set of specific economic and social targets that developing countries are to meet by 2015. Let's compare how India and Egypt are doing compared to China and other developing countries. Let's figure out what succeeds—what contributes to progress and what impedes it." Each ambassador agrees to work with economists in his delegation and back home. In half a year they will compare notes. If their conclusions are promising, they will present them to top leaders in Cairo and New Delhi and to UN and Western development agencies and NGOs.

CONTENDING CONCEPTS AND EXPLANATIONS

DEFINING THE CHALLENGES

How to improve incomes, health, and education for a rapidly expanding world population? The number of humans passed 6 billion in A.D. 2000—up from 4 billion in 1970. World population is expected to reach 8 billion by 2030 and then stabilize at 9 billion by 2050. Of the 6 billion in 2000, nearly half lived on less than $2 per day. To improve their living standards and care for their offspring will require huge increases in productivity and improved systems of distribution.[1]

First, the good news. The challenges to planetary well-being were daunting, but recent history offered some grounds for hope. From 1980 to 2000, average incomes (measured in 1995 dollars) rose in developing countries from $990 to $1,350. Infant mortality was cut in half—from 107 per 1,000 live births to 61. Adult illiteracy declined from 47 to 25 percent. The two largest populations, those of China and India, managed to feed themselves. Minerals and other resources did not run out. More oil and gas were found. Fiber optics substituted for copper. Smallpox and river blindness were eliminated.

Next, the bad news. As the 21st century began, many challenges endured, some becoming more acute in less developed countries (LDCs):

Poverty: One billion people were very poor—living on less than $1 a day. Another 2 billion got by on less than $2 a day. Two-thirds of the world's very poor lived in East Asia and South Asia (defined and discussed later

1. See United Nations Development Programme, *Human Development Report 2002* (New York: Oxford University Press, 2002)[hereafter *HDR 2002*] and World Bank, *World Development Report 2003* (New York: Oxford University Press, 2003).

How the Poor Define Poverty*

"Poverty is hunger, loneliness, nowhere to go when the day is over, deprivation, discrimination, abuse and illiteracy."

—*single mother from Guyana*

"Poverty is the squatter mother whose hut has been torn down by the government for reasons she cannot understand."

—*slum dweller in the Philippines*

Some other answers included "being blind or crippled," "lacking land," "being without a grinding mill," "being unable decently to bury the dead," "having to put children to work."

*HDR 1997, various pages.

in connection with Table 12.2) and one-fourth in sub-Saharan Africa. Economic output fell in many former Soviet republics, casting millions into poverty.

Income inequality: The income average of the richest twenty countries was thirty seven times higher than in the poorest twenty. The ratio of their inequality doubled between 1960 and 2000.

Gender inequality: Women were treated worse than men in most countries. The **gender-related development index (GDI)** placed Mozambique, Burundi, and Niger at the bottom, with Australia, Belgium, and Norway on top. The U.S. ranked sixth in both GDI and Human Development. China was 77th in GDI and 96th in Human Development. India ranked 105th in GDI and 124th in Human Development.

Health: Average life spans extended, but health problems grew worse in many places because of HIV/AIDS, tuberculosis, and malaria. In some others, health problems worsened due to obesity and diabetes among all age groups, plus the infirmities of aging populations. In 2000, average infant mortality in developing countries was ten times higher than in high-income OECD countries.

Violence: Some 46 countries were involved in armed conflict in the 1990s. They included 17 out of 33 of the poorest countries. Besides war between and within countries, there was much violence by individuals—against their neighbors, their spouses, and themselves (suicide).

The biosphere: Hundreds of cities in LDCs suffered from unhealthy air. One-third of the world's people faced moderate to severe water shortages. More than a billion lacked safe drinking water. Soils were eroding, forests disappearing, coral reefs shrinking, fisheries declining, many fauna and flora were more vulnerable to extinction.

Humanity's strengths and vulnerabilities differ by region, as outlined in Table 12.1. Within each region, of course, are the special characteristics of each county, town, village, and family.

What Path from Poverty?

Western countries modernized gradually over 500 years. As we saw in the previous chapter, they pursued top-down and then bottom-up development—followed by a synthesis of the two approaches. Japan started in the late 19th century but then advanced rapidly. So did Russia—tsarist and then Soviet. The Western and Japanese experience spawned a theory of modernization.

Table 12.1 Population, Economic, and Health Indicators by Region

Region	Population, 2000 (millions)	GNI Per Capita Dollars, 2001	PPP Gross National Income, Per Capita Dollars, 2001	GDP Growth Rate, 1990–2001 (percent per year)	Life Expectancy at Birth, 2000	Adult Illiteracy, 2000 (percent)	Under-5 mortality rate (per 1,000) 2000
Low-income countries	2,511	430	2,040	3.4	59	37	115
Middle-income	2,667	1,850	5,710	3.4	69	14	39
Low- and middle-income	5,178	1,160	3,930	3.4	64	25	85
East Asia and Pacific	1,825	900	4,040	7.5	69	15	45
Europe and Central Asia	475	1,960	6,990	−0.9	69	3	25
Latin America and the Caribbean	524	3,560	7,070	3.1	70	12	37
Middle East and North Africa	301	2,000	5,230	3.0	68	35	54
South Asia	1,380	450	2,300	5.5	62	45	96
Sub-Saharan Africa	674	470	1,620	2.6	47	39	162
High-income countries	955	26,710	27,680	2.5	78	low/n.a.	7
World total (t.) or weighted average (w.)	6,133 t.	5,140 w.	7,570 w.	2.7 w.	66 w.		78 w.

SOURCE: Data from World Bank, *World Development Report [WDR] 2003* (New York: Oxford University Press, 2003), Tables 1 and 3.

Modernization Theory

Modernization theory asserts that, as societies are organized more rationally and scientifically, economic, cultural, and political changes occur together in predictable ways. They contribute to **development**—changes that enlarge choice and the well-being of more and more people in that society. The typical trajectory takes the following path: agrarian society → growing literacy → industrialization → urbanization → development of mass media → occupational specialization → specialized education → mass political participation → increasingly similar gender roles → high HDI. But stages overlap and stages can be reversed.[2]

Modernization theory grants that external forces have been and still are important. Still, the deepest obstacles to development lie within society—mutual distrust, exploitative patterns of land ownership, corruption, militarism, criminality, and—not least—sexism. Other factors include natural disasters, political instability, communal strife, civil war, and capital flight. These factors reinforce one another and contribute to a **syndrome of underdevelopment**. People feel powerless and exploited—and they are. In PD terms, experience teaches them: "Always defect."

2. Postmodern countries face different questions: Will computerization enslave or liberate? Will life become more creative or more regimented? How to be trim (not how to subsist)? Ronald Inglehart, *Modernization and Postmodernization: Cultural, Economic, and Political Change in 43 Societies* (Princeton, N.J.: Princeton University Press, 1997).

Government can be too strong or too weak. After 1947, India's rulers attempted to control and regulate economic life. The "license raj" (big government) tied India in knots of red tape. When government shrinks, however, social services may disappear, leaving ordinary people vulnerable to exploitation by aggressive entrepreneurs.

Many leaders engage in **rent seeking**—exploitation of government for personal gain. Russia's former Communist leaders privatized the country for their own benefit in the 1990s. The Russian state had a government but one too weak to provide many essential services. "Failed states" such as Somalia had no overall government—just clan rivalry.

Both states and markets operate more efficiently where people feel themselves part of a civic union—a political community in which they have duties as well as rights.[3] Civic virtue—a spirit of mutual aid—shows up in political engagement such as voting, keeping informed on public affairs, and showing concern for other citizens and for public goods.

In most LDCs there is a chasm between rich and poor. The rich have access to education and other perquisites of power; the poor do not. The bases of inequality include barriers that keep people "in their place"—social castes, ethnic and religious groups, and genders. But the whole cannot advance optimally if major parts lag behind.

Gender Bias. Well over 100 million women are missing in India, and in China. Why? Many have been aborted or killed after birth. Baby girls have long been unwelcome in China and India because they contribute less than boys to farming and are costly to marry off. China's one-child-per-family policy adds to reasons to do away with girls.[4] In parts of India and China, however, a shortage of potential brides emerged in the 1990s, leading to an upsurge in kidnapping of teenage females.

Gender bias impedes both human development and material advancement.[5] It traps not just women but entire societies in a vicious circle of poverty, illness, and population growth against limited resources. Discrimination against women transmits poverty from one generation to another, because a mother's health and education shape the life chances of her children. The role of women in development is discussed in more detail later in the chapter.

Multiple forms of exploitation can cause conflict and impede development. Exploitation exists in many settings and contexts—between family members, sexes, ethnic groups, rulers and ruled, bosses and workers, countries, and regions. Exploitation and conflict arise from a common source: viewing others as rivals in a zero-sum struggle for power and

3. Robert D. Putnam, *Making Democracy Work: Civic Traditions in Modern Italy* (Princeton, N.J.: Princeton University Press, 1993) 156–157.

4. In 1994 the Indian government moved to ban disclosure of an embryo's sex to parents unless it was malformed. Another problem in India is "bride-burning." More than 5,000 brides were killed yearly in the 1990s because their parents failed to deliver an adequate dowry. A quite different custom was banned by British imperialists in 1834: *sutti*—self-immolation of widows, but the practice still occurs in rural areas.

5. *The World's Women 1970–1990: Trends and Statistics* (New York: United Nations, 1991). These realities had been evident for decades. See Irene Tinker and Michele Bo Bramsen, eds., *Women and World Development* (Washington, D.C.: Overseas Development Council, 1976).

Why Women's Work Is Never Done

Repression of women is both cause and consequence of poverty in Africa. Consider the Masai people living near Tanzania's game preserves. Men used to raid cattle and fend off intruders, but—the old ways gone—many now sit drinking a local brew and playing board games. "Men in this community live as supervisors," said a thirty-five-year-old Masai elder, Paritoro Ole Kasiaro. "Men leave the women to do all the everyday activities." Women look after cattle, carry water in jugs from a stream, and ride donkeys to fetch cornmeal from distant shops. They must even maintain the mud and dung hut.

Unlike most Masai men, Kasiaro has attended school and travels eighty miles to meetings of the regional council. In 1990 he became an advocate of women's rights and tried to help local women sell jewelry to passing tourists. If they gained income, Kasiaro believed, women would probably buy cornmeal for children. Many men, by contrast, would spend extra cash on liquor. But men controlled the tribe's capital and refused to underwrite their women. To get started, women had to sell their own necklaces.

Kasiaro in 1991 had three underfed wives and three scrawny children; he himself often went hungry; his cattle were dying of disease. He had a fourth wife, age ten, already paid for by his father to her father—before she was born! His life was ruled by custom. He admitted beating a wife when the roof leaks: "Other men will laugh if I don't."*

*Jane Perlez, "Women's Work Is Never Done (Not by Masai Men)," *The New York Times*, December 2, 1991.

wealth. This outlook leads to one-sided value-claiming. If the stronger side exploits the weaker, the exploited may see the relationship as unfair and resist. Exploitation can keep a society backward and provoke civil strife.

Policies that promote mutual gain are more likely to generate prosperity and peace than strategies of exploitation. The fittest societies thrive on complexity, interdependence, and cooperation for mutual gain.

Four Alternative Routes to Development

Most LDCs obtained their independence only in the second half of the 20th century. They assayed four main routes to development: (1) welfare without industrial growth, (2) import substitution, (3) self-reliant communism, and (4) export-led participation in the world economy. The first three glorified autarky—economic self-sufficiency without foreign trade or aid. By the 1990s, nearly all states had embraced variants of the fourth approach.

1. Welfare Without Industrial Growth

Low incomes need not mean poverty. Lacking material abundance, Barbados, Costa Rica, Sri Lanka, and Cuba achieved good HDI scores by investing heavily from limited resources in education and public health. But "doing more with less" does not appeal to LDCs with rapidly growing populations who want higher material standards of living. Even Sri Lanka

Why Did Costa Rica Prosper While Most of Latin America Languished?

Why is Latin America, so rich in natural resources, so poor? Most Spanish and Portuguese explorers and settlers were exploitative and intent on claiming values—not creating them. They used Indians and Africans to do the dirty work on large estates and mines. Owners became rich while workers subsisted. Why did Costa Rica not fit this pattern? One explanation is that it was settled by Basques and others from northern Spain willing to work for themselves and with one another. A nation of "brothers and sisters"—not of rulers and ruled—Costa Rica became a near model of middle-class prosperity, democracy, and peace. A large Basque migration also imparted a liberal dynamism to Chile, but their relative numbers and impact were less than in Costa Rica.*

*Lawrence E. Harrison, *Underdevelopment as a State of Mind: The Latin American Case* (Lanham, Md.: Madison Books, 1985), 55–56. Asked about Harrison's thesis, former Costa Rican president Oscar Arias Sanchez in 1997 said it had some validity but was an oversimplified explanation.

became disenchanted with socialism in the 1970s and opted for Singaporean-style capitalism. One reason for ethnic conflict in Sri Lanka was that a stagnant economy pushed an expanding population to fight over a shrinking pie. By the time Sri Lanka opted for growth, ethnic strife had become civil war.

Few Cubans rejected the welfare state but many would have preferred a liberalized political and economic system. Under Fidel Castro, however, they had to endure authoritarian rule or flee.

2. Against Dependency: Import Substitution and a New Economic Order

Dependency theory (a variant of world-systems theory) blames external forces for underdevelopment. It says that structures of dependency have developed since 1500 that permit the imperialist core (Europe and the U.S.) to exploit and retard the less developed periphery (the South). Instead of joining the system of world trade, the most radical *dependencia* theorists urged LDCs to "de-link" from the system of world trade and unequal exchange. But many Latin American, South Asian, and African countries attempted a milder approach—**import substitution**: From the 1950s through the 1970s, they tried to become self-sufficient by reducing imports and building up native industries behind high tariff walls. They hoped to earn hard currency by exporting primary commodities and food, but international demand and prices fluctuated wildly. The outcome: Agriculture subsidized inefficient industries that could not compete on world markets. Everyone suffered except government ministers: Quantitative controls on imports permitted them to squeeze the system for private gain. India attempted a version of this policy. So did Egypt.

Many Third World governments in the 1970s called for a **New International Economic Order (NIEO)** to restructure the world economy and redistribute its wealth. A majority of UN members endorsed calls for an NIEO in which LDC commodity exports would be protected from price fluctuations and rich countries would transfer more resources to the poor. Western governments resisted the NIEO demands and called for North–South cooperation—not confrontation.

Many Third World leaders hoped that the sharp rise in oil prices after 1973 would serve as a tool to redistribute the world's wealth. As it happened, however, oil producers gave away very little of their new wealth. Saudis and Kuwaitis got richer while many LDCs became poorer—some becoming a "Fourth World" of near terminal poverty.

Pressures for an NIEO collapsed in the 1980s. Why? Third World unity was rent by the split into petroleum haves and have-nots. Why did LDC

CONGRATULATIONS! WORKING LIKE DOG FOR LOW PAY IS NOW NORMAL!

OK, ENOUGH CELEBRATION. BACK TO WORK!

PERMANENT NORMAL TRADE RELATIONS

US TRADE DEFICIT SOARS

DANZIGER 5 30 2000
TRIBUNE MEDIA www.danzigercartoons.com

Chinese-made goods, produced by low-cost labor, filled American stores and added to the U.S. trade deficit. The strong flow of consumer goods from China to the U.S. was only partially offset by the sale of Boeing aircraft and other high-tech American products to China. Demanding a more level playing field, U.S. trade unions and manufacturers pressed Congress and the White House to insist on better working conditions for workers in China and other developing countries. Many Chinese, however, preferred sweatshops to no jobs or working in rice paddies. Admission to the World Trade Organization in December 2001 obliged China to open its markets to a wide range of foreign products and services. Some observers hoped PRC membership in the WTO would ameliorate social and economic problems.

solidarity shatter? Dependency theorists blamed manipulation by the world system of finance. Liberals and neoliberals blamed the Third World for internal corruption and for excessive borrowing. Some advised lower wages and less welfare.[6]

Dependency theory became discredited. There was little evidence to show that LDCs suffered when rich countries grew. Rather, boom times in the North often spawned economic growth in the South. Prices for LDC commodities did not fall relative to prices for goods made in the North.[7] Most regions of the Third World sold more goods to the U.S. than they imported. The North did not try to hide its science and technology from the South. Manufacturers from rich countries moved their factories to LDCs, while U.S. and European universities opened their labs to LDC students.

Still, dependency thinking lingered in the 1990s. Many LDCs feared that freer trade would benefit the rich and hurt the poor. Some LDC governments worried that the World Trade Organization (WTO) would promote the sale of manufactured goods produced in core developed countries while doing little for the periphery. As we saw in the last chapter's discussion of NAFTA, free trade can gore some oxen and fatten others. Thus, Ecuador and other Latin American banana exporters cheered in 1997 when the WTO declared illegal European Union quotas and licenses favoring bananas from former British and French colonies in the Caribbean and Africa. Governments in Grenada and Dominica,

6. Ngaire Woods, "Economic Ideas and International Relations: Beyond Rational Neglect," *International Studies Quarterly* 39, no. 2 (June 1995): 161–180 at 174–176.

7. Andres Velasco, "Dependency Theory," *Foreign Policy*, (November/December 2002): pp. 44–45. Articles in the same issue reviewed Marxism and writings about the military–industrial complex.

Table 12.2 Contrasting Policy
Frameworks: East and South Asia

East Asia	South Asia
Investment in human capital	Widespread illiteracy
Macroeconomic stability	Budget deficits/ foreign debt
Relative price stability	High inflation
Liberal approach to trade	Protectionist mentality (declining in India since late 1990s)
Inflow of foreign investments	Foreign aid and loans
Merit-based competition	Feudal patronage
Sound governance	Corruption and inefficiency
Land reforms	Peasants without much land
Efficient tax collection	Tax evasion, loan defaulting
High savings/ investment rates	Lower rates
Invitation to foreign direct investment (FDI)	Hostility to FDI
Public–private sector partnerships	Business as client of government
No open hostility except for PRC–ROC confrontation	Pakistan–India arms race and festering Kashmir dispute

however, demanded preferential treatment for small LDCs. They warned that the collapse of the banana trade could produce instability across the Caribbean basin and force islanders to raise or smuggle banned substances.

3. Self-Reliant Communism

The Communist regimes in Moscow, Eastern Europe, and Asia sought for decades to develop apart from the First World. In the late 1940s and early 1950s, Soviet leader Josef Stalin urged them all to industrialize to be self-sufficient and generate a working class with a Communist consciousness. Communist China's Mao Zedong in the 1950s urged his countrymen to walk on "one leg"—their own, spurning foreign dependence. Seeking autarky, Communist Albania and North Korea became hermit states, with dire consequences.

Perceiving in the 1970s that self-reliance meant backwardness, however, the USSR, Eastern Europe, and China began to cultivate trade ties with the West. Unable to beat it, they tried to join the system of First World commerce. They drove nails into the coffins of dependency theory as well as Marxism.[8]

4. Export-Led Participation in the World Economic System

Most of East Asia embraced an export-led strategy of economic development based on manufactured goods competitive in foreign markets, adapting the Japanese approach described in Chapter 11. Japan went first, followed by Singapore, Hong Kong, Taiwan, and South Korea—known as the four little **Tigers**. These four began to emulate the Japanese model in the 1950s and 1960s; mainland China followed suit in the late 1970s. Each country modified the model to fit its own needs. Together they produced an "East Asian miracle" of rapid growth that contrasted with South Asia's stagnation.[9] Unlike India, the East Asians did not try to buck the system of world trade. Rather, they adapted to the system and used it for their own ends. (Singapore, of course, is really located in Southeast rather than East Asia.)

In the mid-1990s it appeared that other Southeast Asian countries—Thailand, Malaysia, and Indonesia—were repeating the East Asian miracle. Chile, Argentina, and Brazil were also developing rapidly. These latecomers were called **NICs—newly industrializing countries**.[10]

How did the four Tigers do so much with so little? They had some tangible advantages—good harbors, substantial foreign aid from the U.S. or Britain, and investment capital from expatriates. But each had a poor

8. Joshua Muravchik, *Heaven on Earth: The Rise and Fall of Socialism* (San Francisco: Encounter Books, 2002); Zbigniew Brzezinski, *The Birth and Death of Communism in the Twentieth Century* (New York: Collier, 1990); Walter C. Clemens, Jr., *Can Russia Change? The USSR Confronts Global Independence* (New York: Routledge, 1990).

9. Could the East Asian miracle be replicated elsewhere? See Walter C. Clemens, Jr., "Are East Asian Models Relevant to the Baltic, "*Issues and Studies*" [Taipei], 28, no. 10 (October 1992): 71–89.

10. See World Bank, *The East Asian Miracle: Economic Growth and Public Policy* (New York: Oxford University Press, 1993) and its bibliography.

resource base with few minerals or cash crops; each depended on imported energy; each was vulnerable to destructive rains. Each had a dense population relative to the area under cultivation. None had a large domestic market. Except for Hong Kong, each Tiger invested heavily in military preparedness.

Nonetheless, each Tiger advanced rapidly from low-income to upper-middle-income ratings. By 1995 all four had high real per capita incomes: Hong Kong, $27,500; Singapore, $22,900; Taiwan, $13,600; and South Korea, $13,100. Despite abundant resources, the other NICs lagged far behind. In 1995 Argentina's real per capita income was $8,100; Brazil's, $6,100.[11] By 2001, Argentina was defaulting on its foreign debts and Brazil struggled to escape Argentina's vortex.[12]

When the Indian ambassador compares his country with China, he finds a stark contrast between the policy frameworks adopted by all countries of **South Asia** (India, Pakistan, Bangladesh, Bhutan, Sri Lanka, Nepal, and the Maldives) and those of **East Asia** (Japan, the Tigers, and China).[13] Table 12.2 outlines the contrasts between East and South Asia.[14]

The East Asians shared five strategies: investment in human capital, outward-looking trade strategies, land reforms and credit reforms to stimulate private initiative, accumulation of physical capital, and comparatively good governance. Let us look at each in turn.

Investment in Human Capital. East Asians invested heavily in high-quality primary education, accompanied by a largely self-financed university system. By contrast, South Asians heavily subsidized higher education, which benefited the elite coming from better-off families. The East Asians started with a higher literacy base and invested much more heavily to broaden and deepen it. In 1960, Malaysia and Singapore were spending 3 percent of GDP on education—Pakistan only 1 percent. The results were stark: By 1990 only 3 percent of China's adolescent boys and 8 percent of its adolescent girls were illiterate, compared to 24 percent of India's boys and 48 percent of India's girls. In 1997, Singaporean pupils scored highest in the world in mathematics and science. Universal education quickly became entrenched in the Tiger countries. Females attend primary school at the same rate as males in each Tiger country, though fewer females attend secondary school and college.[15]

Outward-Looking Trade Strategies. East Asians began manufacturing low-tech consumer goods, competing on the basis of low wages, high productivity, and an enlightened export policy. Except for freewheeling

11. *Handbook of International Economic Statistics 1996* (Washington, DC.: CIA Directorate of Intelligence, 1996), Table 4.

12. Two Argentine books analyzed the problem. The titles in English were *The Awful Charm of Being Argentine* and *Reality: Awakening from the Argentine Dream*. The second book described a society perpetually suspended in the gap between its mediocre present and its potential glory. For analysis, see Santiago Real de Azua, "Anxious in Argentina," *Foreign Policy*, November/December 2002, pp. 88–89. For the psychological roots, see V. S. Naipaul, *The Return of Eva Peron* (New York: A. A. Knopf, 1980).

13. Afghanistan abuts South Asia, but was so convulsed by war and dictatorship from late 1970 until 2002 that it cannot be meaningfully compared with other countries of South and East Asia.

14. See Mahbub ul Haq, *Human Development in South Asia 1997* (New York: Oxford University Press, 1997), 66–78.

15. As families in Taiwan became smaller and as average incomes increased, Taiwanese invested heavily in the education of daughters as well as sons. William L. Parish and Robert J. Willis, "Daughters, Education, and Family Budgets: Taiwan Experiences," *Journal of Human Resources* 23, no. 4 (fall 1993): 863–898.

Tiger Women

Did East Asia's "miracle" happen because women were exploited or because they were liberated? Both sexes worked long and hard to make the miracle happen. Exports grew thanks to millions of young women laboring in textiles and other "female industries." Literacy helped both men and women to adjust to urban and factory life. Women moved part way out of their traditional roles, but they were still subject to discrimination. Patriarchal traditions worked against females in the Tiger countries. Conditions for women were harshest in South Korea and best in Hong Kong. In South Korea the wage gap between men and women was quite large in the 1960s but closed somewhat by the 1980s.

Literacy is no panacea. In Thailand more than 90 percent of the population could read in the 1990s. But many girls (and some boys) became prostitutes, largely because their parents or they sought more money. Many prostitutes contracted HIV infections, but some government officials focused on tourist dollars generated by prostitution and on their private bank accounts.

16. In 1990 Taiwan rose to tenth place among exporters of machine tools and robotics. In the mid-1990s a Taiwan-based consortium began to produce airplane parts with British Aerospace.

17. In the same twenty years Japan multiplied the value of its exports by only 15; West Germany, by 12; and the U.S., by 9. Oil exporters such as Iraq and Indonesia increased the value of their exports by about 19; Saudi Arabia, by 11. Calculated from data in *Handbook of Economic Statistics, 1991: A Reference Aid* (Washington, D.C.: Central Intelligence Agency, 1991), 130–131. From the 1970s through 1990 tiny Hong Kong exported more than any other Tiger. U.S. exports led the world, but were only 4.8 times more than Hong Kong's in 1990; Japan exported 3.5 times more than Hong Kong then and 4.3 times more than Taiwan. Ibid., 134–135.

Hong Kong, the East Asian governments protected and favored certain industries.

The four Tigers raised their combined share of world trade from 1.5 percent in 1965 to 8 percent in 1994—almost equal to Japan's 9.1 percent. Each Tiger based its wealth on export of manufactured goods—computers, telecommunications equipment, and robotics.[16] In the years from 1970 to 1990, South Korea increased its exports 78 times over; Taiwan, 47 times over; Singapore, 34 times over; and Hong Kong, 33 times over. Europe's most prosperous small states, Switzerland and Sweden, increased their exports 13 and 9 times over, respectively.[17] Like Japan, each Tiger exported far more than it imported. In 1997, the World Economic Forum rated Singapore and Hong Kong the most competitive economies in the world, followed by the United States By 2002, the U.S. came first; Singapore ranked 4th and Hong Kong 17th on the Growth Competitiveness Index (GCI); 9th and 19th on the Microeconomic Competitiveness Index (MICI).

Land Reforms and Credit Reforms to Stimulate Private Initiative. Land reforms took place in Japan, South Korea, and Taiwan under U.S. pressure in the decade after World War II; China gave back land to the peasants in the late 1970s. Land reforms in India made some progress, but not in Pakistan, where rural elites in the early 21st century still maintained feudal structures of power.

Farmers need credit but must pay their loans if the economy is to be solvent. Rich landlords often default on their loans in South Asia, while many banks there are reluctant to give credit to poor farmers. One success story, however, is the **Grameen Bank**, launched in Bangladesh in 1976. It provides loans (averaging $100) sequentially to poor people, mostly rural women. Peer pressure has kept the default rate to a mere 2 to 3 percent. Having helped 2 million Bangladeshis, the bank began in the late 1990s to serve other LDCs.

Accumulation of Physical Capital. East Asian governments managed to tax incomes and encourage savings; South Asia did less well. Gross savings in East Asia was 34 percent of GDP in 1993 compared to 21 percent in South Asia. East Asians were not born savers. South Koreans saved only 1 percent in 1960; Singaporeans saved minus 3 percent.

Good Governance. In most of East Asia, government bureaucracies were efficient; in South Asia, the opposite was true. Corruption in some East Asian countries was rampant, but it was even more widespread in South Asia.

Korea, and Singapore, family planning programs helped reduce birth rates by one-third to one-half between 1965 and 1985. But family planning services do not exist in many countries.

It pays to invest in women. Income in the hands of a mother has an effect on a child's health many times greater than income controlled by the father.[26] It pays to educate women. If mainly boys are educated, high rates of fertility and infant mortality tend to persist. Various studies show that an additional year of schooling for women reduces child and maternal mortality and increases women's earnings by up to 20 percent.[27] From Indonesia to West Africa, girls' education brings them larger earnings. But many governments and many families are reluctant to invest in girls. Some families want their daughters to do housework; others fear they will profit less from their daughters' earnings than from their sons'.

At the onset of the 21st century, men still control more resources than women in most countries, though the gap is closing. The poorer the society, the larger the gap. The gap is largest in sub-Saharan Africa, next largest in West and South Asia and in North Africa; it is closing more rapidly in Latin America, Southeast Asia, and East Asia.[28]

Comparing India and Egypt with China and Others

If the two ambassadors compare India and Egypt with China, they might wish to broaden the field. They could gain both positive and negative lessons from looking at an East Asian "Tiger" such as South Korea and India's two main neighbors, Buddhist–Hindu Sri Lanka and Pakistan, the first Muslim entry into the nuclear weapons club. Tables 12.3 and 12.4 compare these six countries and, where possible, place them against the averages for developing countries and the OECD—a stark reminder of how far they would need to travel to reach First World standards.

South Korea shot up within a few decades from an impoverished dictatorship to a high-income democracy with less inequality than China or the United States. Its achievements resembled those of Taiwan, Singapore, and Hong Kong.

Starting in the late 1970s, Sri Lanka tried to join the world of international trade but remained more a welfare state than a model of free enterprise. It stayed poor, in part due to civil war, from 1983 to 2002. Nearly universal literacy—female as well as male—helped Sri Lanka deal with various problems, but was no panacea. Nearly half the population lived on less than $2 a day and nearly one-fourth was malnourished. Infant mortality declined sharply, but tuberculosis was rampant. China grew at a rapid clip in the 1980s and 1990s. Inequality in wealth was high—nearly the U.S.

26. In Brazil, the health effect was twenty times greater. See Marya Buvinic, "Women in Poverty: A New Global Underclass," *Foreign Policy*, no. 108 (fall 1997): 38–53 at 47.

27. Ibid.; T. Paul Schultz, "Investments in the Schooling and Health of Women and Men: Quantities and Returns," *Journal of Human Resources* 23, no, 4 (fall 1993): 694–734; see also World Bank, *World Development Report [WDR]* 1991 (New York: Oxford University Press, 1991), 55. Sri Lanka is a low-income country, but it has low female illiteracy and low infant mortality.

28. T. Paul Schultz, ed., *Investment in Women's Human Capital* (Chicago: University of Chicago Press, 1995). Female access to education is higher in Latin America than in Africa or most of Asia, but machismo still permeates Latin America. Many women attend school, but they experience discrimination and concentrate in only a few academic fields. For background, see Nelly P. Stromquist, ed., *Women and Education in Latin America* (Boulder, Colo.: Lynne Rienner, 1991).

Table 12.3 Haves and Have-nots: Selected Cases

	Republic of Korea	Sri Lanka	China	Egypt	India	Pakistan	Developing Countries	OECD
GDP per capita PPP US $2,000	$17,400	$3,500	$3,900	$3,600	$2,400	$1,900	$3,800	$23,600
GDP per capita growth 1900–2000	4.7%	3.9%	9.2%	2.5%	4.1%	1.2%	3.1%	1.7%
Gini Index (of inequality)	32	34	40	29	38	31	*	**
% less than $1 per day	< 52	7	18	3	44	31		
% less than $2 per day	< 2	45	53	53	86	85		
Undernourished as % of population, 1997–1999.	..	23	9	4	23	18	17	
Tuberculosis cases per 100,000 in 1999	52	40	36	18	107	14	72	17

* no meaningful average available, but Rwanda ranks 29; Mexico, 52; Nicaragua, 60
** no meaningful average available, but Denmark ranks 25; Norway, 26; the U.S., 41
SOURCES: UNDP, *Human Development Report 2002* (New York: Oxford University Press, 2002), Tables 3 and 7; World Bank, *World Development Report 2003* (New York: Oxford University Press, 2003), Table 2.

level on the Gini Index (0 = absolute equality; 100 = absolute inequality). Despite China's rapid economic growth, over half the population still lived on less than $2 a day. Official PRC statistics showed that relatively few Chinese were undernourished or suffered from tuberculosis, but Beijing often downplayed unpleasant facts—even China's growing HIV/AIDS crisis.

The weakest growth was in Pakistan and Egypt—less than average for all LDCs. The growth rate for OECD countries was low in the 1990s, pulled down by Japan and much of Europe, but these countries had already achieved high levels of income, health, and education.

Literacy—including female literacy—appears to be a necessary though not sufficient condition for economic and social well-being. For the six countries surveyed, the higher the level of literacy, the greater the life expectancy—the higher the GDP per capita, the fewer people living on less than $2 a day. The only exception to this pattern was India, which scored 2 percentage points higher than Egypt on literacy, but still placed lower on several social indicators. One datum stands out in the three poorest countries—Egypt, India, and Pakistan: Less than half of women over 15 were literate in 2000. Not only did these three states have the lowest HDI scores and per capita incomes, but they also suffered the highest rates of infant mortality. Some regions of India, Karela, for example, recorded much higher literacy than the national average. Two Indian cities, Bangalore and Hydrabad, became

Table 12.4 Gender, Literacy, Health, and Empowerment: Selected Cases

	Republic of Korea	Sri Lanka	China	Egypt	India	Pakistan	Developing Countries	OECD
HDI rank 2002	27	89	96	115	124	138		
GDI rank	29	70	77	99	105	120		
Life expectancy	75	72	73	67	63	60	64	77
Literacy (over age 15)	98	92	84	55	57	43	74	99
Female	96	89	76	44	45	28		
Male	99	94	92	67	68	58		
Female economic activity as percent of male	53	43	73	35	42	35		
Infant mortality, 1970 .. 2000	43 .. 5	65 .. 17	85 .. 32	157 .. 37	127 .. 69	117 .. 85	108 .. 68	40 .. 12
Percent of seats in lower house (or single house) held by women in 2000	6	4	22	2	9	n.a.		Norway, 36; U.S.,14

SOURCE: UNDP, *Human Development Report 2002* (New York: Oxford University Press, 2002), tables.
n.a. = not applicable, no functioning parliament.

computer programming "back offices" for the United States. Still, less than half of India's women and just two-thirds of its males were literate.

Pakistan had the lowest rate of female literacy and the lowest scores in most other indicators. The country with the strongest economic growth, China, also recorded the highest level of female economic activity. In addition, some 22 percent of the seats in China's legislature were filled by women in 2000. While this indicator did not show much real female empowerment (since the legislature usually rubber-stamped Communist Party decisions), it reflected an official belief that women *should* be active in politics—a view not widely endorsed in the other countries surveyed.

The plights of India and Egypt were sharpened by their respective rivalries with China and Israel. That so many Indians and Egyptians cannot read or write is ironic because each country claimed to be a leader of the Third World and because each received mountains of aid from the USSR and the West. Egypt and Pakistan joined most of the Muslim world in having low rates of literacy and low levels of gender equality. The dimensions of the tragedy were underscored by the Arab intellectuals who authored the *Arab Human Development Reports* in 2002 and 2003. Since most Muslims are not Arabs, the report does not directly apply. Still, many facets of the report are relevant to non-Arab Muslims in Indonesia, Pakistan, India, Iran, Turkey, Central Asia and Afghanistan, Malaysia, Nigeria, and other parts of Africa.[29]

29. Most educated Arabs can read the *Quran* in the language used at the time of Mohammed. For Indonesians and all the other non-Arabs listed, Arabic is a foreign language.

More than a year after the Taliban's controls were removed, two Afghan women wore the traditional burka as they walked past shattered buildings in Kabul in January 2002. Some kept the burka from fear of reprisals or brazen males. For others, the head-to-toe covering was simply part of the culture—a way of life. Some women wore the burka and learned to act outside the home in ways that blended traditional with modern ways.

The Arab intellectuals lamented that their countries lagged behind most regions of the world in participatory governance.[30] "The freedom deficit undermines human development. . . . " How does freedom relate to women? "Gender inequality is the most pervasive manifestation of inequity . . . [It] typically affects half the population." Female literacy rates expanded threefold in Arab countries from 1970 to 2000, and female enrollment in primary and secondary schools more than doubled. But these achievements failed to overcome gender-based social attitudes and norms that exclusively stress women's reproductive role and reinforce the gender-based asymmetry of unpaid care. The result: More than half of Arab women were still illiterate in 2000. Rates of fertility, infant mortality, and maternal mortality were high. Twice as many Arab women died in childbirth as in Latin America, and four times more than in East Asia.

Most Islamic countries in the late 20th and early 21st centuries were authoritarian and male-dominated. To be sure, women achieved the pinnacle of power in Bangladesh, Pakistan, and Turkey; a female Palestinian took part in negotiations with Israel. But women in most Islamic countries have limited access to education and participation in public life. In 1994, Muslim leaders in Bangladesh demanded execution of a feminist writer who called for revision of the *Quran's* treatment of women. Some Saudi women tried to exploit the Gulf War to establish their right to drive a car, but failed.

Arab women suffered also from unequal citizenship and legal entitlements such as voting rights and legal codes. They had the lowest

30. *Arab Human Development Report 2002* (New York: United Nations Development Programme/Arab Fund for Economic and Social Development, 2002). The material quoted or summarized here is from pp. 2–3, backed up by analysis and statistics in the 165 pages that follow. A follow-on report was published in 2003.

participation in the world in parliaments, in cabinets, and in the work-force. Their pay was much lower than that for men and they became un-employed earlier and more often. As the *Arab Human Development Report* noted, society as a whole suffers when a huge proportion of its productive potential is stifled in such ways.

Some 65 million adult Arabs were illiterate in 2000—two-thirds of them women. Ten million children aged 6 to 15 were out of school in 2000. If current trends persisted, this number would increase 40 percent by 2015. Knowledge was undersupplied to people. And there were too few educated Arabs to supply knowledge to others and to contribute to eco-nomic and scientific development. Only 0.6 percent of Arabs could use the Internet in 2000 and just 1.2 percent could access a computer. Investment in R&D was no more than 0.5 percent of GDP in Arab coun-tries (though Saddam Hussein may have spent more on military R&D). These numbers are the more shocking because, while Egypt and many other Arab countries had low incomes, the oil-rich countries sometimes swam for years in petro dollars easily diverted to education, PCs, and research.

About the time that the printing press and the Reformation began to transform the West, Muslims lost not only their intellectual drive but their basic curiosity.[31] Centuries after Gutenberg, no Islamic country had a printing press.[32] A Hungarian brought the first press into the Ottoman realm in the late 18th century. Yale missionaries set up the first press in the Arab world in the 1820s with fonts specially made in Germany.

Poverty feeds on ignorance, and ignorance on poverty. The vicious circle of poverty and ignorance also contributes to unemployment and terrorism. Devout Muslim parents and those unable to afford secular or Christian schools for their children send them to madrasas—religious schools where they are housed, fed, and taught to memorize the *Quran*. About 6 million Muslims study in madrasas around the world and an-other 12 million in small Quranic schools attached to village mosques. Nearly all madrasas teach pupils to reject non-Islamic ways, but some madrasas are activist, indoctrinating and sometimes training their pupils for jihad. The madrasas do not teach skills useful in modern economies. Their pupils go into the world hostile to modernity and with little hope of gainful employment.[33]

How remote Egypt and Pakistan are from First World development is seen in the fact that they do not even appear in the countries studied by the World Economic Forum. The Global Competitive Index placed South Korea 21st in the world; China, 33rd; India, 48th, and Sri Lanka,

31. Bernard Lewis, *What Went Wrong? Western Impact and Middle Eastern Reponse* (New York: Oxford University Press, 2002).

32. Already in the 16th century, Spaniards had installed a printing press in Mexico, and Portuguese brought the first presses to Goa and Nagasaki. What may have been the world's first printed newspaper, "Publick Occurences, Both Foreign and Domestick," was printed in Boston in 1690, but was shut down by Boston's governor after the first issue. The first British paper commenced in 1702; the first one was permitted in Boston in 1704. The *Daily Courant in England* serialized *Robinson Crusoe* in 1714. The first French daily paper did not begin till 1777.

33. Husain Haqqani, "Islam's Medieval Out-posts," *Foreign Policy*, November/December 2002, 58–64, with bibliography at 64.

59th. The Microeconomic Competitive Index ranked them 23rd, 38th, 37th, and 47th, respectively. Eight countries with Muslim majorities do make each index, the highest ranked being Malaysia (58 percent ethnic Malay) at 27th on the GCI and 26th on the MICI. The lowest-placed Muslim country was Bangladesh—74th out of 80 on both indexes. The literacy deficit and other problems in Egypt, Pakistan, and India were not unique. As the 21st century began, much of Asia, the Middle East, and Africa struggled with illiteracy, gender inequality, poor nutrition, corruption, and—making everything worse—bad governance. Latin America and the former Soviet Union also shared many of these problems. A cause and a consequence of this malaise was the spread of HIV/AIDS—highlighted in the box. This was one plague that had not yet seized the Muslim countries.

The Future of HIV/AIDS

The Joint UN Programme on HIV/AIDS (UNAIDS) estimated that 65 million people contracted the illness in the 1980s–1990s and that 25 million had died by 2002. Up to that time, most cases were in Africa, but it would soon reach epidemic proportions in the three giants of Eurasia—China, India, and Russia. Depending on the severity of the epidemic, here are informed estimates of cumulative AIDS deaths, 2000–2015:

	Mild Epidemic	Intermediate Epidemic	Severe Epidemic
China	19 million	40 million	58 million
India	21 million	56 million	85 million
Russia	3 million	9 million	12 million

Looking ahead to 2025, Russia is likely to be the hardest hit of the three Eurasian giants. By 2025 a mild epidemic is likely to trim three to four years off life expectancy in each Eurasian giant. A severe epidemic could slash eight years off life expectancy in China; thirteen in India; and seventeen in Russia.

The toll on public health will have enormous social consequences. Without an HIV epidemic, the productivity of each Russian worker would probably rise by 50 percent between 2000 and 2025. With an intermediate epidemic, it will probably fall to below 2000 levels. If the epidemic is severe, one-tenth of Russia's workforce could be affected and productivity will fall still further. Based on the African experience, however, all these estimates may be too low because a quarter of the workforce (including the army) suffers from HIV infection in some African countries.*

Each country may well lose economic clout and influence. How could morale and public spirit not suffer? The dark shadows could be partially lifted by public awareness programs, safer sex practices, cheaper drug therapies, or a medical breakthrough—a vaccine to prevent HIV. In the early 21st century, however, none of these prospects looked strong. A few governments such as in Thailand had mounted strong education programs that slowed the epidemic. But the governments in Russia, China, and India—as in much of sub-Saharan Africa—seemed reluctant to recognize a looming catastrophe. The South African president talked as though to recognize the HIV epidemic would be to submit to Western imperialism. He opposed distribution of antiretroviral drugs, even when generic drugs made in India were becoming available for about $600 a year—too expensive for people living on a few dollars a day but affordable for governments that collected taxes and received foreign aid.

By 2003 the Caribbean islands had the second highest rates of infection after Africa—more than 2 percent of all adults throughout the region, but more than 6 percent in Haiti.

* Nicholas Eberstadt, "The Future of AIDS," *Foreign Affairs* 81, no. 6 (November/December 2002), 22–45.

What to Do: UN Millennium Development Goals, 2000–2015

Responding to the multiple challenges facing the developing countries, the UN General Assembly in 2000 set out what it called **UN Millennium Development Goals**, to be reached by 2015. There were eight goals, eighteen targets and forty-eight indicators to measure progress in a framework adopted by a consensus of experts from the UN Secretariat, International Monetary Fund (IMF), OECD, and the World Bank. Indicators that measure progress toward each target are on the student Web site. The UN Department of Economic and Social Affairs, Statistics Division, provided live links to evaluate progress on each indicator at http://millenniumindicators.un.org/unsd/mi/mi_goals.asp.

Goal 1. Eradicate extreme poverty and hunger

Target 1: Halve, between 1990 and 2015, the proportion of people whose income is less than one dollar a day

Target 2: Halve, between 1990 and 2015, the proportion of people who suffer from hunger

Goal 2. Achieve universal primary education

Target 3: Ensure that, by 2015, children everywhere, boys and girls alike, will be able to complete a full course of primary schooling

Goal 3. Promote gender equality and empower women

Target 4: Eliminate gender disparity in primary and secondary education, preferably by 2005, and to all levels of education no later than 2015

Goal 4. Reduce child mortality

Target 5: Reduce by two thirds, between 1990 and 2015, the under-five mortality rate.

Goal 5. Improve maternal health

Target 6: Reduce by three quarters, between 1990 and 2015, the maternal mortality ratio

Goal 6. Combat HIV/AIDS, malaria and other diseases

Target 7: Have halted by 2015 and begun to reverse the spread of HIV/AIDS

Target 8: Have halted by 2015 and begun to reverse the incidence of malaria and other major diseases

Goal 7. Ensure environmental sustainability

Target 9: Integrate the principles of sustainable development into country policies and programs and reverse the loss of environmental resources

Target 10: Halve by 2015 the proportion of people without sustainable access to safe drinking water

Target 11: By 2020 to have achieved a significant improvement in the lives of at least 100 million slum dwellers

Goal 8. Develop a global partnership for development

Target 12: Develop further an open, rule-based, predictable, non-discriminatory trading and financial system. Includes a commitment to good governance, development, and poverty reduction—both nationally and internationally

Target 13: Address the special needs of the least developed countries. Includes: tariff and quota-free access for least-developed countries' exports; enhanced program of debt relief for heavily indebted poor countries (HIPCs) and cancellation of official bilateral debt; and more generous **official development assistance (ODA)** for countries committed to poverty reduction

Target 14: Address the special needs of landlocked countries and small island developing states

Target 15: Deal comprehensively with the debt problems of developing countries through national and international measures in order to make debt sustainable in the long term

Target 16: In cooperation with developing countries, develop and implement strategies for decent and productive work for youth

Target 17: In cooperation with pharmaceutical companies, provide access to affordable essential drugs in developing countries

Target 18: In cooperation with the private sector, make available the benefits of new technologies, especially information and communication

HOW CAN OUTSIDERS HELP?

Goal 8 and its targets set out ways the rich could help the poor. Many countries—including the U.S. and the four "Asian Tigers"—have benefited from foreign investment, loans, trade, technology and cultural transfer, brains, and labor. But history cautions that external influences can help or hurt developing economies. Aid may be a mixed blessing that helps some parts of society but harms others. Aid can prop up dictators and enrich corrupt officials; it can prolong fighting. There are dilemmas: Without relief, people die. With relief, more survive but need food, housing, and jobs tomorrow. Aid may be fruitful and then go sour. Recipients may be grateful or resentful. They may become partners, rivals, or foes. Outside aid can never substitute for domestic resource mobilization. If a country's internal structure or policies are distorted, outside aid may perpetuate what should be changed.[34] Aid can focus on meeting immediate humanitarian needs or shaping long-term development. It can also influence attitudes and policies at home, in the recipient country, and even among spectators.

Narrowly defined, **foreign aid** means **grants** (outright gifts) in currency or in kind, such as food, or **concessional loans** (loans at less than commercial interest rates). But foreign aid takes many forms. Some aid is tangible—such as "turn-key" factories (set up and ready to operate), seeds, irrigation pipes, and armored personnel vehicles (new or second-hand). Some is intangible—a "demonstration effect" (images gathered from foreign troops, tourists, or television) and knowledge (how to farm, speak English, use the Internet, control crowds, win elections, thwart coups). The nonprofit Experiment in International Living organizes home visits in many countries—an educational experience for host and visitor alike.

Many forms of aid do not show up in government ledgers. LDCs that preserve their tropical forests help sustain the earth's climate; they also preserve plants and fauna useful to all peoples. The Rockefeller Foundation sponsored research that led to a **"Green Revolution"** that increased wheat and rice harvests by use of high-yield seeds, backed by pesticides, fertilizer, irrigation, and scientific management. Oxfam and other NGOs transferred about $5 billion a year to LDCs in the 1990s.

Education can aid or hinder development. The founder of modern China, Sun Yat-sen, studied in Honolulu in 1879–1882 and began to learn about the West.[35] One of the men most important in shaping Soviet leader M. S. Gorbachev's "new thinking" also learned about democracy in the United States. Twenty-seven years before Gorbachev's rise to power, Alexander N. Yakovlev studied Franklin Roosevelt's New Deal at Columbia University in 1958–1959 on the first officially approved U.S.–Soviet exchange.[36] Over time, many Chinese studied in the West and the USSR. Leading figures in the nuclear weapon and missile programs of China, Iraq, and other countries studied physical sciences and engineering in the U.S., Russia, or Europe. By the 1990s, Taiwan's president and most cabinet members had doctorates from U.S. universities. Many children and grandchildren of Communist China's elite could also be found on U.S. campuses.

Aid was mutual as foreign influences enriched U.S. life. The North transfers much knowledge to the South, but the flow of educated humans is mostly South to North. By the early 21st century, hundreds of thousands of students from around the world were studying in the U.S.—the largest

34. Sarah J. Tisch and Michael B. Wallace, *Dilemmas of Development Assistance: The What, Why, and Who of Foreign Aid* (Boulder, Colo.: Westview, 1994), 127.

35. Upon graduation in 1882, Sun Yat-sen received a second prize in English grammar from Hawaiian King Kalakaua. He visited Hawaii five more times, making contacts and raising funds for his political agenda. Sun and his followers added to the pressures that led to the abdication of China's last Manchu emperor in 1911. But when Dr. Sun died in 1925, China verged on civil war. Sun's wife—a graduate of Wesleyan College in Georgia—aligned with the Communists, while her younger sister—a graduate of Wellesley in Massachusetts—married the Nationalist leader Chiang Kai-shek.

36. Still later, using his privileged acess to Communist Party and KGB archives, Yakovlev documented the crimes of Lenin, Stalin, and others in his book *A Century of Violence in Soviet Russia* (New Haven, Conn.: Yale University Press, 2002). While Yakovlev studied at Columbia, I left Columbia for a year to research Soviet disarmament policy under Lenin and Stalin at Moscow State University where my adviser, professor Boris E. Shtein, had recently returned from Stalinist repression. Yakovlev's story, like that of Sun Yat-sen and other Chinese leaders, illustrates how individuals and fortune shape IR—a deep challenge to neorealism and other determinist explanations.

numbers from India, China, and the Asian Tigers. Not only did they add to the diversity and quality of U.S. intellectual life, but they helped pay the costs of American education. Many scientists and physicians originally educated in LDCs choose to stay in the West, though a reverse flow to Taiwan and India picked up as opportunities there brightened.

Churches and Western NGOs sent missionaries and educators to poor countries long before World War II. But the origins of Western governmental aid to developing countries lay in the European Recovery Program proposed by George C. Marshall in 1947. The ERP helped Europe rebuild in a few years. Why not transfer its principles and techniques to the Third World? A mix of motives came to underlay ODA—humanitarian concerns, colonial ties, commercial ambitions, guilt and pride, and a desire for markets but also for stability. But moral vision also inspired much aid to LDCs in which donors had few security or trade interests.[37]

When the USSR began to court India and Egypt in the mid-1950s, foreign aid became a tool in Cold War competition. The Kremlin sought to appear the true friend of the Third World. The Soviet camp had advantages: Its ideology appealed to many Third World leaders. It was not tarnished by memories of Western imperialism. It could bob and weave without any need to persuade a demanding legislature or public. Its financial resources were limited compared to the U.S., but Moscow never had to justify its aid by the bottom-line logic of market capitalism. The Soviets could contribute to a huge sports stadium in Indonesia to please President Sukarno whether or not it made economic sense. Some Soviet technologies were well suited to Third World needs.

But Western economic resources were five to seven times larger than those of the USSR and its East European allies. Also, the U.S., Western Europe, and Japan controlled decisions of the World Bank and IMF, both located in huge buildings not far from the White House. Both institutions, as we saw in the previous chapter, were part of the Bretton Woods system designed in 1944 to help Europe after World War II. In the 1950s, however, the World Bank and IMF became instruments of ODA to the Third World.

Both institutions, the World Bank and the IMF, did much good but also harm—mostly due to intellectual hubris that led to poorly conceived policies. The World Bank altered its strategies like fads. For decades it lent money for big infrastructure projects such as dams; then it directed funds toward poverty relief; later it conditioned loans on **structural adjustment policies** (freer markets, less debt, reduced welfare, and more democracy). The World Bank was at least twenty years behind informed opinion in gearing its projects to environmental as well as economic objectives. Its

37. David Halloran Lumsdaine, *Moral Vision in International Politics: The Foreign Aid Regime, 1949–1989* (Princeton, N.J.: Princeton University Press, 1993).

policy flip-flops reflected the policies of influential governments (especially the U.S.) and personal beliefs of World Bank presidents.[38]

For its part, the IMF gradually discarded the logic of Maynard Keynes that favored limited interventions by governments or international agencies to compensate for market failures. Instead, the IMF fell under the sway of fundamentalists who believed that free markets are always right. Instead of responding to the immediate needs in liquidity crises, the IMF held back loans until governments cut back on welfare programs and permitted wages to fall and prices to rise. Instead of encouraging and helping LDCs to expand economic production, the latter-day IMF forced them to contract economic activity. The IMF seemed oblivious to politics. When Third World governments sought to meet the IMF's Draconian demands, their actions often triggered domestic upheavals sweeping them from power. Having caused great damage to places like Turkey and Argentina, the IMF became proactive in post-Soviet Russia. The IMF's market fundamentalists encouraged the privatization by which former Communist ministers and bureaucrats seized what had been publicly owned industries as their private property. The IMF thus promoted another form of crony capitalism—the antithesis of Adam Smith's "invisible hand."

How much aid do the rich give the poor? In 2000, the total ODA from 28 OECD countries was $54 billion. This was just over one-fifth of 1 percent of their combined GDP (0.22—down from 0.33 in 1990). This $54

38. Thus, U.S. ties with Jakarta helped Indonesia's military regime become a favorite World Bank client in the late 1960s and remain so, despite a poor record on human rights and the environment.

Robert S. McNamara became president of the World Bank after serving as U.S. Secretary of Defense. On his compulsions, see Deborah Shapley, *Promise and Power* (Boston: Little, Brown, 1993); on fads, see Paul Mosley et al., *Aid and Power: The World Bank and Policy-based Lending*, 2 vols. (London: Routledge, 1991).

I'M SORRY... IT'S AN AFRICAN THING... I DON'T UNDERSTAND...

RWANDA
BURUNDI

THE WEST

DANZIGER

The Christian Science Monitor
Los Angeles Times Syndicate

Africans suffered from many problems foreign aid and investment might mitigate, but the region received less aid and investment per capita than any other. To be sure, many problems were homegrown. Thus, South Africa's president Thabo Mbeki opposed distribution of drugs to treat HIV/AIDS, even after they became available at reduced prices, challenging the scientific consensus on what causes AIDS. But even such apparently homegrown issues as ethnic strife and political–economic corruption resulted in part from Western policies before and after African states became independent.

Who Really Helps the Poor?*

It is not so easy to answer this question. The percentage of GDP a country gives in foreign aid provides only a rough gauge. The Center for Global Development and the journal *Foreign Policy* developed a **Commitment to Development Index (CDI)** based on six factors:

• Aid: In the quantity of aid donated per capita and the quality of aid, Denmark scored best; the U.S., worst.

• Trade: The U.S. was the most open to LDC exports; Norway, the most closed.

• Investment in LDCs: Switzerland led; Greece trailed all others.

• Migration: Switzerland and New Zealand were the most open; France and Japan the most closed.

• Peacekeeping: Greece and Norway did the most; Switzerland and Japan, the least.

• Environment: Switzerland did the most good; the U.S., the most harm.

Overall best, Netherlands, Denmark, Portugal; overall worst, Japan, followed by the U.S.

*"Ranking the Rich," *Foreign Policy* (May/June 2003), 56–66, based on 2001 data.

---

39. These were the words of Colombia's attorney general as quoted in *El Tiempo* (Bogota) in October 2002, but the first reports appeared in May—just as President Bush was asking Congress for additional funds for Colombia's drug warriors.

---

billion amounted to $67 per capita. Private donations channeled through NGOs added about one-tenth more to these totals. Japan gave the most—$14 billion; followed by the U.S., $10 billion; and Germany, $5 billion. Denmark gave the most as a percentage of GDP—1.06 percent, followed by Norway and Sweden—0.80 percent. Japan gave 0.28 percent. The U.S. gave the least of 28 donor countries in the OECD Donor Assistance Committee (DAC)—0.10 percent. The $54 billion given by all donor countries approximated the amount by which U.S. security outlays increased in the year after "9/11."

Total U.S. ODA for 2003 was less than $10 billion—close to what the government would spend on missile defense in 2003. Of this amount, only $2.6 billion was truly for development and child survival programs. Food aid was another big item—$865 million in 2003, but this could be seen also as aid to U.S. farmers, who tended to grow more than could be profitably sold to U.S. or foreign buyers. Instead of depressing U.S. prices, agricultural products were purchased by Washington and distributed overseas. Sometimes this food provided emergency relief. Often, however, it discouraged local farmers or even drove them out of business.

Besides this development aid, the U.S. government provided nearly $7 billion for international security assistance. This sum included nearly $2.25 billion for the "economic support fund"—bribe money for Israel and Egypt not to shoot at each other after their 1979 treaty. Another pair of star-crossed partners, Turkey and Greece, used to get large sums to balance each other's military prowess. Starting in the late 1990s, however, Colombia became the third largest recipient of U.S. military aid (after Israel and Egypt) in the hope that military force could stop the cultivation and smuggling of cocaine. Having expended $1 billion to Colombia, the U.S. slowed the flow after revelations in 2002 that the Anti-Narcotics Police there had diverted at least $2 million for "superfluous purposes" and "fattening" their wallets.[39] Details of these two budgets are provided in Table 12.5.

Many features of America's ODA were quite sound. In the 1990s the **U.S. Agency for International Development (USAID)** began to offer cash loans—some as low as $10—for small businesses, many run by women. USAID developed the Lessons Without Borders program, which shared public health techniques developed for Bangladesh with U.S. inner cities, for example, in Baltimore. The Clinton team sought more funds for family planning and protection of the global environment, but the Bush administration cut off U.S. funding for any program that directly or indirectly

Table 12.5 U.S. Aid for Development and for International Security, 2001–2005 in $millions

	2001	2003	2005
International development and humanitarian assistance			
Development assistance and child survival and disease programs	2,124	2,621	2,713
Food aid	835	865	896
Refugee programs	714	734	760
Andean counterdrug initiative	—	636	659
Multilateral development banks (MDBs)	1,603	1,428	1,477
Assistance for the independent states of the former Soviet Union	559	798	826
Peace Corps	267	287	303
International narcotics control and law enforcement	417	223	230
Assistance for Central and Eastern Europe	542	633	655
USAID operations	544	579	611
Voluntary contributions to international organizations	296	334	346
Other development and humanitarian assistance	304	462	482
Total, international development and humanitarian assistance	8,205	9,600	9,958
International security assistance			
Foreign military financing grants and loans	3,568	3,716	3,847
Economic support fund	2,300	2,254	2,334
Nonproliferation, antiterrorism, de-mining, and related programs	311	350	363
Other security assistance	189	208	216
Total, international security assistance	6,368	6,528	6,760

SOURCE: *U.S. Federal Budget 2003*, *Analytical Perspectives* (included in Function 150, International Programs)

supported abortion. USAID officials knew what the problems were in South Asia and elsewhere. They wanted to strengthen literacy and public health, for example, and reported some successes. But they had very limited funds at their disposal.

More than 150 nonprofit NGOs formed a coalition known as InterAction to support USAID in the 1990s. InterAction claimed that for every dollar its organizations received from the U.S. government, they raised $3 from the U.S. public. The coalition included the American Friends Service Committee, American Red Cross, Church World Service, Islamic African Relief Agency USA, National Wildlife Foundation, and U.S. Committee for UNICEF. The nonprofit Sierra Club and profit-oriented solar power groups lobbied for USAID funds to promote sustainable development.

Such groups had little clout on Capitol Hill compared to other lobbies, but many did useful—often heroic—work in the field. Two physcians in a Christian hospital in Yemen were shot and killed in 2002 by a man who claimed he was fulfilling an Islamic duty.

Many forms of foreign aid and influence cost the U.S. and other donors little or nothing. Some examples are goods sent abroad, which are usually purchased in the donor country so that "foreign aid" adds to the donor's GDP; salaries for persons from the donor country; surplus food stocks in the donor country used for food aid; and educational programs financed by "counterpart funds" (local currencies owed to the U.S. but expended locally). The effectiveness of much U.S. aid was undercut by "**strings**." Except for Israel, recipients of U.S. aid were usually required to "buy American"—even if a tractor made elsewhere might be cheaper or more suited to their needs. Recipients were often obliged to hire U.S. advisers at high prices.

Americans also got a kickback if aid helped LDCs find money for arms purchases in the U.S. The dollar value of U.S. arms sales to the Third World generally matched or exceeded that of U.S. foreign aid. The value of arms sales worldwide declined from $46 billion in 1997 to $25 billion in 2001, but the lion's share—$10 billion—went to U.S. merchants.[40] Washington justified its sales as ways to "strengthen stability" and gain market share. So long as LDC demand is strong, suppliers compete.[41] The other top suppliers in 2001 after the U.S. were the U.K., Russia, France, China, Israel, Ukraine, Slovakia, Belgium, Greece, and South Korea. Pyongyang, condemned in Washington for its arms sales and other irresponsible actions, did not make the top ten.

Saudi Arabia was the world's number one arms buyer in 2001. Next came three East Asian countries—China, Taiwan, and South Korea—none a major recipient of foreign aid. Then came Egypt, Israel, and India—buying expensive arms while also collecting much ODA. Oil-rich Kuwait was 8th—followed by impoverished Pakistan and Sri Lanka. The Saudis and Kuwaitis were just tossing back to Americans some pocket change left from oil sales. The Chinese were buying mainly from Russia at bargain prices. Taiwan and South Korea could afford what they bought and had good cause to buy it. But Egypt, India, Pakistan, and Sri Lanka should have placed their priorities elsewhere.

The list reminds us how the security dilemma can provoke an arms race. Numbers 2 and 3, China and Taiwan, armed against each other. To some extent, so did Egypt and Israel; and so did 7 and 9, India and Pakistan. This waste of resources resembled the former competition between

---

40. International Institute for Strategic Studies, *The Military Balance, 2002–2003* (London: Oxford University Press, 2002), 339–340.

41. Even peace-preaching Stockholm bribed Rajiv Gandhi's India to buy Swedish arms rather than French.

the U.S. and USSR, which armed on a scale far above any of the major arms buyers in 2001.

When Egypt or Israel buys a tank or a plane from the U.S., this should trim the marginal cost of this equipment for U.S. forces and reduce the net flow of funds from the U.S. to the Middle East. If perchance General Dynamics or Lockheed-Martin finds ways to avoid paying taxes, of course, the burden of aid to Egypt and Israel will still fall to "Mary" and "Joe" taxpayer.[42]

The importance of foreign aid in the late 20th and early 21st century was diminished by several factors. First, donors gave less than during the Cold War. Second, foreign direct investment (FDI) by the North in the South mushroomed in the 1980s and 1990s—rising to some $200 billion in the mid-1990s. FDI did little for Angola or even India, however, because private investors focused on China and nine NICs such as Malaysia and Argentina. Third, a rising tide of foreign trade generated cash transfers that eclipsed foreign aid. In the mid-1990s, foreign aid made up only one-third of the net flow of resources to LDCs from the OECD countries. The other two-thirds came from trade and investment.[43]

What was the impact of foreign aid, direct investment, and debt service on China, India, and the other four countries we have analyzed? Table 12.6 lays out the data for 2000.

Each country except China received considerable ODA during the Cold War. In the 1990s, however, South Korea became an exporter of foreign aid—$4.50 per capita in 2000 (compared to $35 per capita in the U.S. and $348 in Denmark). Of the six countries surveyed, China received the least ODA per capita but recorded by far the fastest GDP growth. Egypt received the most aid per capita but had the lowest GDP growth except for Pakistan.

ODA contributed more to the GDP of Sri Lanka and Pakistan than did **foreign direct investment (FDI)**. In rapidly growing South Korea and China, however, FDI played a larger role. In South Korea, FDI rose from 0.3 percent of GDP in 1990 to 2 percent in 2000. In China it accounted for just 1 percent of GDP in 1990, but grew to 3.6 percent in 2000. For Egypt in the 1990s, FDI declined from 1.7 to 1.3 percent. In India it rose slightly, from 0.3 to 0.5 percent. In Pakistan, it declined from 0.6 percent in 1990 to 0.5 percent in 2000. In short, the two poorest countries—India and Pakistan—did not attract much FDI. If Egyptians, Indians, Sri Lankans, or Pakistanis wanted more FDI, they would have to make their countries more attractive to foreign investors. They would have to reduce the risks of armed violence, enhance public

42. Sterling, Michigan, November 8, 2002: The U.S. Army awarded General Dynamics Land Systems (part of General Dynamics—New York Stock Exchange symbol GD) a $141 million contract modification for 100 M1A1 hardware kits for the Egyptian tank coproduction program.

43. In the 1990s some LDCs depended on aid; others did not. For much of sub-Saharan Africa, ODA made up over 20 percent of GDP in the mid-1990s. For Mozambique and Rwanda, it exceeded 95 percent of GDP. For Cambodia, Laos, and Vietnam, aid was over one-third of GDP. At the other extreme, ODA for China and India amounted to less than 1 percent of GDP—a pittance next to foreign trade for both countries and FDI for China. World Bank, *World Development Report 1997* (New York: Oxford University Press, 1997), 218–219.

Table 12.6 Flows of Aid, Private Capital, and Debt in 2000: Selected Cases

	ROK	Sri Lanka	China	Egypt	India	Pakistan
ODA per capita in U.S. $	$−4.2	$14.6	$1.6	$19.6	$1.5	$5.0
ODA as % of GDP	(.0)	1.7	0.2	1.3	0.3	1.1
FDI as % of GDP	2.0	1.1	3.6	1.3	0.5	0.5
Debt service as % of GDP	5.1	4.5	2.0	1.8	2.2	4.6
Debt service as % of exports of goods and services	10.9	9.6	7.4	8.4	12.8	26.8

SOURCE: UNDP, *Human Development Report* (New York: Oxford University Press, 2002), tables.

health, and (except for Sri Lanka) increase literacy. Besides the issues highlighted in the tables, each needed also to restructure its tax codes and enforcement of contracts.

Table 12.6 also highlights the burden of debt service for LDCs—repayment of principal with interest. Often, LDCs pay out more in interest than they receive in loans—External debt for the average low- or middle-income country amounted to about one-third of GDP in the 1990s. Debt service consumed about one-fourth of LDC export earnings. In the mid-1990s, some lenders offered to reduce or cancel debts of the poorest countries, conditioned on internal reform.

Most LDCs faced high levels of tariffs still maintained by most OECD countries. The overall picture in the early 21st century was that the U.S. and other rich countries cut tariffs to very low levels among themselves but kept high tariffs on cheap manufactures and some agricultural products from the Third World.

A few numbers tell a bizarre tale. Total U.S. imports in 2001 reached $1.1 trillion. Total tariff revenues were $19 billion—an average of 1.6 percent. Of total imports, cheap shoes and clothes accounted for only 7 percent, but they accounted for nearly half of total U.S. revenues from tariffs. Why? Because they faced an average 12.4 percent in duties. Other high-tariff consumer goods met duties of 8.4 percent, but they accounted for only 2 percent of total imports and, thus, few tariff revenues. Everything else—more than 91 percent of imports—encountered tariffs averaging less than 1 percent.

Some examples: A cheap plastic handbag faced a duty of 17 percent; a leather handbag costing less than $20, a duty of 10 percent; a handbag of reptile leather, 5 percent. The upshot was that the U.S. collected more tariff revenue from Bangladeshi goods than from French, even though

Bangladesh exported only $2 billion in goods a year to the U.S., and France, $30 billion. Struggling Nepal faced tariffs on its skirts, scarves, and suits fully sixty times higher than those applied to Ireland's chemicals and silicon chips. Reducing these burdens on LDCs such as Bangladesh and Nepal would do more for their economies than funneling a little more ODA their way. The U.S. might lose some jobs, but makers of cheap apparel were going abroad anyway.[44]

Besides trade and FDI, the overall balance sheet should also include remittances from guest workers and emigrants in the North to relatives in the South. For countries such as India, Morocco, and Turkey, such remittances exceeded ODA.

What was the effect of foreign aid? Never in history did rich countries transfer so much wealth to poor countries as in the second half of the 20th century. Was this money well spent? Critics say that "the Marshall Plan succeeded but foreign aid to LDCs failed." They neglect two factors. First, nearly all participants in the ERP were advanced economies before World War II. They could rebuild on strong foundations missing in LDCs that knew very little of modernity. Second, U.S. transfers to Europe were initially 2.3 percent of U.S. GDP. Over four years they averaged 1.2 percent. In 2000 dollars, the ERP funds expended over three to four years would amount to more than $100 billion in 2000 dollars—targeted on a comparatively small group of people. ODA in the early 21st century is about one-fifth of 1 percent of OECD GDP—intended to help more than 3 to 4 billion people! The impact of American aid was narrowed by the fact that most of it went to Israel, Egypt, and Colombia.

Given the limited quantities of ODA disbursed, nobody can prove that "foreign aid has been tried and failed." Rather, we must say that foreign aid has not received a fair trial. Some countries seem to have used it to good advantage, for example, South Korea and Taiwan. Others had little to show for it except for the Mercedez-Benz in the president's driveway. His deposits in a Swiss numbered bank account were not on display.

WHAT PROPOSITIONS HOLD? WHAT QUESTIONS REMAIN?

Wealth creation and development are complex processes. Each region has its own needs and assets. Table 12.7 suggests maxims valid for most countries.

44. Edward Gresser, "Toughest on the Poor: America's Flawed Tariff System," *Foreign Affairs 81*, no. 6 (November/December 2002): 9–14. The same issue presents a more upbeat appraisal of U.S. policies, based on the one step backward, two steps forward principle. See C. Fred Bergsten, "A Renaissance for U.S. Trade Policy," ibid., 86–98.

Table 12.7 Guidelines for North, South, East, and West

How to Stay Poor	How to Develop Equitably
1. Claim values. Quarrel and fight among yourselves and with outsiders.	1. Create values. Make peace at home and with outsiders.
2. Waste and pollute. Live for today and for yourself.	2. Use resources wisely. Seek sustainable development.
3. Accept fate.	3. "Image" alternative futures.
4. Don't study, invent, plant, save, or invest.	4. Prepare for the future.
5. Multiply so that demand for resources exceeds supply.	5. Adjust population to resources.
6. Ignore public health and preventive medicine.	6. Pursue higher HDI. Promote public health.
7. Keep women down and out.	7. Educate and liberate women.
8. Grow, use, make, market, and sell drugs. Fight over them and markets.	8. Discourage drug cultivation and use, including tobacco and alcohol.
9. Let organized crime flourish.	9. Promote law, order, public safety, and private ownership.
10. Shun science and its applications.	10. Cultivate science and its applications.
11. Keep most people in ignorance and illiteracy.	11. Promote mass literacy and numeracy.
12. Exploit and oppress minorities.	12. Give equal opportunity to minorities.
13. Keep land in the hands of a few.	13. Carry out land reforms to promote peace and efficiency.
14. Teach distrust of anyone outside the family.	14. Promote trust and teamwork among all elements of society.
15. Cultivate autarky. Don't specialize or trade. Block imports and pursue import substitution.	15. Cultivate comparative and competitive advantage. Use an export strategy to join international free trade.
16. Avoid risky ideas, inventions, undertakings. Foster an official worldview.	16. Promote moderate risk taking, new enterprises, and new forms of social organization.
17. Reward regime supporters with bribes and kickbacks.	17. Develop a meritocracy. Fight corruption.
18. Depend on central planning; distrust free enterprise.	18. Promote market-friendly government to encourage private enterprise.
19. Shun the outside world or, alternatively, count heavily on outside help.	19. Combine self-reliance with outside aid and investment. Don't count on outsiders for what you can do yourself.
20. Trust in large and showy projects such as high dams and power stations to win votes and transform nature.	20. Distrust any promised panacea. Make modest adjustments to nature.

The Ambasssadors Write Back to Cairo and to New Delhi

Dear Mr. President:

Our country is unique. We must preserve all that is good in our traditions and our emerging way of life. And so I write to share with you some thoughts about how our country can respond constructively to mounting challenges at home and abroad.

Why is economic growth in our country so much less than in East Asia—Japan, the "Tiger" countries, and China? The difference does not lie in natural resources. All of us support dense populations on a thin resource base compared to the U.S., Canada, Russia, or Argentina. The difference is not in foreign aid—China received far less than we have. The difference is not that China, like Costa Rica, has no army. It has the biggest in the world plus a growing nuclear missile arsenal.

Nor is the difference in what complexity theorists call self-organization. Chinese political life still endures a Communist dictatorship. The Communist Party brooks little dissent or free expression. Instead, it throttles even the Falun Gong meditation movement. It keeps tight control on minorities in Tibet and other borderlands.

Chinese intellectual life is still tightly regulated. Our scientists and humanists have far more freedom than in China. Many Chinese intellectuals now access the outer world by the Internet or by foreign travel, but they must struggle to escape state control.

Investors do not favor China because it is strong on law and order. Contracts there are not sacred. Software and other inventions are pirated. Corruption and crime are rampant and growing in China, despite show trials and executions. Drug use is inceasing, breeding crime along with HIV infections. But something in East Asian culture encourages people to work, save, and invest. East Asians are future-oriented. They are more hopeful they can achieve wealth by their own labor and ingenuity than people in many other cultures. Far more of our people seem resigned to "what is" than in East Asia. Few East Asians are Christian, but many seem to have internalized a variant of the "Protestant ethic."

Perhaps our people need their own Luther or Calvin to drive out fatalism. Calvin's teachings encouraged thrift and industry. But Luther did something more important: He unleashed a twin revolution in literacy and free thought that helped Europeans and Americans to think deeply, learn, master, expand, and conquer. The twin revolution fostered a belief in the equal dignity of every person—female as well as male—a belief still foreign to our culture but quite relevant to economic development.

Few Chinese embrace Martin Luther but many, if not most, accept one feature of his revolution: learning for all. Female as well as male literacy is much higher among adults in China and the rest of East Asia than in India, Africa, or most Muslim lands. Far more East Asian children—girls and boys—go to school and continue their education for many years than in our country. In Chinese cities there is no stigma to being a professional or a working woman.

Literacy campaigns and schools are cheap compared to dams, roads, power generators, and war planes. Unless we raise literacy and other forms of learning we will fall further behind economically and in other ways. If our women live without learning, their own and their family's health will suffer. Unless we liberate women, we must do without the energies and skills of half the population.

For now we have a potential advantage next to the Chinese. Nothing in our culture demands that a Big Brother control politics, the mind, or the spirit. Religious fanatics in our midst would impose a theocracy, but they can and must be sidelined. If the Chinese dictatorship is overthrown, chaos may follow. If it melts away, as happened in Taiwan, China will have freedom as well as education. Its upward climb will ascend ever steeper.

Even more fundamental to development than literacy and freedom is peace. We must avoid armed violence within our society and with our neighbors. We should do all we can to understand and meet the demands of have-nots within and to calm the security fears of our neighbors. Peace is the sine qua non for development—followed by literacy and freedom.

These are some general conclusions about our development prospects. An annex to this letter spells out some specifics.

With respect and esteem,

Ambassador to the United Nations

Annex I: Action Plan for the South

Promote Growth with Social Welfare

Neither growth nor social welfare can succeed alone. In Pakistan, for example, growth raised incomes of the poor but social services and schooling lagged. Try to strengthen each link in a virtuous circle: stimulate economic growth ↔ reduce poverty ↔ expand schooling ↔ empower women ↔ improve health ↔ stimulate economic growth.

We should:

*1. **Tap the poor's most abundant asset—labor**. Utilize market incentives, social and political institutions, improved infrastructure, and technological innovation.*

*2. **Provide the poor with basic social services**. Growth will languish without schooling, nutrition, health care, and family planning to enable poor people to take advantage of the jobs and other opportunities generated by economic growth.*

*3. **Promote public health**. Invest more in local clinics than in central hospitals. Train paramedics ("barefoot doctors"). Teach literacy. Make sure that written directions are clear (and certainly not in a foreign language). Promote family planning. Show the benefits of washing and sanitation. Dig wells and latrines and maintain them. Prevent AIDS. Facilitate private sector involvement (as in Tunisia, where eleven large government hospitals were converted into semiautonomous institutions with incentives to improve performance).*

*4. **Invest more resources in women**. There is an economic case for society to subsidize schooling for women more than for men, because the returns are greater: fewer births, less infant and child mortality, fewer maternal deaths, improved nutrition and schooling for children, plus female participation in the workforce.*

*5. **Establish a social safety net**. Provide cash transfers to the destitute, sick, and elderly and establish a social safety net for others hurt by the shocks of economic development. Provide compensation and retraining for those who lose their jobs.*

*6. **Promote agriculture**. Encourage and subsidize land reform, free market pricing, local credit unions, producers' cooperatives, roads, access to markets, storage facilities, agricultural research stations, and farm extension services. Study the pros and cons of diversified food crops versus single "cash" crops such as tea and jute. Utilize traditional wisdom as well as modern science and technology, safeguard biodiversity including traditional herbs and medicines, integrate low technology with intermediate and high technology, and minimize use of chemical fertilizers and pesticides.*

*7. **Treat knowledge as an essential (though insufficient) condition for development**. Promote literacy and quality education. Train skilled workers. Induce scientists to work in their native lands. Organize development projects so that they generate skills as well as roads and bridges.*

8. Maximize investment and minimize debt. *Invest for growth in infrastructure, agriculture, and industry. Use multiple vehicles—loans, bonds, and direct investment—by private investors, national banks, and agencies. Encourage local capitalists and landowners to invest at home—not in Swiss or Bahamian bank accounts. Remember that a small loan can transform a life.*

9. Join the world economic system. *Autarky is a dead end. Use comparative and competitive advantage to find a niche. Diversify. Do not depend on selling the same goods (sugar, coffee, shoes, shirts) that many others produce. Do not count on producers' cartels to regulate supply and prices of commodities such as coffee. (Even the oil producers in OPEC have been unable to control supply and demand.) Seek aid but do not count on charity.*

Practice Market-Friendly Government

1. Intervene reluctantly. *Let markets work unless they visibly fail. Do not protect domestic manufactures that could be imported more cheaply unless local production offers substantial spillover benefits.*

2. Apply checks and balances. *Use markets to discipline interventions. Thus, South Korea's government withdrew its support for the heavy chemicals industry when market performance showed that the policy was failing.*

3. Intervene openly. *Make interventions simple and subject to rules rather than official discretion. For example, use tariffs rather than quotas.*

4. Cultivate good governance. *Appoint officials on the basis of merit. Eliminate corruption. Develop cabinet stability. Define budgets on time and stick to them. Produce and share meaningful statistics.*

Annex II: Guidelines for the North (OECD countries):

1. Security. *Think of development, investment, and trade as investment in security.*

2. Arms deals. *Do not promote arms acquisitions by LDCs. Just one arms deal can divert funds that could build 100 or more schools and clinics.*

3. Self-rule. *Promote stable democracy. Demand "good governance" and respect for human rights as conditions for any form of aid.*

4. Nutrition. *Couple relief aid with steps to improve agriculture and self-reliance. Avoid food distributions that reduce incentives for local growers or perpetuate settlement in flood-prone regions. Circumvent dictators who repress their weak and hungry subjects.*

5. Joint ventures. *Implement joint ventures for mutual gain. "Fordism" works better for all parties than exploitation. Complementary strengths make it possible to mix and match technology, investment capital, know-how, and labor. But do not permit another Bhopal. Foreign companies in LDCs should observe the same ethical and safety standards as at home.*

6. Stabilize currency. *Help LDCs develop a freely convertible, stable currency control inflation, provide incentives to work and save, and attract investment.*

7. Trade. *First World countries can make or break an LDC economy by opening or closing their doors to its products.*

8. Sustainable development. *Seek economic growth with environmental protection. Help LDCs obtain nonpolluting technologies. Arrange debt swaps, for example, conservation of Amazon jungles for cancellation of foreign debt.*

KEY NAMES AND TERMS

autarky
Commitment to Development Index
   (CDI)
concessional loan
dependency theory
development
East Asia
foreign aid
foreign direct investment
   (FDI)

Gender-related Development Index
   (GDI)
Grameen Bank
grant
Green Revolution
import substitution
modernization theory
New International Economic Order
   (NIEO)
newly industrializing country (NIC)

official development assistance (ODA)
rent seeking
South Asia
"string"
structural adjustment policy
syndrome of underdevelopment
Tiger
UN Millennium Development Goals
U.S. Agency for International Development (USAID)

QUESTIONS TO DISCUSS

1. What is "development?" Is there a best route to development?
2. Who is poor? By what measure?
3. In what sense is underdevelopment a syndrome?
   Illustrate with examples.
4. Is the U.S. model of development appropriate to the
   Third World?
5. Is the East Asian model appropriate to South Asia? To
   Latin America? To Africa?
6. Is it possible to live well on a low income? Look up
   statistics and compare Sri Lanka and India; Cuba and
   Haiti; Botswana and Niger.
7. What is the relevance of literacy to development?
8. If Swiss and Japanese women stay at home, why
   shouldn't Nigerian and Pakistani women?
9. Is the IMF right to demand structural adjustment as a
   condition for loans?
10. Compare transparency in banking and diplomacy.
    What are the pros and cons?
11. Why might a government be reluctant to invest in fe-
    male education?
12. If Germany prospered with less aid than Britain or
    France after World War II, does that mean that India
    would be better off with less aid?
13. What sorts of foreign aid are useful? Which are coun-
    terproductive?
14. Lax standards led to an explosion of a Union Carbide
    chemical pesticide factory at Bhopal, India, that killed
    over 3,300 residents and maimed tens of thousands in
    1984. Who was responsible? Company officials in Con-
    necticut? Local employees? The U.S. or Indian or local

Bhopal government? Should the trial be held in the U.S.
or India? Was the U.S. government obliged to extradite
Union Carbide officials to India? The Supreme Court of
India called on Union Carbide to pay $470 million to
settle all claims—a pittance by U.S. standards.

RECOMMENDED RESOURCES

BOOKS

Alam, Shahid M. *Poverty from the Wealth of Nations: Integration and Polarization in the Global Economy Since 1760.*
   New York: Palgrave, 2000.

Bacevich, Andrew J. *American Empire: The Realities and
   Consequences of U.S. Diplomacy.* Cambridge, Mass.:
   Harvard University Press, 2002.

Babb, Sarah. *Managing Mexico: Economists from Nationalism
   to Neoliberalism.* Princeton, N.J.: Princeton University
   Press, 2001.

Beckford, George L. *Persistent Poverty: Underdevelopment in
   Plantation Economies of the Third World.* 2d ed. Kingston,
   Jamaica: University of West Indies Press, 1999.

Birdsall, Nancy, and Frederick Jaspersen, eds. *Pathways to
   Growth: Comparing East Asia and Latin America.* Baltimore, Md.: Johns Hopkins University Press, 1997.

Blumberg, Rae Lesser, et al., eds. *EnGENDERing Wealth and
   Well-Being: Empowerment for Global Change.* Boulder,
   Colo.: Westview, 1995.

Conrad, Joseph. *Heart of Darkness* [1902]. New York: Penguin, 1995.

Dreze, Jean, Amartya Sen, and Athar Hussain, eds. *The Political Economy of Hunger: Selected Essays.* New York: Oxford University Press, 1995.

Harrison, Lawrence E., and Samuel P. Huntington, eds. *Culture Matters: How Values Shape Human Progress.* New
   York: Basic Books, 2000.

Recommended Resources (continued)

Hughes, Neil C. *China's Economic Challenge: Smashing the Iron Rice Bowl.* New York: M. E. Sharpe, 2002.

Lerner, Daniel. *The Passing of Traditional Society: Modernizing the Middle East.* Glencoe, Il.: Free Press, 1958.

Michalopoulos, Constantine. *Developing Countries in the WTO.* New York: Palgrave, 2001.

Mirsepassi, Ali. *Intellectual Discourse and the Politics of Modernization: Negotiating Modernity in Iran.* Cambridge, U.K.: Cambridge University Press, 2000.

Moore, Thomas G. *China in the World Market: Chinese Industry and International Sources of Reform in the Post-Mao Era.* New York: Cambridge University Press, 2002.

Munger, Frank, ed. *Laboring Below the Line: The New Ethnography of Poverty, Low-Wage Work, and Survival in the Global Economy.* New York: Russell Sage Foundation, 2002.

Naipaul, V. S. *A Bend in the River.* New York: A. A. Knopf, 1979.

Prevost, Gary, and Carlos Oliva, eds. *Neoliberalism and Neopanamericanism: The View from Latin America.* New York: Palgrave, 2002.

Roberts, J. Timmons, and Amy Hite, eds. *From Modernization to Globalization: Perspectives on Development and Social Change.* Malden, Mass.: Blackwell, 2000.

Sheff, David. *China Dawn: The Story of a Technology and Business Revolution.* New York: HarperBusiness, 2002.

Stiglitz, Joseph. *Globalization and Its Discontents.* New York: W. W. Norton, 2002.

Stone, Randell W. *Lending Credibility: The International Monetary Fund and the Post–Communist Transition.* Princeton, N.J.: Princeton University Press, 2002.

Stromquist, Nelly P. *Education in a Globalized World: The Connectivity of Economic Power, Technology, and Knowledge.* Lanham, Md.: Rowman & Littlefield, 2002.

———., ed. *Women in the Third World: An Encyclopedia of Contemporary Issues.* New York: Garland, 1998.

Svedberg, Peter. *Poverty and Undernutrition: Theory, Measurement, and Policy.* New York: Oxford University Press, 2000.

Thorp, Rosemary. *Progress, Poverty and Exclusion: An Economic History of Latin America in the Twentieth Century.* Washington D.C.: Inter-American Development Bank, 1998.

Tokman, Victor E., and Guillermo O'Donnell, eds. *Poverty and Inequality in Latin America: Issues and New Challenges.* Notre Dame, In.: University of Notre Dame Press, 2001.

WEB SITES

Andres Velasco on Dependency Theory
http://www.cid.harvard.edu/cidinthenews/articles/FP_11-1202.pdf

Asia–Pacific Economic Cooperation (APEC)
www.apecsec.org.sg

CARE (NGO relief organization with branches in many countries)
www.care.org

Institute of Development Studies
www.ids.ac.uk

International Monetary Fund
www.imf.org

The Third World Network
http://www.twnside.org.sg/index.htm

USAID
www.info.usaid.gov

U.S. Peace Corps
www.peacecorps.gov

World Bank
www.worldbank.org

PART 4

Building a Better World

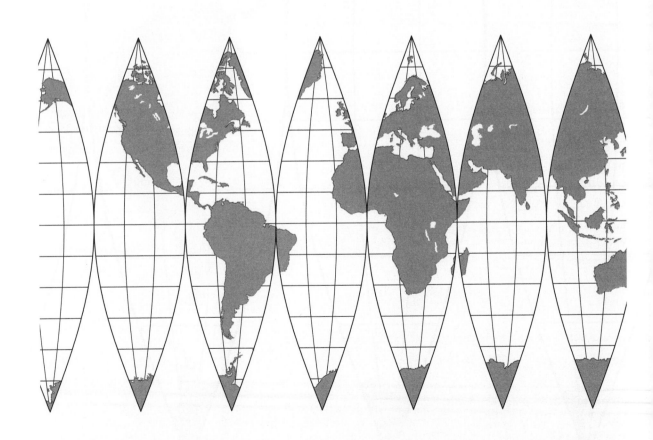

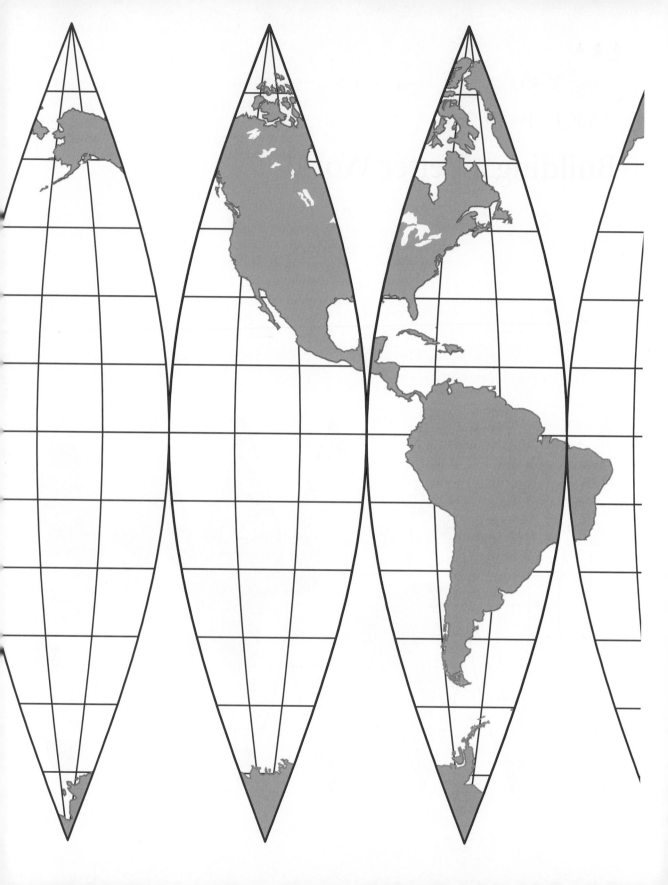

ECOPOLITICS:
THE HEALTH OF NATIONS

THE BIG QUESTIONS IN CHAPTER 13

- Why should a foreign minister care about the environment?

- Is it possible to have both economic development and environmental protection?

- Are there limits to growth?

- How do international environmental conflicts arise?

- People and resources: Was Malthus right?

- Do population pressures multiplied by resource deficits lead to war?

- How is it that big projects often have complex side effects?

- Is it possible to have "sustainable development"?

- What is the Aswan syndrome?

- Why care about climate control if "some like it hot"?

- How do the big issues of mutual gain and exploitation relate to environmental policy?

What Is a Good Trade-off? . . . . *The year is 2012, the place is Rio de Janeiro. As Brazil's Foreign Minister, you chair a meeting of negotiators from nearly 200 countries charged with updating the conventions on climate change adopted at the Earth Summit held in Rio twenty years earlier (1992) and tightened at Kyoto in 1997. The industrialized countries of the Northern Hemisphere signed the Kyoto Protocol in 1997, pledging them to reduce their emissions of "greenhouse gases" by more than 5 percent below their 1990 levels by the year 2010. The U.S. in 2001 rejected the protocol and has fallen far short of this target, but the European Union and Japan have met the goals set in Kyoto.*

In August 2002, ten years after Rio 1992, the follow-up World Summit on Sustainable Development was held in Johannesburg, South Africa. The Brazilian delegation, backed by the World Wildlife Fund and Greenpeace, called on all countries to commit to altering their development matrixes so that by 2012 at least 10 percent of their energy came from renewable sources such as solar, wind, biomass, geothermal, ocean waves, and small dams. The proposal was scuppered by the oil exporters and the United States. Indeed, just after the Johannsesburg summit ended, the World Petroleum Congress met in Rio de Janeiro and reveled in forecasts that demand for oil would rise by 1.9 percent annually from 2002 to 2020—just below the 2.2 percent annual increase recorded from 1973 to 2000.

Led by Germany, most industrial states in 2012 are now emitting fewer hydrocarbons into the air than they did in 1992. While the North's emissions decline, however, those of the South rapidly increase. Heavily dependent on coal furnaces, China has now surpassed the U.S. level of emissions. India, Brazil, and Indonesia have all exceeded Germany's level. The North says it is now time for Brazil, China, India, and other newly industrialized countries to pull in their belts too and cut their emissions.

Brazil's government believes in development—not underdevelopment. It offers tax incentives to transnational corporations such as Volkswagen to help open up Amazonia, the world's largest remaining tropical forest. Most of Brazil's industrialists, miners, big farmers, and timber harvesters resist emissions controls. "It's too early," they say. "First let us catch up with the North." So far, the South has added little to global concentrations of greenhouse gases. In fact, Amazonia has sponged up the carbon released by other countries. "Emissions controls," the industrialists say, "will harm development or profits or both." Still, Brazilians also have reason to want emissions controls. Sao Paulo and other cities are choking on pollution. Scientists say that emissions add to global warming, which leads to rising sea levels that eat away at Rio and other cities along Brazil's Atlantic coast. The wetter, warmer climate spawns more insect-borne disease.

The Amazon forest is shrinking as development races ahead. Who can say how much Amazonia is worth to the global environment? What is a good trade-off? What can you and your colleagues from India and China get from the North in exchange for your taking steps to protect the "global commons"? Brazil's Environment Agency suggests that you promise the UN to spend $1 billion per year on emissions controls and conservation if the North compensates Brazil with $1 billion for maintaining its forests. But can Brazil expect compensation for not fouling its own nest? And if the money arrived, how could your government persuade private business interests to redirect their energies?

CONTENDING CONCEPTS AND EXPLANATIONS

WHY SHOULD A FOREIGN MINISTER CARE ABOUT ECOLOGY?

Why should the Brazilian foreign minister and the U.S. secretary of state concern themselves with air and water quality? These are not the security and sovereignty issues of high politics that occupy top diplomats. Are these not low politics—the mundane economic and social concerns that foreign ministers should leave to junior officials or other departments? The answer is no, for IR, like all of life, depends upon the biosphere—the thin sliver of minerals, flora, fauna, and gases that make human existence possible. Humanity—its biological needs, institutions, and behavior—is part of an emergent structure sustaining many interdependent organisms.[1]

1. Murray Gell-Mann, *The Quark and the Jaguar: Adventures in the Simple and the Complex* (New York: Freeman, 1994), 99–100.

Life is easy to destroy but difficult to create. Species disappear at an accelerating rate. One-fifth of all plants and animals could be doomed by 2020 absent more effective steps to save them.[2] Today's willful act may be tomorrow's deficit—trees burned, marginal lands plowed, irrigation canals untended or destroyed. Human-made change helped destroy the biological foundations of ancient Sumerian, Cambodian, and Mayan civilizations. As their way of life teetered, Mayans worried about war, ecological disasters, deforestation, and starvation. "The population rose to the limits the technology could bear. They were so close to the edge, if anything went wrong, it was all over."[3] At the start of another millennium, does any of this have a familiar ring?

Stability of habitat is important to humans because it is the system in which they have evolved. Environmental loss endangers their spirits, minds, and bodies. Humans risk closing the door to their future as well as wiping out their past. Endangered species may contain as-yet-undeveloped medicines, foods, drugs, timber, fibers, pulp, soil-restoring vegetation, and petroleum substitutes.[4] How does all this concern the IPE? Governments and other IPE actors have sometimes led the assault on the habitat. Not only war and power politics but also development, trade, and tourism can degrade the environment. International relations and the IPE have been part of the problem. Can they be part of a constructive response?

THE BIOSPHERE AS A LEVEL OF IR ACTION AND ANALYSIS

The biosphere should be seen as the broadest level of IR action and analysis. IR shapes the environment and is shaped by it. This is one point on which many exponents of realism, idealism, and interdependence agree. A realist focused on power and geopolitics must take the environment into account. The realist historian Thucydides analyzed the interface between habitat and power—how the settlement patterns of Greece resulted from stronger tribes pushing out weaker peoples from the most fertile lands.

The health of nations also concerns the realist. Thucydides recorded how war spawns not just battle deaths but starvation and disease. He described how the army of one city-state would besiege another polis and then retreat, "laying waste to the fields" as it went. Famine and plague caused more deaths than combat, he wrote.

Disease arising from war has often been far more lethal than enemy action. In the Crimean War (1854–1856), for example, ten times as many British soldiers died of dysentery as from Russian weapons.[5] Influenza in

2. See Edward O. Wilson, *The Diversity of Life* (New York: Norton, 1992), 35–36, 346. Wilson's estimate on disappearing species is challenged by some skeptics.

3. Linda Schele, quoted in David Roberts, "The Decipherment of Ancient Maya," *Atlantic Monthly*, September 1991; see also Linda Schele and Mary Ellen Miller, *The Blood of Kings: Dynasty and Ritual in Mayan Art* (New York: George Braziller, 1986), 14–29.

4. Industrial societies now exploit but a tiny percentage of naturally occurring species. Throughout history, people have utilized about 7,000 plant species for food, but today we rely heavily on about 20 species, such as wheat and rice. Yet 75,000 species have edible parts; some may be superior to those now used, for example, the winged bean of New Guinea, called a "one-species supermarket."

5. William H. McNeill, *Plagues and Peoples* (New York: Anchor Books, 1989), 251.

the wake of World War I killed two or three times as many people as the fighting. Better hygiene and preventive medicine reduced the toll from war-induced disease in the 20th century, but more Iraqis suffered from malnutrition and shortages of medicines in the years after the Gulf War than from the fighting in 1991. Humanity remains vulnerable to environmental dangers triggered by international conflict. Even weather modification is a possible weapon.

Weapons testing and war can damage entire ecosystems. When Saddam Hussein's armies set fire to hundreds of Kuwaiti oil wells in 1991, the blackened air over the Persian Gulf poisoned neutral Iran as well as Kuwait and Iraq; bird and sea life were severely affected. The heavy smoke may also have altered the timing and power of the monsoons that water the Indian subcontinent. Time-lapse satellite images showed that nearly 30 percent of Kuwait's desert was affected by military activity in 1991. Military vehicles disturb the thin layer of pebbles that guards the soil and traps water for plants. Winds then whip the exposed grains into sand storms and dunes—bad for life and livelihood.

Regardless of power considerations, idealists stress the moral and legal reasons to protect all life. Some idealists make the case for **intergenerational equity**—that each generation should leave to future generations natural and cultural resources equal to those that it has enjoyed.[6]

The interdependence school builds on both realism and idealism to underscore the mutual sensitivities and vulnerabilities of all humans and the biosphere. All peoples and countries have become interdependent—with one another and with their environment. In this context they may seek either to claim values or create them with others. In this sphere, as in others, mutual gain policies work better over time than exploitation.

Ecology (environmental science) and IR can learn from one another.[7] No less than ecology and economics, IR is concerned with how humans interact with their *ekos* (or *oikos*, Greek for "habitat"). Government leaders and diplomats are responsible first of all for their own country, but many share with environmentalists the goal of making the planet a safer and more salubrious place to live, not just for those alive today but for their descendants; and not just for one or a few peoples, but for all.[8]

WHEN IS ENVIRONMENTAL PROTECTION A SECURITY ISSUE?

Narrowly defined, a security threat presents a direct and immediate danger. But a security threat can also be indirect and long-term—the result of incremental change in several spheres. Two threats probably

 National Interest and the Biosphere

The U.S. Supreme Court backed the interdependence school when it upheld in *Missouri v. Holland* (1920) the right of the federal government to engage in environmental diplomacy. Asserting "states' rights," the state of Missouri sought to prevent a U.S. game warden from enforcing the Migratory Bird Treaty (1918) and regulations made by the secretary of agriculture to implement it. But Justice Oliver Wendell Holmes argued that "wild birds are not the possession of anyone; and possession is the beginning of ownership." Birds could be in Missouri today but elsewhere tomorrow. "Here is a national interest of very nearly the first magnitude. . . . It can be protected only by national action in concert with that of another power. . . . But for the treaty and the statute there soon might be no birds for any powers to deal with." There is nothing in the U.S. Constitution compelling "the Government to sit by while a food supply is cut off and the protectors of our forests and our crops are destroyed." Therefore, the treaty and statute were sustained.

6. See Edith Brown Weiss, *In Fairness to Future Generations: International Law, Common Patrimony, and Intergenerational Equity* (Tokyo: United Nations University; Dobbs Ferry, N.Y.: Transnational Publishers, 1989).

7. Walter C. Clemens, Jr., "Ecology and International Relations," *International Journal* [special issue, "Earth Politics"] 28, no. 1 (winter 1972–1973): 1–27. See also *International Journal* [special issue, "Environment and Development: Rio and After"] 47, no. 4 (autumn 1992).

8. Harold Sprout and Margaret Sprout, *Toward a Politics of the Planet Earth* (New York: Van Nostrand Reinhold, 1971), 28.

imperil most humans: ozone-layer depletion and climate change. The buildup of trace gases due to industrialization has opened holes in the stratospheric ozone layer—the zone between 15 and 45 kilometers above the earth's surface that contains ozone, a form of oxygen (O_3)—permitting more ultraviolet rays to strike the earth, raising the incidence of skin cancer and blindness among humans and threatening even plankton in the sea. Climate change, also brought on by industrialization, may produce large-scale economic disruption. But many environmental changes impinge directly on some regions and affect others only indirectly. Desertification, for example, may lead to starvation in Africa but not threaten Europe unless Africans attack Europeans or African refugees swarm into Europe.[9]

International environmental conflicts (IECs) may arise from utilization of natural resources that some actors believe cannot be sustained.[10] The depletion may take place directly—within a state (logging in Indonesia) or in a commons (whaling by Norway)—or indirectly (as when sulphur from Russian factories rains down on Norwegian forests). One negative side effect may spawn another, as when deforestation in El Salvador produced "environmental refugees" who crowded into Honduras, sparking a war in 1969. Serious conflicts between states erupt when upstream states close the faucets for tailenders. See "Four IECs Over Water" for four examples of water-related IECs.

Some analysts expect IECs to intensify as states and transnational corporations (TNCs) struggle over increasingly scarce resources.[11]

9. Marc A. Levy, "Is the Environment a National Security Issue?" *International Security* 20, no. 2 (fall 1995): 35–62.

10. Jon Martin Trolldalen, *International Environmental Conflict Resolution: The Role of the United Nations* (Washington, D.C.: World Foundation for Environment and Development, 1992), 57–60.

11. Lands once deemed worthless, such as the Spratly Islands, have provoked clashes between China and Vietnam. For conflicting interpretations, see Denny Roy and Michael G. Gallagher in *International Security* 19, no. 1 (summer 1994): 149–168 and 169–194.

Four IECs Over Water

1. Anticipating that a dam on the Bafing River built with international financing would raise land values, Mauritania's Arab rulers expelled Blacks from the river area, declaring them foreigners—"Senegalese." Blacks in Senegal then destroyed 17,000 shops belonging to Arabs and deported their owners to Mauritania.

2. Turkey controls the flow of the Euphrates River into Iraq and Syria, and diverts it for its multibillion-dollar Ataturk Dam irrigation project. Syria backs Kurdish rebels against Turkey, in part to get leverage in the water talks.

3. Israel controls water valuable to Jordan and to Palestinians on the West Bank and Gaza Strip. Prior to 1993, Israel allotted its settlers on the occupied West Bank four times more water than it did to non-Israeli residents; Israelis were allowed to dig wells that depleted water under non-Israeli farms.

4. Slovakia in the early 1990s rechanneled part of the Danube River and harnessed its power, turning vast wetlands into wastelands, despite Hungarian objections. Budapest had agreed to the project in Communist times, but non-Communist Hungary backed out. Slovakia ignored treaties prohibiting either side from diverting the Danube in ways that altered the common border, impacted negatively on established water conditions, or profited one side only. Slovakia turned down third parties' proposals to restore the region through a debt-for-nature swap. The International Court of Justice in 1997 treated the river's diversion as an accomplished fact but piously urged both sides to protect the environment.

Fig. 13.1 Ideational Factors Between the Environment and Human Action

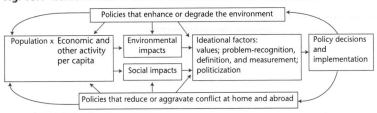

Others believe that a growing abundance removes any need to fight. A third view says that everything hinges on how people think and act. Whether resource shortages provoke conflict depends on **ideational factors**—values, beliefs, institutions, property relationships. These factors shape the behaviors that contribute both to environmental problems and to war, as outlined in Figure 13.1.[12] Global interdependence, however, means vulnerability. Air and water pollution do not recognize the sovereignty of state borders. What begins as a local problem may ripple widely—often unpredictably—through the entire chain of being. As the naturalist John Muir put it: "When you try to touch one thing by itself, you find it hitched to everything else in the universe."

If Amazonia is deforested or polluted, this presents an immediate but localized problem for indigenous people. But deforestation also affects the global environment: It shrinks a sponge (or "sink") that absorbs carbon from the entire world, and it releases gases as trees decompose or burn. Even if new trees are planted, decades are usually needed before the new forest acquires a significant ability to store carbons. Biodiversity is even harder to restore. If Sao Paulo and Rio are polluted, a local problem becomes a worldwide problem as gases rising from the polluted cities add to global concentrations. If global weather becomes more volatile, Brazil too is likely to suffer. As Map 13.1 illustrates, economic and social developments in Brazil affect the global environment, which in turn affects Brazil.

HOW CAN IR ENHANCE THE ENVIRONMENT?

Environmental diplomacy addresses the interface between habitat and IR. It is practiced not only by governments and international governmental organizations (IGOs) such as the UN, but by private parties—scientists, the media, nongovernmental organizations (NGOs), and TNCs.[13] Environmental diplomacy can utilize many levers: growing

12. Thomas F. Homer-Dixon, Jeffrey H. Boutwell, and George W. Rathjens, "Environmental Change and Violent Conflict," *Scientific American,* February 1993, 38–45.

13. A major text is Lynton Keith Caldwell, *International Environmental Policy: Emergence and Dimensions,* 2d ed. (Durham, N.C.: Duke University Press, 1990).

Map 13.1 Brazil in the Global Feedback Loop

1. The Amazon Basin, like other forests, traps carbons, but when trees are cut, burned, or left to rot, they release greenhouse gases. The Amazon may hold half of the world's biological riches. It extends into nine countries, but 68 percent of the Amazon Basin lies in Brazil. However, 75 percent of Peru and Bolivia lie in Amazonia, and 45 percent of Colombia.

2. Deforestation takes place rapidly as the area is "developed," with or without government permission or encouragement. Large tracts of Amazonia are owned by foreign companies that receive tax breaks and other financial incentives for building roads and developing Amazonia.

3. Some 400 ethnic groups—estimated at half a million to 2.5 million indigenous people—live in the Amazon Basin. Development of their habitat often leads to cultural genocide and to physical massacres, as among the Yanomami peoples in the northern part of Amazonia. The Basin in the 1990s had 20 million inhabitants. Besides indigenous peoples, there were gold prospectors, coca farmers, rubber tappers, and urban populations.

4. Large dams in the Amazon Basin include Balbina, Tucurui, and Samuel. In other parts of Brazil are the large dams Itaparica and Itaipu. They generate power but have dislocated many people, added to deforestation, and degraded natural wonders such as Iguazu Falls.

5. Automobiles and industry create serious air pollution in Sao Paulo, Belo Horizonte, and other Brazilian cities.

6. Most of Brazil's Atlantic coast forest, "Mata Atlantica," has been cut down, opening the way to severe erosion. Rio de Janeiro has been extended into the water on fragile foundations. If ocean waters rise, due in part to global warming, Brazil's Atlantic coast will suffer further erosion.

7. Sources of conflict in the Amazon Basin include drug-trafficking vs. antinarcotics operations; oil exploration, mining, and other forms of development vs. native peoples and environmentalists; guerrilla insurgents of Colombia and Peru vs. governments and other defenders of the status quo. Outside actors often magnify the conflicts. They include the U.S. armed forces (antidrug missions), the World Bank, the UN Environmental Programme, the Organization of American States, the Inter-American Development Bank, and Raytheon Corporation.

8. SIVAM (*Sistema de Vigilencia d Amazonia*) is a system of land-based radars and satellites to monitor land clearings approved by the Brazilian Congress in 1996 for development by the Raytheon Corporation and financed by loans from the U.S. Export–Import Bank.

9. Rivalry and some arms competition with Argentina, designated by President Bill Clinton in 1997 as a "non-NATO U.S. ally," and praised by him for officially recognizing that it too should act to reduce carbon emissions, continues.

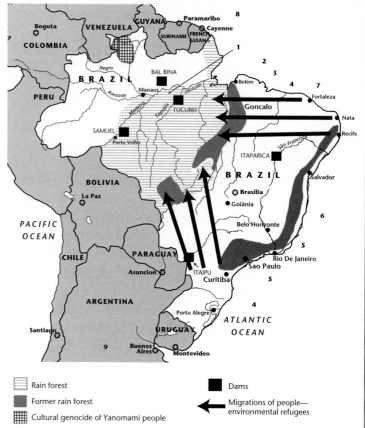

Legend:
- Rain forest
- Former rain forest
- Cultural genocide of Yanomami people
- Dams
- Migrations of people—environmental refugees

MAP NOTE: Latin America and the Caribbean lost 3 percent of their forest cover in 1991–1995, more hectares than any other region. While 68 percent of Argentina has been "converted," only 28 percent of Brazil had been converted by 1995. But 6 percent of the forests in both countries were converted in the 1980s.

SOURCES: *Oxford Atlas of the World* (New York: Oxford University Press, 1994), 47; "Challenges Facing the Amazon Basin," *Strategic Comments* 3, no. 8 (London: International Institute for Strategic Studies, October 1997); interview with Dr. Maria G. M. Rodrigues, Boston University, 1997; and Lester R. Brown et al., *Vital Signs 1997* (New York: Norton, 1997), 96–99; www.amazonia.net; www.unu.edu/env.html; author's interviews in Brazil and Argentina in 1976 and 2002.

knowledge and consensus among experts on environmental problems and options, informed public opinion and environmental awareness, harmonization of policy by various IR actors, carrots and sticks (soft and hard power), declarations of intent (moral force), and bilateral and multilateral agreements (legal force).

Table 13.1 Examples of Environmental Problems, Conflicts, and Negotiated Remedies

Environmental Problem	International Conflict	Negotiated Remedy
Stratospheric ozone layer depletion for LDCs	LDCs resist pressures to reduce their emissions	1987 Montreal Protocol, with grace period due to gas
Greenhouse gases and global climate change	Debate on severity of the problem and who should sacrifice what	1992 Rio Global Climate Change Convention and 1997 Kyoto Protocol
Acid deposits across borders	Polluters resist pressures from their victims	1979 Geneva Convention for Europe; 1991 Canada–U.S. Air Quality Agreement
Deforestation	Brazil and Indonesia tell the North to change its own practices	Debt-for-nature swaps; 1992 Rio Statement on "All Types of Forests"
Nuclear radiation leakage from reactors	Europeans complain that Moscow told them too late and too little about the 1986 Chernobyl meltdown	1986 IAEA Conventions on Early Notification and on Assistance in Case of a Nuclear Accident
Depletion of fish stocks	Canada vs. U.S.; each country vs. outsiders; Ottawa and Washington claim right to regulate fishing over the continental shelf	Bilateral Canadian–U.S. agreements; 1982 UN Law of the Sea; 1992 Rio Convention on Biological Diversity
Dumping of waste at sea and in LDCs, with or without their agreement	Defenders of global commons and LDCs oppose dumpers (mainly from the North)	1989 Basel Convention to Control Transboundary Movements of Hazardous Wastes and Their Disposal

Many environmental agreements are bilateral. In 1869 and 1875, for example, Germany and Switzerland signed treaties to regulate fishing in the Rhine River. More than 130 such agreements had been reached around the world by the 1990s.[14] But many environmental accords are multilateral. A few are outlined in Table 13.1.

Environmental diplomacy often follows a two-stage process: First, diplomats draft and sign a framework convention (treaty) stating general objectives but omitting specific methods and commitments. Second, as consensus builds, diplomats adopt supplementary **protocols**—follow-up agreements to specify and tighten commitments. Step by step, this process builds a **regime**—agreed-on rules or understandings. The process permits countries to "sign on" at the outset even before specific commitments are clear. If supplementary commitments seem too onerous, actors need not sign the additional protocol.

The first UN Conference on the Human Environment, held in Stockholm in 1972, led to establishment of the UN Environmental Programme in Nairobi, Kenya. Ten years later, a follow-up meeting was held in Nairobi. In 1992, a third gathering convened in Brazil. The 1992 UN Conference on Environment and Development in Rio de Janeiro—dubbed the **Earth Summit**—became the largest political gathering in history. The conference was attended by some 170 states—over 100

14. See Edith Brown Weiss, ed., *Environmental Change and International Law: New Challenges and Dimensions* (Tokyo: United Nations University Press, 1992), 479–490.

represented by their heads of state or government—and evaluated by 1,500 accredited observers from NGOs and by 8,000 journalists. The official meetings were paralleled by meetings attended by 30,000 private citizens from NGOs around the globe.

The 1992 Earth Summit endorsed a series of documents: the Rio Declaration, or "Earth Charter," a list of 27 basic principles to govern economic and environmental behavior of states; Agenda 21, action goals in major areas affecting the environment and the economy (nearly 400 pages of small type); the Framework Convention on Climate Change (26 articles and two annexes); the Convention on Biological Diversity (42 articles and two annexes); and the Authoritative Statement of Principles on Sustainable Development of All Types of Forests (15 principles).[15]

The Rio accords were long on generalities and short on specific obligations. For critics, the glass was half empty. For Rio enthusiasts, it was half full; they argued that such meetings raise consciousness and set the stage for more precise action programs.

MALTHUSIANS, CORNUCOPIANS, AND SUSTAINABLE DEVELOPMENT

The **Malthusian perspective** contends that there are finite limits to growth as expanding human populations deplete resources.[16] This view has its roots in an essay by Thomas Malthus, published in 1798. Malthus predicted that population (growing exponentially) would outstrip food production (growing "arithmetically") unless checked by moral restraints or by war, famine, and disease.[17] The **cornucopian outlook**, by contrast, sees life as a horn of plenty that swells with use. Human ingenuity uses the earth to sustain more people than ever—most of them living longer and in greater comfort than their predecessors. Cornucopians are progrowth: Material well-being is the key that makes everything else possible—including environmental protection. Cornucopians say that Malthus did not anticipate that technology would facilitate vastly larger populations.[18]

"In technology we trust" is the optimists' motto. Technological optimists have wagered that insecticides can wipe out malaria; that nuclear power promises not just weapons but clean energy at a reasonable price; that the Green Revolution can transform agriculture by "miracle seeds" backed by abundant fertilizer and irrigation; that modernization plus affluence will stem population growth; that genetic engineering will produce improved life forms. Each approach, however, spawned negative side effects and much criticism.[19]

15. Michael Grubb et al., *The Earth Summit Agreements: A Guide and Assessment* (London: Earthscan, 1993); for texts, see Stanley P. Johnson, ed., *The Earth Summit* (London: Graham & Trotman/Martinus Nijhoff, 1993).

16. See the report to the Club of Rome by Donella H. Meadows et al., *The Limits to Growth* (New York: Universe Books, 1972).

17. Malthus warned: "As population doubles and redoubles, it is exactly as if the globe were halving in size, until finally it has shrunk so much that food and subsistence fall below the level necessary for life." Malthus believed that, due to the law of diminishing returns, food production tends not to keep up with the geometric progression of growth of population. Updated in Eduard Pestel, *Beyond the Limits to Growth: A Report to the Club of Rome* (New York: Universe Books, 1989).

18. The Malthusians' viewpoint and Cornucopian economist Julian L. Simon's views may be found in Simon, *Population Matters: People, Resources, Environment, and Immigration* (New Brunswick, N.J.: Transaction, 1990), 374–380. For more recent appraisals, see Arnulf Grübler et al., eds., *Technological Change and the Environment* (Washington, D.C.: Resources for the Future, 2002).

19. Critics say that the Green Revolution has helped the rich become richer, because only they can afford the necessary fertilizer. If big farms become more efficient, poor farmers are displaced. Over time, however, heavy dependence on fertilizer and water leads to diminishing returns. See also Jane Rissler and Margaret Mellon, *The Ecological Risks of Engineered Crops* (Cambridge, Mass.: MIT Press, 1996).

Are there no limits to growth? Can demand assure supply? Malthusians fear that there is no technical solution to some problems posed by population growth. So far Malthus's predictions have materialized only in specific regions. But if humans multiply beyond a certain threshold, their support system may crash, leading to a sharp reduction in population.[20]

The limits-to-growth school argues that clean air, clean water, and biodiversity must be protected—now, not later. They fear that environmental problems can grow so quickly against fixed limits that policy makers may have little time to avert disaster.[21] A more recent variant of the argument is that, even if we do not run out of basic resources, burning carbons as we do will destroy the biosphere. Cornucopians say that humans can devise answers to shortages and live in peaceful abundance. They advise no costly steps against uncertain risks. They prefer to wait and see. If carbons cause a severe problem, human ingenuity will provide a solution.[22]

SUSTAINABLE DEVELOPMENT VS. EXPLOITATION

Is it possible to bridge the gap between the Malthusian and Cornucopian viewpoints? The concept of **sustainable development** calls for economic growth but stipulates that resources be used in ways that can be sustained over time.[23] Think of natural resources as capital assets and their benefits as income. Sustainable development leaves capital assets (soil, water, forests) intact so that future generations can enjoy undiminished income and quality of life. **Carrying capacity** is the level of resource utilization that can be sustained without degrading the resource. This level depends both on nature and on humans—how they utilize the resource can weaken or buttress its carrying capacity. Critics say that sustainable development is a nice-sounding slogan but solves nothing. At best it offers a goal but gives no practical advice on how to achieve it. As we see in the sidebar on page 483, sustainable development is easier said than done. It can mean different things to different people.

Sustainable development requires a value-creating approach to wealth, politics, and the environment. The concept of mutual gain can be adapted to husbanding the biosphere. A short-term emphasis on claiming values for quick, one-sided profits can make development unsustainable. The values at stake are multiple—the resource itself, the interests of the developers, and those of third parties affected by development. A zero-sum approach to a resource may kill it: A policy that excludes other actors from a resource may lead those actors to sabotage it. In development, as in other spheres, aggressive exploitation can backfire.[24]

20. Positive and negative feedback loops link growth in human population, resource depletion, pollution, and climate change. Each factor aggravates both environmental problems and the aggressive behaviors that exacerbate other shortfalls. A positive feedback loop generates runaway growth: If population increases, requiring ever higher levels of consumption, resources will be depleted. Negative feedback loops tend to hold a system stable for a time. But change in one element propagates change through the system until it comes back to push that element in an opposite direction, which may produce a crash. See Jay W. Forrester, *World Dynamics* (Cambridge, Mass.: Wright-Allen Press, 1971), 94–95; and Meadows et al., *Limits to Growth*, 31–37.

21. Imagine a pond where one water lily grows. This plant doubles in size each day. If it expands unchecked, it will cover the pond in thirty days, choking off other forms of life. For days the plant seems small, so you decide not to cut it back until it covers half the pond. But on the 29th day, only one day remains to save the pond! Meadows et al., *Limits to Growth*, 29.

22. Many Cassandras have predicted a doomsday that never arrived, for example, an end to oil. Even though oil resources have been depleted in some countries, new finds and alternative fuels more than meet global demand. So far the planet resembles a gigantic cave in which, as we reach the limit of one chamber, the door to another opens—even grander than the one just passed.

23. William C. Clark and R. E. Munn, eds., *Sustainable Development of the Biosphere* (New York: Cambridge University Press, 1986); World Commission on Environment and Development, *Our Common Future* (New York: Oxford University Press, 1987).

24. Some UN documents refer to exploitation in a positive and a negative sense on the same page. *Exploitation* comes from the Latin for "unfold." The term long had a positive connotation—tapping a resource. In the 18th century, however, some economists asserted that the exploitation of German peasants by large landowners was unfair. Later, Karl Marx argued that capitalists exploit workers, deriving "surplus value" from their labor. He predicted that this exploitation could not be sustained, for it would trigger a revolution.

HOW THE LOGIC OF COLLECTIVE ACTION CAN DEGRADE THE ENVIRONMENT

As noted in Chapter 1, a collective (or public) good is one that all persons in a given community may share, such as common pasture or breathable air. It is a good that, if available to any group member, cannot feasibly be withheld from other members—even those who do not pay for it. Some public goods are part of the natural environment; some are provided by government or other human agencies. Economic activity and externalities—unplanned side effects—can add to or deplete public goods.

Some actors try to exploit public goods and obtain a "free ride" based on others' efforts. This "logic of collective action" leads to the underfunding of public goods such as clean air and to behavior injurious to the commons.[25] The lure of parasitism is even stronger across borders. To cope, governments use incentives—rewards for tree planters and penalties for polluters. To curb international free riding—for example, dumping wastes—governments set up special regimes. To "green" or "ecologize" production can make a country cleaner and more efficient while fostering innovative technology. But neighbors who refuse to ecologize also benefit from the cleaner environment while their own industries produce, unburdened by pollution abatement costs.

Our case studies show how power politics, the drive for economic development, and the logic of collective action have abetted exploitation of the biosphere. But we shall also see that farsighted diplomacy—by private citizens and NGOs as well as by governments and IGOs—has done much to conserve the planet.

COMPARING THEORY AND REALITY: IS SUSTAINABLE DEVELOPMENT FEASIBLE?

Life can be a gamble. Faust wagered his very soul for earthly pleasure. International actors—governments, TNCs, the World Bank, even the World Health Organization[26]—have often bet that technology can overcome economic and environmental restraints. Each technology has promise, but each entails huge risks. Let us focus first on water power.

DAMMED WATERS AND DAMNED PEOPLE: THE ASWAN SYNDROME

Mastery of water resources has long been a source of power—political as well as economic and social. It was key to the "hydraulic civilizations" of ancient Egypt, Sumeria, India, Sri Lanka, and China. Water politics

25. Mancur Olson, *The Logic of Collective Action* (Cambridge, Mass.: Harvard University Press, 1965, 1971); and Olson, *The Rise and Decline of Nations: Economic Growth, Stagflation, and Social Rigidities* (New Haven, Conn.: Yale University Press, 1982).

26. The World Health Organization and its use of chemical sprays against malaria-carrying mosquitoes are discussed in Chapter 14.

water to their spawning grounds, they could not easily climb ladders or concrete barriers—a problem foreseen by Henry David Thoreau in the 1840s as he watched Massachusetts rivers being harnessed for hydropower. He expected people to wake up in a few hundred years and remove the barricades, but doubted there would be fish left to respond.

Resettlement. The social and economic costs of moving people from the river banks flooded by the dam are usually greater than planners expect or budget for. A way of life often perishes with them as they move into mass-produced housing in regions that often have no jobs for newcomers. Nearly 100,000 Nubians (half of them in the Sudan) lost their traditional way of life when damming the Nile forced them to move elsewhere. Governments on every continent have dammed waters and damned people.[32] Like the Nubians, long-established communities have been uprooted—from Paraguay to Senegal to Siberia.[33] Millions more are in danger—from Canada to India and China.[34] Threatened communities try to resist powerful governments but usually lose—especially where democracy is weak.[35]

Culture. Lake Nasser flooded many ancient Egyptian and Roman ruins, though UNESCO moved the Abu Simbel temple to higher ground. Archeologists in China and elsewhere have rushed to save what they can—usually just a fraction of what falls to the bulldozer and then to the reservoir.

Vulnerability. If a dam breaks, catastrophic flooding can follow. The Aswan High Dam would give Israel or any other foe of Egypt an inviting target. The global pattern was ominous: When rains were moderate, the dam prevented or mitigated floods. If the dam breached or if water had to be released after big storms, floods were often more severe than before.

Dependency. For some years President Nasser and many Egyptians gained pride and confidence from the Aswan High Dam—thumbing their noses at the West and upstream states. But Egypt came to depend on the USSR for money, advice, and technology. Displeased by Soviet behavior, President Anwar Sadat broke most ties with Moscow.[36] Egypt then depended on the U.S. for new turbines and for wheat when Egypt's farms failed to feed the country's growing numbers. Larger powers such as India and China could try to defy the conditions imposed by Western aid givers, but even they needed Western technology. Smaller African countries needed outside financing as well as technology for large dams.

32. S. Robert Aikken, "Hydro-Electric Power and Wilderness Protection," *Impact of Science on Society* 36, no. 1 (1986): 85–96; Fred Pearce, "Building a Disaster: The Monumental Folly of India's Tehri Dam," *Ecologist* 21 (May–June 1991): 123–128; and Ricardo Canese, *La problematica de Itaipu: analisis de los cuestiones financiereas, economicas y energeticas* (Asuncion: Casillia de Correo, 1989).

33. Michael M. Horowitz, "Victims Upstream and Down," *Journal of Refugee Studies* 4, no. 2 (1991): 164–181; and Anthony Oliver-Smith, "Involuntary Resettlement, Resistance and Political Empowerment," ibid, 132–149. On Siberia, see Valentin Rasputin's novel, *Farewell to Matëra.*

34. What benefits one region may harm another. Many New Yorkers may welcome a larger supply of electricity from Canada. But Hydro-Quebec's La Grand project at James Bay would inundate a Vermont-sized area—home to Crees, Inuits, and abundant wildlife. In 2002, the Cree Grand Council permitted Hydro-Quebec to dam two rivers in exchange for $3.4 billion to be paid out over 50 years.

35. The Indian novelist Arundhati Roy took up the cause of people displaced by India's Sardar Sarovar (Narmada River) Project. See her *The Cost of Living* (New York: Modern Library, 1999); see also Jean Dreze et al., *The Dam and the Nation: Displacement and Resettlement in the Narmada Valley* (New Delhi: Oxford University Press, 1997).

36. Walter C. Clemens, Jr., "Behind Sadat's Eviction Order," *New Leader,* October 2, 1972, 6–8.

Nationalist Horizons. Egypt in the 21st century will need more water, but so will Ethiopia, the Sudan, and the countries of equatorial Africa. Upstream states could close the spigot. In 1980, Sadat warned that Egypt would fight if Ethiopia interfered with Egypt's historic rights to Nile water. Later, however, Egypt threatened to dig 3,000 wells to tap the desert if Ethiopia dammed the Blue Nile. In the mid-1990s, Egyptian leaders talked of building a second main branch of the Nile by diverting water into a channel leading west and north. The ideal solution—technically and politically—would be an international storage system to meet overlapping needs of the riverine states, but such an undertaking would require unprecedented cooperation and joint planning.[37]

Grandiosity. Governments overlook cheaper, less grandiose answers to their problems, such as birth control. A serious effort at population planning—inexpensive and environment-neutral—would have done more to keep food stocks in line with population than the costly dam. Egypt did not initiate serious population control campaigns until decades after building the high dam.

Alternative Energy. Counting on one big project, Egypt and other governments tend to ignore solar, wind, geothermal energy or the hydropower available from many small dams. Though an American had engineered Egypt's first solar plant in 1913, a people who once worshiped the sun neglected the earth's major heat source. Solar and wind-power stations were being installed with aid from the World Bank and the Netherlands in the early 21st century, but were expected to help at first only marginally with Egypt's demands for power.

The Aswan syndrome was there for all to see by the 1970s. A high dam is no panacea. There is no free or cheap lunch. Wishful thinking left Egypt and its neighbors with a host of unresolved problems. Nonetheless, the leaders of China, Brazil, India, Nepal and other countries chose to ignore the evidence. So did the World Bank.

Many dams have been financed by the World Bank. Greenpeace activists in 1994 demanded "no more dollars for destruction" by "World Bankenstein."[38] The arc of the World Bank's learning curve was quite high before it began to take a critical look at high dam. Bank president Lewis Preston conceded in 1994 that the bank's greatest mistake had been to undervalue environmental considerations. Better late than never, the World Bank in the 1990s gave more weight to ecology. In the 1980s, the World Bank offered $450 million in loans to India to dam

37. Whittington and Guariso, *Water Management*, 221. Three of the upstream states, however, cooperated in water surveys by the World Meteorological Organization.

38. Some 150 environmental groups in thirty countries organized a campaign, 50 Years Is Enough, directed against the World Bank and International Monetary Fund. The organizers wanted to hold the two agencies accountable to the people whose lives they affect in the developing world. Greenpeace did not wish to destroy the World Bank; it sought to reduce its resources and power.

The Three Gorges Dam promised to be one of the largest and most costly public works ever built—with some of the most serious externalities, such as pollution. The waters rising behind the dam sucked into the Yangtze not just archeological treasures but the scrap heaps and other residues left by factories and human settlements. Rare river dolphins and other marine life as well as humans were threatened.

the Narmada River. Later, a more environmentally conscious bank pressed India to explain how it would cope with the dam's consequences—environmental disruption and displacement of at least 250,000 people. This led India in 1993 to reject the final $170 million loan installment.[39]

The World Bank cosponsored a global survey by the World Dam Commission, published in 2001, entitled *Dams and Development.* Besides the environmental and social problems such as those described here, the WDC also noted the tension betweeen corruption and self-rule. If decisions on dams are taken behind closed doors, opportunities for corruption abound.[40]

If all the people affected by a dam had a say, many dams would never be built. If we think of riparian settlements as stakeholders, surely they should have a vote.[41]

Communist governments have often trusted in large projects to improve on nature.[42] China's National People's Congress in 1992 approved what could be the world's largest water works—the Three Gorges Dam on the Yangtze River. Chinese officials hoped the project, to be built over twenty or more years, would generate power equal to one-eighth of China's 1991 output and prevent floods. An associated project would sluice water by aqueduct 1,500 miles northeast to Beijing.

But many Chinese and foreign observers saw the Three Gorges project as an enterprise with risks and likely costs far outweighing the potential

39. Hamish McDonald, "Closing the Floodgates: New Delhi Rejects a World Bank Loan to Build a Dam," *Far Eastern Economic Review* 156, no. 15 (April 15, 1993): p. 15. Another analyst feared that the Sardar Sarovar Dam would flood 150 villages and force 1.5 million people off their lands. See Damien Lewis, "Drowning by Numbers," *Geographical Magazine* 63, no. 9 (September 1991): p. 34 ff.

40. LDC governments ask engineering companies: "Please study our circumstances and say if we need a dam. Tell us if there are other, less costly ways to produce energy and cope with floods." Not only do some "consultants" shape their advice to win contracts for their own firms, but they cement the deal by bribing local decision makers.

41. World Commission on Dams, *Dams and Development: A New Framework for Decision-Making* (London: Earthscan, 2001). India did not permit the WDC to examine the Narmada project up close.

42. Stalin turned Russia's Volga River into a succession of polluted, heavily sedimented lakes behind vast hydroelectric dams. Cotton irrigation projects in Soviet Uzbekistan virtually destroyed the Aral Sea. A dam completed in the 1980s degraded the water of St. Petersburg. For the broad picture, see D. J. Peterson, *Troubled Lands: The Legacy of Soviet Environmental Destruction* (Boulder, Colo.: Westview, 1993).

Political Obstacles to No-Regrets

Natural gas may burn cleaner than other forms of energy. China wants to tap the natural gas resources of the Caspian, but pipelines require political stability in China's northwest. Should outsiders muffle their concern for the Uighurs and other minorities in hopes that China can obtain natural gas and burn less coal?

The Three Gorges hydroelectric project could also reduce China's dependency upon coal. But some dam labor is forced, more than one million people will be displaced, and biodiversity and natural beauty will suffer. What is the right price for fewer CO_2 emissions?

Whatever the moral and political issues, economic pressures and potential profits pushed for development.

gains. Public debate on the dam was banned after 1989. Prevented from publishing critical analysis within China, some Chinese scientists published their views abroad. Of 2,600 delegates to the 1992 Congress, 177 voted against the dam and 664 abstained.

Top Chinese leaders presided over the initial diversion of the Yangtze in late 1997. The project was expected to flood 24,000 hectares of arable land and displace more than 1 million people; inundate 350 miles of a canyon that was a centerpiece of Chinese art, history, and culture for thousands of years; and destroy the habitat of a unique dolphin and other endangered species. The dam's design was untested. Accumulated sediments behind the dam could limit its storage capacity. Like Aswan, this could also be a prime bomb target. Cost estimates for the dam ratcheted up from $12 billion in 1993 to more than $25 billion in 1997, and kept climbing. Conservationists urged China instead to fix leaking toilets, raise water prices, and build smaller, safer dams.[43]

Technology can make life better. But governments have often opted for big, showy projects rather than seeking **appropriate technology** suited to the task. In 1997, People's Republic of China President Jiang Zemin stated that the Yangtze diversion "vividly proves once again that socialism is superior in organizing people to do big jobs." Prime Minister Li Peng said the event showed the "greatness . . . of China's development." The New China News Agency compared the dam with the Great Wall, built 2,000 years earlier. Undaunted by possible side effects, one of the dam's chief engineers asserted: "Basically no technical problem is insoluble."

But each step toward damming the Yangtze revealed new problems. As waters rose along parts of the river in 2002, they swept into the reservoir not just people's homes but their latrines, along with the industrial and mining wastes cached along the banks, creating a gigantic cesspool. Meanwhile, thousands of ostensibly resettled people returned to their homes, not yet inundated, on the banks of the river. They complained that where they were sent there were few jobs, poor housing, and a very cool reception from the locals.

Why did Chinese leaders insist on carrying through the Three Gorges project? Was it unthinkable to halt a project to which earlier giants of Communist politics had given their blessing? Were China's needs so great that Beijing felt it must gamble that the likely gains would outweigh the dangers? Anxieties about floods and food shortfalls give rise to wishful thinking and "gigantomania." The availability of "free money"—public funds or foreign loans—can mean personal profit and more prestige. But

43. Seth Faison, "Set to Build Dam, China Diverts Yangtze While Crowing About It," *The New York Times,* November 9, 1997, 1, 12; Peter Gwynne, "Yangtze Project Dammed with Faint Praise," *Nature,* April 30, 1992, 736; "The Biggest in Question," *Economist,* March 28, 1992, 97; and Philip M. Fearnside, "China's Three Gorges Dam: 'Fatal' Project or Step Toward Modernization?" *World Development* 16, no. 5 (May 1988): 615 ff.

China was not alone. India, Brazil, and many other governments were swept up by the Aswan syndrome.

HOW TO NEGOTIATE TO PROTECT THE ENVIRONMENT

Let us examine how diplomats have tried to protect the ozone layer and control the buildup of greenhouse gases. Each case is vital, because the biosphere depends upon layers of gases enveloping the planet. To understand and regulate these processes is a challenge for scientists, diplomats, economists, and ethicists. By what principle should rights (for example, to pollute and to breathe) and duties (to protect and to share) be allocated?[44]

A "Simple" Problem: Protecting the Ozone Layer

More than twenty states signed the Vienna Convention on Substances that Deplete the Ozone Layer in 1985. Protocols followed. The Montreal Protocol on Substances That Deplete the Ozone Layer—the **Montreal Protocol**—was signed by some fifty countries in 1987 and entered into force in 1989. The parties agreed to freeze and then reduce production and consumption of chlorofluorocarbons (CFCs) and other chemicals believed to damage the ozone layer. The protocol gave LDCs more time to comply than it did to industrial countries.[45]

The Montreal accord was aided by a scientific consensus on the nature of an environmental problem.[46] DuPont Corporation, the major U.S. producer, initially denied that CFCs presented any danger. DuPont later shifted its stance as evidence pointed to holes in the ozone layer; as Congress threatened to limit CFC production in the U.S.—leaving Dupont's foreign competitors untouched; and as DuPont researchers found a possible substitute for CFCs that promised the firm a competitive advantage worldwide.

The 1987 protocol's restrictions on CFC production were ratcheted up after scientific evidence accumulated about the seriousness of ozone depletion. In 1990 the parties reconvened in London and agreed to eliminate completely the production of eight ozone-depleting chemicals by the year 2000 in industrialized countries and by 2010 in developing countries. In 1990 more countries jumped on the bandwagon: Ninety-three countries, including China and India, signed the London protocol.

The Montreal–London accords imposed heavier near-term obligations on industrialized states than on developing countries. First,

44. For background, see Committee on Science, Engineering, and Public Policy, National Academy of Sciences, National Academy of Engineering, and Institute of Medicine, *Policy Implications of Greenhouse Warming* (Washington, D.C.: National Academy Press, 1991).

45. Each industrial country signatory pledged to reduce by 1990 its production and consumption of CFCs to less than 1986 levels; by 1994 to cut CFCs by 20 percent under 1986 levels; and by 1999 to no more than half of 1986 levels. The Montreal Protocol recognized the special situation of LDCs (so-called Article 5 countries) in which per capita consumption of the controlled substances was less than 0.3 kilograms per year. They would have ten more years in which to comply.

46. See Thomas E. Graedel and Paul J. Crutzen, "The Changing Atmosphere," *Scientific American*, September 1989, 58–68 at 63; and Stephen H. Schneider, "The Changing Climate," ibid., 70–79. Some observers suggested that ozone depletion was a greater issue for fair-skinned, affluent Northerners than for the dark-skinned peoples of the LDCs. Most specialists agreed, however, that greater ultraviolet radiation threatens all living things—even sea plankton.

heavy polluters had to reduce emissions earlier than light polluters. Second, production ceilings were pegged to 1986 consumption levels rather than to a per capita basis. Third, in 1990, the industrialized countries agreed to establish a multilateral fund of $240 million to help LDCs convert existing chemical plants, install new ones, and import substitutes.

The ozone limitations had mixed results. The U.S. and Western Europe stopped production of CFCs in 1995 but agreed only that year to phase out another ozone-depleting agent, methyl bromide by 2010. Ozone holes over Antarctica persisted in the late 1990s.[47] In September 2002, however, the UN Environment Programme (UNEP) and the World Meteorological Organization (WMO, another UN Specialized Agency) reported evidence that the process of ozone-depletion had been reversed. Worldwatch Institute in Washington reported that, globally, production of ozone-depleting CFCs fell by 81 percent in the 1990s. Australian scientists in Tasmania predicted that the Antarctica ozone hole would begin to shrink within five years.

As of 2002, some 183 governments had signed the Montreal Protocol. Still, the UNEP/WMO study gave four reasons why the ozone layer would remain vulnerable for at least a decade. First, criminals smuggled and sold banned chemicals for CFC-dependent refrigerators and air conditioners. Second, new, unregulated chemicals for fire extinguishers and cleaning fluids could damage the ozone layer. Third, particles released by volcanic eruptions could exacerbate ozone depletion. Last but not least, global warming on the earth's surface might be accompanied by cooling of the upper atmosphere and thereby speed chemical processes that deplete the ozone layer.

The UNEP/WMO report suggested an important victory for environmental diplomacy and strengthened the resolve of negotiators seeking to cope with global warming—perhaps the "most monumentous environmental problem in human history."[48]

Dealing with Climate Change

Ice ages and warming trends have occurred without human intervention. But human activities probably contribute to the greenhouse effect—global warming due to carbon dioxide (CO_2) buildup in the atmosphere, where it absorbs infrared radiation from the sun-warmed surface of the planet and returns the radiation to earth. By the late 1990s, carbon dioxide concentrations had risen by 30 percent and methane concentrations had doubled since preindustrial times.

47. *Scientific American,* September 1995, 18–19; *Chemical and Engineering News* 73, no. 29 (July 17, 1995): 7–8; *Nation,* July 8, 1996, 11–16; *UN Chronicle* 33, no. 1 (spring 1996): 73–74; *Forum for Applied Research and Public Policy* 11, no. 2 (summer 1996): 55–64; *Amicus* 18, no. 3 (fall 1996): 35–39; and *Nature,* November 21, 1996, 256–259.

48. Robert Repetto and Jonathan Lash, "Planetary Roulette: Gambling with the Climate," *Foreign Policy,* no. 108 (fall 1997): 84–98 at 84; see also James K. Sebenius, "Designing Negotiations Toward a New Regime: The Case of Global Warming," *International Security* 15, no. 4 (spring 1991): 110–148.

How much climate change should we expect? How much of the change is due to human action (anthropogenic)? What are the consequences of climate change? Is there a scientific consensus on these issues? Seeking answers to these questions, the UN in 1988 established the **Intergovernmental Panel on Climate Change (IPCC)**, an international scientific body that receives input from some hundred governments, including the United States. The panel issued its third assessment in 2001—a report written by more than 400 scientists and reviewed by more than 400 government experts. The panel estimated in 2001 that average global surface temperatures had risen by 0.6 ± 0.2°C over the 20th century and would probably rise, depending on the scenario, by a minimum of 1.4° up to 5.8° over the period from 1990 to 2100. Such an increase would be two to ten times larger than that observed in the 20th century and unprecedented in the past 10,000 years. Just for the 35 years between 1990 and 2025, the projected increase was 0.4° to 1.1°C. Ocean temperatures would also increase and sea levels rise (from 0.09 to 0.88 m). Depending on the region, precipitation would increase or decrease by 5 percent to 20 percent. There would also be changes in the frequency and intensity of extreme weather phenomena.[49]

What does this mean for humans and the rest of the biosphere? The IPCC concluded that:

• Recent regional climatic changes had already affected many physical and biological systems and, most likely, human systems as well.

• Natural systems such as polar regions are vulnerable to climate change, and some will be irreversibly damaged.

• Projected changes in climate extremes could have major consequences.

• People with the least resources have the least capacity to adapt and are the most vulnerable. For example, small low-lying island states are threatened by rising sea levels and warmer ocean temperatures that cause coastal erosion, loss of fresh water resources, and degradation of coral reef ecosystems. The already limited arable land will shrink and become more saline. Income from tourism will be disrupted.

• Policy makers should know that adaptation, sustainable development, and enhancement of equity can be mutually reinforcing.

Policy making is complicated, however, by many factors. First, some facts are still in dispute. Some scientists challenge the IPCC consensus.

49. Intergovernmental Panel on Climate Change, *IPCC Third Assessment Report—Climate Change 2001*, IPCC Website.

Second, if more warming occurs, it could produce gainers as well as losers: "Some like it hot." Warming could make Siberia and Canada more habitable even as the Maldive Islands and some North Carolina beaches disappear beneath the waves. Not surprisingly, vulnerable lands such as the Maldives formed an Alliance of Small States in the 1990s to promote curbs on CO_2 emissions. Some farms could benefit from more rain but then face more mosquitoes and pests.

Third, if policy makers wish to curb emissions, what should they curb? Warming may result from many basic energy uses—transportation, industry, agriculture, and forestry. No single action or substitute can remove the problem.

Fourth, who should pay to curb greenhouse gases? The industrialized North has been the main source of warming gases, but the weight of the South is gaining. One estimate is that half the additional emissions in the early 21st century will come simply from expanding populations; the other half, from increases in living standards dependent upon fuel consumption. Some developed countries have learned to produce more with less, but most LDCs are reluctant to invest in pollution controls. An Indian study asserted that the First World wants to make LDCs a "sink for the West's dirt."[50]

Fifth, the costs of coping with global warming are uncertain, but cutting emissions could mean less catastrophic flooding, fewer droughts, less erosion, less insect-borne disease, and fewer deaths due to heat.

Sixth, few vested interests resisted ozone-layer protection, but opponents to emission controls include some government officials, producers of carbons, heavy industries, and agribusinesses. A potential blocking coalition straddles North and South.

The threat of ozone depletion was analogous to North Korean and Iraqi attacks on their neighbors in 1950 and 1990. The threat emerged quickly and was well defined. Climate control is a long-term, multifaceted problem—for the U.S., more like containing the USSR. It requires a grand strategy to guide actions in the face of distant, uncertain dangers and changing public sentiment.

Designing a New Regime

Uncertainty about danger does not mean that concerned parties should take no action. Even if global warming is a mirage, fewer carbon emissions would benefit public health. The question is how to design a regime—a "law of the air"—that creates value for the conflicting interests at stake.

50. The study asserted that the West wanted to plant trees in the Third World so that the West could "expand its fleet of cars, power stations, and industries while the Third World grows trees." It chided the Netherlands for funding 250,000 hectares of trees in Bolivia, Peru, and Colombia to offset carbons from two new coal-fired electricity plants near Amsterdam. It derided the notion that such projects were "intergenerational compensation." If cows add to warming, the study advised Westerners to consume less meat and milk. Anil Agarwal and Sunita Narain, *Global Warming in an Unequal World: A Case of Environmental Colonialism* (New Delhi: Centre for Science and Environment, 1991), 23.

How to Allocate Emissions Quotas?

Squatters' Rights—The Status Quo. Allocate quotas according to a baseline such as CO_2 production in a certain year, for example, 2004. This principle, however, would penalize industrial states already efficient in energy use, such as Japan, as well as LDCs in early stages of industrialization, such as India.

Egalitarianism. Entitle every person everywhere to the same level of emissions in some way similar to the Montreal Protocol, which allocated CFC emissions quotas equally per capita among the industrialized countries. But if China and India had a right in 2002 to pollute as much per capita as Germany or Russia, carbon emissions could accelerate virtually unbounded.

If entitlements were assigned to each country on a per capita basis in 2004, the South's allowance would shrink as human numbers increased. But if entitlements multiply as populations grow, a limit on global emissions would be pushed into the dim future. One solution would treat the entitlement as a national inheritance to be shared with the newborn. If national allowances were established, governments would have to decide how to allocate permits domestically—to what firms, to what individuals?

Historical Responsibility. Grant each country an all-time quota. Countries such as India that have as yet produced few carbons relative to their current populations would be entitled to pollute heavily for years to come. Countries such as Britain would face imminent restrictions because they have been heavy polluters for more than a century.

This approach would do little to curb future emissions by LDCs, and it penalizes today's rich countries for having blazed the paths of the Industrial Revolution.

Sourcing Global Warming. Set quotas by country of origin. This would mean sharp limits on major oil producers such as Saudi Arabia, Venezuela, and Mexico as well as the U.S. and Russia; also for Brazil, Colombia, and Thailand, where deforestation adds greatly to global warming. Saudi Arabia, of course, might respond that it is servicing demand elsewhere. Consumers rather than suppliers should be penalized. Brazil might demand rewards for the forest it has conserved—more valuable than the forest that has been consumed.

Willingness to Pay. Let emissions rights be sold to the highest bidders. But this approach might not be fair to the small or the poor. The dikes protecting small Holland may burst if large Germany buys high quotas; a poor upstart might be unable to compete with richer, established competitors. Critics said this was a clever device to let rich countries off the hook.

For starters, an actor could initiate a **no-regrets policy**—a policy deemed useful even if other actors do not reciprocate and even if global warming turns out not to be a problem. Some examples follow:

Agriculture: Introduce adaptable crops. Conserve soil. Save trees and reforest.

Building: Move construction away from areas vulnerable to storms and tides.

Design: Introduce energy-saving buildings, transportation, and industrial processes.

Fuel: Use natural gas instead of coal or oil. Phase out fossil fuels gradually and replace them with noncarbon energy sources—solar, geothermal, nuclear, hydroelectric.

Taxes: Penalize waste and pollution. An energy tax could discourage gas-guzzling autos while reducing smog and easing budget deficits.

Recycling: Capture and reuse methane from mines and landfills.

Like the ozone protocols and the U.S. Clean Air Act, a regime to limit carbon emissions could utilize entitlements—permits to pollute to a specified limit. An entitlement regime would require heavy polluters to reduce emissions and permit light polluters to increase emissions. Light polluters might choose to sell their allocations to the highest bidder.

But on what basis would entitlements be assigned? What principles would be fair—and acceptable—to North and South? As we see in the sidebar, each proposed principle has its drawbacks. But a mix of trade-offs and linkage possibilities may be discovered in the give-and-take of actual negotiations. Governments usually consider fairness issues in two stages. First, they weigh the pros and cons of alternative principles in the abstract. Then they see how the issues play out in bargaining. At each stage, LDCs ask: "Does this approach give us room to develop? Are we assured sufficient aid to cover the extra costs of developing with low carbon emissions?" Developed countries weigh potential gains against likely costs at home and abroad. The Global Environmental Facility (GEF) makes grants or loans for projects that respond to global environmental threats that might not otherwise be a top development priority for the country in question. Created in 1991, the GEF is administered by the World Bank in cooperation with the UN Environmental Programme and the UN Development Programme.

The 1992 Earth Summit in Rio produced a Framework Convention on Climate Change (FCCC), ratified by 167 states. At U.S. insistence, the FCCC did not set binding targets or timetables, but it did leave the way open for detailed protocols. President George Bush (the elder) was cool even to a framework agreement, contending that emission curbs could block economic growth. The FCCC acknowledged that rich and poor states share "common but differentiated" responsibilities for addressing climate change. But Rio set no limits on LDC emissions. Rather, it stipulated that developed countries take the first steps to curb their emissions and also subsidize LDC emission curbs.

Seeking to convert the Rio principles into an action program,[51] more than 160 countries sent delegations to the December 1997 conference held in Kyoto, Japan. After many long days and nights, conferees endorsed the Kyoto Protocol, requiring reductions in emissions of CO_2 and five other greenhouse gases (methane, nitrous oxide, hydrofluorocarbons, perfluorocarbons, and sulfur hexafluorides) by thirty-eight industrial countries and the European Union (EU) to be reached between the years 2008 and 2012. No specific targets were set for developing countries, though they were encouraged to make voluntary reductions.[52]

51. Officially, this was known as the Third Session of the Conference of the Parties to the United Nations Framework Convention on Climate Change.

52. Pat Murdo, "Kyoto Pact on Greenhouse Gas Reductions," *JEI Report* [Japan Economic Institute of America], no. 47 (December 19, 1997), and coverage in major newspapers and magazines.

Given the diversity of interests, what negotiating techniques helped achieve an agreement that so many states could endorse?

First, the protocol defined obligations only for the major industrialized countries. Developing countries could approve the protocol in 1997 and decide later if they wished to accept curbs on their own emissions. This approach made it easier for developing countries to sign the protocol, but could make it harder to win ratification by industrialized countries. Some 130 developing countries drew a line at Kyoto and refused to accept even voluntary commitments to reduce emissions. The potential importance of these countries to climate change was undeniable. In 1997 they accounted for only one-third of the world's emissions of greenhouse gases, but contained 80 percent of the world's population. As their economies developed, their emissions would soon exceed those of the West and Japan.

The poor South could prove more vulnerable to climate change than the rich North. Governments in many developing countries had already taken steps before Kyoto to raise prices on fuels that discharge carbons. But many LDCs focused on near- and medium-term economic issues. Thus, Malawi's Minister of Forestry, Fisheries, and Environmental Affairs asked: "How can we devote our precious resources toward reducing emissions when we are struggling every day just to feed, clothe, and house our citizens?"[53]

Second, the protocol represented a compromise on emissions targets for industrialized countries. The U.S. delegation had urged a commitment to cut emissions to equal 1990 levels by the 2008–2012 period; the EU had wanted a 15 percent cut below 1990 levels by 2010; Japan proposed an overall cut of 5 percent or less. Since the U.S. population and GDP had grown much faster than Europe's or Japan's in the 1990s, it would be much harder for the U.S. to reduce its emissions to 1990 levels or below. But since the U.S. produced 22 percent of the world's CO_2 emissions, environmentalists called for strong U.S. action.

A compromise was facilitated by eight **reduction differentials**. They ranged from an obligation to cut emissions by 8 percent (for the EU) to a zero reduction (for three states) to a license to increase emissions by 10 percent (for Iceland). The U.S. agreed to cut emissions to 7 percent below its 1990s levels; Japan, already far more energy-efficient than the U.S. or Europe, had to cut its emissions by only 6 percent (the same target set for Canada, Hungary, and Poland); Australia had wanted the right to increase its emissions by 18 percent but settled for a rise of only 8 percent.

53. F. V. Mayinga Mkandawire, quoted in Calvin Sims, "Poor Nations Resist Role on Warming," *The New York Times*, December 13, 1997, A7.

There was also some personal diplomacy: U.S. Vice President Al Gore phoned Japanese Prime Minister Ryutaro Hashimoto at 2 A.M. and asked Japan to accept a burden of one percentage point more—6 percent rather than 5 percent—for the sake of an overall accord. Conference chair Raúl Estrada-Oyuela put some items to a vote when resistant delegations such as Iraq were absent. To win approval of the protocol, he deleted references to developing nations in the wee hours of December 11, one day after the original ten-day session was to have ended.

Agreement was facilitated by three forms of emissions credits. First, heavy emitters could purchase part of the quota allowed to light emitters. The fifteen members of the EU could trade emission permits with one another to reach their combined 8 percent reduction. The U.S. could buy and sell permits with others in an "umbrella group" that included Japan, Canada, Russia, New Zealand, and Australia.

Second, industrialized countries could offset their emissions by planting forests or taking other steps to bolster carbon sinks. Third, they could also win credits by investing in projects that help developing countries to reduce emissions.

Washington asked for and got an understanding that emissions by armed forces would not be counted when they were engaged in police or humanitarian missions approved by the UN. "We did not want to create a disincentive for future humanitarian operations," said a Pentagon official.

For better or worse, the Kyoto Protocol set the deadline for compliance more than a decade ahead and said nothing about enforcement. Some environmentalists condemned Kyoto for doing too little; others praised it as movement in a constructive direction, setting the stage to tighten obligations for all parties.

American critics complained that U.S. representatives at Kyoto gave away the store. Getting nothing in return, they exempted major actors such as China and Mexico from obligatory reductions. Second, U.S. diplomats at Kyoto agreed to major reductions with no workable system to verify compliance by all parties. Third, they jeopardized U.S. sovereignty by inviting intrusive action by the World Bank and other international agencies.[54] Defenders of the Kyoto Protocol said that such criticism was unfair and simplistic. Environmental well-being is not a zero-sum contest and involves far more parties and issues than did the Soviet–U.S. arms competition.

Senators from coal-rich states and some business leaders said the cost of complying with Kyoto would be onerous, especially since

54. Richard Burt, *Washington Times*, December 29, 1997, A12.

industrializing countries such as South Korea could make steel and other manufactures with no obligation to ecologize production. But other business executives argued that the new regulations would make U.S. firms more energy-efficient and hence more competitive at home and abroad.[55] They said it was feasible to produce electricity far more efficiently (wasting only half instead of two-thirds the energy consumed in generation).[56]

The upshot was that the Clinton administration was unable to ratify the Kyoto Protocol, and President Bush, soon after he took office in 2001, denounced it as unworkable. The Bush White House complained that the protocol placed intolerable burdens on the U.S. while requiring nothing of LDCs. Moreover, it was based on flawed or uncertain science.

Canada's oil-producing province of Alberta campaigned against the protocol. A cold, sparsely populated country like Canada needed to burn carbons. Given its small population, Canada would produce few emissions compared to the U.S. or Europe. The oil and gas lobbies lost, however, and in December 2002 Canada became the hundredth country to ratify. Australia refused to ratify but in 2002 indicated it might reconsider.

A "double trigger" was needed for the protocol to enter into force. The first trigger was ratification by 55 governments—a requirement met in 2002. The second trigger was that the ratifying governments had to include developed countries responsible for at least 55 percent of that group's 1990 carbon dioxide emissions. With the ratification in December 2002 by Poland and Canada, the ratifying countries accounted for 43.7 percent of 1990 emissions. Since Russia was judged responsible for 17.4 percent of emissions in 1990, its ratification—widely expected in 2003—would satisfy the second requirement for entry into force.

The author of *The Skeptical Environmentalist*, Danish statistician Bjorn Lomborg, provided a rationale for rejecting Kyoto. He estimated that the likely costs of global warming for the next century would be no more than $5 trillion—roughly half of U.S. GDP in 2000. This kind of damage would be quite manageable, because the world's GDP would rise in the next 100 years by at least $800 trillion. Furthermore, if problems became truly painful, the technology for coping with carbon emissions was already at hand.[57] Lomborg's critics, in turn, were also skeptical. The $800 trillion figure was a reasonable extrapolation from recent trends, but the $5 trillion damage estimate was pulled from thin air. In January 2003 the highest scientific review board in Denmark censured Lomborg for violating the norms of good scientific behavior.

55. See commentary by Michael J. Gage, "Smart Firms Embrace Kyoto Accord," *Los Angeles Times*, December 31, 1997. President of CalStart, a consortium developing advanced transportation technologies, Gage quoted Michael Porter, cited in Chapter 11.

56. Charles E. Bayless and Thomas R. Casten, "Leave CO_2 to the Entrepreneurs," *The Washington Post*, December 31, 1997, 21. For the opinion of some 2,000 economists, see Bette Hileman, "Tackling Global Warming Won't Hurt Economy," *Chemical and Engineering News* 75, no. 7 (February 17, 1997): 9–10.

57. Bjorn Lomborg, *The Skeptical Environmentalist: Measuring the Real State of the World* (New York: Cambridge University Press, 2001). The $5 trillion estimate is in Lomborg and Oliver Rubin, "Limits to Growth," *Foreign Policy*, November/December 2002, 42–44. The rebuke was by the Danish Committees on Scientific Dishonesty, under the Danish Research Agency. Lomborg replied that the rebuke lacked specifics, but conceded he had not read everything on the environment.

Bush Says Kyoto Treaty Doesn't Limit Greenhouse Gases from China or India

Soon after taking office in 2001, the Bush administration flat-out rejected the Kyoto Protocol. Meanwhile, the administration struggled to open new lands and sea beds to oil exploration, while Congress failed to tighten fuel efficiency standards for sport-utility and most other vehicles. China and India made some progress in tapping renewable sources of energy, but the U.S was the only country to experience a decline in total wind-generating capacity in the decade before 2003. Every dollar that subsidized conventional energy took from the funds available for renewables. See Worldwatch Institute, *State of the World 2003* (New York: W. W. Norton, 2003), 86–109 at 106.

Like Lomborg, the Bush administration seemed to think climate change was manageable. The White House pledged only to lower the greenhouse intensity of U.S. economic activity (the level of emissions per unit of economic output) by 18 percent from 2002 to 2012. This would cut U.S. emissions by 4.5 percent from what would otherwise be their level in 2012. Thus, total U.S. emissions would increase, but America would pollute less for every unit of GDP.

The White House said this "reduction" would be achieved by a "combination of voluntary, incentive-based, and existing mandatory measures." The president's action plan included dozens of measures—most of them implemented voluntarily, nudged along by information and education programs and research. Thus, the Department of Energy (DoE) would give nuclear power plants information and technical assistance to help them reduce greenhouse gas emissions. One of the few actions backed by DoE regulation was a periodic review of efficiency standards for most household appliances. In 2002, the Environmental Protection Agency (EPA) boasted that most of the measures favored by the president had already been "implemented." For example, the EPA was already promoting voluntary improvement of energy performance in commercial buildings. Among the few measures not yet implemented were tax credits for residential solar power systems and electricity generated by wind- and biomass-based generators.[58] The EPA averred that "no one will forego [*sic*] meeting basic family needs to protect the global commons." For this reason, perhaps, the government did not tighten minimum miles per gallon standards for sports utility vehicles but did relax

58. U.S. Environmental Protection Agency, *U.S. Climate Action Report: Third National Communication of the United States of America Under the United Nations Framework Convention on Climate Change* (Washington, D.C., 2002) at www.gcrio.org/CAR2002/.

emissions standards on air conditioners. It also reopened Yellowstone National Park to snowmobiles (a favorite companion of bison, park rangers wearing gas masks, and cross-country skiers).

Sacrifice and even prudence were out. Just as the war on terrorism could be waged by using tax rebates to splurge on consumer goods, so the campaign to deal with climate change could be conducted by letting people do whatever they could afford. Indeed, "adaptation" became the code word in U.S. policy. "The United States is a world leader," the EPA claimed, "in addressing and adapting to a variety of national and global scientific [*sic*] problems that could be exacerbated by climate change, including malaria, hunger, malnourishment, property lossses due to extreme weather events, and habitat loss and other threats to biological diversity." The U.S. government made no commitment, however, to help LDCs cope with extreme weather events, habitat loss, or the "black carbon aerosols (soot)" that the U.S. National Research Council warned probably contributed to global warming as well as to "negative health impacts" in developing countries.

While most R&D conducted by the Department of Energy got more money in fiscal year 2003, the White House asked for an 8 percent cut in research on energy conservation.[59] Perhaps conservation was virtuous, as the vice president once put it, but not in need of more scientific investigation. In December 2002, the U.S. Forest Service proposed the experimental logging of half a million acres on two forests in the Sierra Nevada to see how it would affect the habitat of the California spotted owl and the ferocity of forest fires.

U.S. policy followed the pattern that Mr. Bush established in his two terms as governor of Texas. There he also lifted environmental regulations and encouraged voluntary actions to sustain the enivornment. When he left Austin for Washington, however, Texas could claim the foulest air and water in the country and the most polluted city— Houston—which displaced Los Angeles for this distinction. Meanwhile, deregulated Enron was the largest contributor to Mr. Bush's two gubernatorial campaigns and his 2000 run for the White House.

Strengthening its case for doing nothing new, the EPA asserted that U.S. energy intensity already compared "relatively well with the rest of the world." The facts showed, to be sure, that the U.S. was twice as efficient as Russia and no worse than China. But Japan, Switzerland, Germany, and major European countries extracted far more gross domestic product (GDP) per unit of energy than did the United States. Italy and Austria were nearly twice as efficient.[60]

59. Federal outlays for science and technology research increased in 2000–2003 (see Table 5.10). R&D relevant to climate change was conducted by NASA; the National Science Foundation; the Environmental Protection Agency; the Departments of Agriculture, Commerce (Oceanic and Atmospheric Research), and Energy. More than half the DoE budget went to science programs, but about $400 million was for renewable energy research; $250 million for nuclear energy; nearly $600 million to energy conservation (down 8 percent for fiscal year 2003); and $500 million to fossil energy (down 16 percent for fiscal year 2003).

60. UNDP, *Human Development Report 2002*, Table 19.

What Prospects for Renewable Energy?

In the early 21st century, the International Energy Agency sponsored a global cooperative effort called SolarPACES to encourage and share information about solar power. The UN International Sustainable Energy Organization calculated that world energy demands would rise by 2 percent annually from 2000 to 2050. Renewable energy sources provided just a few percent of the world's needs in 2000. But if renewable energy use increased by 5.2 percent a year, it could surpass the use of finite energy sources by 2020.

Cynics replied: "We've heard all this before. Wind power failed even on the windswept Hawaiian island of Molokai." Sustainable energy advocates countered that (like foreign aid) renewable energy had not been given a fair trial. If more R&D went to renewables, if government subsidies for renewables matched those for carbon fuels, wind and solar power would soon prove their worth. Also, the true costs of a carbon-based economy needed to be factored in—pollution, illness, and death, destructive and unpredictable weather, plus the international tensions and fighting over oil and gas fields. Oil and gas created few jobs while coal required dirty and dangerous work. Solar power and wind power would probably create more jobs as well as help small farmers and other small producers to stay in business.

At the 2002 Earth Summit, the U.S. delegation helped to kill Brazil's demand for a formal commitment by all states to use more renewable energy. Though most Latin American countries endorsed Brazil's call, most relied on carbon fuels and did little to harness wind or solar power. Environmentalists in Brasilia had little clout next to champions of another large dam and thermal power stations. Sunny Mexico, its capital smothered by smog, devoted almost no resources to solar energy. Impoverished El Salvador, however, tried to extract power from biomass.

The Logic of Collective Action

The world's largest polluter thus stood against the tide of world opinion. The Bush administration promised to offer an alternative approach to the Kyoto Protocol but, after two years, failed to do so. Washington seemed to say: In environmental affairs, as in most other domains, "the strong do what they can and the weak suffer what they must."[61]

The less developed "Southern Seven" and the OPEC countries may also follow the logic of collective action. When they return to Rio in 2012 and consider once more the issues of global warming, they may decide to squeeze the rich, as in the following letter:

61. Athenians to Melians in Thucydides, *Peloponnesian War*, Book 5, 89.

Hard Bargaining by the Southern Seven and by OPEC:
Rio de Janeiro, September 1, 2012

Memo to the OECD countries from the Southern Seven:

The governments of Argentina, Brazil, China, India, Indonesia, Malaysia, and Thailand hereby reaffirm our commitment to protecting the environment so long as economic growth continues. In the long run, economic well-being depends upon a healthy environment. In the short and medium run, however, environmental protection can be costly.

We propose to stabilize our CO_2 emissions and maintain our forests at levels reached in 2020. Having contributed little to global warming, we ask compensation for our sacrifices. Each OECD country should contribute 0.05 percent of its GDP to the Global Environmental Fund to be distributed to the Southern Seven for "clean and green" technology.

Also pursuing their narrow self-interest, Saudi Arabia and Venezuela write to the OECD on behalf of OPEC. Their letter follows:

Rio de Janeiro, September 1, 2012

Memo to the OECD countries from OPEC:

OPEC members, like other enlightened countries, seek both environmental and economic well-being. Since our populations are small and we have just begun to industrialize, it is premature for us to limit our CO_2 emissions. Since we have literally fueled the industrial transformation of North and South, we ask for three forms of compensation: (1) freedom from any commitment to limit our carbon emissions; (2) a development fund established by OECD countries to equal the revenues we lose due to reduced carbon use elsewhere; and (3) free access for our scientists and engineers to energy-related R&D of any UN member country.

These two memos represent the self-seeking "logic of collective action." But if each actor focuses on winning for itself, the globe's life support system will become more vulnerable. Enlightened self-interest requires joint sacrifices and efforts to promote mutual gain. Following are some policy implications derived from our study.[62]

WHAT PROPOSITIONS HOLD? WHAT QUESTIONS REMAIN?

For most of the 20th century, Cornucopians proved to be more correct than Malthusians. Human ingenuity managed to sustain an expanding world population that lived longer than ever. By the early 21st century there were many signs that an "environmental revolution" had begun. The signposts included:

• Germany, Japan, and Spain boosted use of renewable energy by more than 30 percent annually in recent years.

• The World Health Organization's campaign against polio reduced the number of cases worldwide from 350,000 in 1988 to 480 in 2001.

• The Netherlands achieved an 86% recycling rate for cars. Denmark imposed a total ban on aluminum cans in favor of reusable glass bottles.

• Defying the U.S. federal government, California announced the world's first mandatory limits on global warming emissions from cars.

62. See also Frances Cairncross, "Environmental Pragmatism," *Foreign Policy*, no. 95 (summer 1994): 35–52.

- Religious institutions were devoting more energy and interest to the quest for sustainable development.
- As noted earlier, ozone depletion may have been reversed.[63]

But would these steps be sufficient in the 21st century to cope with the consequences of what promised to be the greatest climate change in 10,000 years? Might not the limits to growth become more acute? Given the best- and worst-case scenarios for the future, was it more prudent to wait-and-see or to pursue preventive policies?[64] Was it better to exploit the opportunities still available or strive to protect a global commons that could yield mutual gain? This book argues for policies aimed at preserving and creating values for all.

How to Strengthen Winning over Blocking Coalitions

The experience gained in environmental diplomacy suggests several approaches to facilitate an accord:[65]

1. Craft the accord to appeal to a broad group of countries and diminish opposition from blocking coalitions. The deal must satisfy not just governments but also industries, NGOs, and other interest groups.

2. Cultivate scientific consensus. Use the UN Environmental Programme, the World Bank, and other institutions to share information and form joint study groups of private (industrial and NGO) experts as well as governmental experts. Provide advice to governments short on environmental expertise.[66]

3. Promote a voluntary action plan of concerned countries without waiting for conclusion of a formal treaty.[67]

4. Remove penalties for constructive unilateral actions that leave states with higher costs than their commercial competitors. By this reasoning, Japan was awarded a lower target than most other industrialized countries at Kyoto.

5. Work toward a consensus on fairness. Set different tasks for different categories of countries (rich and poor, past and future polluters). This was done for industrialized countries at Kyoto but not for developing economies.

6. Utilize techniques found useful in other negotiating arenas such as a single negotiating text. Avoid an all-or-nothing approach. Fractionate. Utilize linkage.

7. Emphasize potential gains and compensate LDCs for some costs of greening their production. Create new values, for example, by assuring market access for "green products" (such as nuts and rubber) and by inventing better "debt-for-nature" swaps.

63. Worldwatch Institute, *State of the World 2003* (New York: W. W. Norton, 2003).

64. Among the negative trends also reported by Worldwatch, the rate of bird extinction was running at 50 times the natural rate due to habitat loss and other consequences of human activity.

65. Adapted from Sebenius, "Designing Negotiations Toward a New Regime," and the "Salzburg Initiative" of 120 representatives from thirty-two countries, summarized in Lawrence E. Susskind, *Environmental Diplomacy: Negotiating More Effective Global Agreements* (New York: Oxford University Press, 1994), 123–141.

66. Peter M. Haas, "Introduction: Epistemic Communities and International Policy Coordination," *International Organization* [special issue: "Knowledge, Power, and International Policy Coordination"] 46, no. 1 (winter 1992): 1–35, and other articles in this issue.

67. Thus, a "Carbon Club" took shape in the early 1990s. Led by Germany, a number of countries, including Austria, Denmark, Australia, and New Zealand, pledged to cut their CO_2 emissions by 20 to 25 percent by 2005.

Recommended Resources (continued)

Keohane, Robert O., and Marc A. Levy, eds. *Institutions for Environmental Aid: Pitfalls and Promise.* Cambridge, Mass: MIT Press, 1996.

Lomborg, Bjorn. *The Skeptical Environmentalist: Measuring the Real State of the World.* Cambridge, U.K.: Cambridge University Press, 2001.

Nadeau, Robert. *The Wealth of Nature: How Mainstream Economics Has Failed the Environment.* New York: Columbia University Press, 2002.

Repetto, Robert C. *Trade and Environmental Policies: Achieving Complementarities and Avoiding Conflicts.* Washington, D.C.: World Resources Institute, 1993.

Repetto, Robert C., and Duncan Austin. *The Costs of Climate Protection: A Guide for the Perplexed.* Washington, D.C.: World Resources Institute, 1997.

Runge, C. Ford, et al. *Freer Trade, Protected Environment: Balancing Trade Liberalization and Environmental Interests.* New York: Council on Foreign Relations Press, 1994.

Shiva, Vandana. *Stolen Harvest: The Hijacking of the Global Food Supply.* Cambridge, Mass: South End Press, 2000.

———*Water Wars: Privatization, Pollution, and Profit.* Toronto: Between the Lines, 2000.

Stavins, R. N., ed. *Economics of the Environment: Selected Readings.* 4th ed. New York: W. W. Norton, 2002.

Stone, Christopher D. *The Gnat Is Older Than Man: Global Environment and Human Agenda.* Princeton, N.J.: Princeton University Press, 1993.

Susskind, Lawrence E. *Environmental Diplomacy: Negotiating More Effective Global Agreements.* New York: Oxford University Press, 1994.

Wilson, Edward O. *The Future of Life.* New York: A. A. Knopf, 2002.

World Resources Institute. *World Resources, 2000–2001: People and Ecosystems* Washington, D.C.: World Resources Institute, 2000.

Worldwatch Institute. *State of the World.* New York: W. W. Norton [annual].

Worldwatch Institute. *Vital Signs: The Trends That Are Shaping Our Future.* New York: W. W. Norton [annual].

JOURNALS

Ambio
Bulletin of the Atomic Scientists
The Ecologist
Energy Policy
Environment
Journal of Environmental Law
International Organization
Issues in Science and Technology
Nature
Public Interest
Science
Scientific American

WEB SITES

Center for International Environmental Law
http://www.ciel.org/
The Earth Times
http://www.earthtimes.org/
EnviroLink Library
http://library.envirolink.org/index.html
Environment Australia Online: Government Environment Departments on the Internet
http://www.erin.gov.au/epg
Environmental Impact Analysis Data Links
http://h2o.usgs.gov/public.eap/env_data.htm#HDR0
Environmental News Network
http://www.enn.com
Global Environment Facility
http://www.gefweb.com/
Green Globe Yearbook (links to many relevant sites, including NGOs and intergovernmental organizations)
http://www.ngo.grida.no/ggynet/
Greenpeace
http://www.greenpeace.org/index.shtml
Pace University, School Law, Virtual Environmental Law Library
http://www.law.pace.edu/env/vell6.html
United Nations Environment Programme
http://www.unep.ch/
United Nations University
http://www.unu.edu
United States Environmental Protection Agency
http://www.epa.gov/
Sustainable Development
http://www.colby.edu/personal/t/thtietn/sustain.html
WWW Virtual Library—Environment
http://earthsystems.org/Environment.shtml

C H A P T E R   F O U R T E E N

ORGANIZING FOR MUTUAL GAIN: THE UNITED NATIONS, EUROPE, AND NONSTATE ACTORS

T H E   B I G   Q U E S T I O N S   I N   C H A P T E R   1 4

- Why do peoples cooperate and organize across borders?

- What is international organization (IO)?

- Does might make right in IR? Is there such a thing as law among nations? If governments obey the law, why?

- Does order come to world affairs because it is imposed from above or because it rises from below?

- What is collective security? Has the principle of "all for one, one for all" ever worked?

- Is there a link between IO and industrialization?

- Is "Europe" a customs union or a supranational state, or something else?

- Is Europe uniting? If so, from below or from above?

- Why expand NATO if the Cold War is history?

- Can IO save lives?

- Is IO anything but power?

- Is the world coming together or flinging apart?

How to Start Your Own Nonstate Actor. . . . The new world disorder challenges both state and nonstate actors. Official peacemakers have tried but failed to bring harmony to the Middle East. Fed up with governments, you decide to organize a new player, the University of the Middle East (UME), to promote coexistence and development in the region. You create your own nongovernmental organization— a nonstate actor in world affairs. You plan to establish UME campuses across the Middle East and North Africa within thirty years. UME students and faculty will spend time at one another's campuses, bringing Zoroastrians, Jews, Christians, Sunnis, Shi'i, Bahais, and others into scholarly and social contact.

Having come from many countries, most of your board members meet each other for the first time at U.S. colleges. In 1998, your planning sessions take place on Sunday evenings—often at an Italian restaurant in Boston's North End. Your president is Hala Taweel, a graduate student at Boston College and sister-in-law to Palestinian leader Yasser Arafat. Other initial participants include Camelia Anwar Sadat, daughter of the Egyptian president who signed the Camp David Accords, and Walid Chamoun, whose Maronite Christian family went to war to rid its native Lebanon of Arafat's forces in the 1970s. The idea for the university comes from an Israeli physicist at Harvard, Ron Rubin, galvanized by the assassination of Israeli Prime Minister Yitzhak Rabin.

You win endorsements from Lea Rabin, widow of Yitzhak Rabin, Nobel peace laureate Elie Wiesel, a leading Iraqi dissident, and several diplomats at the UN. Soon the project raises donations and gets free office space near Boston College. By 2002 the project has brought nearly 200 students from 14 countries to "institutes" in the U.S. and in Spain for educators and civil society activists. Soon you will convene an institute on sustainable development.

The UME Project continues despite "9/11" and its aftermath. Meanwhile, al-Qaeda strategists sit in a snug cave in Yemen and a crowded apartment in Manila and plan how to foment chaos. They too have formed a nonstate actor. Like other revolutionaries, they believe "the worse, the better."

The UME Project strives to change the world from the bottom up. But how far can it get in a world criss-crossed by jihad, antiterror campaigns, and struggles for "regime change"? Education promises a better life in the future, but what about now?

Fear and hope energize people at every level of society. At the UN we can imagine that the Secretary-General discusses some deep questions with his close aides: "Our job is to help UN member states organize for peace and mutual gain," he says. "But we must also be practical. Should we focus on peace and security or on human development, or both? If the Americans insist on doing things their way, should we go along or try to mobilize the other 96 percent of humanity?"

A parallel discussion takes place over dessert and coffee in Brussels, where a German and a French diplomat ponder the future of the European Union and NATO. The German asks: "Should we try to transform the EU into a United States of Europe, a body far more integrated than our present institutions? If so, should our united Europe become a military superpower or continue as a junior partner to the U.S.? Should we Europeans keep the UN as it is—a vehicle for ad hoc cooperation—or push/pull it toward world government?"

Without supranational government, how can we deal with cross-border problems? International organization is a work in progress. Partial but practical answers to this question are being worked out at the World Health Organization, the International Committee of the Red Cross, the Chernobyl Children's Project, as well as the University of the Middle East and thousands of other nonstate actors. Let us see how some of these groups have organized to meet human needs and how their efforts can become more effective.

CONTENDING CONCEPTS AND EXPLANATIONS

IS WORLD GOVERNMENT THE ANSWER?

What kind of order, if any, awaits humanity in the 21st century? Does a stable peace require a world government imposed from the top down, like the pax romana of imperial Rome? Or must we await the emergence of law and order from the bottom up?

Writing to Sigmund Freud in 1932, Albert Einstein noted that there was no world government—no **supranational authority** above all other IR actors. "At present we are far from possessing any supranational organization competent to render verdicts of incontestable authority and enforce absolute submission to the execution of its verdicts." Einstein assumed that "the quest for international security involves the unconditional surrender by every nation, in a certain measure, of its liberty of action, its sovereignty." No other road, he thought, could lead to security.[1]

Why did past efforts for peace achieve so little? Einstein thought that "the craving for power which characterises the governing class in every nation is hostile to any limitation of the national sovereignty." The powerful minority indoctrinates the masses, many of whom already possess a "lust for hatred and destruction."

Freud replied that he concurred with the gist of Einstein's thinking, but added that early peoples overcame brute force by uniting against it. This was also the origin of law—communal power against individual violence. But if a community joined forces only against one threat, it would quickly dissolve. "Thus the union of the people must be permanent and well organised; it must enact rules to meet the risk of possible revolts; must set up machinery ensuring that its rules—the laws—are observed and that such acts of violence as the laws demand are duly carried out. This recognition of a community of interests engenders among the members of the group a sentiment of unity and fraternal solidarity which constitutes its real strength." For today's world, Freud argued, "there is but one sure way of ending war, and that is the establishment, by common consent, of a central control which shall have the last word in every conflict of interest." This would require "a supreme court" and "its investment with adequate executive force." Writing in 1932, Freud thought that the League of Nations met the first task but not the second. Freud hoped that war could be prevented, but he saw positive value even in destructive instincts. He was not sure that they could—or should—be extirpated. The Einstein–Freud exchange resonates today. Humanity still lacks a supranational authority; human instincts are unchanged. Western civilization (and most others) represses but also applauds violence.

Functionalism and Neofunctionalism: From Low to High Politics?

Functionalism offers a very different path from world government. It contends that the best route to peace is to multiply "technical" cooperation in low politics, where political obstacles are fewer. National loyalties can gradually be diffused and redirected.

1. The exchange is published in Robert A. Goldwin and Tony Pearce, eds., *Readings in World Politics*, 2d ed. (New York: Oxford University Press, 1970), 86–99.

Table 14.1 Assumptions of Functionalism and Neofunctionalism

	Functionalism	**Neofunctionalism**
Image of the world	Interdependence of states	Globalization operating across state borders
Driving force	Need for technical cooperation by states	Need for supranational authority to coordinate technical cooperation
Attitude to politics	Apolitical, technical orientation; high politics consensus may arise from low politics cooperation	Ready to confront tough political issues, beginning on a regional scale

Functionalism thinks of IO as a response to the Industrial Revolution and the IPE. The first modern international government organization (IGO), the Central Commission for Navigation of the Rhine, was established in 1815 to facilitate traffic by steamship (first built in 1802) as the river passed through seven jurisdictions. Similar IGOs were later established for the Danube, Congo, and Prut rivers and the Suez Canal.

New communication technologies have spawned regulatory IOs such as the International Telegraph Union (1865) and, a century later, the International Telecommunications Satellite Organization (1965). A global public utility outside the UN ambit, Intelsat, provided infrastructure as well as rules for satellite communications.[2]

Relations between states are characterized by interdependence—mutual vulnerability. Across state borders, there is globalization. To deal with interdependence and with globalization, states relax their defense of sovereignty: They collaborate to send and receive mail across frontiers, control epidemics, and regulate aviation. From such cooperation, habits of trust and mutual dependency may develop and spill over into the arenas of high politics. Functionalism counts on "technical self-determination" by experts rather than on the whims of politicians.[3] Early functionalists urged that nations cooperate in arenas with little political resonance. But **neofunctionalism** favors cooperation in politically charged domains where there is also scope for technocrats. Jean Monnet, a founder of the European Community, was a neofunctionalist. He sought to build regional institutions that enshrine cooperation and spill over from one activity to another. For the differing assumptions of functionalism and neofunctionalism, see Table 14.1.

Both proponents and skeptics of functionalism find grist for their mills. Advocates point to the vast increase in the number and scope of international and transnational organizations since the mid-19th century. Nearly every country has become more permeable. Some analysts speak

2. Craig N. Murphy, *International Organization and Industrial Change: Global Governance Since 1850* (New York: Oxford University Press, 1994).

3. The theory was articulated by David Mitrany in 1943. See Mitrany, *A Working Peace System* (Chicago: Quadrangle, 1966); see also Ernst Haas, *Beyond the Nation-State: Functionalism and International Organization* (Stanford, Calif.: Stanford University Press, 1963).

The UN Security Council in a January 20, 2003, session attended by Colin L. Powell and other foreign ministers voted to tighten the noose on terrorist actions and finances. Powell, his arm raised in the foreground, was pleased with the vote. But by March 2003, the U.S. and UK saw that they could not obtain a specific Security Council authorization for military action against Iraq. Therefore they invaded Iraq, claiming to be implementing Resolution 1441.

of an "end to geography" because of financial integration and the impact of the information technology revolution.[4] Functionalism and neofunctionalism benefit from and contribute to globalization.

But skeptics question the spillover effect. They contend that, when push comes to shove, states still defend their sovereign prerogatives. Germany and France fought one another in 1914 and 1940 despite extensive trade and other linkages. Ideology often prevails over interdependence, tribalism over pragmatism, and territoriality over globalism.

Skeptics lost as UN Security Council decisions on war and peace in Iraq and Korea came to depend heavily on reports by the International Atomic Energy Agency. In the 1950s, the IAEA was seen as another "merely functional" IO. In the late 20th and early 21st century, however, the IAEA was responsible for inspecting Baghdad's and Pyongyang's compliance with nuclear arms control obligations.

Before proceeding further, let us specify some terms.

WHAT IS A NONSTATE ACTOR?

International organization (IO) consists of IGOs and nongovernmental organizations (NGOs). Early in the 20th century there were some 30 IGOs; by 1950, about 125; today in the early 21st century, there are hundreds.

IGOs can be classified by membership and objectives. The United Nations (UN) seeks universal membership and has many goals. The World Trade Organization (WTO) is also open to all states that qualify but has one main focus. The North Atlantic Treaty Organization (NATO) and the Association of Southeast Asian Nations (ASEAN) are regional organizations with narrower objectives. Some IGOs offer parallel or alternative routes to the same goal. For example, the UN promises universal security; NATO, regional security.

4. Richard O'Brien, *Global Financial Integration: The End of Geography* (New York: Council on Foreign Relations for the Royal Institute of International Affairs, 1992).

How to Make a Better World? Nonstate Actors Speak Out

What if moderators at the Davos World Forum, where top political and economic figures retreat each year to view the IPE from the Swiss mountaintops, asked present and past leaders to give their recipe for a better world? Following might be some of their comments:

Bill Gates: "Universalize the Internet. My company will install the best software in every library."

Soros Foundation Founder *George Soros:* "Open communication."

Ted Turner: "Let CNN bring the world to you."

McDonald's CEO: "Spread the Golden Arches—a sure sign of hygiene and stability. No country with the Golden Arches has ever fought another with the Golden Arches."

Media mogul: "McDonald's, Coca-Cola, and Marlboro are synonymous with the product. World-class brands unite humanity."

Olympic organizer: "Let sports transcend differences."

MTV magnate: "Dance to elevate consciousness."

Gore Vidal: "Beware of military–industrial–media conglomerates striving to control mind and spirit."

Taliban: "Purify. Pray. Jihad. Keep women at home."

Sierra Club president: "Cultivate an environmental ethic."

Montana Militia guerrilla: "Arm to resist black UN helicopters."

Henry Ford: "Go global. I opened a plant in Canada soon after my first U.S. plant. Pay workers a decent wage. Mutual gain."

Lenin: "Let imperialists fight over markets and transfer capital plus technology to Asia and Africa."

Not all of these views have equal weight. Some are incompatible with others. Which do you find most persuasive?

There are tens of thousands of NGOs seeking diverse goals. An NGO for IR scholars is the International Studies Association (ISA). ISA membership is worldwide. While it is headquartered at a U.S. university, some of its officers are residents and citizens of other countries. The ISA meets in many countries. It cooperates with both NGOs and IGOs and sometimes with the U.S. and other governments.

Nonstate actors in IR are players that are not states. They include IGOs, NGOs, TNCs (transnational corporations), and other actors. Their importance to IR was long obscured by the fact that traditional international law recognized only states as its "subjects." In the 20th century, however, international law began to give legal standing—rights and obligations—to individuals, IGOs, and other transnational entities. Thus, the Organization for Economic Cooperation and Development (OECD)—the club of rich industrial nations—and the UN have prescribed codes of conduct for TNCs even though such enterprises are not full legal personalities under international law.[5] But international law and courts lag behind reality in their failure to deal directly with transnational actors with the power to build and destroy. Should not a TNC that pillages a rain forest and destroys a native people's way of life be culpable before some authority other than the local government?

International society, like domestic, depends upon consensus and voluntary cooperation as well as on coercive force and law. The parallels are diagrammed in Figure 14.1.

5. TNCs are not full legal personalities because they have no legal right to take part in formulation of the norms that are to govern them. When home countries endorse codes of conduct for TNCs and international agencies enact follow-up procedures, the process can generate international law. These norms have a semi-legal character: They are neither entirely non-binding internationally nor entirely unenforceable domestically. See Burns H. Weston et al., *International Law and World Order: A Problem-Oriented Coursebook*, 2d ed. (St. Paul, Minn.: West, 1990), 612; see also Philip C. Jessup, *Transnational Law* (New Haven, Conn.: Yale University Press, 1956); and Wolfgang Friedmann et al., *Transnational Law in a Changing Society: Essays in Honor of Philip C. Jessup* (New York: Columbia University Press, 1972).

Fig. 14.1 Determinants of Domestic and International Society

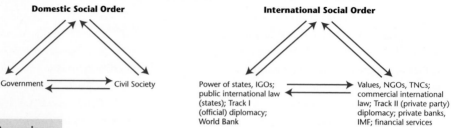

Domestic Social Order

Government ⟷ Civil Society

International Social Order

Power of states, IGOs; public international law (states); Track I (official) diplomacy; World Bank ⟷ Values, NGOs, TNCs; commercial international law; Track II (private party) diplomacy; private banks, IMF; financial services

The Specialized Agencies of the UN

- International Labor Organization (ILO)
- Food and Agriculture Organization of the United Nations (FAO)
- United Nations Educational, Scientific and Cultural Organization (UNESCO)
- World Health Organization (WHO)
- International Bank for Reconstruction and Development (IBRD)
- International Finance Corporation (IFC)
- International Development Association (IDA)
- International Monetary Fund (IMF)
- International Civil Aviation Organization (ICAO)
- International Telecommunication Union (ITU)
- International Center for Settlement of Investment Disputes (ICSID)
- World Meteorological Organization (WMO)
- International Maritime Organization (IMO)
- World Intellectual Property Organization (WIPO)
- International Fund for Agricultural Development (IFAD)
- Multilateral Investment Guarantee Agency (MIGA)
- United Nations Industrial Development Organization (UNIDO)
- Universal Postal Union (UPU)
- International Atomic Energy Agency (IAEA)

Nonstate actors exist on every level:

Individuals. Persons from many walks of life alter IR. Pablo Picasso expanded our awareness of war with his painting *Guernica.* Mother Teresa organized a global network of hospices. Ted Turner in 1997 pledged a billion dollars to assist UN programs.

Determined individuals—private citizens—did as much or more than governments or IGOs to establish the Red Cross, organize assistance for refugees, and ban land mines. Nobel Peace Prizes were awarded for these and other private efforts. Individuals can also destroy. An Israeli hard-liner derailed the Oslo peace process by shooting Prime Minister Yitzhak Rabin. Osama bin Laden changed the entire world.

State and Society. Ethnic groups and interest groups can shape foreign policy and IR, fueling or moderating conflict. Often they cross borders and join like-minded groups to promote change. For example, many nonstate and state actors in the late 1990s demanded a full accounting by Switzerland and other countries regarding deposits made by Jews and then by Nazis before and during World War II.

Interstate (Intergovernmental). The UN and other IGOs owe their existence to states and are part of the state system. Still, they are nonstate actors. The UN has few of the coercive powers associated with states. The European Union (EU), by contrast, started as an IGO but takes on some aspects of a state.

The UN has six principal organs in a system outlined in Figure 14.2. The chart shows some but not all the many UN specialized agencies, commissions, programs, and operations. The World Bank and IMF were discussed in previous chapters. In this chapter we focus on the work of Security Council, the UN secretary–general, and the *World Health Organization (WHO)*—largest of the sixteen UN Specialized Agencies (listed in the sidebar). These agencies are also nonstate actors, even

Fig. 14.2 The United Nations System

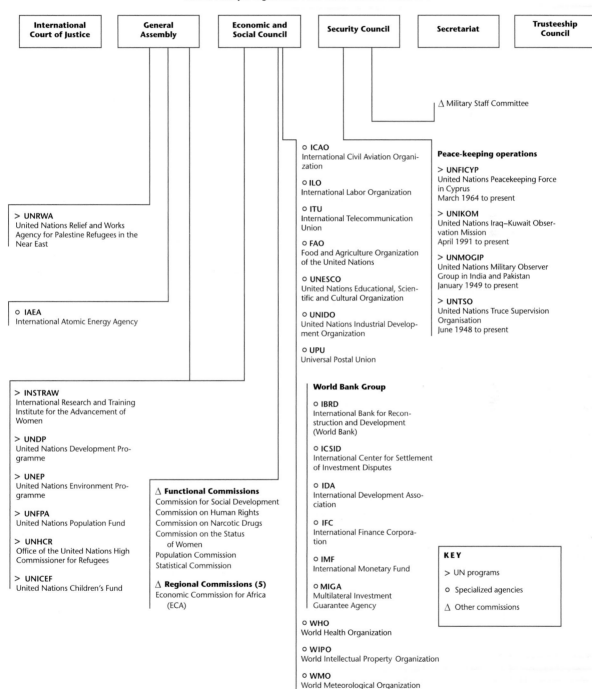

The Six Principal Organs and Other Units Discussed in the Text

| International Court of Justice | General Assembly | Economic and Social Council | Security Council | Secretariat | Trusteeship Council |

△ Military Staff Committee

o **ICAO**
International Civil Aviation Organization

o **ILO**
International Labor Organization

o **ITU**
International Telecommunication Union

o **FAO**
Food and Agriculture Organization of the United Nations

o **UNESCO**
United Nations Educational, Scientific and Cultural Organization

o **UNIDO**
United Nations Industrial Development Organization

o **UPU**
Universal Postal Union

World Bank Group

o **IBRD**
International Bank for Reconstruction and Development (World Bank)

o **ICSID**
International Center for Settlement of Investment Disputes

o **IDA**
International Development Association

o **IFC**
International Finance Corporation

o **IMF**
International Monetary Fund

o **MIGA**
Multilateral Investment Guarantee Agency

o **WHO**
World Health Organization

o **WIPO**
World Intellectual Property Organization

o **WMO**
World Meteorological Organization

Peace-keeping operations

> **UNFICYP**
United Nations Peacekeeping Force in Cyprus
March 1964 to present

> **UNIKOM**
United Nations Iraq–Kuwait Observation Mission
April 1991 to present

> **UNMOGIP**
United Nations Military Observer Group in India and Pakistan
January 1949 to present

> **UNTSO**
United Nations Truce Supervision Organisation
June 1948 to present

> **UNRWA**
United Nations Relief and Works Agency for Palestine Refugees in the Near East

o **IAEA**
International Atomic Energy Agency

> **INSTRAW**
International Research and Training Institute for the Advancement of Women

> **UNDP**
United Nations Development Programme

> **UNEP**
United Nations Environment Programme

> **UNFPA**
United Nations Population Fund

> **UNHCR**
Office of the United Nations High Commissioner for Refugees

> **UNICEF**
United Nations Children's Fund

△ **Functional Commissions**
Commission for Social Development
Commission on Human Rights
Commission on Narcotic Drugs
Commission on the Status of Women
Population Commission
Statistical Commission

△ **Regional Commissions (5)**
Economic Commission for Africa (ECA)

KEY

> UN programs

o Specialized agencies

△ Other commissions

though most of their funding is from governments. The WHO, for example, is staffed mainly by health professionals who focus on their professional tasks and have no coercive power.

Once established, IGOs often take on lives of their own, sometimes defying the states that created them. Their bureaucracies are entrenched in Geneva, Vienna, Nairobi, Bangkok, and elsewhere. Sill, the total professional staff at UN headquarters in New York numbers a few thousands while the WHO staff in Geneva is less than a thousand—tiny numbers for bureaucracies that service the entire world.[6]

Transnational. NGOs such as the ISA are transnational nonstate actors. So are many religions. Large TNCs such as General Motors command more resources than most states. Communications networks such as Cable News Network (CNN) and the Internet are nonstate actors. CNN presents similar images of reality to viewers in Moscow and Washington.[7] Institutions such as the Rockefeller Foundation, Volkswagen Foundation, and Soros Foundation do much to change IR.

Relations between NGOs and governments are varied and complex. Some NGOs serve governments and get money from them; some partner with governments in a common cause; some are gadflies pushing governments in certain directions; some resist governments; still others are indifferent. More than 100 nonstate terrorist groups and crime syndicates operated across the globe and shaped IR early in the 21st century—ten just in Northern Ireland, eight in Palestine, five in Kashmir, four in Congo, and four in the Sudan. Many of these groups laundered money to buy arms or to bolster their cash reserves.

Biosphere. Life's support system is the fifth action level of IR. As we saw in the previous chapter, both the richness and fragility of the biosphere induce new forms of IO to protect the environment. Conservation movements, in turn, generate countermovements dedicated to exploiting nature's abundance.

Which level of IR action is most important depends upon the issue at stake, the time, and the place. The interactions among each level, as we have already seen, are conditioned by many factors.

COMPARING THEORY AND REALITY: VISIONS OF PEACE, JUSTICE, WELFARE

INTERNATIONAL LAW AND WORLD PEACE

Even without a supranational authority, governments for thousands of years have agreed to rules to regulate their behavior—international

6. UN regional offices in the Americas in the 1990s were located in Washington, Havana, Mexico City, Caracas, Bogota, Lima, Asunción, Santiago, and Montevideo. There were another nine offices in Africa, three in Asia, three in the Middle East, and four in Europe. Redundancy and lax financial controls made the global network costly and inefficient.

7. As a State Department official in Washington and his Russian counterpart in Moscow talked by phone, they both looked at the same live CNN broadcast of Russian commandos storming the Russian parliament. Strobe Talbott, "Globalization and Diplomacy: A Practitioner's Perspective," *Foreign Policy*, no. 108 (fall 1997): 69–83 at 69–70.

law. Not until the 20th century, however, was there a strong effort to outlaw war. International law—formal treaties and informal regimes—sought rather to delimit how and when force could be used. Compliance depended mainly on self-interest, for governments valued reciprocity and order over chaos. When vital interests or big gains were at stake, however, they often departed from established norms. Temptations to defect and go for the hare (rather than cooperate for the stag) have repeatedly injected chaos into the world arena.

Does Might Make Right?

What should—what can—other nations do if one state seizes another's territory by force? Medieval Europe accepted the right of conquest. When a prince seized territory, other parties treated this as an accomplished fact. But recognition by the pope was required to consecrate title and legalize sovereignty. The pope, however, lost influence after the Reformation.

1648. Ignoring the pope, Europe's larger powers in the Treaty of Westphalia claimed the right to withhold and bestow recognition of title. Their approach mirrored balance-of-power thinking: Any change in the number or size of states concerned all states, because such change could upset the equilibrium of power.

1789. The French Revolution injected a new element into the equation: national self-determination. Napoleon claimed that France brought liberty to those who wanted it. France annexed Holland, Flanders, and other territories on the ground that these *réunions* represented the free will of the population.

1815. France's annexations were annulled at the Congress of Vienna. Still, plebiscites (popular referenda) became a regular feature of IR, often used to legalize territorial change. In 1860, for example, the Kingdom of Italy annexed the Neapolitan provinces of Sicily, the Marches, and Umbria after plebiscites in each.

Outside of Europe, however, Europeans considered that might made right. When Europeans carved up Africa in the 19th century, they informed one another of their claims—not to obtain recognition, but to prevent friction. Outside of Europe, the white race and Christianity offered no protection: In 1900, Britain annexed the Boer republics in southern Africa by right of conquest. Might made right for major non-Western powers too. Russia took Siberia and Central Asia by conquest; China conquered Tibet in 1909; Japan forcibly annexed Korea in 1910.

Plebiscites After World War I

The principle of national self-determination was widely implemented in creating the states that emerged from the German and Austro-Hungarian empires after World War I. Plebiscites permitted local populations to choose whether to live in Germany or to join Denmark, Belgium, France, or Poland. There were also plebiscites in the Aaland Islands, in some Austrian borderlands, and in Vilnius. But there were no plebiscites for German speakers living in the Sudetenland, incorporated into Czechoslovakia, or in South Tyrol, compelled to accept Italian rule. As Woodrow Wilson's advisers warned in 1919, failure to grant self-determination to the Sudetens would later (in 1938) prove "fatal to the new state" of Czechoslovakia. The 1922 vote in Vilnius was skewed by Polish military control and caused conflict with Lithuania until 1939–1940, when the USSR conquered both eastern Poland and Lithuania and transferred Vilnius to the "Lithuanian Soviet Socialist Republic."

8. The USSR persuaded Poland, Romania, and the three Baltic states to implement the treaty among themselves before it was ratified by the original signatories. Text in *Dokumenty vneshnei politiki SSSR* (Moscow: Politizdat, 1967), 12, 66–70.

9. Godfrey Hodgson, *The Colonel: The Life and Wars of Henry Stimson, 1867–1950* (New York: Knopf, 1990), 158–168.

10. For the Neutrality Act of November 4, 1939, and modifications urged by the Senate on October 25, 1941, see U.S. Senate, Subcommittee on Disarmament, *Disarmament and Security: A Collection of Documents, 1919–55* (Washington, D.C.: Government Printing Office, 1956), 812–824.

The Stimson Doctrine vs. the Right of Conquest

1919. Woodrow Wilson tried to change the rules. He hoped to prevent aggression by creating the League of Nations, which would provide collective security—a system of one for all, all for one against aggression. The League's capacity for collective security, however, was gutted by U.S. nonparticipation and by loopholes in the League of Nations Covenant.

1928. Trying to fill this gap, French Foreign Minister Aristide Briand and U.S. Secretary of State Frank Kellogg drew up the Treaty of Paris, or **Kellogg–Briand Pact**, renouncing war as an "an instrument of national policy." Most countries signed the pact, but it had no teeth—no provisions for enforcement.[8]

1931. Japan flouted both the Covenant and the Kellogg–Briand Pact when its army occupied Manchuria in northern China. Tokyo announced that Manchuria had become "Manchukuo"—a Japanese puppet state.

1932. Kellogg's successor as secretary of state, Henry Stimson, was deeply alarmed by the Japanese moves, but his options were constrained by U.S. isolationism and military weakness. Stimson arose at 6 A.M. on January 2 and penned what became known as the **Stimson Doctrine**: the U.S. refused "to recognize any situation, treaty or agreement . . . brought about by means contrary to the Pact of Paris"—in other words, by war.[9]

Stimson's unilateral action helped create international law by consensus. The League of Nations Assembly in March 1932 resolved that it was "incumbent" upon League members "not to recognize any situation, treaty or agreement which may be brought about by means contrary to the Covenant . . . or the Pact of Paris." In 1933 a treaty signed at Rio de Janeiro committed six major Latin American countries not to recognizing territorial aggrandizement by force. In February 1933 the League of Nations Assembly condemned Japan and urged members not to recognize Manchukuo. Japan withdrew from the League and, in 1937, resumed its march into China.

The French ambassador to Washington, Paul Claudel, recalled a Chinese saying likening words to "spears of straw and swords of ice." Neither the Stimson Doctrine nor League denunciations sufficed to save China or faith in the League's system of collective security. Washington proclaimed U.S. "neutrality."[10]

When Nonrecognition Counts

But words are not always "spears of straw." When Soviet forces annexed Estonia, Latvia, and Lithuania in July 1940, the U.S. State Department

efforts . . . to reach a peaceful solution of the crisis." He tried, but got nowhere with Baghdad. Nor did the Soviet, French, and various Arab emissaries who also offered to mediate.

Next came an ultimatum. On November 29 the Security Council offered Iraq "one final opportunity": If Iraq did not comply with all UN resolutions by January 15, 1991, the Security Council authorized UN members "to use all necessary means to uphold and implement" the resolutions and "to restore international peace and security in the area."

Iraq's Foreign Minister Tariq Aziz met U.S. Secretary of State James Baker in Geneva on January 9, 1991, but each side remained intransigent. Meanwhile, the U.S. Congress pondered what to do. President Bush had dispatched a force of half a million to the Persian Gulf (a force equal in numbers to that once deployed against North Vietnam). To order this force to fight, could the president simply use his power as commander in chief, or did Congress have to declare war? On January 12, 1991, both houses of Congress skirted the constitutional issue. They "authorized" the president "to use U.S. Armed Forces pursuant" to UN Security Council resolutions after "all appropriate diplomatic and other peaceful means" had failed to gain Iraq's compliance.

When the UN coalition opened fire on January 16, the White House proclaimed that the "liberation of Kuwait [had] begun." On February 27, President Bush stated that Kuwait had been liberated and that Operation Desert Storm had ended. The U.S. had led a multilateral force, but supplied most of the men and women and matériel; other states—Kuwait, Saudi Arabia, Japan—subsidized much of the war effort (but left U.S. taxpayers with the tab for medical care and other long-term payments to veterans).

What Did the Gulf War Mean for World Order?

The Gulf War provided history's most successful implementation of collective security. But it left many questions hanging. Could other weak countries count on the UN to assist them against an aggressor? Could the UN ever be sufficiently strong to drive back an invader without depending on a leading power? Would—should—the lone superpower ever subordinate its forces to a UN command?

Following the Gulf War, France persuaded the UN Security Council to broaden its concept of security. Paris insisted on a right to intervene for humanitarian reasons, backed if necessary by military force.[14] This led to a revolution in UN practice as the Security Council began to justify forceful interventions for humanitarian reasons under Chapter VII as a way to

14. The *droit d'ingérence* ("right to intervene") was stressed by Dr. Bernard Kouchner, a founder of Doctors Without Borders. See Kouchener, *Le Malheur des autres* (Paris: Odile Jacob, 1991). Kouchner later became President François Mitterand's state secretary for humanitarian policy.

cope with threats to international peace and security.[15] Thus Security Council Resolution 688, adopted on April 5, 1991, condemned Iraq's repression of its own civilian population, claiming that the consequences of this repression threatened international peace and security. The resolution demanded that Iraq facilitate "immediate access by international humanitarian organizations to all those in need of assistance in all parts of Iraq."

Resolution 688 marked a watershed: Not only did it link domestic repression with threats to international peace, but it compelled Iraq to help NGOs to carry out humanitarian relief for Iraqi citizens. The resolution passed with only ten affirmative votes. China and India abstained, while Cuba, Zimbabwe, and Yemen voted against it. The vote mirrored a growing pattern of assertive support for human rights by the West (usually backed by Russia) and opposition to external probes by developing countries with much dirty (perhaps bloodied) linen to hide. Resolution 688 was short on specifics, but London, Paris, and Washington claimed its authority to establish "safe havens" for Kurds in northern Iraq. The West also barred Iraqi planes from no-fly zones shielding Kurds in the north and Shi'i in southern Iraq. The U.S.-led Operation Provide Comfort air-dropped hospitals for use by Kurdish refugees. UN officials got Iraq to sign a memorandum allowing "humanitarian centers" to be established in both northern and southern Iraq, backed by small contingents of UN guards.[16] After two years, however, Hussein terminated the understandings by which UN guards supported humanitarian activities within Iraq. No Western government wanted to fight Hussein on his home ground on this issue.

Most UN members slowly pulled away from the 1991 coalition, leaving the U.S. and UK to face Iraq. Patiently and relentlessly, Saddam Hussein practiced a kind of salami tactics. Wherever and whenever he could, he sliced off a section of the UN rules imposed in 1991. In 1998, the UN withdrew its inspectors. The Clinton administration fired some rockets at Iraq, but no UN inspectors went there again until 2002.

What did the events of "9/11" mean for the UN and the United States? Now that the sole superpower had been directly attacked, would it act alone or with the UN? At first the Bush team leaned toward acting alone. Unlike his father in 1990–1991, President George W. Bush asked very little of the UN. As we saw in Chapter 4, the U.S. delegation requested and got two Security Council resolutions in September 2001. They gave Washington carte blanche to fight terror however it wished—including an attack on the Taliban regime that controlled most of Afghanistan. The U.S. did not want to be burdened by any need to consult

15. For a survey of the changing military requirements of UN peacekeeping, see Mats R. Berdal, "Whither UN Peacekeeping?" *Adelphi Paper* (October 1993): 281.

16. Despite the two no-fly zones, Hussein blockaded the Kurdish north and actively attacked Shi'i in the south. The West supported Kurdish autonomy, if only to hurt Hussein, but opposed creation of an independent Kurdistan split off from Iraq. (Turkey worried lest support for Iraq's kurds strengthen Kurdish separatists within Turkey.) But Hussein cleverly played off one Kurdish group against another.

IO vs. Money Laundering

The war on terror added to incentives to stop cross-border money laundering——a multibillion enterprise that enriches drug cartels, finances terrorists, and helps major corporations to escape income taxes.

In the late 1990s a number of concerned governments formed the Financial Action Task Force on Money Laundering (FATF), based in Paris. The OECD and the Group of Seven industrialized countries brought together finance ministers, central bankers, and supervisory officials to address these issues. A group of smaller nations such as Barbados, Dominica, and Malaysia formed the Working Group on Harmful Tax Competition to help them meet OECD demands for greater transparency. In 1999 and 2000, the FATF issued reports identifying seventeen states and fifteen territories not cooperating in the struggle against money laundering. It found that the U.S. had not implemented about half of forty-four basic recommendations by the FATF. The U.S. government was soft on insurance companies, currency exchange bureaus, and electronic money transfers.

After 9/11 the U.S. reversed directions and pressed all countries to stop money transfers that could fund terrorist activities. Washington backed FATF sanctions against the Philippines, Ukraine, and other countries. To thwart transnational financing for terror networks, however, required the inputs of many governments, banks, and investment institutions. On the other hand, Washington—the White House, the Treasury Department (!), and many in Congress—continued to protect the right of U.S. businesses to use "correspondent banks" and mail drops in the Caribbean and other tax havens. U.S. law permitted companies to deduct 15 percent of their export earnings if they exploit such dodges. The Boeing Corporation, for example, saved one-tenth of its entire 1998 revenues by using offshore offices. These practices gave U.S. firms an unfair advantage, said the WTO, because they used these fronts to escape income taxes. In August 2002, a three-judge panel of the WTO authorized the EU to impose penalty tariffs on U.S. exports by as much as $4 billion a year.*

*For background, see "Correspondent Banking: A Gateway for Money Laundering," a report by the minority staff, Permanent Subcommittee on Investigations, Committee on Governmental Affairs, United States Senate, February 5, 2001.

---

allies, as happened in the 1999 NATO bombings of Serbia. American air and ground units, assisted by some UK troops, worked with anti-Taliban forces in Afghanistan to overthrow the Taliban and install a new, basically democratic government in Kabul. As the fighting died down, the American presence remained strong only in the capital. UN and NGO workers arrived and began to help with what Bush had disdained—"nation building." By 2004 little progress had been achieved.

The big test of the UN came in 2002 when the Bush administration accused Iraq of colluding with al-Qaeda and retaining weapons of mass destruction. Bowing to State Department pleas, the Bush administration "tried" the UN in the run-up to the Iraq war but found it wanting. In September 2002 the president went to New York and warned that the UN must enforce Iraq's disarmament obligations or become irrelevant like the League of Nations in the 1930s when it failed to stop aggression. Following two months of negotiations, the U.S. delegation in November 2002 obtained UN Security Council Resolution 1441 (detailed above in Chapter 6) giving Iraq one more chance to clear up "material breaches" of its obligations.[17] Baghdad had to open the entire country to a new system of UN and IAEA inspectors. Hawks complained that Bush had been suckered. The inspectors might not find well-hidden WMD in Iraq, and now the U.S. had weakened its right to act without UN approval. As Washington and London interpreted 1441, however, they could decide on their own whether Iraq had breached is new obligations. Thus, when France and Russia threatened in early 2003 to veto military action, U.S. and UK forces invaded Iraq in March without any UN mandate.

Quickly destroying Saddam's regime in March–April 2003, Washington was loath to invite back the UN inspectors to look for WMD or give the UN any share in managing postwar Iraq except to facilitate humanitarian relief. Having assured France and Russia that their long-standing financial claims on Iraq would not be neglected, the U.S. and UK got the Security Council in May 2003 to acknowledge them as the "occupying power" in Iraq—with the rights and duties this entailed. The Americans and Brits promised to restore order and turn over governance to the Iraqi people as quickly as feasible, warning this could take a year or two. The occupying authority also claimed the right to dole out contracts for reconstruction of Iraq (beginning with the Bechtel Corporation and Halliburton, which immediately offered subcontracts to firms in other countries). Washington also persuaded the Security Council to continue the "oil-for-food" program supervised by Secretary-General Kofi Annan. This provided a legal framework for putting Iraqi oil onto the world market and getting funds to feed and rebuild Iraq.

Washington also sidestepped the UN when dealing with Pyongyang. With Iraq, the U.S. tried and then ignored the UN. With North Korea, Washington did not even try. Pyongyang had a credible deterrent while Saddam Hussein did not. Yes, the UN Security Council might well order sanctions against North Korea for violating its arms control obligations. Sanctions, however, could mean war and devastation for South Korea. So the U.S. bypassed the UN and tried to mobilize Chinese, Japanese, South Korean, and Russian pressures on North Korea.

The Bush administration liked having a free hand. The **Bush Doctrine** declared that the U.S. should and would act alone or with a "coalition of the willing" to preempt attacks by potential foes amassing WMD. All IR actors must choose, said Washington, whether or not to join the war against terrorism.

Even if the U.S. wished to play world cop, even a hyperpower would be stretched too thin if it tried to deal with every eruption of chaos from Indonesia to the Ivory Coast. World security required IO.

17. "Material breach" is a term that UK diplomats used in early 1991 to justify U.S. and UK military actions against Iraq for alleged violations of its cease-fire obligations. Washington wanted the Security Council to use this term again in 1998 after Iraq blocked UN arms inspectors. But the relevant UN resolution in 1998, used the less weighty charge of "flagrant" violation.

THE UN AS PEACEKEEPER: THE COLD WAR AND AFTER

Chapter VI of the UN Charter authorizes the Security Council to attempt "pacific settlement of international disputes," for example, by mediation—provided the parties agree. At the other end of the scale, Chapter VII authorizes the Security Council to make binding decisions on the use of force when it judges that there is a threat to peace and security, a breach of the peace, or an act of aggression, as in Korea 1950 and in Kuwait 1990. Between these poles is a large middle range. The UN Secretariat and UN members developed over the years a variety of techniques to straddle what is authorized under Chapters VI and VII—between what is voluntary/nonviolent and what is obligatory/coercive.

Peacekeeping is an extension of Chapter VI authority. It is the introduction of troops between parties, with their consent, to prevent the use of force or to supervise a cease-fire. Peacekeepers buy time in which to resolve conflicts. The UN has sent many observer missions and peacekeepers into the field. The first such mission was improvised in 1948 by the UN mediator in Palestine to supervise the truce between Israel and its

---

TIME LINE: The Ten Costliest UN Peacekeeping Missions, 1948–1990

1948–

UN Truce Supervision Organization **(UNTSO,** $311 million, **1948–1990)**—supervised initial Israeli–Arab truces

1956–1967

First UN Emergency Force **(UNEF I,** $214 million)—stood between Egypt and Israel after the Suez War; withdrawn at Egypt's request just before the Six-Day War

1960–1964

UN Operation in the Congo **(ONUC,** $400 million)—sought to establish law and order in the Belgian Congo (later, Zaire); included more than 20,000 troops and civilians

1964–

UN Peacekeeping Force in Cyprus **(UNFICYP,** $636 million to 1990)— supervises the cease-fire between Greek Cypriot and Turkish Cypriot plus Turkish forces

1965–1966

Representative of Secretary-General in the Dominican Republic **(DOMREP,** $275 million)—observed the cease-fire between the two de facto authorities

1973–1979

Second UN Emergency Force **(UNEF II,** $447 million)—facilitated military disengagement in the Sinai; included more than 6,000 troops from Austria, Canada, Finland, Indonesia, Ireland, Nepal, Peru, Poland, Senegal, and Sweden

1974–

UN Disengagement Observer Force **(UNDOF,** $452 million)—supervises Golan Heights pullbacks

1978–

UN Interim Force in Lebanon **(UNIFIL,** $1,762,900,000)—by far the most expensive UN peacekeeping mission through 1990)—confirms withdrawal of Israeli forces and helps restore peace and stability in Lebanon

1989–1990

UN Transition Assistance Group in Namibia **(UNTAG,** $384 million)—promoted early independence for Namibia and supervised free and fair elections

SOURCE: *The Blue Helmets: A Review of United Nations Peacekeeping,* 2d ed. (New York: United Nations, 1990), Appendix 2.

What Can the UN Secretary-General Do for Peace?

The UN secretary-general has always been caught in a crossfire between conflicting expectations. In 1945 the West wanted him merely to be an "office manager" while smaller countries hoped that he would acquire an independent political role—a counterweight to the great powers. The Charter specified that the winning candidate be recommended by the Security Council—subject to a veto—and then appointed by the General Assembly. The Charter described him as UN "chief administrative officer," but Article 99 gave him the right to "bring to the attention of the Security Council any matter which in his opinion may threaten . . . international peace and security."

The first two men to hold the job, Trygve Lie (1945–1952) and Dag Hammarskjöld (1953–1961), were Scandinavians. Hammarskjöld had modest aspirations when he took the job, but soon saw himself as an explorer: "Working at the edge of the development of human society is to work on the brink of the unknown," he said. Hammarskjöld tried to transform the UN into a dynamic tool of collective security. Believing that Hammarskjöld favored the West, Moscow demanded in 1960–1961 that the Secretariat be headed by a troika—a Communist, a neutral, and a Westerner. This idea was rejected, but the next secretary-general was an inward-focused Burmese, U Thant. In 1971 Washington and Moscow settled on a candidate from neutral Austria—Kurt Waldheim, whose Nazi background, made public later, left him vulnerable to Soviet blackmail. In 1981 Beijing demanded that the next secretary-general come from the Third World. The most acceptable candidate was Javier Pérez de Cuéllar from Peru. He was followed in 1991 by the first African to hold the job, Boutros Boutros-Ghali, succeeded in 1997 by Kofi Annan, another African.

Many threats to world peace arose after 1945, but the UN secretary-general explicitly invoked Article 99 only once to convene the Security Council. Hammarskjöld did so in May 1960 to call the Security Council into session as trouble erupted in the newly independent Belgian Congo. Other secretaries-general used Article 99 without invoking it directly to convene the Security Council—U Thant during the 1971 India–Pakistan war; Waldheim during the 1979 Iranian hostage crisis; and Pérez de Cuéllar during the 1989 Lebanese turmoil.

Critics fault the secretary-general for not convening the Security Council during the buildups to the Arab–Israeli wars of 1967 and 1973 and the Iraq–Iran war of 1980. Others say the secretary-general needs up-to-date intelligence from reconnaissance satellites on military flash points. But both BBC and other news media provide ample warnings of mounting crises. What the UN needs is more willpower—beginning with the permanent members of the Security Council.

18. Six missions were charged to the regular UN budget; nine of them to special accounts, which some members—led by the USSR, France, and the U.S.—delayed paying for years. Two operations were paid by parties directly concerned (Yemen, by Saudi Arabia and Egypt; West Irian, by Indonesia and the Netherlands); the Cyprus operation was partially financed by the voluntary donations of many countries.

The USSR and France refused to pay for UN operations in Congo authorized by the General Assembly. When asked for an advisory opinion, the International Court of Justice (see Figure 14.2) held that General Assembly peacekeeping operations should be treated like any other "expenses of the Organization." Nonetheless, the USSR and France held back.

neighbors. The timeline shows the scope of the ten costliest UN peacekeeping activities from 1948 to 1990 and describes their function. The cumulative cost of these operations, 1948 through 1990, amounted to about $5 billion—less than Israel's defense budget for the year 1990. Nearly 800 UN personnel died in all these operations. They included UN mediator Count Folke Bernadotte, assassinated by Israelis in 1948, and UN Secretary-General Dag Hammarskjöld and seven aides, who perished in a plane crash in the Congo in 1961. These costs and casualties, though tragic, were minimal relative to the losses they helped to prevent.[18]

When the Cold War ended, the great powers relied more on the UN to maintain the peace. In the 1990s, the UN conducted operations unprecedented in scope in six states or regions torn by civil strife—Angola,

Cambodia, Somalia, the former Yugoslavia, Rwanda, and Haiti. When civil war and drought brought famine to Somalia, private relief agencies distributed food. As disorder mounted, the UN Security Council initiated a series of actions under Chapter VII of the Charter.[19] In December 1992, the Security Council recommended steps "to establish a secure environment for humanitarian relief" and welcomed a U.S. offer to lead such an operation. At first the intervention calmed Somalia and made food distribution easier, but when U.S. forces sought to capture a Somali warlord, violence escalated. Somalis were killed; so were UN peacekeepers— Pakistanis and then Americans. After U.S. TV viewers saw charred U.S. corpses dragged through Mogadishu, President Bill Clinton announced an early pullout of U.S. troops, leaving Pakistani and Indian forces to represent the UN.

In 1992–1993 British, Canadian, and French forces in blue helmets operated under a UN flag in the former Yugoslavia. Their job was to ensure delivery of food and medical supplies to besieged communities in Bosnia. But they had neither a UN mandate nor the military strength to overpower Serb and Croat forces obstructing their path. Instead, they had to bargain: Often they paid a road tax—diverting supplies to armed Serbs and Croats—in order to deliver anything to Bosnian Muslims.

The limited UN contingent and NGO aid workers became an obstacle to forceful action to stop Serbian and Croat attacks on Muslim communities. When NATO wanted to bomb Serb artillery pounding Sarajevo, the poorly armed British, Canadians, and French were held hostage and used as human shields to protect Serb and Croat positions.

Both in Somalia and Bosnia some private aid agencies did not want outside military support. They claimed that military escalation made their task more difficult. Still, the NGOs could not stop the fighting. Only when NATO invoked and used hard power did Serbs stop shelling Sarajevo and pull away their cannon and mortars from the surrounding hills.

The Balkan wars of the 1990s taught Washington and London that the UN was ill-equipped for peace enforcement. The UN could not impose peace on the South Slavs with a comparatively small, lightly armed force intended only for peacekeeping. Neither the UN nor Europe had the will—or the means—for peace enforcement in the Balkans.[20] As we saw in Chapter 9, attempted mediation by UN and European Union representatives achieved little. They lacked both soft and hard power.

U.S. and UK officials wanted the UN to take on only operations that entailed no fighting except in self-defense. A new pattern took shape after the 1995 Dayton Accord on Bosnia. UN interventions were based on

19. In January 1992 the Security Council imposed an arms embargo on Somalia; in April it established the UN Operation in Somalia (UNOSOM) to monitor a cease-fire and protect humanitarian relief supplies. Within a few months the UN secretary-general called for a comprehensive approach to support humanitarian relief and recovery, a cease-fire, a peace process, and national reconciliation.

20. For a narrative description of the tensions in Kosovo during the Bosnian War, see Christopher Thornton, "Across the Border," *Sewanee Review* 108, no. 4: 596–602.

Table 14.2 Size of UN Peacekeeping Forces as of June 2002

Force, Location, Date Established	June 2002
UNTSO, Palestine, 1948	143
UNMOGIP, India–Pakistan, 1949	44
UNFICYP, Cyprus, 1964	1,242
UNDOF, Golan Heights, 1974	1,003
UNIFIL, Lebanon, 1978	3,629
UNIKOM, Iraq–Kuwait, 1991	1,098
MINURSO, Western Sahara, 1991	243
UNMIBH, Bosnia, 1995	1,530
UNMOP, Prevlaka, 1996	27
UNOMIG, Georgia, 1993	106
UNAMSIL, Sierra Leone, 1999	17,474
UNMIK, Kosovo, 1999	4,548
UNMISET, East Timor, 2002	5,847
MINUGUA, Guatemala, 1997	14
MONUC, D.R. Congo, 1999	4,233
UNMEE, Ethiopia/Eritrea, 2000	4,152

Definitions

UNTSO UN Truce Supervision Organisation
UNMOGIP UN Military Observer Group in India and Pakistan
UNFICYP UN Peacekeeping Force in Cyprus
UNDOF UN Disengagement Observer Force
UNIFIL UN Interim Force in Lebanon
UNIKOM UN Iraq–Kuwait Observation Mission
MINURSO UN Mission for the Referendum in Western Sahara
UNMIBH UN Mission in Bosnia and Herzegovnia
UNMOP UN Mission of Observers in Prevlaka
UNOMIG UN Observer Mission in Georgia
UNAMSIL UN Mission in Sierra Leone
UNMIK UN Interim Administration Mission in Kosovo
UNMISET United Nations Mission of Support in East Timor
MINUGUA UN Verification Mission in Guatemala
MONUC UN Organization Mission in the Democratic Republic of the Congo
UNMEE UN Mission in Ethiopia and Eritrea

"contracting out" UN jobs, per "consent of the willing." NATO forces replaced those nominally subject to a "UN" commander. Thus, in Bosnia, UN "Blue Helmets" were replaced by a larger and more robust implementation force (IFOR) of 60,000 troops from NATO and sixteen other states—later reduced to 35,000 troops in a stabilization force (SFOR). These forces, one-third of them from the U.S. in the 1990s, kept the local guns silent and permitted economic reconstruction to begin. But even IFOR and SFOR did not compel full compliance with the Dayton Accord. Ethnic differences remained virulent. Few "ethnically cleansed" refugees could return home. The entire operation suffered from Washington's self-imposed deadlines, repeated annually, to pull out after one or two years on the job.

In the mid-1990s, the UN also mandated forces from the **Commonwealth of Independent States (CIS)**—mostly Russians—to guard the borders of Georgia and Tajikistan, and an Italian-led force to restore order in Albania. When the Georgians requested the Russians to leave, however, many remained.

Table 14.2 lists UN peacekeeping operations still in the field in 2002. The table also shows their size—from fourteen in Guatemala to more than 5,000 in East Timor and over 17,000 in Sierra Leone. Figure 14.3 displays the variations in force size from 1993 to 2001. The number of UN forces worldwide declined from 76,000 in 1994 to 19,000 in 1997, before rising to 47,000 in September 2001. Some eighty-eight countries contributed peacekeepers to UN missions in 2001—led by Bangladesh, 6,049; Pakistan, 5,552; and Nigeria, 3,446. At the other extreme, Cape Verde, Estonia, Albania, and Côte d'Ivoire contributed one or two each.

UN outlays for peacekeeping from 1947 through 2001 are detailed in Table 14.3. In 1991–1992, the yearly bill for UN peacekeeping missions jumped from $500 million to over $3 billion but fell to less than $2 billion in the late 1990s, before rising to about $2.5 billion in 2001. UN peacekeeping operations in the 1990s raised the cumulative bill to nearly $26 billion for the period 1948–2001. This was more than pocket change but less than the defense budget of Saudi Arabia or Germany for the year 2001.

Many states were penny-wise and pound foolish. By December 2002, UN members owed the UN more than a billion dollars for peacekeeping. They left the secretary-general with empty pockets just as demand for UN services soared around the world. The U.S. led the list of debtors. By 2003, the U.S. owed the UN $700 million for peacekeeping plus $530 million toward the regular budget—over $1.3 billion (down from $2.3 billion in August 2001).

Fig. 14.3 UN Peacekeeping Operations, 1993–2001: Troops, Civilian Police, and Military Observers

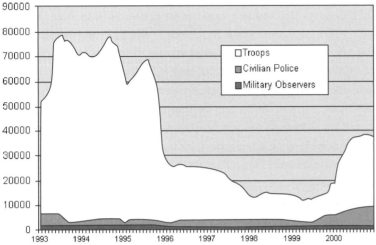

Table 14.3 UN Peacekeeping Expenditures, 1947–2001 ($U.S. millions)

Year	Expenditures	Year	Expenditures	Year	Expenditures	Year	Expenditures
1947	0	1965	45	1983	141	2001	2,500*
1948	4	1966	45	1984	141	2002	2,630*
1949	7	1967	37	1985	141	2003	2,170*
1950	7	1968	24	1986	242		
1951	6	1969	24	1987	240		
1952	6	1970	24	1988	266		
1953	6	1971	24	1989	635		
1954	6	1972	24	1990	464		
1955	6	1973	37	1991	490		
1956	9	1974	131	1992	1,767		
1957	26	1975	153	1993	3,059		
1958	30	1976	153	1994	3,342		
1959	26	1977	153	1995	3,364		
1960	76	1978	202	1996	1,522		
1961	126	1979	186	1997	1,226		
1962	126	1980	141	1998	907		
1963	127	1981	141	1999	1,100		
1964	91	1982	141	2000	1,800*		

* Estimated expenditures
SOURCE: Global Policy Forum. Data compiled by Michael Renner, World Watch Institute; http://www.un.org/Depts/dpko.

Besides combat deaths and financial costs resulting from UN peace-keeping, there were health risks. At least 14 percent of UN peacekeepers in the early 21st century came from countries with high rates of HIV/AIDS infections. Some 20 percent of troops from Nigeria, Tanzania, and Côte d'Ivoire were believed to carry the infection. The rapid rise of HIV/AIDS in Cambodia coincided with the UN peacekeeping mission there. Ten Uruguayan peacekeepers tested negative before their deployment in Cambodia and positive upon return to Uruguay. Infection rates were high among samples of prostitutes in three countries where peacekeeping operations took place in 2002—nearly 30 percent in Sierra Leone and Congo; 73 percent in Ethiopia. The UN Department of Peacekeeping Operations discouraged countries from sending infected troops on UN missions but, as of 2002, did not mandate testing.[21]

Did Intervention Do Any Good?

The Security Council in the 1990s allowed a prominent place for humanitarian intervention backed by force. These operations brought the UN into unknown terrain. They broke new legal ground, but their practical effects were limited. Sometimes they did too little, too late. UN failures, as in Somalia, grabbed headlines. But every mission that prevented fighting (for example, in the Former Yugoslav Republic of Macedonia) could be judged at least a partial success. Meanwhile, the learning curve went up as UN officials and governments fathomed the reach of IO in the post–Cold War era.

Most UN peacekeeping missions lasted only a few years, but some appeared to be open-ended. Of eight longstanding UN operations (lasting more than five years), U.S. and many UN officials thought in the 1990s that two promoted stability—UNDOF (Israel–Syria) and UNIKOM (Iraq–Kuwait); three achieved partial success—UNTSO (Middle East), UNFICYP (Cyprus), and UNAVEM (Angola); and three contributed only marginally to security—UNMOGIP (Kashmir), UNIFIL (Lebanon), and MINURSO (Western Sahara). Still, U.S. officials saw no reasonable alternative to continuing these operations, because they bought time during which conflicts could be resolved peacefully.

Despite George W. Bush's avowed aversion to "nation building," in 2002–2003 there were 7,500 U.S. troops in Afghanistan (Operation Enduring Freedom). Taking part in UN or other peacekeeping missions were some 5,000 Americans in Kosovo; 2,000 in Bosnia; and smaller forces in East Timor, Egypt, Ethiopia, Macedonia, Georgia, Hungary, Kuwait, Kyrgyzstan, the Western Sahara, Saudi Arabia, Tajikistan, Turkey,

21. U.S. General Accounting Office, *HIV/AIDs and U.N. Peacekeeping*, GAO-02-194, 24.

Uzbekistan, plus two observers in the UNTSO. Vastly overshadowing all these numbers, however, were the U.S. forces in Iraq.

ORGANIZING FOR HUMAN WELFARE

Apart from security and economic development, IOs can also foster human welfare. From myriad agencies, let us look briefly at one that promotes public health and another that offers humanitarian relief in wartime.

Serving the Health of Nations

Health issues can be high politics. Bubonic plague, probably carried by ships from Asia, wiped out a third of Europe's population in the 17th century. In an age of global interdependence, jet planes carry lethal diseases far more rapidly than the ships that brought the "Black Death." The **WHO** is committed to the "attainment by all peoples of the highest possible level of health." Successor to public health agencies founded in 1907 and 1919, the WHO became a UN specialized agency in 1948, and in 2003 the largest UN specialized agency, with a budget of $2.5 billion and with 3,000 employees worldwide, half of them medical personnel. For the past five years its director-general had been the "liberals' Margaret Thatcher"—Dr. Gro Harlem Brundtland, former prime minister of Norway and a physician trained in public health at Harvard University. The WHO cooperates with scores of other IGOs, such as the UN Development Programme, and with even more NGOs—from the African Medical and Research Foundation to World Vision International. It is part of "global governance"—pragmatic cooperation between governments, IOs, TNCs (such as drug companies), and NGOs. Let us examine how the WHO has dealt with several threats to public health.

Smallpox. From its founding, the WHO urged its member states to vaccinate against the ancient scourge of smallpox. But it was difficult to store and transport the vaccines to LDCs. The cost of a lifesaving vaccination was about 10 cents. Still, national governments in India and Africa failed to invest the necessary funds or personnel. Epidemics continued until help came from the outside. Dr. Viktor Zhdanov, a Soviet delegate to the World Health Assembly, began to mobilize broad-scale action in 1958.[22]

In 1966, the World Health Assembly resolved to eliminate the disease entirely. It set up the Smallpox Eradication Unit that, assisted by other UN agencies, brought together the personnel and equipment needed to vaccinate throughout India and Africa. The WHO funded conferences, training courses, fellowships, and consultantships. It also established standards

22. Smallpox had nearly been wiped out in the USSR, but epidemics in Iran and Afghanistan spilled over into Soviet Central Asia. Dr. Zhdanov reminded the World Health Assembly gathered in Minneapolis that U.S. President Thomas Jefferson had written to Dr. Edward Jenner, the English physician who introduced the vaccination, commending his discovery as a boon for the future of all peoples. Many epidemiologists trained by Dr. Zhdanov in Moscow took part in the WHO program. The USSR also contributed some 25 million doses of vaccine. WHO efforts multiplied after 1958, but the eradication program dragged until 1966 for lack of funds and personnel. In 1958 there were five WHO officials working on leprosy and twenty-eight on malaria, but none responsible solely for smallpox.

for vaccine quality. It recommended freeze-dried vaccines for remote tropical areas and glycerated vaccines where refrigeration was possible.

In less than a decade—at a tiny cost but with broad East–West–South cooperation—the WHO eradicated smallpox from the planet. The savings made simply by not having to check smallpox vaccination certificates at international airports exceeded the cost of the entire eradication program. No value can be placed on the lives saved.[23]

In the early 21st century, however, this boon came to look like a threat. Russia and the U.S. had been authorized to keep some smallpox spores. Other governments might have done so secretly. If a rogue government or a terrorist group managed to weaponize smallpox, most people would be defenseless. The Bush administration began in 2002 to vaccinate soldiers and medical personnel, even though some people might die from the vaccination.

Primary Health Care. In 1977, the World Health Assembly decided that the main social goal of governments and the WHO should be worldwide attainment by the year 2000 of a level of health permitting all people to lead socially and economically productive lives. Affordable "primary health care" should include community education on health problems and prevention; promotion of adequate food, safe water, and sanitation; maternal and child care; prevention and control of endemic diseases; immunization against the main infectious diseases; treatment of common diseases and injuries; and provision of essential drugs.

The WHO estimated that such care could be provided in developing countries for $10 to $15 per person per year (excepting food, water, and sanitation). But in sub-Saharan Africa outlays were only $7 per capita; in South and Southeast Asia they were only $4. By contrast, in developed market economies they reached nearly $600.[24]

In the 1980s only a third of sub-Saharan Africans had access to safe drinking water or adequate sanitation. Roughly half of South and Southeast Asia had safe drinking water, but only a fifth to a tenth had adequate sanitation. Lack of safe drinking water and sanitation lead to gastrointestinal diseases—a major child killer. Dehydration can be controlled by oral rehydration therapy (ORT) using a saline water solution that costs pennies—provided mothers possess it and know how to use it. The UN Children's Fund (UNICEF), a UN Specialized Agency that works with the WHO, campaigned to make ORT available worldwide. For the cost of a few warships, all the children in the world could be inoculated against six preventable diseases—diphtheria, whooping cough, tetanus, polio, measles, and tuberculosis. The knowledge and medicines exist. The core

23. In 1980 the WHO recommended that vaccination be stopped since the disease had been eradicated. See F. Fenner et al., *Smallpox and Its Eradication* (Geneva: World Health Organization, 1988). In 1996, two centuries after Jenner invented the vaccine, the World Health Assembly recommended destruction of the world's remaining stocks of the virus and maintenance of the seed virus at a laboratory in the Netherlands. *The World Health Report 1997* (Geneva: World Health Organization, 1997), 89.

24. *Global Outlook 2000: An Economic, Social, and Environmental Perspective* (New York: United Nations, 1990), 285–305.

administrative structures exist. The missing ingredient is money—or the will to provide it.

Malaria. Another WHO project achieved dramatic results initially, only to boomerang. Malaria once infected 90 percent of the people in Borneo. In 1955 the WHO sprayed the island with DDT to kill the carrier mosquitoes.[25] It provided a quick-fix that saved many human lives and was then applied in many countries. But new strains of mosquitoes emerged, bringing with them new forms of malaria. Some experts concluded that screening porches and windows offered a more effective and less destructive approach to malaria control than pesticides.[26]

By the early 21st century there were more than 300 million cases of malaria, and the disease killed more than 1 million people each year. The WHO worked with national health ministries and donors to obtain financial support for some seventeen African and three Asian countries where malaria remained endemic. Striving to foster community-based control efforts, the WHO trained entomologists from Asia and Africa in vector control. It provided technical assistance to refugee camps in Azerbaijan and ten other countries affected by malaria. WHO malaria experts collaborated with the UN Development Programme in Myanmar; with the World Bank in Bangladesh, Laos, Madagascar, and Vietnam; with the European Union in Indochina; and with European aid agencies in Eritrea, Ethiopia, and Uganda.

But though the WHO provided technical assistance, it had no budget for projects such as its Roll Back Malaria campaign. The WHO had to convince governments, rich donors, and private foundations to support its recommendations. The population most vulnerable to malaria was children in Africa, where resistance to old-line drugs such as chloroquine was growing. Therefore, the WHO recommended a drug called artemisinin which, in combination with DDT and bed nets, resulted in dramatic declines in death rates. But treatment with artemisinin, at roughly $2, was 10 times the cost of the older drugs. Dr. Brundtland failed in 2002 to persuade official Washington to support use of this drug in Africa.

HIV/AIDS. Besides malaria, the WHO faced two other rapidly spreading diseases at the onset of the 21st century: tuberculosis and HIV/AIDS. The HIV pandemic spread worldwide in less than twenty years—a reminder that globalization can increase mutual vulnerability. The WHO and other agencies attempted to track the disease and disseminate information on how to prevent and cope with it. Working in the Joint UN Programme on HIV/AIDS (UNAIDS), begun in 1996, the WHO sought to coordinate a global, regional, and country-level response to HIV. Unlike

25. Besides killing the mosquitoes that spread malaria, DDT also killed flies and cockroaches—the favorite food of house lizards (geckos), which then perished. The cockroaches and geckos killed by DDT were then eaten by house cats. When the cats also died, the rat population soared, bringing with them a sylvatic plague carried by fleas on the rats. Britain's Royal Air Force then conducted Operation Cat Drop, parachuting fresh cats into remote jungle habitats.

26. A. V. Kondrashin and K. M. Rashid, eds., *Epidemiological Considerations for Planning Malaria Control in the WHO South–East Asia Region* (New Delhi: World Health Organization, South–East Asia, 1987).

smallpox, however, the mechanisms by which HIV spread were poorly understood and there was no magic shot to prevent it.

In the early 21st century, the WTO organized the Global Fund to Fight AIDS, TB & Malaria. But Dr. Brundtland's critics said that the WHO had not brought enough pressure to bear on developed countries and was too cozy with the pharmaceutical industry. In 2003 there were more than 25 million people infected with HIV in sub-Saharan Africa, but just over 100,000 were being treated with anti-AIDS drugs even after the WHO made a deal with pharmaceutical companies to accelerate access to treatment and after prices dropped by up to 90 percent. Dr. Richard Horton, editor of the British medical journal *Lancet,* criticized the WHO for relying on the private sector to provide health care. Consider, he said, a family in a village that has no water supply, suffers Guinea worm infection, is ravaged by malaria, faces an encroaching HIV/AIDS epidemic, and has absolutely no access to health services. What vision did Dr. Brundtland and her team have for that family? "Only 1 percent of people in Africa who need antiretroviral drugs presently get them," said Dr. Horton. "We need to mobilize a constituency to do something about it, and WHO needs to take the lead there."[27]

Infant Formula. Another partial victory for public health occurred when the WHO and UNICEF helped mediate and partially resolve a debate between NGOs and TNCs over infant formula. Two sets of nonstate actors, some allied with governments, faced off. Nestlé and other TNC makers of infant formula touted their product in LDCs using sales personnel dressed as nurses to give free samples to new mothers. Once mothers used the formula, they became physiologically dependent on it when their babies did not suckle.

Public health experts warned that conditions in many developing countries—illiteracy, contaminated water, and lack of refrigeration—made infant formula dangerous to public health. Leading pediatricians estimated that 10 million cases of infant malnutrition and 1 to 3 million deaths occurred yearly in LDCs in the 1970s as a result of mothers ceasing to breast-feed their children.[28]

The World Health Assembly in 1974 warned member countries to review sales promotion of baby foods and to regulate advertisements. But many NGOs took a harder line and demanded a code of conduct. The British group War on Want published a pamphlet called *The Baby Killers* (1974), which was translated in Switzerland under the German title "Nestlé Kills Babies." Nestlé inadvertently publicized the issue when it

27. *All Things Considered,* National Public Radio, January 6, 2003.

28. Kathryn Sikkink, "Codes of Conduct for Transnational Corporations: The Case of the WHO/UNICEF Code," *International Organization* 40, no. 4 (autumn 1986): 815–840.

sued for defamation. In the U.S., the Infant Formula Action Coalition (INFACT) organized a consumer boycott of Nestlé. After Senate hearings, a meeting between Senator Edward M. Kennedy and infant formula companies produced a request by both sides for a WHO meeting on the issue. The World Health Assembly and UNICEF in 1981 adopted the Code of Marketing for Breast-milk Substitutes (the vote was 118 for, 3 abstentions, and 1—the U.S.—against). The code was nonbinding on member governments, but eliminated direct advertising and reduced free sampling and blatant misrepresentation.

The TNCs fought back. Nestlé, Abbot Laboratories, and Upjohn lobbied Washington. The Reagan administration and several LDC governments took no immediate action, but by 1984 over forty countries were moving to insert the code into their domestic legislation. Switzerland and Norway, both major exporters of formula, voted for the marketing code. India passed laws regarding distribution of free samples that were tougher than the code.

Battles may be won but the war can continue. In the 1990s, a major reason to use infant formula emerged: Mothers infected with the human immunodeficiency virus (HIV) often transmitted the disease by breastfeeding. And Israel's Ministry of Health complained in August 2002 that it was unable to enforce the international ban on advertising of baby formula, even though Israel had signed the convention, because of lobbying by the industry. The ministry said the code was being enforced in Norway and some other European countries, but not in the U.S.[29]

Complex Humanitarian Emergencies—The Red Cross in Tajikistan

At the onset of the 21st century, many millions of people needed relief from natural or man-made disasters. Worldwide, there were at least 50 million refugees—forced out of their homes by armed conflict, political persecution, or environmental calamities. Some 27 million (including 4 million Palestinians) lived outside their home countries; the other 23 million were "internally displaced." The total number of people on the move may have approached 1 billion—people moving from rural areas to cities; people migrating to new places in hope of a better life. Some moved legally, but many did so with false or no legal documents.[30]

Why? The end of the Cold War ushered in many **complex humanitarian emergencies**—compounds of dire poverty, hunger, environmental disaster, communal conflict, civil war, displacement of people, and failing

 Factors Facilitating the Code of Conduct

- The emotional appeal of a campaign for breast-milk over infant formula
- A strong consensus on the issues among experts
- A global coalition of NGOs such as the International Baby Food Action Network and INFACT (started in Minneapolis with twenty volunteers and one paid staffer)
- Nestlé's vulnerability to a boycott just as it embarked on a campaign to seek a wider market share for its many products in the U.S.
- The desire of Nestlé and other producers to appear upright and wholesome
- Mediation by UNICEF between Nestlé and its NGO critics
- Rising sales of infant formula to an expanding population regardless of negative publicity

29. The *Jerusalem Post* (August 7, 2002) cited a report by an Israeli physician that ads for Simulac, made by Abbot Pharmaceuticals, claimed that babies fed on this product acquired higher IQs and developed better than those fed on something else.

30. The Worldwatch Institute, *Vital Signs 2001* (New York: W. W. Norton, 2001), 142–143.

Homegrown NGOs for Humanitarian Relief

In 1994 several U.S. teenagers visiting Europe saw how Belarusian victims of the 1986 Chernobyl nuclear disaster were receiving respite and support in Ireland thanks to an NGO called the Chernobyl Children's Project, Ltd. The Americans returned to Boston, and soon five Catholic parishes were organizing a program to host ten children from Belarus in summer 1995. The children stayed with host families for a month. The Americans borrowed the Irish project title but replaced "Ltd." with "Inc." The families take the children to the beach and show them some New England sights. But the children also get a thorough checkup at the New England Medical Center and its Floating Hospital for Children. Other hospitals, physicians, dentists, and eye professionals volunteer their time and resources. Some corporate sponsors underwrite basic costs. Since language is an issue, locals who know both Belarusian (or Russian) and English also get involved. I translated one night in June as a Brighton, Massachusetts, family

met its two guests. They belonged to a group of 160 children, exhausted but excited after a long plane ride to JFK and a bus trip to Boston. Some looked OK, but many were on crutches or visibly ill in some other way. I wept with anger at a political–economic system that permitted such an accident to happen and then did so little to prevent further damage, but also with joy at the generosity and high hopes visible on all sides. By 2003 nearly 1,000 children had spent a month in the Boston area.

Starting right after the 1986 accident, the Cuban government treated more than 15,000 Ukrainian victims of Chernobyl, hosting large groups for forty-five days at a time at a beachfront facility. The American way, from the bottom up, and the Cuban, from the top down, had pluses and minuses.

So near and yet so far. Would the Americans and Cubans ever get to know each other again as they were getting to know Belarusians and Ukrainians?

economic and political institutions, often complicated by armed intervention from neighboring countries. Challenges for outside non-state actor aid agencies multiply when local warlords obstruct or abuse humanitarian relief. The more fighting, the less money there is for relief or development.

For more than a century the Red Cross has tried to lessen the horrors of war, but things were easier when governments were the main combatants. They knew the laws of war and paid some heed to public opinion. They usually permitted the Red Cross to aid prisoners of war, the wounded, and refugees.

In the 1990s relief agencies confronted much fighting by private entrepreneurs. Countries once held together by superpowers were breaking up. Local warlords sought profit or territory for their ethnic group, scorned world opinion, and ignored Red Cross and Red Crescent markings. In 1996 nineteen relief workers were murdered in Chechnya and Africa. Relief agencies often faced clans contesting control of the same city. A local commander's promise of safe passage meant little to an armed teenager at a checkpoint. Warlords in Liberia starved regions to attract food relief, then stole the food plus the trucks that delivered it. Hutus who led the 1994 genocide in Rwanda

ICRC Activities in Tajikistan in 1996

ICRC activities in Tajikistan included the following:

• Visits to 110 detainees held by the Tajik opposition, with arrangements for them to exchange messages with their families

• Nutritional rehabilitation for 5,500 detainees in Tajik prisons (240,000 vitamin tablets, medicines, 165 tons of flour, 10 tons of oil, 113 tons of beans and rice, 2,196 food parcels, 113 tons of high-energy biscuits and milk, 1,347 pairs of shoes, 4,357 blankets)

• Food, plastic sheets, stoves, and fuel for 30,000 people affected by the conflict

• Medical supplies for eight hospitals and six first-aid facilities caring for government and rebel soldiers

• Evacuation of thirty-five amputees to Baku to be fitted with artificial limbs at the ICRC's prosthetic center there

• Seminars and dissemination of printed materials and videotapes on the law of war for officers and soldiers, military academies, the Tajik Institute for Management and Service, the State Medical University, and the Red Crescent Society

ICRC expenditures for Tajikistan in 1996 amounted to just over $17 million—not much compared to outlays for war or even for peacekeeping. Two-thirds went for relief; the rest for protection, tracing of relatives, health, dissemination of information, operational support, and overhead (5 percent). WHO teams also worked in Tajikistan trying to control outbreaks of typhoid fever and malaria.

used refugee camps in Zaire as bases for military raids back into Rwanda.

Complex humanitarian emergencies renewed old questions for the International Committee of the Red Cross (ICRC).[31] Its leaders wondered: If Red Cross workers made war less painful, would this cause more war? Should they ignore politics and act as though each side deserves assistance? Should they welcome or spurn the security that UN or other outside forces could give relief workers?

These questions came to a head in February 1997, when two ICRC aid workers were among sixteen hostages taken by rebels in Tajikistan's civil war. The other hostages included two UN military observers, four workers for the UN High Commissioner for Refugees, five Russian and Tajik journalists, and a translator. The rebel leader abducted the hostages to press the Tajik government for safe passage so a guerrilla force led by his brother could return from Afghanistan.

Responding to the abductions, the ICRC suspended its activities in Tajikistan and evacuated most of its foreign staff to Uzbekistan. The UN told most of its workers to stay indoors. Tajik President Imamali Rakhmanov met with his own security officials, the Russian ambassador, the head of the Red Cross mission, and a UN envoy. Rakhmanov's government, dominated by former Communists, was fighting a coalition of Islamic and nationalist forces. The ICRC tried to give aid to both sides, but neither the Tajik government nor the rebels saw the ICRC as a neutral intermediary.

31. The ICRC was founded in 1864 to provide humanitarian aid in wartime. To assure its neutrality, the committee's twenty-five members are all Swiss nationals. It works with national committees of the Red Cross and Red Crescent throughout the world.

Nothing was easy. ICRC relief convoys took back roads into rebel-controlled territories. One route wove 2,500 kilometers along the borders of neighboring Uzbekistan and Kyrgyzstan at up to 4,300 kilometers above sea level, on extremely poor roads, obstructed by military checkpoints manned by the government, the opposition, and CIS border guards.[32] Was the Red Cross in the forefront of a new world order, or did it wage a futile struggle amid growing chaos?

32. *ICRC Annual Report 1996* (Geneva: International Committee of the Red Cross, 1997), 219–223.

Europe: from Functionalism to Supranationalism? *Back in Brussels, the German diplomat leaves his French colleague and strolls back to his flat. Their discussion raised more questions than answers. Yes, Europeans resent the American "hyperpower"—especially in its bullying mode—but should they strive to become a "United States of Europe"? For now, Europeans get a nearly free ride in security matters. Americans pay two or three times more per capita for defense than Europeans. Even if they tried, could Europeans ever form a unified state able to act with one voice? Our histories and diverse languages keep us nation-states. Even now we must have interpreters in Brussels able to translate not just from German to French but from German to Portuguese and all the other official languages of the EU. After the next wave of expansion, we will need interpreters able to go from German to Estonian and from Estonian to Lithuanian and from Lithuanian into French and Portuguese. Of course we should agree on a single official language, but the French would never accept English. And if we make French and German official along with English, the Italians and Spanish will protest. Are we not destined to remain a Tower of Babel?*

So far we have given up very little power to the central organs of the EU. The total EU budget is only 100 billion euros. The European Monetary Union is a straitjacket. At Germany's insistence, all participants must keep their debt levels below 3 percent of their gross domestic product (GDP) and balance their budgets by 2006. In 2002, however, Germany, France, and Italy all breached this debt ceiling. In January 2003, the EU Commissioner for Economic and Monetary Affairs, Pedro Solbes, scolded all three and warned Germany it could be fined if it did not conform within four months. Señor Solbes noted that George W. Bush could push the U.S. budget from surplus (1.5 percent of GDP) into deficit (3.5 percent of GDP) without having to consult eleven other countries, as those sharing the euro as their common currency must do. Bush did not have to uphold a stability pact that caps deficit spending.

Germany's economic doldrums were worsened by the European Central Bank's benchmark interest rate, which it reduced to 2.75 percent in November 2002. This rate might be good for the twelve euro nations as a whole but was probably too high to stimulate growth in Germany. In short, all these rules prevented the German government from priming the pump as needed to stimulate the economy.

What should Berlin do in the long run? Should it strive to dominate, lead, or pull up the rest of Europe? And what is the rationale for EU enlargement? We must be careful not to ruin a rather fit organism by expanding beyond its natural limits. We already have sharply different views within the EU as well as eleven official languages. As we take in more members, it will be even harder to make decisions. We could adapt the UN Security-Council model and have a Big Five with veto power. But the other EU members would never go along.

Expansion brings problems. Portugal and Greece were and still are much poorer than the core EU members. If we take in Poland and nine other Eastern European states in 2004, each will present its own bundle of issues to be resolved. Where do we stop? Bulgaria and Romania are not only poorer but quite distant, from the core. Turkey is poorer still, even more distant; and burdened with a poor record on human rights. On the other hand, Ankara tries to meet EU standards and Turkey is a long-standing member of NATO.

The more countries we admit from Southern and Eastern Europe, the more that Germany and other rich countries will be flooded by "economic" migrants and disgruntled minorities such as Roma. Yes, we need more young people—manual laborers as well as engineers. But Western Europe is not the United States. When will we install an ethnic Turk, born in Germany, as our foreign minister? When will the French elect the offspring of an Algerian or Senegalese mullah as mayor of Marseilles?

Perhaps Europe should expand gradually, testing and then filling its natural boundaries. Its expansion so far has been well planned and implemented—moving from a few core states to wider circles of states on their periphery.

Visions and Realities of a Uniting Europe

Images of a united Europe inspired visionaries for centuries, but made little progress until after World War II. Four factors contributed to European unity in the late 1940s–early 1950s: revulsion against war, fear of Soviet expansion, payoffs from the Marshall Plan for European recovery, plus a desire to counterbalance U.S. power.

As the Marshall Plan wound down, six of its leading participants— France, Germany, Italy, Belgium, the Netherlands, and Luxembourg ("the Six")—established in 1951 the **European Coal and Steel Community (ECSC)** to coordinate production and sales of coal and steel. This organization became, overnight, the world's closest approximation to a supranational organization. The Six empowered the ECSC High Authority to issue regulations binding on individuals and firms and to collect taxes directly from governments. But the ECSC had no coercive power to implement its decisions.

Jean Monnet, first director of the ECSC, sought to build on its momentum to expand European integration. He wanted to make low politics work for high politics. His neofunctional approach scored a quick victory. The six ECSC states in 1957 signed the **Treaty of Rome**, establishing the **European Economic Community (EEC)**. The EEC aimed to create a customs union—a single economic region in which goods, services, people, and capital could move as freely as they do within national borders. The Six also established the **European Atomic Energy Community (EURATOM)**.

The EEC became simply the EC—European Community—as its functions went beyond economics. By 1986 the original six members had become "the Twelve" with the addition of the UK, Denmark, and Ireland (1973); Greece (1981); and Portugal and Spain (1986). The Twelve in 1987 agreed to a package of laws known as the **Single European Act (SEA)**, which obliged them to create by 1992 a European market without internal barriers or discrimination and gave new powers to the **European Parliament** (see sidebar). Under the act, most decisions could be taken by a simple majority rather than by unanimity, as before. Buoyed by "Europhoria," many members also looked forward to a **European Monetary Union (EMU)**.

In 1993, the EC became the "first pillar" of the European Union. The EU included the EC and two other pillars: one for forging a common

How the European Union Functions

Think of EU governance as "bureaucracy tempered by diplomacy." The European Commission is the EU executive—the only EU body with the right of initiative—the right to propose new laws. It works with member states to implement and enforce EU policy and laws. It represents the EU in international trade negotiations. "Guardian of the treaties," it upholds the interests of the EU as a whole and warns members if they are violating their obligations to the union. With one or two commissioners from every member state, the executive expanded to 20 commissioners in 1995.

Policies drafted by the Commission must be agreed to by the European Parliament and then approved by the **European Council of Ministers** (chaired by rotation, each country having a six-month term).

The European Parliament (625 members in 1999–2004) serves for five years and is the only EC body directly elected. It scrutinizes draft EU legislation, questions the Commission and Council of Ministers on their work, and debates topical issues. Since the parliament is an advisory body rather than a true legislature, critics say that the entire EU apparatus lacks democratic accountability. The **European Court of Justice** interprets EU acts and treaties and supports EU law over local laws of member states.

These four institutions take guidance from semi-annual summit meetings of Europe's heads of government—the **Council of the EU**.

Three EU institutions have some supranational competence: the European Commission, the European Parliament, and the European Court of Justice. But both the Council of Ministers and Council of the EU are intergovernmental.

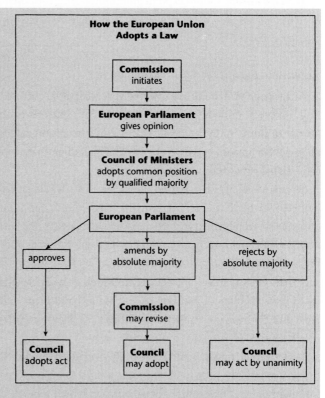

How the European Union Adopts a Law

Commission initiates → European Parliament gives opinion → Council of Ministers adopts common position by qualified majority → European Parliament

- approves → Council adopts act
- amends by absolute majority → Commission may revise → Council may adopt
- rejects by absolute majority → Council may act by unanimity

Dubya Does Europe

ON THE OTHER HAND, HE'S DONE WONDERS FOR EUROPEAN UNITY...

BUSH IS WRONG!

TRADE
DEATH PENALTY
KYOTO TREATY
STAR WARS

6.11.2001
DANZIGER
TRIBUNE MEDIA www.danzigercartoons.com

The Bush administration helped unite Europeans: Most disliked American unilateralism. For more than half a century the U.S. had led NATO with minimal offense to the sensitivities of its medium and lesser powers. But the Bush team opened a gulf. Europeans were dismayed by the administration's brusque rejection of the Kyoto Protocol, the AMB Treaty, and other agreements. Many Europeans regarded the death penalty as barbaric, and some knew it was widely used in Bush's home state. France and Germany strongly opposed the U.S.–UK war on Iraq. Secretary of Defense Donald Rumsfeld pointed to similarities in the positions of Germany, Cuba, and Libya.

foreign policy and another for overseeing justice and home affairs. Unlike NAFTA (North American Free Trade Agreement) and other regional trade organizations, the EU makes trade policies for all its members. To simplify, from 1993 on, we speak of the EU even though its first pillar is the EC.

In the early 21st century, the EU was not yet a "supranational" authority or superstate. It was more like an "international regime" or "international organization."[33] Member states retained more sovereignty than they surrendered.

Still, the EU embodied a process of supranational decision making—a network of pooled sovereignty. Each unit in the network had strong incentives to interact with other units in the group rather than with outsiders. Common norms were emerging. The process depended on intergovernmental bargains. Each country remained basically sovereign, but there was a "cumulative pattern of accommodation in which the participants refrain from unconditionally vetoing proposals and instead seek to attain agreement by compromises upgrading common interests."[34]

Functionalists looked at these trends and pointed to the influence of transnational interest groups, supranational officials, logrolling to exchange favors (as in the U.S. Congress), and spill-over effects. They saw EC institutions as independent forces shaping national preferences.

In contrast to functionalists, the school of **intergovernmentalists** stressed the residual power of governments in the EU. It pointed out that individual governments retained sovereignty in most domains and stayed aloof from any all-European endeavors they disliked. Agreements to tighten common institutions resulted from negotiations dominated by the most powerful states—Germany, France, and Britain—each constrained

33. See Robert O. Keohane and Stanley Hoffmann, "Institutional Change in Europe in the 1980s," in *The New European Community: Decision-making and Institutional Change*, ed. Robert O. Keohane and Stanley Hoffmann (Boulder, Colo.: Westview, 1991), 1–39 at 10, 15–17.

34. Ernst B. Haas, "Technocracy, Pluralism and the New Europe," in *A New Europe?* ed. Stephen R. Graubard (Boston: Houghton–Mifflin, 1964), 64, 66.

by strong internal opposition to European integration.[35] Meanwhile, Europe had no shared vision. And one of the best-kept secrets in Brussels was that most "EU" decisions were settled informally in the shadowy Committee of Permanent Representatives before they ever reached ministers.[36]

How Far Can Europe Unite?

Many European businesspeople welcomed the euro, the single European currency accepted by most of continental Europe in 2002. The euro could integrate an all-European economy operating on a continental scale like the United States. With the euro, shoppers and sellers could compare prices more readily.

A more integrated European economy could encourage mobility of labor and production, thereby weakening existing governments. If companies did not like the taxes or other conditions in State *A*, they could more easily move to State *B*. Companies that adapted to the new environment could benefit while others, slow to change, perhaps could not.

But national loyalties remained. Firms linked to particular countries (for example, Sweden and France) continued to compete against one another for defense contracts.[37] Conflicts could arise from efforts by a European central bank to impose a common fiscal discipline. But what if some countries suffered unemployment and wanted fiscal policies that stimulated production while other countries focused on curbing inflation? Like the U.S. Constitution, the European Monetary Union has no provision allowing disaffected units to secede. If Italy wished to pull out of the EMU, might it have to throw down a gauntlet, as South Carolina did before the U.S. federal government in 1861?[38]

Europe led the world in regional integration, but many obstacles blocked unity in the early 21st century. They arose from different languages, cultures, levels of economic development, and geography. Cosmopolitan elites speaking English felt at home anywhere; most people spoke only their own tongue and felt at home only at home. But there were eleven official languages in 2002—a number soon to be increased.

In 2002, the EU invited ten countries to join in 2004—Cyprus and Malta plus eight from Eastern Europe: Poland, Hungary, the Czech Republic, Estonia, Latvia, Lithuania, Slovakia, and Slovenia. Two weaker candidates, Bulgaria and Romania, were not given invitations but were encouraged to pursue their applications, with prospective joining dates in 2007. The 13th candidate, Turkey, was offered negotiations beginning in 2005 but only if it met human rights and other criteria.

Eneko Landaburu, head of the European Commission's team dealing with enlargement, stated in December 2002 that negotiations with

35. See Mark A. Pollack, "Delegation, Agency, and Agenda Setting in the European Community," *International Organization* 51, no. 1 (winter 1997): 99–134; and Lee Ann Patterson, "Agricultural Policy Reform in the European Community: A Three-Level Game Analysis," ibid., 135–165.

36. Lionel Barber, "Search for One Voice," *Financial Times*, October 30, 1997, 14, an essay prompted by the book of Belgium's retiring permanent representative, Philippe de Schoutheete, *Une Europe pour tous* (Paris: Odile Jacob, 1997).

37. Europeans created two new organizations in the late 1990s to integrate their defense market and procurement, but most European countries favored their own industries. If they shopped abroad, the UK and the Netherlands often bought U.S. weapons, but France preferred to find European suppliers. See U.S. General Accounting Office, *Defense Trade: European Initiatives to Integrate the Defense Market*, GAO/NSIAD-98-6 (Washington, D.C.: Government Printing Office, October 1997).

38. See Martin Feldstein, "EMU and International Conflict," *Foreign Affairs* 76, no. 6 (November/December 1997): 60–73.

Map 14.1 European Union Expansion

Existing members (15 in 2002)

States included in 2002 EU "New Neighbors Initiative"

Potential New Members

Ten states formally invited in 2002 for future membership and expected to sign accession agreements in 2004 (includes Malta and Cyprus)

Two states encouraged to pursue applications, with prospective joining dates in 2007

13th candidate state, Turkey, offered negotiations beginning in 2005 if it meets human rights and other criteria

Turkey, a mostly Muslim country of nearly 70 million, would likely last many years. He pointed out that Spain had negotiated with the EU for seven years before it was invited to join; Poland and the other Eastern European countries, four years. Perhaps Bulgaria and Romania could join by 2007. By 2002, Bulgaria had completed talks on twenty-three of the thirty "chapters," or policy areas, where all candidates were required to bring domestic laws and regulations into line with those of the EU. Romania, less advanced, had closed only 16 chapters. Turkey was much further from meeting EU standards than any of these countries. The EU reserved the right to impose safeguards against new members for three years after accession to protect the bloc's internal market. For example, the EU might block food exports from a country that failed to live up to EU standards on food hygiene.

The future of Cyprus was also unclear, because in 2002 the island was still partitioned. Absent a settlement between the Greek Cypriot and Turkish Cypriot communities before 2004, it seemed likely that only the Greek-speaking part would be integrated into EU structures. Turkish Cypriot leader Rauf Denktash smelled a Greek conspiracy to block Turkey's accession to the EU and turn Cyprus into a "Christian fortress around Turkey."

Where does Europe end? In late 2002, the EU endorsed a Danish plan for a "New Neighbors Initiative" focused on Ukraine, Moldova, and Belarus. It called for steps to help these countries to stabilize their economies and develop their democracies. The initiative also looked forward to closer association with the other countries that comprised the former Yugoslavia. If the EU ever decided to admit Ukraine, however, this would antagonize Moscow unless Russia too were admitted. Apart from all the other differences, Russia's sheer size would distort the EU beyond recognition and make decision making even more difficult. The governments of all ten countries invited to accede had worked for years to bring their own laws and practices into conformity with EU standards. All wished to be part of the West—culturally, economically, and politically. They also viewed membership in the EU, like NATO, as protection against Russian domination. As part of the accession deal, the East Europeans negotiated a package of EU trade concessions and assurances of financial assistance. But Eastern Europe's farmers would receive subsidies only one-fourth as generous as those received by present EU farmers. In 2000 and 2001, EU funds for Eastern Europe ("PHARE") were about $1.6 billion. Besides these funds, the EU budget set aside $4 billion in 2002 to facilitate the accession of the Eastern European countries. These outlays were expected to rise to $15 billion by 2006.

Despite the 2002 invitations, the ten candidate countries still had to pass two hurdles—approval by the parliaments of all fifteen present EU states; and second, approval by a referendum of their own citizens, many of whom did not understand or agree with their government's reasons for joining the EU. Some Balts, for example, asked why they should join another "union" so soon after leaving the much despised Soviet "Union."

Other European Organizations

The economic integration of Europe depended first of all on peace—within the region and between Europe and the outside world. Both goals were supposed to be served by more than a dozen overlapping and interlocking organizations, pictured in Figure 14.4. Let us review briefly how the main units originated and their status early in the 21st century.[39]

The North Atlantic Treaty Organization or NATO

A military alliance founded in 1949, NATO was established to deter and resist a westward march by Soviet forces. It became one of the most successful multilateral alliances of all time. As some diplomats liked to say, "NATO kept the Russians out, the Americans in, and the Germans down." U.S. forces were still in Europe more than half a century after World War II while Germany, reunited in 1990, was a solid member of the European and transatlantic community. After Spain joined in 1982, NATO had sixteen member states. Russian troops withdrew from the former East Germany and most of Eastern Europe in the early 1990s and lost their erstwhile capacity for a Blitzkrieg against the West.

A step ahead of the EU, NATO expanded to the east and south at the turn of the century. In 1999 NATO admitted three former Soviet allies—Poland, Hungary, and the Czech Republic. Many analysts warned that NATO's expansion could provoke a strong Russian backlash and suggested other ways to bolster European security.[40] But the Kremlin protested only mildly when NATO in 2002 took in not just three more former Soviet allies (Slovakia, Bulgaria, and Romania) but also three former Soviet "union-republics" (Estonia, Latvia, and Lithuania) as well as former Yugoslav republic, now independent, Slovenia. The Kremlin had been somewhat mollified by its ever larger consultative role in NATO and by President Putin's buddy–buddy relationship with President Bush after 9/11.

The Bush team had little use for the UN or even for NATO. Many analysts had expected NATO to shrivel after the demise of the long-feared Soviet Union. Still, the alliance took in new members and, in 1999, waged its first war—against Serbia over Kosovo. From that point on, however, NATO withered. To be sure, the alliance declared the 9/11 attacks on the U.S. an attack on all NATO members, but America did not want its war against the Taliban to be complicated by the NATO command structure, as happened in Kosovo. Furthermore, most NATO members did not have the long reach needed to attack Afghanistan. So Washington fought most of its war against the Taliban with little help

39. For further discussion, see Strobe Talbott,"From Prague to Baghdad: NATO at Risk," *Foreign Affairs* 81, 6 (November/December 2002), 46–57; also Celeste A. Wallander, "NATO's Price: Shape Up or Ship Out," ibid., 2–8, and the dour appraisal by Daniel Treisman, "Russia Renewed?" ibid., 58–72.

40. Walter C. Clemens, Jr., "An Alternative to NATO Expansion," *International Journal* 52, no. 2 (spring 1997): 342–365.

Fig. 14.4 Membership in Selected European and Transatlantic Groupings in 2003: Who Belongs to What?

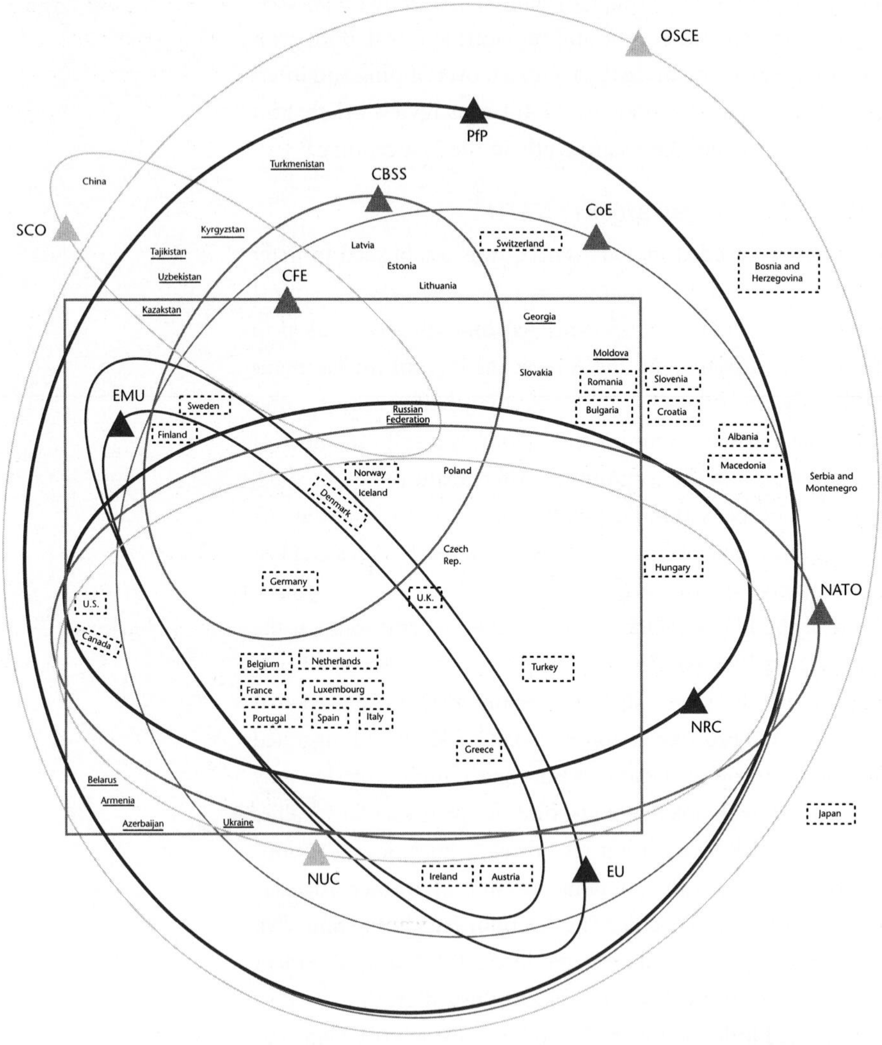

CBSS   10-nation cooperation for security, economic, and environmental goals in the Baltic region

CFE   Conventional Forces in Europe Treaty (discussed in chapter 6)

CoE   Council of Europe

CIS   Commonwealth of Independent States, 12 former Soviet republics, indicated here by an underline, e.g., Belarus.

EMU   European Monetary Union (eurozone): all EU except UK, Sweden, Denmark

EU   European Union

NATO   North American Treaty Organization

NRC   NATO-RF Council for consultation between NATO and RF

NUC   NATO-Ukraine Commission similiar to NRC

OSCE   Organization for Security and Cooperation in Europe

PfP   Partnership for Peace includes most of OSCE in training and rescue missions, sponsored by NATO

SCO   Shanghai Cooperation Organization, six nation consultations, initiated by China, to resolve border disputes, resist U.S. domination, and counter Islamic radicalism

Stability Pact for South Eastern Europe initiated by EU, includes dozens of states and IGOs dedicated to stability, democracy, and economic prosperity in the Balkans. Members designated by a dotted box, e.g. Austria

Sources: Public Affairs Office, CIA; *Foreign Affairs;* http://www.cia.gov/cia/publications/factbook/

Rise of New Europe in Euro Pop

While eurocrats shuffle papers in Brussels, the annual *Eurovision Song Contest* permits Europeans to hear and see performers from more than two dozen countries—from the UK to Malta and Israel. Euro-sophisticates mock *Eurovision* for its schmaltz, but this is Europe's oldest continuously running TV program. Initiated in 1956, it brought the Swedish group Abba to the world in 1974. In the early 21st century some 150 million TV viewers watched and voted for winners by phoning their choices via special hot lines.

"Globalization comes to a screeching halt when it approaches the borders of Euro pop," observed *The New York Times*.

An Estonian group won first prize in 2001; a Latvian singer (of Russian descent) won in 2002: but the 2003 winner came from still further east—Turkey. A year before Donald Rumsfeld praised the "new Europe" (after Paris and Berlin turned against Washington), a Belgian viewer told the BBC: "There's a new Baltic dynasty. They have the chance to impose their own musical tastes on the continent. We're witnessing the start of a seismic shift in Europop tectonics."

Known as Latvia's ``favorite Russian,'' Marija Naumova won in the 2002 contest, held in Tallinn, singing a Russian song, "I Wanna," in English with a Latin beat. Many Russians in Latvia do not know Latvian, but Marija (a lawyer by training) speaks flawless Latvian and also sings in Estonian, Russian, French, and English. Driving back to Riga from Tallinn in a motorcade fit for a queen, Naumova was welcomed by the Latvian PM (A specialist on folk music) and 5,000 well-wishers. A Latvian newspaper enthused: "Forget forestry and shipping. Now we will be known for our music and as a site for tourism."

The years since the fall of the Soviet empire had been good for the Baltic republics. To be sure, many in the old Europe and the U.S. did not know where they were. (``Are the Baltics different from the Balkans?'' some asked.) But Estonia, Latvia, and Lithuania were the only former Soviet republics invited to join NATO or the EU. To be sure, their numbers were small: Only 1 million people spoke Estonian; 2 million, Latvian, and just over 3 million, Lithuanian. But Balts won more medals per capita than any other countries in recent Olympics. The Baltic nations had been repressed longer and more intensively than any other peoples in Europe. But now they stood squarely where they felt they belonged—in the new Europe and the world-at-large.

While the Baltic republics were admitted to the EU in 2002, Turkey was kept waiting. But Sertab Erener, the Turkish diva, may have moved her country a few steps closer to the EU. She beat all comers at *Eurovision 2003*, including a pair of Russian girls who had been favored, by singing ``Every Way That I Can,'' an exotic belly-dancing tune, in English. The homeland of English and the Beatles, however, placed last in 2003.

except from the UK. When Washington and London wanted to attack Iraq, they got only criticism from Paris and Berlin—which Defense Secretary Donald Rumsfeld wrote off as "old Europe." He liked the "new Europe"—former Communist countries, stretching from Estonia to Bulgaria, that endorsed the war against Saddam. To be sure, the former Soviet clients contributed little, except for Poland, which offered postwar security forces in Iraq. But neither did they interfere.

Meanwhile, "old Europe" had no common security and defense policy. The biggest countries in Europe were unwilling to invest in force modernization. The overall quality of NATO forces could diminish further as Eastern European forces, poorly equipped and funded, were added. Bigger was not necessarily better.

The Bush administration liked having a free hand. It looked content to enlist a "coalition of the willing" for whatever operations it chose to mount. As we see in the next chapter, it rejected and even sought to undermine the International Criminal Court, and it did nothing to restore U.S. acceptance of the compulsory jurisdiction of the **International Court of Justice**, jettisoned in the 1980s by the Reagan administration. As we see in Figure 14.2, the ICJ is one of the six principal organs of the UN.

The Organization for Security and Cooperation in Europe

More than fifty countries—all NATO partners, all of Europe, and all successor states to the USSR—belonged to the **OSCE**. This organization evolved from the "Helsinki Process" launched in the mid-1970s to promote East–West cooperation on security, trade, and human rights issues. Periodic meetings reviewed the state of human rights in both East and West—a revolutionary development that weakened authoritarian rule in the Soviet sphere. The Kremlin in the 1990s wanted the OSCE to supplant NATO, but Western governments deemed the OSCE too large and unwieldy. Its decisions required unanimity—leaving Russia and all other members with a veto.

The Partnership for Peace (PfP)

Originally conceived in the early 1990s as a stepping-stone to NATO membership for former Communist states, the **PfP** included most OSCE members except for the warring South Slavs, Ireland (jealous of its neutrality); Tajikistan (torn by civil war); and mini-states such as the Vatican. The PfP conducted training exercises that brought NATO forces together with those of the eastern countries for peacekeeping and rescue operations. But the PfP also demonstrated that U.S. and other NATO forces could operate not only in the Baltic and the Black Sea (Russia's soft underbelly) but even in Kazakstan.

The Commonwealth of Independent States (CIS)

The **CIS** was meant to promote security and economic cooperation among the Soviet union-republics that became independent in 1991—what Moscow referred to as the "near abroad." But three stayed away—Estonia, Latvia, and Lithuania. Azerbaijan and Georgia kept their distance but finally joined—making a commonwealth of twelve independent states. By the mid-1990s, however, Moscow's heavy hand alienated every other member. In 1997 Ukraine began to align with Kazakstan against Russia. Washington backed Kazaks and others against bullying by Moscow. Having failed in most of its security and economic objectives, the CIS lost its raison d'être in the early 21st century.

Nobody was imposing a supranational government on Europe. The region was riddled by deep divisions. By comparison with most of the world, however, Europe and North America were oases of calm. Viewed in tandem with Japan and a few other Pacific rim countries, they constituted a trilateral zone of stability, peace, and cooperation. A century hence, other regions might well be integrating along the lines of the EU and NAFTA. But it was unclear what model, if any, would prevail—one world or a planet divided by regions, income, faith, or pigmentation.

WHAT PROPOSITIONS HOLD?
WHAT QUESTIONS REMAIN?

HOPE OR DESPAIR?

IO helps meet human needs that local communities and nation-states cannot manage. A wide variety of international and transnational organizations help people to cope with the dangers and opportunities inherent in interdependence and globalization.

Does the growth of IO give reason for despair or for hope? One perspective says the glass is half empty; the other, that it is half full. Realists say that IO is merely another instrument in the struggle for power: Hard-liners will manipulate the Red Cross and other nonstate actors as tools or obstacles to their goals. The realist asks: "Should we use or avoid IO to enhance our power?"

Idealists take hope from the growth of international law and organization. They work to ground IR in law and morality. They ask: "How can we use or reform IO to achieve our ideals?"

Students of interdependence perceive a shared vulnerability among IR actors that permits both pain and gain. They see global trends that contain a potential for disaster, but also for greater security, prosperity, justice, and environmental well-being. They ask: "How can we improve IO to generate values for all parties?"

INTERNATIONAL ORGANIZATION
AS AN EMERGENT FORCE

Prosperity in the 19th and 20th centuries depended on IOs that helped to regulate commerce and technology and expand markets. Human life became more complicated, more intertwined, and mutually dependent. Survival in the 21st century may depend upon IOs that protect the environment and prevent wars in which weapons of mass destruction might be used.

"Monsanto, Out of Our Food" was the message on a banner erected by Greenpeace activists on Monsanto offices in Brazil in January 2003. The banner aimed to protest bioengineered foods and was inspired by the World Social Forum meeting in Porto Alegre. The forum met annually to counter the generally proglobalization message of the World Economic Forum, usually held in Davos, Switzerland.

People and ideas, of course, could not be easily pigeonholed. Economist Jeffrey Sachs helped write some Davos reports, but he also worked for the World Health Organization and pressed the U.S. and other governments to do more for LDCs.

Governments cannot meet all the needs of modern societies. They delegate, encourage, or permit other actors to pick up and carry on a wide assortment of tasks. Governments have grown accustomed to a range of other actors operating at their side—or even against them—in the world arena.

Everything has increased—world population, the number of states, and the work of IGOs and NGOs. Why? The efflorescence of nonstate actors in the 20th century resulted from and contributed to globalization. The complex network of IGOs and NGOs can be seen as an **emergent structure** far more than the sum of its parts—the product of coevolution as diverse actors meet their diverse needs. Like a coral reef that sustains and shelters many life forms, IO has evolved and expanded to protect and help people actualize their potential. A coral reef represents "order for free," because it takes shape spontaneously, without planning. Most components of IO, by contrast, represent human intelligence and volition. The total emergent structure of IO, however, is also "order for free." No one foresaw or planned how its many components would come together.

Like sea anenomes and fish, some IOs do not survive—do not fit with changing conditions. Others, such as the IMF and World Bank, have repeatedly reinvented themselves to promote the goals of their leading members and to meet the needs of developing countries. Governments have tried to guard their sovereign rights against the expanding competencies of IGOs and NGOs. Also, some NGOs and IGOs have seen each other as rivals. Experience shows, however, that there is room—perhaps a need—for diverse organizations to meet the multiplicity of human needs. Governments, IGOs, and NGOs have learned to work together in many fields, from women's rights to environmental protection to security.

A top-down approach to world government is not feasible. Governments are not about to sign a treaty transferring authority to a supranational institution. Not even the EU has forged a common foreign or defense policy. How then can still more distant civilizations generate a unified government? And if they did, Juvenal's old question still looms: *Quis custodiet ipsos custodes*—"Who shall guard the guardians?"

Collective security has worked rather well twice and could succeed again, but only if a great power spearheads the effort and no other great power objects.

Peacekeeping can be useful if the disputants consent—the costs are trivial relative to dislocations of war. It can help or weaken solidarity among units from different countries.

To impose peace on parties that still wish to engage in conflict requires a very strong force and a long-term commitment. In principle, a strong UN or NATO coalition should be able to subdue poorly equipped guerrillas. In many instances, however, results were disappointing. Outsiders may halt local violence; to remove its deep roots is much harder. And if outsiders succeed in one place, must they extinguish fires everywhere?

Should You Start Your Own Nonstate Actor? .... *Can a handful of pragmatic idealists succeed in founding a University of the Middle East, where people from diverse backgrounds study how to coexist and develop for mutual gain? The obstacles are formidable. Mounting tensions between Israel and its neighbors are whipped by fear, myopia, greed, cultural differences, have and have-not economies, and radical asymmetries of power—all flayed by entrepreneurs of hate and violence.*

But huge obstacles have been overcome by other individuals and NGOs. Despite the Cold War, Soviet and Western scientists founded the Pugwash Conferences on Science and World Affairs; later, Soviet and U.S. doctors formed International Physicians for Prevention of Nuclear War. Costa Rican President Oscar Arias Sanchez helped mobilize other Latin leaders to press for peace in Central America.[41] Despite U.S.–PRC tensions, the son of Chinese President Jiang Zemin studied at Drexel University and obtained a doctorate. An "American University" has long functioned in Egypt and in Lebanon (though a similar institution was taken over by the Turkish government); another was planned for Kuwait.

The spirit of the times is on your side. Nonstate actors are getting stronger and filling more niches of human need. Education and peace are prerequisites for development. Politics between governments may not suffice to end the wasteful violence that besets the Middle East. Money will be a problem, but some potential financiers may welcome your effort to replace hate and war with sanity and amity.

Get to yes. Show that you can create values for mutual gain. Join the growing emergent structure of private and public organizations whose pooled efforts help all humanity to live safer and more fulfilling lives. Your success is not assured, perhaps not even likely, but it is worth seeking.

---

41. The Nobel Peace Prize was awarded to the IPPNW in 1985, to Arias in 1987, and to the Pugwash Movement in 1995. Other Nobel laureates mentioned in this chapter were the International Red Cross (1917, 1944, 1963), Frank Kellogg (1929), George C. Marshall (1953), the UN High Commissioner for Refugees (1954, 1981), Dag Hammarskjöld (1961), UNICEF (1965), Anwar Sadat and Menachem Begin (1978), Mother Teresa (1979), Elie Wiesel (1986), UN Peacekeeping Forces (1988), Mikhail Gorbachev (1990), the International Campaign to Ban Land Mines (1997), Doctors Without Borders (1999), the UN and Kofi Annan (2000), Jimmy Carter (2002), and Shirin Ebadi (2003). For a complete list, see www.nobel.no/index.html.

KEY NAMES AND TERMS

Bush Doctrine	European Court of Justice	nonstate actor
Commonwealth of Independent States (CIS)	European Economic Community (EEC)	Organization for Security and Cooperation in Europe (OSCE)
complex humanitarian emergency	European Monetary Union (EMU)	Partnership for Peace (PfP)
emergent structure	European Parliament	Single European Act (SEA)
euro	European Union (EU)	Stimson Doctrine
European Atomic Energy Community (EURATOM)	functionalism	supranational authority
	intergovernmentalists	Treaty of Rome (1957)
European Coal and Steel Community (ECSC)	International Committee of the Red Cross (ICRC)	UN General Assembly
European Commission	International Court of Justice (ICJ)	UN Security Council
European Council	international organization (IO)	Uniting for Peace Resolution
European Council of Ministers	neofunctionalism	veto
		World Health Organization (WHO)

QUESTIONS TO DISCUSS

1. What have been the driving forces behind IO? How are they likely to evolve in the 21st century?
2. How did the Stimson Doctrine differ from previous international practice? Did it do any good? How did it relate to collective security?
3. To what extent did UN policy toward North Korean and Iraqi expansion represent collective security?
4. Review the record: What have been the successes and failures of UN peacekeeping efforts? Has the cost been justified?
5. Is Europe uniting as a result of supranationalism or functionalism, or both? What are the obstacles to further union?
6. Has IO done anything for human welfare? Assess the work of the WHO.
7. Consider the role of the ICRC in complex humanitarian emergencies. Should it continue its work? What reforms would you suggest?
8. Do you perceive an emergent structure of IO? If so, is this good or bad?
9. Review the of Nobel Peace Laureates mentioned in this chapter and elsewhere in the book. Evaluate what they did for peace. Given what we now know, did they deserve the prize? Why or why not?

RECOMMENDED RESOURCES

BOOKS

Aall, Pamela R., et al. *Guide to IGOs, NGOs, and the Military in Peace and Relief Operations.* Washington, D.C., United States Institute of Peace, 2000.

Beck, Robert J., et al., eds. *International Rules: Approaches from International Law and International Relations.* New York: Oxford University Press, 1996.

Boutros-Ghali, Boutros. *Building Peace and Development 1994.* New York: United Nations, 1994.

Claude, Inis L. *Swords into Plowshares: The Problems and Progress of International Organization.* 4th ed. New York: Random House, 1984.

Crocker, Chester A., et al., eds. *Turbulent Peace: The Challenges of Managing International Conflict.* Washington, D.C.: United States Institute of Peace, 2001.

Durch, William J., ed. *The Evolution of UN Peacekeeping: Case Studies and Comparative Analysis.* New York: St. Martin's, 1993.

Esman, Milton J., and Shibley Telhami, eds. *International Organization and Ethnic Conflict.* Ithaca, N.Y.: Cornell University Press, 1995.

Fleitz, Frederick H., Jr. *Peacekeeping Fiascoes of the 1990s: Causes, Solutions, and U.S. Interests.* Westport, Conn.: Praeger Publishing, 2002.

Haas, Ernst B. *The Uniting of Europe: Political, Social and Economic Forces, 1950–1957.* Stanford, Calif.: Stanford University Press, 1958.

Hunter, Robert E., and Donna Farley. *The European Security and Defense Policy: NATO's Companion or Competitor?* Santa Monica, Calif.: RAND Corporation, 2002.

Iriye, Akira. *Global Community: The Role of International Organizations in the Making of the Contemporary World.* Berkeley: University of California Press, 2002.

Jacobson, Harold K. *Networks of Interdependence: International Organizations and the Global Political System.* 2d ed. New York: Knopf, 1984.

Keohane, Robert O., and Stanley Hoffmann, eds. *The New European Community.* Boulder, Colo.: Westview, 1991.

Lederach, John Paul, and Jenner, Janice M., eds. *A Handbook of International Peacebuilding: Into the Eve of the Storm.* San Francisco: Jossey-Bass, 2002.

Lopez, George A., and Nancy J. Myers, eds. *Peace and Security. The Next Generation.* Lanham, Md.: Rowman & Littlefield, 1997.

McCormick, John. *Understanding the European Union: A Concise Introduction,* 2d ed. New York: Palgrave, 2002.

Minear, Larry, and Thomas G. Weiss. *Mercy Under Fire: War and the Global Humanitarian Community.* Boulder, Colo.: Westview, 1995.

Mingst, Karen A., and Margaret P. Karns. *The United Nations in the Post–Cold War Era.* 2d ed. Boulder, Colo.: Westview, 2003.

Oneal, John R., and Bruce M. Russett. *Triangulating Peace: Democracy, Interdependence, and International Organizations.* New York: W. W. Norton, 2001.

Otunnu, Olara A., and Michael W. Doyle, eds. *Peacemaking and Peacekeeping for the Next Century.* Lanham, Md.: Rowman & Littlefield, 1998.

Oudenaren, Johan Van. *Uniting Europe: European Integration and the Post–Cold War World,* Lanham, Md.: Rowman & Littlefield, 2000.

Pérezde Cuéllar, Javier. *Anarchy or Order: Annual Reports, 1982–1991.* New York: United Nations, 1991.

Recommended Resources (continued)

Ross, George. *Jacques Delors and European Integration.* New York: Oxford University Press, 1995.

Schaeffer, Robert K. *Understanding Globalization: The Social Consequences of Political, Economic, and Environmental Change.* Lanham, Md.: Rowman & Littlefield, 1997.

Simai, Mihaly. *The Future of Global Governance: Managing Risk and Change in the International System.* Washington, D.C.: U.S. Institute of Peace Press, 1994.

United Nations Publications. New York: United Nations [title varies—annual listings]

JOURNALS

American Journal of International Law
American Political Science Review
Daedalus
The InterDependent (United Nations Association of the United States)
International Organization
International Studies Quarterly
Journal of European Public Policy
UN Chronicle
West European Politics

WEB SITES

European Union
    httn://europa.eu.int/
Food and Agriculture Organization (FAO)
    http:/www.fao.org/
International Committee of the Red Cross
    http://www.icrc.org/
International Energy Agency
    http://www.iaea.or.atlworldatom
International Labor Organization (ILO)
    http://www.imo.org/
International Maritime Organization (IMO)
    http://www. imo. org/
Universal Postal Union
    http://www.unu.int/
World Health Organization (WHO)
    http://www.who.ch
World Intellectual Property Organization
    http://www.wino.org/
World Meteorological Organization
    http://www.wmo.ch '
World Trade Organization (WTO)
    httP://www.wto.org/

in the doctrine of domestic jurisdiction large enough for tanks and warplanes to enter.

THE DUTY AND RIGHT TO INTERVENE

At the end of the 20th century, some observers insisted that the international community could intervene in any society for three reasons:

1. To maintain international security, since civil unrest often spills across borders

2. To uphold human rights, especially the right to life

3. To alleviate suffering caused by famine or other humanitarian crises

Such intervention may be *requested* by a host government seeking assistance, *imposed* upon a government threatening its own people or others, or *provided* to "failed states" where anarchy and banditry have displaced government.[4]

The realities of global interdependence helped to push the dogma of state sovereignty onto the ash heap of history. Broad recognition of transcendent human rights received sustenance from many sources:

The emergence of an international mind-set. Nearly unstoppable radio and television waves help people know about famine and massacres in remote places.

Brave individuals. The words and deeds of **Ralph Bunche**, Martin Luther King, Jr., Mother Teresa, and Andrei Sakharov—all winners of the Nobel Peace Prize—echoed around the globe.

Bold leaders. Presidents Jimmy Carter, Oscar Arias Sanchez, Mikhail Gorbachev, and François Mitterrand raised the priority given to human rights in the world arena.

Nongovernmental organizations (NGOs). Organizations such as the International Red Cross, Oxfam, and Doctors Without Borders (*Médicins Sans Frontières*) intervened where governments did not tread.[5]

Legal precedent. Individuals, along with corporations and international organizations, have become "subjects" of international law. The European Court of Human Rights (not to be confused with the European Court of Justice) hears complaints by individuals against their own governments.[6]

A growing consensus on human rights norms. Since 1945 most governments formally acknowledge a wide range of human rights. They

The First African American to Win the Nobel Peace Prize

Ralph Bunche was for years the second most powerful official in the United Nations, but at times could not get a room in the best hotels in the U.S. South. The first African American to win the Nobel Peace Prize (1950), he understood that "there could be no national security without civil rights, and there could be no international peace without human rights."* Though the only Black to graduate from UCLA in 1927, Bunche was class valedictorian. He was in the forefront of building Black consciousness in the 1930s and 1940s. As the key UN official dealing with international crises, he practically invented UN peacekeeping.

*Charles P. Henry, "Civil Rights and National Security: The Case of Ralph Bunche," in *Ralph Bunche: The Man and His Times*, ed. Benjamin Rivlin (New York: Holmes & Meier, 1990), 50–66 at 63. The other essays in the volume examine Bunche as scholar activist, Africanist and decolonizer, and world statesman.

4. See essays by Robert H. Jackson, Jack Donnelly, Robert Pastor, and Philippe Garigue and others in *International Journal* [special issue: "Humane Intervention"] 48, no. 4 (autumn 1993); Boutros Boutros-Ghali, *An Agenda for Peace*, 2d ed. (New York: United Nations, 1995); Morton H. Halperin and David J. Scheffer, eds, *Self-Determination in the New World Order* (Washington, DC.: Carnegie Endowment for International Peace, 1992); and Lori Fisler Damrosch, ed., *Enforcing Restraint: Collective Intervention in Internal Conflicts* (New York: Council on Foreign Relations, 1993).

5. See annual reports at http://www.msf.org.

6. Since 1971 it has become possible for individuals to complain to a UN committee regarding any "consistent pattern of gross violations of human rights and fundamental freedoms." The mechanism by which they may complain ("the 1503 Procedure"), however, does not ensure confidentiality.

Is there a human right to walk in one's fields without risk of losing a leg from a land mine? In the 1990s, several NGOs focused international attention on the dangers of antipersonnel land mines. More than a thousand NGOs formed a coalition that worked with Canada, Mozambique, Norway, South Africa, and other governments to establish a treaty banning such weapons. The International Campaign to Ban Land Mines won the Nobel Peace Prize in 1997. But Washington did not sign. The Pentagon wanted to keep land mines in Korea to thwart a DPRK attack.

accept not only the right of each people to live but also to "develop." The tides of human consciousness and law press for liberation.

COMPARING THEORY AND REALITY: REVOLUTIONS IN AWARENESS AND ACTION

BREAKING THE BONDS OF SLAVERY

No problem illustrates better the transformation of international belief and action on human rights than slavery—human bondage in which the slave is regarded as the property of the owner.[7] Serfs, by contrast, are in semibondage, supposed to have some rights. Slavery is the ultimate exploitation of humans by humans, often imbedded in a structure of coercive repression. Slavery can extinguish mind and soul as well as physical freedom.

Slavery was found in Babylon and other ancient cultures. Some Greek, Roman, and Arabic writers described other races as subhuman—fit to be enslaved. But Europeans also enslaved and enserfed other Europeans.[8]

When Europeans landed in America in the 16th century, most cultures took slavery for granted. Spanish explorers claimed the New World by a grant from Pope Alexander VI and from King Ferdinand and Queen Isabella.[9] Upon landing, the Spaniards read to the natives (in a tongue unknown to them) an order to submit. If the natives obeyed, they would be treated charitably. If they resisted, they would be killed or enslaved. Any deaths and losses would be the natives' fault, for they had been

7. Martin A. Klein, ed., *Breaking the Chains: Slavery, Bondage, and Emancipation in Modern Africa and Asia* (Madison: University of Wisconsin Press, 1993); and Paul Gorden Lauren, *Power and Prejudice: The Politics and Diplomacy of Racial Discrimination*, 2d ed. (Boulder, Colo.: Westview, 1996).

8. "Slave" intertwines with Slav—captured and enslaved by West Europeans in the early Middle Ages. German landowners in the Baltic region treated Estonians and Latvian serfs as virtual slaves selling individuals and breaking up families.

9. In 1493 Pope Alexander VI, "by the authority of Almighty God," purported to "give, grant, and assign" to the Spanish king all lands found 100 leagues west and south of the Azores and Cape Verde unless they were already ruled by a Christian prince. But Spain and Portugal in 1494 moved the line westward in a way that put Brazil (discovered later) in Portugal's domain.

warned. Having justified themselves, the Spaniards enslaved or massacred the natives.

One of the first protests against such practices took place in 1511 in today's Dominican Republic. With the son of Christopher Columbus present in church, Father Anton Montesino chastised the island's Spanish rulers: "You are living in deadly sin for the atrocities you tyrannically impose on these innocent people. . . .What right have you to enslave them? What authority did you use to make war against them who lived at peace on their territories, killing them cruelly with methods never before heard of? . . .Aren't they human beings? Have they no rational soul?"[10]

When colonial authorities complained to King Ferdinand, he ordered an end to such preaching. But a former landowner become monk, **Bartolomé de Las Casas**, took up where Montesino left off. His *Brief Relation of the Destruction of the Indies* (published in Seville in 1523) described the massacre and torture (for example, slow grilling over a fire, gagged to muffle screams) of huge numbers of natives in today's Dominican Republic, Mexico, and Guatemala.

Some legal scholars joined Las Casas, but others defended Spanish rule. Juan Gines de Sepulveda in 1547 asserted that the Native Americans were "innately servile." Spain's Council of the Indies listened to both sides. Some twenty-six years later it ordered that Spain's role in the New World be one of pacification. The Spanish crown did not ban force, but it disowned the ruthless methods of the *conquistadores.*

As the New World's native peoples perished, Europeans brought in slaves from Africa. Slavery became an integral part of the international political economy: Slaves from Africa cultivated sugar, tobacco, and cotton—producing capital for England's Industrial Revolution. The U.S. Declaration of Independence (1776) asserted that "all men are created equal," but the U.S. Constitution (1787) permitted slave imports until 1808. Slavery was not banned in the U.S. until the 1860s.

By the mid-19th century the major European powers had abolished slavery in their own realms and had begun to attack slavery everywhere. The 1890 Brussels Conference adopted a treaty abolishing the slave trade and establishing elaborate international machinery to suppress it. Even tighter restrictions were written into the 1926 Slavery Convention and its protocol, as amended in 1953. A Supplementary Convention in 1956 banned not only slavery but similar practices such as debt bondage, serfdom, coerced marriage for payment, inheritance of widows, coerced marriage of minors, and branding.

 A Right to Life: "No Contamination Without Representation"

Faced with radioactive pollution of the planet, idealist Eleanor Roosevelt and realist theologian Paul Tillich agreed in the 1950s on the following:

"The sovereignty of the human community comes before all others—before the sovereignty of groups, tribes, or nations. In that community, man has natural rights. He has the right to live and to grow, to breathe unpoisoned air, to work on uncontaminated soil. . . ." [emphasis added].

"If what nations are doing has the effect of destroying these natural rights, whether by upsetting the delicate balances on which life depends, or fouling the air, or devitalizing the land, or tampering with the genetic integrity of man himself, then it becomes necessary for people to restrain and tame the nations."

This declaration came from an appeal to halt nuclear testing by the National Committee for a Sane Nuclear Policy (SANE), published in *The New York Times,* November 15, 1957. Six months later another SANE petition began: "The World's Peoples Have a Right to Demand No Contamination Without Representation."

10. These words were recorded by Bartolomé de Las Casas. His writings and those of Sepulveda are reprinted in Marvin Lunenfeld. ed., *1492: Discovery, Invasion, Encounter: Sources and Interpretations* (Lexington, Mass.: D. C. Heath, 1991), 199–228.

Individuals Responsible for Apartheid: The Banality of Evil

Confronting one of his accusers, police officer Jeffrey Benzien said: "If I say to Mr. Jacobs I put the electrodes on his nose, I may be wrong. If I say I attached them to his genitals, I may be wrong. If I say I put a probe in his rectum, I may be wrong. I could have used any one of those methods." The "probe," one accuser said, was sometimes a broomstick. Accuser Jacobs vividly recalled the "wet bag" at which the policeman was adept: A cloth placed over the head led the victim to the brink of asphyxiation. The now humble officer wondered in 1997 what kind of person could have done such things, but he also believed his work had curbed terrorism. Benzien said he followed orders. One of his superiors admitted that he once held down one of Benzien's victims.*

*See Suzanne Daley, "Apartheid Torturer Testifies, As Evil Shows Its Banal Face," *The New York Times*, November 9, 1997, 1, 12.

The Universal Declaration of Human Rights approved by most UN members in 1948 provides: "No one shall be held in slavery or servitude; slavery and the slave trade shall be prohibited in all their forms." Virtually the same language is used in the 1966 International Covenant on Civil and Political Rights, the American Convention on Human Rights, the African Charter of Human and Peoples' Rights, and the European Convention on Human Rights.

Apartheid—racial segregation and a racial pecking order—was the law of South Africa until the 1990s. The UN Convention on the Suppression and Punishment of the Crime of Apartheid (1973) imposed individual responsibility on government officials for upholding apartheid. As we see in the sidebar, one such individual sought amnesty by confessing to South Africa's Truth and Reconciliation Commission in November 1997.

Despite promises and exhortation, many UN member states permit de facto slavery. A UN study warns: "New forms of servitude and gross exploitation have come to light only in recent years, as violators seek to circumvent laws or to take advantage of changing economic and social conditions."[11] Human rights advocates demand international mechanisms to prevent the sale of children, child prostitution, child pornography, and child labor. Some demand stiffer laws in each country and urge international police cooperation to interrupt and punish the transport of persons in danger of being enslaved. Others suggest that the long-term solution lies in extending the reach of democracy, improving education and living standards, and supporting social empowerment.

No government espouses slavery. The most blatant forms of slavery have disappeared. But practices akin to slavery continue. They are highlighted in many pages of the U.S. State Department's annual Country Reports on Human Rights detailing the condition of women, children, and labor around the world.[12]

LAWS OF WAR: PRISONERS AND NONCOMBATANTS

Human rights protection crept in through a back door—the rules of war. Europeans long believed they could treat prisoners of war as slaves. As Hugo Grotius, a father of international law, wrote in the early 17th century: "Not only do the prisoners of war themselves become slaves, but also their descendants forever. . . .By the law of nations those become our slaves who are born of our slave women. . . .The effects of this law are unlimited. . . .There is no suffering which may not be inflicted with impunity upon such slaves."[13]

11. *Slavery* (UN publication, Sales No. E.84/XIV.1 [1982]).

12. http://www.state.gov/g/drl/rls/hrrpt/2002/

13. Grotius, quoted in an editorial comment by Theodor Meron, *American Journal of International Law* 85 (1991): 116.

are constitutionally responsible rulers, public officials or private individuals." Signatory states are required to pass laws that give effect to the convention.

The Genocide Convention entered force in 1951 and by the 21st century had been ratified by more than 120 countries.[24] But the convention was nearly toothless because it failed to establish a permanent international court to hear genocide cases.[25] Who could try and punish genocidists? The treaty grants jurisdiction to courts in the very country where the genocidal acts took place—as if an Iraqi court under Saddam Hussein might try him for actions against Kurds and Shi'i![26] The treaty also permits genocidal acts to be tried "by such international penal tribunal as may have jurisdiction with respect to those Contracting Parties which shall have accepted its jurisdiction." Here we have another unrealistic provision. Only if such a court existed and only if Baghdad accepted its jurisdiction in advance could Iraq's leaders be tried before it.[27]

Weakening the convention still further, many signatories entered all manner of "reservations." For its part, the U.S. did not even ratify the convention until 1988—eight years after Communist China. Seeking to protect states' rights, Washington entered five "reservations" so sweeping that Greece, Italy, Ireland, and Mexico called them invalid because they violated the "object and purpose" of the convention.

Many jurists say that any state may try a genocidist because genocide is a crime against humanity—like piracy, the slave trade, and skyjacking—all subject to universal jurisdiction.[28] Any state may try pirates, regardless of where the act took place. But when Israeli agents abducted a Nazi genocidist from Argentina and delivered him to Israeli justice in 1960, the UN Security Council asserted that Israel had violated Argentina's territorial integrity and called on Israel to make "reparation."[29]

Governments are reluctant to formally accuse one another of genocide.[30] Pragmatists fear that charges of genocide will only inflame tensions and open a Pandora's box. Who is to be accused—the prime minister, the field commander, the squad leader, or "all of the above"? And will top leaders be tried even if they are also the ones who negotiate a peace treaty?[31] Whoever is tried, can't their lawyers argue that the accused acted on "orders" or in "self-defense"? If the point is to stop bloodletting, why try to prosecute or punish?

In 1993 Bosnia-Herzegovina went to the International Court of Justice (ICJ) and charged Serbia with violating the UN Charter, the Genocide Convention, and the 1949 Geneva Convention on Protection

24. Even after the UN General Assembly voted for the convention, individual states had to sign and then ratify it. If a state did not sign before the treaty entered force, it could accede. Following are a few patterns:

Country	Sign	Ratify	Accede
China	1949	1983	
Croatia			1992
Estonia			1991
Iraq			1979
Latvia			1992
North Korea			1989
USSR	12/16/49	1954	
U.S.	12/11/48	1988	
Yugoslavia	12/11/48	1950	

SOURCE: *Multilateral Treaties Deposited with the Secretary-General* (New York: Office of Legal Affairs, United Nations, annual).

25. See the report by Benjamin C. G. Whitaker to the Sub-Commission on Prevention of Discrimination and Protection of Minorities of the UN Economic and Social Council (UN Doc.E/EN.4/Sub.2/1985/6).

26. Iraq acceded to the convention in June 1979.

27. After the collapse of the Nazi regime, however, German courts tried and punished many ex-Nazis for war crimes.

28. Most jurists agree that the Genocide Convention belongs to the peremptory norms (*ius cogens*) of international law.

29. When Israel apologized, Argentina accepted this as reparation. Israel tried and executed Adolf Eichman under its 1950 law to punish "crimes against the Jewish people" and "crimes against humanity" committed in Europe before and during World War II. See Louis Henkin, *How Nations Behave: Law and Foreign Policy,* 2d ed. (New York: Columbia University Press, 1979), 269–278.

30. The U.S. assistant secretary of state in 1959 referred to evidence that in Tibet "the Chinese Communists have committed acts violating the norms established by the Genocide Convention of 1948." But Washington did not then recognize the Chinese Communist regime.

31. In the early 1970s and again in the early 21st century, there were suggestions that Henry Kissinger be tried as a war criminal guilty of crimes against humanity. Not only had he helped prolong the Vietnam War but he had dragged Cambodia into the fighting, leading eventually to mass executions by the Communists who seized power in the ensuing chaos. There were also calls for Russian President Vladimir Putin to be tried because of his genocidal policies in Chechyna.

UN and EU observers and UN "Blue Helmets" (most of them from Europe) did little to stop or even to protest ethnic cleansing in the former Yugoslavia in the years 1992–1995. No permanent court existed at that time to hear cases brought under the Genocide Convention. After the 1995 Dayton Accord however, NATO troops maintained a negative peace. A special tribunal was created to hear cases arising out of the Yugoslav conflict. Later, the International Criminal Court was established—over vigorous U.S. objections.

Jeff Danziger
The Christian Science Monitor
Los Angeles Times Syndicate

32. The 1949 convention was adopted by more than 150 states, including Yugoslavia in 1950 and the U.S. in 1956 (both with reservations): The convention seeks to protect civilians in the territory of a belligerent state or in occupied territory. It bans "willful killing, torture . . . willfully causing great suffering or serious injury . . . unlawful deportation or transfer . . . taking of hostages and extensive destruction and appropriation of property, not justified by military necessity and carried out unlawfully and wantonly." Enforcement provisions are somewhat stronger than the Genocide Convention. Each signatory is obliged to enact laws to provide effective penal sanctions against persons who violate the convention, to search for such persons, and to try them in its own courts or to hand them over to other signatory states for trial.

33. Snezana Trifunovska, "International Involvement in the Former Yugoslavia's Dissolution and Peace Settlement," *Nationalities Papers* 25, no. 3 (September 1997): 517–536.

of Civilians in Time of War.[32] Bypassing many questions about its jurisdiction, the court ruled (13–1) that it could provide provisional relief under the Genocide Convention. The ICJ enjoined Serbia to constrain any military or irregular forces it directed or supported from committing genocidal acts against Bosnian Muslims or "any other national, ethnic, racial or religious group."

Prodded by numerous reports of ethnic cleansing, the UN investigated events in the former Yugoslavia. A Commission of Experts noted that the same act could be both a war crime and a crime against humanity. It found that policies aimed at ethnic cleansing had used murder, torture, rape, forcible removal, and wanton destruction of property. "Those practices constitute crimes against humanity and . . . war crimes. Furthermore, such acts could also fall within the meaning of the Genocide Convention." Acting under Chapter VII, the Security Council in 1993 established the **International Criminal Tribunal for the Former Yugoslavia (ICTY)** at The Hague to "prosecute persons (not governments) responsible for serious violations of international humanitarian law" in the former Yugoslavia.[33] A similar tribunal was set up in 1994 to try genocide cases in Rwanda—the **International Criminal Tribunal for Rwanda (ICTR)**. In each case the UN member states undercut investigations and the court by withholding adequate funding. There were too few judges, too few courtrooms, and—in Rwanda—too few cells for the accused. For several years it seemed that only a few medium-ranking Serbs, Croats, and Bosnians would face

Dutch police in The Hague drive by the building where Slobodan Milošević and others indicted for war crimes in the former Yugoslavia were tried.

trial at the ICTY. NATO troops enforcing the Dayton Accords were reluctant to arrest the big fish, so they roamed free. In 2001, however, former Serbian leader Slobodan Milošević was extradited to The Hague by the government that replaced him in Belgrade, and his trial began in 2002.[34] The Rwanda tribunal faced similar problems. The trials proceeded slowly and both tribunals had trouble obtaining sufficient judges. In 2002 the Yugoslav tribunal was holding six trials simultaneously, including that of Milošević. Appeals were heard for money to compensate victims of genocide and those persons tried but, after long delays, found innocent.

The need for an international criminal court had been recognized before World War II and after. Draft statutes were prepared but got nowhere.[35] In the 1990s, however, events in the Balkans and in Africa revived efforts to create a permanent **International Criminal Court (ICC)** to deter mass murderers and, if deterrence failed, to pass judgment on them.[36] Spurred by NGOs and many small- and medium-sized states, a strong movement took shape to establish a permanent ICC to try those accused of genocide, war crimes (including rape), and other crimes against humanity when national judicial systems fail to do so. The Rome Statute of the International Criminal Court was adopted by 120 countries on July 1, 1998. The Clinton administration pressed for and got many changes in the statute to reduce the possibility that U.S. peacekeepers would be brought before the ICC for the purpose of anti-American

34. Milošević skillfully acted as his own lawyer and managed to make many political statements inspiring to Serbian nationalists. His heart ailments, however, interrupted the hearings from time to time.

35. Manley O. Hudson, "The Proposed International Criminal Court," *American Journal of International Law* [hereafter *AJIL*], 32, no. 3 (July 1938): 549–554; Vespasian V. Pella, "Toward an International Criminal Court," *AJIL*, 44, no. 1 (January 1950): 37–68; Quincy Wright, "Proposal for an International Criminal Court," *AJIL*, 46, no. 1 (January 1952): 60–72; George A. Finch, "Draft Statute for an International Criminal Court," ibid., 89–98.

36. James Crawford, "The ILC's Draft Statute for an International Criminal Tribunal," *AJIL*, 88, no. 1 (January 1994): 140–152; Walter C. Clemens, Jr., "What the World Needs Now: A Genocide Court," *Christian Science Monitor*, July 26, 1994, 17.

propaganda. For starters, the ICC would not be a court of first resort. It may claim jurisdiction only if national courts fail to act in cases where there are serious grounds to believe a criminal act has been committed. Though not entirely satisfied with the statute, the Clinton administration signed the Rome treaty in December 2000.

But the ICC statute, like the Kyoto Protocol, was deemed fatally flawed by the George W. Bush team. The world's hyperpower refused to accept the court's jurisdiction.[37] On May 6, 2002, the Bush administration purported to "unsign" the statute—an action unprecedented in international law. The Bush team maintained that the ICC could arbitrarily indict U.S. soldiers conducting legitimate military operations around the world. National sovereignty would be ceded to an international organization with no adequate protection for U.S. nationals. Most countries ratified the ICC, however, and it entered force on July 1, 2002. The court's first bench of judges, headed by Phillipe Kirsch of Canada, was sworn in on March 11, 2003.

Unfazed, the U.S. government sought to ensure that U.S. military personnel would never go before the court. It successfully lobbied the U.N. Security Council in 2002 to immunize U.S. military personnel from any prosecution for one year. It pressured several countries to sign bilateral agreements pledging they would not surrender U.S. military personnel to the ICC. Congress adopted the American Servicemembers' Protection Act of 2002, prohibiting U.S. cooperation with the ICC and banning military assistance to most countries that ratified the Rome statute. Just a few years before, Congress had approved U.S. participation in the Yugoslav and Rwanda tribunals and passed laws designed to permit the turnover of any defendants found within the United States. Observers could be forgiven if they charged the White House with rank hypocrisy and with actions subversive to the "new world order" that an earlier President Bush had proclaimed.

THE UNIVERSAL DECLARATION AND COVENANTS

In 1948 the UN General Assembly also adopted the Universal Declaration of Human Rights. It elaborated civil and political rights such as those enshrined in the U.S. Declaration of Independence and the U.S. Constitution. But it also acknowledged economic and social rights such as "the right to work" and to "just and favorable remuneration."

This distinction between political and economic rights reflected the Western idea of limited government versus Communist demands for government control of the economy. The U.S. was willing to endorse the

37. For many aspects of the problem, see the American Academy of Arts and Sciences symposium: Sarah B. Sewall and Carl Kaysen, eds., *The United States and the International Criminal Court: National Security and International Law* (Lanham, Md.: Rowman & Littlefield, 2000). Many relevant articles also appeared in *AJIL*.

As a U.S. representative to the United Nations, Eleanor Roosevelt helped forge the consensus that in 1948 endorsed the Universal Declaration of Human Rights.

right to work and to fair remuneration as *goals* but not as government obligations. Communists downplayed "mere" political rights in societies where the rich controlled the media. They said that the right to organize politically is meaningless for people who live in abject poverty.[38]

The Universal Declaration of Human Rights owed much to **Eleanor Roosevelt**, who led the U.S. negotiators and chaired the UN drafting commission. She also helped bridge differences between Western and other concepts of human rights.[39]

But the Universal Declaration represented a moral—not a legal—commitment by its signatories. Nearly two decades later, in 1966, the UN General Assembly adopted two follow-up "covenants"[40] that established legal obligations for states that joined them: The **International Covenant on Civil and Political Rights** bound each signatory state to uphold for individuals the rights of expression, of peaceful assembly, of association with others in trade unions, and of taking part in public life and elections. Ethnic and other minorities had "the right, in community with the other members of their group," to enjoy their own culture, religion, and language.

The **International Covenant on Economic, Social, and Cultural Rights** emphasized "the right to work" and to "fair wages and equal remuneration for work of equal value." It spelled out the right of "everyone to the . . . highest attainable standard of physical and mental health," to education, and to participation in cultural life.

38. Before Gorbachev, all Soviet leaders insisted that human rights are subordinate to the needs of the class struggle. They downgraded "bourgeois" political rights (such as a free press) as irrelevant in the Soviet Union's classless society, where no contradictions divide leaders from the people. The Soviet system, they said, provides economic rights unknown in the capitalist world. Gorbachev asserted that, "all human interests take precedence over class and all other interests."

39. Jason Berger, *A New Deal for the World: Eleanor Roosevelt and American Foreign Policy* (New York: Social Science Monographs, Columbia University Press, 1981), 67–74.

40. "Covenant" suggested to Jews and Christians a sacred pact like the one between God and his Chosen People.

Each covenant began by affirming that "all peoples have the right to self-determination" and "may dispose of their natural wealth for their own ends." The political–civil rights covenant obligated each signatory state to ensure to *"all individuals within its territory* [emphasis added]" the rights specified without "discrimination of any kind, such as race, sex, language, religion, opinion, national or social origins, property, birth or other status." The economic–social covenant also banned discrimination but gave "developing countries" the option of restricting the economic rights of non-nationals.

Despite signing these covenants, many Asian and African governments continued to assert in the 1990s that their economic conditions and unique cultures exempted them from Western conceptions of human rights. In August 1997 North Korea announced it was withdrawing from the Political Covenant after it was reprimanded for human rights deficiencies and for failing to report on its implementation of the accord. The eighteen-member UN human rights committee responded on October 30, 1997, that no signatory can withdraw from the covenant, which has no provision for termination or denunciation—a deliberate omission, not a mere oversight.

WOMEN'S RIGHTS AS HUMAN RIGHTS

Half of humanity has been subject to discrimination for millennia. Like men, women have been enslaved. But, far more often than men, they have also been raped or compelled to live as concubines or prostitutes, and generally treated as the inferior sex.[41]

Power politics has aggravated the condition of women in many ways. Persecution of witches was endorsed by Jean Bodin (1530–1596), an exponent of mercantilism and state sovereignty, because he saw witchcraft as a form of birth control. Fewer babies would curtail the state's wealth and the armed forces it needed for sovereignty.[42] Moving in the other direction, literacy for both genders became the norm in 17th-century Sweden. But though religious reformers wanted all people to read, many religions condoned male supremacy into the 21st century.

As we saw in earlier chapters, gynocide—killing female embryos, babies, and even adults—is widely practiced in India and China. Many African girls are still subject to clitorectomy in the name of local "culture." Apart from physical abuse, gender discrimination is still widespread, for example, in wage differentials.

Women's political participation has been curtailed in many societies. The first European country to grant women the right to vote was

41. The ambiguous status of women is reflected in etymology. Old English *cwene* gives us "queen," but it also meant "woman," "prostitute," "wife."

42. J. Ann Tickner, *Gender in International Relations: Feminist Perspectives on Achieving Global Security* (New York: Columbia University Press, 1992), 81.

Finland—in 1906. Women did not win the right to vote in the U.S. until 1920; in Switzerland, 1971. The view that democracies do not fight other democracies (Chapter 10) could not really be tested when half the *demos* had no vote.

The UN has treated women's rights as a subset of human rights, to be protected like other rights by law. In 1952 the UN adopted a Convention on the Political Rights of Women. It asserted that women are entitled to vote in all elections on equal terms with men and to hold public office on terms equal with men. However, the U.S. Senate did not assent to this mild commitment until 1976.

In 1979 the UN General Assembly adopted the **Convention on the Elimination of All Forms of Discrimination Against Women (CEDAW)**, which entered force in 1981. The convention banned any gender-based

Governments, rich and poor, often neglect gradually rising threats that do not immediately challenge their hold on power. The leaders of India, as in China and Russia, for years ignored the dangers posed by HIV-AIDS to public health. Here we see sex-trade workers in New Delhi in 1997 demanding more government attention to preventing and coping with HIV.

In Bangladesh alone some 20,000 children worked in brothels in 2002—readily exposed to HIV infection. Fearful their offspring might be abducted, some Bangladeshis sent their children to school in specially protected vans. The U.S. State Department reported in 2001 that several thousand women and girls were trafficked annually from Bangladesh for sexual exploitation, primarily in India, Pakistan, and the Middle East. Some boys were also trafficked to the Middle East to serve as camel jockeys. The government in Dhaka passed laws against trafficking and prosecuted a few offenders, but border police and immigration officials could often be persuaded to look the other way.

A UN official stated that the trafficking of women and children had become "the largest slave trade in history." The trade generated $7 billion a year in the early 21st century. The International Labor Organization estimated in 2003 that 1 million children worked in the sex industry in Asia—mainly in Thailand, India, Taiwan, and the Philippines. A UNICEF official calculated that, just in Asia and the Pacific, more than 30 million children had been trafficked in the decades from 1970 to 2000. A combination of poverty, globalization, organized crime, and discrimination against women encouraged the trade. While some parents guarded their children, others sold their offspring to traffickers who promised them a better future.

Some 50,000 persons were trafficked into the U.S. annually in the early 21st century—mostly Asians and persons from the former Soviet empire. Traffickers sought ways to bypass immigration controls tightened after 9/11. For more information, see http://www.humantrafficking.com.

43. By 1993 more than 120 countries had ratified or acceded to the convention. The U.S. signed it in 1980 but then did not ratify it. Many non-Western countries endorsed the convention. China signed and ratified it in 1980; Cambodia signed it in 1980 and ratified it in 1992; the USSR signed it in 1980 and ratified it in 1981; Afghanistan signed it in August 1980 (nine months after the Soviet invasion), but then did ratify it; Egypt signed it in 1980 and ratified it in 1981. Three Muslim countries did not sign it but did accede to it—Bangladesh in 1984, Iraq in 1986, and Libya in 1989.

44. Iraq claimed that the *Shar'ia* gave "women rights equivalent to the rights of their spouses so as to ensure a just balance between them." Several governments protested that the *Shar'ia* reservation was "incompatible" with the treaty.

distinction impairing women's "human rights and fundamental freedoms" in any field. It required parties to embody gender equality in their laws and to eliminate prejudices and practices based on the alleged superiority of either sex.[43] Iraq and Libya acceded to the convention but entered reservations that put the "laws of personal status derived from the Islamic *Shar'ia*" above the convention.[44]

Enforcement of the 1979 convention is lax. Signatories are required to report on laws or other measures adopted to implement the treaty. The reports are reviewed by a committee of twenty-three experts selected by the signatories, and passed on to the General Assembly. Disputes over implementation may be passed to the International Court of Justice, but this has never happened. The only UN body to have been officially censured for gender discrimination is the Commission on the Status of Women—censured for having too many women on it!

The 1949 Geneva Convention on treatment of civilians forbade rape, but ethnic cleansing in ex-Yugoslavia included rape and gynocide. Not only did Serbs drive victims (Muslims and Croats) from their homes, but they often raped them—sometimes locking them into "rape camps." One rapist told his victim: "Now you'll give birth to Serb and get rid of your Croat past." Mothers watched and heard as their young daughters were raped. Many women were killed after the rape orgies. Those who survived physically would not soon get over the trauma. Some gave life to an alien's child or aborted it. Bosnians and Croats also raped, but their actions seemed to lack the strategic purposes of Serbian rapes.

Similar horrors befall women worldwide, for example, in Brazil, Kenya, Pakistan, Peru, and Turkey.[45]

Western governments have led efforts to stamp out trafficking in women and children. International agreements were signed to suppress this traffic in 1904, 1910, 1921, 1933, 1937, and 1948–1951. Despite such accords, this traffic continues.[46]

Efforts to promote women's rights face a huge gap between promises and performance. Some feminist legal scholars doubt that women's lives can be improved by human rights discourse, since it has essentially male roots and the "add women and stir" process rarely achieves genuine equity. Recognition grows that the theory and practice of world politics reflect mainly "male" values. Even the UN Secretariat is notorious for gender abuses.

So long as the treatment of women is regarded as a private rather than a public issue, it will be difficult for international treaties to help women. This attitude adds a layer to the norm of noninterference in domestic affairs.

CAN INTERNATIONAL PRESSURE ENHANCE HUMAN RIGHTS OBSERVANCE?

Should those who enjoy relative freedom be concerned about human rights violations elsewhere? Should not foreign policy makers focus on their state's security and trade balances and leave human rights to Amnesty International and the International Red Cross? As we see in the sidebar, two Soviet Nobel Prize winners said "no!"[47] But what can the relatively free do to help the partly free and unfree?

Pressure and Preaching: The China Case

Presidents Carter and Clinton tried to nudge China to become not just a dependable trading partner but also a supporter of human rights. Until the late 1990s, Congress threatened every year to cut off most-favored nation (MFN) treatment for Chinese exports unless Beijing conformed to U.S. demands. Congress also barred exports to the U.S. made by prison labor. The Voice of America funneled in criticisms of Beijing's policies to Chinese listeners, undercutting regime efforts at mind control.

The European Parliament (EP) also condemned China's human rights practices. Far more radical than the rest of Europe's governments, the EP joined with the U.S. Senate in 1989 to denounce Chinese policies in Tibet. In February 1994, the EP passed a thirty-three-point resolution that called for establishment of a multiparty state in China, demanded

Why Human Rights Can Affect War and Peace

Aleksandr Solzhenitsyn suffered in (and later described) the "gulag [prison camp] archipelago" of the USSR. He warned: "Coexistence on this tightly-knit earth should be viewed as an existence not only without wars—that is not enough—but without violence, or anyone's telling us how to live, what to say, what to think, what to know and what not to know."

Soviet scientist and human rights campaigner Andrei Sakharov cautioned Washington not to cultivate "a country where anything that happens may be shielded from outside eyes—a masked country that hides its real face." The minimum condition for easing restrictions on East–West trade, Sakharov said, should be unrestricted emigration from the USSR.

45. *Human Rights Watch Global Reports on Women's Human Rights* (New York: Human Rights Watch, 1995), chaps. 1 and 2.

46. In the 1990s, girls and women were kidnapped, forced, or lured from Burma into Thai brothels. Occasional crackdowns by Thai police put hundreds of prostitutes in cramped detention for months. Some were released for return to Burma—many HIV-infected. The U.S. Congress was often more outspoken than the State Department in pressing for protection of women in Thailand and other countries. NGOs were even more forthright.

47. Aleksandr Solzhenitsyn won the Nobel prize for literature; Andrei Sakharov, for peace. Sakharov's statement was made to Western reporters on August 20, 1973; Solzhenitsyn's, in his September 1973 statement nominating Sakharov for the peace prize.

release of political prisoners, condemned infanticide, and called for banning goods produced by forced labor. The EP said that economic reforms in China should be accompanied by "the gradual introduction of internationally recognized social standards." It reminded Beijing that China had signed the Universal Declaration of Human Rights. It also hoped the Chinese legal system would become independent of political authority. It said any expansion of trade with the European Union should be conditioned on China's ending its system of labor camps. And it urged Beijing to open negotiations with Tibet's Dalai Lama.[48]

Like the U.S. and other governments, Beijing zealously defended its "domestic jurisdiction" and argued that the Communist government upholds the most basic human rights—to work and eat. Westerners, said Beijing, had no right to preach morality after centuries in which they had treated the Chinese as subhuman. Beijing welcomed technology and capital from outside, but condemned Western efforts to spread ideological and moral "pollution."

Neither preaching nor pressure made a discernible impact on PRC authorities. Beijing scorned Western criticisms. China needed the U.S. market, but U.S. consumers and exporters also needed China.[49] Beijing counted on U.S. greed to press Congress to renew MFN treatment for China. U.S. business executives chided their own government for making the U.S. look unreliable as a commercial partner.

Why did the USSR succumb to human rights pressure while China remained defiant? As noted in the previous chapter, Moscow accepted the Helsinki human rights commitments in 1975 as part of a larger package that promised the Soviet bloc greater security and trade. But China perceived little threat to its security and counted on MFN status no matter what. The Soviet authorities liked to swear their devotion to human rights—partly to claim that the USSR belonged with the West—but PRC leaders did not. The Soviets probably assumed that the Helsinki commitments could be controlled, but Beijing was cautious. China acceded to seven human rights accords in the 1980s, but usually with enfeebling reservations.[50] Beijing made a sham of human rights.

Some liberals within China saw the expansion of Chinese contacts with the outer world as the best basis for human rights. On the other hand, some Chinese dissidents complained that the West did not protest human rights abuses in China as it did in the old Soviet empire. Westerners, they said, believed that Chinese valued the individual less than Russians. Few governments in the world have a worse human rights

48. Real power lies elsewhere in the European Union. Still, earlier EP recommendations helped block European trade with Morocco and Syria. David Wallen, "Europe Condemns China," *South China Morning Post*, February 12, 1994, 1–2.

49. In another gesture, five U.S. journalists were given a tour of a labor reform camp where Liu Gang, an organizer of the Tiananmen Square protests, was kept and, relatives said, tortured. The cells and cafeteria shown to the journalists were nearly deserted, and they could see Mr. Liu only through a smoked glass window as he walked in the yard with a guard. Patrick E. Tyler, "Chinese Take Journalists on Guided Tour of Prison" and "China Dissident Reports Release," *The New York Times*, March 6, 1994.

50. Beijing acceded to the torture convention but said it would not be bound by Article 20, permitting an outside commission to investigate possible violations. This meant that China would judge and punish its own torturers. In 1982 Beijing acceded to the protocol protecting refugees, but rejected the treaty's obligation to submit disputes to the ICJ. Beijing also registered broad reservations when it joined the 1949 Geneva convention on protection of victims in war and the 1979 convention banning discrimination against women.

record than China. By the late 1990s, things were better than during Mao Zedong's Great Leap Forward (1958–1962) and the Cultural Revolution (1966–early 1970s), but China's observance of human rights in the 1990s was bad—just marginally better than Iraq's. There had been no public massacres since Tiananmen Square in 1989, but since then there had been no large demonstrations to shoot at.[51]

No Political or Civil Rights. Despite some opening up in the 1990s, the Chinese had virtually no freedom of speech, press, assembly, or association—and certainly no opposition party (though closely supervised multicandidate elections took place in villages). Few legal safeguards existed. No due process was observed. Authorities used torture to extract confessions. Prison labor was extensive. Organs of executed persons were sold for transplants.

Social and Economic Rights Were Minimal. The new reforms threw millions out of secure jobs and onto the streets with no safety net. Forced abortions were common.

Cultural Genocide. An ancient and major civilization, Tibet, was being extirpated. Sinification of Tibetan, Muslim, and other minority regions took place by inundating the local populations with Chinese migrants and by imposing Mandarin as the language of education, government, and economics.

Religious Persecution. Nonapproved religious groups were banned and persecuted.

Indifference to Law. China succeeded in its export-based economic transformation, but Beijing played unfairly.

Despite repression, China opened up. More money, fewer controls, and freer access to information since the 1980s led to more choice.

President Clinton asserted that China's human rights practices were on "the wrong side of history," but he lifted a ban on export of U.S. nuclear power reactors to China after President Jiang Zemin in 1997 pledged not to sell missiles to Iran. Jiang also placed an order for fifty Boeing aircraft worth about $3 billion—some twenty planes more than expected. Business leaders feted the PRC leader at the Waldorf Astoria, but Jiang returned home having made no commitments on human rights or Tibet. The long-term impact of his trip, however, could yield surprises. He had met leading members of Congress who also called for a change in China's human rights policies. He had seen and heard human rights demonstrators who followed him to the New York Stock Exchange and then to Massachusetts. Jiang hinted that to see the "specifics" of U.S. democracy was different from reading about them.

51. The following analysis is based on many sources, including U.S. Department of State, *Country Reports on Human Rights Practices for 1996* (Washington, D.C.: Government Printing Office, 1997), 616–643.

He allowed, in a talk at Harvard University, that Chinese leaders had made some mistakes. Five years later, Jiang was still China's president and a good interlocutor when President George W. Bush phoned on January 10, 2003, to ask him for help in dealing with North Korea and "the Bomb."

THE ZIGS AND ZAGS OF U.S. POLICY TOWARD HUMAN RIGHTS

Human rights have played an important if secondary role in U.S. foreign policy since 1945. Since the mid-1970s the Department of State has issued a yearly survey on human rights worldwide—the *Country Reports on Human Rights Practices*. In the Reagan–Bush years these reports were soft on Latin American dictators, China, and the U.S.'s European allies. In the 1990s, however, the *Country Reports* became more objective, exceeding 1,000 pages filled with facts both positive and negative. Thus the 1993 report said of one friendly country: "A wide range of individual freedom is provided for by the Mexican Constitution and honored in practice." But the State Department also reported "the use of torture," "extrajudicial killings," and "electoral flaws" in Mexico.[52]

Starting in 1984, Congress required that the *Country Reports* contain information on workers' rights in countries benefiting from duty-free access to the U.S. market.[53] The yearly surveys have detailed policies by Indonesia, Taiwan, and other friendly countries to block collective bargaining. Beginning in 1992, Congress also demanded that the *Country Reports* provide more information on children, indigenous peoples, and—for recipients of U.S. aid—data on their efforts to curtail military expenditures.

"Doctor, heal thyself." While Washington prodded others, its own performance left much to be desired. Critics wondered how a rich country could permit extreme poverty, racism, and serious public health shortfalls.[54]

Table 15.1 summarizes the official U.S. position, and those of several other governments, on the major human rights conventions. For comparison, we should note that Finland is a party to every human rights convention except those governing regions outside Europe. So, too, is Russia, though its compliance is ragged.

Of industrial democracies, the U.S. showed the most reserve toward human rights treaties. Some senators refused to approve specific conventions on the grounds that their obligations could violate "states' rights" or lead to anti-U.S. propaganda by governments that did not practice

52. U.S. Department of State, *Country Reports on Human Rights Practices for 1992* (Washington, D. C.: Government Printing Office, 1993), 400–451.

53. This stipulation was part of the Generalized System of Preferences Renewal Act of 1984.

54. These problems are especially acute on Native American reservations.

Time is probably on your side. The revolution in human rights awareness has gained momentum since the 16th century. It has impacted China only since the early 20th century. But totalitarian controls in China are eroding, as they did earlier in the USSR. Make the most of this opening. If Nelson Mandela could become president of South Africa in the late 20th century, who knows what might be possible in China in the 21st? Engage individuals and groups at all levels to discuss and promote human rights. Some Chinese have a vested interest in stability, but others want change. They include many women, ethnic minorities, labor leaders, and intellectuals—artists, humanists, scientists, and reporters. Businesspeople chafe at restrictions. Politicians who want unification with Taiwan must demonstrate that human rights are respected in mainland China.

Expect setbacks, but persist.

Individuals make history. After spending twenty-seven years in jail for opposing apartheid, Nelson Mandela (born in 1918) won the presidency of South Africa in 1994. Here he dances at a celebration following his inauguration. The previous year he received the Nobel Peace Prize together with then President F. W. de Klerk. Mandela served just one term as president, 1994–1999, but remained one of Africa's most influential statesmen.

KEY NAMES AND TERMS

apartheid
Bricker Amendment
Ralph Bunche
Bartolomé de Las Casas
Convention on the Elimination of All
    Forms of Discrimination Against
    Women (1979)
Convention on the Prevention and
    Punishment of the Crime of
    Genocide (1948)

Country Reports on Human Rights
    Practices
crimes against humanity
Geneva Conventions of 1949
International Covenant on Civil and
    Political Rights (1966)
International Covenant on Economic,
    Social, and Cultural Rights
    (1966)
international criminal court (ICC)

International Criminal Tribunal
    for the Former Yugoslavia (ICTY)
International Criminal Tribunal for
    Rwanda (ICTR)
International Military Tribunal at
    Nuremberg
Eleanor Roosevelt
slavery
Universal Declaration of Human
    Rights (1948)

QUESTIONS TO DISCUSS

1. To what extent is banning slavery like limiting weapons? How does it differ? Consider the mechanisms and the goals of such limitations. Which levels of action have been most fruitful?

2. How does democide (see Chapter 10) differ from genocide? How does cultural genocide differ from physical genocide? Compare U.S. (Australian, Canadian) government policies toward indigenous peoples with ethnic cleansing in the former Yugoslavia.

3. What right do outsiders have to demand a halt to clitorectomy in cultures where it has long been a tradition?

4. Should outsiders press for an end to child labor (for example, in the carpet factories of Pakistan and India) if families will be plunged deeper into poverty?

5. You are the UN High Commissioner for Human Rights. How do you approach Algeria (or another government) widely believed to be suppressing human rights? The government there blames local terrorists for disturbances and says that outsiders have no right to meddle.

6. As a member of Amnesty International and a stockholder in Boeing Corporation, do you want the U.S. State Department to continue its public reports on human rights in China?

7. Should the U.S. join the International Criminal Court?

8. Should the U.S. accept the compulsory jurisidiction of the International Court of Justice?

RECOMMENDED RESOURCES

BOOKS

Amnesty International (for general and regional reports, see library listings under this heading).

Barnett, Michael N. *Eyewitness to a Genocide: The United Nations and Rwanda.* Ithaca, N.Y.: Cornell University Press, 2002.

Brysk, Alison. *Globalization and Human Rights:* Berkeley: University of California Press, 2002.

Chandler, David. *From Kosovo to Kabul: Human Rights and International Intervention.* London: Pluto Press, 2002.

Donnelly, Jack. *International Human Rights.* Boulder, Colo.: Westview, 1993.

Forsythe, David P. *The Internationalization of Human Rights.* Lexington, Mass.: Lexington Books, 1991.

Helton, Arthur C. *The Price of Indifference: Refugees and Humanitarian Action in the New Century.* Oxford, U.K.: Oxford University Press, 2002.

Human Rights Watch Global Report on Women's Human Rights: New York: Human Rights Watch, 1995. [For general, regional, and thematic reports, see library listings under Human Rights Watch.]

Morgan, Theodore H. *Beyond Sweatshops: Foreign Direct Investment and Globalization in Developing Nations.* Washington, D.C.: Brookings Institution, 2002.

Ratner, Steven R. and Jason S. Abrams. *Accountability for Human Rights Atrocities in International Law: Beyond Nuremberg.* 2d ed. New York: Oxford University Press, 2001.

Rieff, David. *A Bed for the Night: Humanitarianism in Crisis.* New York: Simon and Schuster, 2002.

Recommended Resources (continued)

Schabas, William A. *An Introduction to the International Criminal Court.* Cambridge, U.K.: Cambridge University Press, 2001.

Terry, Fiona. *Condemned to Repeat? The Paradox of Humanitarian Action.* Ithaca, N.Y.: Cornell University Press, 2002.

U. S. Department of State. *Country Reports on Human Rights Practices.* Washington, D.C.: Government Printing Office [annual].

JOURNALS

American Journal of International Law
Ethics & International Affairs
Human Rights Quarterly
UN Chronicle

WEB SITES

AAAS Directory of Human Rights Sites on the Internet
   http://shr.aaas.org/dhr.htm
Amnesty International
   http://www.amnesty.org

DIANA: An International Human Rights Database
   http://diana.law.yale.edu/
Human Rights Internet
   http://www.hri.ca/
Human Rights Watch
   http://www.hrw.org/
Human Rights Web
   http://www.hrweb.org/
International Committee of the Red Cross
   http://www.icrc.org
International Helsinki Federation for Human Rights
   htttp://www.ihf-hr.org/
Lawyers Committee for Human Rights
   http://www.lchr.org
Organization of American States
   http://www.oas.org/
U.S. Department of State, Country Reports on HR Practices 1997
   http://www.state.gov/www/global/human_rights/1997_hrp_report/97hrp_report_toc.html
UN High Commissioner for Refugees
   http://www.unhcr.ch/
University of Minnesota Human Rights Library
   http://www.umn.edu/humanrts/

ALTERNATIVE FUTURES: LESSONS FROM THE PAST

T H E   B I G   Q U E S T I O N S   I N   C H A P T E R   1 6

- Can the world become a better place for life? If so, how? On whom or what does improvement depend?

- What can we learn from IR history? Under what circumstances did it pay for IR actors to pursue a hard line? A win–win orientation? Conditional cooperation?

- Under what circumstances did it pay IR actors to mask their concerns and objectives in negotiations?

- Under what circumstances, if any, was openness a better guide to IR tactics and strategy?

- Looking at the first quarter of the 21st century, what kinds of IR scenarios are most plausible? What are the most likely "if–then" alternatives?

- Can unipolarity be beneficent, or will it lead to dictatorship?

- Must we assume a collision between today's hegemon and a rising power such as China or the European Union?

- Is the South likely to get poorer or begin closing the gap with the North?

- Is IR likely to be dominated by governments, nonstate actors, or cooperation among a variety of international actors? If by non-state actors, which kind—NGOs, TNCs, or others?

- Do we have more reason to fear or welcome the global future?

- How do mutual gain and conflict/exploitation relate to environmental policy?

"History Is the Future.". . . . This is a favorite saying of the UN Secretary-General. But she also stands by another belief: "The future is ours to fill." Humanity's future depends on the past but also on what we do in the present.

She turns to you, a former diplomat turned historian, for advice. You have put aside day-to-day crises and standard operating procedures to write and teach history, utilizing insights gained in arenas where South confronts North and East meets West. The Secretary-General asks you to review IR in the past 100 or 200 years. Can the world be made safer, more just, more prosperous, more salubrious? What can we learn from the past to guide our policies in the 21st century? Are there lessons for individuals? For governments? For IGOs, NGOs, TNCs, and other international actors?

How do these lessons play out in the alternative futures discernible as we enter the 21st century? Are there any constants in IR? Is change even possible?

IS IT POSSIBLE TO BUILD A BETTER WORLD?

Realists reply no. They maintain that human nature does not change. People in the 21st century will behave much like Athenians and Spartans in the 5th century B.C. They will continue to fear one another and, in preparing to attack or defend, provoke arms races and wars. No one analyzed IR better than Thucydides when he dissected the Peloponnesian War. We cannot expect to understand IR or prescribe policy better than the ancient Greeks. There are limits to knowledge. Despite scientific advances in many fields, we still cannot fathom leaders such as Saddam Hussein. There are also limits to what humans can regulate. Despite the growth of international law, the 20th century experienced two global wars and many smaller ones. The Damocles sword of nuclear war hangs by a thread ready and able to end life in the 21st century. Lusting for wealth and power, humans use technology to lay waste to the fishing grounds, the forests, the very water and air on which life depends. As Mephistopheles noted, men use reason only to be more beastly than any beast.

But there are also reasons to believe in the possibility of a better world. The quality of life has improved dramatically since the 18th century. The planet sustains a steady increase in its human inhabitants. At the dawn of the 3rd millennium, the average human is healthier and better educated than at any time in history.[1] Infant mortality has fallen sharply even in many poor countries. Average life spans have dramatically increased. Literacy and basic education are the norm across most of the planet. As resources dwindle, humans learn to conserve them or invent replacements.

What lies behind this capacity for life? Science. Technology. Morality. Organization. Power. Learning.

Scientific Knowledge. Understanding the processes that condition life, humans can extend it. Social science, however, lags behind physical science.

Technology. Applied science provides food and shelter for huge populations; it permits people to travel and communicate globally. Knowledge and technology are great equalizers. Their diffusion permits India, once ruled by the British raj, to become a center of computer software development, and China to compete with the West and Russia in launching commercial rockets.

1. More education did not mean more genius. The 20th century had its Einstein, Picasso, T. S. Eliot, Andrei Sakharov, and Leonard Bernstein. But were they a match for Leonardo, Shakespeare, or Mozart? How did the Left Bank of Paris compare with the agora of ancient Athens? How did 20th-century religious figures compare with those that emerged in ancient India and the Middle East?

Are We Our Cousins' Keepers? A Test Case

Ali Jawarish, age eight, was killed in November 1997 by an Israeli rubber bullet shot to the forehead as he played near older Palestinian boys throwing stones at Israeli soldiers guarding Rachel's Tomb, a holy site inside the Palestinian self-rule area of Bethlehem. Ali's parents donated his organs to the Israeli national organ bank. Soon his heart, liver, a lung, and one kidney were transplanted into two twelve-year-old Israeli boys. Mohammed Jawarish, Ali's father, said he wanted his son's death to give life to others.

2. Ernst B. Haas, *Nationalism, Liberalism, and Progress: The Rise and Decline of Nationalism* (Ithaca, N.Y.: Cornell University Press, 1997). See references in Haas, Chapter 1, to relevant works of other social scientists such as Max Weber, Karl W. Deutsch, James N. Rosenau, Herbert A. Simon, Janice Stein, Raymond Tanter, Larry Laudan, Peter Berger, and Robert L. Rothstein.

Morality. Since the 18th century, many people have believed that science, technology, and wealth can and should be used to improve the lives of all people, not just privileged elites. Many humans recognize human solidarity across the divides of gender, border, race, religion, language, culture, and class. There is a growing consensus on morality. Most governments endorsed the Universal Declaration of Human Rights, even though few fully conformed to it.

Organization. The modern state helped people organize on a large scale—to establish law and order, tap divisions of labor, produce for broad markets, improve physical security, and establish a welfare safety net. IGOs such as the Universal Postal Union and NGOs such as the Red Cross help states to meet basic needs on a global scale. But the nation-state framework has often proved inadequate for dealing with many challenges. The technology of war has outpaced organization for peace. Electronic money transfers have undermined the ability of governments to control their currency and collect taxes. HIV and drug trafficking have mocked national borders.

Experience suggests that humans can and will devise better ways to cope with the dangers and opportunities inherent in mutual vulnerability and globalization.[2]

Power. Human nature may not have changed, but diverse constellations of power may have helped prevent war—a multipolar balance during the 19th century, bipolarity during the Cold War era, and unipolarity in the 1990s. No one has mastered the art or science of peace. Still, it is possible that science, technology, morality, and organization can combine to produce better ways to restrain aggression and promote cooperation.

Learning. Underlying each domain is the ability to adapt and to learn. While physically weak compared to other life forms, humans have brains, nervous systems, and dexterity that enable them to adapt to extreme conditions. Humans have learned from trial and error, including bitter and tragic failures, how to organize to live better.

Today's students of IR can proceed from theoretical insights that the ancient Greeks could only guess at. Game theory deepens our understanding of adversarial relationships—that rivals may have interests in common as well as in conflict, so that, under some conditions, rivals may gain from cooperation. Modern psychology helps explain why actors often misread one another and even their own interests. Chemistry helps explain emotions. Sociobiology compares and contrasts human behavior with that of other life forms. Complexity theory helps us understand coevolution. The better we understand ourselves and the biosphere, the greater our chances of coping with challenges and opportunities.

Diplomatic skills, communication, conflict resolution, and mediation techniques can be taught. The slim book *Getting to Yes* puts forth not just an outlook on adversarial relations but a compendium of negotiating techniques found useful by negotiators in a variety of cultural settings.[3] The science and art of collaborative decision making illuminates IR as well as business problems.[4]

What can we learn from the past? Let us analyze the cases studied throughout this book. Under what conditions has it paid for policy makers to pursue hard-line policies, a win–win approach, or conditional cooperation? For now we focus on the payoffs for the policy initiator. Later we can consider the outcomes for other actors affected by those policies.

WHICH APPROACH WORKS BEST: WIN–LOSE, WIN–WIN, OR CONDITIONAL COOPERATION?

The experiences recorded in this book confirm the utility of approaching foreign policy in a spirit of conditional cooperation and openness to elicit informed participation by all concerned parties. These conclusions emerge from the cases summarized in Tables 16.1–16.4—a highly simplified interpretation of complicated, sometimes contradictory, events. Still, the overall patterns are striking. We see that hard-line policies spawned many failures: the Versailles system, defeat for the perpetrators of six major wars, Khrushchev's Cuban gambit, and Communist repression of human potential.

By contrast, a win–win orientation helped cultivate fitness in the U.S. for most of the 20th century and in Japan after 1945. Two major IR achievements hinged on conditional cooperation. The Marshall Plan helped produce a secure and prosperous transatlantic community, while U.S. and Soviet management of the Cuban confrontation was a victory for sobriety and peace.

Conditional cooperation helped the U.S. and USSR limit both offensive and defensive arms. The Nuclear Nonproliferation Treaty helped limit the nuclear club, but India, Israel, and others refused a have-not status despite U.S. and Soviet blandishments. Conventional arms control foundered on a zero-sum of mentality of both buyers and sellers.

Conditional cooperation generated several short-lived détentes between Moscow and Washington, setting the stage for an end to the Cold

---

Is Learning Possible? Defining the Problem

How can we learn and become sensitive to mistakes before the roof crashes in? How can decision makers become more responsive to the need to abandon a familiar path or logic and choose a new one before catastrophe strikes? Can IR players—governments, IGOs, NGOs, TNCs—learn? If they do not learn, can they at least adapt? Both adaptation and learning are part of bargaining. An early stage of bargaining is defining the problem—how one set of problems is "nested" with others. The definition entails linkage: Which aspects of the problem should be fused and which decomposed?

Actors must see that past practices and beliefs are no longer adequate to deal with looming problems. Even antagonists may find themselves condemned by interdependence to negotiate better solutions.

To facilitate learning we should cast aside dogmas. The decision-making process within governments and international organizations should be made transparent to reduce errors and achieve maximum consensus. The standard operating routine should include hearing out advocates of conflicting views—each making the best case possible.*

*See Ernst B. Haas, *When Knowledge Is Power: Three Models of Change in International Organizations* (Berkeley: University of California Press, 1990), 72, 209–212.

---

3. Roger Fisher and William Ury, *Getting to Yes: Negotiating Agreement Without Giving In* (New York: Penguin, 1983), available in many languages.

4. Howard Raiffa et al., *Negotiation Analysis: The Science and Art of Collaborative Decision Making* (Cambridge, Mass.: Harvard University Press, 2002).

Table 16.1 Approaches and Outcomes in Part 1: Hard Realities, High Ideals, and Global Interdependence

Cases Analyzed	Approach			Outcomes	Interpretation/Other Key Variables That Made a Difference
	Hard-Line	Win–Win	Conditional Cooperation		
How to Win at Peace					
Appomattox and after		◆		−	Soft peace terms abused → repressive occupation of South → lose–lose
Versailles and after	◆			−	Tough terms weakly enforced → German resentment and revisionism → WWII
ERP (Marshall Plan)		◆	◇	+	Need to rebuild + fear of USSR = mutual gain policy → security community
Confrontation					
Cuban confrontation	◆			−	U.S. missile buildup + Khrushchevian risk taking → confrontation
Cuban stand-down (1962)			◆	+	Sobering dangers → top leaders make concessions → war averted
Why Fight?					
World War I	◆			−	Irresponsible leaders + cult of offensive + nationalism → war
World War II	◆			−	Nationalist militarists in Tokyo, Rome, and Berlin vs. irresolute West
Korean War	◆			−	Egomaniacs + rising confidence in communism vs. irresolute West
U.S.–Vietnam War	◆			−	U.S. determination to prevent falling dominoes + LBJ insecurity
Soviet–Afghan War	◆			−	Instability in Afghanistan + Soviet determination not to lose a Communist regime
The Gulf War	◆			−	Egomaniac in Baghdad + Iraqi grievances vs. irresolute West
How To be Fit					
The U.S. in the 20th century		◆		+	Rich resources + freedom + Fordism = mutual gain; deep problems remain
The USSR	◆	◇		−	Rich resources + dictatorship = industrialization + poverty
Japan		◆		+	Industrial policy + consensus = affluence, but modest creativity

NOTE: ◆ = dominant approach; ◇ = partial approach; empty cell = little attention; + = positive outcome for initiator; − = negative results for initiator.

War in the late 1980s. Hope for mutual gain encouraged closer economic ties between Beijing and Taipei, but win–lose hostility kept political differences alive between North and South Korea.

Positive-sum expectations underlay the relative ethnic harmony of the U.S., Singapore, and Switzerland. In sharp contrast, top Soviet, Sri Lankan, and South Slav leaders followed a hard-line approach to ethnic problems, making conflict likely. Ethnic harmony probably requires confidence that all groups can win.

Conditional cooperation permeated the successful mediation at Camp David, Lancaster House, and Oslo. But the Dayton Accord rested heavily

Table 16.2 Approaches and Outcomes in Part 2: From Anarchy, Order?

Cases Analyzed	Approach			Outcomes	Interpretation/Other Key Variables That Made a Difference
	Hard-Line	**Win–Win**	**Conditional Cooperation**		
Arms Control					
SALT 1 and ABM (1972)			◆	+	Offense can beat defense → make the best of mutual vulnerability
INF (1987)			◆	+	Overkill + desire for détente → destruction of new weapons systems
START 2 (1990s)			◇	+/−	Overkill + end of Cold War → U.S. and Russia move toward a smaller deterrent
NPT (1968 into 1990s)			◇	+/−	Nuclear club tries to close the door but three or more states persist
Conventional arms trade		◇		−	Desire for stability vs. profit motive + new weapons technologies + new world disorder → reduced but continued arms transfers
Conflict Management					
Geneva Spirit (1955)	◇		◆	+	GRIT → brief détente cut short by Eisenhower's heart attack + other conflicts
Moscow Spirit (1963)	◇		◆	+	GRIT → détente cut short by JFK's death, Khrushchev's ouster, and Vietnam
Moscow Spirit (1972)	◇		◆	+	GRIT + triangular diplomacy → détente, damaged by 1973 Arab–Israeli War
East–West détente (1989)			◆	+	GRIT + weakening of Soviet regime + Gorbachev style → end of Cold War
Soviet–PRC détente (1989)			◆	+	Soviet pullback of forces + Gorbachev style = new Sino–Russian relationship
PRC–ROC (1980s–1990s)	◇		◆	+/−	PRC GRIT + eventual ROC reciprocation = much commerce and less conflict
ROK–DPRK (1970s–1990s)	◆			−	Rival regimes (and once homogeneous people) enmeshed in hostile distrust
Nationalism and World Order					
Unity of U.S.		◆	◇	+	Voluntary union of many cultural and ethnic groups + residue of slavery
Disunity of USSR	◆			−	Coerced union of many disparate groups fails when coercion weakens
Unity of Singapore	◇	◆	◇	+	Authoritarian government imposes unity from above on small city-state
Disunity of Sri Lanka	◆			−	Affirmative action for Sinhalese majority vs. Tamil demands = civil war
Unity of Switzerland		◆	◇	+	Oldest democracy + local autonomy + power sharing (+ wealth) = harmony
Disunity of South Slavs	◆			−	Enforced union + death of unifying leader + nationalist agitation + war
Mediation					
Camp David (1978)	◇		◆	+	Sadat's confidence + Begin's intransigence + Carter's mediation + U.S. soft and hard power = Egyptian–Israeli peace that omits Palestinians
Lancaster House (1979)			◆	+	Carrington's mediation + isolated minority regime = peace in Zimbabwe
Oslo (1993)			◆	+	Holst's good offices facilitate Israeli-Palestinian accord to coexist
South Slavs (1991–1995)	◇	◇		−	UN and EU mediators and UN forces too weak to stop bloodshed
South Slavs (1995–1998)	◆		◇	+/−	Holbrooke mediation + NATO troops = negative peace and no ethnic harmony

NOTE: ◆ = dominant approach; ◇ = partial approach; empty cell = little attention; + = positive outcome for initiator; − = negative results for initiator.

on dictation and hard power. U.S. dictation left many parties resentful, but stopped most of the fighting.

Many steps toward peace—from the "Spirit of Geneva" in 1955 through the 1990s—suffered from hard-line sentiments that impeded cooperation. Playing it safe or keeping some guns in reserve stoked the security dilemma and mutual distrust.

The dictators' exploitation of their own peoples and others assured their ultimate collapse. China's dictatorship softened after Mao but still menaced any who dared dissent.

Confidence in the possibility of win–win outcomes helped the West and Japan to achieve mass affluence. Dealing with foreigners, however, Japan sometimes played hardball. Mimicking Japan, President Clinton's synthesis offered vigorous support of U.S. exports. Trying to protect Airbus, the EU Commission took a hard-line approach to the Boeing–McDonnell Douglas merger. Behind NAFTA and the WTO, however, there were win–win assumptions plus expectations of reciprocity.

Win–lose assumptions underlay most efforts at autarky. Asia's "Tigers," however, embraced the win–win rationale of free trade even when they protected their domestic markets. China followed the Tigers' path, but shielded an even larger proportion of its economy from competition. Autarky and protectionism sometimes did more harm than good for their practitioners. "Infant industry protection often becomes senile industry protection."[5] For decades, governments and their cronies in South Asia also played a version of hardball: They dominated economic life and throttled free competition. Lack of transparency fostered reckless business decisions and economic waste as well as corruption. In the mid-1990s, better late than never, they began to open up.

Transitions were painful in the former Second World. In most former Soviet republics, influential individuals and groups seized what were formerly state monopolies. These parasite-robber commissars became millionaires overnight, leaving most people worse off than under communism. Russia, Azerbaijan, and Kazakstan counted on oil wealth. None produced many goods for export, with the exception of arms—still a Russian specialty. By contrast, Poland and Estonia acted like Tigers and embraced a win–win approach to world trade.

A hard-line approach in ecopolitics views even the biosphere in zero-sum terms. Builders of large dams and those who clear-cut tropical forests do not respect the intricate balances of nature cultivated over time. Some groups profit from pillage, but at a high cost to long-term sustainability.

5. Steven Radiolead and Jeffrey Sachs, "Asia's Reemergence," *Foreign Affairs*, 76, no. 6 (November 1997): 44–59 at 51.

Table 16.3 Approaches and Outcomes in Part 3: International Political Economy

| Cases Analyzed | Approach | | | Outcomes | Interpretation/Other Key Variables That Made a Difference |
	Hard-Line	Win–Win	Conditional Cooperation		
Democracy vs. Dictatorship					
Democratic peace		◆	◆	+	Established democracies + mutual respect (+ trade) → positive peace
Dictatorial tyranny	◆	◆	◇	−	Dictatorships start and lose most major wars of the 20th century
Indian democracy				+/−	Corrupt system is inept but avoids tyranny, disintegration, and famine
Chinese dictatorship	◆	◇		+/−	Corrupt system mobilizes and educates but also commits democide
Economic Prosperity					
Economic growth (Western)		◆		+	Free enterprise + literacy + "invisible hand" + technology = Industrial Revolution
Economic growth in Japan	◇	◆		+	Drive to learn/adapt + discipline + industrial policy → rapid ascent
Clinton synthesis	◇	◆		+	Free enterprise + industrial policy + free trade → growth, low inflation
NAFTA		◆		?	Complementary economies at different stages + proximity → hope
WTO		◆	◆	?	GATT experiences → trust in free trade vs. residual protectionism → hope
Boeing-MCD merger	◆		◇	?	Free trade/antimonopoly policies vs. desire for market share → compromise
Models of Development					
Import substitution	◆			−	Inability to compete in world markets → attempted autarky → isolation
NIEO	◆			−	Dependency on fluctuating commodity prices → request to share the wealth
Communist autarky	◆			−	Reluctance to depend on capitalist or other foreign systems → isolation
Tigers		◆		+	Work, education, savings, investment + some foreign aid = Asian miracle
Leninist capitalism	◇	◆		+	Tiger formula minus foreign aid + strong central controls = PRC miracle
South Asia	◆	◇			Central controls + poor education and public health = slow growth
Transitions					
Russia	◆	◆		+/	Russia in 1990s is not Germany in 1950s; robber baron capitalism + lack of entrepreneurial traditions + poor safety net + mafias = low productivity + income inequality + poor health
Kazakstan	◇	◇	◇	−	Conditions as in Russia + dictatorship + hope for salvation by oil
Poland		◆			Free enterprise not forgotten + some foreign capital + belief in work
Estonia		◆			Conditions as in Poland + Protestant ethic + ties with Nordic countries

NOTE: ◆ = dominant approach; ◇ = partial approach; empty cell = little attention; + = positive outcome for initiator; − = negative results for initiator.

Table 16.4 Approaches and Outcomes in Part 4: Building a Better World

Cases Analyzed	Approach			Outcomes	Interpretation/Other Key Variables That Made a Difference
	Hard-Line	Win–Win	Conditional Cooperation		
Ecopolitics					
Aswan syndrome	◆	◆		+/−	Trust in the technological quick-fix → some economic gain + serious environmental and other problems
Amazonian syndrome	◆	◇		−	Trust in natural abundance and development
Ozone diplomacy			◆	+	Expert consensus on dangers/remedies + willingness to apportion costs
Global warming diplomacy	◇		◇	?	Potential disasters vs. limited consensus on dangers/ remedies/costs
Does Might Make Right?					
Stimson Doctrine	◆			+/−	Moral–legal pressure → legitimacy denied to Japan, Germany, Soviet conquests
Collective security in Korea	◆			+	UN approval + U.S.-led forces = denial of DPRK annexation of South Korea
Collective security in the Gulf	◆			+	UN approval + U.S.-led coalition = denial of Iraqi annexation of Kuwait
Keeping/Making Peace					
Peacekeeping (1948–1990)	◇	◆		+/−	UN missions → prevent renewed war in many but not all conflict zones
Mixed missions (1991–1997)	◇	◇	◇	+/−	Many UN missions fail in rebuilding failed states and enforcing peace
Functionalism					
EU as a common market		◆	◆	+	Functional cooperation + common market + peace = world's richest trading bloc
EU as a political union	◆	◇	◇	−	Diversity of interests and cultures = political divergence/impotence
Humanitarian Relief					
Tajikistan		◆		+/−	Neutral relief efforts difficult in civil/international strife
Law and Human Rights					
Slavery in the 1990s	◆			+	Slavery stopped but practices akin to slavery continue
Nuremberg Tribunal	◆			+	Personal culpability for war crimes + no sure enforce- ment = no deterrence
Genocide	◇			−	No sure enforcement → genocide in Indochina, Bosnia, Rwanda
Laws of war			◆	+	Geneva Conventions usually observed by govern- ments but often not by warlords
Universal declaration		◆		+/−	Moral pressure → raised consciousness, but no legal force
Covenants		◆		+/−	Legal obligations undermined by reservations and weak or no enforcement
Women's rights		◇		?	Legal obligations undermined by reservations and weak or no enforcement
Helsinki Final Act (1975)	◆	◆	◆	+	Moral pressures + Soviet desire for trade and legiti- macy = growing voice for human rights in USSR and less repression
Human rights in China	◇			−	Outside pressures + FDI + trade = little effect on awakening giant

NOTE: ◆ = dominant approach; ◇ = partial approach: empty cell = little attention: + = positive outcome for initiator: − = negative results for initiator.

Environmental diplomacy usually plays catch-up after the damage is manifest. Protecting the ozone layer required sacrifices first by industrial economies and later by LDCs. The obstacles to an accord on global warming were more complicated. Bottom-line greed reinforced the logic of collective action.

Hard power plus resolve are needed to restore or enforce peace. The 1932 Stimson Doctrine was tough but, lacking any material punch, did not discomfit aggressors except for the USSR, which was denied legitimacy in the Baltic. Indeed, Washington's principled stand against Soviet annexation of the Baltic republics contributed to their eventual liberation. By contrast, tangible and intangible power merged in the U.S.–UN responses to the Korean War and to Iraqi expansion.

The win–win approach proved weak or inadequate in dealing with hard-liners: Southern leaders after the U.S. Civil War; merchants and buyers of conventional arms; protection of human rights by toothless conventions; mediation or peacekeeping when some parties insist on zero-sum policies.

Win–win can be a useful approach to peacekeeping when all parties want peace. But peacekeeping failed between adversaries not content with the status quo, such as the South Slavs. To maintain peace in the Balkans required much hard power. Similarly, both Afghanistan and Iraq in 2003 teetered on anarchy for lack of security they could not provide for themselves.

A win–win strategy helped to build European economic cooperation but failed to generate a common foreign/defense policy. The win–win orientation of the International Red Cross and other relief agencies did not dissuade warlords in Tajikistan and other battle zones from their *kto kovo* mind-set.

A firm line gave a coup de grâce to slavery in most parts of the world. It also inflicted punishment on some top Nazi and Japanese leaders for war crimes. Conditional cooperation—an expectation of reciprocity— often moves governments to respect the laws of war regarding prisoners and civilians. Without enforcement, however, most human rights conventions are flouted by dictatorships and sometimes by democracies. Moscow's hope for trade and other benefits induced the Kremlin in the 1970s and 1980s to pledge respect for human rights. But China received massive foreign investment and trade privileges in spite of its poor human rights performance.

To sum up, win–win policies helped to foster domestic fitness in the U.S. and Japan; advance ethnic harmony in several multiethnic countries;

sustain the democratic peace and unite democracies against dictator-ships; spur economic growth within and among free market countries.

An orientation toward mutual gain served the interests of each party better than exploitation. Value-creating policies assisted actors with roughly comparable assets, such as the U.S. and USSR. But unequal part-ners also generated mutual gain, for example, the small and large coun-tries that participated in the European Recovery Program. Similarly, in-dustrialized and industrializing countries apportioned the restraints needed to protect the ozone layer.

Hard-line policies that aimed to exploit failed in every case studied.[6] In 2001, however, two new purveyors of zero-sum politics loomed up and confronted each other. The George W. Bush administration took office and asserted unilateralist policies not seen in Washington since the 1920s or perhaps 1898. For nine months the Bush administration systematically alienated friends and potential partners such as China. But on 9/11/01 it suffered a severe blow from another exponent of zero-sum politics, the al-Qaeda network for jihad. The pampered sons of American and Arabian oligarchies, George W. and Osama bin Laden, faced one another in a fight to the death.[7] The one represented a blend of Western material-ism and Christian fundamentalism; the other an intolerant and militant form of antimaterialist Islamic fundamentalism. Bush turned to foreign partners and the UN for help against bin Laden's network, but U.S. policy remained far more unilateralist than multilateralist. Both Bush and bin Laden defied most of the lessons of 20th-century history summarized in this book.[8] Time would tell whether either leader would succeed. Perhaps Secretary of State Colin Powell and other forces for multilateral coopera-tion would manage to return U.S. policy to the principles that helped it to lead—not dictate or bully—in earlier decades. If not, the chances for a scenario of fragmented chaos, described below, would improve.

A second conclusion drawn from our case studies is that, in peace-time, openness and multiparty dialogue are more likely to produce suc-cessful policies than decisions hatched in secrecy. The best support for this hypothesis is again the Marshall Plan—conceived behind closed doors but initiated, planned, and implemented openly. Yes, most agree-ments on security issues were negotiated in secret—even those that gen-erated mutual gain, such as the Cuban stand-down, SALT, INF, START, and the Camp David and other mediated accords. While the details were negotiated in secret, the logic of most arms control accords was discussed openly in the West. Most of the numbers and types of weapons at stake were public information. As a result, Western publics and NGOs could be

6. For a more detailed analysis, see Walter C. Clemens, Jr., *America and the World, 1898–2025: Achievements, Failures, Alternative Futures* (New York: Palgrave, 2000); also Robert A. Pastor, ed., *A Century's Journey: How the Great Powers Shape the World* (New York: Basic Books, 1999).

7. Demetrios James Caraley, ed., *September 11, Terrorist Attacks, and U.S. Foreign Policy* (New York: Academy of Political Science, 2002); *The War on Terror* (New York: W. W. Norton for the Council on Foreign Relations, 2002).

8. See also Joseph S. Nye, Jr., *The Paradox of American Power: Why the World's Only Superpower Can't Go It Alone* (New York: Oxford University Press, 2002) and, from another perspective, Andrew J. Bacevich, *American Empire: The Realities and Con-sequences of U.S. Diplomacy* (Cambridge, Mass.: Harvard University Press, 2002).

and were active participants in the arms control process. Except for a few privileged scientists and journalists, Communist publics remained in the dark about arms control issues and numbers, informed only after treaties were signed—and even then, only in generalities. Absence of public participation permitted militarization of the USSR beyond any reasonable security need, ultimately weakening the Soviet regime. If open diplomacy plays to the crowds, of course, it can become a propaganda contest harmful to mutual trust. Both secrecy and propaganda helped to sour most Soviet–U.S. détentes. Thus, President Eisenhower's major proposal at the 1955 Geneva summit was a call for "open skies"—permission for spy planes to cross Soviet and Western territory. The idea had intrinsic merit, but it was conceived at a U.S. Marine base by experts in psychological warfare and aimed to embarrass the Soviets.

The only Soviet–Western détente that endured more than one or two years was that pursued by Gorbachev and the Reagan–Bush administrations. It was also the most open and constructive, with little propaganda meant to embarrass the other side.

Openness also proved useful in welding national unity in free societies, cultivating a strong economy, and unleashing science. By contrast, Communist governments have tended to deny the realities of ethnic discontent, falsify production and health statistics, and keep scientific advances secret. Secrecy also shields corruption. In the late 20th and early 21st century businesspeople the world over came to decry corruption, as practiced in Nigeria, Indonesia, China, and—after Enron and similar scandals—the United States.

Secrecy is useful if you wish to evade arms limitations or prepare a surprise attack. Openness is good if you wish to rally collective security against aggressors. Saddam Hussein's deceptions kept UN arms inspectors running in circles but helped over time to bring about his downfall.

Secrecy is good if you wish to keep a government bureaucracy or banking system dominated by nepotism and other favoritisms. Openness is better if you wish to clean house, attract long-term credits and investments, and inspire support for bodies such as the UN.

Secrecy is useful if you want to violate human rights without public embarrassments. Openness is good if you campaign against such violations.

An open society—where all citizens may think and express themselves freely and enjoy access to all forms of information—is a prerequisite for other social goals at home and internationally—scientific and technological progress, improved living standards, mutual gain enterprises at home and abroad, détente, arms control, peace, environmental preservation, and justice.[9] Even before 9/11, however, the Bush administration took unprecedented steps to hide its decision making and deep objectives from public view. After 9/11, these tendencies multiplied. Even as the executive branch became more secretive, it stepped up collection of data on the lives of ordinary citizens. While Big Brother became bigger in Washington, al-Qaeda broadcast its objectives but counted on secrecy to mount surprise attacks.

INTO THE 21ST CENTURY: ALTERNATIVE FUTURES

Let us stretch our minds across the first quarter of the 21st century. Our view starts from the pyramid of power outlined in Chapter 5—a unipolar world combining a sole superpower with successive levels of great, medium, regional, and rising powers. Six scenarios follow, though many variations are possible. Each scenario assumes that technology continues to reduce distance and time, that many means of locomotion and of destruction become cheaper and more widely acceptable, and that mutual vulnerabilities increase. Our first five scenarios assume that governments dominate the world scene; the sixth scenario posits that the processes of globalization elicit world governance by combinations of national, international, and transnational agents. Each scenario blends elements of conflict and mutual gain. To maximize credibility, each scenario is portrayed as a fact—not what "could," "would," or "should" be. The most familiar scenarios—those closest to the pyramid of power in the 1990s—are listed first.[10]

I. Unipolar Stability

U.S. hegemony is rooted in tangible and intangible assets that show no sign of weakening—a splendid geographical setting occupied by a diverse and well-educated population with freedom to create.[11] The unipolar world continues for decades. It proves to be the most peaceful, stable, and prosperous era in human history. It is a world in which most states deal with global interdependence in a manner that generates mutual gain. It begins to embody the principle: "From each according to her or his ability, to each according to her or his need." There is more value-creation than aggressive exploitation or parasitism.

Unipolarity is more conducive to peace among the great powers than the multilateral balancing of the 19th century, the rival alliances of 1914, or Cold War bipolarity. Great power stability, of course, does not prevent disorder between and within lesser states drifting toward chaos. Outside

9. As Andrei Sakharov put it in his Nobel Peace Prize acceptance speech in 1975: "Détente can only be assured if from the very outset it goes hand in hand with continuous openness on the part of all countries, an aroused sense of public opinion, free exchange of information, and absolute respect in all countries for civic and political rights. In short: in addition to détente in the material sphere, with disarmament and trade, détente should take place in the intellectual and ideological sphere."

10. For more detailed scenarios, see Clemens, *America and the World*, 205–222.

11. See Zbigniew Brzezinski, *The Grand Chessboard: American Primacy and Its Geostrategic Imperatives* (New York: Basic Books, 1997).

Acting as both cause and effect, the single European currency boosted intra-European commerce and political cooperation. It simplified economic transactions not just for Europeans but also for foreign tourists who no longer had to calculate exchange rates each time they crossed a border. Question: If the euro is good for Europe, and if multilateral cooperation increases, should Americans renounce the dollar and use the euro as well? Or should both sides adopt the "nata"—north Atlantic trading agent?

powers, usually with UN blessing, intervene in some but not all trouble spots. The U.S. is a new kind of hegemon on the world stage. This pax americana is more stable than the ancient pax romana, because it rests more on persuasion and cooption than on commands or coercion. The sole superpower seldom acts alone. Washington needs, seeks, and usually gets the support of other actors for its key goals, as it did in forging a policy to contain Iraq and North Korea in the 1990s.

A deal takes shape: Washington does not abuse its power and other countries do not gang up against the lone superpower. This deal is feasible because the U.S. remains closer to the UK, Germany, Japan, China, Russia, Brazil, India, Ukraine, and Kazakstan than any one of them is to another. The other major powers have no deep reason, as in 1914, to chain-gang or, as in 1938–1939, to pass the buck.

Economic prospects for most of the world are positive. The world is sufficiently rich and well informed to find paths to sustainable development. The World Bank formulates dependable guidelines by which countries can develop and improve their HDI and gender equality scores as well as their GDPs. Russia begins to realize its economic potential. New giants arise—China, Brazil, Argentina, Indonesia, Kazakstan. But none has the wish or the means to challenge the global hegemon.

Europe and Japan remain powerful trading states. Europe, however, is at most a confederation. Real union is infeasible due to language and cultural differences. Most Europeans are more likely to converge against one of their own, Germany, than against the United States. To avert this, Germany abjures advanced weapons and remains dependent upon the nuclear forces of its NATO partners.

Alliance with the U.S. is still the linchpin of Japan's security. The country's place in the pyramid of power declines as China's strengthens. Japan faces severe limits. Its archipelago remains crowded. The population becomes grayer with fewer workers to support retirees. Japan's foreign markets shrink as Korea and other neighbors fill the same demands at lower prices. Most Pacific rim economies slow their torrid pace as fresh inputs of labor, capital, and energy become more costly. HIV infections impose a heavy economic burden in several countries. Many workers die young or require expensive drugs to live. Authoritarian rule curtails the once vibrant growth of Singapore and Hong Kong.

II. Fragmented Chaos

Extrapolations often go wrong. How could chaos replace stability? Humans stand at the brink: Mutual vulnerability means that a serious change in any part of the system can ripple and multiply throughout the whole.

First, the biosphere fails to support human life in some places where it flourished in the 1990s. The affluent Pacific rim sits on a ring of fire—volcanoes and fault lines—that devour life and property. Storms and droughts increase due to climate change abetted by pollution and deforestation. Both environmental and economic barriers impede growth. It is

America could abet chaos if U.S. policies were too aggressive or too nonchalant. The Bush administration's focus on the "axis of evil" led it to neglect a series of other problems that could destabilize world peace, prosperity, and environmental quality. In 2003 America attacked an Iraq that lacked any serious nuclear weapons capability while North Korea and Iran openly developed nuclear arms and Pakistan and India regularly threatened nuclear war on each other. Environmental problems could sweep the globe.

Mr. Bush Travels Through the World Other Than Iran, Iraq and North Korea

and are partners with Kuwait in developing an infrastructure built on desalinized water.

North–South differences narrow. More Asian, African, Middle Eastern, and Latin American countries enter the path of rapid and sustainable development. New strains of hybrid wheat, rice, maize, and other crops permit nearly every region to become self-sufficient in basic foods—without heavy irrigation or chemicals. Few countries still depend on jute, cocoa, or any other single commodity. Investment in health and education rises dramatically as developing and industrialized countries shift resources from defense to development needs. Biodiversity in the Amazon and other tropical regions is protected and becomes profitable.

VI. Global Governance Without World Government

A transnational civil society is evolving. Like civil society within countries, it shields individual humans and groups from the raw powers of government and market. The transnational civil society develops in tandem with complex interdependence across many countries and regions. Common values—political choice, trust in free markets, respect for human rights—are shared by more than half of humanity. Territoriality weakens as a principle of organization. There is no world government by a supranational authority. National governments remain but they share power with a medley of nongovernmental agencies—business and labor groups as well as NGOs. Together they form expanding networks of institutions designed to meet a wide range of human needs.[14]

National governments confer among themselves and with responsible specialists from subnational, international, and transnational agencies. This is functionalism writ large—decision making informed and managed by experts, mediated and supervised by representatives of elected governments.

Twenty-first century humanity can build upon the efforts of governments, industrial, and NGO leaders in the late 20th century to forge a consensus on shared concerns. To cope with epidemics, government experts form a committee drawn from national medical boards, the WHO, the International Red Cross, and the recently formed International Academy of Health Sciences. To deal with economic issues—currency fluctuations, debt, volatile commodity prices—government experts form a committee drawn from the World Bank, the IMF, leading commercial

14. See Wolfgang H. Reinicke, "Global Public Policy," *Foreign Affairs* 76, no. 6 (November–December 1997): 127–138; *Our Global Neighborhood: The Report on the Commission on Global Governance* (New York: Oxford University Press, 1995); Mihaly Simai, *The Future of Global Governance: Managing Risk and Change in the International System* (Washington, D.C.: United States Institute of Peace Press, 1994); John D. Donahue and Joseph S. Nye, Jr., eds., *Governance Amid Bigger, Better Markets* (Washington, D.C.: Brookings Institution, 2001).

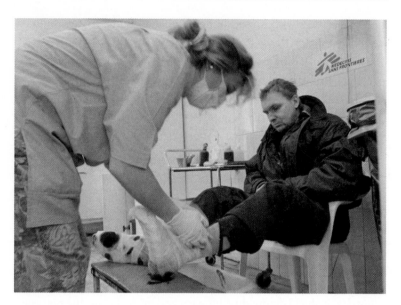

Unable to get care from Russia's doctors after medicine was privatized in the 1990s, a homeless man in Moscow is treated for frostbite by a physician from Doctors Without Borders. Founded by a group of French physicians in 1971, *Médicins Sans Frontières* (MSF) became the world's largest independent international medical relief agency. It aided victims of armed conflict, epidemics, and disasters, whether natural or man-made. It also helped those who lacked health care due to geographic remoteness, ethnic marginalization, or—as in the Russian case—a breakdown of the social welfare net. MSF teams provided primary health care, performed surgery, vaccinated children, rehabilitated hospitals, operated emergency nutrition and sanitation programs, and trained local medical staff. Operating independently of governments, the organization depended on volunteer health professionals (over 2,000 annually) and private donations. It received the 1999 Nobel Peace Prize.

Six MSF volunteers were working in Iraq as the U.S–UK coalition entered the country in 2003. On April 10, MSF addressed the UN Security Council and raised concerns about two MSF volunteers missing since April 2, about humanitarian conditions in Iraq, and about rising casualties from the fighting. MSF also worried that America's "hearts and minds" strategy might fuel Arab suspicions that all humanitarian activities were subordinated to the U.S.–UK coalition.

banks, and the recently formed International Academy of Economic and Social Scientists.

To deal with threats to peace and security, governments depend heavily on the UN Security Council and the UN secretary-general. Some governments retain nuclear arsenals, but the Security Council has its own rapid reaction force, backed by designated units from most UN members. The UN secretary-general has a panel of mediators available to disputants. A committee of elders drawn from Nobel Peace Prize laureates advises the Security Council and the secretary-general. The International Peace Academy has graduated many diplomats skilled at conflict resolution.

By 2010 the University of the Middle East has received significant help from some governments and foundations. By 2020 it has trained a generation of men and women more concerned with peaceful development than with sectarian passions. By 2025 these people have launched several projects that knit Israel and its neighbors in mutual gain.

World governance is more than the "common marketization" of IR. It is global public policy responding to the dangers and opportunities inherent in globalization.

Which Scenario Is Best? Which Is Most Feasible?

It is easy to say which scenarios are the worst. Scenarios II and III—fragmented chaos and a collision between hegemon and challenger—

could destroy many lives and waste valuable assets. The more violence, the greater the suffering and the more difficult the tasks of reconstruction. Wise planners will act to block the roads that lead in these directions.

Any scenario that promotes peace and prosperity is acceptable. But Scenario VI—world governance—has two advantages. First, it postulates development of a truly transnational society. Without such a society, the state system may eventually break down.[15] World governance both requires and contributes to a well-integrated global society.

Second, global governance is more likely to cultivate a rich emergent structure able to cope with complex challenges than any scenario that leaves basic tasks mainly to governments. Fitness requires an ability to cope with complexity. Cooperation between governments and non-governmental bodies is more likely to embody the flexibility and reach needed to deal with emerging needs.

LEARNING TO SHARE ONE WORLD

How deeply did 9/11 alter IR? The events of that day and their aftermath sharpened existing trends and confirmed basic truths in each way of looking at world affairs. For starters, they reinforced elements in the realist paradigm. States remain the fundamental actors in IR, even though nonstate actors are important. Power counts: Whether other states approved or objected, most got out of the way when the global colossus decided to attack its tormentors. Regimes, law, and other forms of international cooperation are not cut in granite. They endure only so long as states' interests overlap. Functional cooperation makes life more convenient, but can vanish if governments feel their vital interests require them to depart from established norms.

But idealists also found support for their outlook. The events on 9/11 underscored how eroded is the myth of national sovereignty. Every state is permeable—from the sole superpower to hermit dictatorships such as Myanmar. World politics is not just a struggle for power. Ideals count—even if twisted. Thus, radical Muslims and their counterparts in other faiths acted to sharpen clashes between civilizations. Other idealists, however, reduce the damage and raised hopes of human solidarity, for example, NGOs such as Doctors Without Borders.

But realism and idealism—even in their various "neo" variants—are too narrow. Above all, 9/11 and its aftermath confirmed the utility of viewing the world through the lens of global interdependence. Awareness of our shared vulnerabilities and capacity to help or harm one another

15. See the alternative paths to world order in Hedley Bull, *The Anarchical Society: A Study of Order in World Politics* (New York: Columbia University Press, 1977), chaps. 10–14.

provides a broader framework for understanding the past and planning the future. It underlines the need to think about means and ends, practicality and morality.

How we respond to mutual vulnerability is up to humans—in and out of government. Nothing is predetermined. On 9/11, a few skyjackers spending under a million dollars shook the world. Neither their chief backer nor (after the fact) their chief foe bent with the wind. Both Osama bin Laden and George W. Bush defied convention and ignored critics. Each endeavored to tap all the assets, tangible and intangible, at his disposal. Each man was impaled, however, on his own narrow vision and his zero-sum approach to problem solving. Neither came close to a one-world vision of global interdependence to reduce anarchy and create mutual gain.

GLOBAL CONSCIOUSNESS: EDUCATION FOR ONE WORLD

To reduce anarchy we need heightened global consciousness, deeper and more rewarding global relationships, and stronger global institutions. The quotations in the epigraph to this book sum up its main conclusions. As Ralph Bunche put it in 1951, people need to perceive and act on their true self-interest. National egocentrism, imagined superiority, and claims to special privilege carry us toward disaster.

If we are to live in peace and create values together, each person needs education in basic principles:

Empathy—to see the world as others do

Historical perspective—to understand that "everything is the result of everything else"

Respect for other cultures—to admire and enjoy the myriad ways of life across the globe

Reverence for life—to deal with a fecund but fragile biosphere

Responsibility—to consider our place in the great chain of being: our debts to those who lived before, to those less privileged than ourselves, and to those who will follow

POLICIES FOR ONE WORLD

The case studies reviewed here—taken from different times and places—end to confirm the book's two underlying hypotheses. Informed by this knowledge, you draft your report.

Memo to the UN Secretary-General:

The dynamics of international relations in the last one or two hundred years are replete with cases validating the efficacy of these two guidelines:

1. The optimal way to enhance each actor's interests is by carrying out strategies aimed at creating values for each party. Value-claiming generates short-term gains that tend to backfire.

2. Policies arrived at openly tend to work better than those conceived and implemented covertly.

These guidelines have an inner logic: The more that policies are discussed at home and with concerned actors abroad, the greater the likelihood of achieving mutual gains valued by each party. The quality of discussion, in turn, depends upon the information and orientation of decision makers and the public. A variable-sum outlook is more constructive than a zero-sum perspective and safer than win–win expectations.

The combined power of these guidelines is best seen in the postwar evolution of the First World—a security and trade community built upon a quest for mutual gain—its contours and defining moments debated openly within and among North America, Europe, and Japan.

Value-creating strategies can be difficult to conceive, plan, and implement due to many factors—bad memories, divergent cultures, asymmetries of power and wealth. We can buy time by negotiating arms control, establishing international regimes, developing trade and educational exchange, utilizing third-party mediation, and fostering dialogue among all segments of global society. If we avoid catastrophe, there is the possibility that a negative-sum or zero-sum struggle may become a variable- or even positive-sum search for overlapping goals. If the relationship between France and Germany can be transformed, why not that between Israel and Syria? If the U.S. and Russia can become real partners, why not India and Pakistan?

Every dogmatism can be a blindfold shutting out light and opportunity from our vision. For Russia to shed communism was not death but a chance for rebirth. Other societies may also find that by shedding their zero-sum dogmas, they are liberated at home and abroad. Wisdom dictates a quest to nurture value-creating policies with other societies, coupled with awareness that strong currents of anarchy remain.

RECOMMENDED RESOURCES

BOOKS

Berger, Peter L. and Samuel P. Huntington, eds. *Many Globalizations: Cultural Diversity in the Contemporary World.* New York: Oxford University Press, 2002.

Brockman, John, ed. *The Next Fifty Years: Science in the First Half of the Twenty-first Century.* New York: Vintage, 2002.

Clemens, Walter C., Jr., *America and the World, 1898–2025: Achievements, Failures, Alternative Futures* (New York: Palgrave, 2000).

Cooper, Richard N., et al., eds. *What the Future Holds: Insights from Social Science.* Cambridge, Mass.: MIT Press, 2002.

Eban, Abba. *Diplomacy for the Century.* New Haven, Conn.: Yale University Press, 1998.

Encyclopedia of the Future. 2 vols. New York: Macmillan Library Reference, 1996.

Fukuyama, Francis. *Our Posthuman Future: Consequences of the Biotechnology Revolution.* New York: Farrar, Straus & Giroux, 2002.

Glover, Jonathan. *Humanity: A Moral History of the Twentieth Century.* New Haven, Conn: Yale University Press, 2002.

Recommended Resources (continued)

Godet, Michael. *From Anticipation to Action: A Handbook of Strategic Prospective.* Paris: UNESCO, 1994.

Hughes, Barry. *International Futures: Choices in the Face of Uncertainty.* 3d ed. Boulder, Colo.: Westview, 1999.

Kahn, Herman. *Thinking About the Unthinkable in the 1980s.* New York: Simon & Schuster, 1984.

Kahn, Herman, et al. *The Next Two Hundred Years.* London: Abacus, 1978.

Kennedy, Paul. *Preparing for the Twenty-first Century.* New York: Random House, 1993.

Kennedy, Paul M., et al., eds. *Global Trends and Global Governance.* London: Pluto, 2002.

Neack, Laura. *The New Foreign Policy: U.S. and Comparative Foreign Policy in the 21st Century.* Lanham, Md.: Rowman & Littlefield, 2002.

Resources for the Future: An International Annotated Bibliography for the 21st Century. ed. Alan J. Mayne. London: Adamantine, 1993.

Singer, Peter. *One World: The Ethics of Globalization.* New Haven, Conn.: Yale University Press, 2002.

Toffler, Alvin. *Future Shock.* New York: Bantam, 1971.

———. *Powershift: Knowledge, Wealth, and Violence at the Edge of the 21st Century.* New York: Bantam, 1990.

WEB SITES

The Centre for Future Studies
http://www.futurestudies.co.uk/home.shtml

Futurology
http://www.kheper.auz.com/future/scenarios/futurology.htm

Future Studies, Future Conflict Studies
http://www.au.af.mil/au/awc/awcgate/awc-futr.htm

Institute for Alternative Futures
http://www.altfutures.com/

GLOSSARY

absolute advantage concept of market strength based on natural endowment; a premise of Adam Smith's trust in an invisible hand

actor in IR a state, TNC, NGO, or other IR player

alliance a military partnership stipulating joint action under specified conditions; more loosely, any partnership

al-Qaeda see Qaeda, al-

Alsace and Lorraine disputed borderlands taken by Germany in 1871 and retaken by France in 1918–1919

anarchy absence of government (though order is still possible)

antiballistic missile (ABM) defense a net of radars and missiles to track and destroy incoming ballistic missiles, but of no use against low-flying cruise missiles or, of course, "suitcase" or truck bombs; constrained by a U.S.-Soviet treaty from 1972 until its abrogation by President George W. Bush in 2002, after which the U.S. began an ABM deployment in Alaska

apartheid system of racial segregation practiced in South Africa until the 1990s

Appomattox Virginia courthouse where Confederate General R. E. Lee surrendered to Union General U. S. Grant in 1865; symbol of a conciliatory peace policy

appropriate technology whatever scale technology is appropriate to the task

Arafat, Yasser chairman of the Palestinian Liberation Organization (PLO) since 1969 and, after 1994, of the Palestinian Authority in the West Bank and Gaza Strip

arbitration binding adjudication by one or more arbiters selected by the disputants

arms control regulation of arms to enhance political, military, economic, or other aims; could entail disarmament

assimilation absorbing minorities into the dominant culture

Association of Southeast Asian Nations (ASEAN) international organization formed in 1967 to promote cooperation among its members, which in 2003 included Brunei, Indonesia, Laos, Malaysia, Myanmar (Burma), the Philippines, Singapore, Thailand, and Vietnam

Aswan syndrome devotion to high dams and reluctance to face negative externalities—uprooted people, silting, salty soil, diminished nutrients downstream, increased vulnerability

attention space the amount of attention a decision maker can devote to any problem; constrained by fatigue and by multiple demands

autarky economic self-sufficiency and nonreliance on imports or aid

authoritarian top-down governance based on strong leadership rather than democracy

autonomy self-rule in local affairs

balance of payments accounting of all transactions between one country and others

balance of power an ambiguous concept that can mean equality of power, inequality, or any distribution of power, with focus on military and economic assets

Baruch Plan U.S. proposal in 1946 to create an international authority to control all nuclear weapons and plants throughout the world; inspection and other provisions rejected by Moscow

Bay of Pigs Cuban coast where anti-Castro exiles, sponsored by the CIA, were defeated by Cuban forces in April 1961

bean count an assessment of power based on counting who has what, for example, how many soldiers, tanks, modems; undervalues intangibles

Berlusconi, Silvio billionaire media mogul who served as Italy's prime minister in the mid-1990s and early 21st century; exploiting his three TV channels for political influence

best alternative to a negotiated agreement (BATNA) a crucial issue in deciding whether to seek a negotiated accord

Big Mac Time (BMT) how many minutes an average worker must work to pay for a Big Mac—far fewer in the U.S. than in Russia or China, thus—an alternative way to measure PPP

bin Laden see Laden, Osama bin

biosphere the zone of life on earth and the atmosphere that shapes and is shaped by IR; the fifth level of IR action and analysis

Blair, Tony leader of the Labour Party since 1994, elected UK prime minister in 1997; close partner to U.S. presidents Bill Clinton and George W. Bush in foreign affairs

Blitzkrieg German for lightning war; combined tank and air assaults followed by rapid infantry advance used by Germany in 1939–1941

bounded rationality the concept that limits on time, energy, and available information constrain the ability of decision makers to process information and act rationally

Bretton Woods system system of international finance established in 1944 based on convertibility of the U.S. dollar into gold and supported by the IMF and World Bank; replaced by floating currencies after 1971

Bricker Amendment U.S. constitutional amendment proposal of the 1950s that called for implementing legislation for treaties (for example, on human rights) before they could become law

buck passing deferring to another actor to take the first step, for example, to cope with expansionist Germany in the 1930s

Bunche, Ralph African-American who served for years as the second most powerful official in the UN Secretariat; awarded Nobel Peace Prize (1950) for mediating Arab–Israeli dispute in 1948–1949; helped create UN peacekeeping

Bush [George W.] Doctrine to defend, attack: U.S. should and will act alone or with a coalition of the willing to preempt attacks by potential foes amassing WMD; defensive offensive

C^4 command, control, communications, and computer processing to coordinate warfare in real time from a distance, used with ISR

capital material wealth being used or usable for the production of more wealth

capitalism private ownership of the means of production; for Marxists, private ownership of the means of production, destined to be replaced by socialism

carrying capacity the level of resource utilization that can be sustained without degrading the original resource

Carter, Jimmy U.S. president who mediated the 1978 Camp David Accord and, as a private citizen, the 1994 U.S.–North Korea understandings on nuclear issues

Carthaginian peace total destruction of Carthage by Rome in 146 B.C.; symbol of a vindictive, repressive policy to the defeated

Caspian Sea landlocked sea bordered by Russia, Kazakstan, Iran, and Azerbaijan, with vast oil reserves

Central Asia Kazakstan, Kyrgyzstan, Turkmenistan, Tajikistan, Uzbekistan, and some adjacent parts of Russia and China, such as Xinjiang, where more than half the population is Uighur or Kazak

chain-ganging movement in unison, as in 1914, when most members of the two alliances quickly joined one another in war

Chechnya political entity in the north Caucasus; declared its independence from Russia after the Soviet breakup; attacked by Russian forces in 1994–1996 and again in 1999

Chernobyl site of 1986 nuclear reactor accident in Ukraine; also the nontechnical name for a type of Soviet-built reactor widely used in Eastern Europe

Chernomyrdin, Viktor prime minister of Russia for much of the 1990s; former official in the oil industry

Chicken collision course in which double defection leads to shared catastrophe

China card leverage that Washington hoped to use against the USSR based on the prospect that the U.S. might draw closer to a major Soviet foe

Christianity, Orthodox and Western civilizations sharing much in common, but Orthodox Christianity based in Constantinople, Moscow, and other Eastern capitals developed differently from, and sometimes in conflict with, Western Christianity

civil society intermediate institutions shielding individuals from government and from raw market forces

civilization the broadest level of cultural identity

civilizationism Samuel P. Huntingon's view that the fault lines of post–Cold War IR are at the meeting places of the world's seven or eight major civilizations

Clausewitz, Carl von early-19th-century Prussian military strategist who argued that war is the continuation of policy by other (violent) means

Clemenceau, Georges French premier who pressed for reparations from and repression of Germany after World War I

coalition of the willing ad hoc partnership of countries willing to help the U.S. outside of any formal alliance or IGO obligations

coevolution the development of an actor in tandem with other actors and their shared environment

cold war multifaceted struggle to defeat the other side using many kinds of hard and soft power but avoiding hot war, unless by proxies

collective (or public) good a good freely available to all, whether produced by human action or nature, thus tempting free riders

collective security a system of "one for all and all for one" requiring each party to respond to an attack on another member as an attack on itself

Commitment to Development Index (CDI) six measures of the effectiveness of development aid

commodity agreement accord by producers of a primary product to limit production and/or set prices

Commonwealth of Independent States (CIS) an IGO in which all former Soviet republics participate, except for the three Baltic states

comparative advantage relative advantage of one producer or country; a major reason for international trade

competitive advantage economic strength based not just on endowment but on many factors, including standards set by local consumers and governments

complex humanitarian emergency problem facing relief agencies in the 1990s, often includes consequences of a failed state, poverty, civil war and foreign intervention, environmental disaster, and famine

complex interdependence a relationship between IR actors characterized by a complex agenda with no hierarchy, interaction on many levels, and bargaining without force

complexity (or agent-based-systems) theory derived from evolutionary science, the theory sees a capacity for self-organization as crucial to the fitness of organisms and entire systems

Concert of Europe periodic meetings of the major powers during the 19th century to deal with threats to stability; a precursor to the UN Security Council

concessional loans loans at less than commercial interest rates; with grants, a form of foreign aid

condominium international order in which two or more actors share power

confederation a system of governance in which most power resides in local units

conflict disharmony, struggle, combat, war—deeper than a dispute; often results from exploitation real or perceived

conflict resolution removing the causes and manifestations of conflict, for example, by peacemaking or peace building

Congress of Vienna 1815 conference that established a new order in Europe after Napoleon's final defeat; symbol of a firm but conciliatory policy to the vanquished

consilience E. O. Wilson's term that many scholarly disciplines should "jump together" to advance theoretical and practical knowledge.

constitutionalism the democratic principle that government power should be distributed and limited by law—not by a politics of personality or manipulation of crises

constructivism idealist approach to IR emphasizing the role of social constructs—the deep beliefs each group of people has about other groups and ways of life

convention in IR a synonym for *treaty*, often used in environmental diplomacy

Convention on the Elimination of All Forms of Discrimination Against Women (CEDAW) 1979 treaty banning gender-based distinctions impairing women's human rights in any field

Convention on the Prevention and Punishment of the Crime of Genocide 1948 treaty adopted by most governments that bans acts committed with the intent to destroy a "national, ethnic, racial, or religious group, as such"

Conventional Forces in Europe (CFE) Treaty 1990 treaty limiting tanks, planes, and other weapons from the Atlantic to the Ural Mountains; tilted against Russia after Moscow's former allies aligned with the West

conventional war war fought by regular forces with tanks, planes, and missiles but without biological, chemical, or nuclear weapons; definition may change over time

conversion the difficult problem of converting military to civilian industry

conversion power ability to translate hard and soft power into fitness and influence

cooperative security programs to promote shared security interests between U.S. and partner–rivals such as Russia

Cooperative Threat Reduction Program cooperation between the U.S. and RF (and earlier, the USSR) to identify, destroy, and dispose of unwanted or banned WMD in the Russian (former Soviet) arsenal. Also called "Nunn-Lugar" for the two senators who sponsored the bill in 1991. The program helped eliminate some 6,000 warheads in the 1990s. The Republican Congress cut funding for the program in 2001 but the U.S. and other industrialized countries pledged in 2003 to continue and expand the program over the next ten years

coordination game a game in which the point is to increase the gains for each player

Cornucopian outlook the belief that human ingenuity ensures that there will be no finite limits on growth, as technology will be used to sustain populations

cost tolerance an intangible asset of power, the ability of a society to endure hardship and persevere in war despite losses

Council for Mutual Economic Assistance (COMECON) Moscow's anwer to the ERP; an IGO formed in 1949 to coordinate trade and economic policies in the Soviet sphere; disbanded in 1991

Country Reports on Human Rights Practices annual survey undertaken by the U.S. State Department to assess human rights practices worldwide (except in the U.S.)

crimes against humanity activities undertaken during wartime or in preparation for war identified by the International Military Tribunal at Nuremberg as actionable before an international court; includes murder, extermination, enslavement, and deportation of any civilian population and persecution on political, racial, or religious grounds

cruise missile pilotless aircraft, radar and computer-guided, armed with nuclear or other warheads

cult of the defensive military doctrine trusting in the superiority of the defense over the offense

cult of the offensive military doctrine trusting that wars can be won quickly by the side that mobilizes and strikes first

culture way of life, material and spiritual; a matrix of behavior

current account a measure linking a country's international transactions with its national income; includes all sales and purchases of currently produced goods and services, interest income, military transactions, travel and transportation receipts, and unilateral transfers

Dayton Peace Accord November 1995 agreements to end fighting in Bosnia and establish a Bosnian state that included the Croat–Muslim Federation and *Republika Srpska;* peace to be upheld initially by NATO forces

DDT an insecticide banned for most uses in the U.S. since 1972 but used in many LDCs

deadlock an impasse; in game theory, a condition in which both parties defect, round after round, causing mutual hurt

debt rescheduling renegotiated terms for loan repayment; usually, attenuation

debt service total principal and interest due on a loan each period

declinism view that great powers decline if they overreach, that is, expand too far and spend too much on empire

demagogue leader who arouses popular passions with rhetoric

demilitarized zone (DMZ) an area without fortifications; between North and South Korea

democide mass murder of people (*demos*), especially one's own

democracy governance by the people, usually indirect, by means of freely contested elections

Deng Xiaoping paramount PRC leader from 1977 to 1997

dependency theory variant of world-systems theory that sees the world as having an imperialist core with a dependent periphery

détente relaxation of tensions

determinism belief that impersonal forces, not individuals with free will, determine historical outcomes

deterrence restraint of other actors achieved by fear of retribution

development in IR, refers to fulfillment of potential by individuals (measured in HDI) or states (economic and political development)

dictatorship governance by an individual or small group with complete authority and unlimited power; may use persuasion as well as force

diplomacy foreign policy, especially by negotiation; includes Track 1 diplomacy—diplomacy by government officials—and Track 2 diplomacy—diplomacy by private citizens and organizations

disarmament the reduction or elimination of armaments

Dobrynin, Anatoly Soviet ambassador to six U.S. presidents; an important go-between during the Cuban missile crisis

dove conciliator, seeking to avoid war, not a "hawk"

Duma (also State Duma) the lower house of parliament in the Russian Federation

Earth Summit 1992 UN Conference on Environment and Development

East Asia home of an "economic miracle" led by Japan, followed by the four "Tigers" and by China; the miracle appeared less certain by the late 1990s

ecology study of habitat, environmental science

economic liberalism theory that individuals seeking their self-interest will raise the common good; against government intervention in economic affairs

economic statecraft use of economic rewards and penalties to shape the behavior of other actors in IR

economic warfare boycotts and sanctions meant to punish other actors or slow their development

ekos (oikos) "habitat," Greek root of economics and ecology

emergent structure a holistic entity more than the sum of its parts; a product of coevolution as diverse actors meet their diverse needs, as in a coral reef or, by analogy, the networks of global governance

endism the view of Francis Fukuyama that history—defined as the clash of ideas—ended with the Cold War

entente an agreement or understanding to collaborate (from the Old French *intent*), as in the Triple Entente before World War I

entitlement right or permit, for example, to release carbons

environmental diplomacy negotiation and actions at the interface between IR and the habitat, for example, the ozone layer

escalation dominance ability to prevail at any step of the escalation ladder, thus discouraging the other side from escalating

escalation ladder   hypothetical steps by which actors move toward greater violence, pausing at intervals that permit the parties to deliberate before intensifying their struggle

ethnic   pertaining to ethnos

ethnic cleansing   forced removal or attempted extermination of an ethnic group

ethnocentrism   centering on one's own ethnic group, its merits and problems

ethnos   a different people with its own ethos (like Spartans to Athenians); sometimes rendered as *ethnie*, a unit smaller than a nation

ethos   the character and moral values of a people

euro   common currency accepted by most EU members since 2002

European Atomic Energy Community (EURATOM)   established in 1957, promotes nuclear energy use in Europe and develops common standards

European Coal and Steel Community (ECSC)   the world's premier supranational organization, founded in 1951 by France, Germany, Italy, Belgium, the Netherlands, and Luxembourg to coordinate their production and sales of coal and steel

European Commission   executive body of the European Community; initiates policies and "guards" previous EC accords

European Community (EC)   collective term for the EEC, the ECSC, and EURATOM; the EC became the first "pillar" of the EU in 1993

European Council   the EU summit: the heads of government meeting twice each year to provide guidance for other EU organs

European Council of Ministers   a forum for policy planning by top ministers who meet at least twice a year; chaired by rotation

European Court of Justice   judicial body of the EC; rules on legality of acts by the European Commission and on compatibility of national and EC laws

European Economic Community (EEC)   established in 1957 by the ECSC states, an agreement to form a common market for the free movement of goods, labor, and capital across national borders

European Monetary Union (EMU)   EC goal of a common currency managed by a central bank, mandated by the Maastricht Treaty adopted in 1991–1992

European Parliament   the only EC body directly elected by voters of the member states; primarily a deliberative body

European Recovery Program (ERP)   see Marshall Plan

European Union (EU)   formed in 1993, the EU includes the EC as one pillar plus a pillar for forging a common foreign policy and another for overseeing justice and home affairs

ExCom (Executive Committee)   fourteen to twenty officials from various branches of government who advised the U.S. president during the Cuban missile crisis

expansionist nationalism   a nationalism seeking to displace or rule other nations, for example, Nazi German nationalism

exploitation   utilization of a resource; value-claiming, hard-line treatment of others as foes in a zero-sum relationship

export-led development strategy   following the Japanese model, a development strategy that aims to build a country's wealth by export of goods cheaper or better than others available in world markets; the strategy aims to utilize the IPE—not withdraw from it

externality   in economics, any cost or benefit of a good not encompassed in its price; a side effect, positive or negative, for an initiator or for third parties

extraction capability   ability to mobilize assets, for example, to tax and conscript for public purposes

factor endowment   production inputs: land and resources, labor, capital, and skills

failed state   country such as Somalia in the 1990s, where central government does not function

falling dominoes theory   expectation that if a critically positioned actor falls to the other side, its neighbors will also fall; helped to motivate U.S. support for Greece, Turkey, and South Vietnam

Faustian wager   risking the future for the present, as with nuclear power, an energy source that can also damage the biosphere

federation   political system in which power is divided between the center and the regions

feminism   in IR, belief that women and their interests have been neglected in the practice and the study of IR

first mover advantage (FMA)   long-term advantage of innovator

First World   the West and Japan, comparatively rich and free

fitness   ability to cope with complex challenges and opportunities

Fordism   mass production plant with wages adequate to allow consumerism

foreign affairs   any matters that concern a foreign minister

foreign aid   any form of assistance across borders—from emergency relief to grants and low-interest loans to education and technology transfer

foreign direct investment (FDI)   capital investments, including plants in a foreign country; can lower production and transportation costs and surmount local tariffs and NTBs

foreign policy   the approach of governments and other IR actors to cross-border relations; includes issues of "high" and "low" politics, indeed, any problem a foreign minister must deal with as part of the job, including "homeland" security

Fourth World   poorest of the poor; includes some Native Americans

Fox, Vicente   president of Mexico, elected in 2000 in the country's first free elections; a former Coca-Cola executive and putative friend of George W. Bush, Fox felt neglected after 9/11

framework convention   a treaty stating general goals, a commitment the parties expect to spell out in subsequent accords

Framework Convention on Climate Change (FCCC)   agreement reached at 1992 Earth Summit, the FCCC provided a foundation for later protocols; stipulated that developed countries take the first steps to curb greenhouse gas emissions and subsidize LDC emission curbs; set no targets or deadlines

free riding   taking advantage of public goods but not contributing one's own share

free trade   exchange of goods and services across borders shaped by market forces without tariffs or other government constraint

freer trade   neoliberal view that the principle of free trade must be modified to meet the internal needs of each country

frontier of possibilities (Pareto Optimum)   area of agreement beyond which one side must lose

functionalism   international technical cooperation on common interests, as in the WHO, that can bypass political differences but build habits of trust

fungibility   convertability; the extent that an asset (for example, gold, dollars, or knowledge) may be traded for another

Gender Empowerment Measure (GEM)   indicator of participation in economic and political activity relative to gender

Gender-related Development Index (GDI)   HDI corrected for gender differences

General Agreement on Tariffs and Trade (GATT)   a forum established in 1947 to promote free trade; more than 125 states took part in early 1990s; superseded by the WTO in 1993–1995

Geneva Conventions of 1949   rules for the humane treatment during wartime of the sick, the wounded, prisoners of war, civilians, and others; accepted by most governments but unknown to or not respected by many guerrilla groups and warlords

genocide   effort to destroy another people or its culture, banned by 1948 Genocide Convention

geonomics   belief that economic strength has eclipsed military strength as a source of influence in IR; rationalizes neomercantilist policies

geopolitics   belief that geography plus military assets is key to survival and influence in IR; underlies belief in the importance of controlling "heartlands" and choke points at sea

Ghandi, Rajiv   prime minister of India in 1987 who used Indian hard power in attempt to make peace between the Sri Lankan government and Tamil insurgents

Gini Index   a measure of income equality

Global Environmental Facility (GEF)   created in 1991 and administered by the World Bank in cooperation with the UNEP and UNDP, the GEF makes grants or loans for projects that respond to global environmental threats

globalization   cross-border ties based on forces that bypass governments, from the Internet to epidemics

Good Friday Agreement   April 1998 agreement between the Republic of Ireland and UK on power–sharing by unionists and republicans in Northern Ireland, and relations between the Republic of Ireland, Northern Ireland, the entire UK; referenda-approved

good offices   using one's position to promote talks between disputants

graduated reciprocation in tension reduction (GRIT)   a publicly announced strategy of initiatives to reduce tensions, steps that, if reciprocated, will be enlarged

Grameen Bank   a development bank established in Bangladesh in 1976; provides small loans mostly to poor rural women; spreading to other LDCs

grants   outright gifts, either in currency or in kind, such as food

green accounting   calculating environmental costs and gains along with economic costs and returns

Green Revolution   improved agricultural yields due to hybrid seeds, fertilizer, irrigation, and management

greenhouse effect   global warming presumed to be caused by trapping of solar radiation in the earth's atmosphere due to buildup of carbon dioxide, methane, and other gases

gross domestic product (GDP)   total value of goods and services produced within a country; does not include depreciation of resources or machines

GDP per capita   average income (omits discrepancies among classes)

gross national income (GNI)   total value added from domestic and foreign sources claimed by residents

gross national product (GNP)   GDP plus net receipts from nonresident sources

Group of Seven (G-7)   First World economic giants: Canada, France, Germany, Italy, Japan, the UK, and the U.S., sometimes joined by Russia

group think   collective opinion shaped by pressures to conform with little room for dissent

Gulf Cooperation Council   organization founded 1981 to coordinate activities of Bahrain, Kuwait, Oman, Qatar, Saudi Arabia, and the United Arab Emirates

Gulf of Tonkin Resolution   August 1964 resolution by which the U.S. Congress sanctioned escalation of U.S. military activity in Vietnam; authorized the president to take "all necessary measures" to repel attack on U.S. forces and "prevent further aggression"

hard power   ability to command others by threat or coerce them by force

hawk   hard-liner, not a "dove"

hegemonic war   fought by a challenger to displace a hegemon or by hegemon to maintain its position

hegemony   leadership, dominion

Helsinki Process   follow-on structures and evaluation of progress in implementing the Conference on Security and Cooperation in Europe Final Act signed in Helsinki in 1975

high politics   issues of state security and sovereignty

Hitler, Adolf   leader of Germany, 1933–1945

Holbrooke, Richard E.   U.S. assistant secretary of state who negotiated the 1995 Dayton Accord

Holst, Johan Jorgen   Norwegian foreign minister who helped mediate the Oslo Accord between Israel and the PLO

hot line   Washington–Moscow crisis communication link established in 1963 using undersea cables; revised in 1971 to use satellite links

hubris   arrogant, overweening pride

human development index (HDI)   an aggregate measure of development based on health, education, and real GDP; designed and applied by the UNDP

human poverty   the lack of choices and opportunity for living a tolerable life; affected at least one-fourth of humanity in 2003

human poverty index (HPI)   an aggregate measure of poverty based on life expectancy, literacy, and access to public and private resources; designed and applied by the UNDP

Hussein, Saddam   president of Iraq, 1979–2003; ordered war against Iran in the 1980s and an invasion of Kuwait in 1990

Huxley, Aldous   author of the dystopia Brave New World (1932)

ICBM (intercontinental ballistic missile)   land-based fixed or mobile missile with a range of 3,000 or more nautical miles

idealism (in IR)   theory that IR is or should be a quest for law and morality in international life

ideational factors   values, beliefs, institutions, and property relationships that shape behavior, for example, toward a potential international environmental conflict

import substitution   strategy to develop an economy shielded from foreign imports

income poverty   a measure of poverty: an income below $1 or $2 in LDCs but with a higher threshold in industrialized countries

indigenous   native, for example, the "First Nations" of Canada

industrial (or technology) policy   government actions to nurture and protect a selected industry or industry in general; an expression of neomercantilism

infant mortality   death rate in the first year per 1,000 live births; an indicator of social and economic conditions

influence   a measure of change in others' behavior achieved by hard or soft power; a result of power but not identical to it

intelligence   information, sometimes secret, gathered about other actors and forces in IR

interdependence   mutual vulnerability or sensitivity, with capacity for pain or gain; suggested here as a paradigm for IR theory

intergenerational equity   obligation of each generation to pass on natural and cultural assets equal to those it enjoyed

intergovernmental organization (IGO)   an IO whose membership consists of governments, for example, the UN and the IAEA

Intergovernmental Panel on Climate Change (IPCC)   an international scientific body to assess climate change

intergovernmentalist   view that the EU is an IGO—an organization among governments more than a supranational body over them

Intermediate Nuclear Forces (INF) Treaty   1987 Soviet–U.S. treaty to eliminate all land-based missiles with ranges between 500 and 5,500 kilometers (about 300 to 3,400 miles); verified by on-site inspectors; required destruction of missiles, but warheads could be recycled

intermingled nationalism   cohabitating nationalisms, often in conflict—unlike intermingled nations, which may coexist peacefully

international   what happens between states, the third level of IR analysis, not the same as transnational or supranational

International Atomic Energy Agency (IAEA)   UN agency established in 1957 to promote peaceful uses of atomic energy; since 1970, monitors compliance with the NPT

International Committee of the Red Cross (ICRC)   NGO founded in 1864 to provide relief to wounded soldiers and other victims of violence worldwide; an agent of humanitarian diplomacy, the ICRC works with national Red Cross and Red Crescent organizations; it is composed of Swiss nationals who, being citizens of a neutral country, can act as intermediaries

International Court of Justice (ICJ)   permanent court at The Hague to hear cases that states bring to it; one of six principal UN organs

International Covenant on Civil and Political Rights   1966 treaty that binds each signatory to uphold the individual's right of expression and participation in public life; not ratified by the U.S. until 1992

International Criminal Court (ICC)   permanent court at The Hague to hear war crimes and crimes against humanity cases; the ICC was established by the Rome Statue in 1998, which entered into force in 2002 and ratified by ninety-some countries in 2003, but actively opposed by the Bush administration

International Criminal Court Tribunal for the Former Yugoslavia (ICTY)   ad hoc tribunal at The Hague established by the UN Security Council in 1993 to hear cases of crimes against humanity or war crimes in the former Yugoslavia, justified also as a response to threats against international peace and security posed by violations of international law

International Criminal Court Tribunal for Rwanda (ICTR)   ad hoc tribunal in Rwanda established by the UN Security Council in 1994 to hear cases of genocide and other crimes against humanity by Rwandans and others in Rwanda and in neighboring countries

international environmental conflict (IEC)   conflict caused or aggravated by dispute over the environment, for example, a dispute over water

international law   treaties and customary behavior; public international law applies mainly to states but is expanding to cover other IR actors, including individuals; private international law governs business across borders and helps decide which state's courts have jurisdiction

International Military Tribunal at Nuremberg   court that tried German leaders in 1945–1946 and confirmed that individuals could be held responsible for crimes against peace, war crimes, and crimes against humanity

International Monetary Fund (IMF)   a UN Specialized Agency founded in 1944 charged with easing the short-term liquidity problems of its members

international organization (IO)   IGOs and NGOs

international political economy (IPE)   interaction of international economics and politics, for example, on trade and investment

international relations (IR)   cross-border interactions, especially political; includes any development, governmental or private, material or spiritual, shaping these interactions

IRBM   intermediate-range (1,500 to 3,000 nautical miles) ballistic missile

Iron Curtain   Winston Churchill's term for the political, economic, and barbed-wire barriers separating Western and Communist Europe during the Cold War

irredentism   nationalist movement demanding the union of a people (irredenta) ruled by another government with their kinsfolk in their own nation-state

ISR intelligence, surveillance, and reconnaissance, used with C^4

Jiang Zemin   president of China in the late 1990s who continued Deng Xiaoping's policies aimed at cultivating a freer economy while retaining Communist political rule; succeeded in 2003 by Ho Jintzo, but retained control of military affairs commission

joint implementation   a way for industrialized and developing countries to cooperate to reduce gas emissions

joker   an item in a negotiating package sure to cause its rejection by the other side

Kant, Immanuel   18th-century Prussian scholar; helped inspire liberal peace theory of late 20th century

Kellogg–Briand Pact   1928 Pact of Paris renouncing war

Keynesianism   use of government monetary and fiscal policies to stimulate, regulate, and cushion a market economy

Khatami, Mohammed   elected president of Iran in 1997, articulated a GRIT-like policy toward the U.S. people

Kim Il-sung   leader of North Korea from 1945 until his death in 1994; initiated the Korean War

Kim Jong-Il   son of Kim Il-sung and his successor as DPRK leader in 1994

kinetic power   power in action, for example, troops marching

Kissinger, Henry   realist scholar and diplomat; secretary of state under presidents Richard Nixon and Gerald Ford

Kyoto Protocol   1997 addition to the FCCC spelling out specific gas emissions targets and deadlines for developed countries but not for LDCs; rejected by the Bush administration in 2001

Laden, Osama bin   charismatic founder of al-Qaeda, scion of wealthy Saudi family laissez-faire   strong form of economic liberalism

Las Casas, Bartolomé de   16th-century Spanish priest who sought humane treatment for indigenous peoples of the Americas

less developed countries (LDCs)   poor countries with low incomes; may or may not be developing economically

levels of analysis   distinct but overlapping arenas for IR action and analysis; in this book, individuals, states, international systems, transnational systems, and the biosphere

leverage   the total political, economic, and military power a party or mediator can mobilize to influence others

liberal internationalism   theory that market democracy offers the surest foundation for peace and prosperity

liberal peace theory   democracies do fight but rarely, if ever, make war on other democracies

logic of collective action   to contribute as little as possible to public goods while benefiting from what others contribute

low politics   foreign affairs apart from high politics, for example, trade, humanitarian action, and environmental protection

MacArthur, Douglas A.   supreme allied commander in occupied Japan, 1945–1950, and commander of UN forces in Korea, 1950–1951

madrasa   school, usually for Sunni Islamic theology

Maginot Line   defensive fortifications shielding some but not all of France's border with Germany in the 1930s; skirted by Germany in 1940

majority rule   the method of governance in which the laws are made and enforced according to the desires of the numerical majority

Malthusian perspective   derived from Thomas Malthus, the belief that there are finite limits to growth as expanding human populations deplete natural resources

Mao Zedong   leader of Chinese Communist Party from 1921 and the PRC from 1949 until his death in 1976

maquiladora   export processing plant in Mexico near the U.S. border that takes advantage of low-priced Mexican labor and proximity of U.S. import markets

market   arena where supply meets demand mediated by price

Marshall, George C.   U.S. army general, secretary of state, and secretary of defense; exponent of the Marshall Plan

Marshall Plan   the European Recovery Program (ERP) proposed and funded by the U.S. to promote Europe's reconstruction, 1947–1951; a model of mutual gain

McNamara, Robert S.   U.S. secretary of defense during the Cuban missile crisis and initial U.S. escalation of the Vietnam conflict

mediation   a process of conflict management in which an outside or third party helps disputants accommodate their differences

mercantilism   doctrine that wealth consists in accumulating gold bullion or similar forms of wealth

Mikoyan, Anastas   first deputy prime minister of the USSR under Nikita Khrushchev and occasional emissary to Fidel Castro

minimum deterrent   the smallest arsenal sufficient for deterrence, perhaps dozens or hundreds of nuclear weapons

Ministry of International Trade and Industry (MITI)   Japanese agency responsible for protecting Japanese industries and promoting targeted exports

MIRV (multiple independently targetable reentry vehicle)   warhead and guidance system for missiles able to carry multiple warheads, each able to target a different object

Mitchell, George J.   former U.S. senator who helped mediate the Good Friday Agreement

modernization theory   a developmental strategy stressing that economic, cultural, and political change occur together in predictable ways

Molotov, Viacheslav   Soviet foreign minister under Josef Stalin and later under Nikita Khrushchev; a supporter of Stalinism and a hard line toward the West

monkey wrench problem   tendency of extraneous events to disrupt the process of détente

Monroe Doctrine   President James Monroe's 1823 admonition to Europeans not to colonize the Americas, coupled with an assurance that the U.S. would not intervene in Europe or Europe's existing colonies; a noninterventionist policy that later set the stage for U.S. interventions "south of the border"; a doctrine that died in the 1960s, if not earlier

Montreal Protocol   1987 agreement to phase out the use of chlorofluorocarbons and halons that deplete the ozone layer

MOOTW (military operations other than war)   Pentagon-speak for everything from peacekeeping to disaster relief to intimidation

Morgenthau, Hans J.   leading U.S. exponent of realism after World War II; author of *Politics Among Nations*

most-favored nation (MFN)   a designation that grants a state the maximum trade privileges afforded to any other; a potential lever in bargaining

MRBM   medium-range (600–1,500 nautical miles) ballistic missile

multiple symmetry   a model that says each rival must match or surpass every asset of its adversary or lose the competition

Mussolini, Benito   Italian dictator, 1922–1943

mutual gain   shared benefit for parties to a transaction; can be equal or asymmetrical; the result of value-creating policies or other circumstances

nation   a people that perceives itself a nation

nation-state   a state consisting largely of one nation, an ideal of nationalists

national interest   hypothetical stake of a nation (i.e., a state) in security or some other value; the realist's basic criterion for action; some interests, however, are ephemeral or pertain only to particular groups

nationalism   dedication to one's nation—its past, present, and future; can energize a people and/or foster conflict

national missile defense (NMD)   planned ABM system to protect the U.S. from an ICBM attack; not fully tested or proved useful, its deployment began in 2002 after the Bush administration withdrew from the 1972 ABM treaty

national self-determination   self-rule by a nation or the right to choose self-rule, for example, by a plebiscite

natural resources   renewable supplies (such as water) and nonrenewable (such as oil)

NBC weapons   nuclear, biological, and chemical agents of mass destruction—WMD

near abroad   Russian term for area formerly occupied by the Soviet border republics such as Ukraine; a concept used to justify Russian interventions in this area

negative peace   absence of war, sometimes fragile

negative-sum (lose–lose)   an interaction in which both sides lose

negotiation   a process by which parties communicate about ways to deal with issues on which they disagree

neofunctionalism   orientation to IO that seeks international cooperation on issues that are politically sensitive

neoidealism   diverse efforts to update classic IR idealism; ranges from civilizationism and endism to feminism, faith in NGOs, and postmodernism

neoliberalism   liberalism modified by Keynseanism and neomercantilism; part of the Western response to Japan

neomercantilism   doctrine that wealth depends on a favorable trade balance; encourages industrial policy and strategic trade

neorealism   theory that structures of material power determine IR; updates classic realism by greater attention to IPE and to scientific method

New International Economic Order (NIEO)   call by LDCs in 1970s for redistribution of wealth and for stabilization of commodity prices

newly industrializing countries (NICs)   states such as Thailand, Malaysia, Indonesia, Argentina, and Brazil that adopted an export-led development strategy in the 1980s and 1990s

nongovernmental organization (NGO)   a nonstate actor in IR such as Greenpeace or Amnesty International; sometimes referred to as international NGO (INGO)

nonstate actor   IR players that are not states; includes IGOs, NGOs, and TNCs

nontariff barriers (NTBs)   rules, subsidies, and other bureaucratic measures to limit foreign imports

nonviolent sanctions and resistance   moral, political, and economic measures to persuade or pressure others to change their behavior; includes embargoes, strikes, and demonstrations

no-regrets policy   actions useful even if other actors do not reciprocate and the possible danger (for example, global warming) turns out not to be a problem

North American Free Trade Agreement (NAFTA)   1994 agreement establishing a free trade area between Canada, Mexico, and the U.S.

North Atlantic Treaty Organization (NATO)   military alliance formed in 1949 to protect the West from attack by the USSR; expanded membership in 1999 and 2002

Nuclear Nonproliferation Treaty (NPT)   1968 treaty to limit the spread of nuclear weapons beyond the Big Five; signed by most states except those most able and determined to join the nuclear weapons club

Nunn–Lugar Act   1992 U.S. congressional act allocating funds to facilitate dismantling and control of former Soviet weapons

official development assistance (ODA)   government aid to developing countries, directly or through the World Bank and IMF

OPEC   Organization of Petroleum Exporting Countries, a cartel that seeks to coordinate production and pricing of oil; established in 1960 by Venezuela, Saudi Arabia, Iran, Iraq, and Kuwait; later joined by more than half a dozen other countries, though Ecuador and Gabon withdrew in 1992

Organization for Economic Cooperation and Development (OECD)   the only IO to include all industrial democracies (the "club of rich nations"); conducts research and fosters discussion of common problems

Organization for Security and Cooperation in Europe (OSCE)   outgrowth of the Helsinki process launched in 1975, an IGO with more than fifty member states—all of Europe, all members of NATO and the former Warsaw Pact, all successor states to the USSR; meets and acts to promote security and cooperation

Organization of American States   a regional IGO established in 1948 aiming to facilitate and coordinate cooperation in many domains among all states of the Americas, but it excluded Cuba from active participation in 1962

Oslo Accord   joint Declaration of Principles in August 1993 by Israel and the PLO providing for an interim period of limited Palestinian self-rule; left many problems for future negotiations

ozone layer   stratospheric gases shielding the earth from ultraviolet rays

pacific settlement of disputes   mediation or other nonviolent intervention by the UN or other actors not party to the dispute; authorized by UN Charter Chapter VI, if the disputants consent

Palestinian Liberation Organization (PLO)   umbrella organization for Palestinian nationalists, founded in 1964; led after 1967 by Yasser Arafat

Panmunjom   meeting place for DPRK and UN negotiators adjacent to Korea's DMZ

parity   rough equality, for example, 1,000 bombers and 1,000 missiles in country A versus 2,500 missiles but no bombers in country B

Partnership for Peace (PfP)   conducts multilateral exercises and peacekeeping missions by most states belonging to the OSCE; a substitute for, or a stepping-stone toward NATO membership

peace building   structural measures to generate a positive peace

peace enforcement   the use of force to uphold or impose peace, for example, the Dayton Accord

peacekeeping   the interposition of lightly armed forces to separate combatants with their consent, may buy time for negotiators to achieve a pacific settlement

Penkovsky, Oleg V.   a colonel in Soviet military intelligence who transmitted valuable information to British and U.S. agents in 1960–1962

perestroika   "restructuring," Gorbachev's economic reforms in late 1980s

ping-pong diplomacy   use of sports to signal interest in normalizing relations between estranged countries

plan   in Communist economics, physical output goals for one, five, or even fifteen years, often including set wages and prices

polarity (uni-, bi-, multi-)   centers of global power—one, two, or many

police action   military intervention with proclaimed purpose of upholding international law, as in the UN action in Korea, 1950–1953

political culture of authoritarianism   trains subjects to want guidance from above; emphasizes duties, not rights; excludes civil society

political culture of democracy   balances rights and duties; follows the majority but respects the minority

politicide   extermination of political foes

population transfer   the systematic movement of a group of people, often against their will

positions vs. interests   distinction between a sometimes rigid bargaining posture and the deep interests that negotiations could enhance

positive peace   not just the absence of war but a stable harmony; may arise from a value-creating order oriented to mutual gain

positive-sum (win–win) an interaction in which both sides win

postmodernism movement that deconstructs IR language and institutions to see what lies beneath the surface

Powell Doctrine belief of retired general and later secretary of state Colin Powell that the U.S. should fight only when it has clear and attainable war objectives, using overwhelming force, and with a clear exit strategy

power latent, mobilized, or kinetic means to influence others; includes hard coercive and soft persuasive power

power-sharing governance that ensures each minority or faction a voice, regardless of its electoral or numerical strength

power transition theory belief that a shifting balance of power induces hegemonic war, a war either to uphold or overthrow the existing hegemon

practices similar to slavery activities banned by the Supplementary Convention on the Abolition of Slavery (1956); includes debt bondage, serfdom, coerced marriage, and branding

preemptive war first strike delivered a short time (minutes, hours, days) before the enemy attacks; ordered when a foe seems to be embarking on an attack

preferential trade agreement reduces barriers between signatories but does not provide for MFN to others; NAFTA and the EEC are examples of such accords

prenegotiation the process of setting the agenda, developing meeting sites and procedures, and generating a constructive ambiance before formal negotiations begin

preventive war a first strike delivered months or even years before the shifting balance of power permits the other side to attack and win

Prisoner's Dilemma (PD) game theory exercise showing how distrust and self-seeking can lead to losses for each player

productivity–compensation balance an outcome whereby a highly paid worker who produces more products per hour than a lower-paid worker costs less per unit of output; relevant to NAFTA

protocol a code of conduct; an addendum to a treaty/convention spelling out and often tightening obligations

proxy war war by clients

psychological warfare efforts to weaken the resolve and confuse the minds of the foe by propaganda, disinformation, and other techniques and to rally support

purchasing power parity (PPP) real GDP per capita

Putin, Vladimir V. former KGB agent, RF president since 2000

Pyongyang capital of the Democratic People's Republic of Korea

Qaeda, al- global network ("the base") established by Osama bin Laden for terrorist operations against the West and "corrupt" Muslims

quota quantitative limit on imports or exports

R&D research and development

rapprochement improved relations between two previously estranged parties

rational actor model assumption that states are united and rational in pursuit of their "national" interests

real GDP PPP

realism (in IR) theory that IR is struggle for power by states

reduction differentials different obligations for different countries, for example, in targets for gas emissions

regime government; in IR, tacit or explicit norms of behavior among states, with or without a formal treaty

rent seeking exploitation of official position for personal gain

reparations compensation for damages caused by the other side, paid in cash or in kind— labor, coal, ships; indemnities may be paid from gold and currency reserves or from future earnings

reservation price (RP) the walkaway price of each disputant; minimum acceptable terms

reverse wave movement to displace democratic with the authoritarian regimes, as in Serbia and several other countries in the 1990s

revisionist state one that seeks to revise or overthrow an unfavorable international order

ripeness hypothetical condition making a dispute amenable to mediation

rogue state a state that deviates from generally accepted standards; vicious, unreliable actor, perhaps willing to use poison gas or biological weapons or other mass destruction weapons

Rome Statute 1998 document establishing the ICC

Rome, Treaty of 1957 treaty creating the EEC; a second treaty signed the same day in Rome established EURATOM

Roosevelt, Eleanor U.S. humanitarian who campaigned against racial and gender discrimination in the U.S. and later chaired the UN commission that drafted the Universal Declaration of Human Rights

rule-based trade regime a system characterized by qualitative rather than quantitative targets in trade

Rumsfeld Doctrine belief of U.S. Defense Secretary Donald Rumsfeld that the U.S. should depend less in war on brute force and more on fast-moving forces armed with smart weapons and supported by advanced C^4 ISR

Russian Federation (RF) official designation of the Russian state that emerged from the USSR, a federation of "Russia" and more than eighty subunits

Sadat, Anwar president of Egypt who agreed to peace with Israel at Camp David in 1978

SAM surface-to-air missile for use against enemy aircraft

secession withdrawal by one unit from an organization or a state, as when Slovakia seceded from Czechoslovakia in 1992

second strike massive retaliatory blow after suffering a first strike

Second World the Communist states, especially those obedient to the USSR; did not always include China

security being safe; includes military security (safe from external attack, achieved by military means or by diplomacy), internal security (safe from subversion), food security (safe from hunger), and environmental security (safe from environmental disaster)

security dilemma phenomenon where State A's defensive actions may elicit countermeasures from State B and thus increase State A's insecurity

security regime rules, informal norms, and decision-making procedures designed to overcome the security dilemma

segmentation partitioning a country by natural borders, ethnicity, and other criteria

self-determination choosing one's own political identity; the alleged right of a nation to have its own state

self-help realist belief that IR actors must depend upon their own strengths for survival and other goals

separatism nationalist or other political movement seeking self-determination, for example, some Tamils in Sri Lanka

Shanghai Communiqué framework for normalizing PRC–U.S. relations drafted in 1972 by Zhou Enlai and Henry Kissinger

Shi'a branch of Islam at odds with orthodox Sunni faith; most Iranians, a majority of Iraqis, and large segments of other Persian Gulf populations are Shi'a; since their troubled origins, when the rightful heir to the caliphate was martyred, many Shi'i have seen themselves as persecuted by Sunnis and others

silting silt buildup behind a dam lowering its life span and energy potential

Single European Act (SEA) 1987 agreement by which all EC members pledged to create a European market without internal barriers or discrimination by 1992

single negotiating text (SNT) one text accepted or amended by each party in negotiations; used at Camp David in 1978 to define areas of agreement and difference

slavery form of human bondage whereby one individual is considered the property of another; common throughout history but generally banned since the 19th century

smart bombs highly accurate weapons, able to outwit defenses

Smith, Adam a father of economic liberalism, authored *The Wealth of Nations* (1776)

social learning capacity of an entire society to draw relevant lessons from experience and change its behavior accordingly

socialism public ownership of the means of production; for Marxists, individual income is decided by the quality and quantity of work performed; the views of non-Marxist socialists differ on many points from those of Marxist socialists

soft power the ability to inspire consensus (agreement) and to coopt (persuade others to share the same goals)

South Asia Bangladesh, Bhutan, India, Maldives, Nepal, Pakistan, and Sri Lanka—a region lagging East Asia in many aspects of economic and social development

South Asian Association for Regional Cooperation (SAARC) regional IGO charged with fostering cooperation among its members: Bangladesh, Butan, India, Nepal, the Maldives, Pakistan, and Sri Lanka

sovereign a supreme power, for example, a king

sovereignty independent, unfettered power of a state in its jurisdiction

spectrum of intervention the range of techniques by an outside party that may intervene in the affairs of one or more other IR actors, from military coercion to financial bribes to the use of good offices to facilitate negotiations

Spirit of Geneva first détente of the Cold War, generated by 1955 summit conference in Geneva of French, Soviet, UK, and U.S. leaders

Stag Hunt Rousseau's allegory about going it alone: A greedy and shortsighted hunter, unwilling to cooperate with other hunters and wait for a stag, chases a hare, spoiling chances for himself and the others to obtain a larger bounty

Stalin, Josef Georgian-born dictator of the USSR from the mid-1920s to his death in 1953, surpassed even Mao Zedong in per capita democide and politicide

standard operating procedures (SOPs) bureaucratic routines meant to promote efficiency but that sometimes yield rigid and/or inconsistent policies

state key actor in IR; a political entity with a sovereign government controlling a demarcated territory and a permanent population and possessing the legal right to deal with other states

state-centric view of IR focused on the state (level 2) and their interactions (level 3) and minimizing levels 1, 4, and 5

stereotyping casting others in a rigid and simplified mode based on preconceptions and resisting evidence to the contrary

Stimson Doctrine U.S. refusal (1932) to recognize any political or territorial change accomplished by force; the doctrine resurfaced when Iraq seized Kuwait

Strategic Arms Limitation Treaty (SALT 1 and 2) froze Soviet and U.S. strategic arms and sharply limited ABM deployment (SALT 1, 1972) and endeavored to limit not just missiles and bombers but the number of warheads they could carry (SALT 2, 1979); SALT 2 was never ratified, but each side generally observed it

Strategic Arms Reduction Treaty (START 1, 2) accords mandating not just arms control but disarmament as well; required Moscow and Washington to reduce arsenals to no more than 6,000 strategic nuclear warheads (START 1, 1990) and cut down to no more than 3,500 strategic nuclear warheads by the year 2003 (START 2, 1991); START 2 never entered force

Strategic Defense Initiative (SDI) "Star Wars" plan developed in the 1980s to build an astrodome-like defensive shield to protect the U.S.

strategic doctrine the theory guiding a country's military planning, for example, a "cult of the offensive" or faith in deterrence

Strategic Offensive Reductions Treaty (SORT) three-page commitment by the U.S. and RF in 2002 to reduce operationally deployed strategic nuclear warheads to between 1,700 and 2,200 by 2012

strategic (or managed) trade government intervention to help a country's firms win market share abroad

strategic weapon a WMD that can hit a country's homeland (for Russia, a plane or missile from NATO, Europe, or China, as well as from the U.S.)

strategy long-range plan; a military plan

Straussian follower of the natural law philosopher Leo Strauss and/or a neoconservative such as Paul D. Wolfowitz in the George W. Bush administration; self-righteousness in a campaign to extirpate evil from the world scene

"string" condition attached to foreign aid, such as "buy American"

structural adjustment policies freer markets, less debt, reduced welfare, and more democracy—often demanded of LDCs by the IMF and other international financial agencies

submarine-launched ballistic missile (SLBM) mainstay of the U.S. deterrent; SLBMs are accurate and can carry many warheads, and their placement on submarines makes them difficult to destroy

Sunni orthodox Islam (from *sunna*—"path of the Prophet"), dominant in most of the Islamic world but divided into many tendencies, often conflicting with each other as well as with Shi'a

Sunshine policy launched in late 1990s, South Korea's policy to appease and open up North Korea, regarded as naïve for its failure to demand reciprocity

supranational authority a government over other governments; a world government

sustainable development economic growth that maintains the carrying capacity of system resources

syndrome of underdevelopment reinforcing patterns of mutual distrust, skewed land ownership, corruption, militarism, criminality, and sexism that instill a feeling of powerlessness among the population

tactics means to a strategic goal; may include one step back to get two steps ahead

Taiwan Strait body of water separating the PRC and ROC, with several ROC-controlled islands

INDEX